Home Made Best Made

Home Made Best Made

HUNDREDS OF WAYS TO MAKE ALL KINDS OF USEFUL THINGS

 Reader's Digest

The Reader's Digest Association, Inc.
Pleasantville, New York / Montreal

READER'S DIGEST GENERAL BOOKS

Editor-in-Chief, Books and Home Entertainment
Barbara J. Morgan

Editor, U.S. General Books
David Palmer

Executive Editor
Gayla Visalli

Managing Editor
Christopher Cavanaugh

Australian Staff for Homemade Best Made

Editors: Phil Rodwell, Michael Wall

Design: Barbara Beckett, assisted by Cathy Campbell

Photographers: John Hollingshead, Rodney Weidland

Stylists: Jan Berry, Kay Francis, Louise Owens, Kathy Tripp, Anne Marie Unwin, Paul Urquhart

Illustrators: David Carroll, Sue Ninham, Keith Scanlon

Interior Decorating Consultant: Louise Owens

Cover design: David Trooper

Library of Congress Cataloging in Publication Data
Home made best made: hundreds of ways to make all kinds of useful things.
    p. cm.
  Includes bibliographical references and index
  ISBN 0-7621-0076-1
  1. Home economics. 2. Handicraft. 3. Cookery. I. Reader's Digest Association.
TX147.H752 1998
640--dc21   97-46894

Printed in the United States of America.

Recipe p. 210 reprinted from DR. PITCAIRN'S COMPLETE GUIDE TO NATURAL HEALTH FOR DOGS & CATS, copyrighted 1982 by Richard H. Pitcairn. Permission granted by Rodale Press, Inc., Emmaus, PA 18098.

Warning: All do-it-yourself activities involve a degree of risk. Skills, materials, tools, and site conditions vary widely. Although the editors have made every effort to ensure accuracy, the reader remains responsible for the selection and use of tools, materials, and methods. Always follow a manufacturer's operating instructions, and observe safety precautions.

Address any comments about HOMEMADE, BEST MADE to
Editor, U.S. General Books, c/o Customer Service, Reader's Digest, Pleasantville, NY 10570.

To order additional copies of HOMEMADE, BEST MADE, call 1-800-846-2100.

You can also visit us on the World Wide Web at http://www.readersdigest.com

Home Made Best Made

STAFF

Project Editor
Nancy Shuker

Project Art Editor
Virginia Wells Blaker

Editor
Judith Cressy

Associate Editor
Alexis Lipsitz

Associate Designers
Barbara Lapic
Ed Jacobus
Wendy Wong

Assistant Editor
Andrew Boorstyn

Special thanks
Eleanor Kostyk
Robert Steimle

CONTRIBUTORS

Editor/Consultant
Zuelia Ann Hurt

Contributing Editor
Linda Hetzer

Editorial Assistant
Howard G. Senior

Photographer
Steven Mays

Illustrators
Ray Skibinski
Ian Worpole
Thomas Sperling

Stylist
Susan E. Piatt

Consultants
Tom Christopher
Ara DerMarderosian, PhD.
Kim Erickson
Helen Taylor Jones
Leslie Glover Pendleton
Susan B. Schoen, VMD

Copy Editors
Gina Grant
Jacqueline Kinghorn Brown
Susan Converse Winslow

Indexer
Felice Levy/AEIOU Inc.

Contents

Looking Good, Feeling Good

Pets and Wildlife

Yard and Garden

Loving Touches

About This Book

ADVANCES in modern technology have certainly made all our lives easier, allowing us to buy, ready-made, almost anything we might need or want, as long as we can pay for it.

Not so long ago, most of the things that people wore and ate, many of their furnishings, and such luxuries as personalized gifts and cosmetics had to be made at home. In accepting the convenience of mass-produced, machine-made products, we gave up some very personal pleasures. One was simple creative pride. A second was the incomparable aroma and taste of home-cooked foods—from breads to broths. Another, particularly important in these ecologically sensitive times, was knowing all the ingredients that went into the dishes served at our tables. A fourth was a handmade touch here and there that marked our home as uniquely and comfortably ours.

The purpose of this book is to help you recapture that sense of creative accomplishment, gain control over your home environment, and cultivate the skills and techniques that allow you to express yourself in your home and garden and in the gifts you make for family and friends. We think you'll have fun trying some of these projects and you'll be proud of the results. As a bonus, you'll also save some money.

In the six chapters of HOMEMADE, BEST MADE, we give you the opportunity to try your hand at cooking, gardening, decorating your home, taking care of yourself and your pets, and making delightful items to give as presents. We don't just tell you how to make things from scratch. In the chapter titled "From the Kitchen," for example, there are hundreds of recipes for making everything from jams to sausage—and there are also dozens of suggestions for using, storing, and wrapping up your creations as beautiful, thoughtful personal gifts. A section on freezing in the same chapter will be particularly useful when you begin to harvest the vegetables you have grown with guidance from the chapter titled "Yard and Garden."

Cross-fertilization is another element of the book. Projects in the various chapters are interrelated, so that skills learned in one place may be applied in others. The knitting that you learn in "Loving Touches" will help you make Easter baskets and rugs as well as sweaters. Stencil patterns in the decorating chapter can also be used in craft projects. The herbs that you learn to grow in the gardening chapter can be used to accent a sauce or to make a soothing balm.

At the start of each chapter, a "Before you Begin" section describes special techniques that may be required in the projects on the ensuing pages. There are lots of little bonuses as well. On nearly every page of every chapter there are hints and tips that simplify the making, serving, storing, and displaying of your homemade items.

Most of the projects require only moderate skills and experience. We have, however, included a few more challenging ones that you may want to postpone until you have honed your techniques on simpler projects. Whatever your abilities and interests, there is plenty here to get you started and keep you busy.

Full-page color photographs and clear illustrations, including straightforward, step-by-step drawings, will guide you every step of the way. For years to come, you'll find yourself turning to HOMEMADE, BEST MADE regularly for inspiration as well as project plans.

from the Kitchen

*I*n the world of food, the word "homemade" conjures up the heady aromas of baking bread and simmering sauces and memories of special-occasion dishes—often vividly recalled on the palate—that can only come from a warm and happy kitchen.

Those sensual impressions may explain why a gift from the kitchen is so satisfying for both the giver and the recipient. The former has the pleasure of creating kitchen magic with fresh foodstuffs, and the latter knows that the gift comes from the heart as well as the stove.

This chapter explores a range of cooking skills and techniques that allow you to create wonderful food gifts, cater your own perfect parties, and properly celebrate happy events—easily and economically. It also tells you how to safely put up delicious jams, jellies, pickles, and chutneys, and how to freeze summer's bounty of fruits and vegetables for later enjoyment.

Recipes range from dips and spreads to pasta sauces and savory pastries; from pâtés and sausages to stocks and yeast breads; from biscuits and muffins to a panoply of cakes and candies; from party drinks and punches to old-fashioned ice cream and modern sorbet. Throughout the chapter, step-by-step drawings explain techniques and special boxes give you helpful hints and tips.

BEFORE YOU BEGIN ...

Nothing says "homemade" better than good food prepared in your own kitchen. The recipes
in this chapter celebrate the diversity of cuisines and cooking styles available to the home cook.
Here are a few general tips to help you get started.

You don't need a large kitchen or a great many tools to cook well. Electric food processors, stationary mixers, and microwave ovens are useful work- and time-savers, but they are not essential to good cooking. Any well-stocked kitchen, however, will have the basic utensils listed below:

1 Two or three sharp knives of varying sizes, which are more safely stored in a wooden block or on a magnetic strip than in a drawer.

2 Wooden and stainless-steel mixing and stirring spoons, tongs, and ladles, plus slotted spoons for lifting solids from liquid. Make sure the handles are long enough to extend well beyond the heat source and that the handles of metal spoons are made of a heatproof material.

3 A set of ¼-, ⅓-, ½-, and 1-cup measuring cups for dry ingredients.

4 A heatproof glass measuring cup for liquids—4-cup capacity is best.

5 Measuring spoons of ¼-, ⅓-, ½-, 1-teaspoon, and 1-tablespoon capacities.

6 Mixing bowls of various sizes (a copper one is particularly good for whisking egg whites if you don't have an eggbeater or a mixer).

7 Several saucepans with lids. At least one should be lined with a nonreactive material, such as stainless steel, enamel, or nonstick coating, to prevent interactions with acidic foods.

8 A double boiler, especially for making custards. You can improvise one by setting a heatproof mixing bowl over a saucepan of simmering water; the bottom of the bowl must sit high enough not to touch the water.

9 Kitchen scissors, rotary peeler, citrus zester, colander, sieve, and grater.

10 For baking you will also need a rolling pin, spatulas, whisks, a range of cake and pie pans and sheets in varying sizes and shapes, and a handheld electric mixer or eggbeater. A candy thermometer can also be useful.

Safe canning

The key to safe canning is processing foods at a high enough temperature for a long enough time. Acids inhibit the growth of microorganisms, so that naturally acidic fruits, such as those used in the jam and chutney recipes in this chapter, and pickle recipes that call for plenty of vinegar can safely be processed by an easy water-bath method in which the filled jars are boiled for the amount of time specified in the recipe. You can buy a water-bath set or simply fit out a large pot—the one you cook corn in, for example—with a tight-fitting lid and a rack or basket that holds the canning jars off the bottom of the pot. The pot must be deep enough that the boiling water covers the tops of the jars by at least an inch. You can buy canning jars at hardware or grocery stores. Glass canning jars and their metal screw bands, which help make the seal, are reusable. The lid that actually seals the jar is not.

The directions for putting up jams, shown below, also apply to chutneys and pickles. Wash canning jars in hot, sudsy water, rinse, and cover with boiling water until ready to fill. Prepare tops according to the manufacturer's directions. Place cool processed jars on a rack or towel with air space between the jars for 12 to 24 hours. Then press the center of each lid. If the depression holds, the seal is good and you can remove the screw band and store the jar. Otherwise, refrigerate the jar and use the contents right away or reprocess the filled jar.

Canned foods should last a year in a cool (40°F to 60°F), dark storage space as long as the seal holds. Discard *any* food from a leaking jar or food from a freshly opened jar that has a questionable odor or appearance. Never taste doubtful food to test it.

PUTTING UP JAMS

1 *Once the jam is cooked, remove from the heat. Stir to distribute the fruit evenly and ladle into warm, clean jars, which have been resting in hot water.*

2 *Fill jars to within ⅛ or ¼ inch of the top, according to the recipe. Remove any air bubbles around the inside of the jar with a sterile spatula.*

3 *Wipe off any drips from the top and the outside of each jar with a clean, damp cloth. Apply lids and screw bands, following manufacturer's instructions.*

4 *Process in boiling water bath for specified time, starting when water boils. At high altitudes, increase the time by 1 minute for each 1,000 ft. above sea level.*

COOKING TERMS

DREDGE: to roll or dip food in a powder, such as flour or sugar, until generously covered

FOLD: to blend ingredients by gently cutting and lifting, so as not to lose any incorporated air

KNEAD: to blend in ingredients and make dough smoother and more elastic by repeatedly pushing it down and folding it

SCALD: to heat milk to a point just below boiling (212°F)

WHISK: to beat ingredients, such as cream or egg whites, briskly with a whisk or fork to incorporate air

ZEST: the colored outer peel of citrus fruits that contains the flavorful oils

Condiments made at home—from chutneys to pickles and jams—make the tastiest and most appreciated gifts.

Using fresh or dried herbs

Fresh herbs are called for in many recipes in this chapter. If fresh herbs aren't available, substitute dried ones. Dried herbs usually have a more intense flavor, so reduce the quantity given in the recipe by two-thirds (1 teaspoon dried herbs for 1 tablespoon fresh). For a more pronounced flavor, taste the dish and add more herbs at the end of the cooking time.

Cooking with yeast

Yeast is the leavening agent for many breads and some cakes. Its live cells react with the sugars in flour. Both compressed and dried varieties are available, but dried yeast, sold in ¼ -ounce packets, is more popular because it is easier to use. To work, yeast must first be activated by dissolving it in a small amount of warm (105° to 115°F) water or milk. A higher temperature is likely to kill the yeast, and a lower one won't activate it. Active yeast will become frothy in about five minutes, proving its viability. Adding a pinch of sugar to the warm liquid "feeds" the yeast and helps activate it more quickly.

Making ice creams

An ice-cream churn—either electric or hand-cranked—produces the best ice cream because it incorporates air into the mixture, making it smooth and adding volume. If you don't have a churn, there is a good alternative method that requires only a freezer. Pour the ice-cream mixture into ice trays or a metal bowl and let it partially freeze for several hours. Remove the ice cream and beat it with an electric mixer to break up the ice crystals. Return the beaten ice cream to the freezer for another hour or so. Repeat the beating and partial refreezing twice more before letting the ice cream harden. Allow fully frozen ice cream to ripen in the freezer for two or more hours before serving. To add fruit pieces or nuts to ice cream, wait until the base mixture is partially frozen. (Most fruits or small nutmeats freeze more quickly than the custard or cream base and, if added too soon, will turn into ice before the cream has frozen.)

Oven temperatures

Ovens can vary in temperature. Test yours with an oven thermometer. If the oven is badly calibrated, have a repairperson readjust it. If the variation is small, learn to compensate by resetting the temperature dial. If your oven runs a little hot, for example, set it at 325°F when a recipe calls for 350°F.

Some cooks describe oven temperatures in general terms—"bake it in a medium oven"—rather than in specific degrees. What they mean is spelled out below:

Very low: 250°F	Medium: 350°F	Very hot: 475°F–500°F
Low: 300°F	Hot: 400°F	

◆ Pickled Preserves ◆

*Bottling fruits and vegetables in brine or vinegar is a
time-honored method of preserving them. These tart condiments
add color and flavor to any meal.*

Mixed vegetable pickle

*Almost any vegetable can be used for this spicy
pickle. It will brighten a cold roast chicken lunch
or a hot baked ham dinner, and add spice to a
simple tuna salad.*

- ◆ **4 kirby cucumbers, halved
  and cut into 1-inch strips**
- ◆ **1 small cauliflower, cut into
  florets, about 4 cups**
- ◆ **8 shallots, peeled and
  trimmed**
- ◆ **2 green peppers, seeded
  and cut into strips**
- ◆ **2 sweet red peppers,
  seeded and cut into strips**
- ◆ **1 pound green beans,
  topped and tailed**
- ◆ **1 bunch baby carrots, scrubbed
  and trimmed, or 3 large carrots, peeled and cut into strips**
- ◆ **2 tablespoons salt**
- ◆ **6 cups white vinegar**
- ◆ **¼ cup sugar**
- ◆ **2-inch piece fresh ginger,
  peeled and halved**
- ◆ **1 teaspoon ground turmeric**
- ◆ **1 tablespoon each mustard
  seeds, peppercorns, allspice
  berries, and dry mustard**

1 Place all the prepared vegetables in a
ceramic or glass bowl. Sprinkle with the salt,
cover, and leave for 24 hours.
2 Rinse the vegetables with cold water and
then drain well.
3 Place vinegar in a nonreactive saucepan
with sugar, ginger, and spices. Bring to a boil,
then add the vegetables. Cook for 3 minutes.
4 Lift the vegetables out with a slotted spoon
and arrange them in an attractive pattern—
make layers of color, for example, or use the

pepper slices to make vertical stripes—in
warm, clean, widemouthed jars.
5 Discard the ginger, strain the hot vinegar,
and pour it over the vegetables, leaving
¼ -inch headspace. Process 20 minutes in a
boiling water bath (p.14).
MAKES ABOUT 3 QUART JARS   TOTAL TIME 24 HOURS
PLUS 1 HOUR

Pickled cauliflower florets

*A welcome addition to an antipasto platter, these
crisp florets are also the perfect accompaniment
to spicy sliced meats for a tasty picnic lunch.*

- ◆ **1 large cauliflower, cut
  into florets, 7 to 8 cups**
- ◆ **white vinegar, sufficient
  to cover cauliflower**
- ◆ **1 tablespoon salt**
- ◆ **1 tablespoon white peppercorns**
- ◆ **1 tablespoon light brown sugar**
- ◆ **1 medium sweet red pepper,
  seeded and finely sliced**
- ◆ **6 small dried red chilies**

1 In a nonreactive saucepan, cover the cauliflower florets with the vinegar. Add the salt,
peppercorns, and sugar.
2 Bring to a boil, add the pepper strips, and
boil for 1 minute. Remove the vegetables with
a slotted spoon and place in two clean, warm,
wide-mouthed jars. Pack snugly, distributing
the pepper strips evenly. Tuck 3 chilies
between the cauliflower florets in each jar.
3 Pour the hot vinegar from the saucepan into
the jars, making sure the liquid covers all the
cauliflower florets. Leave ¼ -inch headspace.
Process 20 minutes in a boiling water bath
(p.14). Will be ready to eat in 2 weeks. Refrigerate once opened.
MAKES ABOUT 2 QUART JARS   TOTAL TIME 30 MINUTES

Pickled onions

A chunk of cheddar, a slice or two of crisp-crusted bread, and a couple of these spicy onions are all you need for a simple and delicious lunch.

- ◆ **4 pounds small white pickling onions**
- ◆ **½ cup salt**
- ◆ **10 peppercorns**
- ◆ **4 fresh red chilies**
- ◆ **4 bay leaves**
- ◆ **4 cups cider vinegar**

1 To peel onions easily, cover them with boiling water, let stand for 5 minutes, and drain.
2 Remove the outer skins and trim the roots and crowns. Avoid removing too many of the onion layers because this can make them soggy during the pickling process. Cover the onions with cold water, add the salt, and mix well. Leave to soak overnight.
3 Drain the onions and pack in widemouthed, sterilized jars (p.168) with the peppercorns, chilies, and bay leaves.
4 Bring the vinegar to a boil in a nonreactive saucepan and immediately pour it over the onions to cover them, leaving ⅛-inch headspace. Process 10 minutes in a boiling water bath (p.14). Will be ready to eat in 4 weeks. Refrigerate once opened.
MAKES ABOUT 4 PINT JARS   TOTAL TIME 1 HOUR PLUS OVERNIGHT

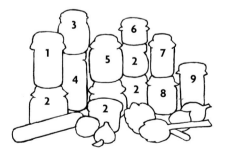

A range of pickles is a wonderful standby to have handy in the pantry: **1** *Globe artichokes in olive oil,* **2** *Marinated pickled olives,* **3** *Pickled red cabbage,* **4** *Mixed vegetable pickle,* **5** *Pickled onions,* **6** *Pickled eggs (quail),* **7** *Pickled spiced plums,* **8** *Pickled eggs,* **9** *Pickled cauliflower florets.*

Thick and hot, this Indian lime pickle is delicious served with curries or cooked meat. You might also try it with chilled shrimp and crusty bread.

Spicy lime pickle
For a milder pickle, reduce the number of chilies.

- ◆ **2 pounds limes, washed**
- ◆ **8 fresh red chilies, chopped**
- ◆ **4 cloves garlic, chopped**
- ◆ **2 tablespoons fresh ginger, chopped**
- ◆ **1 tablespoon ground coriander**
- ◆ **1 tablespoon ground cumin**
- ◆ **2 teaspoons ground cardamom**
- ◆ **2 teaspoons black mustard seeds**
- ◆ **1 teaspoon freshly ground black pepper**
- ◆ **1 teaspoon salt**
- ◆ **1 teaspoon turmeric**
- ◆ **1½ cups white wine vinegar**
- ◆ **½ cup vegetable oil**

1 Cut each lime into 6 wedges, then halve the wedges and place the pieces in a nonreactive saucepan with all the other ingredients.
2 Bring to a boil; then reduce the heat and simmer until the fruit is tender and the pickle thick, about 50 minutes.
3 Ladle into warm, clean jars, leaving ¼ -inch headspace. Process 15 minutes in a boiling water bath (p.14). Will be ready to eat after 2 weeks. Refrigerate once opened.
MAKES ABOUT 4 HALF-PINT JARS   TOTAL TIME 1½ HOURS

Pickled red cabbage
The sharp mustard flavor of this pickle makes it a complementary side dish for roast pork.

- ◆ **1 red cabbage**
- ◆ **3 tablespoons kosher salt**
- ◆ **4 cups white vinegar**
- ◆ **1 teaspoon each mustard seeds and black peppercorns**
- ◆ **1 tablespoon fresh ginger, chopped**
- ◆ **2 bay leaves**

1 Discard the outer cabbage leaves and wash the remainder well. Cut the cabbage into quarters and shred. (It should make about 10 cups.) Place in a bowl and sprinkle with the salt. Cover and leave overnight.
2 Rinse the cabbage in a colander and drain.
3 Place the vinegar, spices, and ginger in a nonreactive saucepan and bring to a boil. Cool and strain, reserving the liquid.
4 Pack the cabbage into two warm, clean jars and cover with the spiced vinegar, leaving ¼ -inch headspace. Tuck a bay leaf into each jar. Process 20 minutes in a boiling water bath (p.14). Will be ready to eat in 2 weeks. Refrigerate once opened.
MAKES ABOUT 2 QUART JARS   TOTAL TIME 1 HOUR PLUS OVERNIGHT

Pickled eggs
Perfect for a picnic, these eggs give cold chicken and a tossed green salad a flavorful lift.

- ◆ **12 medium eggs**
- ◆ **4 cups cider vinegar**
- ◆ **10 black peppercorns**
- ◆ **2 small dried red chilies**

1 Hard-boil the eggs in barely simmering water for 10 minutes. Drain, then plunge into cold water and leave for 10 minutes.

2 Meanwhile, in a nonreactive saucepan, boil the vinegar with the peppercorns.
3 Crack the eggshells all over, peel the eggs, and pack them in warm, clean, widemouthed jars. Place a chili in each jar. Cover with the hot vinegar, leaving ¼-inch headspace. Process in a warm water bath for 20 minutes. Will be ready to eat in 4 weeks. Refrigerate once opened.

MAKES ABOUT 2 PINT JARS TOTAL TIME 1 HOUR

VARIATION Try 2 dozen quail eggs boiled and peeled in the same way, but use white vinegar rather than cider vinegar for the pickling process. The quail eggs are a little more tedious to peel, but they make a most attractive addition to an antipasto platter.

Pickled spiced plums

These aromatic plums bring the spices of the Orient to a traditional roast of pork or lamb.

- **1⅔ cups sugar**
- **2⅔ cups water**
- **1 cup cider vinegar**
- **4 sticks cinnamon, broken**
- **1 tablespoon each whole cloves and whole black peppercorns**
- **2 to 3 strips orange zest**
- **2 pounds small, firm, ripe red or purple plums**

1 Place the sugar and water in a saucepan and bring to a boil, stirring to dissolve the sugar. Reduce the heat and simmer for 10 minutes.
2 Add the vinegar, cinnamon sticks, cloves, peppercorns, and orange zest, cover the pan, and simmer gently for 15 minutes.
3 Meanwhile, wash the plums; then prick in several places with a sterilized skewer or darning needle.
4 Place in warm, clean, widemouthed jars. Add the hot spiced syrup to cover, leaving ¼-inch headspace. Process 25 minutes in a boiling water bath (p.14). Will be ready to eat in 4 weeks. Refrigerate once opened.

MAKES ABOUT 2 QUART JARS TOTAL TIME 1 HOUR

Marinated pickled olives

Look for firm, unblemished fresh olives at specialty food stores or a farmer's market. Either green or black olives can be used in this two-stage preserving process. After pickling, the olives are marinated for an additional week before eating to allow the flavors to develop more fully.

- **3 pounds fresh green or black olives**
- **¼ cup kosher salt**
- **4 cups water**

MARINADE INGREDIENTS
- **2 cups olive oil**
- **1 cup water**
- **½ cup dry white wine**
- **4 large cloves garlic**
- **4 bay leaves**
- **4 dried whole red chilies, each about 2 inches long**
- **1 teaspoon dried oregano**
- **1 teaspoon cracked black pepper**
- **6 thick slices lemon**
- **3 sprigs fresh thyme**

1 Wash the olives and remove the stems. Using a sharp knife, slit each olive in two or three places through to the stone. Place in clean, widemouthed jars, filling each jar three-quarters full. Cover with cold water and weight down the olives with an upside-down saucer to keep them submerged. Cover the jars and their saucer covers with plastic wrap and store in a cool, dark place—5 days for green olives, 3 days for black olives. Change the water in each of the jars daily.
2 After the olives have soaked the required number of days, prepare the brine. In a saucepan, heat and stir the salt and 4 cups water until the salt dissolves. Remove pan from the heat and let the brine cool.
3 Drain the olives, return them to clean jars, and pour the brine over them. Seal and store in a cool, dark place for 8 to 12 weeks, or until the olives are no longer bitter; black olives take less time than green ones to sweeten, so start checking them in 8 weeks.

4 To prepare the marinade, in a nonreactive saucepan, combine the oil, water, and wine and bring to a boil. Remove pan from the heat and add the garlic, bay leaves, chilies, oregano, and pepper. Let stand for 30 minutes. Strain (reserving the marinade); pick out and reserve the garlic, bay leaves, and chilies.
5 Place a lemon slice in each of three sterilized quart jars (p.168). Add the olives, then arrange the garlic, bay leaves, chilies, remaining lemon slices, and thyme sprigs in an attractive pattern in the jars. Cover with the marinade and seal. Store in the refrigerator for up to a month. Wait 1 week before eating. Refrigerate once opened.

MAKES ABOUT 3 QUART JARS TOTAL TIME 2 HOURS
PLUS 3–5 DAYS AND 8–12 WEEKS

Pickled baby corn

Nothing is prettier—or a nicer gift—than a glass jar filled with these bright yellow miniature ears of corn, pickled in a spicy brine. The pickles strike a cheerful note when garnishing cold meat platters and sandwich plates, and serve as a crisp accent wherever pickles are appropriate.

- **½ cup sugar**
- **2 cups cidar vinegar**
- **1½ cups water**
- **1 teaspoon kosher salt**
- **1 teaspoon mixed pickling spices**
- **3 cans (14 ounces each) baby corn, drained**

1 In a 3-quart nonreactive saucepan, combine sugar, vinegar, water, and salt. Tie pickling spices tightly in cheesecloth. Add to the vinegar mixture. Over medium-high heat, bring mixture to a boil, stirring to dissolve sugar. Cook 4 to 5 minutes.
2 Pack corn upright into warm, clean jars. Remove spice bag from vinegar mixture. Pour boiling syrup over corn, leaving ¼-inch headspace. Process 15 minutes in a boiling water bath (p.14). Will be ready to eat in 1 week. Refrigerate after opening.

MAKES 3 PINT JARS TOTAL TIME 20–30 MINUTES

◆ Chutneys for Your Table ◆

Chutneys originated in India and are redolent of the spices of Asia. Virtually any vegetable and many fruits—fresh or dried—can be used in chutney, so you might like to vary these recipes to use the produce that is in season or most readily available.

Mango chutney

With its strong ginger flavor, this chutney enhances a spicy, homemade curry.

- ◆ **5 pounds green mangoes, peeled**
- ◆ **1 teaspoon kosher salt**
- ◆ **1¼ cups cider vinegar**
- ◆ **1¼ cups apple cider**
- ◆ **1 tablespoon fresh ginger, chopped**
- ◆ **2 teaspoons ground red pepper**
- ◆ **1 large onion, chopped**
- ◆ **1½ cups dark brown sugar**

1 Dice the mangoes, sprinkle with the salt, and leave for 24 hours. Rinse and drain.
2 Combine the mango pieces and remaining ingredients in a nonreactive saucepan and simmer over low heat for 30 to 40 minutes.
3 Ladle the chutney into warm, sterilized jars (p. 168), leaving ¼ -inch headspace. Process 10 minutes in a boiling water bath (p.14). Will be ready to serve in 4 weeks. Refrigerate once opened.
MAKES ABOUT 6 HALF-PINT JARS TOTAL TIME 1 HOUR PLUS 24 HOURS

Rhubarb chutney

The tang of lemon permeates this quick-to-make mild chutney.

- ◆ **2 pounds rhubarb**
- ◆ **1½ cups golden raisins**
- ◆ **4 cups sugar**
- ◆ **2 lemons, seeded and finely chopped**
- ◆ **1 teaspoon salt**
- ◆ **2 tablespoons fresh ginger, chopped**
- ◆ **2 cups cider vinegar**

1 Wash and trim the rhubarb stems and cut into 1-inch lengths. In a nonreactive saucepan, combine rhubarb with all the other ingredients and bring to a boil. Reduce the heat and simmer over a very low flame, uncovered, for 1 hour or until the chutney has thickened, stirring occasionally to prevent burning.
2 Ladle the chutney into warm, sterilized jars (p.168), leaving ¼ -inch headspace. Process 10 minutes in a boiling water bath (p.14). Ready to serve in 4 weeks. Refrigerate once opened.
MAKES ABOUT 5 HALF-PINT JARS TOTAL TIME 1 ½ HOURS

Green tomato chutney

Pick unripened tomatoes from your own vines, or order them from the local grocer.

- ◆ **4 pounds green tomatoes**
- ◆ **2 medium onions, peeled**
- ◆ **1 large green apple, peeled and cored**
- ◆ **¾ cup golden raisins**
- ◆ **1 teaspoon salt**
- ◆ **½ teaspoon ground red pepper**
- ◆ **1 teaspoon ground allspice**
- ◆ **1 teaspoon curry powder**
- ◆ **1 cup brown sugar**
- ◆ **2 cups cider vinegar**

1 Coarsely chop tomatoes, onions, and apple.
2 Combine in a nonreactive saucepan with the rest of the ingredients. Simmer gently for about 45 minutes or until the chutney has thickened, stirring occasionally. Stop cooking if the chutney begins to dry out.
3 Ladle the chutney into warm, sterilized jars (p.168), leaving ¼ -inch headspace. Process 10 minutes in a boiling water bath (p.14). Will be ready to serve in 4 weeks. Refrigerate once opened.
MAKES ABOUT 6 HALF-PINT JARS TOTAL TIME 1 ½ HOURS

Dried-apricot chutney

Because dried apricots are available year-round, you can make this versatile chutney in any season to complement everything from cold ham to hot curried chicken. Be aware that using dried apricots rather than fresh ones also gives a much more intense flavor.

- ◆ **½ pound dried apricots**
- ◆ **3 medium green apples, peeled, cored, and chopped**
- ◆ **¾ cup raisins, coarsely chopped**
- ◆ **3 medium onions, peeled and chopped**
- ◆ **2 cloves garlic, finely chopped**
- ◆ **zest and juice of 1 lemon**
- ◆ **1 teaspoon each salt, mustard seeds, and ground allspice**
- ◆ **½ teaspoon each ground red pepper and ground cloves**
- ◆ **2½ cups cider vinegar**
- ◆ **2 cups brown sugar**

1 Roughly chop the apricots, place in a bowl, and cover with cold water. Cover the bowl and leave apricots to soak for 12 hours.
2 Drain the apricots. In a nonreactive saucepan, combine apricots with the remaining ingredients, except the sugar. Simmer gently over low heat for 30 to 40 minutes.
3 Add the sugar and bring slowly to a boil. Reduce the heat to a fast simmer and continue to cook until the chutney has thickened—about 10 minutes.
4 Ladle the chutney into warm, sterilized jars (p. 168), leaving ¼ -inch headspace. Process 10 minutes in a boiling water bath (p.14). Will be ready to serve in 4 weeks. Refrigerate once opened.
MAKES ABOUT 5 HALF-PINT JARS TOTAL TIME 1 ½ HOURS PLUS 12 HOURS

Winter chutney

Both fresh and dried ingredients are combined to make this simple but delicious chutney.

- ◆ **1 cup chopped and pitted dried dates**
- ◆ **1 cup chopped dried figs**
- ◆ **1 large green pepper, seeded and finely chopped**
- ◆ **1 large onion, finely chopped**
- ◆ **4 medium tart green apples, such as Granny Smiths, peeled, cored, and chopped**
- ◆ **1½ cups cider vinegar**
- ◆ **1 cup dark brown sugar**
- ◆ **2 teaspoons salt**
- ◆ **½ teaspoon ground red pepper**
- ◆ **½ teaspoon dry mustard**

1 In a large nonreactive saucepan, combine all the ingredients and bring to a boil. Reduce the heat to very low and simmer gently for 1 hour.
2 Ladle the chutney into warm, sterilized jars (p. 168), allowing ¼-inch headspace. Process 10 minutes in a boiling water bath (p. 14). Will be ready to serve in 4 weeks. Refrigerate once opened.
MAKES ABOUT 6 HALF-PINT JARS   TOTAL TIME 1½ HOURS

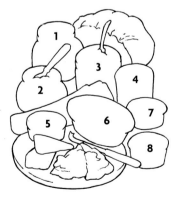

Almost any fruit or vegetable can be transformed into a delectable chutney like the ones shown here:
1 *Spicy tomato chutney,* **2** *Mango chutney,* **3** *Lemon and lime chutney,* **4** *Green tomato chutney,* **5** *Winter chutney,* **6** *Zucchini chutney,* **7** *Rhubarb chutney,* **8** *Dried-apricot chutney.*

Zucchini chutney

Serve this mild and very versatile chutney with cold cuts or barbecued meats.

- ◆ **2 pounds zucchini**
- ◆ **1 tablespoon salt**
- ◆ **1 teaspoon mustard seeds, 6 whole allspice, 6 pepper-corns, and 6 cloves, tied in a cheesecloth bag**
- ◆ **1 sweet red pepper, chopped**
- ◆ **5 yellow onions, chopped**
- ◆ **2 cloves garlic, finely chopped**
- ◆ **1 teaspoon turmeric**
- ◆ **½ teaspoon ground cloves**
- ◆ **1½ cups brown sugar**
- ◆ **4 cups cider vinegar**

1 Cut zucchini into ½-inch slices, sprinkle with the salt, and drain in a colander over a bowl overnight.
2 Combine zucchini and all remaining ingredients in a nonreactive saucepan and bring to a boil. Reduce heat and simmer for 1 hour.
3 Discard the cheesecloth bag. Stir the chutney and ladle into warm, sterilized jars (p. 168), leaving ¼-inch headspace. Process 10 minutes in a boiling water bath (p. 14). Ready to serve in 4 weeks. Refrigerate once opened.
MAKES 3–4 HALF-PINT JARS   TOTAL TIME 1½ HOURS PLUS OVERNIGHT

Lemon-and-lime chutney

This tangy citrus-fruit chutney makes a fine accent to milder-than-curry Middle Eastern lamb and couscous dishes .

- ◆ **4 large lemons**
- ◆ **2 limes**
- ◆ **2 medium yellow onions, chopped**
- ◆ **1 teaspoon salt**
- ◆ **2½ cups cider vinegar**
- ◆ **¾ cup golden raisins**
- ◆ **1 tablespoon mustard seeds**
- ◆ **1 teaspoon ground ginger**
- ◆ **½ teaspoon ground red pepper**
- ◆ **2 cups sugar**

1 Wash and wipe the unpeeled lemons and limes. Chop finely, removing any seeds. Place the lemons, limes, and onions in a bowl, sprinkle with the salt, and leave for 12 hours.
2 Place the undrained contents of the bowl in a nonreactive saucepan and simmer gently until the fruit is soft. Add the vinegar, golden raisins, spices, and sugar. Bring to a boil and simmer for about 45 minutes, or until the chutney thickens.
3 Ladle the chutney into warm, sterilized jars (p. 168), leaving ¼-inch headspace. Process 10 minutes in a boiling water bath (p.14). Ready to eat in 4 weeks. Refrigerate once opened.
MAKES ABOUT 5 HALF-PINT JARS   TOTAL TIME 1½ HOURS PLUS 12 HOURS

Spicy tomato chutney

The flavor of a curry will be more intense if a spoonful of this aromatic chutney is stirred in while it simmers. Serve some more of the chutney at the table as a condiment for the curry.

- ◆ **5 pounds ripe red tomatoes**
- ◆ **5 medium yellow onions**
- ◆ **1 tablespoon salt**
- ◆ **1 tablespoon fresh ginger, chopped**
- ◆ **2 teaspoons turmeric**
- ◆ **1 tablespoon cumin seeds**
- ◆ **3 cloves garlic, finely chopped**
- ◆ **2 tablespoons dry mustard**
- ◆ **1 teaspoon mustard seeds**
- ◆ **1 teaspoon ground red pepper**
- ◆ **1 cup cider vinegar**

1 Cut the tomatoes into quarters and roughly chop the onions.
2 In a nonreactive saucepan, combine the tomatoes and onions with the remaining ingredients and bring the mixture to a boil. Reduce the heat and simmer gently, stirring occasionally, for 50 to 60 minutes, or until the chutney has thickened.
3 Ladle the chutney into warm, sterilized jars (p. 168), leaving ¼-inch headspace. Process 10 minutes in a boiling water bath (p.14). Ready to eat in 4 weeks. Refrigerate once opened.
MAKES ABOUT 8 HALF-PINT JARS   TOTAL TIME 1½ HOURS

Spiced Cherries

The tart and spicy flavor that permeates these cherries makes them a delicious—and unusual—accompaniment to rich game dishes, such as duck and venison. They also go well with hot baked ham. In a glass jar, the cherries make a pretty gift; all you need for wrapping is a pretty ribbon bow and a gift card.

- ◆ **3 cups sugar**
- ◆ **1½ cups cider vinegar**
- ◆ **1½ cups water**
- ◆ **2 sticks cinnamon**
- ◆ **2 teaspoons whole allspice**
- ◆ **1 teaspoon whole cloves**
- ◆ **2 quarts tart red cherries, pitted**

1 In a 6-quart nonreactive saucepan, combine sugar, vinegar, and water. Tie cinnamon sticks, allspice, and cloves tightly in cheesecloth. Add to vinegar mixture. Over medium-high heat, bring to a boil, stirring to dissolve sugar. Cook for 4 to 5 minutes.
2 Add the cherries and return the vinegar-spice mixture to a boil. Cook for 2 to 3 minutes or until cherries are just softening.
3 Remove pan from heat and discard spice bag. Carefully spoon cherries into hot, clean jars. Top with syrup, leaving ¼-inch headspace. Process 15 minutes in a boiling water bath (p.14). Ready to eat in 2 weeks. Refrigerate once opened.
MAKES ABOUT 4 PINT JARS   TOTAL TIME 45 MINUTES

PRACTICAL IDEAS

IT'S FINE TO EXPERIMENT

Chutney recipes are very adaptable, so don't worry if you lack any particular ingredient. If you don't have the dark brown sugar called for in a recipe, for example, use light brown. Experiment with various vinegars. If you can't find mangoes in your local market, try apples or pears instead. You may like the improvised results even better than the original recipe. (Keep notes for future reference.) Chutney recipes are among the few for which trial produces very little error.

◆ Good Tastes in Oil ◆

Olive oil brings out the best flavor of certain vegetables. Although it is no longer considered safe to put up such foods in oil for the pantry (oils can be a breeding ground for bacteria), there is no need to give up these time-honored taste combinations.

Globe artichokes in olive oil

The best time of year to make this recipe is at the tail end of winter—February and March—when small, tender baby artichokes first appear at the grocery store. Herbs to consider using include bay leaves, rosemary, dill, or marjoram. Olive-oil-packed artichokes are delicious in salads and served with strong-flavored cheeses, such as feta or haloumi.

- ◆ **2 pounds fresh young globe artichokes (about 6 small)**
- ◆ **1 large lemon, halved**
- ◆ **4 cups white wine vinegar**
- ◆ **1 tablespoon each kosher salt, dill seeds, and black peppercorns**
- ◆ **2 bay leaves**
- ◆ **2 sprigs fresh herbs**
- ◆ **2 cloves garlic, sliced**
- ◆ **2 small fresh red chilies**
- ◆ **3 to 4 cups extra virgin olive oil**

1 Use scissors to remove the tough outer leaves of the artichokes and to trim off the pointed tips of each leaf. Cut each artichoke in half lengthwise and rub with a lemon half to prevent browning. Place in a bowl of cold water with any juice remaining in the lemon halves. Leave for 1 hour.

2 In a nonreactive saucepan, combine the vinegar, salt, dill seeds, peppercorns, and bay leaves; bring to a boil.

3 Drain the artichokes, add to the boiling vinegar, and simmer for 10 minutes.

4 Drain and dry the artichokes and place in sterilized, widemouthed jars (p.168). Add an herb sprig, half the garlic slices and 1 chili to each jar. Cover with the oil, seal, and store in the refrigerator for up to a month. Will be ready to eat in a few days

MAKES ABOUT 2 QUART JARS   TOTAL TIME 1½ HOURS

Roasted sweet peppers in olive oil

Serve as part of an antipasto platter or as a snack with thick, crusty bread. Use any leftover oil for making salad dressings or marinades.

- ◆ **4 pounds firm sweet red peppers (about 8 medium)**
- ◆ **2 tablespoons coriander seeds**
- ◆ **1 tablespoon peppercorns**
- ◆ **5 cloves garlic**
- ◆ **5 bay leaves**
- ◆ **1 to 2 cups virgin olive oil**

1 Grill the peppers on a ridged griddle or barbecue or broil or cook over a gas flame until

Roasted sweet peppers in olive oil taste smoky and sweet, quite different from the raw vegetable. Mix red, green, and yellow peppers for added color.

the skins begin to blacken.

2 Place in a plastic bag to sweat, then peel off the charred skin. Cut the peppers in thick slices, discarding the stalks and seeds.

3 Pack in sterilized jars (p.168) with the spices, garlic, and bay leaves arranged decoratively.

4 Pour in enough olive oil to cover. Use a sterilized skewer to expel air bubbles from the oil.

5 Seal and store in the refrigerator for up to 1 month. Ready to eat within a few days.

MAKES 3 HALF-PINT JARS   TOTAL TIME ½ HOUR

◆ A Spot of Jam ◆

What better way to use your own seasonal fruit than by making it into jam?
It's the perfect method for keeping summer on the table year-round. Use ripe fruit for the best flavor,
even if you must add pectin to ensure that the jam sets properly.

Strawberry jam

If you pick your own strawberries, avoid woody ones because they have less flavor.

- ◆ **2 quarts fully ripe strawberries**
- ◆ **¼ cup lemon juice**
- ◆ **7 cups sugar**
- ◆ **3 ounces liquid fruit pectin**

1 Wash and hull the strawberries. Use a potato masher to crush the berries. You should have 4 cups of crushed berries.
2 In a heavy 6- or 9-quart nonreactive saucepan, combine crushed strawberries, lemon juice, and sugar. Bring the mixture to a full rolling boil over high heat, stirring constantly. Boil, still stirring, for 1 minute.
3 Add liquid fruit pectin; boil and stir 1 minute. Remove from heat; skim off any scum or foam.
4 Ladle hot mixture into warm, sterilized jars (p.168), allowing ¼ -inch headspace. Process 10 minutes in a boiling water bath (p.14). Ready to eat in 2 weeks. Refrigerate once opened.
MAKES ABOUT 8 HALF-PINT JARS TOTAL TIME 1 HOUR

Rhubarb and ginger jam

Lovers of ginger will really enjoy this rich red jam.

- ◆ **5 pounds rhubarb stems**
- ◆ **8 cups sugar**
- ◆ **zest and juice of 3 lemons**
- ◆ **4 tablespoons fresh or crystallized ginger, finely chopped**

1 Wash and trim the rhubarb stems and cut into 1-inch lengths. In a large bowl, layer the rhubarb with the sugar. Add the lemon zest and juice, cover with a cloth, and let stand overnight.
2 In a heavy saucepan, combine the contents of the bowl and the ginger. Bring to a boil and

continue to cook until the jam reaches the gelling point (p.27), 45 to 55 minutes. Use a slotted spoon to remove any scum that rises to the top.
3 Remove the pan from the heat. Stir to disperse the fruit, then ladle into warm, sterilized jars (p.168), allowing ¼ -inch headspace. Process 10 minutes in a boiling water bath (p.14). Ready to eat in 2 weeks. Refrigerate once opened.
MAKES ABOUT 8–9 HALF-PINT JARS TOTAL TIME 1½ HOURS PLUS 12 HOURS

Fig and lemon jam

Dried figs work well in this recipe. The pine nuts are a change from the more traditional almonds.

- ◆ **1 pound dried figs**
- ◆ **4 cups water**
- ◆ **3 cups sugar**
- ◆ **zest and juice of 2 lemons**
- ◆ **½ cup pine nuts, lightly toasted**

1 Wash and roughly chop the figs and place in a bowl with the water. Let stand 12 hours.
2 In a heavy saucepan, combine the figs and water and bring to a boil. Reduce the heat to low and simmer for 35 minutes.
3 Add the sugar, lemon zest, and juice. Stir until the sugar dissolves. Bring to a boil, reduce the heat slightly, and cook for 10 to 15 minutes or until the jam has reached the gelling point (p.27). Use a slotted spoon to remove any scum that rises to the top.
4 Add the pine nuts and stir well. Remove the pan from the heat and stir to disperse the fruit.
5 Ladle into warm, sterilized jars (p.168), allowing ¼ -inch headspace. Process 10 minutes in a boiling water bath (p.14). Will be ready to eat in 2 weeks. Refrigerate once opened.
MAKES 3 HALF-PINT JARS TOTAL TIME 1¼ HOURS PLUS 12 HOURS

Quince jam

Quinces are available in late winter each year. Make this superb jam, and you will have the taste to savor long after they have disappeared.

- ◆ **5 pounds firm quinces (5 to 7)**
- ◆ **8 cups water**
- ◆ **juice of 3 lemons**
- ◆ **8 cups sugar**

1 Wash and peel the quinces, then core and roughly chop them.
2 Place in a heavy saucepan with the water. Bring to a boil and simmer gently for 35 to 45 minutes or until the fruit is soft and pale pink.
3 Add the lemon juice and sugar, and stir until the sugar has dissolved. Increase the heat and boil rapidly until the jam reaches the gelling point, about 10 minutes. Use a slotted spoon to remove any scum that rises to the top.
4 Ladle into warm, sterilized jars (p.168), allowing ¼ -inch headspace. Process 10 minutes in a boiling water bath (p.14). Will be ready to eat in 2 weeks. Refrigerate once opened.
MAKES ABOUT 8 HALF-PINT JARS TOTAL TIME 1½ HOURS

Seasonal bounty to enjoy year-round: **1** *Dried-apricot and almond jam,* **2** *Rhubarb and ginger jam,* **3** *Pear, apple, and citron jam,* **4** *Strawberry jam.*

Plum and pecan jam

Red plums give this jam a wonderful rich color, but the flavor is just as good if you use the yellow or green varieties of plums.

- 4 pounds plums
- 4 cups sugar
- zest and juice of 1 lemon
- 1 cup water
- ½ cup pecans, roughly chopped

1 Wash the plums and cut in half, discarding the stones. Place in a large bowl and sprinkle with half the sugar. Cover with a cloth and let stand for 12 hours.
2 Place the contents of the bowl in a heavy nonreactive saucepan and add the zest, juice, and water. Place the pan over moderate heat and simmer for about 20 minutes, or until the plums are tender when tested.
3 Stir in the remaining sugar, bring to a boil, and cook rapidly for 30 to 35 minutes or until the jam reaches the gelling point (box, right, and facing page). Use a slotted spoon to remove any scum that rises to the top.
4 Add pecans. Stir to distribute fruit and nuts. Ladle into warm, sterilized jars (p.168), allowing ¼ -inch headspace. Process 10 minutes in a boiling water bath (p.14). Will be ready to eat in about 2 weeks. Refrigerate once opened.
MAKES ABOUT 7 HALF-PINT JARS   TOTAL TIME 1 ½ HOURS PLUS 12 HOURS

Brandied carrot jam

Once called "poor man's marmalade," this jam is a bright orange color. The brandy helps it to keep.

- 2 pounds carrots (9 to 10 large)
- sugar, 1 cup for every 1 cup carrot pulp
- juice and zest of 1 lemon
- 3 tablespoons blanched slivered almonds
- 2 tablespoons brandy

1 Wash, peel, and roughly chop the carrots. In a large saucepan, barely cover with water and cook for 8 to 10 minutes, or until just soft.

SUCCESSFUL JAMS AND MARMALADES

THREE components are necessary for making jams and marmalades successfully: pectin, acid, and sugar, which must always be in correct proportions. **Pectin** occurs naturally in fruits and is released when the fruit is boiled. Some fruits have more pectin than others, which is the reason high-pectin fruits, such as apples, are added to some jams where the pectin would otherwise be low. Other high-pectin fruits include currants and tart red plums; fruits with more moderate pectin include raspberries, blueberries, peaches, and apricots. The pith of citrus fruits contains pectin. With other fruits, the peel and seeds are included in recipes because of their pectin. Commercial gelling pectins—powdered and liquid—are available from health-food stores and some supermarkets. It's a good idea to have some on hand to avoid anxiety about jam not gelling. Follow package instructions, because the two kinds work differently. In general, powdered pectin is added before the sugar, liquid pectin, after all other ingredients. Using commercial pectin may cut down on cooking time.

Acid helps extract pectin and aids in gelling. It also improves flavor and color of jams and marmalades. Acid is added in the form of either lemon juice or tartaric acid.

Sugar—beet or cane—helps to make the mixture gel, brings out the flavor of the fruit, and acts as a preservative.

To test jellies and jams for the **gelling point**, you can use the plate test (facing page) or a candy thermometer. First, however, you must establish the exact gelling point for your elevation. To do that, find out what the boiling point for water is in your area. Hold a candy thermometer vertically in a pot of boiling water and read the temperature at eye level. Add 8°F for the gelling point. At sea level—and usually up to 1,000 feet above—the boiling point is 212°F: the gelling point is 220°F.

Make jams and marmalades in small batches. If you double a recipe, the fruit mixture will cook at a different rate and the timing may be off, preventing the mixture from gelling properly.

---

2 Drain the carrots, and puree in a blender. Measure the pulp, add the appropriate amount of sugar, and stir to combine. Add lemon juice.
3 In a heavy nonreactive saucepan, bring mixture to a boil, reduce heat, and cook, stirring occasionally, for 40 to 45 minutes or until jam has reached the gelling point (box, left, and facing page). Use a slotted spoon to remove any scum that rises.
4 Add lemon zest, almonds, and brandy; stir well to disperse the nuts. Ladle into warm, sterilized jars (p.168), allowing ¼ -inch headspace. Process 10 minutes in a boiling water bath (p.14). Will be ready to eat in 2 weeks. Refrigerate once opened.
MAKES ABOUT 4 HALF-PINT JARS   TOTAL TIME 1 ½ HOURS

Pear, apple, and citron jam

Citron peel is available at specialty stores. Candied peel of other citrus fruits can be substituted.

- 6 medium pears
- 6 medium apples
- juice and zest of 2 lemons
- 4 cups sugar
- 2 tablespoons ginger, finely chopped
- ¼ cup candied citron peel, finely chopped

1 Wash, peel, core, and finely chop the pears and apples and place in a bowl. Pour the lemon juice over the top, tossing thoroughly to keep the fruit from discoloring. Stir in the zest and sprinkle the sugar over the fruit. Cover and leave for at least 12 hours.
2 In a heavy nonreactive saucepan, combine the fruit mixture with the ginger. Bring to a boil and then simmer, stirring occasionally, for 30 minutes, or until the mixture reaches the gelling point (box, left, and facing page). Use a slotted spoon to remove any scum that rises to the top.
3 Add the citron peel and stir to distribute the fruit. Ladle into warm, sterilized jars (p.168), allowing ¼ -inch headspace. Process 10 minutes in a boiling water bath (p.14). Will be ready to eat in 2 weeks. Refrigerate once opened.
MAKES 6 HALF-PINT JARS   TOTAL TIME 1 ½ HOURS PLUS 12 HOURS

Dried-apricot and almond jam

Use best-quality dried apricots when making this jam. The almonds give it texture.

- ◆ **1 pound dried apricots**
- ◆ **6 cups water**
- ◆ **zest and juice of 2 lemons**
- ◆ **6 cups sugar**
- ◆ **½ cup blanched slivered almonds**

1 Wash and roughly chop the apricots and soak in the water for about 8 hours.
2 Put the apricots and any unabsorbed liquid in a heavy nonreactive saucepan with the lemon zest and juice, and bring to a boil. Reduce the heat and simmer, covered, for 20 to 30 minutes or until the apricots are soft.
3 Add the sugar and bring to a boil again, stirring until the sugar has dissolved. Reduce heat and simmer, uncovered, stirring occasionally, for 30 minutes or until the jam reaches the gelling point (below). Use a slotted spoon to remove any scum that rises to the top.
4 Remove the pan from the heat and stir in the almonds. Ladle into warm, sterilized jars (p.168), allowing ¼ -inch headspace. Process 10 minutes in a boiling water bath (p.14). Ready to eat in 2 weeks. Refrigerate once opened.

MAKES ABOUT 6 HALF-PINT JARS   TOTAL TIME 1 ½ HOURS PLUS 8 HOURS

Lime curd

Delicious as a pie filling or a between-layer spread for cakes, lime curd can also be served with cream cheese on a bread round to make an unusual open-faced tea sandwich.

- ◆ **zest and juice of 4 limes**
- ◆ **1 ½ cups sugar**
- ◆ **½ cup unsalted butter**
- ◆ **4 large eggs, beaten**

1 In the top of a double boiler, combine the zest, sugar, butter, and eggs. Stir over low heat until the butter has melted and the sugar has dissolved.
2 Once the sugar has dissolved, add the lime juice. Increase the heat a little and cook, stirring constantly, until the curd has thickened enough to coat the back of a metal spoon, 8 to 10 minutes.
3 If not using immediately, ladle the mixture into warm, sterilized jars (p.168) and seal. The curd can be stored unopened in the refrigerator for 1 month. Once opened, use within 2 weeks.

MAKES 2 HALF-PINT JARS   TOTAL TIME 30 MINUTES

VARIATIONS For lemon or orange curd, simply replace the lime juice with the same quantity of lemon juice and lemon zest or orange juice and orange zest.

Apple butter

Makes a most welcome gift for friends, who may not have tasted apple butter since childhood. Use ripe, tart cooking apples, such as Granny Smiths or Northern Spies, for the best flavor.

- ◆ **6 pounds apples**
- ◆ **6 cups apple juice**
- ◆ **3 cups sugar**
- ◆ **2 teaspoons ground cinnamon**
- ◆ **1 ½ teaspoon ground cloves**
- ◆ **½ teaspoon ground allspice**

1 Wash, quarter, and core the apples. In a large, heavy saucepan, combine the apples and apple juice and bring to a boil. Reduce the heat, cover, and simmer for 30 minutes, stirring occasionally.
2 Press the cooked apples through a food mill or sieve and return the purée to the pan. Stir in the sugar and spices and cook, stirring, until the sugar dissolves and the mixture boils. Reduce the heat and simmer, uncovered, very gently over low heat for 1 ½ to 2 hours or until the mixture is very thick. Stir often to prevent sticking.
3 Ladle into warm, sterilized jars (p.168), allowing ¼ -inch headspace. Process 10 minutes in a boiling water bath (p.14). Will be ready to eat immediately. Unprocessed jars will keep, refrigerated, for a month.

MAKES ABOUT 4 HALF-PINT JARS   TOTAL TIME 3 HOURS

MAKING JAMS AND MARMALADES

1 *Place the washed and prepared fruit and any liquid in a large—6-quart or more—flat-bottomed, nonreactive saucepan or kettle with a tight-fitting lid. Bring the mixture to a boil and then cook as directed in the recipe.*

2 *Add the sugar and bring the mixture back to a boil. Keep stirring until you are sure all the sugar has dissolved. Using a long wooden spoon, which is nonreactive to acids, protects your hands from the heat of the mixture.*

3 *To check gelling readiness, remove the pan from the heat and drop a teaspoonful of jam onto a cold saucer. The surface should wrinkle when pushed with a finger. If not, return the pan to the heat, cook a bit longer, and retest.*

4 *Once the mixture has gelled, remove from the heat and use a slotted spoon to remove any scum that has risen. Stir to distribute the fruit, then ladle into warm, sterilized jars (p.168) and process in a boiling water bath (p.14).*

◆ A Wealth of Marmalades ◆

*Citrus comes gloriously into its own in this selection of both traditional and inventive spreads
for the breakfast table. If you have your own citrus trees, you will have no trouble using up surplus
fruit when you dedicate it to experimenting with these delightful recipes.*

Kumquat marmalade
*This marmalade is delicious on toast and also
makes a fine accompaniment to a baked ham.*

- ◆ **2 pounds kumquats**
- ◆ **2 cups water**
- ◆ **4 cups sugar**
- ◆ **juice of 2 lemons**

1 Wash and slice the kumquats, reserving the
seeds. In a heavy nonreactive saucepan, combine fruit with 1½ cups water and bring liquid
to a boil. Reduce the heat and simmer, covered,
for 10 minutes. Allow kumquats and water to
stand, covered, overnight. Place the kumquat
seeds in a small bowl, cover with ½ cup water,
and let stand overnight.
2 Strain the liquid from the seeds and add to
the saucepan. Discard the seeds. Bring the
kumquat mixture to a boil, then lower the heat
and simmer for 30 minutes.
3 Add the sugar and lemon juice and stir until
the sugar has dissolved. Simmer for 1 hour or
until the jam reaches the gelling point (p.27).
Use a slotted spoon to remove any scum.
4 Ladle into warm, sterilized jars (p.168), allowing ¼ -inch headspace. Process 10 minutes
in a boiling water bath (p.14). Will be ready to
eat in 2 weeks. Refrigerate once opened.
MAKES ABOUT 4 HALF-PINT JARS   TOTAL TIME 2 HOURS
PLUS OVERNIGHT

Lime-shred marmalade
*Lime and lemon combine for a delicious tangy
marmalade.*

- ◆ **6 to 8 firm limes**
- ◆ **3 cups water**
- ◆ **4 cups sugar, warmed**
- ◆ **juice of 1 lemon**

1 Remove the zest from half the limes with
a sharp knife, cut into fine shreds, and reserve.
Line a medium bowl with cheesecloth.
Roughly chop the limes and place in the lined
bowl. Catch any juice you can in a cup and set
aside. Gather the cheesecloth corners together
and tie with string to make a bag.
2 Place zest, water, and lime juice in a bowl.
Add the bag, cover, and leave for 12 hours.
3 In a heavy nonreactive saucepan, bring
the contents of the bowl to a boil, reduce
the heat, and simmer for 1 hour.
4 Remove and discard the cheesdecloth bag.
Add the sugar and lemon juice. Stir over low
heat until the sugar has dissolved. Bring to a
boil, reduce heat slightly, and cook for 45 minutes, or until the gelling point is reached (p.27).
Use a slotted spoon to remove any scum
that rises.
5 Ladle into warm, sterilized jars (p.168), allowing ¼ -inch headspace. Process 10 minutes
in a boiling water bath (p.14). Will be ready to
eat in 2 weeks. Refrigerate once opened.
MAKES ABOUT 3 HALF-PINT JARS   TOTAL TIME 1 ½ HOURS
PLUS 12 HOURS

Three-fruit marmalade
*Here is a traditional marmalade that combines
the three most popular citrus flavors.*

- ◆ **1 large grapefruit, orange, and
  lemon, thinly sliced and cut
  into quarters**
- ◆ **3 cups water**
- ◆ **12 cups sugar**

1 Remove seeds from each fruit and tie up in
cheesecloth. In a nonreactive saucepan, combine the cut-up fruit, water, and seeds. Bring to a
boil and cook for 10 minutes. Remove from heat.
Set aside, covered, in a cool place overnight.

2 Bring contents of pan to a boil again; cook
over moderate heat until rind is tender, about
40 minutes. Remove from the heat, cover, and
set aside in a cool place for a second night.
3 The next day, reheat the contents of the pan
and add the sugar. Stir over moderate heat
until the sugar dissolves. Bring to a boil and
cook rapidly for 20 to 30 minutes, or until
gelling point is reached (p.27). Use a slotted
spoon to remove scum that rises to the top.
4 Stir to disperse the fruit, ladle into warm,
sterilized jars (p.168), allowing ¼ -inch headspace. Process 10 minutes in a boiling water
bath (p.14). Will be ready to eat in 2 weeks.
Refrigerate once opened.
MAKES ABOUT 8 HALF-PINT JARS   TOTAL TIME
1 ¼ HOURS PLUS 2 OVERNIGHTS

Apricot and orange marmalade
*The addition of apricot to the traditional citrus
fruit flavors makes a rich-tasting and most
unusual marmalade.*

- ◆ **2 pounds oranges (about 4)**
- ◆ **2 lemons**
- ◆ **1 pound dried apricots,
  finely chopped**
- ◆ **6 cups water**
- ◆ **10 cups sugar**

1 Wash oranges and lemons. With a sharp
knife, remove zest with some pith attached. Cut
the zest into thin strips. Finely chop orange and
lemon pulp. Tie the seeds in a cheesecloth bag.
2 In a heavy nonreactive saucepan, combine
the zest, pulp, seeds, apricots, and water, and
bring the mixture to a boil. Cook 10 minutes.
Remove pan from the heat and leave, covered,
in a cool place for 12 hours.
3 Measure amount of the mixture. Over high
heat, bring the mixture to a boil, reduce the

Seville orange marmalade is one of the great breakfast classics. The thick skin of this variety gives the marmalade a slight bitterness that many people like.

heat, and simmer gently for 1 hour.

4 Discard the cheesecloth bag. Add the sugar—1 cup for each cup of the mixture—and stir until dissolved. Bring back to a boil and cook for 20 minutes, or until the marmalade has reached the gelling point (p.27). Use a slotted spoon to remove any scum that rises.

5 Ladle into warm, sterilized jars (p. 168), allowing ¼ -inch headspace. Process 10 minutes in a boiling water bath (p.14). Will be ready to eat in 2 weeks. Refrigerate once opened.

MAKES ABOUT 10 HALF-PINT JARS   TOTAL TIME 2 HOURS PLUS 12 HOURS

Seville orange marmalade

This recipe works just as well with firm thin-skinned oranges, such as Valencias.

- ◆ **2 pounds Seville or Valencia oranges (4 to 6)**
- ◆ **4 cups water**
- ◆ **juice of 3 lemons**
- ◆ **8 cups sugar**
- ◆ **¼ cup Scotch whiskey (optional)**

1   Wash the oranges and slice thinly, catching any juice and reserving the seeds. Place the oranges and juice in a large bowl and add the water. Tie seeds in a cheesecloth bag and add to the bowl. Cover and let stand for 18 hours.

2   In a heavy nonreactive saucepan, combine the contents of the bowl with the lemon juice and simmer, uncovered, for 20 to 30 minutes or until the orange zest is tender.

3   Add the sugar, stirring until it has dissolved. Bring to a boil and cook for 30 to 40 minutes, or until the marmalade reaches the gelling point (p.27). Use a slotted spoon to remove any scum that rises to the top.

4   Ladle into warm, sterilized jars (p.168), allowing ¼ -inch headspace. Process 10 minutes in a boiling water bath (p.14). The flavor develops even more with added time, but the marmalade is ready to eat in 2 weeks. Refrigerate once opened.

MAKES ABOUT 8 HALF-PINT JARS   TOTAL TIME 1 ½ HOURS PLUS 18 HOURS

Pear and orange marmalade

This marmalade appeals to those who prefer a less bitter flavor than that of Seville orange marmalade. The sweetness of the pears tempers the acidity of the oranges nicely.

- ◆ **4 medium oranges**
- ◆ **1 lemon**
- ◆ **3 cups water**
- ◆ **3 pounds pears**
- ◆ **12 cups sugar**

1   Wash and finely slice the oranges and lemon and cut into quarters. Place the sliced fruit in a bowl and add the water. Cover with a cloth and let stand overnight.

2   Peel, core, and dice the pears and add to the orange and lemon slices. Add the sugar, cover with a cloth, and let stand overnight.

3   In a heavy nonreactive saucepan, bring the contents of the bowl to a boil. Simmer gently, uncovered, over very low heat for 1 hour, or until the pear pieces are soft and the marmalade has reached the gelling point (p.27). Use a slotted spoon to remove any scum that rises to the top.

4   Ladle into warm, sterilized jars (p.168), allowing ¼ -inch headspace. Process 10 minutes in a boiling water bath (p.14). Will be ready to eat in 2 weeks. Refrigerate once opened.

MAKES ABOUT 10 HALF-PINT JARS   TOTAL TIME 1 ½ HOURS PLUS 2 OVERNIGHTS

◆ A Clear Case for Jellies ◆

*Gleaming through a glass jar, homemade jelly—ready for morning toast or to baste a good
piece of meat—makes a lovely and personal gift. You will need a jelly bag, available from cookware
and department stores, to help turn summer's fruits into winter's treats.*

Red currant jelly
*Brush this jelly over a pork loin just before it
finishes roasting.*

- ◆ **3 pounds red currants**
- ◆ **2 cups water**
- ◆ **1 cup sugar for every
  1 cup currant juice**

1 Wash the red currants. In a heavy nonreactive saucepan, combine the currants with the water and cook, uncovered, over moderate heat until the fruit is very soft, 10 to 15 minutes. Remove from the heat and leave until cold.
2 Strain through a wet jelly bag overnight.
3 Measure the resulting juice and pour it into the saucepan. Bring the juice to a boil. Add the appropriate amount of sugar and stir until it has dissolved. Boil for 10 to 12 minutes or until the jelly has reached the gelling point (p.27). Use a slotted spoon to remove any scum that rises to the top.
4 Ladle hot jelly into warm, sterilized jars (p.168), allowing ¼-inch headspace. Process 10 minutes in a boiling water bath (p.14). Will be ready to eat in 2 weeks. Refrigerate once opened.
MAKES 3 HALF-PINT JARS   TOTAL TIME 1 HOUR PLUS OVERNIGHT

Apple and ginger jelly
*Apple seeds are rich in pectin, so gelling an apple
jelly is never a problem.*

- ◆ **5 pounds green apples (8 to 10)**
- ◆ **½ cup lemon juice**
- ◆ **1-inch piece fresh ginger,
  peeled and bruised**
- ◆ **6 cups water**
- ◆ **¾ cup sugar for every
  1 cup juice**

1 Wash and roughly chop the apples (no need to peel or core). In a heavy nonreactive saucepan, combine the apples, lemon juice, ginger, and water. Simmer over moderate heat until the fruit is very soft, 25 to 30 minutes. Remove from the heat and leave until cold.
2 Strain through a wet jelly bag overnight.
3 Measure the resulting juice, pour into a saucepan, and bring to a boil. Add the appropriate amount of sugar and stir to dissolve. Gently boil for 5 to 10 minutes, or until the

*Apple and ginger jelly adds just the right taste of spice
to raisin-bread toast.*

jelly reaches the gelling point (p.27). Use a slotted spoon to remove any scum that rises.
4 Ladle hot jelly into warm, sterilized jars (p.168), allowing ¼-inch headspace. Process 10 minutes in a boiling water bath (p.14). Ready to eat in 2 weeks. Refrigerate once opened.
MAKES ABOUT 5 HALF-PINT JARS   TOTAL TIME 1 HOUR PLUS OVERNIGHT

Grape jelly

When grapes are plentiful, preserve their flavor in this delightful jelly, staple of peanut-butter-and-jelly sandwiches. For a change, you can use green grapes, which, surprisingly, yield a jelly that is a delicate pale pink.

- ◆ **3 pounds Concord grapes**
- ◆ **3 ¼ cups water**
- ◆ **¾ cup sugar for every 1 cup juice**

1 Wash the grapes and remove the stems. In a heavy nonreactive saucepan, combine the fruit with the water and mash with a potato masher. Bring the mixture to a boil and cook, covered, for 10 to 15 minutes. Remove from the heat and leave until cold.
2 Strain the cooked grapes through a wet jelly bag overnight.
3 Measure the resulting juice and pour it into the saucepan. Bring the juice to a boil over moderate heat. Add the appropriate amount of sugar and stir until it has dissolved. Increase the heat to a rapid boil and boil for 12 to 16 minutes or until the jelly has reached the gelling point (p.27). Use a slotted spoon to remove any scum that rises to the top.
4 Ladle hot jelly into warm, sterilized jars (p.168), allowing ¼ -inch headspace. Process 10 minutes in a boiling water bath (p.14). Ready to eat in 2 weeks. Refrigerate once opened.
MAKES ABOUT 4 HALF-PINT JARS   TOTAL TIME 1 HOUR PLUS OVERNIGHT

Herb jelly

Serve this flavorsome herb jelly as an accompaniment to hot or cold roast meats and poultry.

- ◆ **5 medium green apples**
- ◆ **1 bunch herb of choice (basil, tarragon, or mint), tied with string**
- ◆ **zest, juice, and seeds of 1 lemon (discard pulp)**
- ◆ **1 cup sugar for every 1¼ cups juice**

1 Wash and roughly chop the apples (don't peel or core). In a heavy nonreactive saucepan, combine the apples, herb, lemon zest, lemon juice, and lemon seeds. Cover the contents with water. Bring to a boil and simmer for 40 to 50 minutes or until the apple is soft. Remove from the heat and let stand until cold.
2 Strain through a wet jelly bag overnight.
3 Measure the resulting juice and pour it into the saucepan. Bring the juice to a boil. Add the appropriate amount of sugar and stir over a low heat until it has dissolved. Boil for 10 to 12 minutes or until the jelly has reached gelling point (p.27). Use a slotted spoon to remove any scum that rises to the top.
4 Ladle hot jelly into warm, sterilized jars (p.168), allowing ¼ -inch headspace. Process 10 minutes in a boiling water bath (p.14). Ready to eat in 2 weeks. Refrigerate once opened.
MAKES ABOUT 4 HALF-PINT JARS   TOTAL TIME 1 HOUR PLUS OVERNIGHT

Rhubarb and mint jelly

Rhubarb is used here as a change from the more traditional apple. The combination of rhubarb and mint makes a distinctive jelly that goes well with roast lamb.

- ◆ **2 pounds rhubarb stems**
- ◆ **1 bunch fresh mint, tied with string**
- ◆ **1½ cups water**
- ◆ **1½ cups sugar for every 2½ cups juice**

1 Wash the rhubarb stems and cut into 1-inch lengths. In a heavy nonreactive saucepan, combine rhubarb with the mint and water. Cook over moderate heat for 35 to 45 minutes or until the rhubarb is very soft and pulpy. The mixture at this point will seem very watery. Remove from the heat and leave until cold.
2 Strain through a wet jelly bag overnight.
3 Measure the resulting juice. Pour it into the saucepan and bring to a boil. Add the appropriate amount of sugar and stir until it has dissolved. Boil for 15 to 20 minutes or until the jelly has reached the gelling point (p.27). Use a slotted spoon to remove any scum that rises.
4 Ladle hot jelly into warm, sterilized jars (p.168), allowing ¼ -inch headspace. Process 10 minutes in a boiling water bath (p.14). Will be ready to eat in 2 weeks. Refrigerate once opened.
MAKES ABOUT 4 HALF-PINT JARS   TOTAL TIME 1 HOUR PLUS OVERNIGHT

MAKING JELLIES

1 *Wash fruit and chop. In a nonreactive saucepan, cover fruit with water and cook for the time specified in the recipe.*

2 *Scald the jelly bag by pouring boiling water through it. Squeeze bag well and suspend it over a large nonreactive pan.*

3 *Ladle fruit pulp into the jelly bag and leave to strain overnight. Don't squeeze the bag: you may produce cloudy jelly.*

4 *Measure strained juice. In a clean non-reactive saucepan, combine with sugar and cook to the gelling point (p. 27).*

◆ Favorite Condiments and Sauces ◆

Keep a selection of these well-loved meal enhancers in your refrigerator or pantry.
Condiments made at home are much more flavorful than the store-bought variety. Be creative:
spread mustard on meat before cooking or stir onion confit into polenta for added flavor.

When poured into attractive containers, many of these condiments and sauces make welcome gifts for friends and add a personal touch to the simplest meal:
1 *Red onion confit,* **2** *Marinated goat's cheese,* **3** *Salsa verde,* **4** *Oven-dried tomatoes,* **5** *Tomato ketchup.*

Salsa verde

This delicious mix of fresh herbs, garlic, capers, and anchovies goes well with grilled seafood.

- ⅔ **cup fresh Italian or flat-leaf parsley**
- ⅔ **cup fresh basil leaves**
- **1 clove garlic, halved**
- ¼ **cup capers, drained**
- **2 tablespoons anchovies, chopped**
- **3 tablespoons red wine vinegar**
- ⅓ **cup extra virgin olive oil**
- ½ **teaspoon Dijon mustard**
- **freshly ground black pepper**

1 Place the parsley, basil, garlic, capers, and anchovies in the bowl of a food processor and process until smooth.
2 Stir in the vinegar, olive oil, and mustard. Season to taste with the black pepper. Serve at once or refrigerate, covered, for up to 2 days.
MAKES ABOUT 1 CUP   TOTAL TIME 20 MINUTES

Tomato and basil salsa

This salsa is the natural dip to serve with tortilla chips and the best topper for tacos. It also makes a colorful side dish to accompany grilled fish or chicken. Serve fresh for maximum flavor.

- **1 pound ripe tomatoes, peeled and finely chopped**
- **1 small red onion, peeled and finely chopped**
- **1 clove garlic, crushed**
- **1 tablespoon extra virgin olive oil**
- ¼ **cup fresh basil, finely chopped**
- **salt and freshly ground black pepper**

1 Toss all the ingredients together in a glass or ceramic bowl. Add salt and pepper to taste.
2 Cover with a lid or plastic wrap, and refrigerate for 2 to 4 hours to allow the flavors to develop. Will keep for 2 to 3 days but is best eaten on the day it is made.
MAKES 2–3 CUPS   TOTAL TIME 15 MINUTES PLUS 2–4 HOURS

Tomato ketchup

The fresh flavor of this kitchen staple is vastly superior to that of any commercial product.

- ◆ **4 quarts ripe tomatoes (about 24), peeled, cored, and chopped**
- ◆ **1 large onion, chopped**
- ◆ **1 large sweet red pepper, chopped**
- ◆ **1 ½ teaspoons celery seed**
- ◆ **1 teaspoon mustard seed**
- ◆ **1 teaspoon whole allspice**
- ◆ **1 stick cinnamon**
- ◆ **1 cup sugar**
- ◆ **1 tablespoon salt**
- ◆ **1 ½ cups vinegar**
- ◆ **1 tablespoon paprika**

1 In a nonreactive saucepan, cook tomatoes, onion, and pepper over medium heat until soft. Press through a food mill or sieve.
2 Return to pan and cook rapidly until thick (volume is reduced by half), about 1 hour.
3 Tie whole spices in a cheesecloth bag and add with sugar and salt to tomato mixture. Cook gently about 25 minutes, stirring frequently.
4 Add vinegar and paprika; cook until thick. Stir frequently to prevent sticking.
5 Ladle mixture into hot, sterilized jars (p.168), leaving ⅛ -inch head space. Process 10 minutes in a boiling water bath (p.14). Ready to serve in 1 week Refrigerate once opened.

MAKES 3 PINT JARS TOTAL TIME 2 ½ HOURS

Oven-dried tomatoes

These bring a lighter flavor to sauces and pasta salads than commercial sun-dried tomatoes.

- ◆ **2 pounds ripe Italian plum or large cherry tomatoes, halved**
- ◆ **¼ cup kosher salt**
- ◆ **¼ teaspoon freshly ground pepper**
- ◆ **2 tablespoons dried marjoram**
- ◆ **olive oil, to cover**

1 Preheat the oven to warm (below 200°F).
2 Remove the seeds from the tomato halves, but not the fibrous tissue. Place tomatoes, cut side up, on a baking sheet lined with aluminum foil. Sprinkle with salt, pepper, and marjoram,

then place in the oven and leave for 12 hours. You want to dry, not cook, the tomatoes; if they are drying out too quickly, prop open the oven door a little. The tomatoes will darken and wrinkle. Small tomatoes may take only 12 hours, but large ones may need up to 24 hours.
3 Pack the tomatoes in warm, sterilized jars (p.168) and cover with olive oil. Seal, allow to cool, and store in the refrigerator for up to a month. The tomatoes are ready to eat immediately. Refrigerate once opened.

MAKES 2 HALF-PINT JARS TOTAL TIME 45 MINUTES PLUS 12–24 HOURS

VARIATION Try drying green, sweet red, or sweet yellow peppers in the same way. Cut the peppers into quarters after seeding.

Red onion confit

A tasty condiment for cheese or roasted meat.

- ◆ **3 tablespoons olive oil**
- ◆ **2 pounds red onions, peeled and sliced**
- ◆ **½ cup sugar**
- ◆ **1 teaspoon kosher salt**
- ◆ **½ teaspoon black pepper, freshly ground**
- ◆ **4 tablespoons balsamic or sherry vinegar**
- ◆ **1 cup red wine**

1 In a nonreactive saucepan, heat the oil. Add the onion slices and cook over moderate heat for about 20 minutes, stirring occasionally.
2 Stir in the sugar, salt, and pepper. Reduce heat to the lowest setting, cover the saucepan, and cook for 10 minutes. Put the saucepan on a heat diffuser if the heat is too high.
3 Stir in the vinegar and wine, and cook, uncovered, 20 to 30 minutes, stirring at regular intervals, until the mixture has the consistency of chutney. Use a spoon to remove any scum that rises to the top.
4 Ladle into hot sterilized jars (p.168), allowing ¼ -inch headspace and process 10 minutes in a boiling water bath (p.14). Will be ready to serve in 4 weeks. Refrigerate once opened.

MAKES 2 HALF-PINT JARS TOTAL TIME 1 ½ HOURS

Orange and almond oil dressing

Try this light dressing on baby spinach leaves and Spanish onion slices for a special salad treat.

- ◆ **3 tablespoons orange juice**
- ◆ **4 tablespoons almond oil**
- ◆ **2 tablespoons canola or sunflower oil or light olive oil**
- ◆ **salt and black pepper, freshly ground**

1 Place the orange juice and oils in a small bowl and whisk together until well emulsified. Add salt and pepper to taste, then whisk again.
2 Pour into a glass jar or bottle with a screwtop lid. Use immediately or refrigerate for up to a week. Bring to room temperature and shake well before using.

MAKES ABOUT ½ CUP TOTAL TIME 10 MINUTES

Flavored oils

Make only small quantities of flavored oils at a time, as they are perishable. Use herbs that don't contain much moisture, such as rosemary, thyme, or summer savory, or spices, such as coriander seeds or chilies.

- ◆ **several sprigs herbs or spices of choice**
- ◆ **olive oil, enough to fill chosen bottle or bottles**

1 Lightly bruise the herbs or the spices by gently pressing down on them with a rolling pin, just enough to release the flavor. In a saucepan, heat the olive oil over a low flame, add the herbs or spices, and leave for several minutes. Lift out the herbs or spices and pack in sterilized bottles (p.168), then fill with the oil.
2 Seal and store in the refrigerator for at least 2 days to let the herbs or spices infuse.
3 Strain into a second set of sterilized bottles; discard the herbs or spices. Add a fresh sprig for decoration, then seal. Store in the refrigerator for up to 1 month. Ready to use right away. Refrigerate after opening.

TOTAL TIME 15 MINUTES PLUS 2 DAYS

Flavored vinegars

For best results, use only a good-quality vinegar to make these flavored versions.

- ◆ **several sprigs herbs of choice**
- ◆ **vinegar, enough to fill chosen bottle or bottles**

1 Lightly bruise herbs with a rolling pin and pack them into hot, sterilized bottles (p.168).

2 Bring the vinegar to a boil and pour over the herbs in the bottles.

3 Seal and place on a sunny windowsill for at least 2 weeks to infuse the flavors, turning each bottle daily.

4 Strain the vinegar into a second set of sterilized bottles and discard the herbs. Add a fresh sprig for decoration, and seal. Store in a cool, dark place; flavored vinegars last up to a year. Will be ready to use in 2 weeks. Refrigerate after opening.

TOTAL TIME 30 MINUTES PLUS 2 WEEKS

VARIATIONS Combine white wine vinegar with hot chilies, or lemon slices and fennel, or orange zest and white peppercorns, or nasturtium flowers and a few nasturtium leaves. With red wine vinegar, try fresh sage leaves, or shallots and green peppercorns. With cider vinegar, try mashed blackberries.

An attractive selection of flavored oils and vinegars to give to your friends or enjoy at your own table:
1 *Lemon zest and peppercorn-flavored vinegar,*
2 *Orange zest-flavored vinegar,* **3** *Herb-flavored oil,*
4 *Nasturtium-flavored vinegar,* **5** *Shallot and green peppercorn vinegar,* **6** *Chili oil.*

Honey mustard

This mustard has a wonderful bite and freshness. Buy your mustard seeds at a health-food store, where they are sold in bulk .

- ◆ **2 cups mustard seeds (black or white, or a mixture of both), 1 cup of which are ground in a spice mill**
- ◆ **¾ to 1 cup white wine vinegar**
- ◆ **½ cup honey**
- ◆ **1 teaspoon salt**

1 Mix all the ingredients together in a bowl until thoroughly combined. Leave for 2 hours.
2 Stir briskly again, adding more vinegar if the mustard has dried out. Ladle into warm, sterilized jars (p.168) and seal. Store in a cool, dark place for up to 1 year. Will be ready to serve in 2 weeks. Refrigerate after opening.
MAKES 2 HALF-PINT JARS   TOTAL TIME 2 ¼ HOURS AND 2 WEEKS

VARIATIONS Use half the honey and add 2 tablespoons freshly chopped tarragon.

Aïoli

Aïoli, a Mediterranean garlic mayonnaise, is traditionally served with poached fish. Made from scratch in the happy days before salmonella put raw egg yolks off-limits, it is still delicious made with pasteurized store-bought mayonnaise.

- ◆ **4 cloves garlic, halved**
- ◆ **1 cup commercial mayonnaise**
- ◆ **pinch of sugar**
- ◆ **½ teaspoon ground red pepper**

Put garlic cloves in a blender or the work bowl of a food processor and process until the garlic is pureed. Add the mayonnaise, sugar and pepper and process just until blended. Serve at once or refrigerate for up to 1 week. Tastes best at room temperature.
MAKES 1 CUP   TOTAL TIME 10 MINUTES

Garlic lovers will relish the warm bite of aïoli as a dip for crisp raw vegetables.

Marinated goat cheese

Goat cheese, or chèvre, *from the deli takes on a flavorful new dimension when marinated in olive oil with fresh herbs. Multiply the recipe to make as many cheeses as you like.*

- ◆ **1 goat cheese (3 to 4 ounces)**
- ◆ **¼ teaspoon mixed peppercorns (black, white, or green)**
- ◆ **⅛ teaspoon coriander seeds, crushed**
- ◆ **sprigs thyme, rosemary, fennel**
- ◆ **1 fresh bay leaf**
- ◆ **1 small red chili**
- ◆ **1 clove garlic**
- ◆ **½ cup olive oil**

1 Pack the goat cheese in a sterilized, wide-mouthed jar (p.168) with the spices, herbs, chili pepper, and garlic tucked around it.
2 Pour in the oil and seal the jar well. Store in the refrigerator up to 1 month. Will be ready in 1 week. Refrigerate once opened.
MAKES 1 CHEESE   TOTAL TIME 10 MINUTES PLUS 1 WEEK

VARIATIONS A range of Mediterranean-style cheeses can be marinated in the same way. Instead of *chèvre*, use about 4 ounces of *bocconcini* (fresh baby mozzarella) or cubes of feta. It is best to make small amounts at a time because none can be kept longer than a month. Marinated cheeses are delicious when served on a mixed-appetizer platter with pita bread, marinated pickled olives (p.19), hummus (p.40), and baba ghanoush (p.40). Remember: once the cheese is eaten, you can use the leftover flavored oil for cooking and for adding interest to salad dressings.

◆ A Touch of Ethnic Spice ◆

There's a world of exiting flavor in these condiments from Asia, Africa, and the Caribbean.
Making them yourself allows you to benefit from the freshest ingredients and to use only those herbs
and spices you find most pleasing to the palate

Vindaloo paste

Indian curry pastes may be available commercially these days, but once you've made your own, you'll see how much more flavor and zip it has. The more exotic ingredients are available in Asian speciality stores. This recipe is enough to curry 1 to 2 pounds of meat. If you wish, make extra to keep in the refrigerator for future use.

- ◆ **2 tablespoons ghee (clarified butter) or vegetable oil**
- ◆ **2 teaspoons turmeric**
- ◆ **2 tablespoons dried coriander seeds**
- ◆ **1 teaspoon each cumin, mustard, and fenugreek seeds, and white peppercorns**
- ◆ **2 teaspoons fresh ginger, chopped**
- ◆ **½ to 1 teaspoon red chilies, freshly chopped**
- ◆ **1 large onion, peeled and chopped**
- ◆ **3 cloves garlic, chopped**
- ◆ **2 to 3 tablespoons cider vinegar**
- ◆ **1 tablespoon thick tamarind pulp (bottled or soaked)**

1 In a small frying pan over medium-low heat, melt the ghee and stir in the turmeric and all the seeds and peppercorns. Continue to cook, stirring with a wooden spoon, for about 5 minutes or until all the spices release their aroma and start to "jump" in the sauce pan.
2 Add the ginger, chilies, onion, and garlic to the spice mixture, again stirring continuously until thoroughly softened and browned. Don't allow any ingredients to scorch. Remove from the heat and cool slightly.
3 Place the vinegar and tamarind in the bowl of a food processor, process in a brief burst, then add the cooled curry paste ingredients and process to a chunky paste. You may need to stop processing from time to time to scrape down the sides of the bowl so that the ingredients are well blended.
4 Store in a sterilized jar (p. 168) with a tight-fitting lid until needed.
MAKES ABOUT ONE-HALF CUP   TOTAL TIME 20 MINUTES

Spicy peanut sauce

Every Southeast Asian country has a version of peanut sauce. This one, from Malaysia, is particularly good with satay beef or chicken.

- ◆ **1 cup peanuts, roasted, unsalted**
- ◆ **1 bunch green onions, greens discarded, white part trimmed and chopped**
- ◆ **2 tablespoons peanut oil**
- ◆ **1 teaspoon shrimp paste, available in Asian specialty stores, or anchovy paste**
- ◆ **2 cloves garlic, quartered**
- ◆ **2 teaspoons fresh ginger, chopped**
- ◆ **4-inch piece fresh lemongrass, inner stalk chopped**
- ◆ **2 to 3 fresh red chilies, stemmed but not seeded**
- ◆ **juice and zest of 2 limes**
- ◆ **1 teaspoon each ground cumin, ground coriander, turmeric, and ground cinnamon**
- ◆ **1 cup coconut cream**
- ◆ **1 tablespoon soy sauce**

1 In bowl of a food processor, pulse the peanuts with the green onions a few times. In a medium frying pan, heat the oil over medium heat. Add the onion-nut mixture and cook, stirring, for 2 to 3 minutes. Stir in the shrimp paste and cook 1 minute more .
2 Process the garlic, ginger, lemongrass, and chilies with the lime juice, then stir into the frying pan and cook for 2 to 3 minutes.
3 Add the lime zest and remaining spices to the pan and stir over medium heat until the spices release their aroma and the mixture forms a thick paste, about 5 minutes.
4 Mix in the coconut cream and soy, then cook for 5 minutes over low heat. If the mixture is too thick, stir in hot water until the desired consistency is reached. Use right away and refrigerate any leftovers.
MAKES ABOUT 2 CUPS   TOTAL TIME 35 MINUTES

Thai hot sauce

Hot-pepper aficionados may take to this Asian hot sauce that combines fire with the sweetness of sugar and raisins. Use in stews, salsas, and gumbos or to add a dash of fire to dips.

- ◆ **2 to 3 tablespoons ground red pepper, or to taste**
- ◆ **3 cups sugar**
- ◆ **3 cups white vinegar**
- ◆ **3 tablespoons salt**
- ◆ **1⅛ cup golden raisins**
- ◆ **2 tablespoons chopped garlic**
- ◆ **2 tablespoons fresh ginger, chopped**

1 Place all the ingredients in a nonreactive saucepan and bring to a boil, stirring constantly. Reduce the heat; simmer 15 minutes. Remove from the heat and cool slightly.
2 Process in a blender and pour into hot, sterilized bottles (p.168). Seal well and store in a cool, dark place for up to 3 months. Will be ready to use in 4 weeks. Refrigerate once opened.
MAKES ABOUT 4 HALF-PINT BOTTLES TOTAL TIME 40 MINUTES

Plum sauce

Serve this flavorsome sauce with pork or chicken, or drizzle over a rack of lamb minutes before the end of cooking time.

- **6 pounds ripe red plums**
- **5 cups light brown sugar**
- **5 cups white vinegar**
- **2 teaspoons salt**
- **2 cloves garlic, finely chopped**
- **4 tablespoons fresh ginger, finely chopped**
- **½ teaspoon freshly ground black pepper**
- **½ teaspoon ground cloves**
- **½ teaspoon mustard powder**

1 Chop the fruit roughly and discard the stones. Place the plum pieces in a nonreactive saucepan, add the remaining ingredients, and cook over very low heat for 1½ hours.

2 Press the cooked mixture through a sieve. Discard the residue, return the sauce to the pan, and bring to a boil.

3 Pour the sauce into warm, clean bottles (p.168). Process 20 minutes in a boiling water bath. Will be ready to use in 4 weeks. Refrigerate once opened.

MAKES ABOUT 8 HALF-PINT BOTTLES   TOTAL TIME 2 ½ HOURS AND 4 WEEKS

PLEASE TAKE NOTE

HEAT CONTROL

When barbecuing meat that has been marinated for some time in a sauce with a high sugar content (such as the Texas barbecue sauce, above right), watch the meat carefully to prevent burning. The sugar will caramelize rapidly, long before the meat is cooked. To control the temperature, keep the meat away from direct exposure to the coals and turn it often.

Want the flavor of chilies without all the heat? Remove the seeds and use only the flesh. You'll still get some fire, but it will be less intense. Always wear gloves when handling fresh chilies and avoid touching your face.

Texas barbecue sauce

Ask your butcher for 5 pounds of pork spareribs in a slab of 6 to 8 ribs. Marinate in all but 1 cup of this sauce overnight. On a covered kettle grill, using the indirect method of barbecuing, cook the ribs for 1 to 1½ hours, basting constantly with the marinade. Serve with the reserved cup of barbecue sauce.

- **1½ cups tomato ketchup (p.34)**
- **1 cup cider vinegar**
- **⅔ cup vegetable oil (preferably peanut or safflower)**
- **⅓ cup Worcestershire sauce**
- **½ cup dark brown sugar**
- **3 tablespoons prepared mild yellow mustard**
- **½ teaspoon freshly ground black pepper**
- **juice of 1 lemon, plus ½ lemon**
- **1 to 2 fresh red chilies, very finely chopped (optional)**

1 Combine all ingredients, including the lemon half, in a medium saucepan over medium heat and bring to a boil. Immediately reduce the heat to low and simmer, covered, for 20 minutes, or until the sugar has completely dissolved and the mixture has thickened slightly.

2 Use as directed above for barbecued spareribs or as a barbecue sauce for other grilled meat or poultry.

MAKES ABOUT 3 CUPS   TOTAL TIME 30 MINUTES

Preserved lemons

Choose small, firm, thin-skinned lemons for preserving. To use, rinse one lemon and remove the peel. Cut the peel into fine strips and use in Middle Eastern stews, Indian curries, or your favorite casserole. Use the juice in sauces and dressings.

- **10 small lemons**
- **¼ cup kosher salt**
- **2 cups lemon juice**
- **2 cinnamon sticks**
- **2 bay leaves**
- **20 whole black peppercorns**

---

1 Scrub the lemons well. Place in a large bowl and cover with water. Let stand for 3 days, and change the water each day.

2 Drain the lemons and cut lengthwise as if to quarter, but leave them intact at the base. Sprinkle the flesh with a little salt.

3 Pack the lemons in sterilized, widemouthed jars (p.168). Divide the remaining salt and the lemon juice evenly between the jars. Top off with boiling water. Add a cinnamon stick, a bay leaf, and peppercorns to each jar. Seal and store in a cool, dark place for up to 6 months. Will be ready to use in 3 weeks. Refrigerate once opened.

MAKES 2 QUART JARS   TOTAL TIME 15 MINUTES PLUS 3 DAYS

Green curry paste

A popular Thai cooking sauce, this paste goes well with poultry, vegetables, and more delicately flavored meats. To release the flavors of the spices and herbs, fry the paste in a little vegetable oil before stirring it in with a dish's ingredients.

- **4 shallots, chopped**
- **1 teaspoon shrimp paste (or anchovy paste)**
- **3 cloves garlic, quartered**
- **2 dried kaffir lime leaves, crushed or 1 teaspoon lime zest**
- **4-inch piece fresh lemongrass, inner stalk chopped**
- **1 tablespoon coriander seeds**
- **1 tablespoon fresh ginger, sliced**
- **1 teaspoon each freshly grated nutmeg, cumin seeds, and white peppercorns**
- **6 green chilies, seeded and quartered**
- **3 to 4 tablespoons coconut cream**

In a food processor, blend all the ingredients until smooth. Use the paste at once or keep, covered with vegetable oil, in a small, airtight container in the refrigerator for up to 4 days. Or freeze the paste in ice-cube trays, pack cubes in a freezer bag, and use cubes as needed in recipes.

MAKES ABOUT ¾ CUP   TOTAL TIME 15 MINUTES

In Thailand, this red curry paste would be ground for a long time by hand with a mortar and pestle. These days, a food processor cuts the preparation time to a fraction and produces delicious results.

Red curry paste

Part of the pleasure of a Thai curry is making the paste yourself—it's far more flavorful than the bottled variety. This popular paste is quite hot, so adjust the chili content to suit your taste. As with the green curry paste, it's a good idea to fry the paste in a little vegetable oil before adding it to the rest of a recipe.

- ◆ **3 to 6 fresh red chilies, stemmed but not seeded**
- ◆ **4 shallots, quartered**
- ◆ **1 red onion, cut into eighths**
- ◆ **4 cloves garlic, quartered**
- ◆ **4-inch piece fresh lemongrass, inner stalk chopped**
- ◆ **¼ cup fresh cilantro leaves**
- ◆ **2 kaffir lime leaves, finely sliced, plus zest of 2 limes**
- ◆ **1 tablespoon toasted coriander seeds**
- ◆ **1 teaspoon each freshly grated nutmeg, cumin seeds, and white peppercorns**
- ◆ **2 teaspoons shrimp paste (or anchovy paste)**
- ◆ **2 tablespoons vegetable oil**

1 Place all the ingredients, except the shrimp paste and oil, in the bowl of a food processor and process until smooth. A mortar and pestle can be used if you prefer to grind it by hand.

2 In a skillet, over medium-low heat, dry-roast the shrimp paste for 2 to 3 minutes, stirring constantly. Add to the curry paste and process to blend in. Use the curry paste at once or place in a small, airtight container, cover with the 2 tablespoons of vegetable oil, and store in the refrigerator. Red curry paste will keep for up to 2 weeks.

MAKES ABOUT 1 CUP   TOTAL TIME 20 MINUTES

Caribbean spicy meat rub

Massage this spice mixture onto the meat the night before barbecuing.

- ◆ **3 tablespoons brown sugar**
- ◆ **2 tablespoons paprika**
- ◆ **2 teaspoons dry mustard powder**
- ◆ **2 teaspoons garlic salt**
- ◆ **1½ teaspoons dried basil**
- ◆ **1 teaspoon each crushed bay leaves, ground coriander, ground savory, dried thyme, freshly ground black pepper, and ground cumin**

1 In a medium bowl, combine all the ingredients until thoroughly blended. Spoon the powdery spice mixture into a sterilized glass jar with a tight-fitting lid (p.168). Keep in the kitchen cupboard with your other spices; there is no need to refrigerate.

2 To add the spicy meat rub to a marinade or braising sauce, combine 4 tablespoons of the rub with 2 tablespoons vegetable oil in a heavy frying pan and stir over low to moderate heat until the aromas of the spices are released. Then blend the rub-and-oil mixture into the other sauce ingredients.

MAKES ABOUT ½ CUP   TOTAL TIME 10 MINUTES

VARIATION This rub can also be used as a tasty ingredient in a sauce for stews or a marinade for tougher cuts of meat, such as beef brisket or lamb shanks.

◆ Dips and Spreads ◆

Having a party is easy when you serve a selection of foods made from these recipes.
Most of them can be made several days ahead, so you can store them until needed. On the day,
buy chips and fresh breads—and you're ready for any celebration.

Guacamole

Its buttery consistency and typically Mexican flavors (fresh cilantro and hot chilies) has made guacamole a universally popular dip. Contrary to what you are often served, a traditional guacamole contains no garlic and has a chunky consistency, not a smooth one .

- ◆ **2 large, very ripe avocados**
- ◆ **¼ cup freshly squeezed lime juice**
- ◆ **1 large ripe tomato, finely chopped and drained**
- ◆ **2 tablespoons cilantro, freshly chopped**
- ◆ **3 tablespoons red onion, finely chopped**
- ◆ **1 tablespoon extra virgin olive oil**

1 Cut the avocados in half and remove the stone. Scoop out the avocado flesh from the skin, place in a small bowl, and cover immediately with the lime juice. Mash the avocado and lime juice together with the back of a spoon until the avocado has an even, rough-textured consistency.
2 Blend the tomato pieces and all remaining ingredients into the mashed avocado as gently as possible.

A NEW LOOK AT DIPS

Be inventive when serving your dips. Use crisp vegetables, along with pita bread, to scoop up hummus. Stuff cherry tomatoes with tapenade or spread guacamole on ham or chicken sandwiches. Try a little baba ghanoush on a baked potato.

3 Cover the bowl tightly with plastic wrap and refrigerate the guacamole until about a half hour before it is needed. Leave, covered, outside the refrigerator to come to room temperature before serving. Garnish with a chopped chili or a few cilantro leaves.
MAKES ABOUT 2 CUPS   TOTAL TIME 15 MINUTES

Hummus

It's easy to see why this dish is loved from Afghanistan to Algeria. It's equally delicious with raw carrot sticks and toasted pita bread wedges.

- ◆ **2 cups cooked chickpeas or 19-ounce can chickpeas, rinsed and drained**
- ◆ **1 tablespoon extra virgin olive oil**
- ◆ **2 cloves garlic, peeled and quartered**
- ◆ **½ teaspoon ground cumin**
- ◆ **¼ cup tahini (sesame paste)**
- ◆ **¼ to ½ cup freshly squeezed lemon juice**
- ◆ **salt and freshly ground black pepper**

1 Drain the chickpeas into a colander and rinse, running cold water over them
2 Place the chickpeas in the bowl of a food processor with the olive oil, garlic, cumin, and tahini; process to a rough-textured paste.
3 With the motor running, pour in the lemon juice a little at a time. Turn off the food processor once the desired consistency is reached. Season to taste with salt and pepper. Cover and refrigerate for at least 2 hours before serving, to allow the flavors to meld. Garnish the top with chopped parsley or paprika just before serving.
MAKES 1½ CUPS   TOTAL TIME 10 MINUTES PLUS 2 HOURS

Tapenade

Spread tapenade on Melba toast or oven-crisped slices of Italian bread, drizzled with olive oil.

- ◆ **1 cup oil-cured Mediterranean or Greek black olives, pitted**
- ◆ **6 to 8 anchovy fillets**
- ◆ **¼ cup capers, drained**
- ◆ **2 cloves garlic, peeled and halved**
- ◆ **2 teaspoons lemon juice**
- ◆ **3 to 4 tablespoons extra virgin olive oil**
- ◆ **freshly ground black pepper**

1 Combine olives, anchovy fillets, capers, garlic, and lemon juice in the bowl of a food processor. Process until finely chopped.
2 Add 3 tablespoons of olive oil, and process off and on until the mixture is a spreadable, grainy paste. Add extra olive oil if necessary. Season to taste with the black pepper.
MAKES ABOUT 1 CUP   TOTAL TIME 10 MINUTES

Baba ghanoush

Charring the eggplant gives a smoky flavor to this much-loved Middle Eastern dip.

- ◆ **1 large eggplant (1¼ pounds)**
- ◆ **¼ cup lemon juice**
- ◆ **1 tablespoon extra virgin olive oil**
- ◆ **2 cloves garlic, peeled and quartered**
- ◆ **¼ cup tahini (sesame paste)**
- ◆ **salt and pepper to taste**

1 Preheat broiler. Prick the eggplant all over with a sharp fork or skewer and broil 6 inches from the heat for about 20 minutes, turning

every 5 minutes or so until the skin blackens and the eggplant is soft.

2 When cool enough to handle, peel the eggplant and place the flesh in the bowl of a food processor with the lemon juice, olive oil, garlic, and tahini. Process with an off-and-on motion until the mixture is well blended and has a spreadable consistency. Season to taste with salt and black pepper.

3 Cover and refrigerate the baba ghanoush for at least 2 hours before serving, to allow the flavors to develop. To add a dash of color, garnish with a sprinkle of chopped parsley or paprika over the top. Serve as a dip with quartered slices of pita bread.

MAKES ABOUT 2 CUPS   TOTAL TIME 30 MINUTES
PLUS 2 HOURS

Tzatziki

Tzatziki is a well-known Greek dish flavored with garlic and cucumber. It makes a particularly refreshing dip in summer, when it goes well with cold vegetables—baby carrots, radishes, and blanched sugar snap peas—as well as quarters of pita bread. You can also serve it as a dressing for sliced tomatoes, fresh summer lettuces, good Greek olives, and a little feta cheese.

- ◆ **1 medium cucumber, peeled**
- ◆ **2 cups yogurt**
- ◆ **1 clove garlic, finely chopped**
- ◆ **1 tablespoon mint, freshly chopped**
- ◆ **2 tablespoons olive oil**
- ◆ **kosher salt and freshly ground black pepper**

1 Dice the cucumber and dry the pieces well between sheets of paper towel.

2 Stir the cucumber into the yogurt, add the remaining ingredients, and season to taste with kosher salt and freshly ground pepper.

3 Place the tzatziki in a bowl and drizzle olive oil over the top.

MAKES ABOUT 2 ½ CUPS   TOTAL TIME 10 MINUTES

A trio of classic dips, clockwise from top left, are hummus, baba ghanoush, and guacamole. All now enjoy popularity worldwide.

◆ Pasta Sauces ◆

This quartet of recipes showcases Italian-style dishes. One, the fresh tomato sauce, is delicious all by itself—but also serves as the building block for a world of other sauces, from a pancetta-and-onion Amatriciana to a delicate fantasy of salmon and cream.

Fresh tomato sauce

When good-quality, fully ripe tomatoes are not available, use canned Italian plum tomatoes. Overripe tomatoes make an especially rich tomato sauce because their flavor is at its most intense. To peel tomatoes, drop them in boiling water for 1 minute to loosen skins, then into cold. If you use canned tomatoes, include the juice in the recipe.

- ◆ **3 pounds ripe fresh tomatoes, or 35-ounce can Italian plum tomatoes, coarsely chopped**
- ◆ **2 tablespoons olive oil**
- ◆ **3 cloves garlic**
- ◆ **2 tablespoons tomato paste**
- ◆ **2 to 3 tablespoons fresh basil leaves, chopped, or 2 teaspoons dried leaves, crushed**
- ◆ **1 teaspoon sugar**
- ◆ **1 teaspoon salt**
- ◆ **¼ teaspoon freshly ground black pepper**

1 If using fresh tomatoes, peel, then coarsely chop.

2 Heat the oil in a large, heavy saucepan over moderate heat and cook the garlic for 1 minute. Add the tomatoes, tomato paste, basil, and sugar, and bring to a boil, stirring constantly. Reduce the heat and simmer for 12 to 15 minutes, or until the sauce thickens.

3 Add the salt and pepper. Spoon over hot, drained pasta, toss lightly, and serve sprinkled with grated Parmesan if desired.

MAKES 3 CUPS   TOTAL TIME 30 MINUTES

Spaghetti topped with fresh tomato sauce is further enhanced by baby black olives and a generous amount of finely shredded basil leaves.

SAUCE VARIATIONS *Amatriciana* Heat 2 tablespoons each olive oil and butter in a sauté pan, and cook 1 cup finely chopped onion and ½ cup chopped pancetta until the meat is just brown but not crisp. Drain, then stir into the warm fresh tomato sauce. Toss with 1 pound cooked pasta, adding ½ cup freshly grated Pecorino or Romano cheese just before serving.

Radicchio or arugula Shred 1 small head of fresh radicchio or 2 bunches of arugula (washed, dried, and stems discarded). Gently cook ½ cup finely chopped bacon until crisp. Add the greens and, when just wilted, add 2 tablespoons freshly chopped basil and 1 cup heavy cream. Heat through, then stir into the warm fresh tomato sauce. Toss with 1 pound cooked pasta just before serving.

Chicken livers Heat 2 tablespoons each olive oil and butter in a sauté pan and gently cook ½ pound cleaned and diced chicken livers, ¼ cup freshly chopped green onions, 1 teaspoon fresh sage, and 2 tablespoons chopped pancetta over moderate heat for 4 to 5 minutes, stirring constantly. Remove with a slotted spoon, drain, and then stir into the fresh tomato sauce. Pour ¼ cup vermouth into the pan and warm briefly, scraping the pan with a spatula to stir in any browned bits that remain. Stir the vermouth mixture into the warm fresh tomato sauce. Toss with 1 pound of cooked pasta just before serving.

Zucchini Cut 1 large zucchini into julienne strips and sauté briefly in 1 tablespoon olive oil. When just tender, add 2 tablespoons freshly chopped mint. Stir the zucchini and mint immediately into the warm fresh tomato sauce. Toss with 1 pound cooked pasta just before serving.

Baked macaroni Finely slice and fry 1 large unpeeled eggplant (about 1 pound) in ¼ cup olive oil; remove from the pan, drain and reserve. Stir 1 ½ cups fresh tomato sauce into 1 pound freshly cooked and drained, pasta. Put half of it in a buttered, shallow ovenproof dish. Layer eggplant slices on top of the pasta in the dish along with 1 cup equal parts grated Parmesan and fresh mozzarella. Cover the cheeses with the remaining pasta; then shake another ½ cup grated mozzarella over the top. Bake at 400°F for 15 to 20 minutes, or until firm and the top is just browned; let the dish stand 10 minutes before serving.

Salmon and cream Cut an 8-ounce salmon fillet, skin removed, into chunks. Sauté over medium-high heat in 2 tablespoons butter for 3 to 4 minutes until just cooked. Stir in 1 cup heavy cream, ¼ cup freshly chopped chives, and 1 teaspoon capers. When just warmed, stir into warm fresh tomato sauce. Toss with 1 pound cooked pasta just before serving.

Shrimp and fennel Clean, finely slice, and lightly fry half of one small bulb of fennel in 2 tablespoons each olive oil and butter. When just golden brown, add 3 tablespoons water, cover, and cook for 15 minutes. To the fresh tomato sauce add 1 pound raw peeled and deveined medium shrimp; cook for 3 to 4 minutes or until shrimp are pink. Stir in 2 tablespoons freshly chopped parsley and the cooked fennel. Toss with 1 pound of cooked pasta just before serving.

EACH SERVES 4–6   TOTAL TIME EACH 15–20 MINUTES

Basic pesto

Pesto no longer requires a mortar and pestle; the flavor is still wonderful from a food processor.

- 1 ½ cups tightly packed fresh basil leaves
- 2 cloves garlic, halved
- ½ cup pine nuts (raw or lightly toasted)
- ½ teaspoon kosher salt
- ½ cup extra virgin olive oil
- ⅓ cup freshly grated Parmesan cheese
- freshly ground black pepper

1 Place the basil, garlic, pine nuts, and salt in the bowl of a food processor and process until smooth. Gradually add the olive oil.
2 Spoon the mixture into a bowl, fold in the Parmesan, and add pepper to taste. Toss with 1 pound cooked pasta and serve immediately. To store, place in a glass jar, cover the surface with olive oil, and refrigerate for up to 1 week. You can also freeze the sauce for longer storage.

MAKES ABOUT 1 CUP   TOTAL TIME 10 MINUTES

Sun-dried tomato pesto

Sun-dried tomatoes and walnuts make an interesting variation on the usual pesto recipe.

- 1 cup tightly packed fresh basil leaves
- ½ cup sun-dried tomatoes in oil, undrained
- ¼ cup chopped walnuts, raw or lightly toasted
- 1 small red chili, seeded and chopped (optional)
- about ½ cup olive oil
- ⅓ cup freshly grated Parmesan cheese

1 Process all ingredients except the olive oil and Parmesan in the bowl of a food processor until smooth. Then gradually add the olive oil.
2 Spoon mixture into a bowl and fold in the Parmesan. Toss with 1 pound cooked pasta and serve immediately. Or store in glass jar, covered with olive oil, in refrigerator for up to 1 week.

MAKES ABOUT 1 CUP   TOTAL TIME 15 MINUTES

Puttanesca sauce

The flavors of anchovy, capers, and olives permeate this pungent homemade Pasta sauce.

- 2 to 3 tablespoons olive oil
- 2 cloves garlic, chopped
- 3 large ripe fresh tomatoes, peeled and chopped
- ½ cup black olives, pitted
- 2 tablespoons capers, drained
- ½ teaspoon dried oregano
- ¼ teaspoon red pepper flakes
- 2 tablespoons parsley, chopped
- 4 flat anchovy fillets, chopped
- freshly ground black pepper

1 Heat oil in a frying pan over moderate heat; add all ingredients except parsley, anchovies, and pepper. Cook, stirring, until the sauce thickens, about 15 minutes. Pepper to taste.
2 Add parsley and anchovies and cook, stirring, for 2 minutes more. Serve the sauce at once over 1 pound cooked pasta.

MAKES ABOUT 1 CUP   TOTAL TIME 30 MINUTES

◆ Savory Pastries ◆

*Make pie crusts ahead of time and keep extra pie shells in your freezer, packed in aluminum
pie pans. Then you can create a simple, delicious main course or a hearty snack at a moment's notice.
Choux puff pastry is quick to make—and the results can be stored for days.*

Basic pie crust

The amounts given here will make a double-crust pie. If you are making a one-crust pie, see the box below for the proper ingredient amounts .

- ◆ **2 ¼ cups all-purpose flour**
- ◆ **½ teaspoon salt**
- ◆ **1 stick (4 ounces)
  cold butter, cut up**
- ◆ **¼ cup vegetable shortening**
- ◆ **5 to 6 tablespoons ice water**

1 Sift the flour and salt together. With a pastry blender or two knives, cut in the butter and shortening until the mixture resembles coarse breadcrumbs.
2 Stir in ice water, a tablespoon at a time, just until the dough begins to hold together. Shape into 2 equal balls, wrap each in plastic wrap, and chill for at least 1 hour before rolling out.
3 To roll out dough, place one ball of dough on a floured board, flatten it slightly, and roll from the center out in all directions. Make a circle large enough to cover the bottom and sides of the pie pan plus a rim that you can fold under and crimp or flute for an edge. For the top crust, take out the second ball of dough and roll a circle large enough to fold over the pan and make a seal with the bottom

crust around the edge. Make slits or decorative holes to allow steam to escape.
4 To bake, follow individual pie recipes or see Baking Blind on page 46.
MAKES 1 DOUBLE PIE CRUST   TOTAL TIME 1 ½ HOURS

Quiche Lorraine

The traditional quiche from the Lorraine province of France is made simply with rich cream and the bacon of the district. It is delicious, but these days quiche Lorraine almost always includes cheese. Choose a good Gruyère or other Swiss-type cheese. Serve with a crisp green salad.

- ◆ **1 basic pie crust (left)**
- ◆ **6 slices bacon, diced
  and lightly fried**
- ◆ **1 ½ cups light cream**
- ◆ **4 eggs**
- ◆ **½ teaspoon salt**
- ◆ **small pinch each ground red
  pepper and nutmeg**
- ◆ **1 ½ cups Gruyère
  cheese, grated**

1 Preheat the oven to 400°F.
2 Line a 9-inch pie pan with basic pie crust and flute the edges. Chill for 15 to 20 minutes. Bake blind (p.46) for 10 minutes. Remove the beans and paper.
3 Sprinkle the cooked bacon over the base of the pie shell. Beat the cream well with the eggs, salt, cayenne pepper, and nutmeg. Layer the cheese over the bacon and gently pour in the cream mixture.
4 Bake, uncovered, for 15 minutes at 400°F, then reduce the oven temperature to 350°F and bake for 15 to 20 minutes more or until the filling is set in the center. Let stand for 10 minutes before serving.
SERVES 6   TOTAL TIME 1 HOUR

VARIATION To make an onion quiche, substitute 2 large onions, sliced and sautéed in butter until soft, for the bacon.

Tomato herb tarts

These individual puff pastry pies with a Mediterranean flavor make a quick and festive lunch.

- ◆ **1 sheet frozen puff pastry**
- ◆ **½ cup cheddar cheese,
  finely grated**
- ◆ **2 tablespoons Parmesan
  cheese, grated**
- ◆ **1 pound ripe tomatoes,
  peeled and sliced**
- ◆ **2 tablespoons each chopped
  parsley, basil, and thyme**
- ◆ **1 tablespoon virgin olive oil**
- ◆ **freshly ground black pepper**

1 Preheat the oven to 400°F.
2 Cut four or more circles from the sheet of puff pastry with a large round cutter or use a sharp knife to cut around an overturned bowl. Place circles on a baking sheet and bake for 10 to 12 minutes or until puffed and golden.
3 Sprinkle the pastry with the cheeses, leaving a small border around the edge.
4 Layer the tomato slices on the cheese, sprinkling each layer with herbs and pepper. Drizzle with the olive oil and return to the oven for 5 minutes, or until the cheese has melted completely. Turn off the oven and let tarts sit a few minutes before removing them.
5 Serve just warm or at room temperature.
4–6 INDIVIDUAL PIES   TOTAL TIME 30 MINUTES

VARIATIONS Try thinly sliced sautéed zucchini with sliced tomato and black olives or your favorite salami and thin slices of roasted green or red peppers.

From left: Leek and ham flamiche, Tomato herb tarts, and Quiche Lorraine. In France, the ingredients used in quiches vary from region to region.

Leek and ham flamiche

A traditional dish from Burgundy, flamiche is a savory pie that is made with either pie crust or, as here, a brioche dough for the base.

- 1 batch standard brioche dough (p.56), risen and chilled
- 3 medium leeks
- 3 tablespoons butter
- 4 ounces cooked lean ham, cut into fine strips
- 1¼ cups heavy cream
- 2 eggs and 1 yolk
- dash grated nutmeg
- salt and black pepper to taste

1 Grease a 10-inch square cake pan.
2 Take two-thirds of the dough and press it into the prepared pan. Cover and leave to rise in a warm place for 15 minutes.
3 Trim tops and bottoms off leeks, slit each lengthwise, and wash in cold running water.
4 Cut across into half-inch slices. In a heavy frying pan, melt the butter over medium-high heat and add the leeks. Sauté 2 to 3 minutes, then cover tightly and cook gently until soft, about 15 to 20 minutes.
5 Transfer to a bowl. Stir in the ham. Spread the cooled leeks and ham over the dough.
6 In a bowl, lightly whisk the cream with the eggs and yolk, adding seasonings to taste. Pour the custard carefully over the leeks.

7 Take the last third of dough and roll out in a rectangle. Cut into strips and lay the strips over the flamiche in a lattice pattern. Press down the ends of the strips to make a seal with the dough in the pan. Trim any overlap and brush strips with beaten egg.
8 Leave the flamiche, lightly covered, to rise in a warm place for 30 minutes. After 15 minutes, preheat the oven to 375°F. Bake the flamiche for 35 minutes, or until the filling has set.
SERVES 6–8 TOTAL TIME 2 HOURS

BAKING BLIND

THE term "baking blind" refers to the practice of baking an unfilled pastry shell before the filling is added. This is appropriate when the filling doesn't require the same amount of baking time as the crust or needs no baking at all.

To bake blind, simply make a single pie shell as you would normally. Then, instead of adding the filling, line the crust with a layer of parchment paper or aluminum foil, bringing the lining up the sides of the pan.

Fill the lined crust to the top with dried beans (such as kidney or broad beans). Some kitchenware shops sell bags of metallic "beans" made specifically for this purpose.

Place the pie shell in a preheated 425°F oven and bake for 12 to 15 minutes. Remove the beans and paper and return the pan to the oven. Bake for 3 to 4 more minutes, or until the pastry starts to brown and shrink away from the sides.

When the bottom of the crust has lost its doughy look, it is done enough so that you can safely add the filling.

Spanakopitakia

These small Greek spinach pastries are a variation on the larger spinach pie, spanakopita. They make wonderful canapés. To prepare the pies ahead for an upcoming event, follow the recipe to the end of step 4, then wrap the triangles in foil or plastic wrap and freeze. When ready to use, simply place the frozen pastries on baking sheets, brush with oil, and bake until golden.

- ◆ **1 small onion, diced**
- ◆ **2 tablespoons olive oil**
- ◆ **1 10-ounce package frozen chopped spinach, thawed and squeezed dry**
- ◆ **⅓ cup feta cheese**
- ◆ **⅛ teaspoon pepper**
- ◆ **1 egg**
- ◆ **⅓ 16-ounce package fresh or thawed frozen phyllo**
- ◆ **1 stick (4 ounces) butter, melted**

1 In a 2-quart saucepan over moderate heat, cook onion in olive oil until tender, about 5 minutes. Remove from the heat; stir in spinach, cheese, pepper, and egg until mixed.

2 With a knife, cut phyllo lengthwise into 2-inch-wide strips. Place strips on waxed paper, then cover with slightly damp dish towels to prevent phyllo from drying out.

3 Place one strip of phyllo on the work surface; brush the top of the pastry lightly with melted butter. Place about 1 teaspoonful of the spinach mixture at the end of the strip. Fold one corner of the strip diagonally over the filling so that the short edge meets the long edge, forming a right angle. Continue folding over at right angles until you reach the end of the strip. You should have a triangular package. Place the package, seam side down, in a 15 ½ x 10 ½ -inch jelly-roll pan; brush the top of the pastry with butter.

4 Repeat step 3 with remaining phyllo strips and spinach mixture. If not serving the spanakopitakia right away, cover them with foil and refrigerate.

5 About 25 minutes before serving, preheat oven to 425°F. Bake 15 minutes or until golden.

MAKES 36 PASTRIES   TOTAL TIME 1 ½ HOURS

VARIATIONS You can fill the triangles of phyllo with other mixtures, such as chopped and sautéed mushrooms or diced ham and Gruyère.

Pissaladière

This simple dish hails from the south of France. The delicate puff pastry makes a nice foil for pungent Mediterranean toppings. Served with a salad, it makes a tasty light lunch. Or simply slice it and serve small pieces as part of an hors d'oeuvres platter with drinks.

- ◆ **1 sheet puff pastry, fresh or thawed frozen**
- ◆ **2 tablespoons olive oil**
- ◆ **2 medium onions, thinly sliced**
- ◆ **½ teaspoon dried thyme**
- ◆ **2 tomatoes, thinly sliced, or 4 Italian plum tomatoes, thinly sliced**
- ◆ **12 oil-cured or Kalamata olives, pitted and sliced**
- ◆ **6 canned anchovy fillets, cut in half lengthwise**
- ◆ **1 egg, beaten lightly**

1 Preheat the oven to 400°F. Grease a baking sheet and place the pastry on it.

2 Heat the olive oil in a heavy sauté pan and cook the onion slices over moderate heat for 10 to 15 minutes, or until translucent and softened. Sprinkle the thyme over the onion.

3 Spread the onion mixture over the top of the pastry, leaving a border of about ¾ inch. Arrange the tomato slices and the olives over the onion.

4 Arrange the anchovy pieces in a lattice pattern over the onion-tomato filling. Brush the edges of the pastry with a little beaten egg to encourage browning. Bake for 20 to 25 minutes, or until puffed and golden. Serve warm.

SERVES 6   TOTAL TIME 1 HOUR

VARIATIONS Try a topping of drizzled olive oil, sliced tomatoes, chopped basil, and grated Gruyère cheese. Or combine drizzled olive oil, chunks of tuna, sliced, pitted Kalamata olives, sliced onions, fresh chopped oregano, and grated cheddar cheese.

Choux pastry

Choux puffs will keep several days in an airtight container. Fill them with seafood or cream cheese with herbs and serve as hors d'oeuvres. Or use them for dessert, with a filling of whipped cream, custard, or fruit. Note that when making pastry, you should avoid using cold eggs—room-temperature egg whites whip up more stiffly.

- **1 cup water**
- **½ cup butter**
- **¼ teaspoon salt**
- **1 cup sifted all-purpose flour**
- **4 eggs, at room temperature**

1 Preheat the oven to 400°F.

2 In a large saucepan over moderate heat, combine the water, butter, and salt, and bring to a full boil.

3 Remove the pan from the heat. Add the flour all at once. Stir vigorously with a wooden spoon for 1 minute, or until the mixture forms a smooth ball, leaving the sides of the pan clean.

4 Add 1 egg at a time and beat the mixture until it becomes smooth and very shiny. Repeat the process with the remaining eggs. With the addition of each egg, the pastry will separate, but continued beating smooths it (below).

5 Using a pastry bag or two spoons, shape the pastry into small mounds on an ungreased baking sheet. The puffs will triple in size during baking, so use only a teaspoonful of mixture for each mound. Space the mounds an inch apart to give them room to expand.

6 Bake for 40 to 45 minutes without opening the oven door. After turning the oven off, leave the puffs in the oven with the door slightly ajar for about 5 minutes more. This allows the puffs to dry internally, ensuring a crisper product.

MAKES 12 LARGE OR 36 SMALL PUFFS TOTAL TIME 1¼ HOURS

VARIATIONS For cream puffs or éclairs, add a teaspoonful of sugar to the water, butter, and salt mixture in step 2. Use about twice the amount of choux pastry to make large puffs. After the puffs have cooled completely, cut off the top of each with a sharp knife. Fill puffs with custard or whipped cream and replace the tops. To shape éclairs, pipe the mixture from an icing bag fitted with a large, round tip or use a sealable plastic food bag with one corner cut off.

Gougère

This delightful cheese pastry is based on choux paste, to which cheese and flavorings are added. Served warm from the oven with a salad, it makes a tasty light lunch.

- **1½ cups water (or ¾ cup water, ¾ cup milk)**
- **½ cup butter**
- **1⅓ cups all-purpose flour**
- **½ teaspoon salt**
- **generous pinch ground cayenne pepper**
- **generous pinch ground nutmeg**
- **4 eggs, at room temperature**
- **1¼ cups grated Gruyère cheese**
- **1 teaspoon Dijon mustard**

1 Preheat the oven to 375°F. Lightly oil a large baking sheet.

2 In a large saucepan, bring water and butter to a boil . Remove from heat and add flour, salt, pepper, and nutmeg all at once. Stir hard with a wooden spoon for about 1 minute, or until the mixture forms a smooth ball, leaving the sides of the pan clean (below).

3 Add 1 egg and beat the mixture well until it becomes smooth and very shiny. Repeat this process with the rest of the eggs. With the addition of each egg, the pastry will separate, but with beating will become smooth again.

4 Add 1 cup of the grated cheese and the mustard, continuing to beat until the mixture becomes shiny.

5 On the prepared baking sheet, spoon out the dough to make 8 equal mounds in a circular shape (dough will connect during baking to form a ring). Sprinkle remaining ¼ cup grated cheese over the top of the dough.

6 Bake for about 45 minutes without opening the oven door. Then turn off oven, open door slightly, and leave the gougère in oven for another 5 minutes to dry out more. Once baked, the gougère will be firm to the touch, although it may fall and settle a little on being removed from the oven. Serve at once.

SERVES 6–8 TOTAL TIME 1½ HOURS

MAKING CHOUX PASTRY

1 *Place water, butter, and salt in a large saucepan; bring to a full boil over moderate heat, then remove from heat. Add flour, stirring with a wooden spoon.*

2 *Continue to stir for about a minute, or until the mixture forms a smooth ball and comes cleanly away from the sides of the pan. It should start to look "dry."*

3 *Add 1 egg; beat vigorously until the mixture looks smooth and shiny. As each egg is beaten in, the pastry will separate and then come together again.*

4 *Once all the eggs are in, the pastry is ready to be piped or spooned onto a buttered baking sheet and baked. Allow room for expansion.*

◆ Pâtés and Sausages ◆

*It's no wonder terrines and pâtés are popular party fare—they're full of rich flavor and can be
made a day or two ahead of time. Add homemade sausages, sliced and served with a spicy mustard,
to your hors d'oeuvres tray and watch your guests keep coming back for more .*

Ham, pork, and veal terrine

*Here is a simple, classic baked pâté that makes
perfect summer picnic fare. Serve with pumper-
nickel bread or crusty French bread.*

- ◆ **1 pound diced cooked ham**
- ◆ **1 pound minced pork**
- ◆ **1 pound minced veal**
- ◆ **1 clove garlic, chopped**
- ◆ **1 teaspoon dried thyme**
- ◆ **½ teaspoon dried marjoram**
- ◆ **¼ teaspoon ground
  nutmeg or mace**
- ◆ **1 teaspoon salt**
- ◆ **⅛ teaspoon pepper**
- ◆ **½ cup dry white wine
  or vermouth**
- ◆ **4 small bay leaves**
- ◆ **6 to 8 slices bacon**
- ◆ **¼ pound fresh chicken livers,
  cleaned, trimmed, and halved**

1 Preheat the oven to 300°F. In a nonreactive
bowl, combine the ham, pork, and veal. Add
the garlic, herbs, spices, salt, and pepper. Mix
with your hands until combined. Mix in the
wine, then cover and refrigerate for 1 hour.
2 On the bottom of a 9 x 5-inch loaf pan
(or terrine), arrange the bay leaves. Line the
pan crosswise with half of the bacon, allowing
the ends to hang over the edges. Pack half of
the meat mixture into the loaf pan. Arrange
the chicken livers along the center, then add
the remaining meat mixture. Cover the loaf
with the remaining bacon, tucking in the ends
and folding the ends of the bottom slices over
the top of the loaf.
3 Set the loaf pan in a baking dish filled with
enough warm water to come halfway up the
sides of the loaf pan. Bake for 2 to 2 ½ hours,
or until the loaf pulls away from the sides of
the pan and the juices run clear when the loaf

is pierced with a clean skewer or toothpick.
4 Leave the terrine to cool in the pan on a
wire rack. Pour off any liquid. When completely cool, turn out on a plate and cover
with plastic wrap. Refrigerate, covered,
overnight before slicing and serving to guests.
SERVES ABOUT 6 TOTAL TIME 2¾ HOURS PLUS
OVERNIGHT

Easy chicken liver pâté

*This smooth pâté goes well with toast points,
crackers, or crudités. Remember that making
pâtés a day or two ahead lets the flavors develop
and the texture become firm.*

- ◆ **½ pound chicken livers,
  cleaned, trimmed, and halved**
- ◆ **2 tablespoons butter**
- ◆ **1 package (3 ounces) cream
  cheese, softened to room
  temperature**
- ◆ **1 to 2 tablespoons brandy**
- ◆ **1 teaspoon salt**
- ◆ **⅛ teaspoon pepper**
- ◆ **½ teaspoon dried thyme**
- ◆ **⅛ teaspoon nutmeg**
- ◆ **shelled pistachio nuts
  (optional)**

1 In a heavy skillet over moderately high heat,
brown livers in butter for 4 to 5 minutes.
2 Transfer livers to an electric blender or a
food processor; add drippings and scraped-up
browned bits, along with the next seven ingredients. Blend for 20 to 30 seconds until the
mixture is smooth. Adjust seasoning.
3 Spoon mixture into a crock, cover, and chill
overnight. Garnish with the pistachio nuts, if
you like.
MAKES 4 SERVINGS TOTAL TIME 15 MINUTES PLUS
OVERNIGHT

Country pork sausages

*No casings are needed for these tasty homemade
sausages, staples of Sunday-morning breakfasts
and hearty brunches.*

- ◆ **2 pounds lean pork, trimmed**
- ◆ **¼ pound uncooked pork fat**
- ◆ **1½ teaspoons kosher salt**
- ◆ **1½ teaspoons dried sage**
- ◆ **½ teaspoon dried thyme**
- ◆ **¼ teaspoon crushed
  black pepper**
- ◆ **1 small onion, finely chopped**

1 Cut the pork and pork fat into ½-inch
cubes, place in a bowl, cover, and chill.
2 In a small bowl, combine the salt, herbs, and
pepper. Sprinkle the mixture over the meat,
add the onion, and mix with your hands.
3 Place half the sausage mixture in a food
processor and process to a medium-coarse
texture. Remove to a bowl and process the
remaining mixture, adding it to the bowl.
Cover the bowl and refrigerate overnight to
firm the mixture and allow the flavor to
develop fully.
4 Divide the mixture into 10 to 12 balls.
With damp hands, form the balls into small
sausage patties, which you can cook right
away or store between sheets of aluminum
foil, wrapped in more foil or plastic wrap. Patties will keep in the refrigerator for up to 2 days
and in the freezer for a longer period. Always
thaw frozen sausage patties before cooking.
5 Cook sausage patties in a preheated heavy
skillet over moderate heat, 13 to 15 minutes,
turning often, until browned on all sides and
cooked through. Drain off the fat as it accumu-
lates and drain cooked patties on paper towels
before serving.
MAKES 10–12 SAUSAGE PATTIES TOTAL TIME 30 MINUTES

Italian pork and fennel sausages

This recipe shows you how to make traditional Italian sausages with casings. If you prefer not to use casings, simply follow Steps 4 and 5 of the Country pork sausages recipe (facing page).

- ◆ **2 pounds lean pork, minced**
- ◆ **1 tablespoon fennel seeds, crushed**
- ◆ **1 bay leaf, crushed**
- ◆ **2 tablespoons parsley, chopped**
- ◆ **3 cloves garlic, crushed**
- ◆ **crushed red pepper to taste (about ¼ teaspoon)**
- ◆ **1 teaspoon salt**
- ◆ **⅔ teaspoon freshly ground pepper**
- ◆ **4 tablespoons water**
- ◆ **2 to 3 yards natural sausage casing (1¼ inch diameter), soaked in salted water for 2 hours (found at many butcher shops)**

1 In a large bowl, mix all the ingredients except the casings with your hands. Cover, then chill for several hours or overnight.

2 Fill a piping bag with the mixture and fit it with a large, plain nozzle about ¾ inch in diameter. Insert the nozzle into one end of the casing. Holding the casing on to the nozzle with one hand, gently force the sausage mixture in, squeezing it down into the casing. It is easiest to make 2 to 3 sausages at a time, tying them off with string, cutting the casing, and starting again. There is usually enough extra casing for a trial run.

3 Arrange sausages between sheets of waxed paper in a plastic container. Cover with more paper and a lid. Refrigerate for up to 3 days before cooking or freeze for longer.

4 To cook, brush thawed sausages with olive oil, prick once or twice with a fork, and grill until cooked through, 15 to 20 minutes.

MAKES 10–12 SAUSAGES   TOTAL TIME ¾ HOUR PLUS OVERNIGHT

Clockwise from back left: Country pork sausages; Italian pork and fennel sausages; Ham, pork, and veal terrine; and Easy chicken liver pâté.

49

◆ Super Stocks ◆

Rich and flavorful, homemade stock is the secret to superior soups, stews, and many sauces.
Make your stocks in large batches and store in the refrigerator for up to four days or in the freezer for up
to six months. If refrigerating, leave the fat layer as insulation but remove before using.

Brown beef stock

Ask your butcher, who has the proper tools, to break the beef bones into pieces small enough to fit into your stockpot, which may be a saucepan.

- ◆ **4 pounds meaty beef bones (including marrow and shinbones or knucklebones)**
- ◆ **2 onions, thickly sliced**
- ◆ **2 carrots, thickly sliced**
- ◆ **2 stalks celery with leaves, sliced**
- ◆ **6 sprigs fresh parsley**
- ◆ **2 small bay leaves**
- ◆ **1 sprig fresh thyme or ½ teaspoon dried thyme**
- ◆ **10 black peppercorns**
- ◆ **1 tablespoon salt**

1 Preheat oven to 400°F. Place the bones, onions, and carrots in a roasting pan and roast until bones turn a rich brown, 30 to 45 minutes.
2 Transfer the mixture to a large stockpot; add the remaining ingredients and 5 quarts cold water, or enough to cover the bones.
3 Add a little water to the roasting pan and stir to scrape up the browned particles. Add this liquid to the mixture in the stockpot.
4 Bring slowly to a boil, skimming the surface with a slotted spoon to remove any scum. Reduce the heat, partly cover, and simmer gently for 3 to 4 hours.
5 Clarify the stock (box, facing page) or strain through a fine sieve lined with cheesecloth into a large bowl. Let cool. Transfer to small containers and refrigerate or freeze.
MAKES 3 QUARTS   TOTAL COOKING TIME 5 ½ HOURS

A clarified brown beef stock, garnished here with sprigs of chervil, is luminously clear and very appetizing, a perfect first course for an elegant dinner.

VARIATION Make your own bouillon cubes by cooking the stock down to 2 cups. Cool, put in ice-cube trays, and freeze. Then wrap each cube in foil and store in a freezer bag until you need it. You'll have 12 cubes, each good for a rich cup of soup.

Fish stock

Use this stock in soups, for poaching whole fish, or in sauces for seafood. Don't overcook fish stock; it will lose its delicate flavor. The scallops are not essential, but they enrich the flavor. Use the cooked fish in salads, dips, or spreads.

- ◆ 1½ pounds whole white fish (such as cod, scrod, or snapper), cleaned, scaled, and boned
- ◆ 1 to 2 stalks celery with leaves, sliced
- ◆ 1 small onion, sliced
- ◆ 1 cup white wine or juice of 1 lemon
- ◆ 1 cup water
- ◆ 3 sprigs fresh parsley
- ◆ 1 sprig fresh thyme or ½ teaspoon dried thyme
- ◆ 1 small bay leaf
- ◆ ½ teaspoon salt
- ◆ ½ teaspoon black peppercorns
- ◆ 6 to 7 cups cold water
- ◆ 3 or 4 fresh scallops (optional)

1 Place the fish fillets, head, and bones in a large saucepan. Add the remaining ingredients, except the scallops. Bring liquid to a boil, skimming the surface with a slotted spoon to remove any scum that rises.
2 Reduce the heat and barely simmer the stock, uncovered, for about 5 minutes, or until the fillets are just cooked. Lift out the fillets with a slotted spoon, drain, and set aside.
3 Continue simmering the liquid for 15 minutes more. (Add the scallops, if using, only during the last 5 minutes of cooking.)
4 Remove the scallops, strain the stock through a fine sieve, and cool. Transfer the fish stock to small containers, cover, and refrigerate or freeze until needed.

MAKES 6–7 CUPS   TOTAL TIME 45 MINUTES

Chicken stock

Use this full-flavored stock as a base for sauces, risottos, and easy soups.

- ◆ 5½-pound stewing hen or 2 pounds chicken wing tips, necks, and backs
- ◆ ½ pound chicken giblets other than livers, trimmed (optional)
- ◆ 3 stalks celery with leaves, sliced
- ◆ 1 large carrot, sliced
- ◆ 1 large onion, peeled and quartered
- ◆ 1 leek, halved lengthwise, cleaned, and sliced
- ◆ 6 sprigs fresh parsley
- ◆ 1 sprig fresh thyme or ½ teaspoon dried thyme
- ◆ 1 bay leaf
- ◆ 1 teaspoon salt
- ◆ ½ teaspoon black peppercorns

1 Place all the ingredients in a large saucepan or stockpot with 10 to 12 cups cold water or just enough to cover the chicken bones. Bring slowly to a boil, skimming the surface with a slotted spoon to remove any scum that rises.
2 Reduce the heat, partly cover, and simmer gently until the stock is well flavored, about 3 hours. (The longer it simmers, the richer the flavor will be.)
3 Strain the stock through a fine sieve into a large bowl and cool. Transfer to several small containers, and refrigerate or freeze until needed. If refrigerating, discard the fat layer just before using.

MAKES ABOUT 2 QUARTS   TOTAL TIME 4 HOURS

TO CLARIFY STOCK

Whisk 2 egg whites and crush the shells. Add both to the stock and slowly, with the lid off, bring to a simmer.

When the whites begin to set, pour the contents of the pan through a cheese-cloth-lined colander or large sieve. Particles will be trapped in the egg white.

Vegetable stock

Save your clean vegetable peelings—they can be used to make a terrific soup base for meatless meals. Use this rich liquid to braise fresh vegetables, such as leeks or cabbage, and as a substitute for chicken or beef stock in most recipes.

- ◆ ½ stick unsalted butter
- ◆ 5 onions, peeled and chopped
- ◆ 2 leeks, halved lengthwise, cleaned, and sliced
- ◆ 2 whole cloves garlic
- ◆ 4 carrots, roughly chopped
- ◆ 4 stalks celery with leaves, roughly chopped
- ◆ 6 to 8 dried mushrooms
- ◆ 1 small bunch fresh parsley
- ◆ 1 sprig fresh thyme or ½ teaspoon dried thyme
- ◆ 1 tablespoon salt
- ◆ ½ teaspoon ground allspice
- ◆ pinch nutmeg or mace
- ◆ 4 quarts cold water
- ◆ 1 tablespoon red wine vinegar and 1 fresh red chili, halved and seeded (optional)

1 In a large saucepan over moderate heat, melt the butter. Add the onions, leeks, and garlic, and cook, stirring, for 5 to 8 minutes or until the onions are golden. Add remaining vegetables, herbs, seasonings, and water.
2 Bring slowly to a boil, skimming the surface with a slotted spoon to remove any scum that rises. Reduce the heat, partly cover, and simmer gently for 2 hours, replenishing water if necessary to maintain level at about 3 quarts. Add the vinegar and chili, if desired, and simmer for 30 minutes more.
3 Strain the stock through a fine sieve into a large bowl, gently pressing the liquid from the vegetables with a wooden spoon. Discard the chili halves. This stock can be clarified in the same way as other stocks (box, left). If clarity is not a priority and a fuller-bodied stock is preferred, purée about ½ cup of the vegetables and stir into the stock. Cool. Transfer the stock to small containers, cover, and refrigerate or freeze until needed.

MAKES ABOUT 3 QUARTS   TOTAL TIME 3 HOURS

◆ Quick Breads ◆

*These nonyeast breads are perfect for last-minute treats,
since you don't have to wait for them to rise. Some savory quick breads,
filled with cheese and vegetables, can even make a meal.*

Zucchini and cheese bread

You can bake this savory bread in a loaf pan or in muffin tins. Serve zucchini and cheese bread as an hors d'oeuvre with cream cheese, smoked salmon, and a few capers, or toast slices to accompany a main dish soup.

- ◆ **2 cups all-purpose flour**
- ◆ **1 teaspoon baking powder**
- ◆ **1 tablespoon sugar**
- ◆ **1 teaspoon salt**
- ◆ **6 tablespoons butter, cut up**
- ◆ **1 cup grated sharp Cheddar cheese**
- ◆ **1 cup milk**
- ◆ **1 large egg**
- ◆ **1 cup grated zucchini, squeezed dry in a towel to remove excess moisture**
- ◆ **1 tablespoon grated onion**
- ◆ **1 teaspoon Dijon mustard**

1 Preheat the oven to 375°F. Grease an 8 x 4-inch loaf pan.

2 In a large bowl, sift the flour, baking powder, sugar, and salt. Cut in the butter with a pastry blender or two knives until the mixture resembles coarse bread crumbs. Stir in the cheese.

3 In a smaller bowl, beat together the milk and egg. Stir in the grated zucchini, onion, and mustard. Add the milk mixture to the dry ingredients. Using a fork, mix just until the dough holds together. Don't overmix or you risk making the bread heavy.

4 Spoon the dough into the prepared pan. Bake for 40 to 45 minutes, or until the bread is well risen and brown and a tester inserted into the middle comes out clean.

5 Transfer the bread to a cooling rack for 10 minutes, then remove from pan.

MAKES 1 LOAF   TOTAL TIME 1¼ HOURS

Corn bread

This is a lovely yellow bread, wholesome and delicious. Serve it with soups or stews.

- ◆ **1½ cups all-purpose flour**
- ◆ **1¼ cups yellow cornmeal**
- ◆ **4 teaspoons baking powder**
- ◆ **2 tablespoons sugar**
- ◆ **1 teaspoon salt**
- ◆ **1 egg**
- ◆ **1¼ cups milk**
- ◆ **¼ cup vegetable oil**

1 Preheat the oven to 400°F. Grease an 8-inch square baking pan.

2 In a large bowl, sift the flour, cornmeal, baking powder, sugar, and salt. In a smaller bowl, beat the egg with the milk and the oil. Make a well in the center of the dry ingredients; pour in milk mixture and stir with a fork until well blended. Don't overmix.

3 Pour the mixture into the prepared pan and bake for 20 to 25 minutes, or until the bread pulls away from the edge of the pan and is slightly brown.

4 Transfer bread to a rack and cool for 10 minutes. Cut into large squares and serve warm with lots of butter.

MAKES ABOUT 9 SQUARES   TOTAL TIME 45 MINUTES

Variations on the staff of life: **1** *Soda bread rolls,* **2** *Beer bread,* **3** *Sesame pumpkin bread,* **4** *Zucchini and cheese bread,* **5** *Olive and sun-dried-tomato bread.*

Beer bread

This versatile bread has a malty aroma.

- ◆ 2½ cups all-purpose flour
- ◆ 2 tablespoons sugar
- ◆ 2 teaspoons baking powder
- ◆ 1 teaspoon salt
- ◆ 1 cup beer
- ◆ ¼ cup plus 2 tablespoons butter, melted

1 Preheat the oven to 350°F. Grease and line an 8 x 4-inch loaf pan with baking paper.
2 In a large bowl, sift flour, sugar, baking powder, and salt. Stir in beer and ¼ cup melted butter, and mix to form a soft dough.
3 Spoon the dough into the prepared pan and pour remaining 2 tablespoons melted butter over it. Bake for 40 to 45 minutes, or until golden brown and loaf sounds hollow when tapped.
4 Remove from pan and cool on rack.
MAKES 1 LOAF   TOTAL TIME 1¼ HOURS

Soda bread

You can add a topping of seeds or oatmeal, if you like. Serve with hearty stews and soups.

- ◆ 2 cups all-purpose flour
- ◆ 2 teaspoons baking soda
- ◆ 1½ teaspoons salt
- ◆ ⅓ cup vegetable shortening or margarine
- ◆ 2 cups whole wheat flour
- ◆ 1⅔ cups buttermilk

1 Preheat the oven to 400°F. Lightly grease a baking sheet. In a large bowl, sift together all-purpose flour, baking soda, and salt. With a pastry blender or two knives, cut in shortening until mixture resembles coarse bread crumbs. Stir in whole wheat flour.
2 Add buttermilk and mix until thoroughly blended. Turn out on a lightly floured board and knead until smooth, 4 to 5 minutes.
3 Divide dough into 8 parts and roll each into a ball. Place on prepared baking sheet, spacing 2 to 3 inches apart. Cut a cross into the top of each ball and add a topping if you like. Bake

about 20 minutes or until crusty brown and rolls sound hollow when tapped at base.
4 Cool on a rack. Serve while still warm.
MAKES 8 ROLLS   TOTAL TIME 45 MINUTES

Sesame pumpkin bread

A good autumn bread with an offbeat flavor.

- ◆ 4 cups all-purpose flour
- ◆ ¼ cup sugar
- ◆ 4 teaspoons baking powder
- ◆ 1 teaspoon salt
- ◆ 1 cup plus 2 tablespoons milk
- ◆ 1 egg
- ◆ 1 cup pumpkin puree
- ◆ ⅓ cup butter, melted
- ◆ 1 tablespoon sesame seeds

1 Preheat the oven to 425°F. Grease and lightly flour a baking sheet. In a large bowl, sift flour, sugar, baking soda, and salt. In a smaller bowl, beat together the 1 cup milk and the egg; stir in the pumpkin puree and butter.
2 Make a well in the center of the dry ingredients; pour in the milk-pumpkin mixture and stir with a fork until well blended. Turn dough out on a lightly floured board and knead lightly until smooth, 4 to 5 minutes.
3 Shape into a round loaf and place on prepared baking sheet. Slash a cross in the top; brush lightly with the 2 tablespoons milk and sprinkle with sesame seeds.
4 Bake for 25 minutes, then reduce heat to 375°F. Bake for 15 minutes longer, or until loaf sounds hollow when tapped. Cool on rack.
MAKES 1 LOAF   TOTAL TIME 1 HOUR

Pecan bread

Delicious with fruit and soft cheeses.

- ◆ 2 cups all-purpose flour
- ◆ 2 teaspoons baking powder
- ◆ 1 teaspoon salt
- ◆ ¾ cup pecans, coarsely chopped
- ◆ ⅓ cup light brown sugar
- ◆ 1 cup milk
- ◆ 1 large egg
- ◆ 3 tablespoons butter, melted

1 Preheat the oven to 350°F. Grease an 8 x 4-inch loaf pan.
2 In a large bowl, sift flour, baking powder, and salt. Stir in pecans and sugar. In a smaller bowl, beat milk and egg. Stir in melted butter.
3 Make a well in the center of the dry ingredients. Add the milk mixture and using a fork, blend only until the dough holds together.
4 Spoon the dough into the prepared pan. Bake for 45 to 50 minutes or until a tester inserted into the center comes out clean.
5 Transfer the pan to a cooling rack for 10 minutes, then remove bread from pan to cool. Serve warm.
MAKES 1 LOAF   TOTAL TIME 1¼ HOURS

Olive and sun-dried-tomato bread

A great accompaniment to soup, this tasty bread is easy to prepare on short notice.

- ◆ 2 eggs
- ◆ ⅔ cup milk
- ◆ 2 cups all-purpose flour
- ◆ 2 teaspoons baking powder
- ◆ 1 teaspoon kosher salt
- ◆ 3 tablespoons oil drained from sun-dried tomatoes or olive oil
- ◆ ½ cup black olives in oil, drained, pitted, and slivered
- ◆ ½ cup sun-dried tomatoes in oil, drained and sliced
- ◆ 1 tablespoon fresh basil or marjoram, chopped

1 Preheat the oven to 400°F. Grease an 8-inch springform pan.
2 Place the eggs and milk in the bowl of an electric mixer. Beat lightly, just to combine. Sift the flour and baking powder together and add to the egg mixture. Beat for 2 minutes; then add the salt and oil and beat for 1 minute more. Stir in the olives, sun-dried tomatoes, and basil or marjoram with a spoon.
3 Pour the batter into the prepared pan and bake for 30 minutes or until a tester inserted into the bread comes out clean.
4 Cool slightly on a wire rack. Serve warm.
MAKES 1 LOAF   TOTAL TIME 45 MINUTES

◆ Yeast Breads ◆

Breads that have yeast as the rising agent delight the senses with their scent and texture.
Many home cooks derive enormous satisfaction from kneading and shaping yeast dough;
their lucky families always have fresh bread to eat.

Pizza dough

Use this dough recipe for one family-size pizza or make it into four small rounds for individual pizzas, allowing each person to customize the toppings to taste.

- ◆ ¼ -ounce packet active dry yeast
- ◆ ¾ cup warm (105° to 115°F.) water
- ◆ 2 to 2 ¼ cups all-purpose flour
- ◆ 1 teaspoon salt
- ◆ 1 ½ teaspoons extra virgin olive oil

1 Place the yeast in a small bowl and add the warm water. Mix rapidly with a fork and leave to stand for 5 minutes, or until frothy.
2 Place 2 cups of flour and the salt in the bowl of a food processor, add the yeast mixture and olive oil, and process until the dough holds together; add additional flour if needed.
3 Turn the dough out on a lightly floured surface and knead for 2 minutes. Shape into a ball. Roll the dough around in a lightly oiled bowl

to coat it with oil; then cover with lightly oiled plastic wrap and leave in a warm place to rise for 1 hour, or until it has doubled in size.
4 Remove dough from bowl and press into a pizza shape. When ready to bake, place on a lightly oiled baking sheet or pizza pan and add toppings of choice. Bake in a very hot preheated oven (425°F) for 20 to 25 minutes.
MAKES ONE 12-INCH PIZZA BASE   TOTAL TIME 1 ¼ HOUR

VARIATION You can use the pizza dough recipe to make your own soft pretzels. After it rises, roll dough out in a rectangle ½ inch thick. Using a pizza wheel, cut dough into 1-inch strips. Dust a baking sheet with cornmeal. Tie the dough strips into pretzel shapes and arrange them on the baking sheet. Cover with plastic wrap and let pretzels rise 30 minutes. Preheat the oven to 400°F. In a small bowl, mix 1 egg yolk with 1 tablespoon of water and brush on the pretzels. Sprinkle with kosher salt and bake for 10 minutes or until golden and crisp.

Country white bread

Shape this basic bread into loaves or dinner rolls.

- ◆ 2 ¼ -ounce packets active dry yeast
- ◆ 2 teaspoons sugar
- ◆ 3 ½ to 3 ¾ cups warm (105° to 115°F) water
- ◆ 11 cups bread flour
- ◆ 1 tablespoon salt

1 Place the yeast and sugar In a small bowl. Add the warm water and mix quickly with a fork. Leave in a warm place for 5 minutes, or until the mixture is frothy.
2 Combine flour and salt in a large bowl, make a well in the center, and add the yeast mixture. Mix well, adding a little more warm water if the mixture is too dry. Turn dough onto a lightly floured surface and knead until smooth and elastic.
3 Grease two bread pans, each 8 ½ x 4 ½ x 2 ½ inches, or a baking sheet, if making rolls.

BREAD BOXES

1 *Buy a dense loaf of bread. Using a sharp, serrated knife, slice off ½ inch of crust for the box lid. Cut ½ inch inside the crust all around. Make incision along one side, ½ inch from the base; work knife back and forth to free bottom.*

2 *Lift out the block of interior bread. Cut the block into thin, neat slices with the same serrated knife. Brick-oven-type breads work well for this: they are a good rectangular shape and slice neatly. (Be sure you get the unsliced version.)*

3 *Make the slices into sandwiches with the fillings of your choice . (Avoid bulky fillings, however, or the sandwiches won't fit back in the box.) Cut the sandwiches into squares, triangles, or rectangular fingers, as desired.*

4 *Carefully stack the sandwiches in the box. Replace the lid and secure it with wide strips of ribbon, taped together at the bottom of the box. Alternatively, wrap a napkin around the box and knot it at the top.*

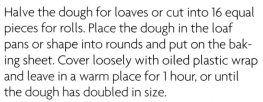

Halve the dough for loaves or cut into 16 equal pieces for rolls. Place the dough in the loaf pans or shape into rounds and put on the baking sheet. Cover loosely with oiled plastic wrap and leave in a warm place for 1 hour, or until the dough has doubled in size.

4 Preheat the oven to 425°F. Remove the plastic and place the pans or sheet in the oven. Bake loaves for 30 minutes, rolls for 15 minutes, or until golden brown.

5 When done, turn the loaves or rolls out on a wire rack and let cool.

MAKES 2 LOAVES OR 16 ROLLS   TOTAL TIME 2 HOURS

Herb sourdough

Sourdough requires a starter—a fermented paste of flour, yeast, and water—that needs to be prepared several days ahead.

STARTER
- **1 teaspoon active dry yeast**
- **1 cup warm (105° to 110°F) water**
- **1 cup whole wheat flour**

DOUGH
- **1¾ cups whole wheat flour**
- **1 cup boiling water**
- **¼ -ounce packet active dry yeast**
- **1 teaspoon sugar**
- **1 teaspoon salt**
- **1 cup warm (105° to 110°F) water**
- **½ cup sourdough starter (above)**
- **4 cups bread flour**
- **½ cup fresh herbs of choice, chopped**

1 To make the starter, place the yeast in a medium bowl and add the warm water. Mix rapidly with a fork and allow the mixture to stand for 5 minutes, or until frothy.

2 Add the whole wheat flour and stir to a paste. Cover bowl with oiled plastic wrap and leave at room temperature for 3 to 7 days.

3 To make the dough, in the bowl of an electric mixer, blend the whole wheat flour with the boiling water. Let this paste cool.

4 In a small bowl, dissolve the yeast, sugar, and salt in the warm water. Add the starter and mix to combine. Blend this mixture into the whole wheat paste, then add enough bread flour to form a smooth dough and the herbs.

5 Turn the dough out on a lightly floured surface and knead for 10 minutes. Roll the dough around in a lightly oiled bowl to coat it with oil, cover with lightly oiled plastic wrap, and leave in a warm place to rise for 1 hour.

6 Preheat the oven to 400°F. Grease a large baking sheet. Halve the dough. Punch each half down and shape into an oval or round.

7 Place the loaves on the baking sheet, cover with lightly oiled plastic wrap, and leave in a warm place for 1 hour or until the dough has doubled in size.

8 Remove the plastic wrap and bake bread for 30 minutes, or until golden. Cool on a rack.

MAKES 2 LOAVES   TOTAL TIME 3 ½ HOURS PLUS 3–7 DAYS

Flowerpot brioche

Traditionally, brioche is made in a large fluted pan, wider at the top than the base. Terra-cotta flowerpots, greased and lined, can be used to make individual loaves.

- **3 cups all-purpose flour**
- **¼ -ounce packet active dry yeast**
- **1 tablespoon sugar**
- **1 teaspoon salt**
- **1 stick unsalted butter**
- **¼ cup warm (105° to 110°F) water**
- **4 eggs**

1 Grease and line six 3 ½ -inch-high terra-cotta pots or one brioche pan with parchment or wax paper.

2 In the bowl of an electric mixer with a paddle attachment, blend flour, yeast, sugar, and salt.

3 In a small saucepan, melt the butter and add the water. Pour the liquid into the flour mixture and mix until the dough becomes crumbly. Add the eggs, one at a time, blending well. Beat dough for 5 minutes or until smooth but sticky.

4 Oil a bowl and scrape the dough into it. Cover with lightly oiled plastic wrap and leave in a warm place for 2 hours, or until the dough has doubled in size.

5 Punch down the dough, knead for 5 minutes, and divide it among the prepared pots or put it all in the brioche pan. Place the pots or the pan on a baking sheet and cover with lightly oiled plastic wrap. Leave in a warm place for 1 hour or until the dough is well risen.

6 Preheat oven to 375°F. Remove the plastic wrap. Place the sheet in the oven and bake the individual brioches for 8 to 10 minutes or the large brioche for 15 to 20 minutes or until light and golden. When done, turn out onto a rack to cool.

MAKES 6 SMALL OR 1 LARGE BRIOCHE TOTAL TIME
3 ¾ HOURS

Seeded whole wheat bread

Any seeds—sesame, pumpkin, flax, or poppy—can be substituted for sunflower in this recipe.

- **4 cups whole wheat flour**
- **6 tablespoons sunflower seeds**
- **1 tablespoon kosher salt**
- **¼ -ounce packet active dry yeast**
- **1 tablespoon plus 1 teaspoon olive oil**
- **1 ¾ to 2 cups warm (105° to 110°F) water**
- **1 tablespoon milk**

1 In a large bowl, place the flour, 4 tablespoons sunflower seeds, salt, and yeast. Add 1 tablespoon olive oil and enough warm water to make a dough.

2 Turn the dough out on a lightly floured surface and knead for 5 minutes or until smooth and elastic. Rub the teaspoon of olive oil over

A few of the breads it's possible to create with yeast:
1 Individual pizzas (Pizza dough), 2 Olive flat bread,
3 Pear and walnut bread, 4 Country white bread, and
5 Flowerpot brioche.

the dough, return the dough to the bowl, and cover with oiled plastic wrap. Leave in a warm place for 1 hour, or until double in size.

3 Punch the dough down and halve it. Knead each half again for 3 minutes and form into a round. Place the rounds on a greased and lined baking sheet and cover with oiled plastic wrap. Leave in a warm place to rise for another 30 minutes.

4 Preheat the oven to 425°F. Brush the loaves with milk and sprinkle with the remaining sunflower seeds. Bake for 30 minutes.

5 When done, turn the loaves out on a rack and let cool.

MAKES 2 LOAVES TOTAL TIME 2 ½ HOURS

Olive flat bread

Here is a perfect bread to offer with drinks and a garlicky dip, such as hummus or aïoli.

- ◆ 2 ⅓ cups all-purpose flour
- ◆ 1 teaspoon salt
- ◆ 1 teaspoon sugar
- ◆ ¼ -ounce packet active dry yeast
- ◆ ⅔ cup lukewarm milk
- ◆ 1 large egg
- ◆ ¼ cup extra virgin olive oil
- ◆ 1 cup black olives, roughly chopped
- ◆ 15 black olives, pitted
- ◆ 1 tablespoon olive oil, for brushing

FOR THE BEST RESULTS

Lightly oil your hands before mixing or kneading dough so that the dough doesn't stick to them.

For a rich, crisp, golden crust on bread, lightly mist the dough with salted water before baking.

Use your hands or the dough hook of an electric mixer to knead bread successfully. Or try a combination, beginning with a mixer and kneading by hand in the later stages.

1 Sift the flour into a large bowl with the salt and stir in the sugar and yeast.

2 Make a well in the center and add the milk, egg, ¼ cup olive oil, and chopped olives. Mix to a dough, then turn out on a well-floured board.

3 Knead lightly for 4 to 5 minutes until smooth and elastic. Roll the dough around in a lightly oiled bowl to coat it with oil, cover with lightly oiled plastic wrap, and leave in a warm place to rise for about 1 hour.

4 Turn the dough out on a floured board and roll it or shape it into a large disk or oval about 3 inches thick. Place on a baking tray. Cover and leave to rise in a warm place for about 15 minutes.

5 Preheat the oven to 400°F. Stud the surface of the dough with olives, brush with olive oil, and bake for about 25 minutes, or until the crust is golden. Serve warm or cold.

MAKES 1 LOAF TOTAL TIME 2 HOURS

Pear and walnut bread

Try this tasty bread drizzled with a mixture of honey and yogurt. Toast it for breakfast or add it to a dessert cheese-and-fruit platter.

- ◆ 1 cup dried pears, rehydrated for 1 hour in warm water to cover
- ◆ ½ cup walnuts, chopped
- ◆ 5 cups bread flour or all-purpose flour
- ◆ 2 teaspoons kosher salt
- ◆ ¼ -ounce packet active dry yeast
- ◆ 1 ½ to 1 ¾ cups warm (105° to 110°F) water
- ◆ 3 tablespoons vegetable oil

1 Drain, then roughly chop the pears. Place them with the walnut pieces in a bowl and mix with the flour, salt, and yeast.

2 Make a well in the center of the dry ingredients and add 1 ½ cups warm water and the oil. Mix well to form a soft dough, adding a little more water if the mixture is too dry.

3 Turn the dough out on a floured surface and knead for 10 minutes, or until smooth and elastic. Halve the dough and shape each piece into

an oval. Place each oval on a greased baking sheet and cover loosely with lightly oiled plastic wrap. Leave in a warm place for 40 minutes or until the dough has doubled in size.

4 Preheat the oven to 425°F. Remove the plastic wrap and cross-slash the top of each loaf. Bake for 10 minutes; then reduce the temperature to 350°F and bake for 25 minutes or until the loaves have browned.

5 When done, turn the loaves out on a rack and let cool.

MAKES 2 LOAVES TOTAL TIME 1 HOUR 45 MINUTES

Focaccia

Focaccia is delicious toasted and topped with Italian-style toppings, such as grilled or marinated vegetables and mozzarella. So embellished, it can make a satisfying one-dish lunch.

- ◆ ¼ -ounce packet active dry yeast
- ◆ 2 cups warm (105° to 110°F) water
- ◆ ¼ teaspoon sugar
- ◆ 4 ½ to 5 ½ cups bread flour or all-purpose flour
- ◆ ¼ cup olive oil
- ◆ 1 tablespoon salt
- ◆ tiny sprigs rosemary
- ◆ olive oil, for drizzling
- ◆ kosher salt

1 Place the yeast in a small bowl, add the warm water and sugar, and mix rapidly with a fork. Leave in a warm place for 20 minutes, or until activated and frothy.

2 Place the flour in a large bowl and make a well in the center. Add the yeast mixture, oil, and salt, then mix well. Knead the dough for 10 minutes, or until smooth. Place in an oiled bowl, cover with lightly oiled plastic wrap, and leave to rise in a warm place for 1 hour.

3 Grease two baking sheets. Halve the dough. Spread each half on a baking sheet, pressing dough out with your fingers to about ½ -inch thickness. Cover the sheets with lightly oiled plastic wrap and leave for 10 to 20 minutes.

4 Press out the dough with your fingers again, cover, and leave for 30 minutes.

5 Preheat the oven to 425°F. Indent the dough

CROÛTES AND CROUTONS

You can treat baked or grilled slices of French baguette as if they were mini pizza bases (*croûtes*) and invent your own toppings. Drizzle with olive oil and spread with your favorite tomato sauce. Top with prosciutto, Gruyère cheese, black olive halves, and a sprinkling of Parmesan cheese. Season with salt and freshly ground black pepper, add another drizzle of olive oil, and bake in a pre-heated 400°F oven for 7 to 10 minutes.

To make croûtes, simply slice a loaf of French bread and brush each slice with olive oil or melted butter. Toast the slices briefly in a preheated 250°F oven, turning once, until pale golden on both sides. Use large croûtes as bases for juicy steaks or grilled quail. Spread small ones with tapenade (p.40), or use as foils for pâtés or for the dips on pages 40 and 41. Use your imagination and the leftovers in the refrigerator to vary the toppings.

For garlic croutons, trim the crusts from bread slices and cut bread into ½-inch cubes. Slice 2 cloves of garlic and sauté in olive oil over medium heat until golden, taking care not to burn them. Lift out and discard the garlic after 2 or 3 minutes. Add the bread cubes to the flavored oil and stir-fry until well coated, golden, and crisp. Drain on paper towels. Use fresh croutons to garnish soups and salads or to add texture to vegetable and meat dishes. Store in airtight containers to keep crisp.

all over with your fingers, press in tiny sprigs of rosemary, drizzle with olive oil, and sprinkle with kosher salt. Bake for about 25 minutes or until firm and golden. Serve warm.

MAKES 2 LOAVES   TOTAL TIME 3 HOURS

Pita bread

Pita is delicious eaten warm with a dip. Or stretch the dough into an oval, sprinkle it with sesame and poppy seeds, and make Turkish bread.

- ◆ **1¼ cups warm (105° to 115°F) water**
- ◆ **1 teaspoon dry yeast**
- ◆ **1 teaspoon sugar**
- ◆ **3 cups bread flour or all-purpose flour**
- ◆ **1 heaping teaspoon salt**
- ◆ **1½ teaspoons olive oil**
- ◆ **¼ cup snipped fresh herbs**
- ◆ **olive oil, for brushing**

1 Pour the warm water into the bowl of an electric mixer and sprinkle in the yeast. Mix rapidly with a fork. Add the sugar and half the flour and blend, using the mixer's paddle attachment. Cover the bowl with lightly oiled plastic wrap and set in a warm place for about 2 hours or until the dough has doubled in size.

2 Return the bowl to the mixer, add the salt, 1½ teaspoons olive oil, and the remaining flour. Blend for 5 to 10 minutes or until the dough is smooth and elastic.

3 Turn the dough out on a lightly floured surface and knead for 10 to 12 minutes or until smooth and elastic. Roll the dough around in a lightly oiled bowl to coat it with oil, cover with lightly oiled plastic wrap, and leave in a warm place to rise for about 1½ hours.

4 Preheat the oven to 475°F. Line a baking sheet with parchment or aluminum foil.

5 Turn the dough out on a lightly floured surface and divide into four balls. Roll out each ball into a circle about 6 inches in diameter and ½ inch thick and place on the prepared sheet. Brush lightly with oil and sprinkle with the herbs. Bake for 8 minutes, or until golden.

6 Turn the pita breads out on a rack to cool.

MAKES 4 PITA BREADS   TOTAL TIME 4 HOURS

◆ Cakes for All Occasions ◆

Our cakes run the gamut from everyday family favorites to company-best desserts. Ranging from light sponge cakes filled with fresh fruit and whipped cream to a rich chocolate cake and a dense and tangy apple cake, they are bound to satisfy every sweet tooth.

Chocolate fudge cake

Lightly crisp on the outside and deliciously soft in the center, this cake is the ultimate treat for chocolate lovers. There's no need to ice it. Simply decorate the top as directed.

- ◆ **2 sticks (8 ounces) unsalted butter**
- ◆ **8 ounces best-quality bittersweet chocolate, coarsely chopped**
- ◆ **¾ cup granulated sugar**
- ◆ **⅓ cup brown sugar**
- ◆ **6 eggs, separated**
- ◆ **3 tablespoons all-purpose flour**
- ◆ **¼ cup ground almonds**
- ◆ **½ teaspoon cream of tartar**
- ◆ **1 tablespoon each sifted unsweetened cocoa and confectioners sugar**

1 Preheat the oven to 350°F. Butter and flour a 9-inch springform pan, then line the bottom with wax paper.

2 In a heavy saucepan, over low heat, melt the butter and chocolate, stirring constantly, until just melted and smooth. Set aside.

3 In a large mixing bowl, whisk the two sugars into the egg yolks until just mixed. While the chocolate is still warm, whisk it into the egg mixture, then stir in the flour and almonds.

4 Warm the egg whites slightly by swirling them in a large bowl over hot water. Add the cream of tartar and, with an electric mixer on high, beat until soft peaks form. Gently fold the whites into the base mixture.

5 Pour into the prepared pan and bake for 35 to 45 minutes, or until the cake is completely set around the sides but is soft and creamy in the center. A toothpick inserted in the cake should come out clean on the edges but coated in the middle.

6 Cool the cake thoroughly in the pan on a rack. Remove the wax paper and set the cake on a plate. Dust with cocoa powder. Arrange small leaves in a decorative pattern on the

Our sweet temptations include, clockwise from back left: Lemon madeleines, Strawberry cream cake, French apple cake, and Chocolate fudge cake.

cake, dust the top evenly with confectioners sugar, and remove the leaves. Serve with whipped cream if desired. This cake keeps well in its pan, covered with foil, for 2 days. Do not refrigerate or freeze.

SERVES 8 TO 10   TOTAL TIME 1 HOUR 15 MINUTES

Strawberry cream cake

This light-as-air sponge cake relies on beaten egg whites rather than leavening for its height. Slow baking at a low temperature produces a cake that retains its height when removed from the oven. For a change of pace, top the cake with sliced peaches instead of strawberries.

- ◆ **1 cup granulated sugar**
- ◆ **7 eggs, separated**
- ◆ **2 teaspoons vanilla extract**
- ◆ **½ cup all-purpose flour**
- ◆ **1 cup potato flour (from health food stores)**
- ◆ **1 cup heavy cream**
- ◆ **1 pound strawberries, halved**
- ◆ **Sifted confectioners sugar**

1 Preheat the oven to 325°F. Butter and flour a 9-inch springform pan, then line the bottom with wax paper.

2 With an electric mixer at high speed, beat the sugar, egg yolks, and vanilla until the mixture is pale and tripled in bulk.

3 Sift the flours together and gently fold into the sugar and egg mixture.

4 In a large bowl, with clean beaters, beat the egg whites until stiff but not dry. Whisk a spoonful into the batter, then fold in the rest. Turn the batter into the prepared pan and bake for 60 to 65 minutes, or until the cake is light golden and a toothpick inserted in the center comes out clean. Turn off the heat and allow the cake to rest in the oven, with the door open, for 10 minutes. Then cool on a rack.

5 In a medium bowl, beat the cream until soft peaks form and sweeten lightly with sugar if desired. Remove wax paper and split the cake. Spread whipped cream over the bottom half. Add the strawberries and the cake top. Dust cake top with confectioners sugar.

SERVES 8   TOTAL TIME 2 HOURS

Lemon madeleines

These sponge-cake shells are no larger than cookies, which makes them perfect for a shower or other afternoon gathering. Madeleine molds are available from cookware suppliers.

- ◆ **3 small or 2 large eggs**
- ◆ **⅓ cup granulated sugar**
- ◆ **1 cup all-purpose flour**
- ◆ **½ teaspoon baking powder**
- ◆ **¼ teaspoon salt**
- ◆ **7 tablespoons butter, melted**
- ◆ **zest 1 lemon, grated**
- ◆ **1 tablespoon lemon juice**
- ◆ **Sifted confectioners sugar**

1 Preheat the oven to 350°F. Generously butter and lightly flour twenty 3-inch long madeleine molds. Set aside.

2 In a large bowl, with an electric mixer on high, beat the eggs and sugar until light and thick—about 5 minutes. Into another bowl, sift together the flour, baking powder, and salt, then gently fold in the egg and sugar mixture. Add the melted butter, lemon zest, and juice, and fold in until combined.

3 Spoon the mixture into the molds and bake for 20 to 25 minutes, or until golden.

4 Remove from the oven and turn out onto a rack. When cooled, dust with confectioners sugar. Store in an airtight container.

MAKES 20   TOTAL TIME 40 MINUTES

VARIATION For a special treat, serve the madeleines with lime curd (p.27) and whipped cream.

FOR THE BEST RESULTS

Use medium-weight metal pans to get a thin, golden-brown surface on a cake. For a thicker, browner edge, use glass or enameled pans.

Chocolate and other rich cakes may retain a slight indent if pressed with a finger when they're done. Most cakes, including sponge and butter cakes, will spring back when tested this way.

Lemon and almond cake

The best way to bake this delicately flavored cake is in a classic bundt pan. A tube in the center of the pan allows the cake to rise high and cook evenly. A ribbed design around the outside of the pan gives the cake a pretty molded appearance when it's turned out. Serve warm, with a dollop of whipped cream, or at room temperature with fresh fruit or berries.

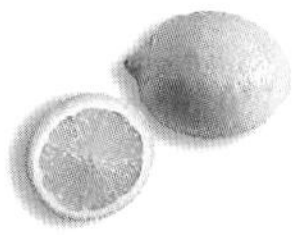

- ◆ **2 cups all-purpose flour**
- ◆ **1 teaspoon baking powder**
- ◆ **2 sticks (8 ounces) unsalted butter at room temperature**
- ◆ **1 cup granulated sugar**
- ◆ **zest of 2 lemons, finely grated**
- ◆ **1 cup buttermilk**
- ◆ **1 teaspoon vanilla extract**
- ◆ **6 egg whites**
- ◆ **¼ teaspoon salt**
- ◆ **1 cup blanched almonds, finely chopped**

FOR THE TOPPING
- ◆ **½ cup sugar**
- ◆ **3 tablespoons lemon juice**

1 Preheat the oven to 350°F. Butter and flour a 9-inch bundt pan or a 9-inch springform pan.
2 Onto a sheet of wax paper, sift the flour with the baking powder twice to aerate thoroughly. Set aside. In the large bowl of an electric mixer, beat the butter, ½ cup of the sugar, and the lemon zest until thick and creamy.
3 Add the flour mixture to the butter and sugar mixture alternately with the buttermilk. Add the vanilla and beat until well mixed.
4 In a medium bowl, with clean beaters, beat the egg whites and salt until stiff peaks form. Gradually add the remaining ½ cup of sugar, beating until the peaks are glossy.
5 Add a large spoonful of the egg whites to the batter and whisk briskly to combine. Lightly fold in the remaining egg whites until no streaks remain. Fold in the almonds.
6 Spoon the mixture into the prepared pan and smooth the surface. Bake for 55 to 60 minutes or until a toothpick inserted in the center comes out clean and the cake begins to pull away from the sides of the pan.

7 For the topping: In a small saucepan, over low heat, stir the sugar and lemon juice until the sugar dissolves and forms a syrup.
8 Place the hot cake, still in its pan, on a rack and pierce the surface all over with a toothpick. Pour the hot syrup over the cake. Let it cool completely in the pan before unmolding. The cake can be stored in an airtight container for 3 to 4 days.
SERVES 8–10   TOTAL TIME 1½ HOURS

Apricot and pecan loaf

This delicious fruit-and-nut loaf is at its best when enjoyed still warm from the oven. Serve it sliced and lightly spread with butter, cottage cheese, or cream cheese.

- ◆ **¾ cup dried apricots, coarsely chopped**
- ◆ **¼ cup boiling water**
- ◆ **1 stick (4 ounces) unsalted butter at room temperature**
- ◆ **1 cup sugar**
- ◆ **1 egg**
- ◆ **1 teaspoon vanilla extract**
- ◆ **2 cups all-purpose flour**
- ◆ **1 teaspoon baking powder**
- ◆ **1 teaspoon baking soda**
- ◆ **¼ teaspoon salt**
- ◆ **1 cup milk**
- ◆ **½ cup pecans, chopped**
- ◆ **½ cup apricot jam**

1 Preheat the oven to 350°F. Butter and flour three 6- x 3½ -inch loaf pans.
2 Place the apricots and boiling water in a small bowl; set aside for at least 10 minutes.
3 In a large bowl, with an electric mixer on high, beat the butter and sugar until creamy. Beat in the egg and vanilla. Into a separate bowl, sift the flour, baking powder, baking soda, and salt.
4 Add the flour mixture and milk alternately to the creamed butter and sugar, beginning and ending with the flour. Fold in the pecans and apricots with their soaking liquid.
5 Spoon the mixture into the prepared pan and bake for 45 to 50 minutes, or until a toothpick inserted in the loaf comes out clean.

6 Remove from the oven and let stand in the pan on a rack for 5 minutes. Turn out on a rack.
7 Heat the apricot jam in a small saucepan with a few drops of water, stirring constantly. Brush the jam over the top of the warm loaves with a pastry brush for a shiny, glazed finish.
MAKES THREE 6-INCH LOAVES   TOTAL TIME 1¼ HOURS

French apple cake

Choose apples with a sweet-tart bite, such as Romes or Granny Smiths, to make this cake.

- ◆ **1 cup all-purpose flour**
- ◆ **1 teaspoon baking powder**
- ◆ **¼ teaspoon salt**
- ◆ **½ stick (4 ounces) butter at room temperature**
- ◆ **⅓ cup sugar**
- ◆ **1 egg**
- ◆ **¼ cup milk**
- ◆ **2 apples, peeled, cored, quartered, and sprinkled with the juice of 1 lemon**
- ◆ **3 tablespoons sugar**
- ◆ **1 teaspoon ground cinnamon**

1 Preheat the oven to 350°F. Butter a 9-inch springform pan.
2 Onto a sheet of wax paper, sift together the flour, baking powder, and salt. Set aside. In a large bowl, with an electric mixer on high, cream the butter and sugar until light colored and fluffy.
3 Add the egg and beat well. Add half the flour, baking powder, and salt mixture. Beat until combined. Add the milk alternately with the remaining flour mixture. The resulting batter will be quite thick.
4 Pour the batter into the prepared pan, spreading it evenly.
5 Cut the quartered apples into thin slices, but not all the way through (see the photograph on page 60).
6 Place the apples on the batter, cored side down, fanning the slices slightly. In a small bowl, stir together the sugar and cinnamon and sprinkle on top. Bake for 60 to 70 minutes or until golden on top.
SERVES 6   TOTAL TIME 2 HOURS

Honey tea cake

This simple cake is perfect for a light tea snack or as a first baking project with children. The nut topping can dress it up, but for children you can serve it with a sprinkling of confectioners sugar.

- ◆ **2 large eggs**
- ◆ **¾ cup honey**
- ◆ **¼ cup water**
- ◆ **¼ cup vegetable oil**
- ◆ **2 teaspoons vanilla extract**
- ◆ **1½ cups all-purpose flour**
- ◆ **1½ teaspoons baking powder**
- ◆ **3 tablespoons non-fat dry milk**
- ◆ **¼ teaspoon salt**

FOR THE ICING
- ◆ **¾ cup chopped pecans or other nuts**
- ◆ **¼ cup confectioners sugar**
- ◆ **1 teaspoon cinnamon**

1 Preheat the oven to 375°F. Butter and flour a 9-inch square baking pan.
2 In the large bowl of an electric mixer fitted with a whisk attachment, beat eggs and honey at high speed for 5 minutes or until light in color. Add water, oil, vanilla, flour, baking powder, dry milk, and salt and beat mixture until just smooth.
3 Pour batter into pan. If you are using the topping, mix together the ingredients and sprinkle over top of batter.
4 Bake for 25 minutes or until a tester comes out clean. Let cool in the pan on a rack.

Portuguese nut cake

This chocolate-frosted flourless cake has a rich, nutty flavor and is bound to be a family favorite.

- ◆ **1 cup granulated sugar**
- ◆ **4 eggs, separated**
- ◆ **2¼ cups ground almonds**
- ◆ **3 ounces semisweet chocolate**
- ◆ **1 tablespoon heavy cream**
- ◆ **½ cup blanched slivered almonds, for decoration**
- ◆ **½ cup pecan halves, for decoration**

1 Preheat the oven to 350°F. Butter an 8-inch springform pan and line the bottom with wax paper.
2 In a large bowl, whisk the sugar and egg yolks until pale and thick. Stir in the ground almonds. In another bowl, with the electric mixer on high, beat the egg whites until soft peaks form. Whisk half the whites into the sugar and egg mixture, then fold in the balance.
3 Pour the mixture into the prepared pan and bake for 50 to 55 minutes or until a toothpick inserted in the cake comes out clean.
4 Remove from the oven and let cool in the pan on a rack. When the cake is cool, remove it from the pan and peel off the wax paper.
5 In a double boiler, over low heat, stir the chocolate until melted. Stir in the cream. Remove from the heat and spread the chocolate mixture thinly over the cake.
6 Decorate the cake with nuts. It can be stored in an airtight container for up to 5 days.
SERVES 8–10   TOTAL TIME 2 HOURS 15 MINUTES

Passion fruit sponge cake

Passion-fruit juice is refreshingly tart. If you need a substitute for it, use a teaspoon of lemon juice.

- ◆ **2 cups flour, sifted**
- ◆ **2 teaspoons baking powder**
- ◆ **2 sticks (8 ounces) butter at room temperature**
- ◆ **1 cup granulated sugar**
- ◆ **3 eggs**
- ◆ **2 tablespoons hot water**
- ◆ **1 teaspoon vanilla extract**

FOR THE ICING
- ◆ **2 passion fruits**
- ◆ **1 cup confectioners' sugar, sifted**

1 Preheat the oven to 375°F. Butter an 8-inch springform pan and line the bottom with wax paper.
2 Onto a sheet of wax paper, sift the flour with the baking powder. In a large bowl, with an electric mixer on high, beat the butter and sugar until thick and creamy. Beat in the eggs, one at a time, until combined. Fold in the flour, then lightly fold in the hot water and vanilla.
3 Spoon the batter into the prepared pan. Bake for 35 to 40 minutes or until a toothpick inserted in the center comes out clean.
4 Cool the cake in the pan on a rack for 5 minutes, then turn out to cool completely.
5 Halve the passion fruits and squeeze the pulp into a fine sieve set over a bowl. With the back of a spoon, force the pulp through the sieve. Blend the confectioners sugar and fruit pulp until the mixture is smooth and spreadable. Pour the icing over the cake and carefully spread to the edges. Let stand until set.
SERVES 8–10   TOTAL TIME 2 HOURS

Kugelhopf

Rum-soaked fruit flavor this German favorite.

- ◆ **½ cup currants**
- ◆ **½ cup raisins**
- ◆ **3 tablespoons rum**
- ◆ **⅓ cup slivered almonds**
- ◆ **2¼ ounces dry yeast**
- ◆ **1 cup warm (105° to 115°F) milk**
- ◆ **3 cups all-purpose flour**
- ◆ **pinch of salt**
- ◆ **3 tablespoons granulated sugar**
- ◆ **3 eggs, lightly beaten**
- ◆ **1 stick (4 ounces) butter, melted**
- ◆ **Sifted confectioners sugar**

1 In a small bowl, soak the currants and raisins in the rum. Set aside.
2 Preheat the oven to 375°F. Generously butter a 9-inch bundt pan and press the almonds into the butter. Refrigerate until needed.
3 In a small bowl, stir the yeast into the milk.
4 Into a large mixing bowl, sift the flour and salt. Make a well in the center and add the yeast mixture, sugar, eggs, and melted butter. With the mixer on low, beat well. Stir in the fruit and rum. Spread the batter into the pan.
5 Cover with a damp cloth and let stand in a warm place for 30 minutes, or until the mixture has risen to 1 to 2 inches below the pan's top.
6 Bake for 45 to 50 minutes, or until a tester comes out clean. Let stand for a few minutes, then turn out on a rack to cool. Dust with confectioners' sugar.
SERVES 6   TOTAL TIME 1½ HOURS

◆ Cookies, Muffins, and Scones ◆

*It takes only minutes to whip up a batch of homemade cookies or a pan of sweet
or savory muffins or scones. Nothing makes family or guests feel more loved or welcome than being
served fresh-baked treats right out of the oven for breakfast or an afternoon kaffeeklatsch.*

Macadamia biscotti

*These popular Italian cookies are twice baked,
which gives them a crisp, hard texture and makes
them perfect for dipping. Biscotti freeze well, so
make an extra batch to have on hand.*

- ◆ **6 tablespoons unsalted butter,
  cut up, at room temperature**
- ◆ **¾ cup granulated sugar**
- ◆ **2 eggs**
- ◆ **1 teaspoon vanilla extract**
- ◆ **2 teaspoons grated lemon zest**
- ◆ **2¼ cups all-purpose flour**
- ◆ **1½ teaspoons baking powder**
- ◆ **½ teaspoon salt**
- ◆ **1 cup macadamia nuts,
  coarsely chopped**

1 Preheat the oven to 350°F. Grease and flour a
baking sheet.
2 In a large bowl, with an electric mixer on
high, beat the butter and sugar until pale and
creamy. Beat in the eggs, vanilla, and lemon
zest. Add the flour, baking powder, and salt.
Blend to combine. Stir in the nuts.
3 Halve the dough and, with lightly oiled
hands, roll each half into a log about 2 inches
thick and 12 inches long. Place the logs on the
baking sheet and bake in the center of the
oven for 25 minutes, or until golden.
4 Remove the baking sheet from the oven and
place on a rack to cool.
5 Transfer the logs to a breadboard. Using a
serrated knife, slice them about ¾ inch
thick at a 45° angle. To avoid crumbling, use
firm, decisive strokes. Place the slices flat on
a baking sheet and return to a 350°F oven for
about 10 minutes, turning once, to dry them.
6 Cool on a rack. The cookies will keep in an
airtight container for 2 to 3 weeks.
MAKES 24–30 TOTAL TIME 1½ HOURS

Sesame Parmesan crackers

*Served warm, these easy-to-make crackers are
good as a savory snack, with or without a dip.*

- ◆ **1 cup all-purpose flour**
- ◆ **2½ tablespoons sesame seeds**
- ◆ **½ tablespoon salt**
- ◆ **¼ cup plus 2 tablespoons
  grated Parmesan cheese**
- ◆ **¾ teaspoon baking soda**
- ◆ **3 tablespoons butter, cut up**
- ◆ **¼ to ⅓ cup chilled water**
- ◆ **poppy seeds (optional)**

1 Preheat oven to 350°F. Grease a baking sheet.
2 In a medium bowl, combine the flour, sesame
seeds, salt, ¼ cup Parmesan cheese, and baking
soda. Using your fingers, add the butter, working
it in until the mixture resembles fine crumbs.
Add enough chilled water to form a stiff dough.
3 On a lightly floured surface, roll out the
dough to ⅛ inch thick. Using cookie cutters,
cut out the crackers. Place on the baking sheet,
brush with water, and sprinkle with the 2 tablespoons of Parmesan cheese and the poppy
seeds. Bake for 15 minutes, or until golden and
crisp. The crackers can be stored in an airtight
container for 1 week.
MAKES 24–36 TOTAL TIME 30–40 MINUTES

Coconut macaroons

*Desiccated coconut, which is available in health-
food stores and the natural-foods section of
supermarkets, produces an excellent macaroon.*

- ◆ **3 egg whites**
- ◆ **1 cup granulated sugar**
- ◆ **2½ cups desiccated coconut**
- ◆ **1 cup macadamia nuts or
  almonds, finely chopped**

1 Preheat the oven to 350°F. Lightly grease
two baking sheets.
2 In a medium bowl, with an electric mixer on
high, beat egg whites into soft peaks. Gradually
add the sugar, beating after each addition until
peaks are glossy. Fold in the coconut and nuts.
3 With wet hands, roll tablespoonfuls of the
mixture into rounds and set on baking sheets.
4 Bake for 20 to 25 minutes, or until lightly
golden. Cool on racks and store in an airtight
container. They will keep for 2 to 3 days.
MAKES ABOUT 35 TOTAL TIME 45 MINUTES

Chocolate-almond bites

This shortbread variation is delicious with coffee.

- ◆ **2 cups all-purpose flour**
- ◆ **½ cup unsweetened cocoa**
- ◆ **2 sticks (8 ounces) unsalted
  butter, at room temperature**
- ◆ **½ cup granulated sugar**
- ◆ **1 teaspoon vanilla extract**
- ◆ **¼ teaspoon salt**
- ◆ **1 cup toasted almonds,
  finely chopped**
- ◆ **sifted confectioners sugar**

1 Preheat oven to 350F°. Grease a baking sheet.
2 Onto a sheet of wax paper, sift the flour
with the cocoa. In a large bowl, with an electric
mixer on high, beat the butter, sugar, vanilla,
and salt until pale and creamy. Beat in the flour
mixture, then the almonds.
3 Shape heaped teaspoonfuls of dough into
balls and arrange on baking sheet. Bake for 20
to 25 minutes or until firm. Cool briefly on the
sheet before removing to a rack.
4 While still slightly warm, dredge the biscuits with confectioners sugar. Store in an
airtight container. They will keep for 5 days.
MAKES 48-60 TOTAL TIME 45 MINUTES

Almond tuiles

The curved roof tiles, called tuiles, *on the farm-houses of southern France are the inspiration behind these curved almond cookies. Shaping them is the trickiest part of the recipe, but a little practice will make the process easier and easier. It is also true that the cookies taste just as good when they are flat.*

- ◆ **6 tablespoons (3 ounces) unsalted butter**
- ◆ **⅓ cup plus 1 tablespoon sugar**
- ◆ **½ cup all-purpose flour**
- ◆ **pinch of salt**
- ◆ **⅔ cup slivered or flaked blanched almonds**

1 Preheat the oven to 400°F and grease two baking sheets.

2 In a large bowl, with an electric mixer on high, beat the butter and sugar until light and creamy. Beat in the flour with the salt, and stir in the almonds.

3 Drop teaspoonfuls of the dough onto one of the baking sheets, leaving plenty of room for spreading. Flatten each drop with a wet fingertip before putting the baking sheet in the oven.

4 Bake 5 minutes or until golden. Remove from the oven and leave for a few moments to cool on the baking sheet.

5 While the cookies are still warm and pliable, carefully lift each one with a spatula and drape it over a rolling pin to give it the characteristic curved shape. Leave for a minute to harden, then carefully remove and finish cooling on racks. (To make yourself more comfortable with this process, start with just three cookies in the first batch; you will soon get the rhythm of removing and handling the hot tuiles in time to shape them.) Store the cooled cookies in airtight containers.

MAKES ABOUT 24   TOTAL TIME 40 MINUTES

Snacks and sweets from the oven are shown clockwise from top right: Macadamia biscotti, Almond tuiles, Sesame Parmesan crackers cut in several different shapes, and Chocolate-almond bites.

Ready-to-bake biscuits

Roll out and cut this traditional biscuit dough. Then freeze for a handy supply of oven-ready biscuits to go with soups, stews, or breakfast eggs.

- ◆ **2 cups all-purpose flour**
- ◆ **1 tablespoon plus 1 teaspoon baking powder**
- ◆ **1 tablespoon sugar**
- ◆ **½ teaspoon salt**
- ◆ **½ cup (4 ounces) butter or vegetable shortening, melted**
- ◆ **⅔ cup milk**

1 In a large bowl, blend the flour, baking powder, sugar, salt, and butter until mixture resembles coarse crumbs. Add the milk, stirring with a fork until the dough comes together.
2 Knead on a floured surface until smooth—about 30 seconds. Roll out dough ½ inch thick and cut into 2- to 3-inch rounds. Gather scraps, roll again, and cut out more rounds.
3 Coat rounds with flour and stack. Wrap well in plastic wrap. Freeze for up to 4 weeks.
4 Arrange biscuits on a baking sheet; thaw about 15 minutes. Bake in a preheated 425°F oven for 15 to 20 minutes or until golden.
MAKES 15　TOTAL TIME 35 MINUTES

Orange and date muffins

These wholesome muffins are great with juice at breakfast and with milk as an afternoon snack.

- ◆ **1¾ cups all-purpose flour**
- ◆ **1 teaspoon baking powder**
- ◆ **1 teaspoon baking soda**
- ◆ **½ teaspoon salt**
- ◆ **½ cup dates, pitted and chopped**
- ◆ **1 stick (4 ounces) unsalted butter, at room temperature**
- ◆ **¾ cup sugar**
- ◆ **1 large egg**
- ◆ **½ cup freshly squeezed orange juice**
- ◆ **1 navel orange, chopped, seeded, and pureed (¾ cup)**

1 Preheat the oven to 400°F. Grease twelve 2½-inch muffin cups.
2 In a medium bowl mix the flour, baking powder, baking soda, and salt. Add the dates and toss to coat. In a large bowl, with an electric mixer on high, beat the butter and sugar until pale and creamy. Beat in the egg, orange juice, and pureed orange. Fold in the dry ingredients—do not overmix.
3 Spoon the mixture into the muffin cups, filling them ⅔ full. Bake in the center of the oven for 20 minutes or until golden. Turn out on a rack to cool.
MAKES 12　TOTAL TIME 35 MINUTES

Blueberry muffins

This classic recipe can be made with fresh or frozen berries, but it's at its very best when made in late summer with fresh farm-stand blueberries or tiny wild blueberries that you pick yourself.

- ◆ **1½ cups blueberries, fresh or frozen (thawed)**
- ◆ **3 cups all-purpose flour**
- ◆ **1 tablespoon baking powder**
- ◆ **½ teaspoon baking soda**
- ◆ **1 teaspoon salt**
- ◆ **¾ cup plus 2 tablespoons sugar**
- ◆ **3 tablespoons butter, melted**
- ◆ **2 eggs, lightly beaten**
- ◆ **1 cup buttermilk**
- ◆ **1½ teaspoons vanilla extract**

1 Preheat the oven to 400°F. Grease twelve 2½-inch muffin cups.
2 Rinse and dry fresh blueberries. Toss fresh or frozen berries with 2 tablespoons of the flour.
3 In a large bowl, combine the remaining flour, baking powder, baking soda, salt, and sugar. In another bowl, whisk together the butter, eggs, buttermilk, and vanilla and fold into flour mixture—do not overmix. Fold in the blueberries.
4 Spoon the mixture into the muffin cups, filling them ⅔ full. Sprinkle with 2 tablespoons sugar. Bake in the center of the oven for 20 to 25 minutes, or until golden. Cool on a rack. Serve warm.
MAKES 12　TOTAL TIME 40 MINUTES

Herb and bacon muffins

Savory muffins—made with meat, cheese, and herbs instead of sugar and spices—are a delightful change for breakfast or brunch.

- ◆ **1¾ cups all-purpose flour**
- ◆ **2 teaspoons baking powder**
- ◆ **½ teaspoon salt**
- ◆ **¼ cup chopped herbs**
- ◆ **¼ cup grated Parmesan cheese**
- ◆ **1 tablespoon sugar**
- ◆ **⅓ cup cooked, crumbled bacon**
- ◆ **1 egg, beaten**
- ◆ **I cup milk**
- ◆ **½ stick (4 tablespoons) butter, melted**

1 Preheat the oven to 400°F. Grease twelve 2½-inch muffin cups or 24 miniature muffin cups.
2 Into a large mixing bowl, sift the flour, baking powder, and salt. Stir in the herbs, cheese, sugar, and bacon. Make a well in the center.
3 In a small bowl, combine the egg, milk, and butter. Add to the dry ingredients. Mix lightly with a fork just until the dry ingredients are moistened. The mixture should be lumpy—do not overmix.
4 Spoon the batter into the prepared muffin cups, filling them ⅔ full. Bake until browned, 12 to 15 minutes for smaller muffins, 15 to 20 minutes for larger muffins. Serve warm.
MAKES 12 LARGE OR 24 SMALL　TOTAL TIME 35 MINUTES

PRACTICAL IDEAS
MAKING AND STORING

Don't overmix muffin mixtures: Only a few light strokes are needed. Any more, and the mixture will produce tough, heavy muffins.

For lighter, flakier scones, use buttermilk or soured milk in place of plain milk in most recipes.

To freeze scones or muffins, wrap individually in foil; store in freezer bags for up to 6 months. To reheat, place thawed, foil-wrapped scones or muffins in the oven at 350°F for 12 to 15 minutes.

Apple and golden raisin muffins
The apple in these muffins provides a natural sweetness that reduces the need for a larger quantity of sugar.

- ◆ **2 cups all-purpose flour**
- ◆ **3 teaspoons baking powder**
- ◆ **1 teaspoon salt**
- ◆ **½ teaspoon ground cinnamon**
- ◆ **¼ teaspoon ground nutmeg**
- ◆ **¾ cup peeled, grated apple**
- ◆ **⅓ cup golden raisins**
- ◆ **⅔ cup dark brown sugar**
- ◆ **¼ cup walnuts or pecans, chopped**
- ◆ **2 eggs, well beaten**
- ◆ **⅔ cup milk**
- ◆ **¼ cup vegetable oil**
- ◆ **1 cup corn, bran, or wheat flakes breakfast cereal**

1 Preheat the oven to 400°F. Grease twelve 2 ½ -inch muffin cups.
2 In a large mixing bowl, combine the flour, baking powder, salt, and spices. Stir in the apple, raisins, brown sugar, and nuts. Make a well in the center.
3 In a small bowl, combine the eggs, milk, and oil. Add the liquid, all at once, to the dry ingredients and stir just until moistened and combined—do not overmix. Fold in the cereal.
4 Spoon the mixture into the muffin cups, filling them ⅔ full. Bake for 15 to 20 minutes, or until puffed and brown. Cool for 5 minutes before removing from cups. Serve warm.
MAKES 10–12 TOTAL TIME 35 MINUTES

Cheese and parsley wedges
Add a golden crust to this savory cottage loaf by sprinkling it with grated cheese before baking.

- ◆ **2 cups whole wheat flour**
- ◆ **1 teaspoon baking powder**
- ◆ **1 teaspoon baking soda**
- ◆ **¾ cup diced Cheddar or ¼ cup grated Parmesan cheese**
- ◆ **¼ cup fresh parsley leaves**
- ◆ **1 teaspoon salt**
- ◆ **¾ cup milk or buttermilk**

1 Preheat the oven to 450°F. In the bowl of a food processor, place the flour, baking powder, baking soda, all but 1 tablespoon of the cheese, parsley, and salt. Process until the cheese crumbles into the flour and the parsley is finely chopped.
2 Add the milk all at once, and process just until a soft dough forms, about 5 seconds.
3 Turn the dough out on a floured surface and knead gently. Shape into a round on a lightly floured baking sheet. With a sharp knife, cut the dough almost through into 8 wedge-shaped pieces. Sprinkle the wedges with 1 tablespoon grated cheese.
4 Bake in the center of the oven for 20 to 25 minutes or until puffed and brown. Remove, wrap in a towel, and cool slightly. Cut through the marked wedges to serve.
MAKES 8 PIECES TOTAL TIME 35 MINUTES

Fruit scone fingers
The dough for these scones is scored into finger shapes before it's baked. You can separate the fingers into individual servings after they have finished baking. Serve with butter and jam for an afternoon snack with coffee or tea or put them out for a breakfast treat.

- ◆ **1 ½ cups all-purpose flour**
- ◆ **1 teaspoon cream of tartar**
- ◆ **½ teaspoon baking soda**
- ◆ **¼ teaspoon salt**
- ◆ **6 tablespoons butter, cut up**
- ◆ **½ cup granulated sugar**
- ◆ **¾ cup raisins**
- ◆ **⅔ cup buttermilk**
- ◆ **1 egg, separated**
- ◆ **1 tablespoon confectioners sugar**

1 Preheat the oven to 375°F. Grease a 9-inch square cake pan and line the bottom with wax paper.
2 In a large bowl, combine the flour, cream of tartar, baking soda, salt, and butter. Using your fingers, work the mixture until it resembles fine bread crumbs. Add the sugar and raisins and mix well.
3 In a medium bowl, whisk the buttermilk and egg yolk. Mix into the dry ingredients until the dough just comes together.
4 Spread the dough evenly in the prepared pan. With a floured knife, score the dough into finger shapes about 1 inch wide and 4 ½ inches long. Brush with egg white and dust with confectioners sugar. Bake for 15 to 20 minutes, or until golden. Serve warm.
MAKES 16 TOTAL TIME 35 MINUTES

Ginger and pecan scones
Roll out and cut this dough with a round cookie or biscuit cutter for traditional scones, or score it into finger-shaped segments as described in the recipe for fruit scone fingers. Serve the ginger and pecan scones with butter or cream cheese, softened for spreading.

- ◆ **2 cups all-purpose flour**
- ◆ **1 tablespoon baking powder**
- ◆ **3 tablespoons sugar**
- ◆ **½ teaspoon salt**
- ◆ **½ stick (4 ounces) unsalted butter, cut up**
- ◆ **2 eggs, lightly beaten**
- ◆ **⅓ cup heavy cream**
- ◆ **¼ cup crystallized ginger, chopped**
- ◆ **½ cup pecans, chopped**
- ◆ **1 egg white, lightly beaten**

1 Preheat the oven to 375°F. In a large bowl, place the flour, baking powder, 2 tablespoons of the sugar, and salt and mix well. Using your fingers, work the butter into the flour until the mixture resembles coarse crumbs. Add the beaten eggs, cream, ginger, and pecans. Mix until the dough just comes together.
2 Turn the dough out onto a lightly floured surface and roll it out gently with a floured rolling pin to ½ -inch thickness. Using a cutter dipped in flour, cut the dough into rounds or other fancy shapes. Place on a lightly floured baking sheet, brush with the beaten egg white, and sprinkle with 1 tablespoon of sugar. Bake for 20 minutes or until golden brown.
3 Turn the scones out on a rack to cool. Serve warm or cold.
MAKES 16 TOTAL TIME 35 MINUTES

• Sweet Tarts and Pies •

*When it comes to crowd-pleasing desserts, tarts and pies are hard to beat. Use the recipe
for basic piecrust pastry (p.44) as the base for a wide range of delights. Or, for variety, try the
rich shortcrust pastry (below) or our crumb crust (facing page).*

Rich shortcrust pastry

*Use this pastry for fruit tarts that require a sweet,
crisp crust. Chill it for easy handling.*

- ◆ **1½ cups all-purpose flour**
- ◆ **1 teaspoon sugar**
- ◆ **¼ teaspoon salt**
- ◆ **2 tablespoons dry milk**
- ◆ **1 stick (4 ounces) butter, cut up**
- ◆ **1 egg**

1 In a medium bowl, mix the flour, sugar, and
salt. Stir in the dry milk and make a well in the
center of the mixture.
2 Place the butter and egg in the well and mix
thoroughly. With your fingers, work the butter
into the flour until the mixture sticks together.
3 Turn the dough out on a floured surface.
With the heel of your hand, knead the dough
lightly until the butter is fully worked in.
4 Flour your hands generously and roll the
mixture into a ball. Wrap in plastic wrap and
chill in the refrigerator for at least 30 minutes.
5 Roll out as for basic piecrust (p.44).
MAKES ONE 9-INCH PIECRUST   TOTAL TIME 50 MINUTES

Key lime pie

*Outside Florida, you can't find true Key limes but
standard limes also serve to make a success of
this elegant summery dessert.*

- ◆ **4 eggs, separated**
- ◆ **¾ cup condensed milk**
- ◆ **zest of 2 limes, finely grated**
- ◆ **½ cup lime juice, or to taste**
- ◆ **1 crumb crust (facing page)**
- ◆ **⅓ cup sugar**

1 Preheat oven to 325°F. In a large bowl, whisk
together the yolks, condensed milk, zest, and
lime juice until smooth.

2 Pour the egg-yolk mixture into the crumb
crust. Bake 20 minutes.
3 In a separate bowl, with an electric mixer on
high, beat the egg whites until they stiffen. Add
the sugar slowly, beating continuously, until it
is all incorporated.
4 Pile the meringue on top of the filling, using
the back of a spoon to spread the meringue to
the crust's edge. The meringue should touch
the crust all the way around to allow for
shrinkage while baking. Bake the pie 20 to 25
minutes or until golden. Cool on a rack , then
chill before serving.
SERVES 6   TOTAL TIME 1 HOUR

PIE AND TART SHELLS

When making pie pastry, handle the dough as
little and as lightly as possible. Overhandling will
make the pastry tough. A light (and cool) hand
produces tender, flaky pastry.

Make sure that the water you add to pie pastry
is as cold as possible—some recipes even
specify ice water. Avoid using too much. If you
can get by with less than the maximum amount
suggested in the directions, so much the better.

Chilling pastry dough before rolling it out helps
make it tender and prevent shrinkage during baking. Several hours is ideal, but at least 30 minutes
is recommended. Once removed from the refrigerator, the dough should be allowed to come to
room temperature (about 30 minutes), to make it
easier to handle and roll.

To spread crumbs evenly in a pie pan, spread the
crumbs in the pan, then press down with another
pan of the same diameter.

Custard tart

*This perennial favorite is silky smooth. Flavor it
the standard way or try one of our variations.*

- ◆ **1 rich shortcrust pastry**
- ◆ **1 cup milk**
- ◆ **1 cup heavy cream**
- ◆ **1 teaspoon vanilla extract**
- ◆ **3 eggs, lightly beaten**
- ◆ **⅓ cup sugar**
- ◆ **pinch of salt**
- ◆ **pinch of ground nutmeg**

1 Preheat the oven to 400°F.
2 Make the pastry for a 9-inch pie pan according to the recipe for rich shortcrust pastry at
left. Bake blind (p.46) for 10 to 15 minutes just
to set the pastry. Remove from the oven and
lower the heat to 325°F.
3 In a medium saucepan over moderate heat,
warm the milk and cream until scalded.
Remove from the heat and add the vanilla.
4 In a medium bowl, place the eggs, sugar, salt,
and nutmeg and whisk lightly to combine. Stir
in about a third of the hot milk. Then pour the
egg mixture into the saucepan with the
remaining milk and mix well.
5 Strain the mixture into a measuring cup,
then pour into the partially baked pastry shell.
Place the tart on a baking sheet to catch any
drips and place in the oven.
6 Bake at 325°F for 30 to 40 minutes, or until a
knife inserted in the center of the custard
comes out clean. Remove the tart from the
oven and let cool.
SERVES 6   TOTAL TIME 1 HOUR 20 MINUTES

VARIATIONS Add a little grated zest of orange
to the eggs in Step 4 for a pleasing hint of
orange; or add a bay leaf or a few cardamom
pods to the scalded milk and leave to infuse
for 30 minutes. Remove before proceeding.

Pumpkin pie is an autumn treat. Ours is a deep-dish version decorated with pecans for extra appeal and flavored with a hint of bourbon for extra flavor.

Pumpkin pie

The winning combination of a creamy and aromatic custard and a crisp short pastry makes this variation on traditional Thanksgiving pumpkin pie an interesting and delightful dessert. If you want to cook your own pumpkin meat, be sure to pick a small, sweet pumpkin, grown for this purpose, rather than the big jack-o'-lantern pumpkins you buy at Halloween.

- **1 shortcrust pastry (facing page)**
- **2 cups solid-pack canned pumpkin puree**
- **½ stick (4 tablespoons) butter, melted**
- **¾ cup brown sugar**
- **2 large eggs**
- **1 to 2 tablespoons bourbon whiskey, or 2 teaspoons vanilla extract**
- **1 tablespoon grated orange zest**
- **½ teaspoon ground cinnamon**
- **1 cup milk**
- **pecan halves, for decoration**
- **whipped cream, as an accompaniment (optional)**

1 Preheat the oven to 425°F.

2 Roll out the pastry and line a 9-inch deep-dish pie pan. Trim the edges. Chill the crust for at least 15 minutes.

3 In a large bowl, with an electric mixer on medium, beat the pumpkin puree, butter, sugar, eggs, flavorings, and milk. Pour the filling into the prepared piecrust. Top with the pecan halves, arranged in a pattern.

4 Bake at 425°F for 10 minutes; then reduce the heat to 350°F and bake 45 to 50 minutes longer or until a tester inserted in the center of the pie comes out clean. Cool completely on a rack (or chill the pie) before serving it with whipped cream, if desired.

SERVES 8   TOTAL TIME 1 HOUR 25 MINUTES

Crumb crust

This quick and easy crumb crust is particularly good with fillings that require little or no baking and must spend some time in the refrigerator.

- **1¼ cups graham cracker crumbs**
- **5 tablespoons unsalted butter, melted**

1 Place the crumbs in a bowl and add the butter; mix with a fork until all the crumbs are well coated.

2 Pour the crumb-butter mixture into a pie pan. Use your fingers to spread it evenly and press it into the sides. Chill until set, about 1 hour. Fill with your choice of filling.

MAKES ONE 9-INCH SHELL   TOTAL TIME 1¼ HOUR

VARIATIONS Use chocolate wafer or ginger-snap crumbs, or replace ½ cup of the crumbs with finely ground almonds or hazelnuts.

NOTE If your crumb crusts tend to crumble, freeze them for 15 minutes before filling.

◆ Sweet Temptations ◆

Homemade confections and chocolates are easier to make than you may think.
These little extras show off your talents as a host and make delightful gifts. Use the best
ingredients you can find—the superior flavor will make the extra expense worthwhile.

Candied citrus peel

Candied peel is a delicious decoration for desserts and ice cream. It's also wonderful dipped in chocolate to serve with coffee.

- ◆ **3 firm, ripe lemons or oranges**
- ◆ **¼ cup granulated sugar**
- ◆ **½ cup water**

1 Using a swivel-bladed vegetable peeler, remove the peel from the fruit, leaving the bitter white pith. Using a sharp knife, cut the peel into strips, according to intended use. If you want to use the candied peel on cakes or tarts, cut it into matchstick strips; if candying to dip in chocolate, cut the peel into larger strips.
2 Place the strips in a small saucepan and cover with cold water. Bring to a boil, drain, and refresh under cold running water. Return to the saucepan, add the sugar and ½ cup water and cook over moderate heat until the liquid has evaporated and the peel is bright and shiny. Spread peel on a sheet of foil to cool, separating the strips.
3 Store in a sealed jar in the refrigerator. The candied peel will keep for up to 6 months.
MAKES ABOUT 1 CUP   TOTAL TIME 30 MINUTES

Chocolate fruit clusters

To gift wrap these treats, pile them into small, pretty boxes or aluminum pans, wrap with cellophane or plastic wrap, and tie with a bright bow.

- ◆ **8 ounces high-quality semisweet chocolate**
- ◆ **1½ cups hazelnuts, coarsely chopped**
- ◆ **½ cup golden raisins**

1 Line a baking sheet with aluminum foil.
2 In the top of a double boiler, over low heat,
stir the chocolate until melted. Remove from the heat and stir in the nuts and raisins. Mix to coat all the pieces.
3 Place heaping teaspoonfuls of the mixture on the prepared baking sheet. Refrigerate until set. The clusters can be stored in an airtight container in the refrigerator for 1 to 2 months.
MAKES ABOUT 30   TOTAL TIME 20 MINUTES

Coconut ice

No cooking is required to make this delicious and pretty old-fashioned sweet. It's very easy to make. You can pack the candy as a gift in tiny baskets lined with foil. Wrap the baskets in cellophane or plastic wrap to keep the candies fresh.

- ◆ **2½ cups desiccated coconut (available at health-food stores or the health-food section of supermarkets)**
- ◆ **½ cup sugar**
- ◆ **¼ teaspoon cream of tartar**
- ◆ **1 cup sweetened condensed milk**
- ◆ **few drops red food coloring**

1 Line an 8-inch square pan with baking parchment or aluminum foil.
2 In a medium bowl, combine the coconut, sugar, and cream of tartar. Add the condensed milk and mix until it forms a mass.
3 Spread half the mixture in the pan. Add a drop or two of food coloring to the remaining mixture and mix well for a uniform color. Spread on top of the white layer. Cover the coconut ice with foil and leave in the refrigerator overnight to set.
4 Cut the coconut ice into bars or squares and store in an airtight container. The bars will keep in the refrigerator for up to 1 month.
MAKES 30–36   TOTAL TIME 10 MINUTES PLUS OVERNIGHT

Chocolate fruit and nut truffles

An irresistible indulgence or a luscious gift for a special occasion, these chocolate truffles will delight your family and friends.

- ◆ **9 ounces bittersweet chocolate**
- ◆ **2 tablespoons heavy cream**
- ◆ **2 tablespoons cognac or rum**
- ◆ **1¼ cups apricots, finely chopped**
- ◆ **½ cup hazelnuts, finely chopped**
- ◆ **2 tablespoons crystallized ginger, minced**
- ◆ **2 tablespoons confectioners sugar, sifted**
- ◆ **30 hazelnut halves**

1 Line a large baking sheet with baking parchment or aluminum foil.
2 In the top of a double boiler over low heat, stir 4 ounces of the chocolate until melted.
3 Remove from the heat and beat in the cream and cognac. Blend in the apricots, chopped hazelnuts, ginger, and confectioners sugar. Stir well to combine.
4 Chill the mixture, if necessary, until firm enough to handle. Form into 1-inch balls and set aside on a sheet of wax paper.
5 In the top of a double boiler over low heat, stir the remaining 5 ounces of chocolate until melted. Remove from the heat.
6 Using a fork, dip each truffle into the melted chocolate, allowing any excess to run off. Place the truffles on the prepared baking sheet. Top each with a hazelnut half and chill.
7 When the chocolate has set, the truffles can be stored in an airtight container in the refrigerator for up to 1 month.
MAKES ABOUT 30   TOTAL TIME 1 HOUR

Lollipops

Imagine your children's delight when you come up with homemade lollipops in whatever flavor they choose. Use oil flavorings, available at health-food stores; alcohol-based extracts evaporate.

- ◆ **1 cup sugar**
- ◆ **½ cup water**
- ◆ **2 tablespoons light corn syrup**
- ◆ **4 to 8 drops food coloring**
- ◆ **2 to 3 drops flavoring oil**
- ◆ **12 lollipop sticks**

1 Line a large baking sheet with aluminum foil and arrange lollipop sticks 4 inches apart.
2 In a heavy saucepan over medium heat, combine sugar, water, and corn syrup and heat until sugar dissolves. Cover and boil mixture 1 minute to wash down any sugar crystals. Remove the cover and boil the syrup until it registers 310°F on a candy thermometer.
3 Immediately remove the saucepan from the heat and set on a rack. Let syrup cool 5 minutes, then stir in food coloring and flavoring.
4 Pour syrup in 2- to 3-inch puddles over one end of each lollipop stick. Allow candy to cool completely. Wrap each lollipop in plastic wrap.
MAKES ABOUT 12 TOTAL TIME 40 MINUTES

VARIATION For variety, make several batches, each one a different color and flavor. You can make surprise pops by allowing one batch to cool and then coating it with a second flavor on one or both sides.

This selection of classic confections will satisfy every sweet tooth: **1** *Turkish delight,* **2** *Chocolate fruit and nut truffles,* **3** *Chocolate fruit clusters,* **4** *Peanut brittle,* **5** *Coconut ice,* **6** *Marshmallows.*

Marshmallows

These homemade treats are quick and easy to make with an electric mixer.

- ◆ **3 tablespoons confectioners sugar**
- ◆ **3 tablespoons cornstarch**
- ◆ **1½ tablespoons unflavored gelatin**
- ◆ **⅓ cup water**
- ◆ **½ cup granulated sugar**
- ◆ **⅔ cup light corn syrup**

1 Line a 13 x 9 x 2-inch baking pan with wax paper. Combine 1 tablespoon each of the confectioners sugar and cornstarch, and sift evenly into the prepared pan.
2 In the bowl of an electric mixer, place the gelatin and ⅓ cup water. Set aside until the gelatin has softened, about 5 minutes.
3 Place the bowl in a larger pan of simmering water and stir until the gelatin has dissolved. Add the granulated sugar and continue to stir until it has dissolved. Remove bowl from the water and add the corn syrup. Beat for 10 to 15 minutes until creamy and thick. Let cool.
4 With a wet spatula, spread the mixture in the prepared pan. Set aside for 20 minutes to cool and set.
5 Lift the set marshmallow onto a cutting board. Lightly dust with confectioners' sugar and cornstarch and cut into squares. Dredge the pieces in confectioners' sugar and cornstarch and store in an airtight container in a cool, dry place. Keeps for 1 to 2 weeks.
MAKES ABOUT 36   TOTAL TIME 1 HOUR

Caramel fudge

Cut into squares and wrapped in colorful cellophane, this creamy fudge makes a great gift.

- ◆ **6 cups dark brown sugar, firmly packed**
- ◆ **1½ sticks (6 ounces) unsalted butter, cut up**
- ◆ **1¼ cups milk**
- ◆ **⅔ cup heavy cream**
- ◆ **1 teaspoon vanilla extract**

1 Line a 9-inch square pan with foil.
2 In a large, heavy saucepan over medium heat, stir the sugar, butter, milk, and cream until the sugar dissolves, the butter melts, and the mixture comes to a boil.
3 Reduce the heat and boil gently, stirring occasionally to prevent sticking, until the mixture reaches the soft-ball stage (240°F on a candy thermometer).
4 Set the saucepan in a larger pan of cold water and allow the fudge to cool until the bottom of the pan is cool enough to touch.
5 Add the vanilla and, with a wooden spoon, beat the mixture until it becomes creamy and thick. As soon as the mixture begins to lighten in color and lose its gloss, pour it into the prepared pan and set aside to cool thoroughly.
6 Using a knife dipped in hot water, score the fudge into squares, then slice through. Pieces can be stored in an airtight container in the refrigerator for up to 2 weeks.
MAKES 50–60   TOTAL TIME 3 HOURS

Peanut brittle

Packed with peanuts, this classic candy is both crunchy and melt-in-your-mouth delicious.

- ◆ **2¾ cups granulated sugar**
- ◆ **½ stick unsalted butter**
- ◆ **⅔ cup water**
- ◆ **1½ cups lightly salted peanuts**

1 Grease and line a 13 x 9-inch pan with foil.
2 In a large, heavy saucepan over moderate heat, cook the sugar, butter, and water, stirring occasionally, until the mixture becomes a golden-brown syrup, about 25 minutes (see below). Remove to a cool surface.
3 Stir in the peanuts and pour mixture into the pan, spreading the nuts evenly.
4 Let peanut brittle set and cool before breaking into bite-size pieces. It can be stored in an airtight container in a cool, dry place for up to 1 month.
MAKES ABOUT 45 PIECES   TOTAL TIME 1 HOUR

MAKING PEANUT BRITTLE

1 *In a heavy saucepan, using a wooden spoon, stir the sugar, butter, and water together over medium heat. Bring to a simmer—the mixture should deepen in color.*

2 *Once the mixture begins to bubble, remove the pan to a cool surface. Stir in the peanuts. (Substitute toasted almonds for the peanuts, to make praline instead of peanut brittle.)*

3 *Pour the mixture into a greased, foil-lined, rectangular pan and leave it to set and cool. This should take no more than 30 minutes, but check for hardness before proceeding to Step 4.*

4 *When set and cool, break the brittle into bite-size pieces with a knife handle. If making praline, use a rolling pin to crush the pieces. Store in airtight jars in a cool, dry place.*

Sweet spiced nuts

These make unusual nibbles. Offer them along with fruit and cheese at the end of a festive meal.

- ◆ **1 egg white**
- ◆ **2 tablespoons cold water**
- ◆ **2 cups nuts of choice**
- ◆ **½ cup sugar**
- ◆ **¼ cup cornstarch**
- ◆ **3 teaspoons cinnamon**
- ◆ **1 teaspoon allspice**
- ◆ **½ teaspoon ground ginger**
- ◆ **½ teaspoon ground nutmeg**
- ◆ **pinch of salt**

1 Preheat the oven to 350°F.
2 In a small bowl, whisk the egg white lightly with the water. Add nuts and toss well.
3 In a medium bowl, combine the sugar and cornstarch with the spices and pinch of salt. Lift the nuts out of the egg-white mixture, leaving the extra in the bowl, and transfer them to the spice mixture, tossing well. Arrange the nuts in a single layer in a jelly-roll pan lined with baking parchment or aluminum foil. Bake for 30 minutes or until golden.

MAKES 2 CUPS   TOTAL TIME 50 MINUTES

Turkish delight

This appealing candy is easy to make at home. Rose water can be found at specialty food stores. When the sugar syrup boils, coat the inside of the saucepan with a brush dipped in water to prevent sugar crystals from forming.

- ◆ **4 cups sugar**
- ◆ **4 ½ cups water**
- ◆ **2 teaspoons lemon juice**
- ◆ **1 ¼ cups cornstarch**
- ◆ **1 teaspoon cream of tartar**
- ◆ **1 ½ tablespoons rose water**
- ◆ **red food coloring (optional)**
- ◆ **1 cup confectioners sugar**

1 Oil a 9-inch square pan. Line with plastic wrap and oil the plastic wrap.
2 In a heavy saucepan over medium heat, combine the sugar, 1 ½ cups of the water, and the lemon juice. Stir until the sugar dissolves

CRYSTALLIZED FLOWERS

1 Line a baking sheet with aluminum foil.
2 In a small bowl, lightly beat 1 tablespoon pasteurized powdered egg white and 2 tablespoons water just until foamy. Apply the mixture to both sides of the flowers with a soft artist's brush. Just moisten the surface. Sift very fine granulated sugar lightly all over the flowers. Repaint any parts where the sugar won't stick and resprinkle.
3 Place the flowers on the prepared sheet, making sure that they don't touch each other. Place in a very low (200°F or less) oven with the door slightly ajar for 10 to 15 minutes. Check from time to time that the flowers aren't discoloring. Alternatively, dry in the refrigerator for 1 to 3 days.
4 Crystallized flowers that are well coated with sugar will keep for 3 to 4 days in an airtight jar.

F LOWERS such as pansies, violets, and rose petals are the most successful for crystallizing. Pick pretty, fresh specimens, free of chemical pesticides, early in the morning.

and the mixture boils. Reduce the heat and simmer gently, without stirring, until the mixture reaches the soft-ball stage (240°F on a candy thermometer). Remove the pan from the heat.
3 In a second large heavy saucepan over medium heat, stir together 1 cup cornstarch and the cream of tartar. Gradually stir in the remaining 3 cups of water until no lumps remain. Stir constantly, until the mixture boils and is a thick, gluey paste.
4 Slowly pour the hot sugar, water, and lemon juice syrup into the cornstarch mixture, stirring constantly. Reduce the heat and simmer, stirring often to prevent sticking, for about 1 hour, or until the mixture has become a pale golden color.

5 Stir in the rose water and tint as desired with food coloring. Pour the mixture into the prepared pan and spread evenly. Cool to room temperature and let stand, uncovered, overnight to set.
6 Sift the confectioners sugar and the remaining ¼ cup cornstarch onto a large cutting board. Turn the Turkish delight out and cut into 1-inch squares with an oiled knife. Roll pieces in the sugar mixture to coat well. Store in an airtight container with sheets of wax paper, dusted with the sugar mixture, separating every layer.

MAKES ABOUT 80 PIECES   TOTAL TIME 2 HOURS

◆ Drinks with Dash ◆

*Whether you're hosting a summer barbecue or holiday get-together, or simply having a few friends
over on a Saturday night, hospitality demands that drinks are festive and plentiful. These welcoming beverages,
with and without alcohol, will maintain your reputation as a perfect host.*

Drinks for all seasons, from Christmas cheer to something cooling on a hot summer night: **1** *Lemon syrup drink,* **2** *Cranberry punch,* **3** *Whiskey eggnog,* **4** *Fruit cup,* **5** *Hot Bloody Mary,* **6** *Red wine and strawberry cup,* **7** *Hot chocolate espresso,* **8** *Sangria.*

Sangria

Instead of serving a variety of drinks at a party, fill a punch bowl or pitcher with this simple but refreshing drink.

- ◆ **2 oranges, sliced**
- ◆ **2 lemons, sliced**
- ◆ **2 cinnamon sticks**
- ◆ **¾ cup brandy**
- ◆ **1 bottle (750 milliliters) red wine of choice**
- ◆ **1 bottle (750 milliliters) sparkling cider, chilled**
- ◆ **ice cubes**

1 In a large jug or bowl, place the orange and lemon slices, cinnamon sticks, and brandy.
2 Pour the wine and cider over the ingredients. Stir in some ice cubes at serving time.
MAKES ABOUT 1¾ QUARTS   TOTAL TIME 10 MINUTES

Cranberry punch

This sparkling red punch is a good choice for a buffet at holiday time, and with its citrus bite, it's a great summer cooler, too.

- ◆ **2 cups cranberry juice**
- ◆ **2 cups unsweetened pineapple juice**
- ◆ **1 cup orange juice**
- ◆ **¾ cup Triple Sec (omit for nonalcoholic punch)**
- ◆ **1 pint strawberries, hulled and sliced**
- ◆ **1 lime, thinly sliced**
- ◆ **4 cups ginger ale, chilled**
- ◆ **ice cubes**

1 In a large glass container, combine the juices, Triple Sec, strawberries, and lime slices. Chill thoroughly.
2 Just before serving, slowly stir in the ginger ale. Pour into a punch bowl or large jug and add ice cubes.
MAKES ABOUT 1½ QUARTS   TOTAL TIME 20 MINUTES
PLUS CHILLING TIME

VARIATION For a less sweet punch, substitute seltzer or club soda for the ginger ale.

Hot Bloody Mary

Warm the cockles of your heart with this heated version of a traditional drink.

- ¼ cup vodka
- ¾ cup tomato juice
- 4 drops hot red pepper sauce
- ¼ teaspoon Worcestershire sauce
- kosher salt
- freshly ground black pepper
- celery or cucumber stick

1 Into a microwave-safe cup, pour the vodka, tomato juice, and sauces. Microwave on medium-high for 30 seconds. Or gently heat the mixture on the stove in a small saucepan, then pour into glasses with handles.
2 Sprinkle with salt and pepper to taste, and garnish with a celery or cucumber stick.
MAKES 1 CUP   TOTAL TIME 10 MINUTES

Whiskey eggnog

This traditional holiday drink is saved from raw-egg safety problems by cooking the custard. Brandy or rum can be substituted for whiskey.

- 4 eggs
- ½ cup sugar
- 3 cups milk
- 1 teaspoon vanilla extract
- ½ cup whiskey
- ½ teaspoon freshly grated nutmeg
- 1 cup heavy cream

1 In a saucepan, beat the eggs and sugar until creamy. In a second saucepan over low heat, heat 2 cups of the milk until hot. Slowly add to the egg mixture, stirring continuously. Cook over low heat, stirring, for 15 to 20 minutes or until the mixture reaches 170°F and has thickened. Stir in the remaining milk, vanilla, whiskey, and half the nutmeg. Chill 3 hours.
2 In a medium bowl, beat the cream until soft peaks form. Fold into the milk mixture.
3 Ladle the eggnog into a punch bowl and sprinkle with the remaining grated nutmeg.
MAKES 6 CUPS   TOTAL TIME 45 MINUTES PLUS 3 HOURS

Citrus vodka liqueur

This is a delicious, warming drink to sip by the fire. Enjoy it in small amounts.

- 1½ cups white wine
- 3 cups vodka
- 2 lemons, sliced
- 1 orange, sliced
- 1 strip lemon zest
- 2 cinnamon sticks
- 3 allspice berries
- 3 whole cloves
- 1 vanilla bean
- 1 sprig rosemary
- ¼ cup sugar

1 In a large, clean, widemouthed jar, place all the ingredients and seal with a tight-fitting lid. Let sit for 4 weeks to allow the flavors to develop. Shake daily.
2 Sterilize several sealable bottles or jars (p.168).
3 Into a pitcher, strain the liqueur through doubled cheesecloth or a fine sieve. Pour the liqueur into the bottles and seal.
MAKES 5–6 CUPS   TOTAL TIME 15 MINUTES PLUS 4 WEEKS

Red wine and strawberry cup

Strawberries steeped in port give this cooling drink a heady fragrance and ambrosial taste.

- 1 pint strawberries, hulled and sliced
- ⅓ cup sugar
- several strips orange zest
- ¾ cup port
- 1 bottle (750 milliliters) red wine
- seltzer, chilled
- mint sprigs, to decorate

1 In a large jar, place the strawberries, sugar, zest, and port. Cover and chill for 24 hours.
2 When ready to serve, transfer to a punch bowl and add the red wine and mint, if desired. Serve in glasses, topped off with chilled seltzer and a sprig of mint.
MAKES ABOUT 8 CUPS   TOTAL TIME 15 MINUTES PLUS 24 HOURS

Iced tea

Here is the perfect summer-afternoon refresher.

- 3 tea bags
- 4 cups freshly boiled water
- sugar (optional)
- crushed ice
- lemon slices
- mint sprigs

1 In a teapot or enameled saucepan, infuse the tea bags in the water for 4 minutes.
2 Pour the tea into a pitcher, discarding bags, and cool. Stir in sugar to taste, if desired. Do not refrigerate or the tea will become cloudy.
3 Divide the tea among 4 tall glasses and fill each to the top with crushed ice. Add a slice of lemon and a mint sprig to each glass.
MAKES 4–5 CUPS   TOTAL TIME 1 HOUR

VARIATIONS Lime slices are equally good as lemon slices in iced tea. Fruit-scented herbal teas can also be used.

Hot chocolate espresso

Not for the worried weight watcher, this creamy drink is pure indulgence, but just right for after ice skating or sledding on a wintry day.

- ½ cup strong hot coffee
- 1 to 3 teaspoons sugar (optional)
- ½ cup cream, or ¼ cup half-and-half and ¼ cup milk
- 1½ teaspoons unsweetened cocoa
- whipped cream
- 1 tablespoon grated milk chocolate
- cinnamon stick

1 In a large cup or mug, mix the coffee and sugar, if desired.
2 In a small saucepan over low heat, warm the cream. Add the cocoa and mix well.
3 Add the cream mixture to the coffee and top with a dollop of whipped cream and the grated chocolate. Serve with a cinnamon stick.
MAKES 1 CUP   TOTAL TIME 10 MINUTES

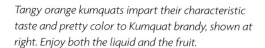

Tangy orange kumquats impart their characteristic taste and pretty color to Kumquat brandy, shown at right. Enjoy both the liquid and the fruit.

Fruit cup

This nonalcoholic punch combines the juices of three fruits for flavor and adds seltzer for bubbles, making it great for summer entertaining.

- ◆ **2 cups fresh orange juice**
- ◆ **2 quarts grape juice**
- ◆ **1 quart pineapple juice**
- ◆ **2 quarts seltzer, chilled**
- ◆ **mint leaves**
- ◆ **lemon or orange slices**
- ◆ **crushed ice**

1 In a serving bowl, mix all the juices together and chill in the refrigerator.
2 Just before serving, crush the ice and add seltzer, mint leaves, and citrus slices to the bowl. Put crushed ice in each glass and ladle the fruit cup over it.

MAKES ABOUT 24 CUPS TOTAL TIME 5 MINUTES PLUS CHILLING TIME

Lemon syrup

Dilute this syrup base with water, seltzer, or club soda, and decorate with lemon or lime slices, as you like. You can also make up a glass with hot water and a tablespoon of brandy to help ease a head cold.

- ◆ **1 cup fresh lemon juice**
- ◆ **zest of 2 lemons**
- ◆ **1 cup sugar**
- ◆ **1 teaspoon cream of tartar**
- ◆ **10 cups boiling water**

1 Sterilize 2 or 3 sealable bottles or jars (p.168).
2 In a large bowl, place all the ingredients except the boiling water. Mix well to combine. Add the boiling water and stir well until the sugar has dissolved.
3 Pour the liquid into the sterilized bottles, seal, and store in the refrigerator for up to 6 months. Ready to use immediately.

MAKES 2½ CUPS TOTAL TIME 10 MINUTES

Kumquat brandy

This is one of the most popular of all fruit liqueurs. The kumquats themselves make a delicious dessert with ice cream if they are used within six months of preparing the brandy.

- ◆ **1½ pounds kumquats, firmly packed**
- ◆ **1 cup sugar**
- ◆ **½ vanilla bean**
- ◆ **2 cups water**
- ◆ **4 cups brandy**

1 Carefully wash the kumquats and prick them 8 times with a needle.

2 In a large saucepan, bring the sugar, vanilla bean, and water to a boil over low heat and simmer for 15 minutes. Add the kumquats, bring the syrup back to a boil, and simmer 5 minutes more.
3 Remove the saucepan from the heat. Using a slotted spoon, ladle the kumquats into a warm 6-cup sterilized jar (p.168).
4 Over high heat, reduce the syrup by half. Cool, then pour the syrup over the kumquats, discarding the vanilla bean.
5 Pour in the brandy and seal. Label and store in a cool, dark place for at least a month before opening.

MAKES 6 CUPS TOTAL TIME 1 HOUR PLUS 1 MONTH

◆ Festive Foods ◆

Preparing desserts and treats for the holidays is a year-end tradition in many homes.
Baking a fruitcake or steaming the pudding yourself means you get the exact flavor you want.
We've included seasonal favorites from around the world to help you celebrate.

Orange shortbread fingers

The tangy flavor of these shortbread fingers makes a pleasant change from traditional Christmas shortbread.

- ¾ cup all-purpose flour
- 3 tablespoons cornstarch
- ¼ cup plus 2 tablespoons sugar
- grated zest of 1 orange
- ¼ teaspoon salt
- 7 tablespoons unsalted butter, cut up

1 Preheat the oven to 300°F. Grease an 8-inch square pan.
2 Into a medium bowl, sift the flour and cornstarch. Add the ¼ cup sugar, orange zest, and salt. Using your fingertips, work the butter into the dry ingredients until the mixture resembles fine crumbs.
3 Knead the mixture until it forms a dough, then press it into the prepared pan. Score the dough into 24 narrow rectangles and prick with the tines of a fork. Sprinkle with the 2 tablespoons of sugar. Bake for 30 minutes or until a pale golden color.

FOR SUCCESSFUL BAKING

To keep dried and glacé fruits from sinking to the bottom of a Christmas cake, toss them in a little flour before adding them to the mixture.

To help prevent overbrowning when making cookies, use vegetable shortening instead of butter to grease the baking sheets . Remove cookies from the baking sheets as soon as they are baked.

Any shortcrust pastry is suitable for mince pies.

4 Remove from the oven and leave the shortbread to cool in the pan until it holds its shape enough to turn out on a rack.
5 When completely cooled, cut the shortbread into fingers along the scored lines. The cookies can be stored in an airtight container for up to 1 week.
MAKES 24 FINGERS   TOTAL TIME 45 MINUTES

Christmas fruit mince

Serve this spicy fruit mixture in pies or miniature tarts for Christmas festivities. Prepare the mince well beforehand to ensure full flavor—and to make the pie-making go faster.

- 3 cups dried currants
- 1½ cups golden raisins
- 1½ cups dark raisins
- ¾ cup candied peel, chopped
- 1 pound cooking apples, peeled, cored, and finely chopped
- 2½ cups brown sugar, firmly packed
- 1 teaspoon ground allspice
- 1 teaspoon ground nutmeg
- 1 teaspoon ground cinnamon
- grated zest and juice of 2 lemons
- ¾ cup brandy

1 In a large bowl, place all the ingredients and mix well to combine. Cover with plastic wrap and leave overnight.
2 Pack the mixture into sterilized jars (p.168) and close tightly. Leave in the refrigerator for 4 to 6 weeks.
3 Stir the mixture well before using.
MAKES ABOUT 10 CUPS   TOTAL TIME 30 MINUTES
PLUS 6 WEEKS

Kourambiedes

These delicious little almond cookies are a traditional treat in Greece. Bake them ahead and freeze. They thaw quickly, so set them out while you are making the coffee that usually accompanies them.

- 2 sticks (8 ounces) unsalted butter at room temperature
- ½ cup granulated sugar
- 1 egg plus 2 egg yolks
- 3 cups all-purpose flour
- ¼ teaspoon salt
- ½ cup almonds, finely chopped
- about 50 whole cloves
- 1 cup confectioners sugar

1 Preheat the oven to 350°F. and grease 2 baking sheets.
2 In a food processor, place the butter, sugar, egg and egg yolks, flour, salt, and almonds and process for 30 seconds or until just combined.
3 Roll the mixture into balls about the size of a walnut and place a clove in each. Arrange on 2 baking sheets. Bake 25 to 30 minutes, or until golden brown.
4 Remove the baking sheets from the oven and transfer the cookies to a rack. Leave to cool slightly, then dredge generously with confectioners sugar. The cookies can be stored in an airtight container for 1 to 2 weeks. To freeze, layer the cookies, without the dusting of confectioners sugar, in a freezer container, separating each layer with wax paper.
MAKES ABOUT 50   TOTAL TIME 1 HOUR

Christmas is a time for the treats we've loved since childhood. Clockwise from top right: Christmas fruit mince, Traditional Christmas cake, Kourambiedes, Christmas pudding, and Orange shortbread fingers.

Cranberry lebkuchen

This tasty cake from Germany keeps well and suits many occasions but is especially nice on a chilly day at holiday time. Serve with a hot cup of tea or a fresh brew of coffee

BASE
- 1⅓ cups honey
- ¾ cup granulated sugar
- 3 tablespoons butter
- 3½ cups all-purpose flour
- 1 teaspoon baking powder
- ½ teaspoon baking soda
- ¾ cup blanched almonds
- 1 cup dried cranberries
- ¼ teaspoon ground ginger
- ½ teaspoon ground cardamom
- 2 teaspoons ground cinnamon
- 1 teaspoon ground allspice

ICING
- 1½ cups confectioners sugar
- 2 tablespoons lemon juice
- 1 tablespoon butter, softened

1 Preheat the oven to 350°F. Grease a 9-inch square pan and line with wax paper.
2 In a large saucepan over low heat, stir the honey and granulated sugar together. Add the butter and stir until melted. Remove saucepan from the heat.
3 Into a medium bowl, sift together the flour, baking powder, and baking soda. Add to the honey mixture. Stir in the almonds, cranberries, and spices, mixing well to combine. The mixture will be sticky.
4 Spoon the mixture into the prepared pan; level and smooth the top. Bake for 25 to 30 minutes or until a toothpick or tester inserted in the cake comes out clean. Cool in the pan on a rack.
5 For the icing: In a small bowl, mix together the confectioners sugar, lemon juice, and butter with a wooden spoon until blended and smooth. Ice the cake while it is still slightly warm. Store the cooled cake in an airtight container for up to 1 week.

SERVES ABOUT 24   TOTAL TIME 1 HOUR 30 MINUTES

Christmas pudding

No traditional Christmas dinner is complete without pudding. It is best if allowed to mature for at least two days before serving, but it can be made up to three months ahead.

- 1½ cups raisins, chopped
- ⅔ cup dates, pitted and chopped
- 1 cup soft dried figs, chopped
- 1 cup currants
- ¾ cup golden raisins
- ½ cup brandy
- 2 sticks (8 ounces) unsalted butter
- 1 cup dark brown sugar, firmly packed
- grated zest of 1 lemon
- grated zest of 1 orange
- 4 eggs, beaten
- 1 cup blanched almonds, chopped
- ¾ cup all-purpose flour, sifted
- 1 teaspoon cinnamon
- ½ teaspoon nutmeg
- 1 teaspoon ground allspice
- 1 teaspoon ground ginger
- 1½ cups fresh white bread crumbs

1 Grease a 2-quart ceramic mold or casserole.
2 In a large bowl, place all the fruit and pour the brandy over it. Stir well to disperse the brandy. Cover with a towel and set aside to macerate 12 to 24 hours.
3 In a large bowl, with an electric mixer on high, beat the butter and sugar until thick and creamy. Beat in the zests and eggs. Fold in the fruit and almonds. Add the flour and spices, combining well, then fold in the bread crumbs.
4 Spoon the mixture into the prepared mold, press down well, and level the surface. Cut a sheet of wax paper 2 inches larger than the top of the mold. Pleat the wax paper twice through the center to allow for expansion as the pudding rises. Place the paper on top of the pudding and cover it with a twice-pleated double thickness of foil. Tie foil securely to the edge of the mold with string.

5 Place the mold on a rack in a Dutch oven or other large covered pot. Pour boiling water into the Dutch oven until it is halfway up the side of the mold. Keep water at a gentle boil. Steam for 4 hours, topping the boiling water to the same level when necessary.
6 Remove the mold from the Dutch oven and set on a rack to cool. When thoroughly cooled, rewrap with fresh wax paper and foil, and store in the refrigerator until ready to serve.
7 Steam again for 2 hours or microwave to reheat before serving.

SERVES 12–16   TOTAL TIME 5 HOURS PLUS 3 DAYS

Traditional Christmas cake

This rich cake can be made at the last minute before Christmas—it doesn't need to mature.

- 2 sticks plus 2 tablespoons (9 ounces total) butter at room temperature
- 1½ cups dark brown sugar
- 4 eggs
- 3 cups all-purpose flour
- ¼ teaspoon salt
- 1 teaspoon ground allspice
- 1 teaspoon cinnamon
- ½ teaspoon nutmeg
- 1½ cups each currants, golden raisins, dark raisins
- 1⅓ cups soft dried figs, chopped
- 1¼ cups dates, pitted and chopped
- 1 cup chopped stoned dried prunes
- 1¾ cups chopped dried apricots
- ¾ cup blanched almonds, chopped
- ⅔ cup plus 4 tablespoons brandy
- 2 teaspoons instant espresso, mixed with 1 tablespoon water

1 Preheat the oven to 300°F. Grease a round 9- or 10-inch cake pan, and line bottom and sides with several layers of wax paper.
2 In a large bowl, with an electric mixer on high, beat the butter and sugar until thick and creamy. Add the eggs, one at a time, beating well after each addition. Sift together the flour,

salt, and spices; then fold into the creamed mixture. Add the fruit, almonds, ⅔ cup brandy, and espresso, folding in well.

3 Spoon the mixture into the prepared pan, leveling the surface. Place the pan in the center of the oven and bake for 30 minutes. Reduce the temperature to 275°F and bake for 3 ½ hours longer or until a tester inserted in the center of the cake comes out clean.

4 Remove the pan from the oven, cover with first a kitchen towel and then a thick bath towel so that the cake will cool slowly.

5 When the cake is cool, prick the top with a skewer and drizzle with the extra brandy. Wrap in wax paper and store in an airtight container. Keep in a cool place for up to 3 months.

SERVES 30   TOTAL TIME 4 ¾ HOURS PLUS COOLING

Stollen

The distinctive oval shape of this traditional German Christmas cake is said to represent the Christ child wrapped in swaddling clothes.

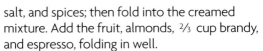

- ◆ **3 to 4 cups all-purpose flour**
- ◆ **1 teaspoon salt**
- ◆ **¼ -ounce packet dry yeast**
- ◆ **½ cup warm (105° to 115°F.) milk**
- ◆ **⅓ cup sugar**
- ◆ **2 sticks (8 ounces) unsalted butter, melted, plus 4 tablespoons, melted**
- ◆ **2 tablespoons cognac**
- ◆ **1 cup blanched almonds, chopped**
- ◆ **1 ½ cups raisins, chopped**
- ◆ **⅓ cup mixed candied citrus peel**
- ◆ **1 tablespoon grated zest of lemon**
- ◆ **sifted confectioners sugar**

1 Into a large bowl, sift 3 cups of flour with the salt. In a small bowl, dissolve the yeast in half the milk. Make a well in the center of the flour and salt mixture; then add the yeast and milk, sugar, 2 sticks of butter, and cognac. Mix well to combine, adding enough additional flour to form a smooth, elastic dough.

2 On a lightly floured surface, turn the dough out and knead for 3 minutes. Lightly oil a bowl

and place the dough in it, turning to coat well with oil. Cover with lightly oiled plastic wrap and let stand in a warm place for about 1 hour.

3 On a lightly floured surface, turn out the dough. Knead in the almonds, raisins, citrus peel, and zest. Allow the dough to rise once more until almost doubled in bulk.

4 Remove the dough from the bowl and shape it into a 10-inch round. Fold the round almost in half, flatten, and shape to form an oval. Place on a greased baking sheet, cover with lightly oiled plastic wrap, and let stand in a warm place for 30 minutes.

5 Preheat the oven to 375°F. Brush the stollen with melted butter. Bake, brushing with butter every 10 minutes, for 45 to 50 minutes or until a tester comes out clean when inserted.

6 Remove from the oven and cool on a rack. When cooled, wrap in several layers of foil and store in the refrigerator—the cake will keep for 3 to 4 weeks. To serve, slice thinly, wrap the slices in foil, and warm in a moderate oven for 15 minutes, or toast the slices . Dust with confectioners sugar before serving.

SERVES 10–12   TOTAL TIME 4 HOURS

PUDDING PREPARATION

Smaller puddings can be made from the Christmas pudding recipe on the facing page. To make puddings to serve three or four, fill four 2-cup molds with the mixture and steam for 2 hours.

Make puddings ahead of time, wrap securely, and store either in the refrigerator for up to 3 months or the freezer for up to 12 months. When planning to resteam a frozen pudding, first allow it to thaw in the refrigerator— 3 to 4 days for a large one, 2 to 3 days for a small one.

A microwave oven is useful for reheating puddings. Set the microwave on medium and heat a large pudding for about 10 minutes. Reheat individual servings on high for 30 seconds.

A Christmas gift pudding, still in its mold and wrapped decoratively, makes a lovely seasonal token for friends or holiday dinner hosts.

Panforte

This traditional Italian chocolate, nut, and fruit cake is a specialty of Siena, Italy. It is best left for a day to firm before cutting. If you can't find candied apricots and pears, substitute dried ones.

- ◆ **¾ cup toasted blanched almonds, chopped**
- ◆ **¾ cup toasted hazelnuts, chopped**
- ◆ **⅓ cup candied pineapple, chopped**
- ◆ **⅓ cup candied apricots, chopped**
- ◆ **⅓ cup candied pears, chopped**
- ◆ **⅔ cup all-purpose flour, sifted**
- ◆ **2 tablespoons unsweetened cocoa, sifted**
- ◆ **1 teaspoon cinnamon**
- ◆ **3 ½ ounces dark chocolate**
- ◆ **⅓ cup granulated sugar**
- ◆ **½ cup honey**
- ◆ **sifted confectioners sugar**

1 Preheat the oven to 300°F. Grease an 8-inch round cake pan and line the bottom with wax paper.

2 In a large bowl, mix the nuts and candied fruits with the flour, cocoa, and cinnamon to coat thoroughly.

3 In a double boiler, over low heat, stir the chocolate until melted. In a medium saucepan, over low heat, dissolve the sugar and honey. Once the sugar has dissolved, bring the syrup to a boil, reduce the heat, and simmer for about 5 minutes. Add the syrup and the melted chocolate to the fruit and nuts and mix well.

4 Spread the mixture quickly and evenly in the prepared pan. Bake for 30 minutes. (The panforte will be soft and appear underdone, but it will firm as it cools.)

5 Cool in the pan on a rack. Turn out the cake, dust with confectioners sugar, and wrap in foil. It can be stored in an airtight container in a cool place for 3 to 4 weeks.

SERVES 8   TOTAL TIME 1 HOUR

VARIATION Panforte can also be made in a square pan lined with edible rice paper and topped with rice paper before baking.

◆ Delightful Desserts ◆

The simplest combinations of ingredients can produce memorable desserts. Poached fruit from the garden, snowy meringues with a sauce of berries, old-fashioned puddings, and silky-smooth custards are delectable dishes that provide a sweet finish to a meal.

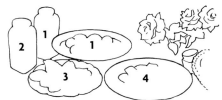

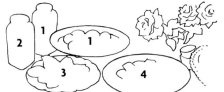

Desserts needn't be heavy to make a satisfying end to a meal. Today's eating style calls for light, flavorful desserts such as these: **1** *Preserved peaches,* **2** *Brandied figs,* **3** *Meringues awaiting a berry and whipped-cream filling, and* **4** *Gratin of brandied figs.*

Fruit compote with sabayon

This beautiful compote of peaches and plums is easy to make and is the perfect hot dessert. The French use a vanilla bean to flavor the syrup; Italians prefer the zest of a lemon or an orange .

- ◆ **1 cup syrup drained from poached (see instructions for poaching figs, below) or preserved fruit**
- ◆ **1 vanilla bean, or the zest of 1 lemon or orange**
- ◆ **4 poached or preserved peaches, drained**
- ◆ **4 poached or preserved plums, drained**

SAUCE SABAYON
- ◆ **2 egg yolks**
- ◆ **1 tablespoon sugar**
- ◆ **⅓ cup sweet sherry**

1 In a medium saucepan, over moderate heat, stir the syrup and the vanilla bean or the lemon or orange zest. Simmer for 5 minutes.
2 Add the prepared fruit to the syrup and warm gently until heated through. Turn fruit once or twice and spoon syrup over it.
3 To make the sauce, in the top of a double boiler over simmering water, mix the egg yolks, sugar, and sherry and whisk briskly until the mixture becomes thick and glossy and registers 170°F. on a candy thermometer. Don't allow the water to boil, or the sauce will curdle.
4 Pour the sauce over the warm fruit and serve immediately with a crisp cookie.
SERVES 4-6   TOTAL TIME 30 MINUTES

Brandied figs

Dried figs can be prepared in this manner as easily as the fresh variety. Serve brandied figs with cream or broiled with sauce and confectioners sugar, as in the gratin recipe below.

- ◆ **2 pounds fresh figs or 1 pound dried, halved lengthwise**
- ◆ **1 cup water**
- ◆ **⅔ cup sugar**
- ◆ **4 star anise**
- ◆ **1 cinnamon stick**
- ◆ **1 cup brandy**

1 In a medium saucepan, over low heat, bring the figs, water, and sugar slowly to a simmer. Poach gently for 2 minutes if using fresh figs, 5 to 8 minutes for dried.
2 Remove the figs with a slotted spoon and, when they are cool enough to handle, layer attractively with the spices in a jar with a tight-fitting lid.
3 Pour in the brandy, add enough cooking syrup to fill to the top, and cover tightly. The flavor develops better if the fruit is allowed to steep for more than a week.
MAKES 2 PINT JARS   TOTAL TIME 30 MINUTES PLUS 1 WEEK

Gratin of brandied figs

This dessert is a boon to a busy dinner-party host. The figs need only be placed under the broiler for seconds before they are served. Prepare the brandied figs ahead, using the recipe above.

- ◆ **8 brandied figs**
- ◆ **sabayon sauce (see recipe for Fruit compote, left)**
- ◆ **sifted confectioners sugar**
- ◆ **fresh mint leaves**

1 Preheat the broiler. Prepare the brandied figs, as above, then remove them from their syrup and drain in a colander. Arrange on four heatproof serving plates.
2 Spoon the sabayon sauce over the fruit, sprinkle lightly with confectioners sugar, and place under a very hot broiler until the top is lightly colored. Decorate with mint leaves.
SERVES 4   TOTAL TIME 30 MINUTES

VARIATION This recipe works well with any poached fruit, such as peaches or pears.

Preserved peaches

Poached fruits are the basis of many easy desserts. Try plums, nectarines, and apricots.

- ◆ **4 pounds small peaches**
- ◆ **3 cups sugar**
- ◆ **4 cups water**
- ◆ **1 cinnamon stick**
- ◆ **4 whole cloves**
- ◆ **1 cup kirsch (optional)**

1 Skin the peaches by scalding them in boiling water for 30 seconds, then dipping them in ice water. The skins will peel off easily.
2 In a large saucepan, over moderate heat, bring the sugar, water, and spices to a boil.
3 Halve and pit the peaches. Pierce each half four times so the syrup will penetrate. Add to the syrup and simmer 5 minutes. Remove with a slotted spoon and pack into warm, sterilized jars (p.168) with the cinnamon stick and cloves.
4 Boil the syrup for 5 minutes to reduce it slightly. Add kirsch, if desired, and pour syrup over fruit. Seal and keep refrigerated for several months.

MAKES 2 LARGE JARS   TOTAL TIME 50 MINUTES

VARIATIONS This recipe is just as appropriate for poaching pears, plums, or apricots. You might want to substitute white wine or sherry for the kirsch when you poach pears. Experiment with mint and thyme as seasonings.

Meringues

Store meringues in an airtight container. If they soften, place in a low oven for 5 minutes.

- ◆ **whites of 3 large eggs**
- ◆ **scant ⅛ teaspoon cream of tartar**
- ◆ **½ cup granulated sugar**
- ◆ **½ cup brown sugar**

1 Preheat the oven to 250°F. Brush baking sheets lightly with oil and dust with flour. Alternatively, line the baking sheets with baking parchment.
2 In a large bowl, using a balloon whisk or an electric mixer, beat egg whites, slowly at first, until frothy. Add the cream of tartar, and beat at high speed until peaks hold their shape.
3 Gradually beat in 2 tablespoons of the granulated sugar and continue beating 2 to 3 minutes. Mix the remaining sugars together. Add half to the egg whites, beating until very thick. Add remaining sugar by folding in lightly.
4 Push even spoonfuls of meringue onto the baking sheets, forming ovals that mound in the middle. Leave 1 inch of space between each.
5 Bake 1½ hours and remove from the oven. Shut off the oven. Turn each meringue over and make an indentation in the bottom by pressing gently with your finger. Return to the oven for about 1 hour to dry completely.

MAKES 24–36   TOTAL TIME 3 HOURS

VARIATION To serve meringues with a topping, form them with a slight hollow on top. In Step 5, omit the indent and simply let the meringues dry in the turned-off oven. Serve with ice cream and sliced berries or other fruit.

Tiramisu

As soon as you taste it, you will know why this is Italy's most famous dessert.

- ◆ **24 soft ladyfingers, split**
- ◆ **¾ cup brewed espresso or strong coffee, cooled**
- ◆ **¼ cup rum**
- ◆ **1 pound mascarpone cheese**
- ◆ **⅓ cup sugar**
- ◆ **2 tablespoons plus 2 teaspoons powdered pasteurized egg whites**
- ◆ **½ cup water**
- ◆ **¾ cup heavy cream, well chilled**
- ◆ **1 teaspoon vanilla extract**
- ◆ **2 ounces grated chocolate**

1 Preheat the oven to 375°F. On a baking sheet, arrange the ladyfingers in a single layer and bake 8 minutes to toast. Arrange half the ladyfingers in the bottom of a 1½-quart shallow baking dish. Combine coffee and rum and drizzle half the mixture over the ladyfingers.

MAKING MERINGUES

1 *Carefully separate the whites from the yolks—even a speck of yolk will prevent the whites from whipping up satisfactorily. Use clean, dry beaters and a glass or metal bowl for beating.*

2 *The mixture is ready when no undissolved sugar remains. Shape each meringue with a wet spoon. With your finger, push the meringue onto the prepared baking sheets; shape into ovals.*

3 *Use the same amount of batter for each meringue. Allow plenty of room around each meringue on the tray for air to circulate. When cooked, they should be barely colored.*

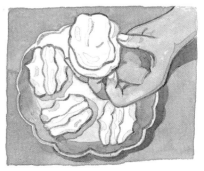

4 *One way to fill the meringues is to press them gently on the bottom to make an indentation as soon as they are taken from the oven. Sandwich pairs with whipped cream, jam, or lime curd.*

2 In a large bowl, whisk together the mascarpone and 2 tablespoons of the sugar until smooth. In the bowl of an electric mixer, whisk together the egg-white powder and water until dissolved. With the mixer on high, beat the mixture, adding the remaining sugar gradually, until the whites hold stiff, glossy peaks. Transfer to another bowl.

3 Add cream and vanilla to the mixing bowl and beat until soft peaks form. Fold the cream into the mascarpone thoroughly; then fold in the egg-white mixture.

4 Spread half the cream mixture over soaked ladyfingers. Top with remaining ladyfingers and drizzle with the coffee-rum mixture. Spread the remaining cream mixture on top and sprinkle with chocolate. Chill, covered, for 2 hours.
SERVES 8–10 TOTAL TIME 45 MINUTES PLUS CHILLING

Vanilla pudding

Serve this old-fashioned family dessert with seasonal fresh fruit.

- ◆ ¾ cup sugar
- ◆ 1½ tablespoons cornstarch
- ◆ pinch of salt
- ◆ 2 cups milk
- ◆ 1 egg
- ◆ 2 tablespoons butter
- ◆ 1 teaspoon vanilla extract

1 In a medium saucepan, combine the sugar, cornstarch, and salt. Stir in the milk until smooth. Cook over moderate heat, stirring continuously, until the mixture boils and thickens. Reduce the heat and simmer, stirring continuously, for 2 minutes. Remove from the heat.

2 In a medium bowl, beat the egg until foamy. Gradually stir in about ½ cup of the hot milk mixture. Pour the egg mixture back into the remaining hot milk mixture. Cook over low heat, stirring continuously, for 2 minutes more.

3 Remove from the heat, stir in the butter and vanilla and immediately pour into a bowl or individual dessert dishes. Cool, then refrigerate.
SERVES 4–6 TOTAL TIME 25 MINUTES PLUS CHILLING

VARIATIONS To make chocolate pudding, add 2 ounces chopped semisweet chocolate to the

milk in step 1. For chocolate-mint pudding, heat the milk with several bruised mint leaves until scalded. Cool and strain. Use the strained milk as directed in Step 2.

Orange rice custard

Serve warm or chilled with fruit or a favorite jam. Marmalade will emphasize the citrus flavor.

- ◆ ½ cup short-grain rice
- ◆ ⅔ cup water
- ◆ ⅛ teaspoon salt
- ◆ 1 cup milk
- ◆ 1 cup heavy cream
- ◆ ⅓ cup sugar
- ◆ 2 eggs
- ◆ 1 teaspoon grated orange zest
- ◆ ⅛ teaspoon ground nutmeg

1 Preheat the oven to 325°F. Butter a 6-cup ovenproof dish. In a medium saucepan over moderate heat, bring the rice, water, and salt to a boil. Cover and simmer 12 minutes. Remove from heat and whisk in remaining ingredients.

2 Pour into the prepared dish and bake for 50 minutes or until set.
SERVES 6 TOTAL TIME 1 HOUR 10 MINUTES

Raspberry coulis

Fresh or frozen berries can be used for this dessert sauce. For variety, make it with strawberries, blackberries, or blueberries. You can also use fresh peaches and apricots (these puree better if lightly poached first).

SERVING SUGGESTIONS

Pour hot chocolate or caramel sauce over crepes filled with sliced bananas and serve with ice cream or whipped cream for a party dessert.

Make a meringue pyramid by stacking up individual ones, using vanilla pudding for mortar. To serve, pour hot chocolate sauce over the structure and sprinkle with toasted slivered almonds.

- ◆ ½ pint fresh raspberries or one 8-ounce package, frozen
- ◆ sugar, to taste

1 Rinse and drain the berries (if using fresh). In a food processor or blender, puree with about 2 tablespoons sugar. Sieve the mixture to remove seeds. Taste and add sugar, if necessary.

2 Chill before serving. The sauce can be refrigerated in a covered container for up to 2 days.
MAKES ABOUT 1 CUP TOTAL TIME 20 MINUTES

Hot chocolate sauce

Make this irresistible sauce at the last minute and pour it, piping hot, over rich vanilla ice cream.

- ◆ ⅓ cup milk
- ◆ ½ cup heavy cream
- ◆ ¼ cup sugar
- ◆ 7 ounces bittersweet chocolate

1 In a small saucepan over low heat, stir together the milk, cream, and sugar.

2 Add the chocolate and stir until melted smooth. Serve at once or keep chilled and reheat slowly to serve.
MAKES ABOUT 1½ CUPS TOTAL TIME 10 MINUTES

Butterscotch sauce

Try this versatile sauce warm over ice cream in summer or over hot gingerbread in the fall.

- ◆ 1½ sticks (6 ounces) unsalted butter
- ◆ 1½ cups brown sugar
- ◆ 1 cup heavy cream
- ◆ 1 teaspoon vanilla extract
- ◆ ⅛ teaspoon salt

1 In a small saucepan over low heat, melt the butter. Add the sugar, salt, and cream, stirring until the sugar has dissolved. Simmer 8 to 10 minutes over low heat, stirring continuously so that the sugar doesn't crystallize. Remove from heat and add vanilla.

2 Serve warm or cool. Can be refrigerated in a covered container for up to a week.
MAKES ABOUT 2½ CUPS TOTAL TIME 15 MINUTES

◆ Ice-Cream Variety ◆

Homemade ice cream is one of life's great gustatory delights. Even if you don't have an ice-cream maker, you can still produce these treats. See page 15 for details.

Mango ice cream

The most exotic of fruits gives this ice cream a tropical taste. Serve within two days of making.

- ◆ **2 ripe mangoes**
- ◆ **1 cup sugar**
- ◆ **2 cups heavy cream**
- ◆ **1 cup milk**
- ◆ **1 teaspoon vanilla extract**

1 Peel the mangoes and cut all flesh from the stones. In a food processor, puree the mango flesh with the sugar.

2 Add remaining ingredients; pulse until combined. Pour into an ice-cream maker and churn according to the manufacturer's instructions.

3 Serve immediately or spoon into a container, cover with plastic wrap, and place in the freezer overnight. Soften in refrigerator for 15 to 30 minutes before serving.

MAKES 4–5 CUPS   TOTAL TIME 45 MINUTES

Lavender ice cream

The secret of this delicately flavored ice cream is lavender honey. If it is unavailable, however, use any honey that has a flowerlike essence.

- ◆ **¾ cup milk**
- ◆ **½ cup lavender or other flower-flavored honey**
- ◆ **2½ cups heavy cream**
- ◆ **4 egg yolks**
- ◆ **2 teaspoons fresh lavender flowers or 1½ teaspoons dried (available at health-food stores)**
- ◆ **1 teaspoon vanilla extract**

1 In a large saucepan, warm the milk, honey, and 1 cup of the cream over moderate heat, stirring continuously until the honey dissolves.

2 In a medium bowl, beat the egg yolks.

Slowly pour half the milk mixture into the egg yolks, stirring continuously. Return the mixture to the saucepan. Cook over low heat, whisking continuously, until the mixture thickens and registers 170°F. on a candy thermometer. Mix in the remaining cream, the lavender flowers, and the vanilla.

3 Chill the mixture in the refrigerator for 8 hours. Remove flowers if desired.

4 Strain mixture, pour into an ice-cream maker, and churn according to the manufacturer's instructions.

5 Serve immediately or spoon the ice cream into a container, cover with plastic wrap, and place in the freezer. Soften in the refrigerator for 15 to 30 minutes before serving.

MAKES 4–5 CUPS   TOTAL TIME 10 HOURS

Berry ice cream

For deeper flavor, use more than one variety of berry—combine blackberries with blueberries, for example. Serve with a sprinkling of fresh berries.

- ◆ **2 cups berries of choice**
- ◆ **½ cup sugar**
- ◆ **½ cup milk**
- ◆ **1½ cups heavy cream**
- ◆ **⅛ teaspoon salt**

1 Rinse berries; in a bowl, combine with ¼ cup of the sugar. Mash with a potato masher.

2 Mix in the milk, cream, salt, and remaining ¼ cup of sugar.

3 Pour into an ice-cream maker and churn according to the manufacturer's instructions.

4 Serve immediately or spoon the ice cream into a container, cover with plastic wrap, and place in the freezer. Soften in the refrigerator for 15 to 30 minutes before serving.

MAKES 3–4 CUPS   TOTAL TIME 45 MINUTES

Mandarin ice cream

The ease and convenience of using canned mandarin segments is equaled only by this ice cream's spectacular taste.

- ◆ **3 cans (11 ounces) mandarin orange segments, drained**
- ◆ **juice of 1 orange**
- ◆ **1 cup sugar**
- ◆ **1 cup heavy cream**
- ◆ **1 cup heavy cream for topping (optional)**
- ◆ **extra orange segments or fresh berries, for decoration**

1 In a food processor, puree the mandarin oranges, then strain the mixture through a fine sieve. Add enough orange juice to make 2 cups of liquid. Add the sugar and stir to dissolve.
2 With a hand mixer or whisk, whip 1 cup cream until it holds soft peaks, then fold in orange juice. Pour orange and cream mixture into a stainless-steel or plastic bowl. Cover with plastic wrap and freeze for 2 to 2 ½ hours or until soft-frozen.
3 Whisk the partially frozen mixture until smooth. Return to the freezer for 3 to 6 hours.
4 Unmold the ice cream and decorate with whipped cream, if desired, and orange segments or fresh berries.
MAKES 4–5 CUPS TOTAL TIME 15 MINUTES
PLUS 8 ½ HOURS

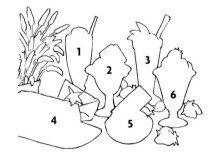

Nothing will win you more compliments than homemade ice creams and sorbets. Flavor a base mixture with anything from berries to nuts. A good selection includes: **1** *Berry ice cream,* **2** *Lavender ice cream,* **3** *Mango ice cream,* **4** *Pecan semifreddo (p.90), and* **5** *Lemon-mint sorbet (p.92),* **6** *Strawberry sorbet (p.90).*

ICE-CREAM TOPPINGS

CHOCOLATE TOFFEE SAUCE In the microwave or in a bowl set over simmering water, melt 3 ounces semisweet chocolate. Add ½ cup heavy cream and ½ cup toffee candy, and stir until melted and well combined. Serve warm.

Make your own toffee candy by following Steps 1 through 3 in the recipe for Hokeypokey ice cream (facing page). Makes about 1 cup.

MANGO AND PASSION FRUIT SAUCE Peel 1 large mango and puree the pulp in a blender. Stir in ½ cup (6 to 8 fruits) strained passion fruit pulp and chill before serving. Makes about 1 cup.

Banana-and-honey ice cream

Serve this ice cream with a biscotti (p. 64) or gingersnaps as a delicious finale to a meal.

- ◆ **6 egg yolks**
- ◆ **2 cups milk**
- ◆ **½ cup honey**
- ◆ **2 teaspoons vanilla extract**
- ◆ **2 cups heavy cream**
- ◆ **3 bananas, mashed (1 cup)**

1   In a double boiler, whisk the egg yolks and milk until well blended. Add the honey and vanilla extract. Stir over moderate heat until the mixture coats the back of a spoon and registers 170°F. on a candy thermometer.

2   Pour the mixture into a bowl and allow to cool. Cover with plastic wrap and place in the refrigerator for 1 hour to chill.

3   Stir in the cream and mashed banana. Pour into an ice-cream maker and churn according to the manufacturer's instructions.

4   Serve immediately or spoon into a container, cover with plastic wrap, and place in the freezer. Soften in the refrigerator for 15 to 30 minutes before serving.

MAKES 5–6 CUPS   TOTAL TIME 2 ½ HOURS

Vanilla ice cream

Try dressing up this perennial favorite with the toppings in the box at left.

- ◆ **2 cups milk**
- ◆ **1 small vanilla bean, split**
- ◆ **8 egg yolks, beaten**
- ◆ **¾ cup sugar**
- ◆ **¼ teaspoon salt**
- ◆ **4 tablespoons vanilla extract**
- ◆ **2 cups heavy cream**

1   In a heavy saucepan, heat the milk until just bubbling. Remove from the heat, add the vanilla bean, cover, and set aside to cool until just warm.

2   Remove the bean and scrape the seeds into the saucepan. In a bowl, place the egg yolks, sugar, salt, and vanilla and whisk until the mixture is thick and creamy. Gradually add the warm milk, whisking continuously.

3   In a heavy saucepan, cook the mixture over low heat, whisking continuously, for 6 minutes or until the mixture coats the back of a spoon and registers 170°F. on a candy thermometer.

4   Into a bowl, strain the mixture and stir as it cools. Whisk in the cream, then cover the bowl with plastic wrap and place in the refrigerator for 1 hour to chill.

5   Pour the mixture into an ice-cream maker and churn according to the manufacturer's instructions.

6   Serve immediately or spoon into a container, cover with plastic wrap, and place in the freezer. Soften in the refrigerator for 15 to 30 minutes before serving.

MAKES 5–6 CUPS   TOTAL TIME 2 ½ HOURS

Citrus ice cream

Refreshing and tangy, this ice cream makes an ideal complement to a fresh-fruit salad.

- ◆ **½ cup citrus juice of choice**
- ◆ **1 egg**
- ◆ **1 cup sugar**
- ◆ **1 cup heavy cream**
- ◆ **1 ½ cups milk**
- ◆ **1 tablespoon grated zest of a citrus fruit**
- ◆ **pinch of salt**

1   In a heavy saucepan, cook the citrus juice, egg, and sugar over low heat, whisking continuously, until the sugar has dissolved and the mixture registers 170°F. on a candy thermometer. Stir in cream, milk, zest, and salt.

2   Let the mixture cool, then place in the refrigerator for 1 hour to chill.

3   Pour the mixture into an ice-cream maker and churn according to the manufacturer's instructions.

4   Serve immediately or spoon into a container, cover with plastic wrap, and place in the freezer. Soften in the refrigerator for 15 to 30 minutes before serving.

MAKES 5–6 CUPS   TOTAL TIME 2 HOURS

PRACTICAL IDEAS
ICE CREAM TIPS

Make your own vanilla extract. Simply place a vanilla bean and 3 tablespoons of vodka in a clean jar with a tight lid. Let stand for 4 weeks and discard bean before using liquid.

Old-fashioned churns freeze ice cream with a combination of ice and rock salt. The paddles that stir the ice cream are turned by hand. As the mixture hardens, the cranking gets tougher. Good arms are required for this ice cream making.

All-electric ice cream makers, expensive and large, both freeze and churn ice cream. Less costly machines have electric churns but rely on a freezer or pre-chilled inserts to freeze ice cream.

Peach ice cream

This treat is full of the succulent flavor of summer. For an equally tasty alternative, substitute 10 to 12 fresh apricots for the peaches.

- ◆ **5 large ripe peaches**
- ◆ **1 tablespoon lemon juice**
- ◆ **½ cup honey**
- ◆ **1¼ cups heavy cream**
- ◆ **¼ cup sugar**
- ◆ **1 teaspoon vanilla extract**

1 Wash the peaches; cut a cross in the base of each one. Drop them into boiling water for 1 minute, then lift out with a slotted spoon and plunge into cold water. Slip off the skins and chop the flesh coarsely, discarding the pits.
2 In a food processor, place peaches, lemon juice, and honey. Pulse to make a coarse puree.
3 In a large bowl, beat the cream with the sugar and vanilla until thickened but not stiff. Stir in the peach puree.
4 Pour into an ice-cream maker and churn according to the manufacturer's instructions.
5 Serve immediately or spoon into a container, cover with plastic wrap, and place in the freezer. Soften in the refrigerator for 15 to 30 minutes before serving.

MAKES 4–5 CUPS TOTAL TIME 1 ½ HOURS

Hawaiian ice cream

Tropical flavors permeate this tangy concoction. Serve it simply with cookies or biscotti.

- ◆ **1⅓ cups milk, scalded**
- ◆ **3 eggs**
- ◆ **1 cup sugar**
- ◆ **½ cup sweetened, flaked coconut**
- ◆ **2 teaspoons vanilla extract**
- ◆ **1-pound can crushed pineapple, drained**
- ◆ **1⅓ cups heavy cream**

1 In a heavy saucepan, whisk hot milk into eggs and sugar. Cook over moderately low heat, whisking continuously, until custard is thickened and registers 170°F on a candy thermometer. Strain custard through a sieve into a

bowl and stir in the coconut and vanilla. Stir in the cream and chill until cold.
2 Pour into an ice-cream maker and churn according to the manufacturer's instructions.
3 Serve immediately or spoon into a container, cover with plastic wrap, and place in the freezer. Soften in the refrigerator for 15 to 30 minutes before serving.

MAKES 4–5 CUPS TOTAL TIME 1 ½ HOURS

VARIATIONS Instead of the pineapple and coconut, add one of the following combinations to the cream and custard: an 8-ounce mixture of chopped fruit-and-nut chocolate bar; 8 ounces crushed Oreo cookies; or 8 ounces mixed dried and glacé fruits and nuts.

Hokeypokey ice cream

The sweet crunch of toffee candy and the smooth taste of vanilla ice cream combine here to produce a unique texture and an irresistible flavor.

TOFFEE INGREDIENTS
- ◆ **5 tablespoons sugar**
- ◆ **2 tablespoons honey**
- ◆ **1 teaspoon baking soda**

ICE-CREAM INGREDIENTS
- ◆ **1⅓ cups milk**
- ◆ **1 cup heavy cream**
- ◆ **1 vanilla bean, split**
- ◆ **½ cup sugar**
- ◆ **¾ cup water**
- ◆ **6 egg yolks**

1 Line a baking sheet with aluminum foil.
2 In a heavy saucepan, place the sugar and honey and, stirring continuously, bring slowly to a boil. Reduce the heat to very low and simmer gently for 4 minutes, stirring occasionally.
3 Remove from the heat, add the baking soda, and stir briskly—the toffee will froth up dramatically. Pour onto the prepared sheet and leave to cool and harden.
4 Break the toffee into small pieces.
5 To prepare the ice cream, in a heavy saucepan, scald the milk and cream with the vanilla bean added. Remove from the heat, cover with a lid, and leave to infuse until com-

pletely cooled. Scrape the vanilla seeds into the milk and discard the bean.
6 In a second saucepan, over low heat, dissolve the sugar and water. Increase the heat and boil the mixture until it registers 260°F on a candy thermometer or a little syrup forms a hard ball when dropped into cold water.
7 Beat the egg yolks in the bowl of an electric mixer until thick and creamy. With the mixer running, pour the hot syrup slowly onto the yolks and continue beating until cool. The mixture should be thick and fluffy.
8 Strain the milk-cream mixture, add to the egg mixture, and blend well. Pour into an ice-cream maker and churn according to the manufacturer's instructions. When half-frozen, stir in 1 cup of the toffee pieces; continue to churn.
9 Serve immediately or spoon into a container, cover with plastic wrap, and place in the freezer. Soften in the refrigerator for 15 to 30 minutes before serving.

MAKES 5–6 CUPS TOTAL TIME 3–6 HOURS

Chocolate custard ice cream

Who can resist chocolate ice cream? This easy-to-make version has custard for extra richness.

- ◆ **1¼ cups milk, scalded**
- ◆ **3 eggs**
- ◆ **¾ cup sugar**
- ◆ **2 ounces unsweetened chocolate, chopped**
- ◆ **2 teaspoons vanilla extract**
- ◆ **¼ teaspoon salt**
- ◆ **2 cups heavy cream**

1 In a heavy saucepan whisk, hot milk into eggs and sugar. Cook over low heat, whisking continuously, until custard is thick and registers 170°F on a candy thermometer. Strain custard through a sieve into a bowl and stir in chocolate, vanilla, and salt. Stir in cream. Chill.
2 Pour into an ice-cream maker and churn according to the manufacturer's instructions.
3 Serve immediately or spoon into a container, cover with plastic wrap, and place in the freezer. Soften in the refrigerator for 15 to 30 minutes before serving.

MAKES 4–5 CUPS TOTAL TIME 2 ½ HOURS

◆ Iced Desserts and Treats ◆

When the weather turns hot, nothing is more welcome than a fruity iced sorbet, a creamy frozen yogurt, or a classic ice-cream cake. Below, you'll find such iced treats and more—including nutty chocolate bananas and refreshing tropical pops.

Pecan semifreddo

The word semifreddo *is Italian for "partly frozen." In texture a semifreddo is more like a frozen mousse or soft ice cream than a true ice cream.*

- ◆ 2½ **cups milk**
- ◆ 6 **egg yolks**
- ◆ ¼ **cup sugar**
- ◆ 1¾ **cups heavy cream**
- ◆ 3 **tablespoons maple syrup**
- ◆ ½ **cup pecans, chopped**
- ◆ ¾ **teaspoon almond extract**
- ◆ 12 **ladyfingers**
- ◆ **grated chocolate, for decoration**

1 Grease a 10 x 4-inch loaf pan. Line the pan carefully with plastic wrap, leaving enough to fold over the top of the ice-cream loaf.
2 In a medium saucepan, heat the milk until hot but not scalded. Remove from the heat.
3 In a medium, heat-resistant bowl, place the egg yolks and sugar and whisk vigorously with a whisk or beat with a hand mixer until pale in color. Slowly beat in the hot milk. Place the bowl over a saucepan of simmering water and cook, stirring continuously, until the mixture thickens enough to coat the back of a spoon and registers 170°F. on a candy thermometer.
4 Remove bowl from heat and cover with plastic wrap to prevent a skin from forming on top. Leave the mixture to cool completely.
5 Beat the cream until soft peaks form. Fold in the cold custard, maple syrup, chopped pecans, and almond extract.
6 Pour the mixture into the lined loaf pan. Carefully place the ladyfingers in rows on top of the ice cream. Fold the plastic wrap over the ice cream and freeze until solid, about 6 to 8 hours. Allow the semifreddo to soften for about 15 minutes in the refrigerator before serving. Turn out on a serving plate so that the ladyfingers form the base. Sprinkle with the grated chocolate and serve immediately or refrigerate until ready to serve, but no longer than 20 to 30 minutes.

SERVES 8   TOTAL TIME 2½–8 HOURS

Ice-cream cake

Much like a frozen chocolate sundae with an Oreo cookie crust, this kid-pleasing concoction is easy and fun to make—so be sure to enlist the children as cook's helpers. For a birthday ice-cream cake, let the honoree choose the two ice-cream flavors.

- ◆ 1½ **cups ground Oreo cookies (use a food processor)**
- ◆ 2 **tablespoons butter, melted**
- ◆ 1½ **pints coffee ice cream, softened**
- ◆ ¾ **cup hot chocolate sauce (p.85), cooled but still pourable**
- ◆ 1½ **pints vanilla, chocolate, or toffee-crunch ice cream, softened**
- ◆ ½ **cup grated chocolate or sliced toasted almonds**

1 Thoroughly combine cookie crumbs and butter with a fork. Press mixture onto the bottom and halfway up the sides of an 8-inch springform pan. Freeze for 30 minutes.
2 Spread coffee ice cream evenly onto the crust and freeze for 30 minutes or until firm. Spread the chocolate sauce quickly on top; freeze for 15 minutes or until firm. Spread vanilla ice cream on top of sauce, smoothing it. Top it all off with a sprinkle of grated chocolate or sliced almonds. Freeze cake, covered with plastic wrap, for at least 1 hour.
3 To unmold your ice-cream cake, wipe the side of the springform pan with a hot, damp cloth, then remove the side of the pan. Cut the cake with a knife dipped in hot water.

MAKES 8–10 SERVINGS   TOTAL TIME 2½ HOURS

Strawberry sorbet

Use ripe, top-quality fruit only. Also try a mixture of raspberries, blueberries, and strawberries.

- ◆ 6 **cups strawberries (or use a combination of berries)**
- ◆ 1¾ **cups sugar**
- ◆ 2 **cups fresh orange juice, strained**
- ◆ 2 **tablespoons Grand Marnier**
- ◆ **edible flowers and leaves for decoration**

1 Wash and hull the strawberries; drain. Halve them and place in a bowl with the sugar and orange juice. Set aside for 1 hour.
2 In the work bowl of a food processor, puree the berries and juice. Add the Grand Marnier and pulse to combine.
3 Pour the mixture into two ice trays or a shallow freezersafe dish. Place in the freezer and leave until almost firm but not hard—an hour or more.
4 Spoon the mixture back into the food processor and pulse on and off until slushy.
5 Pour the mixture back into the trays or dish. Return to the freezer.
6 Once again, when the mixture is almost firm, repeat the pulsing process.
7 Return the mixture to the trays or dish, cover with plastic wrap, and allow to freeze until solid.
8 Soften for 15 minutes in the refrigerator and spoon into chilled serving dishes or glasses. Garnish the sorbet with edible flowers and leaves, if desired.

MAKES ABOUT 6 CUPS   TOTAL TIME 10 HOURS

Tropical pops

Choose a mixture of seasonal fruits, such as pineapples, papayas, peaches, grapes, mangoes, apples, or oranges. Work over a bowl when peeling the fruit to catch any juices.

- **6 cups fruit, peeled and cored, if necessary, and cut into bite-size pieces**
- **3 cups mixed tropical fruit punch or fresh orange juice**

1 Place the fruit in the bowl with any juices. Stir well and spoon the mixture into ½-cup or 1-cup plastic cups or any small, shaped molds, until three-quarters full.
2 Cover fruit with punch or juice, leaving space for expansion, and partially freeze. Insert a wooden stick in the center; freeze overnight.
MAKES 24 ½-CUP OR 12 1-CUP POPS   TOTAL TIME 10 MINUTES PLUS OVERNIGHT

Nutty chocolate bananas

For fun, dye wooden skewers a range of bright colors with food coloring for these frozen treats.

- **8 small bananas**
- **8 ounces dark chocolate**
- **3 tablespoons vegetable shortening**
- **1 cup each coarsely chopped walnuts and macadamia nuts, roasted**
- **8 wooden skewers, sharp ends cut off**

1 Line a baking sheet with plastic wrap.
2 Push a skewer into one end of each banana to halfway along its length. Place on the sheet, cover with plastic wrap and freeze solid.
3 Melt chocolate and vegetable shortening in a bowl over simmering water. Remove from heat. Hold each banana over the bowl, spoon chocolate over it until well coated, and sprinkle with nuts before the chocolate hardens.
4 Return bananas to the freezer until the chocolate is frozen. Wrap individually in plastic wrap and keep frozen until ready to serve.
MAKES 8   TOTAL TIME 1 HOUR 45 MINUTES

Strawberry ice pops

These pops are easy, healthy, and delicious.

- **2 pints strawberries**
- **½ cup apple juice concentrate**
- **8 pop sticks**

Mash the strawberries coarsely, leaving some chunks. Stir in the apple juice concentrate.

Treats kids love: clockwise from top left, nutty chocolate bananas, tropical ice pops, strawberry ice pops.

Spoon into ice-cube molds or small cups and partially freeze, then push a wooden pop stick into each and freeze until needed.
MAKES ABOUT 8 ⅓-CUP POPS   TOTAL TIME 10 MINUTES PLUS 6 HOURS

Lemon-mint sorbet

Served in chilled wineglasses and topped with a sprig of fresh mint, this refreshingly light dessert is just right for a hot summer evening.

- 1 cup sugar
- 2 ½ cups water
- ½ cup fresh mint leaves, packed
- ½ cup lemon juice

1 In a saucepan, over moderate heat, stir the sugar and water until the sugar has dissolved. Bring the syrup to a boil and simmer for 3 minutes. Remove from the heat, add the mint leaves, and set aside for about 1 hour to cool.
2 Into a bowl, strain the syrup and stir in the lemon juice.
3 Pour the mixture into ice trays or a shallow freezersafe dish, and freeze for about 4 hours.
4 Run a fork back and forth through the sorbet to break it up. Cover the trays or dish with plastic wrap and freeze for another 4 to 8 hours. Let the sorbet soften in the refrigerator for 15 minutes before serving.
MAKES 3–4 CUPS TOTAL TIME 13 HOURS

Honeydew sorbet

Serve this fresh-tasting sorbet with slices of honeydew melon or cantaloupe. Using an ice cream maker speeds up the making of this sorbet.

- 6 cups honeydew melon or cantaloupe, cubed
- ¾ cup sugar
- 3 tablespoons melon liqueur, such as Midori

1 In a food processor, puree the melon, sugar, and liqueur until the sugar has dissolved.
2 Refrigerate until thoroughly chilled.
3 Pour into an ice-cream maker and churn according to the manufacturer's instructions.
4 Spoon the sorbet into ice trays or a shallow freezersafe dish, cover with plastic wrap, and freeze until firm. Let soften in the refrigerator for 15 minutes before serving.
MAKES ABOUT 4 CUPS TOTAL TIME 1 HOUR 15 MINUTES

Frozen mocha chip yogurt

This rich and delicious frozen treat nicely finishes a light supper. You may substitute low-fat yogurt if you prefer.

- 3 cups plain yogurt
- 1 ½ tablespoons instant espresso powder
- ¾ cup sugar
- 1 cup heavy cream
- 2 ounces bittersweet chocolate, chopped
- 1 teaspoon vanilla extract

1 In a fine strainer or one lined with cheesecloth, place the yogurt and set over a bowl to drain for 1 hour in the refrigerator.
2 Discard the whey from the bowl. In a separate bowl, place the espresso powder, sugar, and cream, and stir until the sugar has completely dissolved. Beat until the mixture holds soft peaks. Add the drained yogurt, chocolate, and vanilla, mixing well to combine.
3 Pour the mixture into an ice-cream maker and churn according to the manufacturer's instructions.
4 Serve immediately or spoon the frozen yogurt into a container, cover with plastic wrap, and place in the freezer. Soften in the refrigerator for 15 minutes before serving.
MAKES 5–6 CUPS TOTAL TIME 2 HOURS 15 MINUTES

Cappuccino granita

This Italian specialty is delightfully cooling on a summer day. Top with chocolate-coated coffee beans (found in gourmet-food stores).

- 1 ¼ cups strong black coffee (not instant)
- ¼ cup granulated sugar
- 5 tablespoons Kahlúa
- 1 cup heavy cream
- 1 tablespoon confectioners sugar
- unsweetened cocoa for dusting

1 In a small bowl, mix the coffee, granulated sugar, and 3 tablespoons of the Kahlúa.
2 Pour the liquid into an ice tray or freezer-

safe dish and place in the freezer. To make the granita icy and flaky, run a fork through the mixture, breaking up the lumps, three times at 45-minute intervals. Cover with plastic wrap and freeze for at least 8 hours.
3 Whip the cream with the remainder of the Kahlúa and confectioners sugar until soft peaks form.
4 To serve, roughly break up the granita with a fork, place spoonfuls in chilled serving glasses, top with the cream mixture, and dust with the cocoa.
SERVES 6–8 TOTAL TIME 10 ½ HOURS

VARIATION For a subtle almond flavor, substitute the same amount of amaretto for the Kahlúa.

Blood-orange champagne granita

If blood oranges are unavailable, you can make this refreshing iced treat with lemon, grapefruit, or any combination of your favorite citrus fruits.

- 1 ½ cups sugar
- 1 cup water
- 2 cups freshly squeezed blood-orange juice
- 2 cups champagne
- pinch of salt

1 In a saucepan, over moderate heat, stir the sugar and water until the sugar has dissolved. Bring the syrup to a boil and simmer for 3 minutes. Remove from the heat and set aside for about 1 hour to cool.
2 In a bowl, place the syrup, juice, champagne, and salt. Stir well to combine.
3 Pour the mixture into ice trays or a freezer-safe dish, cover with plastic wrap, and place in the freezer. To make the granita icy and flaky, run a fork through the mixture three times at 45-minute intervals.
4 Cover the granita with plastic wrap and freeze for 8 hours or overnight. Soften in the refrigerator for 15 minutes before serving in chilled glasses or bowls.
MAKES 12 SERVING TOTAL TIME 10 MINUTES PLUS 10 ½ HOURS

Peach granita

Mangoes or nectarines can be substituted for the peaches. Serve with slices of chilled fresh fruit.

- 1 cup water
- ½ cup sugar
- 4 ripe peaches, peeled, pitted and coarsely chopped
- 1 tablespoon peach schnapps or fruit liqueur

1 In a small saucepan over moderate heat, stir the water and sugar until the sugar has dissolved. Bring the syrup to a boil and simmer for 3 minutes. Remove from the heat and set aside for about 1 hour to cool.

2 In a food processor or blender, puree the peaches. Add the sugar syrup and schnapps or liqueur and stir to combine.

3 Pour the mixture into ice trays or a shallow freezersafe dish, cover with plastic wrap, and place in the freezer. To make the granita icy and flaky, Run a fork through the mixture three times at 45-minute intervals.

4 Cover with plastic wrap and freeze for at least 6 hours or until solid. Soften in the refrigerator for 15 minutes before serving in chilled bowls or glasses.

MAKES ABOUT 4 CUPS   TOTAL TIME 8 HOURS

Frozen chocolate-nut yogurt

Reach for this energizing snack any time of day.

- 6 ounces bittersweet chocolate
- 1¼ cups heavy cream
- ½ cup dried apricots or dried cherries, finely chopped
- ½ cup golden raisins
- 2 cups vanilla yogurt
- ⅔ cup chocolate chips
- ½ cup almonds, finely chopped
- ½ cup hazelnuts, finely chopped

1 Line a mold, bowl, or loaf pan with plastic wrap, leaving plenty to fold over the top.

2 In a microwave or a double boiler over low heat, melt the chocolate, stirring from time to time. Remove from heat and stir in ¼ cup cream. Cover apricots (or cherries) and raisins with hot water, and let soak 15 minutes. Drain and pat dry.

3 Whip the cream until stiff peaks form. Add the yogurt and chocolate and mix well to combine. Fold in the remaining ingredients.

4 Spoon the mixture into the mold, then fold the plastic film over the top and freeze. Soften to room temperature before cutting into slices or wedges.

MAKES 5 CUPS   TOTAL TIME 40 MINUTES PLUS 6 HOURS

Kiwifruit sorbet

Light and refreshing, this sorbet is ideal as a light dessert after a rich main course. Serve it in a dish that complements the pretty color.

- 1 cup water
- 2 cups sugar
- juice of 2 lemons
- 6 large, ripe kiwifruit, peeled and coarsely chopped
- mint sprigs for decoration

1 In a small saucepan, combine the water, sugar, and half the lemon juice . Stir over a moderate heat until the sugar has dissolved. Bring the syrup to a boil, and simmer for 3 minutes. Remove from heat and let cool.

2 In the bowl of a food processor, puree the kiwifruit. Blend in the remaining lemon juice. Stir the purée into the cool syrup.

3 Spoon mixture into ice trays or a shallow freezersafe dish. Cover with plastic wrap, and place in the freezer. Run a fork through the mixture three times at 45-minute intervals.

4 Cover with plastic wrap and freeze for at least 6 hours or until solid. Soften in the refrigerator for 15 minutes before serving in chilled bowls or glasses. Garnish with mint.

MAKES ABOUT 4 CUPS   TOTAL TIME 8 ¾ HOURS

MAKING SORBETS AND GRANITAS

1 *Puree fruit and liquids in a food processor or blender. Any juicy fruits, including tomatoes, are suitable for sorbets and granitas, but be careful with alcohol—too much will inhibit freezing.*

2 *Pour the mixture into ice trays or a shallow freezersafe dish and freeze until grainy and partly frozen. Run a fork through a granita from time to time to achieve an even texture.*

3 *Spoon partly frozen sorbet into the processor and pulse to break up lumps. Return to ice tray or dish and refreeze. Repeat Steps 2 and 3 at least once more, then freeze at least 6 hours.*

4 *Soften in the refrigerator for 15 minutes before serving. To serve, run a fork through the sorbet or granita to break it up. Spoon into chilled serving dishes or glasses and garnish with fruit if desired.*

◆ The Frozen Pantry ◆

Freezing beautifully captures the color, texture, and flavor of fresh vegetables and fruits. If a fruit or vegetable is in season and plentiful, purchase a few extra to put away in your freezer. If you're a gardener, don't let surplus crops go to waste—preserve them to enjoy year-round.

Vegetables

Most vegetables can be frozen with excellent results. See the box on the facing page for instructions on water-blanching and steam-blanching in preparation for freezing, plus a guide to yields. Prepare vegetables as directed below, then pack them snugly in resealable freezer bags or sturdy containers that can be tightly closed. The bags are ideal because they allow you to expel excess air, which prevents frost from accumulating, and to readily vary the portions from one serving to four. Once thawed, cook frozen vegetables, covered, in a small amount of boiling water. Don't refreeze.

Asparagus, green beans, carrots
Wash, trim, and cut into lengths suitable for chosen containers or into 2-inch pieces. You can also slice carrots 2 inches thick. Sort asparagus according to the thickness of the stalks; water-blanch thin stalks for 2 minutes, thick stalks for 4 minutes. Blanch green beans for 3 minutes. Blanch whole carrots for 5 minutes, slices for 2 minutes. Rinse briefly under cold water, drain thoroughly, and pack. Seal, label, and freeze.

Beets
Wash and trim, leaving 1-inch stems (be careful not to pierce the skins). Sort according to size and cook small beets in boiling water for 25 to 30 minutes, large for 45 to 50 minutes or until tender when pierced with a fork. Drain and cool. Peel off the skins. Slice or cube, as desired, and pack. Seal, label, and freeze.

Enjoy a bounty of fresh vegetables at their nutritional peak—whether from your own garden or the neighborhood farmers' market—all year long by freezing.

Broad beans and lima beans

Shell young, tender beans and discard any damaged ones. Water-blanch small beans for 1 minute, medium beans for 2 minutes, and large beans for 3 minutes. Cool quickly, drain thoroughly, and pack. Seal, label, and freeze.

Broccoli, cauliflower

Wash and peel stalks if woody. Cut stalks and florets into 1½-inch pieces. Steam-blanch for 5 minutes. Cool quickly, drain thoroughly, and pack. Seal, label, and freeze.

Brussels sprouts

Trim off coarse leaves and stems and sort by size. Water-blanch small sprouts for 3 minutes, large sprouts for 5 minutes. Cool quickly, drain, and pack. Seal, label, and freeze.

Corn

Use young cobs only. Remove the husks and silks. Water-blanch for 4 minutes. Cool quickly. Drain well. Wrap each ear individually, airtight, in freezer paper or foil, molding it to the shape of the ear. Pack several together in a freezer bag, expelling as much air as possible.

To freeze corn kernels, blanch the ears as above and cool. Cut the kernels off the cobs and pack in meal-size containers. Seal, expelling as much air as possible; label and freeze.

Green beans

Wash and trim off ends and any blemishes. You can water-blanch small green beans whole, but you may want to cut larger beans into pieces. Blanch whole beans for 3 minutes, pieces for 2 minutes. Cool quickly, drain, and pack. Seal, expelling all the air; label and freeze.

Mushrooms

Wipe with a damp cloth to remove any dirt. Do not peel or rinse. Button varieties can be frozen whole, raw. Spread on a baking tray and place in the freezer. When hard, pack into bags,

label, and return to the freezer. Wild mushrooms, such as Portobello and shiitake, should be sliced and sautéed in butter and packed in small containers with their cooking liquid.

Peas

Shell sweet peas, discarding any damaged ones. Water-blanch for 1½ minutes. Destring pods of sugarsnap peas and water-blanch for 2 minutes. Cool quickly, drain thoroughly, and pack. Seal, expelling as much air as possible; label and freeze.

Pumpkin and hard squashes

Wash fruit, peel, and cut in half; remove any seeds and strings. Cut into slices or cubes. Steam-blanch until tender. Mash. Cool and pack into containers, leaving a ½-inch space at the top of the container. Label and freeze.

Spinach and greens

Wash the leaves thoroughly; remove any thick stems and imperfect leaves. Water-blanch for 30 to 60 seconds, or until just wilted. Cool quickly by running cold water over the leaves. Drain thoroughly, pressing out excess moisture. Pack in a plastic bag. Seal, expelling as much air as possible; label and freeze.

Sweet peppers

Wipe firm sweet peppers and cut out the stems, removing all seeds. Cut in halves, slices, or rings. Blanch halves for 2 minutes, slices for 1 minute. Cool quickly, drain, and pack. Seal, expelling all the air; label and freeze.

Vegetables, mixed

Dice larger vegetables or cut them into bite-size pieces. Blanch according to directions for each individual vegetable, remembering that a shorter blanching time may be required to compensate for the smaller piece size. When they are cool, mix your choice of vegetables and pack in plastic freezer bags in one-meal quantities. Seal, label, and freeze.

PREPARING VEGETABLES FOR FREEZING

Most vegetables freeze well, with the exception of salad greens and vegetables with a high water content—such as celery, cucumbers, radishes, onions, and zucchini and other summer squashes. (the last three can be frozen if grated or chopped and cooked). Tomatoes freeze best in the form of tomato sauce. All vegetables destined for the freezer must be blanched in order to retain color and fresh flavor. Vegetables may be blanched in boiling water or by using the steam method described below.

TO WATER-BLANCH Bring at least 12 cups of water to a boil in a large saucepan. Place 1 pound prepared vegetable pieces in a wire-mesh basket and plunge into the boiling water. When the water returns to a boil, cook the vegetables for the time indicated on these pages. Lift the basket, and place immediately into a large bowl of cold or ice water to cool; it may be necessary to change the water or add more ice. Drain thoroughly.

TO STEAM-BLANCH Place vegetables in a single layer inside a steamer basket in a large saucepan containing 2 inches of boiling water. Cover, and steam the vegetables for the time indicated on these pages. Cool, but don't rinse, the vegetables.

You will need the following amounts of fresh, unblemished vegetables to yield 4 cups frozen:

ASPARAGUS	2½ to 3 pounds
BEANS, BROAD	2½ pounds
BEANS, GREEN	1½ to 2½ pounds
BEETS, TRIMMED	2½ to 3 pounds
BROCCOLI	2 to 2½ pounds
BRUSSELS SPROUTS	2 to 2½ pounds
CARROTS	2½ to 3 pounds
CAULIFLOWER	2½ pounds
CORN	2½ pounds
MUSHROOMS	1 to 2½ pounds
PEAS, GREEN	2½ pounds
PUMPKIN, SQUASH	3 pounds
SPINACH	2½ pounds
SWEET PEPPERS	3 pounds
SWEET POTATOES	1½ pounds
TOMATOES	2½ pounds

Fruit

You'll have a supply of flavorful fruit for dessert toppings and pastry fillings all through the winter months if you buy the season's best at its peak in the summer and fall and freeze it.

Sugar-packed fruit

Because there is no added liquid with this method, sugar-packed fruit is best for baking and for sauces.

- ◆ **4 cups prepared fruit of choice, dipped into acidulated water (box, right)**
- ◆ **½ to ⅔ cup sugar**

1 Drain the dipped fruit thoroughly on paper towels so it is as dry as possible.
2 Place the fruit in a bowl. Add just enough sugar to coat the pieces evenly, then gently mix to dissolve the sugar.
3 Pack snugly into two 2-cup freezer containers or bags and expel all air. Seal tightly, label, and freeze.
MAKES 4 CUPS   TOTAL TIME 15 MINUTES

Syrup for frozen fruit

Use a light, medium, or heavy syrup to freeze fruit, depending on the fruit's tartness. Sour cherries and plums will benefit from a medium or heavy syrup, for example, while fresh grapes and cantaloupe require only a light syrup. You will need 1 to 1½ cups syrup for each 4 cups of prepared fruit.

SYRUP	SUGAR	WATER	YIELD
light	**2 cups**	**4 cups**	**5 cups**
medium	**3 cups**	**4 cups**	**5½ cups**
heavy	**4¾ cups**	**4 cups**	**6½ cups**

1 In a medium saucepan, bring the water to a boil. Add the sugar, stir to dissolve, and simmer for 2 minutes.
2 Remove the pan from the heat, cool, and chill until cold. Use as directed in recipes.

VARIATIONS Add a vanilla bean, cinnamon stick, or strips of lemon peel to the syrup in step 1 to flavor it if desired. Strain the cooled syrup before chilling.

Fruit packed in syrup

The fruit you pack in syrup and freeze can be used just as you would any commercially canned or frozen fruit—drained or not. It's delicious served with ice cream, pound cake, or homemade custard. Home-packed fruits are superior in flavor—nothing beats the summer-fresh taste of fruit from your own freezer.

- ◆ **1 quantity sugar syrup (see previous recipe)**
- ◆ **6 cups prepared fruit of choice, dipped in acidulated water (box, right)**

1 Prepare and chill the syrup.
2 Pour ½ cup chilled syrup into each of three 2-cup freezer containers. Place the fruit pieces in the containers, pressing to remove any air bubbles.
3 Pour in enough remaining syrup to cover the fruit, leaving a half-inch space below the rim, then cover tightly. Seal, label, and freeze.
MAKES 6–7 CUPS   TOTAL TIME 10–15 MINUTES

Sugar-free frozen fruit

This method is ideal for all fruit, particularly strawberries, raspberries, blueberries, and other small fruits you might use as garnishes. Once thawed, the fruit can also be pureed with a little sugar and used as a simple sauce to serve over ice cream or with other desserts.

- ◆ **4 cups prepared fruit of choice, dipped in acidulated water (box, right)**

1 Drain the dipped fruit thoroughly on paper towels. Arrange on a freezer tray and freeze until just firm.
2 Transfer the fruit to two 2-cup freezer containers or bags and expel all air. Seal tightly, label, and freeze.
3 Thaw in the sealed container in the refrigerator or put the still-closed container in a bowl of cool water on the counter. Serve while still slightly icy.
MAKES 4 CUPS   TOTAL TIME 10 MINUTES

PREPARING FRUITS

F RUIT browns quickly when handled, so prepare it as quickly as possible. Keep it in a bowl of acidulated water (about 8 cups water with 1 to 2 tablespoons of lemon juice or mild vinegar added). This is known as dipping. After dipping, drain the fruit thoroughly on paper towels to remove as much moisture as possible. This step prevents ice from forming around the pieces and keeps them from sticking together.

For 4 cups of prepared fruit, purchase the following amounts of unblemished fruit:

APPLES	2½ to 3 pounds
APRICOTS	1¼ to 1½ pounds
CHERRIES	2 to 3 pounds
MANGOES	2½ to 3 pounds
PEACHES, PLUMS	2 to 3 pounds
RASPBERRIES	1 pound
STRAWBERRIES	1¼ pounds

Peel, core, and slice the apples. Stem and pit the cherries. Pit and slice or halve apricots, peaches, plums, and mangoes. Remove stems on berries. Peel melon and cube the flesh or make it into balls with a melon baller.

General freezing

Besides fruits and vegetables, meat, fish, poultry, homemade casseroles, baked goods, and even herbs can be successfully frozen. To find frozen foods in a hurry, label the packets before you freeze them with the contents and the date.

Bread

Bread should be fresh but thoroughly cooled before freezing. Seal in doubled heavy freezer bags. Loaves will keep for up to 6 months, rolls up to 3 months.

Cakes

Cakes keep longer if frozen without icing or filling. (Custard filling and icing containing egg white should never be frozen.) Wrap in plastic, then in foil. Sponge layers should be frozen separately and will keep for about 4 months. To thaw: leave at room temperature about 2 hours (small cakes, 1 hour).

Muffin mixture

To freeze plain unbaked muffins or cupcakes, line a muffin pan with paper liners, add the batter, and freeze, uncovered. Remove the frozen cups from the pan and seal in heavy freezer bags. Will keep about 2 months.

To bake: Replace cups in the original baking pan and bake in a preheated oven for slightly longer than freshly made batter.

Cheese

Hard cheeses, such as Cheddar, Swiss, Edam, and Gouda, should be packed tightly in a double layer of plastic wrap, with all air forced out. Will keep 6 months. To thaw: leave overnight in the refrigerator.

Cream cheese can be frozen for 6 weeks. Don't freeze cottage cheese or ricotta.

Choux pastry

Line baking sheets with baking paper. Form the desired shapes on the sheets and freeze, uncovered. When frozen, pack pastries into plastic freezer bags or containers (the containers may help keep the pastries from being crushed in a full freezer). Will keep for up to 3 months. Do not thaw before baking

Eggs

Raw whole eggs and yolks: Mix with a fork to break up; add ½ teaspoon salt for every 6 whole eggs or a pinch of salt for every 6 yolks. Freeze in small containers.

Whites: Do not beat or add salt before freezing. You can freeze individual whites in ice trays; then pack in plastic bags. Whole eggs, yolks, and whites will keep for 6 months.

Fish

Fish should be frozen within 24 hours of catching. Scale and wash small fish and seal in plastic bags, expelling as much air as possible. Store large fish whole, or cut into fillets or steaks, and sealed in plastic bags. Small fish and fillets or steaks can be cooked still frozen; large, whole fish should be thawed for about 24 hours in the refrigerator. White fish will keep for about 3 months; oily fish, about 2 months.

Herbs

Wash and spin-dry sprigs of bushy herbs; then pack in plastic freezer bags. You can take as many or as few leaves as you need and return sprig to freezer. Pack chopped leaves of herbs such as chives or parsley in plastic containers or ice-cube trays, covered with water. Will keep about 2 months.

Meat

Wrap fresh meat well in plastic wrap, expelling air. Pack in meal-size amounts; layer chops and steaks with wax paper. Beef will keep 8 months; lamb, 6 months; pork, 6 months.

Poultry

Pack whole or halved birds in freezer bags, expelling as much air as possible. Pack poultry pieces in a single layer in bags. Whole birds will keep for 6 months, pieces for about 4 months.

ICE BOWLS TO GRACE YOUR TABLE

Arrange flowers, leaves, herbs, or citrus slices around the inside of the larger bowl, and place the smaller bowl inside. (Choose decorations that will complement what you plan to serve in the bowl.) Tape the two bowls together so that they are flush and will not move apart. Gently pour cooled boiled water into the gap between the bowls to about ½ inch from the top. (Cooled boiled water makes a clearer, more sparkling ice bowl.) Add more decorations if needed, arranging them gently with a dull knife or skewer. Freeze overnight.

Remove the bowls from the freezer and allow to stand at room temperature on a plate or a towel for 10 to 20 minutes or until they separate easily; running water over the bowls to speed the process may ruin the ice bowl. Remove the tape, lift out the inner bowl, and invert the larger bowl to release the ice bowl. Return it to the freezer until needed.

To make an ice bowl, use two glass or stainless-steel bowls of the same shape. One should be small enough to fit inside the other with about a 1-inch space between the two.

Around the Home

Achieving a beautiful and gracious home isn't difficult—all it takes is a little time, imagination, and, in most cases, a modest amount of money. For this chapter, we have tapped many experts for decorating ideas and techniques that will allow you to create the special touches that make a room your own.

You'll learn the secrets of achieving stylish wall and floor finishes quickly and inexpensively. Because you can do it all yourself, you'll save money while producing exactly the look you want.

Once you are satisfied with the walls and floors, complete your decorating with furniture and furnishings you create yourself—use clever painting techniques to rejuvenate tables, chairs, and picture frames, or harness your sewing machine to whip up cushions, chair covers, window swags, and round tablecloths.

Make a handsome screen for a bedroom or living room; construct your own display shelves to show off a favorite picture and a cherished photograph. Disguise an unused fireplace with a charming fire board or screen. There are decorating ideas for every room in the house along with recipes for homemade cleaning and polishing products that will keep your house healthy as well as sparkling.

BEFORE YOU BEGIN ...

The decorating projects in this chapter offer some homemade alternatives to mass-produced accessories, giving you the opportunity to add a personal touch to your home. Before you begin, take time to consider the impact your project will have on the existing decor.

EVERYTHING in your house contributes some element of color, pattern, and texture to the overall appearance. To make the most of the finishing touches presented in this chapter, consider color and proportion carefully before embarking on a project. Think about the impact of new colors or features on the total look of a room.

The object of interior decorating is to emphasize the good features of a room and to minimize or even disguise any less desirable ones. Color, pattern, and texture, used skillfully, can change the information received by the eye about a room's depth, height, and width.

Playing with proportion

A ceiling can be made to appear higher—and the room airier—by painting it a shade paler than the floor and walls. You can take the illusion even further by hanging floor-length striped curtains from a broad valance that covers the gap between the window and the ceiling. For maximum effect, the curtains' stripes should match the wall color.

If a ceiling appears too high, extending its color down to picture rail level will make the walls appear longer and the ceiling lower. Applying horizontal stripes to the walls will produce a similar effect if the stripes aren't interrupted too frequently by doors and windows. In a small room, any horizontal feature below waist height draws the eye down and makes the walls seem farther apart.

Color power

Color is the most significant element in decorating. Modern paint stores, with computerized color matching, offer just about every color and shade imaginable. While at first glance this array may overwhelm you, you can choose colors you like quite simply by associating them with very basic things, such as happy moods, pleasant emotional responses, and fond memories. Even the colors you have selected for your clothing can be a starting point for the those you choose to live with.

Keep in mind that dark, rich colors intensify an area and make it appear cozy and intimate. Light shades, conversely, promote a feeling of airiness and space. Pick and combine colors that you love; your personal taste in mixing and matching colors will pay dividends in originality and style.

Pattern and texture

Pattern performs a function similar to that of color but takes a little more practice to use successfully. Generally, the size of a pattern should relate to the size of a room, with large patterns reserved for large spaces and small, simple patterns used in living areas of modest size. Mixing patterns within color schemes can add interest and individuality.

The contours of a textured surface affect not only the way we expect that surface to feel but also the color of the surface: the most prominent parts catch the light and are brightest while the rest is in a slight shadow.

DESIGNING WITH COLOR, TEXTURE, AND PATTERN

Color is a powerful decorating tool. Use it boldly, but give thought to the views from one space to another. An entrance hall's color, for example, not only sets the welcoming note but also has a direct impact on adjoining rooms.

Texture adds an extra dimension to walls and fabric by inviting touch while also introducing subtle distinctions between light and shade. It gives depth and interest to many colors that might otherwise seem undistinguished.

Patterns provide a reassuring element in any decor because of their reliance on regular repetition. Pattern can be introduced in ornaments and other accessories as well as in larger, more obvious forms, such as fabrics and wallpaper.

Good decorating provides an appealing backdrop for things you love and the way you live. Here, blue and white china pieces stand out against a neutral wall of white paint and upholstery and brown-toned books, vase, and shelves.

MAKING DO

If a specified material isn't available, look around the house for a substitute. Here are some easy replacements:

NATURAL SEA SPONGE: Make your own version from standard synthetic sponges (p.108).

LOW-TACK TAPE: You can make a substitute for masking tape by cutting off a length of the tape you have and pressing it against and lifting it off a smooth fabric surface, such as sheeting, several times to reduce its strength.

MDF: A grade-A plywood of the same thickness can substitute for medium-density fiberboard. While the edges of MDF can be cut and painted as is, plywood edges need an additional finish. Use the fusible edging strip designed for plywood and apply it with a household iron.

Relatively little equipment or money is required to add personal finishing touches to your house. Paint and paintbrushes and rollers are at the top of the list, followed by scissors and pens. Other materials, such as fabric and small pieces of lumber, are a modest investment that pays off well in comfort and beauty.

The magic wand: a coat of paint

Painting is one of the easiest and most satisfying jobs a home decorator can undertake. The key to success is careful preparation. Make sure all surfaces are repaired and sanded smooth to receive new paint. If a surface is pitted or uneven, you may need to fill cracks or depressions with an appropriate filler, such as spackling compound or wood putty, and then sand again when this has dried.

All traces of dust or grit from the sanding must be removed. Wipe down a wall with a lightly dampened soft cloth; wipe down wood with a tack cloth, a rag dampened with turpentine or mineral spirits and a little varnish, which picks up wood dust.

No substitute for quality

The size paintbrush you use depends on the job you are doing. For example, when applying the base color or varnishing a picture frame, choose a brush slightly smaller than the width of the frame. Detailed work is best done with small artist's brushes. Quality paintbrushes produce the best finish. Always use good nylon brushes unless instructed otherwise. Natural bristles don't work well with water-based paints, but nylon serves well with either latex or alkyd (oil-based) paints.

Use a natural sea sponge rather than a man-made one to apply paint to walls. Sea sponges give a soft effect, while synthetic ones produce harsher outlines that may mar the seamless effect you are after.

Decorative stencils

If you are a beginner at stencil cutting (pp. 276 and 277), start with a simple pattern, such as the pear on page 161. When making a stencil, always cut out the design segments carefully. The "bridges" that link the various cutout parts of the design must be kept intact. They not only keep the stencil in one piece, but they also read as "lines" on the completed work. Without the bridges, the finished image will often lack definition.

Stencil cutting is an exacting and time-consuming task that requires patience to achieve the best results. As it is likely that you will want to save stencils for further use or to freshen a design at a later time, proper cleaning and storage are important. After using the stencil, remove any masking tape. Place the stencil on a table covered with several layers of newspaper and paper towels and wipe it with a soft cloth moistened with mineral spirits to remove any vestiges of paint. Store the stencils on a flat surface between two sheets of stiff cardboard.

Fitting and applying the design

After choosing a stencil design, measure the length of the surface onto which it will be applied and divide this figure by the width of the stencil to find out how many times the design is to be repeated. Mark the surface where each repeat has to be placed. You may need to adjust the spacing between the repeats to ensure that the pattern fits neatly into the corners. Depending on the design, it is possible that using just a portion of the stencil at the corners may provide an attractive, symmetrical way to adapt the pattern to your space.

The traditional method of applying the paint when stenciling is called pouncing. A stiff stenciling brush is used to stipple paint over the surface. If you do not have a stencil brush (available at art-supply stores), trim the bristles of a round paintbrush to about ½ inch in length to achieve the required stiffness.

While you are stenciling, wipe the back of the stencil with a damp cloth or paper towel every now and then to remove excess paint, which may bleed around the edges of your image.

Gilding the lily at home

The ancient art of applying paper-thin metal leaf to ornamental objects produces an elegant appearance rarely matched by other forms of decoration. In its most highly refined form, gilding involves the application of real gold or silver leaf to a surface.

There are, however, base metals, such as Dutch metal or aluminum, which are easier to apply and which will still produce a beautiful effect. Dutch metal, which consists of copper and zinc, is a common substitute for gold leaf and is the metal used for gilding frames in this chapter (p.152). Once you are adept at applying Dutch metal, you may want to consider working with gold leaf, a craft that requires special equipment and a very deft hand.

Gilding is not difficult to master as long as you maintain a lightness of touch with your materials. Even your breath can disturb and distort a sheet of leaf once its upper surface is exposed. It is important that your fingers don't come into direct contact with the leaf, as it is likely to disintegrate. Wear a pair of cotton gloves and manipulate the leaf using the rouge paper (between each sheet of leaf) onto the object being gilded. Similarly, once the gilt has been applied, avoid touching the surface with bare fingers until it is varnished.

Remember that gilding takes a little practice, so you may want to take a few trial runs before beginning in earnest. You will often find when you brush down the leaf at the end of the gilding process that the surface will have cracks, through which you will see the red paint layer that is applied before the leaf. This is quite normal and, in fact, adds to the beauty of the finish.

Something different: découpage

Although a sable brush is called for in the materials list for the découpage mirror frame (p.154), imitation sable, which is less expensive, works just as well for a one-time project.

Never work in circles when sanding between applications of découpage. Use the left-to-right, top-to-bottom cross-hatching motion that is also the proper procedure for varnishing. If you have protected your finished frame with a satin-finish, oil-based varnish and want to give it a burnished glow, wait until it is completely dry (this process can take up to a week), and using a soft cloth (a clean cotton sock is ideal), polish the frame with light strokes.

Although it takes time, patience, and some dexterity with the scissors, this traditional craft can make wonderful and very personal gifts. Try covering a wooden jewelry box with a friend's favorite flowers or follow a family motif with childhood photographs on a box to store memorabilia.

MAKING A STENCIL FOR A CURVED BORDER

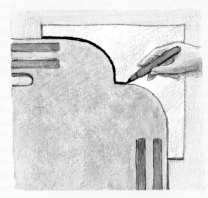 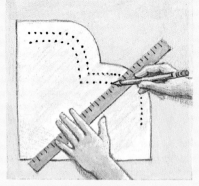 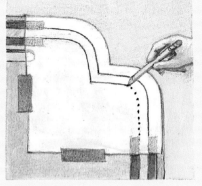 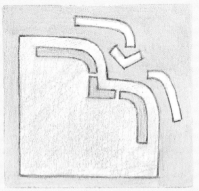

1 Place the stencil acetate underneath the area needing a curved border. With a fine-tip permanent marker, trace the curved shape, stopping about 2 inches beyond any adjoining straight edge. Use a craft knife to cut the curved edge.

2 Use a ruler to mark two rows of dots equidistant inside the curved edge of the acetate. Follow measurements given in project instructions (the fire screen, p.149, for example) for spacing inside the edge and between rows of dots.

3 Use a French curve and ruler to connect the dots into two parallel curved border lines inside the curved edge. Lay the acetate on the curved area of the project to check that the curved border is properly spaced to meet the side lines.

4 Draw lines ⅛ inch apart at 4- to 6-inch intervals to connect the parallel border lines with the bridges. Cut out the stencil areas with a craft knife, leaving the bridges to hold the sides of the stencil together. Paint in the gaps later.

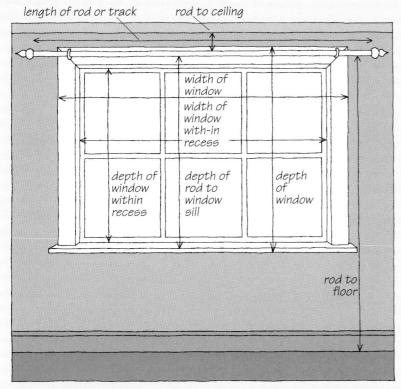

length of rod or track *rod to ceiling*

width of window

width of window with-in recess

depth of window within recess *depth of rod to window sill* *depth of window*

rod to floor

Window measurements

The simple skill of dressing up a window

If you are lucky enough to enjoy a view, you may wish to select window dressings that enhance rather than obscure it. This is especially important in rooms where light is at a premium. A silk swag (p.120) over simple sheer curtains or a puffy fabric cloud valance (p.121) meets these needs perfectly. They not only can enhance a well-proportioned window but can also disguise faults in an unattractive one. Both window treatments frame the view while allowing plenty of light to enter the room.

A window that doesn't have an attractive view will benefit from having a decorated roll shade, such as the child's stenciled shade on page 124. You can make full tab curtains using the instructions for the shower curtain on page 137 and decorate a handsome curtain rod to hold the curtains, as on page 126.

When measuring for window coverings (Diagram above), make a rough sketch of your window and on it note the following measurements: length of the curtain rod or track; distance between the outer edge of the window frame and the end of rod; drop from the rod to the window stool (the indoor sill); drop from the rod to the floor; distance from the rod to the ceiling; distance from the rod to the top of the window frame; total depth of the window; depth of the window within the recess; total width of the window; width of the window within the recess. If you are not sure of how much fabric you will need for curtains, take the diagram to your fabric retailer, who can help you with the necessary calculations. Use the measurements for ordering blinds as well.

Glossary

Artist's acrylic: A water-based artist's paint available in tubes. It can be used alone or as a colorant in water-based glazes, scumbles, and washes.

Dutch metal: Thin sheets (leaves) of copper and zinc used for gilding; a substitute for the more expensive, harder to handle gold leaf. When purchased, leaves of gilding are separated by sheets of rouge paper in a book format.

Eggshell finish: A medium-luster finish in latex- or oil-based paint. Its consistency is thicker than that of other lower-luster finishes, a desirable quality for painting special finishes on large surfaces. Because eggshell-finish paint has a longer drying time, you have more time to work with it.

Fusible webbing: A fabric interfacing used to stiffen appliqués, prevent their raveling, and hold them in place while you sew around them. Applied with an iron, the webbing has a bonding agent activated by heat.

Gesso: A white liquid composed of fine white chalk, called whiting, mixed with a size glue that is made from rabbit skin. Gesso is used to prime canvas for floorcloths (p.116). It is also used as a primer, or undercoat, for faux finishes and under gilding on frames.

Glaze: A homogeneous mixture of paint that produces a transparent layer of color over a colored base coat of paint. Several glaze coats in different colors can be built up to create a brilliance and depth of color. Ready-made glazes for water-based and oil-based paints are available at paint stores; stay with the same base type for all paint and glaze layers.

Ragging: A painting technique, sometimes known as dragging, in which crumpled rags or papers are rolled over a wet layer of paint to expose the previously painted color underneath. Use lots of rags or papers and change them frequently.

Scumble medium: A type of glaze that produces "broken color work." In effect, the scumble-glaze layer breaks up and cracks to reveal the contrasting base-coat color underneath. Both water- and oil-based scumble mediums are available at art-supply stores. You add the appropriate acrylic or oil paint colorant.

Sponging: A painting technique that employs a sponge to apply one layer or more of paint in one color or more. The sponge is dabbed randomly over the surface to produce an irregular spotted effect.

Stippling: A painting technique similar to sponging, except a stencil brush or a stipple brush is used to apply the random spotted effect. These brushes have stiff, blunt-end bristles.

Tack cloth: A piece of cheesecloth impregnated with linseed oil. This special cloth, available at home centers or hardware stores, picks up fine, hard-to-see particles of dust left behind after sanding wood. It produces a clean surface for the next procedure.

White craft glue: A white glue made from polyvinyl acetate (PVA). It dries to a transparent finish, desirable for many craft techniques in which you don't want the glue to show.

White modeling compound: A pliable doughlike mixture for making paintable flat decorations, such as Christmas tree ornaments or the dinosaur magnets on page 318. You can buy the compound at crafts stores or make your own by mixing equal parts salt and flour with enough water to make a manageable dough.

◆ Painted Wall Finishes ◆

Why settle for a plain, painted wall when paint can be used in so many creative ways?
Some beautiful effects can be achieved with the easily mastered techniques described here. As you
become more confident, who knows where your creative imagination may lead.

Fresco effect

A fresco finish gives a subtle, aged look to a wall.
The softly muted blend of shades adds a warm
touch to many surroundings and is suitable for
both rustic and modern decors. It's wise to prac-
tice on a board or a small area to refine your
technique before working on a complete wall.

- **two large paintbrushes**
- **flat latex paints in off-white and bright yellow ocher**
- **natural sea sponge**
- **cleaning rag**

1 Paint the surface with two coats of off-white paint and allow to dry.

2 Apply the yellow ocher to a 3-foot-square area with a brush, working quickly and evenly.

3 Before the ocher paint dries, use a second, dry paintbrush to rub the color into the surface, achieving a mottled effect. Wipe the brush regularly on a clean rag as you progress to keep the bristles as dry as possible. Repeat the procedure if the effect is too patchy.

4 Make a mixture of one part off-white paint to one part water. Wet the sponge in the mixture and, working quickly, apply to the entire painted surface with a rubbing motion. Wet the sponge repeatedly in the paint-water mixture as you progress.

5 While the painted surface is still wet, wring all the moisture out of the sponge. Working with a circular motion, rub the sponge over the

entire surface. Do not apply pressure to the sponge or the paint will spread unevenly. Work your way over the entire surface until a mottled effect is achieved. Wring the sponge periodically to remove excess moisture. When covering large areas, the job can be done more quickly and consistently if two people work side by side with separate sponges.

Give your walls the look of aged plaster without wait-
ing 100 years for time to show its effect. Two people
working together can complete a "frescoed" room in
just a couple of days. Many base colors look good, but
among the most effective are the earthy, ocher tones of
the Mediterranean and the American Southwest.

Ragged wall

For this dappled finish, two paint colors are used. When the base coat is dry, the second color (or glaze) is thinned with water, painted on, and then partially removed with a cloth in a consistent pattern. For best results, use paints with an eggshell finish and test a variety of ragging techniques on a small area before attempting an entire room. Two people should work together.

- ◆ **large paintbrush**
- ◆ **latex paint for base coat (gray or color of your choice)**
- ◆ **latex paint for the ragging glaze (green-gray or color of your choice thinned with equal amount of water)**
- ◆ **plenty of cotton rags, such as old sheets, cut up**

1   Using the gray paint, apply two base coats, allowing 4 hours drying time between coats. Let dry for 24 hours after the second coat.

2   Working on only a small area at any one time (3 square feet), the first person applies the second color over the base coat, using a cross-hatching technique (below).

3   The second person follows immediately and, working quickly with folded, rolled, or crumpled strips of cloth, blots off part of the paint in an irregular pattern that will look consistent over a whole wall. (Using different textures of cloth will create different surface

Ragging gives a subtle, muted effect, rather like an unobtrusive wallpaper but without the seams. Soft pastel tones work well for this treatment.

textures.) Gently twist or swipe the cloth for different effects. Pick up and use fresh cloths often. Catch paint drips immediately because they will show as lines on the finished work. For best results, rag a room as one continuous process from start to finish. Never rework part of a wall, because the new work will stand out as different from the rest. Repainting the entire wall is the only way to achieve a satisfactory result, if you aren't satisfied with the first effort. Allow glaze to dry.

A sponged ceiling gives a room a warm, intimate feeling. You can take breaks when doing this finish—start and stop lines are easy to disguise.

Sponged wall

Sponging is one of the quickest and easiest finishes to apply. It produces a stylish effect, and mistakes can easily be rectified. We used a dark jungle green as the base for our sponged finish, but choose any deep color, observing the ratios of paint to water given here. Test your technique on a board or a small section of wall before you try to sponge the entire room.

- ◆ **paintbrush**
- ◆ **flat-finish latex paints in jungle green and off-white**
- ◆ **natural sea sponges**

1 Paint the wall with jungle green. Allow to dry. The wall may appear dark when dry, but the final effect will be much lighter.
2 Make a mixture of one part off-white paint to one part water. Using the sponge, rub the mixture over the entire surface. It doesn't matter if dark green highlights appear. They will give character to the finished project.

Even a novice can achieve an excellent result with sponging. Although the look is mottled, it's not meant as a disguise for poorly prepared surfaces. For the best finish, prepare your walls with care.

3 Make a mixture of one part jungle green to one part off-white paint. Dab the sponge in the mixture, so that the sponge is almost dry; then dab onto the wall, working with an even pressure. Make sure you vary the angles at which you press the sponge on the wall to avoid making an obvious pattern. Take care to use a corner of the sponge to apply paint right up to the edge of the wall. Leave to dry.
4 Add more white to the original mix to lighten it a few shades. Using a clean sponge, apply this new shade as a second coat and allow to dry.
5 Add more white to the mix. Using a clean sponge, apply the new shade as a third coat and allow to dry. This last shade, the lightest of the three, will provide the dominant color of the finished surface.

◆ Reviving with Paint ◆

You can give new life to old furniture with a painted finish. The special effect of sponge painting is impressively easy to achieve, even for a beginner, and simple stencils, applied over a painted finish, can customize a piece for a particular person or to match a decor.

Stenciled child's rocker

You can personalize the top rail of this rocker with a child's name where "my chair" is seen here. Letters, numbers, and punctuation marks spill out over the rocker in several bright colors to make a cheerful design.

- **sandpaper**
- **tack cloth**
- **one quart yellow latex paint**
- **paintbrush**
- **artist's acrylic paints in red, blue, green, purple, and orange**
- **two to five small stencil brushes**
- **palette or clean plastic meat tray**
- **paper towels**
- **precut stencil of 1-inch-high letters, numbers, and punctuation marks**
- **scissors**
- **masking tape**

1 Sand the surfaces of the rocker smooth to prepare it for the new paint. Wipe all the sanded surfaces clean with the tack cloth.

2 Paint the chair yellow or the color of your choice. Let it dry. Repeat with a second, and possibly a third, coat of paint so that an even color is achieved.

3 Cut the large stencil into several mini-stencils (box, p.108).

4 To stencil, work with one paint color at a time and a dry brush. Apply a small amount of paint to the palette and dab the brush tip in it. Swirl the brush in a circular motion lightly over a paper towel to disperse the paint evenly.

A brightly painted rocker, stenciled with a youngster's name, would make a fine present for a birthday or other special occasion.

WORKING WITH PRECUT STENCILS

A ready-made stencil can be cumbersome to work with, particularly in a scattered arrangement, such as the rocker on page 107. On a large sheet, individual letters and numbers are difficult to fit around slats, posts, and rails of the chair.

An easy solution is to cut the stencil into smaller, more flexible units—mini-stencils of four to six letters or numbers each.

Use masking tape around the edges of the mini-stencils to provide a buffer for the stencil brush. Since the tape is pliable, it allows the mini-stencil to be tucked in between slats for painting and gives you equal access to all the letters, numbers, and punctuation marks.

5 Position the selected letter, number, or punctuation stencil in the desired location on the rocker and use the same circular motion to stencil in the color. Be sure to keep the stencil flat against the surface with masking tape (below) while stenciling, so that paint doesn't seep under the stencil's edges. You may even find it helpful to block off adjacent letters with tape before stenciling the selected one.

6 Repeat Steps 4 and 5 until the desired effect is created. Change to a clean, dry brush when you switch stenciling colors.

7 When the stenciling is finished and the paint is completely dry, finish the rocker with several coats of polyurethane, following the manufacturer's directions.

Sponged chest

In this sponging process we used two shades of the same color, but you can easily use three or four to achieve yet another effect. Experiment on a scrap board before you begin, to be sure you end up with an effect that you like. The possibilities are almost limitless, so keep track of the steps you take and the paints you use at each part of the process.

- ◆ **sandpaper**
- ◆ **tack cloth**
- ◆ **one quart light sage green latex paint**
- ◆ **paintbrush**
- ◆ **one quart medium sage green latex paint**
- ◆ **large and small natural sea sponges**
- ◆ **bucket of water**
- ◆ **paper plates**
- ◆ **rubber gloves**
- ◆ **polyurethane**

1 Remove the drawer hardware and knobs. Sand smooth the surfaces of the chest, including any wooden knobs, to prepare it for the new paint. Check the interior of the drawers. If these areas are painted, you may decide to freshen them up, too. Sand the drawer interiors smooth before painting.

2 Wipe all the sanded surfaces clean with the tack cloth. Paint the drawer interiors, if desired, with the brush. Let dry completely before proceeding to the next step.

3 Using the paintbrush, coat the exterior of the chest with the lighter color. Let dry. Repeat with a second, and possibly a third, coat so that an even color is achieved.

4 Put on the rubber gloves for the sponging process. Soak the sponges in the water and squeeze them out so they are just damp.

5 Dip the bottom of the sponge lightly into the medium-color paint and blot it around on a paper plate a couple of times to disperse the paint and remove the excess.

6 Working randomly over each surface, dab the sponge onto the furniture with a light rolling motion. The sponging will appear darker at first but will lighten up as the sponge needs more paint. This is why you need to work randomly: so you can balance out the color.

7 Repeat Steps 5 and 6 until the furniture is completely covered. Use the small sea sponge in hard-to-reach areas and on small details, such as the knobs.

8 Allow the paint to dry completely. Finish the chest with several coats of polyurethane, following the manufacturer's instructions.

This pretty sponged chest could start out as an old weathered bureau or an unpainted piece of new furniture. Either way, the result is fresh and charming.

SUBSTITUTION FOR NATURAL SPONGES

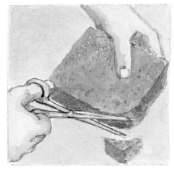

1 *If you can't find natural sponges to use in your painting, you can adapt a synthetic sponge from the supermarket. First cut off any sharp corners with a pair of scissors.*

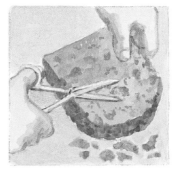

2 *Cut out rounded recesses from the corner area, then make additional irregular cuts across the flat surface. The desirable quality of a natural sponge is its rounded edges.*

3 *Apply paint sparingly to the sponge; then dab and roll the surface of the sponge around in various directions, just as you would with a natural sponge.*

◆ Traditional Floor Stenciling ◆

*In Colonial times, stenciling was widely used as an inexpensive means of adding color
and pattern to a room. Though there are now many other alternatives for decorating, stenciling is still
valued for its inherent charm and the individuality and character it gives a home.*

A stenciled border around a floor is easy to apply. Use the design provided on this page or choose a precut stencil at a crafts supply shop. Stenciling will not adhere to varnish or wax. Stripped and sanded wooden floors can be stenciled as is, or the floor can be covered with a coat of thinned latex paint before stenciling. A stripped and sanded floor can also be painted with two or three coats of latex paint in a complementary color before being stenciled.

- ◆ **acetate stencil**
- ◆ **craft knife**
- ◆ **low-tack spray adhesive**
- ◆ **self-healing cutting board**
- ◆ **pencil, ruler, and eraser**
- ◆ **small stencil brush**
- ◆ **artist's brush**
- ◆ **latex paint to suit color
  of floor and walls**
- ◆ **tracing paper (if not
  using photocopier)**
- ◆ **masking tape, if needed**
- ◆ **polyurethane varnish**
- ◆ **brush for applying
  polyurethane**

1 Using a photocopier, enlarge the design below—or your chosen design—to the desired size. (To enlarge it without a photocopier, see page 276.)
2 Spray the back of the design with adhesive to prevent any movement during cutting; then place on the acetate. Using the craft knife, carefully cut out the shapes over the cutting

IDEAS FOR STENCILING

When stenciling furniture, take pains to work knobs and hardware into the design. The overall pattern will look much more graceful and appropriate to the piece.

To center a pattern on a wall or a floor, tack a pushpin into each corner of the surface and stretch two strings diagonally from corner to corner. Where the strings cross is the center. Mark it and then line up your pattern

The interiors of some pieces of furniture—desks and armoires, for example—are good candidates for stenciling. An interior stencil can be a pleasant surprise every time you look inside for a piece of stationery or a pillowcase .

Brighten a basement by stenciling its concrete floor. Just be sure the floor is freshly scrubbed and dry before you start. Protect the finished stenciling with three coats of clear polyurethane.

Highlight windows that have a view with a stencil pattern around the frame. Pick up a motif from the view, such as acorns if you see an oak tree from the window. Or choose a motif from other elements in the room.

board. Work from the center out and turn the acetate as you go to make cutting easier. If you cut one of the bridges (the acetate between

two cutout areas), you can repair it with a small piece of masking tape on either side.
3 Before you apply any paint, you must establish how to fit the stencil to the given space (p.102). Measure the width of the stencil and measure your floor; then work out how much space to leave between each repeat. With our design, you'll achieve the trimmest appearance if you allow the circle at the center of the stencil to fall at each corner of the room.
4 Starting with that premise, measure the floor and figure out how many repeats of the stencil pattern will fit along each side of the floor and what an even spacing between the stencils will be. Mark the floor lightly with a pencil where each stencil will start.
5 Tape the stencil in place and apply the paint with a stencil brush: use very little paint and dab it on lightly with the tip of the brush only. Lift the stencil carefully. Using the artist's brush and a little paint, connect the four sections of the center circle. Allow to dry.
6 Repeat Step 5 until you have completed the area you wish to stencil. Once it is finished and dry, erase any pencil marks.
7 Protect the floor with three coats of matte or gloss polyurethane. Allow each coat to dry for 24 hours before applying the next.

A simple border, stenciled around the edge of a floor, gives a room an individual touch in keeping with Early American decor. You can choose other stencil patterns to pick up motifs in wallpaper or fabric.

Classic border stencil for floors

◆ Reversible Rags Under Foot ◆

*These charming braided and knitted rag rugs will cushion
your feet. The feathery edges and pop-up ends of the torn fabric strips
used to create them enhance their casual country feeling.*

*For braiding, choose one of two ways to fold the
fabric—once along the width or twice along the
width, with the torn edges meeting at the center.*

FOR ALL RAG RUGS
- **threads to match fabrics**
- **button and carpet thread
  to match fabric**
- **darning needle, size 1**
- **blunt needle**
- **sharp needle, size 9**
- **large quilter's-type safety pins**
- **scissors; tape measure**
- **rubber bands to secure rolled
  balls of fabric strips**

Braided heart rug

*This rug measures about 30 x 25 inches. To make
a coordinating table mat, begin with a starting
line of 8 inches, with a 12-inch spread and lace
for five or six rounds.*

- **3 ½ yards of 44-inch-wide fabric
  in each of three different prints**
- **cutting board**

Gauge for all braids
1 to 1 ⅛ inches wide x 5 repeats = 4-inch braid.

Preparing the rag strips
1 Follow the directions for "Tearing rag strips"
on page 281, using 10 inches for the A measurement and 5 inches for the B measurement; tear
up to 1 ½ inches from selvages.
2 Fold each color of the rag strips, wrong side
inside, and roll into a ball. To join on a strip of
the same or another color, lap the ends of the
folded strips about ½ inch and sew with a
running stitch in matching sewing thread. Limit
size of balls to about 10 strips so they don't
become too large and heavy.

Braiding
1 To start the braid, fold each strip's end in a
pleat, arrange the pleats side by side, and tack
the three ends together (p.114).
2 Braid for about 20 yards.
3 To join the braids in a heart shape, bend the
beginning end of the braid back on itself, forming a starting line of 12 inches on the downward side. With the carpet thread and darning

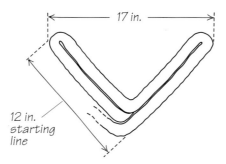

needle, tack the beginning end to the braid
above. Using a blunt needle, lace the carpet
thread through the abutted sides of the braid.
End off at the top of the loop. With the continuing braid, form another 12-inch loop on the
other side; pin these loops 17 inches apart on a
cutting board. Lace the second side together
with carpet thread from the top.
4 Continue wrapping the braid around this
center looped form for eight rounds, ending at
the bottom of the heart.
5 To finish the braid ends, cut a 2 x 3-inch strip
of fabric. Fold one long edge under. Trim the
braid ends and tack them together. Wrap a
band around the ends as shown in Step 4 on
page 114. Tack the band to the heart.

*Braided rag rugs made of soft cotton fabrics are won-
derful country accent pieces. Using fabrics in shades of
one or two colors and mixing printed fabrics with
solids in the braids create a delicately muted look.*

Braided rectangular rug

This rug measures 22 x 38 inches, excluding 3 to 4 inches of fringe on each end.

◆ **2 yards of 44-inch-wide fabric in each of six different prints**

1 Using the heart rug directions, start braiding three strips of the same color together about 4 inches from the end and braid for 38 inches.
2 Make three to four identical-length braids from each fabric and finish both ends as described below to form a tassel.
3 Arrange braids in a repeating pattern of colors, lace, and tack bands together.

Braided oval rug

This rug measures about 28 x 40 inches.

◆ **seven prints and solids (A-G) that gradually shade from beige to rust to dark brown in 44-inch-wide fabrics:**
◆ **fabrics A and G: 1½ yards**
◆ **fabrics B and C: 3¾ yards**
◆ **fabric D: 2¾ yards**
◆ **fabrics E and F: 2 yards**

1 Using the heart rug directions, braid fabrics A, B, and C together for 7 yards. Starting with a 15-inch center line, lace five rounds together.

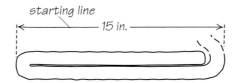

starting line — 15 in.

2 Braid fabrics B, C, and D together for about 9 yards and lace for four rounds.
3 Braid fabrics D, E, and F for about 3 yards and lace for one round.
4 Braid fabrics E, F, and G for about 6½ yards and lace for two rounds, ending on the long side. End the braid at the beginning of the curve of the oval end.
5 To finish the rug, you can conceal the end of the braid, as in the heart rug, or you can leave the braid end as a tassel, as in the rectangular rug. To conceal the end, tack the three braid ends together. Fold under one long edge of a 2 x 3-inch fabric strip and place it under the braid ends. Fold under the other long end and bring the folded ends together, concealing the braid ends. Wrap the short ends around the braid ends and slip-stitch them together.

THE BASICS OF BRAIDING RAG STRIPS

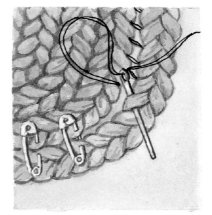

1 *Before you begin, roll the torn lengths into balls, folding the strips with the right sides out as you go. Secure the balls with rubber bands. To begin a braid, pleat the starting ends of three strips and hand-sew them together with several stitches.*

2 *To braid, fold the far right strip snugly over the center strip and place it in the center. Fold the far left strip snugly over the new center strip and place it in the center. Repeat these two steps for the desired length.*

3 *To lace, with carpet thread doubled, sew through a braid; then use a blunt needle to lace thread through the abutted sides of the braid, first one side, then the other. Pull thread as tight as possible without distorting the rug .*

4 *To finish braid ends, fold in the long edges of a 2 x 3-inch fabric strip, wrap it tightly around the braid, and slip-stitch the end. To conceal the braid ends, tack blunt ends together, wrap fabric strip around ends, and stitch as shown above.*

A rag rug in blue and white, a favorite color combination, makes a handsome addition to a kitchen or bathroom. Knitted from torn strips of washable cotton fabric in easy stockinette stitch, the rug is practical, too.

3 Using one fabric color, cast on 22 sts. 1st row: K 22. 2nd row: P 22. Repeat these two rows (stockinette st) for 44 rows, or until work measures 12 inches. Cast off by slipping one loop at a time onto a crochet hook and pulling the next loop on the needle through it until reaching the end; cut the fabric 2 inches from last loop and pull the end through the loop.
4 Repeat Step 3 to make two more squares.
5 Using the second fabric color, repeat Step 3 to make three squares.

To assemble the rug
1 Block each square to 12 inches.
2 Working with two squares at a time, safety pin together three rows as shown below; alternate the colors in each row and turn all squares of one color with purl side up and a cast on or off edge against the side of the contrasting square. Sew the squares together from each side with carpet thread and a darning needle, using either the running or the whip stitch.

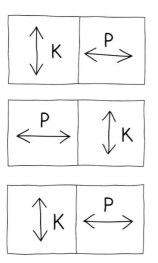

Knitted checkerboard rug

Knit any number of 12-inch squares to achieve the rug size wanted. Purchase 1¼ yards of fabric for each square. Shown here is a 2 x 3-foot rug.

- **3 ¾ yards of 44-inch-wide fabric in each of two colors (we used blue and white)**
- **knitting needles, size 15**
- **crochet hook, size K**

Gauge

5 ½ sts and 11 rows = 4 in. of stockinette st, using size 15 needles. If you have fewer sts than stated, use smaller needles; if more sts, use larger needles. For abbreviations, see page 256.

To make the squares

1 Follow the directions in "Tearing rag strips" on page 281, using 2 inches for the A measurement and 1 inch for the B measurement.
2 Fold the rag strip, right side inside.

3 Sew rows together from each side, making sure the corners are secure and tight.

◆ Painted Floorcloths ◆

Painted canvas rugs have been a practical solution to decorating floors since the 1700s.
The basic process is surprisingly easy. Use one of the four designs presented here or devise one of your
own, matching colors or picking up favorite design motifs from fabrics or wallpaper in the room.

To start a floorcloth, give the canvas a coat of gesso (artist's primer) and two coats of background paint color. Choose one of the lighter colors in the design for the background color.

- **plastic drop cloth**
- **artist's canvas (see Basic Tips on Canvas, right)**
- **acrylic gesso (available at art-supply stores). Mix 3 ½ cups gesso with 1 cup water to cover 50 square feet.**
- **paint roller with medium-rough cover and paint tray**
- **background paint: flat exterior latex or eggshell latex**
- **3-inch nylon paintbrush**
- **long metal ruler and T square, HB pencil, art gum eraser**
- **scissors**
- **white craft glue**
- **sewing machine with heavy-duty needle, white polyester thread**
- **paint for the design: latex paint, artist's acrylics, spray paint**
- **artist's brushes for painting design**
- **stencils, stencil paints, stencil brushes (optional)**
- **masking tape**
- **sponge**
- **water-based varnish**
- **2-inch nylon paintbrush**
- **paste wax, rags**
- **liquid nonskid rubber backing**
- **paint roller with foam cover**

1 Spread the drop cloth. Arrange the canvas smooth side up. Prime the canvas by rolling the gesso mixture generously on the surface, working from the center out. Don't allow the fabric to ripple; smooth out any ridges with the roller. Let the canvas dry overnight.

BASIC TIPS ON CANVAS

Artist's canvas, or cotton duck, is available at art-supply stores in various weights. Even-numbered weights range from 4, the heaviest, to 12, the lightest. Number 10 is a good average weight. It's available up to 120 inches wide and can be purchased in any length. The canvas you buy should be at least 8 inches longer and wider than the size of the rug you plan to make. This accommodates a hem plus the shrinkage that occurs when the gesso primer is applied.

Purchase enough yardage to make the floorcloth without seams. The scale of our four designs would easily produce rugs 2 feet by 2 feet 9 inches or 3 feet by 4 feet.

Ask the retailer to wind your yardage on a fabric roll. Folds and creases are unforgiving in this fabric.

While canvas has no right or wrong side, one side will be smoother. Use that one for painting.

Draft geometric designs, such as the checkerboard and herringbone patterns, to scale first on graph paper. When the pattern works out to what you want, buy canvas and produce a full-size floorcloth to match the proportions.

2 Brush on one coat of background color, working from the center out. Paint up to but not over the edges. Allow to dry.

3 Turn the canvas wrong side up. Using the T square, ruler, and pencil, draw the rectangular dimensions of the floorcloth on the back. Draw a second rectangle ⅝ inch outside the first. Draw a 45-degree line across each outer corner (Diagram 1). Trim the canvas along the outer pencil lines and diagonal corners.

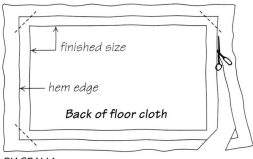

DIAGRAM 1

4 Fold the trimmed corner inward so that it touches the pencil line (Diagram 2); glue.
5 To hem: Working on one edge at a time, fold a ⅝-inch hem to wrong side of the canvas. Topstitch ¼ inch from the edge (Diagram 3.)

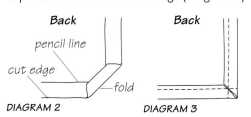

DIAGRAM 2   DIAGRAM 3

6 Lay canvas right side up. Apply a second coat of background color. When dry, use a pencil to draw the design on the surface; then paint. If the design has linear motifs, use tape to mask sections while adjacent sections are being painted. Any stenciling should be done last.
7 When the design is painted and dry, use a damp sponge to wipe it free of dust. Following the manufacturer's directions, apply the varnish as a sealer. Repeat the sealing process three to five times, until the surface feels smooth.
8 With soft rags, apply a thin coat of wax. Hand-buff with a clean cloth to a high sheen.
9 Turn the floor cloth wrong side up. Apply glue under the loose hem edge; let dry.
10 Follow the manufacturer's instructions to apply liquid nonskid rubber to the back of the rug, inside the hem lines.

Four floorcloth designs

Checkerboard rug *Start with the cream color for the background; then add the colorful squares and triangles. Work out the border first by marking even intervals around the perimeter and drawing lines at 45 degrees with a ruler to make the triangles. Use the inner points of the triangles to mark the width of the squares.*

Herringbone rug *This design is based on a parquet or brick flooring pattern. Start with the cream-colored background paint and the brown border. Then work out the design with a ruler and even measurements, or cut a cardboard template to the size of one of the "bricks" and trace it repeatedly to create the pattern.*

Celestial rug *Mask the white borders with tape before painting the lighter blue background color and then the border. When dry, remove the tape and paint the framing lines and white dots, then the stars and moons—stencils make this easy. Add the shadows to the stars and moons freehand with black paint.*

Abstract rug *This design relies on intersecting areas of color for its effect. Paint the cream background; then add the other colors. Mark out the circles using two pencils and a piece of string—tie a pencil to each end of the string, hold one steady at the center point and draw the circle outline with the other.*

◆ Catch the Sun with Falling Leaves ◆

Red and yellow autumn leaves become sun catchers and glimmer like jewels when you use
a faux stained glass technique that is easy enough for even young children to manage. Vary the colors
of the leaves to capture their seasonal changes or to evoke a holiday mood.

Oak

These birch, oak, and maple leaf sun catchers are about life size. Feel free to make them even larger, if you like. Buy supplies for making sun catchers at an art-supply or crafts store.

- ◆ **8 x 10-inch styrene sheet for leading or clear plastic sheet**
- ◆ **1-ounce bottles glass paint: sunny yellow, gold sparkle, berry red, orange poppy, amber, and ivy green**
- ◆ **1-ounce bottle simulated liquid leading in pewter or bronze**
- ◆ **paper towels; cotton swabs**
- ◆ **paper clip**
- ◆ **nut pick or wooden toothpicks**

1 Using a photocopier, enlarge the leaf drawings to the size you want. Or enlarge them by hand, using the directions on page 276. The

Leaves in the vibrant colors of autumn glisten in the sunlight as they appear to cascade down a window .

HELPFUL LEADING TIPS

Holding the tip of the bottle above the surface allows you to achieve straighter, smoother lines. Try to keep the lines an equal width.

All lines must meet so that a paint color will not seep into an unwanted area.

Keep it simple. Simple patterns are usually more attractive than complex ones and are always easier to make.

birch leaf is 2 ½ x 3 ½ inches; the oak, 3 ¼ x 5 inches; the maple, 4 ¼ x 3 ½ inches.
2 Lay a blank sheet of styrene, smooth side up, over the leaf drawing.

Leading

1 Use the end of a paper clip to puncture a hole in the nozzle of the bottle of simulated liquid leading.
2 To start the flow of the leading, touch the tip of the bottle to the styrene. Squeeze the bottle slightly and raise the tip about ¼ inch above the surface just as the leading starts to flow.
3 To lead, hold the bottle at a slight angle with the tip raised and follow the perimeter line. Then add the interior lines. The leading

will stretch and follow the direction in which you move your hand.
4 Let the leading dry for 24 hours.

Coloring

1 Make sure your work surface is level so the liquid paint colors will not run together or puddle. Before you start, mix each color thoroughly by rocking the bottle back and forth. Do not shake it; this will cause unwanted bubbles to develop.
2 Repeat Step 1 of leading.
3 Hold the selected color at the same angle as you did the leading bottle. Release a small pool of the color in the center of a leaded area by squeezing the bottle, but more gently than with the leading because the paint is thinner. Without squeezing the bottle, use its tip to fill the area. Make sure a thin layer of paint fills the area completely. Use a nut pick or toothpick to push the color against the leading and into the narrow areas and points of the leaves.
4 To mix colors, squeeze dots of one color; add swirls of a second color. Use the nozzle to mix the colors. Or squeeze rows of alternating colors; use the toothpick to blend them.
5 Allow the paint to dry for 24 hours.
6 Carefully peel the leaf from the blank styrene. Press it on any clean glass surface and it will cling. Pick windows where light will filter through the color.

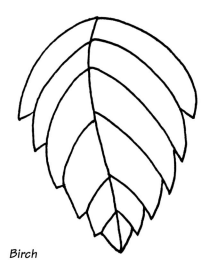

Birch

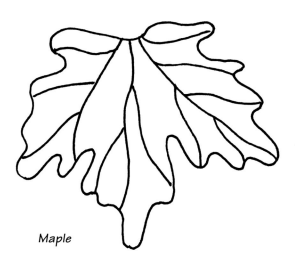

Maple

MAKING SUN CATCHERS

1 *To start the flow of the leading, touch the tip of the bottle to the styrene or plastic. Squeeze the bottle lightly and raise the tip about ¼ inch above the surface as the leading starts to flow.*

2 *To lead, hold the bottle at a slight angle with the tip raised. Follow the perimeter line of the shape; then add the interior lines. The leading will stretch and follow the moves of your hand.*

3 *If you make a mistake or are unhappy with the way a leading line looks, the wet leading can be removed with a cotton swab; the line can then be redrawn. Let the leading dry for 24 hours.*

4 *Release a small pool of the color in the center of a leaded area by squeezing the bottle more gently than you did the leading. Use the nozzle tip to fill the area with color; use a toothpick for corners.*

❀ Dressing Up Windows ❀

*Creating beautiful window coverings can be surprisingly simple. A special window treatment
is a versatile and easy way to spruce up your room. Often the best choice is a minimal treatment
that frames a wonderful view and allows the sun to come streaming in.*

Cloud valance

Shown here on a 36-inch-wide window with the brackets mounted outside the frame, this valence with five wraps and two tails required the yardages listed below. To customize it for any-size window, divide the mounted rod's length by 8 inches to determine the number of wraps. Allow 24 inches for each wrap and add 1 yard for each tail. Total these numbers for your yardage.

- ◆ **5 ½ yards of 54-inch-wide chintz (peach)**
- ◆ **5 ½ yards 54-inch-wide open-weave linen or lace (natural)**
- ◆ **thread to match chintz**
- ◆ **13 yards ⅛-inch metallic gold piping**
- ◆ **long metal ruler, tape measure**
- ◆ **right-angle triangle, chalk**
- ◆ **scissors, two large safety pins**

Making the valance

1 Arrange a single layer of linen under a layer of chintz, folded with right side inside, so that all three selvages align; pin selvages as necessary to hold layers together smoothly.

2 On the chintz, draw a chalk line just inside

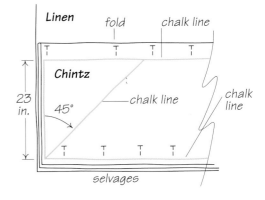

A symmetrically draped length of open-weave linen lined with chintz gracefully tops a window with a view.

one selvage for the full length of the layers. Mark a line 23 inches above the first to create a rectangle on the full length. At each end, draw a bias line, at a 45-degree angle, to create the valance's tapered ends (Diagram, facing page).

3 Cut out the three layers; remove the pins.

4 Place a chintz layer with its right side against the linen's wrong side; stay-stitch together ¼ inch from the cut edges on all sides.

5 Install the zipper foot on the machine. Starting about 36 inches from a corner on a long side, stitch the piping over the stay-stitching, rounding off the corners slightly. Clip the edge of the piping as necessary to allow it to turn corners. Lap the cut ends of the piping at their meeting and stitch across.

6 With right sides together, pin the other chintz piece to the linen and stitch just to the left of the previous stitches. Leave an 18-inch opening in the center of a long side for turning.

7 Turn the valance right side out and slip-stitch the opening closed. Press the edge next to the piping with a dry iron.

Hanging the valance

1 Mark the center of the rod with chalk. Mark the center of the valance with large safety pins. Starting at the center of the rod, wrap the center cloud with the linen side out and the pins at the bottom of the loop. Wrap the right half of the valance around the rod, from front to back, about 12 inches above the pins. Wrap two more clouds, with 12-inch-deep loops, toward the right end of the rod. (If your valance has an even number of clouds, begin with the pin marks at the top back side of the rod.)

2 Return to the center. Wrap two loops around the left side of the rod, this time from back to front so you can retain the same angle. When you complete the last wrap on the left end, wrap the fabric from the front to the back.

3 Hang the rod on the brackets and lift the left and right ends of the valance over the brackets, to the outside. Arrange the vertical ends and the pouf of the cloud wraps into an attractive, even placement.

NOTE It is easier to work with the rod on a flat surface rather than hung at the window. A bed, a table, or a sheeted floor are good locations.

Finished shirred rod and finials

Shirred rod and finials

Remnants from the cloud valance on page 120 can be made into a coordinating set of rod and finial covers at no extra cost. If you want to make only the shirred rod and finial for another window treatment, purchase 2 yards of chintz and ½ yard of linen or lace.

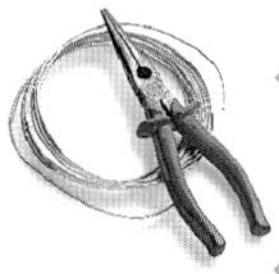

- ◆ **remnants of chintz and linen from the cloud valance (p.120) or new fabric, as described above**
- ◆ **threads to match fabrics and braid**
- ◆ **beige buttonhole twist, needle**
- ◆ **ruler, compass, paper, pencil, chalk**
- ◆ **two 18-inch pieces of 22-gauge wire, wire cutters, pliers**
- ◆ **two 8-inch circles of extra-high-loft quilt batting**
- ◆ **1⅜-inch wooden pole cut 2 inches longer than the outside distance between the mounted pole brackets**
- ◆ **pair of pole brackets**
- ◆ **pair of 2¾-inch ball finials**
- ◆ **18 inches of ⅜-inch-wide stiff metallic gold braid**
- ◆ **½-inch-circle self-sticking hook-and-loop fastener tape (such as Velcro)**

1 To cover the rod, cut—or stitch together from scraps—a piece of fabric 5½ inches wide by 2½ to 3 times the rod's length (the more fabric you use, the fuller the shirring).

2 Sew a ¼-inch double hem on each end. Fold the strip lengthwise, right side inside, and sew a ¼-inch seam. Do not press. Turn the strip right side out and shirr it onto the pole.

3 To pad the finials, thread the needle with buttonhole twist and sew hand-gathering stitches about ½ inch and then ¼ inch inside the edge of the batting circle as shown in Dia-

VARIATIONS ON A THEME

Y ou can turn the shirred rod into a valance for a complete window treatment. Here are three variations. Before you begin, determine the amount of fabric needed for your window.

This version has the same ruffle depth above and below the rod. To the 5½-inch-wide measurement given for the shirred rod cover, add an additional 10 inches. Stitch and turn the cover as described. Center the long seam on the center back and press the tube. Topstitch 2½ inches inside each creased edge to form a heading above and below the rod. Shirr the center of the tube onto the pole and hang it with the top and bottom ruffles straight across. Or, for another effect, twist the whole cover in a spiral.

For a valance that will hang 10 inches below the rod with a narrow ruffle above, add an additional 25 inches to the original 5½-inch-wide measurement. Press the stitched tube so the long seam is 3 inches from the top crease. Stitch 2½ and 5 inches from the top crease to form the rod's casing.

gram 1. Center a finial over the circle and pull up the two sets of threads, wrap the threads around the neck of the finial several times and secure with a slipknot.

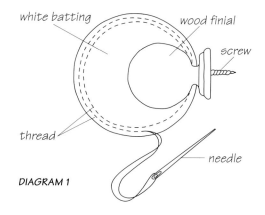

white batting
wood finial
screw
thread
needle

DIAGRAM 1

4 For each finial cover, draw a 13 ½-inch circle on paper and use the pattern to cut four circles from chintz and two from linen.

5 Pin the right side of one chintz circle against the wrong side of one linen circle. Cut a 1 ½-inch X-opening in the center of another chintz circle; pin right sides together over the linen circle (already pinned to the other piece of chintz).

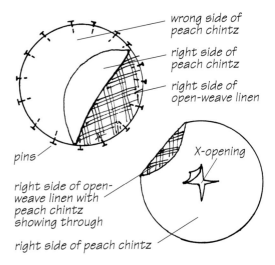

wrong side of peach chintz

right side of peach chintz

right side of open-weave linen

pins

X-opening

right side of open-weave linen with peach chintz showing through

right side of peach chintz

6 Stitch a ¼-inch seam around the entire circle. Trim the seam allowance and turn the cover right side out through the X. Press the seam and edge-stitch it if necessary. Repeat steps 5 and 6 for the second cover.

7 To gather the circle, chalk-mark dashes 2 ¾ inches inside the circumference. Thread the needle with buttonhole twist, doubled. With the linen side up, sew ½-inch-long hand-gathering stitches over the marks. Center the circle, linen side out, over the padded finial and pull up the gathering stitches as firmly as possible; secure with a slipknot.

8 Wrap a piece of wire around the neck of the finial; grab the ends with the pliers and

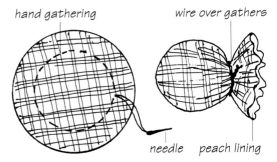

hand gathering

wire over gathers

needle   peach lining

turn the finial to twist the wire tightly against the gathers. Cut away excess wire and press the twist against the neck. Adjust gathers evenly. Repeat with second finial cover.

9 Cut two pieces of stiff braid 2 inches longer than the neck measurement. Turn one end under ½ inch and hand tack. Wrap the braid around the finial's neck with finished end on top. Cut the hook and loop fastener dot in half and apply half as a closure to each braid collar.

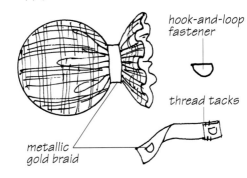

hook-and-loop fastener

thread tacks

metallic gold braid

10 Screw the finials into the ends of the rod and hang the window treatment on the rod.

Curtain and swag

A tied swag makes a bold statement over sheer curtains gathered on a rod. Sew the swag in a single layer of fabric that has no right or wrong side, such as taffeta, using Method A. For other fabrics, sew two layers of the same or contrasting fabrics together using Method B. You can alter the depth, or fullness, of the swag by cutting away any desired amount from the fabric's width. Test the fullness by loosely hanging it across the rod before trimming.

- **two lengths of sheer or lace fabric: measure from bottom of rod to floor plus circumference of rod plus ½-inch seam allowance plus 8 inches for hem**
- **one or two lengths of fabric for swag: measure width of window plus 18 inches for each knot plus two times length of the tails**
- **matching threads**
- **dressmaker's pins, tape measure**

Curtains

1 On the bottom edge of each panel, press under 4 inches and then 4 inches again for a double hem. Edge-stitch the hem in place.

2 Clip through the selvages on each side of both panels, about every 2 inches. Press under 1 inch and then 1 inch again along each side. Edge-stitch each side hem in place.

3 To make the casing, on the top edge of each panel, press under ½ inch. Fold the pressed top edges to the wrong side again by an amount equal to half the circumference of the rod and edge-stitch the hem in place.

4 Insert the rod through the casing of each panel and hang the curtains so the hems are toward the wall.

NOTE If you select a heavy, nonsheer curtain fabric, you may want to measure and sew the hem last, after allowing the curtains to hang on the rod overnight or longer. Its own weight may stretch the fabric out, making a hem measured before the curtain has hung for a while too shallow.

Swag-sewing Method A

1 Fold the full or trimmed length of the fabric in half crosswise, with the wrong side out, and pin the sides together for about 24 inches. Fold the cut ends over to align with one long side, forming a 45-degree angle. Trim the two ends along this diagonal fold and remove the pins.

2 Press ¼ inch under around all four sides and then press under ¼ inch again, forming a narrow double hem. Edge-stitch the hem around all four sides.

Swag-sewing Method B

1 Make sure each piece of fabric is exactly the same length and the cut ends are square with the sides. If necessary, trim the longer to match the shorter piece. Trim the ends of each fabric diagonally, following Step 1 of Method A. Make a tiny clip at the center fold on each long side of the fabric before removing the pins.

2 Open out the fabrics and lay them right sides together, with the angled ends matching. Pin the layers together, starting at the center clips on each long edge and continuing toward the diagonal ends.

3 Stitch ½ inch from the edge around all four sides of the swag, leaving about 6 inches open on one long edge for turning.

4 Press the seam allowance open by pressing one side of the allowance at a time toward the swag. Diagonally trim about ⅛ inch from the seam allowances at the corners.

5 Insert your hand through the opening in the seam and turn the swag right side out. Press the edges so that the seamline is exactly in the center and the bottom layer of fabric cannot be seen from the top.

6 Slip-stitch the opening closed.

Draping the swag (A and B)

1 Center the length of the swag at the center of the rod with the shorter edge along the top. Carry an end of the swag toward each end of the rod and drape it from the front over the top, allowing it to hang downward behind the rod, as shown in Diagram 1.

2 To drape the swag so that the top edge is straight along the top of the rod and the bottom edge swings downward at the center (photo), align the top swag edge with the rod and arrange pleats across the width of the swag near the ends of the rods. Gently pull downward on the bottom pleats to release

DIAGRAM 1

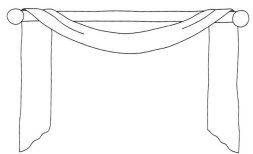

DIAGRAM 2

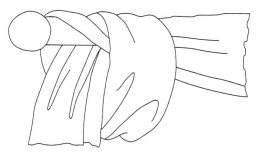

more length along the bottom edge of the swag to form the desired drape.

3 To secure the drape, wrap each end around the rod in a knot, as shown in Diagram 2. Gently arrange the front of the knot into a puff, covering the end of the rod if you like. If you used a contrasting fabric for the second side of the swag in Method B, this fabric will be visible on the tail sections of the swag, below the knots.

Sheer curtains allow light into a room while providing privacy and perhaps hiding an unappealing view. You can top the sheers in a striking way by making a decorative silk swag, loosely knotted at the corners of the window. The swag can match the color of the bedspread in a bedroom or be created from a strip of the fabric used to slipcover the sofa in a living room.

Child's window shade

Stencil a shade for a child's room with this design—or one of your own.

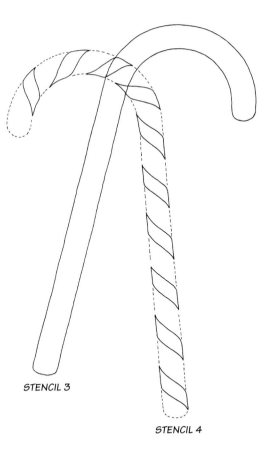

- ◆ **fabric pull-shade**
- ◆ **latex paint (optional)**
- ◆ **artist's acrylics: cream, red, light blue, dark blue, white, yellow, pink, light green, dark green**
- ◆ **paintbrush, for background**
- ◆ **masking tape**
- ◆ **pencil, ruler, fine-tip permanent marker**
- ◆ **stencil acetate**
- ◆ **craft knife and cutting surface**
- ◆ **small stencil brush**

STENCIL 3

STENCIL 4

Dress up a child's bedroom window in a creative and playful way by stenciling a conventional pull-shade with "toyland" images.

124

STENCIL 1

STENCIL 2

1 If you can't find a fabric pull-shade in the color you want, paint the background with the latex paint. A light color will show the design to best advantage.

2 Start with the drum design at the bottom of the shade. Use a pencil and ruler to outline a rectangle, 15 x 5 ¼ inches, for the body of the drum. Mask the rectangle with tape and paint it red with the paintbrush. Let dry for about 20 minutes and remove the tape.

3 Mask out a rectangle 5 ½ x 1 ⅝ inches on the top and bottom edges of the red drum body. Using the stencil brush, paint each of these bands light blue. Let dry for about 20 minutes and remove the tape.

4 The dark blue triangles on each light blue band (photograph, facing page) and the white swags on the drum can be painted freehand. For more accurate painting, enlarge Stencil 1 and Stencil 2 (above) on a photocopier 200%, then 200% again, then 140%. (To enlarge without a photocopier, see p.276; enlarge so that the triangles have 2-inch sides, and each rope swag is 5 ¾ inches wide.) Lay acetate over each enlargement and trace with the marker. Cut out the acetate with a craft knife to make a stencil.

5 On each light blue band, lay Stencil 1 and paint the triangles in dark blue (Step 1, below). Let dry, then move the stencil along to paint the triangles in between the ones just painted. Wipe stencils with a paper towel before reversing and before applying another color.

6 Apply Stencil 2 to the large red rectangle and paint the swag white (Step 2, below). When dry, paint on three yellow circles, at the tops of the swags. Apply extra coats of white and yellow if needed.

7 For the candy canes, enlarge Stencils 3 and 4 (facing page) 175%. Cut the stencil acetates as you did in Step 4. Stencil 3 is for the cane, and Stencil 4 is for the cane's stripes. When tracing Stencil 4, include only the solid lines, not the dotted lines. There are two color combinations: red on pink, and dark green on light green, all painted separately.

8 Place Stencil 3 above the drum, and paint it pink. Repeat in various locations. Reverse the stencil from time to time so the canes face the opposite direction, and leave space for green canes. When dry, use Stencil 4 for the red stripes. Apply the green canes the same way.

Curtain rods

A curtain rod can be a decorative item in itself. Here are suggestions for rods that can easily be adapted to suit your decor.

Verdigris-finish curtain rod

An ordinary wooden curtain rod can be given the appearance of weathered copper with an easy painting technique.

- ◆ **wooden rod cut to measure 2 inches beyond rod brackets.**
- ◆ **fine sandpaper**
- ◆ **all-purpose primer-sealer**
- ◆ **small paintbrush**
- ◆ **dark brown semigloss alkyd enamel**
- ◆ **brass picture-hanging wire**
- ◆ **wire cutters**
- ◆ **alkyd-base scumble mixture, available at art-supply stores**
- ◆ **verdigris-green alkyd-based paint**
- ◆ **cotton rags**

1 Sand the rod to give it a smooth finish.

2 Paint the rod with primer-sealer. When dry, sand again, and apply two coats of dark brown semigloss paint, allowing the paint to dry thoroughly between coats.

3 When the paint is dry, wrap equal lengths of brass picture wire neatly around either end of the rod, 1 ¼ inches in from the ends.

4 Secure the ends of the wire and snip them with wire cutters.

5 Mix the scumble mixture and verdigris-green paint according to manufacturer's directions. Using the small paintbrush, and working on only one side of the rod, apply the scumble mixture over the brown paint and the wire.

6 Take a wad of cotton rag and dab at the wet paint to create soft mottled marks. Irregularities in the application only add to the effect, so don't worry about being neat.

7 When the paint is dry, turn the rod over and paint and dab the scumble mixture on the surface, as above. When dry, set in brackets.

NOTE Wooden rod brackets and curtain rings can also be painted verdigris-green to match.

STENCILING THE WINDOW SHADE

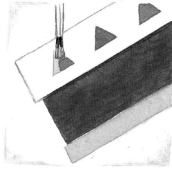

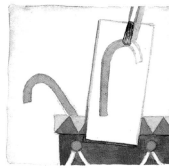

1 *On the light blue bands, lay Stencil 1 at left of top band and paint the four triangles dark blue. Let dry. Move the stencil over and paint four more triangles to complete the band. Repeat for bottom band, but invert the stencil.*

2 *Use Stencil 2 to make rope swags on the drum. Lay the stencil on the red rectangle so the ends of the swags touch either side. Leave space at top so that yellow circles can later be painted to connect the swags. Stencil swags in white.*

3 *For candy canes, place Stencil 3 above the drum and paint pink. Repeat as desired, reversing the stencil so some canes face the other way. When dry, apply decorative red stripes using Stencil 4. Apply green canes the same way.*

Bamboo curtain rod

Dress up a bamboo rod by hanging a tassel, made from brown string or raffia, at each end.

- **length of bamboo to fit rod brackets**
- **4-inch-square heavy cardboard**
- **brown string, or natural raffia from crafts shop**
- **scissors**
- **white craft glue**
- **masking tape**

To make each tassel

1 Wind string (or raffia) back and forth tightly around cardboard until it's covered.
2 Insert a length of string under the wound string and secure tightly with a knot.
3 Remove the string from the cardboard. Bind with string 1 inch from the tied end to make the neck of the tassel.
4 Using scissors, cut the looped ends at the bottom of the tassel and splay out. Trim.
5 Thread additional string through the top of the tassel and knot several times. Attach the tassel to the rod, about 1½ inches from end.
6 Apply glue to the rod to cover about ⅜ inch on either side of the string that attaches the tassel. Wrap more string around the rod to cover the glued areas. Use masking tape to hold the string in place while the glue dries.

Candy-striped curtain rod

Provide a child's room with a whimsical circus theme by making this cheerful rod.

- **length of wooden rod to fit 1 inch beyond rod brackets**
- **flat white latex paint**
- **paintbrush**
- **red ribbon 2½ times the rod's length**
- **old newspapers**
- **spray adhesive**
- **two balls 4-ply knitting yarn (one red, one white)**
- **cardboard**
- **compass, pencil, ruler**
- **white craft glue**
- **fine sandpaper**
- **scissors**

To make the rod

1 Sand rod ends smooth and paint rod with two coats of white paint. Allow to dry.
2 Lay newspapers on the floor. Lay ribbon flat, right side down, on the newspaper. Spray one end of the ribbon with adhesive.
3 Lay rod at a 45-degree angle to the ribbon.
4 Roll rod over the length of the ribbon, ensuring that the ribbon goes around the rod tightly in an even spiral.
5 Finish covering the pole, spraying the ribbon and rolling the rod, a section at a time.

6 When the ribbon is attached, thread on the curtain rings (before attaching pom-poms).

To make pom-pom rod ends

1 You need two pom-poms, one for each rod end. For each pom-pom, use a compass to draw two cardboard circles with diameters three times that of the rod. Cut them out.
2 With a pencil and ruler, mark each circle into eight equal wedges. Cut out a circle, slightly larger than the diameter of the rod, in the center of each cardboard circle.
3 Put the two circles together and wrap yarn around them—through the center, around the outer edge, and back through the center—alternating the wedges in red and white.
4 Once the circles are covered with yarn, spread glue over about ⅜ inch of rod at one end. Push the rod end through the card's center hole. Let the glue dry. Repeat for the pom-pom at the other end.
5 For each pom-pom, work the tip of the scissors between the cards at the outer edge of the circles, and snip through the wool all around. Thread a length of wool between the cards, and tie several times. Cut off cardboard. Trim excess wool and fluff pom-pom.

A selection of decorative curtain rods to suit any room: (top to bottom) candy-striped rod with pom-pom ends; verdigris-finish rod; bamboo rod with string tassels; tortoiseshell-finish rod (technique, p.152).

◆ Pillow and Tassel Finishes ◆

If you are looking for additional color and texture in a living room or bedroom, you can achieve a delightful effect by making a variety of tassels to decorate pillows or bolsters. Tassels are also fun to use as pulls for window shades, on curtain tiebacks, and on lampshades.

Simple tassel

Tassels can be made with many different threads, yarns, and ribbons. These instructions are for the 3-inch tassels on the curtain and pillows at right.

- ◆ **5 x 3-inch piece heavy cardboard**
- ◆ **one ball ecru DMC cebelia crochet cotton no. 5**
- ◆ **large-eyed tapestry needle**
- ◆ **scissors**

Follow the basic method shown on page 128, using the following specifications. In Step 1, wind the cotton 150 times around the 3-inch width of the cardboard. In Step 2, use a 20-inch length of cotton for the tie at the top. In Step 3, use a 36-inch length of cotton to wrap the neck about 1 inch from the top of the tassel.

Four tassels can be made on one piece of cardboard. Instead of cutting the thread when the first tassel has been wound, take the thread about 1 inch farther along the card and wind the next tassel. Snip the connecting threads before removing tassels from the cardboard.

*A selection of elegant soft furnishings: **1** pillow with simple tassels, **2** curtain tieback, **3** flanged pillow with clustered tassel, **4** neck roll with simple tassel **5** flower pot decorated with clustered tassel, **6** mitered pillow with piping and simple tassels, **7** piped pillow with twisted cord and simple tassel.*

Clustered tassel

A clustered tassel—made up of a number of separate uncut tassels—makes a special impact when several colors are combined. (See the tassel on the flowerpot on page 127.) These directions are for 2-inch tassels.

- ◆ **5 x 2-inch piece of heavy cardboard**
- ◆ **one ball red DMC cebelia crochet cotton**
- ◆ **one ball coffee DMC cebelia crochet cotton**
- ◆ **two skeins gold DMC cotton perle no. 5**
- ◆ **two skeins ecru DMC cotton perle no. 5**
- ◆ **large-eyed tapestry needle**

Make four tassels in each color, following Steps 1 to 3 of the step-by-step method illustrated below. Each set of four tassels can be made together on the same piece of cardboard, as described in the instructions for the simple tassel on page 127.

In Step 1, wind the yarn around the cardboard 80 times. In Step 2, cut two 1-yard lengths of yarn for the tie at the top of each tassel. In Step 3, cut a 20-inch length of yarn for wrapping the neck of each tassel ½ inch from its top. Do not cut the loops, as specified in Step 4; simply fan them out a little. Knot the

four ties in each color together 1 to 2 inches above the top of the tassels, staggering the distance of each tassel from the knot. Then knot the four sets of ties together about 1 inch above the first knots. Loop all the threads back on themselves and knot again.

Flanged pillow

A flange is a flat border around a pillow. This elegant pillow, pictured on page 127, is made from two coordinating fabrics, the outer one featuring a floral border. The finished size is 20 inches square. A ½-inch seam allowance is used.

- ◆ **1¼ yards fabric A**
- ◆ **¾ yard fabric B**
- ◆ **16-inch zipper**
- ◆ **18-inch pillow form**

1 To make the front of the cushion, cut an 11-inch square from fabric A. From fabric B, cut four strips 21 inches by 6 inches.
2 With right sides together and the raw edges even, pin the strips of fabric B to the edges of the square of fabric A. Leaving ½ inch open to either side of each corner, stitch the strips to the square. With the strips, form miters at the corners (p.306).
3 Repeat the process for the two other strips, then stitch the remaining corners to form a mitered square. Press seam allowance

of the inner edge to the wrong side.
4 Center mitered square of fabric B on top of square of fabric A (below). Pin together and then topstitch the mitered square onto the square of fabric A.

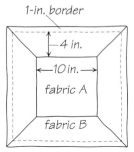
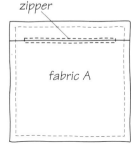

Front of pillow   *Back of pillow*

5 For the cushion backing, cut two pieces from fabric A, one measuring 21 inches by 18½ inches, the other 21 inches by 3½ inches.
6 For the zipper opening, pin the 2 pieces of backing together on a long edge, right sides together. Mark a space for a 16-inch zipper at the center of the edge. Sew a 2½-inch seam at either end and press open. Pin and then stitch the zipper into the opening (above).
7 With right sides together and zipper open, stitch front and back of pillow together. Turn cover right side out and topstitch 1 inch inside the outer edges for the flange.
8 Insert pillow form. Decorate, if desired, with a clustered tassel, as pictured on page 127.

BASIC METHOD FOR TASSEL-MAKING

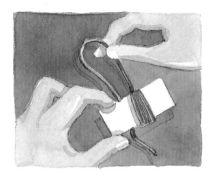

1 *Cut cardboard width to the desired tassel length. Hold end of thread at edge of card and wind around card until tassel is desired thickness, or wind for number of times specified in instructions.*

2 *To tie, thread a length of yarn into a tapestry needle; pass needle and thread under the wound yarn. Unthread needle, pull yarn to the top of the tassel and knot securely.*

3 *Remove from the cardboard. Use yarn to tie the neck with a knot. Knot again on opposite side. Wind each end of the tie around the neck, then thread into a needle and tuck into the neck.*

4 *Cut loops at the bottom of tassel and trim even. To plump up the skirt, use tongs to hold tassel over the spout of a steaming kettle for about 30 seconds. Use a needle to comb out the skirt.*

Neck roll

The elongated shape of a neck roll adds variety to a group of rectangular pillows. Neck rolls suit either living room or bedroom decor.

- ◆ **24 x 20 ½ -inch piece of fabric**
- ◆ **1 ½ yards ¼ -inch piping cord**
- ◆ **2 yards string and a safety pin (for casing)**
- ◆ **6-inch-diameter x 13-inch-long neck-roll form**
- ◆ **2 simple tassels (p.128)**

1 Cut piping cord into two equal lengths.
2 With wrong side of fabric facing you, measure in from the corners on each long side and mark the fabric at 4 ¾ inches and 5 ½ inches.

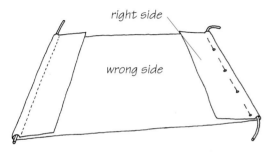

right side

wrong side

Center a piece of piping cord between the marks on each end and fold the ends of the fabric over the cord. Using the zipper foot, stitch next to the cord (above).
3 Open out the ends. Pin the long edges, right sides together. Stitch a 1-inch seam (below). Press the seam open.

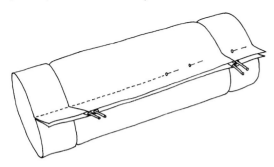

4 To make the hem casings: With wrong side of fabric facing you, fold in and press ½ inch on either end. Then fold and press again, making a 1-inch hem on each end. Edge-stitch the hems, leaving about 1 inch open near the seam.

TO MAKE A TWISTED CORD

THE perfect way to finish a tassel is with a twisted cord. Made in the same materials as the tassel—or in contrasting thread or yarn—the cord can be used to attach the tassel to a pillow or it can just act as decorative trim.

Start a twisted cord with three to five strands of thread or yarn. and cut them so that the strands are about three times the length required for the finished cord. Knot the strands together at both ends. Attach one knotted end to a firm anchor, such as a cup hook. Push a pencil between the threads at the other end and stretch the strands taut by pulling the pencil against the knot. Turn the pencil over and over to twist the strands. Keep turning the pencil until the strands are very tightly wound.

Remove the pencil while holding the strands taut with one hand. With the other hand, firmly pinch the twisted strands at midpoint, then carefully bring the two knotted ends together. Release the midpoint and the strands will twist back on themselves, forming a cord. Work along the cord with your fingers in small sections to tighten the twist as necessary and to keep the cord smooth. Knot the ends together.

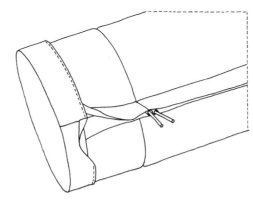

5 Cut the string in half. Knot the end of one piece of string around a closed safety pin, insert the pin in one hem opening, and work it all the way around the hem casing, pulling the string with it. Exit the opening. Draw the two

---

ends of the string tight. Tie securely and trim.
6 Turn the cover right side out and insert the neck-roll form. Insert and tie the cord in the second hem casing as described in Step 5. Attach a tassel to either end of the bolster.

Piped pillow

Piping gives a simple pillow a tailored look, and tassels add the final touch. Our instructions are for a pillow made with two coordinated printed fabrics and a mitered border. But piping is equally attractive on solid-color pillows, with or without a mitered border. The color of the piping can match or contrast with the pillow color. The finished size of the pillow in the photograph is 16 inches square. A ½ -inch seam allowance is used.

- ◆ **⅓ yard fabric A**
- ◆ **1 yard fabric B**
- ◆ **2 ¼ yards ¼ -inch piping cord**
- ◆ **glue or thread, for cord ends**
- ◆ **18-inch pillow form**
- ◆ **tassels to match fabric**

1 For the pillow front, cut a 10-inch square from fabric A. From fabric B, cut four strips 17 inches by 4 ½ inches.
2 With right sides together and the raw edges even, pin the strips of fabric B to the edges of the square of fabric A. Leaving ½ inch open to either side of each corner, stitch the strips to the square. With the strips, form miters at the corners (p.306).
3 For the piping, cut 1 ⅝ -inch-wide bias strips of fabric A—enough to equal 2 ¼ yards when the ends are sewn together. To make and attach the piping, follow the instructions on page 134.
4 For the pillow back, repeat Steps 1 and 2.
5 With right sides together and using the zipper foot, stitch front and back of pillow together. Leave a 14-inch opening on one side.
6 If necessary, diagonally trim the seam allowances at the corners to reduce bulk. Turn the pillow cover right side out. Make matching tassels (facing page) and attach them at the corners. Insert the pillow form and slip-stitch the opening closed.

◆ A Bedside Story ◆

To bring a personal touch to your bedroom, simply add attractive highlights to existing items. Stencil designs onto a lampshade or trim your linens with appliquéd floral motifs.

Rose sheets

We've used a pretty chintz fabric to decorate plain sheets and pillowcases. Fusible webbing is applied to the back of the fabric before it's cut out and ironed into position. A zigzag machine stitch then finishes the edges of the appliqué.

- **solid-color top sheet**
- **pair of solid-color pillowcases**
- **1 yard floral fabric**
- **2 yards fusible webbing with paper backing**
- **thread to match flowers on fabric and sheets**
- **small, sharp fabric scissors**

1 Press the sheet, pillowcases, and fabric to remove all creases.

2 Select the flowers you want to use from the floral fabric. Apply small pieces of webbing to the wrong side and slightly beyond the edges of each motif. Carefully cut around the flowers and leaves as desired. Remove the paper backing from the webbing. Repeat until you have as many motifs as you need.

3 Position the flower and leaf motifs along the top border of the sheet and wherever appropriate on the tops of the pillowcases. When you are happy with the design, press to fuse the motifs in place using a hot iron. If you want to place an appliqué near the closed end of a pillowcase, remove the stitches from the end seam before zigzag stitching and restitch it afterward.

4 Wind the bobbin with thread to match the sheets and thread the top of the machine with thread to match the flowers. Using a narrow, close-set zigzag stitch and the appropriate foot for your machine, stitch carefully around each of the motifs. To end off, overlap for several stitches and trim thread ends close.

Use pastel-shaded stencil designs, appliqués in floral motifs, and a soft blue paint on furniture to suggest a calming, relaxed atmosphere in the bedroom.

APPLIQUÉ METHOD

1 Apply fusible webbing to back of fabric behind the selected motifs and cut around them. Remove paper backing from webbing.

2 Position the motifs as you wish on the border of the sheet and on the pillowcases and then fuse them into position using a hot iron.

3 Use the appropriate foot on your sewing machine to zigzag stitch the motifs into position, working carefully around each one.

A plain pine bedside cabinet becomes something special when paint is applied unconventionally. This one is done with dragging, stippling, and stenciling.

Star stencil pattern

Star shade

You can transform a plain lampshade with a stencil and a little paint (p.130). Enlarge the pattern above and cut your own acetate star or buy a star stencil at a crafts store.

- **wooden lamp base with cream paper lampshade**
- **fine sandpaper**
- **latex semigloss paint: cream**
- **artist's acrylic paint: blue**
- **star stencil**
- **paintbrush**
- **small stencil brush**
- **low-tack masking tape**

1 Sand the lamp base smooth.
2 Paint the lamp base with two coats of cream paint, sanding between coats.
3 Tape the star stencil on the lampshade. With only a small amount of blue acrylic paint on the tip of a stencil brush, stencil the stars, dabbing the brush lightly. For a varied pattern, apply the paint in a random fashion, filling in parts of the stencil only.

Bow stencil pattern

Bedside cabinet

An unfinished pine bedside cabinet can be turned into a distinctive piece of furniture with a decorative painted finish. We've used two scumbling techniques—dragging and stippling. You can buy scumble medium at art-supply stores.

- **fine sandpaper**
- **latex undercoat or primer**
- **nylon brush**
- **white flat latex paint**
- **tack cloth**
- **blue scumble mixture:**
  one part blue flat latex paint,
  one part scumble medium,
  one part water
- **pink scumble mixture:**
  one part pink flat latex paint,
  one part scumble medium,
  one part water
- **2-inch natural-bristle brush**
- **small stencil brush**
- **¼ -inch and ½ -inch**
  low-tack masking tape
- **stencil acetate**
- **fine-tip permanent marker pen**
- **craft knife, ruler**
- **wax, or satin water-based**
  varnish

1 Sand the cabinet smooth and remove dust with a soft cloth. Then, using the nylon brush, seal the surface with the undercoat.

2 When dry, sand the cabinet again to settle the grain raised by the undercoat.

3 Using the nylon brush, give the cabinet two coats of white paint. Sand each coat when dry and wipe with the tack cloth to remove any dust adhering to the surface.

4 Lay a strip of ½ -inch-wide masking tape around the top of the cabinet 1¼ inches in from the edge. If your cabinet has a drawer and door, as pictured here, mask a ½ -inch border on each of them as well. If you are painting a small chest of drawers, mask borders on the sides of the chest.

5 With the nylon brush, apply the blue scumble mixture to the areas inside the tape and, while the paint is still wet, drag the small, dry bristle brush through the glaze. This dragging creates an attractive streaked effect. Allow to dry thoroughly; then remove the tape.

6 Lay a strip of ½ -inch-wide tape on the dragged area, matching the outer edges of the tape and dragged surface. Center a ¼ -inch-wide tape between this tape and the edge of the cabinet (Step 3, below). Apply a small amount of blue scumble mixture to the stencil brush and stipple the paint—dabbing the brush tip lightly—onto the areas between the two tapes and from the outer tape to the edge of the cabinet top. Allow to dry; remove tape.

7 Isolate the white ¼ -inch border with parallel strips of masking tape. Using the stencil brush, apply pink scumble mixture between the strips of tape. Allow to dry. Remove tape.

SURFACE EFFECTS

For our cabinet, we used a dragging technique on the main body of each surface and stippling on the borders. These techniques can be reversed.

The exact effect you achieve will vary according to the pressure you apply to the brush and the type of brush you use. If you do not have a natural-bristle brush, experiment with what you have on hand. To do the dragging, for example, try using steel wool or a fine-toothed comb.

Try extending the theme of the cabinet and lamp by repeating one of the scumble techniques on another element in the room.

8 Use the stencil brush and white paint to stencil motifs on the blue surfaces. We used a bow stencil on top of the cabinet and on the door, and a star stencil on the drawer and door. To make the stencils, use a photocopier to enlarge the motifs shown on facing page to the desired size (to enlarge without a photocopier, see p.276). Trace the designs on acetate (see p.101) and cut out with a craft knife.

9 When all the paint is dry, seal the surface with two coats of wax or varnish. Polish after each coat of wax has dried, or sand after each coat of varnish has dried.

APPLYING SCUMBLING AND STENCILS

1 Prepare all surfaces by painting them white and sanding. Apply a strip of masking tape around the top, about 1¼ inches in from the edge. Apply tape to sides, door, and drawer in the same way.

2 Use a nylon brush to apply blue scumble mixture to the area inside the tape. Drag a small, dry bristle brush through the wet paint to create a streaked effect. Allow to dry, then remove the tape.

3 Lay tape inside edge of dragged area. Center a ¼ -inch tape between this tape and the edge of the table. Stipple blue between the tapes and to the edge of the cabinet. Dry; remove tapes.

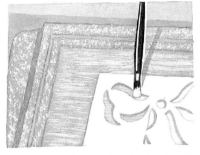

4 Lay ½ -inch tape along both sides of the white ¼ -inch border; stipple with pink mixture. Dry; remove tape. Stipple stencils in white onto blue surfaces as desired. Let dry. Apply wax or varnish.

◆ Dream on in Comfort ◆

*While you sleep, wrap yourself in comfort and style under a duvet cover you have made
yourself in your own choice of fabric. By day there is no need to conceal it with a bedspread. Shams and
pillows can just pile up at the headboard, looking fashionable and inviting at the same time.*

Duvet cover

*The yardages and instructions are for a 76 x 86-
inch cover, which will accommodate a full or
queen-size comforter. To adjust to a twin or king
size, see box "Resizing the duvet," on page 136. For
a coordinating shower curtain, see page 137.*

- ◆ **7 ¾ yards 54-inch-wide fabric A**
- ◆ **2 ½ yards 54-inch-wide fabric B**
- ◆ **threads to match fabrics**
- ◆ **12 yards ¼ -inch-diameter
  piping cord**
- ◆ **¼ yard 1-inch-wide sew-on
  hook-and-loop fastener tape**
- ◆ **scissors, pencil, chalk**
- ◆ **tape measure, long metal ruler**

1 For the front panels, cut one piece 53 x 88
inches and two pieces 12 ½ x 88 inches from
fabric A.

2 For the back panels, cut one piece 53 x 87
inches and two pieces 12 ½ x 87 inches from
fabric A.

3 For the flap, cut two pieces 77 x 15 ½ inches,
with the long edges on the lengthwise grain line,
from fabric B. From the same fabric cut enough
⅝ -inch-wide bias strips to equal 12 yards when
seamed together (for piping) and five 6 x 13-inch
ties, centering any repeat within the width.

4 Wrap the wrong side of the bias fabric
around the piping cord and stitch next to the
cord with the zipper foot, as shown below.

5 On the wide (center) front panel, stitch the
piping to each long edge, stitching just to the
left of the first line of stitching. At either end,
remove some cord (1 ½ inches, top, and ½
inch, bottom) from inside the piping to eliminate it from the hem and seam areas.

6 With right sides together, sew the side front
panels to the center panel, with center panel
on top, stitching just to the left of the piping
stitch line. Press the seams toward the center.

7 Repeat Steps 5 and 6 to join back panels.

8 On the front top, press ½ inch and then 1
inch to the wrong side. Cut the hook-and-loop
fastener tape into seven pieces, each
1 ¼ inches long. Separate hook and loop
pieces. Working on the right side of the top
hem area, pin one loop piece at the center, one
piece 2 inches inside each end and the others
spaced equally between these three.

9 With the fastener-hem side up, use the regular presser foot on the sewing machine to
edge-stitch the fold and inner edges of the
hem, catching the fastener tape as you go.

10 To sew the piping to the sides and bottom
edges of the duvet front, put the zipper foot

*Two coordinating prints make a pretty duvet cover to
protect a comforter or a quilt that has seen better
days. If you pick a no-iron, washable fabric for the
duvet, you will have no trouble keeping it fresh.*

MAKING AND APPLYING PIPING

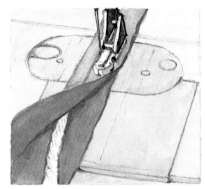
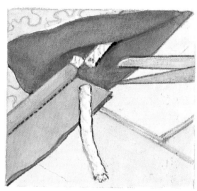

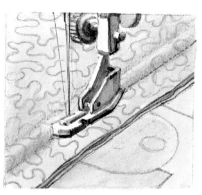

1 *To make piping, center the cord on the
wrong side of a bias strip. Fold the bias
strip over the cord, aligning the raw
edges. With the zipper foot on the right
side of the needle, machine-stitch close
to the cord. The bias strip has enough
give to lie flat around the cording.*

2 *To apply cording where its ends will
meet—around a pillow cover, for example—and keep a smooth line, stop the
sewing machine, needle in fabric, 2 inches
from the meeting point. Take out 1 inch of
stitching from either end of cording. Trim
cord ends so they just abut.*

3 *Fold under ½ inch of the overlapping
bias strip and layer it over the other
cording end. Finish stitching, using the
zipper foot as your guide. You now have
piping completely around one side of the
pillow cover and are ready to stitch the
other side of the cover to it.*

4 *With right sides together, the corded
side on top and the raw edges aligned,
stitch the two sides of the pillow cover
together. Use the zipper foot on the right
side of the needle and stitch just to the
left of the piping stitching, so that it will
not show on the right side.*

back on the machine. Remove the stitching from 2 inches of the piping's end, trim away 1 inch of cord, and wrap the loose fabric end down over the cord's end. Refold and restitch the piping end. Pin and stitch the piping to the right side of the front along the sides and bottom, slightly rounding off the bottom corners and clipping the piping seam allowance as necessary to make the turns. When nearing the opposite top corner, trim and encase the end of the piping as on the other side so that it ends even with the hem fold.

11 Right sides together, and the front on top, pin and stitch the front and back of the duvet together on the sides and bottom. Turn it right side out and press along the piping.

12 Return to the regular presser foot. Pin the right sides of the flap together. On the bottom long edge, make a tiny clip at the center. On each side, make a tiny clip 7 ½ inches down from the top. Draw a diagonal line from each side clip to the center clip. Trim the flap on the drawn lines.

13 Stitch the sides and angled bottom seams of the flap.

14 On the right side of the back flap piece, arrange and pin the hook pieces of the fastener tape 1 ½ inches inside the long top edge in positions that match the tape on

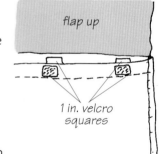

flap up

1 in. velcro squares

the duvet front. Edge-stitch around each piece.

15 Trim the flap corners diagonally and the seam allowance to ¼ inch. Turn the flap right side out and press. Topstitch the side and bottom edges ¼ inch from the edge.

16 Right sides together, pin and stitch the front of the flap to the top edge of the duvet back. Press the seam toward the flap.

17 Press under ½ inch on the remaining top flap edge; cover the stitched seam and place pins on the right side to hold it in place.

18 From the right side, topstitch in the ditch of the top seamline to secure the flap layers together; topstitch again ¼ inch from the seamline on the flap side.

19 Chalk-mark five 1-inch-long buttonholes, letting each start 1 ½ inches inside the diagonal bottom edges of the flap. Place one buttonhole at the center, one 3 inches inside each side, and the others spaced equally between. Machinestitch the buttonholes following the grain line of the fabric. Slash open the centers of the buttonholes with scissors.

20 Cut five 5 x 13-inch ties from fabric B, centering any repeat in the width. Fold each lengthwise, right sides in, and stitch a seam, leaving a 1-inch center opening; press the seam open. Center the seam within the width and stitch across the ends of each piece, trim the corners diagonally, turn the ties right side out, and press. Tie each with a loose slipknot in the center, arranging the seam on the back. Pin one tie about 1 ½ inches above the bottom of the flap at the center, one about 3 inches inside the ends, and the others spaced evenly between. Tack them to the duvet top.

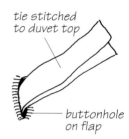

tie stitched to duvet top

buttonhole on flap

PRACTICAL IDEAS

RESIZING THE DUVET

Follow the instructions for the duvet cover but purchase the following fabric amounts and change the main pieces to the following measurements:

Twin: The finished size is 52 x 86 inches. Buy 5 yards of a print and cut the front 53 x 88 inches and the back 53 x 87 inches. Buy 2 yards of a floral stripe and cut two rectangles 53 x 14 ½ inches. Make 7 yards of piping and five knotted ties.

King: The finished size is 103 x 91 inches. Purchase 10 ½ yards of a print and cut the center front panel 53 x 93 inches and two side panels 26 ½ x 93 inches. For the back, cut a center panel 53 x 92 inches and two side panels 26 ½ x 92 inches. Buy 4 yards of a floral stripe and cut two rectangles 104 x 15 ½ inches. Make 14 yards of piping and nine knotted ties.

21 Insert the quilt or comforter into the duvet. Fasten the top closures and push the knotted ties through the buttonholes.

Decorative pillowcases

Use some of the leftover duvet cover fabric to decorate two pillowcases. You can also make matching throw pillows (pp.128–129).

1 Cut two strips of duvet fabric 3 inches wide and as long as the circumference of the pillowcase plus 1 inch for seam allowance. Press the long edges under so that they meet on the wrong side.

2 Directly below the hem on each pillow, remove 2 inches of the seam's stitches.

3 Tuck ½ inch of the end of the strip into the seam opening. On the right side of the pillowcase, pin one pressed edge just below the hem, ending with the second end tucked into the seam opening. Edge-stitch each edge of the strip and restitch the seam closed. Repeat for the second pillowcase.

Shower curtain

The envelope flap and ties on this curtain coordinate with the duvet cover, although the fabrics have been reversed. The finished curtain is 72 x 76 inches, excluding tabs. For a custom look, hem the curtain to end 1 inch above the bathroom floor.

- ◆ **5 yards 54-inch-wide fabric A**
- ◆ **2 ½ yards 54-inch-wide fabric B**
- ◆ **thread to match fabric**
- ◆ **long metal ruler, pencil, tape measure**
- ◆ **scissors**
- ◆ **12 plastic hooks to hold liner, available at sewing centers**

1 From fabric A, cut one panel 53 x 81 inches and two panels 14 ½ x 81 inches. Cut the smaller panels so that their width will continue and match any repeat in the fabric of the wide panel when the seams are sewn.

2 Pin and stitch one narrow panel to each side of the wide panel with a ½ -inch seam; press the seams open.

A shower curtain in a fabric and design that match the duvet cover on page 135 extends a delightful decor from the bedroom to the bath.

3 Along the bottom edge, press under ½ inch and then the 4-inch hem allowance. Edge-stitch the inner edge of the hem. (Alternate: The bottom and side hems can be stitched with the machine's blind-stitch attachment.)

4 On the sides, press under 2 inches twice for a double hem; edge-stitch the hem edge. Make sure bottom edges are even with hemline.

5 Top width should measure 72 inches. From fabric B, cut two rectangles on the lengthwise grain line 14 ½ x 73 inches for the flap. Place them with the right sides together and randomly pin the layers together. On the bottom long edge, make a tiny clip at the center. On each side, make a tiny clip 6 ½ inches down from the top. Draw a diagonal line from each side clip to the center clip. Trim the rectangles on the drawn lines.

6 Right sides together, pin and stitch the sides and angled bottom seams of the flap. Press the seams open. Diagonally trim the corners and trim the seam allowances to ¼ inch.

7 Turn the flap right side out and press. Top-stitch ¼ inch inside the sides and bottom. Follow Step 19 for the duvet cover (facing page) to

CURTAIN WITH ANOTHER VIEW

By adjusting the measurements for the shower curtain, you can use the same instructions to sew tab curtains for a window. Just measure your window's width and length after hanging the rod and make two finished panels to fit, omitting the flap and ties. You'll end up with a lush pair of curtains that are twice as full as the window's width.

If you want tiebacks, measure around the hung curtains with a tape measure and make fabric strips this length by the same method used for the ties. Small utility rings tacked to the ends will allow you to attach the tiebacks to cup hooks installed on the wall.

make buttonholes on the shower curtain flap.

8 Cut 12 tabs 5 x 6 inches, with the stripe area of the repeat centered in the width.

9 Fold the tabs in half lengthwise, right side in, and stitch a seam; press open. Turn each right side out. Center the seam on the back and press. Fold each tab in half, cut edges together, and stitch ⅜ inch from cut edges.

10 Arrange the tabs evenly across the top edge of the flap, right sides together. Place one tab aligned to each side edge; pin the others, allowing about 4 ¾ inches between tabs. Stay-stitch the tabs to the top seam.

11 Pin the right side of the flap to the wrong side of the curtain with the top cut edges aligned; stitch. Trim seam allowance to ¼ inch.

12 Press the flap to the front side of the curtain with the tabs upward. Topstitch ⅜ inch inside the top seam.

13 Follow Step 20 for the duvet cover (facing page) to make the ties. Tack the ties to the shower curtain and push them through the buttonholes on the flap.

14 Sew hooks for hanging the shower curtain liner to the base of each tab on the back side of the curtain.

VARIATION Make a tab shower curtain without the flap and then make matching tab curtains for the bathroom window. Use water-resistant plastic poles with finials for the shower and curtain rods.

• New Life for Patio Tables and Chairs •

A new tablecloth—with or without a contrasting topper—can spruce up any round table. Matching new seats and backs for your director's chairs give you a customized dining area on the porch or patio for cheerful, informal meals.

Round tablecloth

Once you've made your own custom tablecloth —in a matter of an hour or so—you will never buy another one at any price. Choose whatever fabric you like and match it with a topper that you can launder more frequently.

FOR UNDERSKIRT:
- ◆ **fabric (see chart for yardage)**
- ◆ **matching thread**
- ◆ **scissors**
- ◆ **1¼ inch piping cord**
- ◆ **tape measure, string, pencil**

FOR SHIRRED TOPPER:
- ◆ **5½ yards of single shirring tape**
- ◆ **eight small safety pins**

Cutting and sewing tablecloths

1 Cut the pieces required for the tablecloths (chart, facing page). As necessary, allow for matching a print's repeat on seam lines.

2 Right sides together, sew one side panel to each long edge of the center panel, creating a large square. Press seams open.

3 With the right side inside, fold the fabric in half in one direction and again in the opposite direction, forming a square of four fabric layers. Pin the layers together.

wrong side

seam

4 Tie a string onto a pencil. Stretch the string from the center fold to the end of the square and slowly swing the pencil from one edge to

Custom-made tablecloth and shirred topper match the homemade director's chair seat and back, brightening up a patio with very little effort.

the other to mark a cutting line.

5 Trim the fabric on the cutting line. Discard the outer piece.

Finishing the underskirt

1 Unpin the trimmed layers.

2 Cut 5-inch-wide bias strips from fabric B for piping and join them (p.142) to form the required length (see Measurement chart, right). Press seams open.

3 Make the piping according to the instructions on page 134.

4 Starting on a straight-grain area, pin and stitch the piping to the perimeter of the table-cloth. Join piping ends as shown on page 134.

5 From the right side, edge-stitch the seam line to hold the allowance in place underneath.

Shirred topper

1 Follow Steps 1 through 6 for cutting and sewing the full-length cloth. With the layers still pinned, make a tiny clip in the cut edge of each fold (four clips). Mark a dot on the fold 20 inches above each clip, and draw a line from the clip to the dot above it.

2 With the right side still inside, fold the fabric in half with the drawn lines aligned, two by two, and pin. Fold this half-circle in half. Repeat Step 1 to draw four more lines halfway between the first set. Unpin the layers.

3 Around the perimeter, press under ¼ inch twice and stitch the resulting double hem.

4 Cut eight pieces of shirring tape 21 inches long. About ½ inch inside one end, use a strong pin to prick out the strings from inside the tape. Fold the tape's cut ends under ½ inch to the wrong side. Center the wrong side of each tape over a marked line, with the loose strings just above the hemline.

5 Edge-stitch one side, across the top, and down the other side of the tape. Pull up the string as tight as possible and make a slipknot at the bottom. (Don't cut the string; you will want to unshirr the topper for cleaning and pressing.) Use a safety pin to tack the looped string to the tape.

NOTE All exposed seam edges, particularly of fabrics that ravel easily, should be finished with zigzag or serger stitches.

Measurement chart

Measurements account for the jumbo piping used on the hem of the full-length tablecloth and ½-inch seam allowances.

Tablecloth sizes for 27-inch-high round tables:
30-inch table: 72-inch topper; 84-inch cloth
36-inch table: 84-inch topper; 90-inch cloth
48-inch table: 90-inch topper; 102-inch cloth

Yardage requirement in 54-inch-wide fabric and 1¼-inch-diameter piping cord:
72-inch topper: 4⅛ yards fabric; no cord; side panels, 72 x 9½ inches
84-inch tablecloth: 4¾ yards fabric; 8 yards cord; side panels, 84 x 15½ inches
90-inch tablecloth: 5⅛ yards; 8¼ yards cord; side panels, 90 x 18½ inches
102-inch tablecloth: 5¾ yards; 10 yards cord; side panels, 102 x 24½ inches
All tablecloths: 1 yard for piping cover

Director's chair renewal

A quilted new seat and back will perk up worn or drab director's chairs in quick order. The quilting reinforces fabrics that you might have thought were not strong enough for this use, allowing you a wider range of choices

- ♦ **½ yard 54-inch-wide fabric for chair back**
- ♦ **1 yard 54-inch-wide fabric for chair seat**
- ♦ **¾ yard 44-inch-wide polyester fleece interfacing**
- ♦ **pencil, water-soluble marking pen**
- ♦ **paper, tape measure, framing square**

1 Use the old cover pieces to make a pattern for the new cover. Remove the stitches from the back post and slat casings on the old cover.

2 Trace each cover piece onto paper. Use the framing square to square off corners (Diagram 1).

3 Outside all lines draw a ½-inch seam allowance. From each pattern piece, cut two of fabric and one of fleece.

4 With right sides together and fleece on one side, pin and stitch each piece, leaving a 4-inch

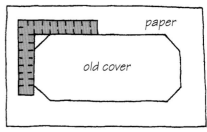

paper

old cover

DIAGRAM 1

opening on one end for turning.

5 Trim the fleece seam allowance next to the stitching. Trim corners diagonally and trim seam allowance to ¼ inch. Turn pieces right side out. Press.

6 Fold each end casing area to the back, following the old cover pattern. Edge-stitch the casing from top to bottom. Stitch again ¼ inch inside the casing edge (Diagram 2).

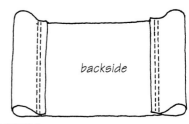

backside

DIAGRAM 2

7 Dress the chair with the new cover pieces. On the seat, use the water-soluble pen to mark a line 2 inches inside the frame and front and back edges, forming a rectangle. On the back, mark a rectangle of the same width with the top and bottom lines 1½ inches from those edges. Remove the cover.

8 Mark two diminished rectangles inside the first (Diagram 3). On the seat, draw them 2 inches apart; on the back, 1½ inches apart. Topstitch each rectangle on the seat and the back. This quilting reinforces the fabric.

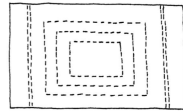

DIAGRAM 3

9 Dress the chair.

◆ Fabric Seats for Chairs ◆

*Bold, bright fabric and paint to match can spruce up a dowdy old chair and turn it
into an eye-catching piece. New fabric can work wonders for an old drop-in chair seat, and a colorful
cushion will make a simple wooden chair both decorative and more comfortable.*

Colorful cushions

*Two café or kitchen chairs present a perfect
opportunity for brilliant color combinations. This
pair has been creatively mismatched to great
effect with vivid colors and patterns.*

- **wood glue**
- **wood putty and putty knife**
- **fine sandpaper (120 grit)**
- **paintbrushes**
- **primer paint (for unfinished
  wood)**
- **1 quart paint for each chair
  (different colors)**
- **plain paper (larger than seat
  cushion), pencil, straight pins**
- **scissors and kitchen knife**
- **2 pieces of 2-inch-thick foam
  (size of the chair cushions)**
- **1½ yards medium-weight
  upholstery fabric for each chair**
- **¼ -inch piping cord (twice the
  circumference of each cushion)**
- **thread to match fabric**

Preparing the chairs

1 Assess the chairs for repairs to joints and
woodwork, and glue as necessary. Use a putty
knife to fill any gaps with wood putty. When
the putty is dry, sand smooth any rough areas.
2 If the wood is unfinished, apply the primer.
If previously painted, sand the finish smooth.
Paint each chair a different color—to match
the fabric you have chosen—and allow to dry.

*Fix up a few secondhand chairs with all your favorite
colors in fabric and paint, and you may be pleasantly
surprised by the cheerful and coordinated effect.*

Making the cushions

1 Trace the seat of each chair onto the paper. Add a ½ -inch seam allowance all around. Using this pattern, cut 2 cushion pieces (per chair), centering a motif, if any.

2 Trim the seam allowance from the pattern; pin the pattern to the foam. Using a kitchen knife, cut a foam piece to match each chair.

3 From the lengthwise grain of the fabric, cut two strips for the cushion boxing. Each piece should be 2¾ inches wide and as long as half the circumference of the cushion plus ½ inch at each end for a seam allowance. With right sides facing, stitch together the ends of the boxing pieces to form a circle; press seams open before proceeding.

4 For ties, cut two pieces, each 1¼ x 12 inches, from lengthwise grain of fabric. Fold strips in half lengthwise, right sides together; stitch ½ inch from edge. Turn right side out; press. Fold ends in and slipstitch closed.

5 Square off crosswise edges of remaining fabric. To make bias strips, fold one selvage to form a 45-degree angle with the crosswise edge; cut along fold. Parallel to the cut edges, mark several strips, 1⅝ inches wide. You should have enough to equal twice the circumference of the cushion plus 12 inches.

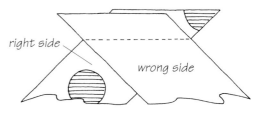

right side *wrong side*

6 Cut strips and join them, as shown above, to form one continuous strip. Press seams open.

7 To make piping (p.136), fold bias strip in half lengthwise, wrong sides together, and lay the cord in the fold. Using a zipper foot, stitch next to the cord.

8 Baste piping to cover top, starting at center back and aligning cut edges. Clip piping at each corner to ease the fit. Using the zipper foot and starting 1 inch from end of piping, stitch piping to cover, placing stitches just left of previous row of stitching. When you have come nearly full circle, cut the piping so it overlaps the starting end by 1 inch (p.136). Remove stitches from the 1-inch overlap and turn under ½ inch of fabric. Trim cord to butt the ends; wrap the folded end of the piping around the cut end. Finish stitching joined piping. Repeat process for cover bottom.

9 Baste boxing to cover top, clipping at the corners. With cover facing you, stitch just to the left of the previous two rows of stitching. Stitch bottom cover to boxing in the same way, leaving an opening of 7½ inches at the back. Turn cover right side out and insert the foam through the opening. Slip stitch closed.

10 Tack center of each tie to a back corner of the cushion. Tie cushion to back posts of chair.

Drop-in seats

Making new seat covers for old dining chairs can freshen up the whole room. You can also give new life to a second-hand chair bought at a garage sale or secondhand-furniture shop with the use of some bright paint and a colorful print fabric to match.

- ◆ **fine sandpaper (120 grit)**
- ◆ **wood putty and putty knife**
- ◆ **wood primer for unfinished wood**
- ◆ **1 quart paint for each chair (different colors)**
- ◆ **paintbrushes**
- ◆ **claw hammer or screwdriver**
- ◆ **scissors**
- ◆ **spray adhesive**
- ◆ **for each chair: ¾ yard upholstery fabric, ¾ yard polyester batting, 24-inch square black felt or nonwoven interfacing**
- ◆ **upholstery tacks and hammer or staple gun and staples**
- ◆ **rawhide mallet**

1 Remove the chair seats by unscrewing fasteners under each corner. Assess, repair, and paint chairs (see "Preparing the chairs," p.140).
2 Use the hammer or screwdriver to remove the tacks or staples that hold the old fabric to the seat frame. Cut a new cover, using the old one as a pattern. Take care to center a motif, if any, or balance stripes, and add a little extra fabric to all edges, The lengthwise grain of fabric should run front to back.
3 Cut new batting to fit the seat, coat it lightly with adhesive, and press the new layer in place over the old batting, pulling it taut.
4 Center the seat on the wrong side of the fabric, bottom side up. Spray adhesive along the edge of the fabric at the back of the seat and press the fabric to the chair bottom, making sure the grain is straight. Starting at the center, tack or staple along this edge about every 2 inches; do not tack the corners.
5 Turn the seat right side up and pull the fabric over the seat until it is taut and even. Turn the seat wrong side up again and, starting at the center front, slip-tack (hammer a tack or shoot a staple through the fabric, going only partially into the frame) every few inches. Repeat this step for each side.
6 Turn the seat right side up and check the placement of the fabric. If an adjustment is necessary, remove the tacks or staples and start over. Otherwise, use the mallet to drive the slip-tacked tacks or staples fully into the frame.
7 Fold the excess fabric at the corners to the inside, making careful tucks so that a neat finish is created (Step 4 below).

8 Trim away the excess fabric beyond the tacks or staples.
8 Trim away the excess fabric beyond the tacks or staples.
9 For the dustcover, cut a piece of felt or nonwoven interfacing 1 inch smaller than the length and width of the bottom of the seat. Center; then tack or staple it to the bottom of the frame, covering the cut edges of the upholstery fabric.
10 Insert the drop-in seat into the chair's frame, tapping it into position with the mallet, if necessary. If the seat was held in place with screws, reattach them.
11 Repeat steps 2 through 10 for each seat you are covering.

PRACTICAL IDEAS
PICTURE-PERFECT FINISH

For a custom cushion, take the pattern of your seat cushion to a foam retailer and have the cushion filler cut to size professionally.

For the tie-on cushions, work out the positions of all the pattern pieces on the fabric before you start to cut into it.

Spray a stain repellent on your new cushions for protection if the fabric you picked was not pretreated by the manufacturer.

REUPHOLSTERING DROP-IN SEATS

1 *Take out drop-in seat and turn it over—it may have webbing strips, as shown, or a solid dustcover. Remove all staples or tacks, and take off the old seat cover.*

2 *Cut a new cover, using the old one as a guide and adding a little extra fabric to all edges. Glue edge of the new cover to the back edge of the seat; tack in place.*

3 *Turn the seat over and pull cover over padding and seat, making sure it is taut and smooth. Slip-tack in place along the front edge first, then along each side.*

4 *To finish the corners, fold under the excess fabric, aligning folds with the corners. Tack securely in place. Tack on a new felt dustcover.*

◆ Decorative Covers and Screens ◆

*It is the little handmade touches that give a home its personal stamp. Pleated chair covers will
"dress" your dining room for dinner, while a folding screen is both practical and attractive. And what
better way to enhance an empty fireplace than with a colorful fireboard or screen?*

Chair slipcovers

*Masters of disguise, slipcovers with simple classic
lines like these can make a room instantly elegant.*

- ◆ **paper, pencil, scissors**
- ◆ **tape measure**
- ◆ **3 to 4 yards of 44-inch or wider
  decorative fabric per chair**
- ◆ **pins**
- ◆ **tailor's chalk**
- ◆ **matching thread**
- ◆ **2 self-cover buttons, 1 inch in
  diameter**
- ◆ **1-inch-wide satin ribbon, 5 inches
  long, per chair**

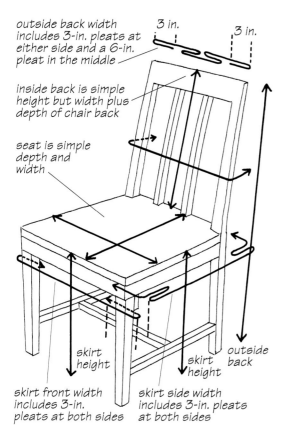

*outside back width
includes 3-in. pleats at
either side and a 6-in.
pleat in the middle*

3 in.   *3 in.*

*inside back is simple
height but width plus
depth of chair back*

*seat is simple
depth and
width*

*skirt
height*   *skirt
height*   *outside
back*

*skirt front width
includes 3-in.
pleats at both sides*   *skirt side width
includes 3-in. pleats
at both sides*

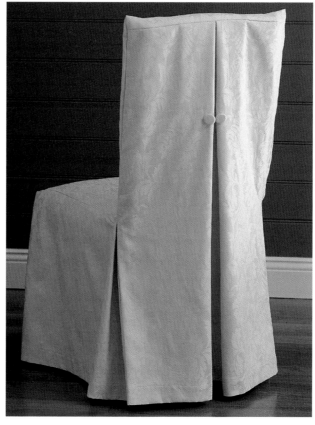

The slipcover is made from six pieces: the
inside back; the seat; three skirt sections (front
and two sides), pleated at the corners; and the
outside back, deeply pleated and falling in a
sweep from the top of the chair to the floor.

Measuring the chair

1 List the six slipcover pieces on a piece of
paper. Leave space to write in measurements.
2 Measure the length and width of each chair
area, following the arrows on the diagram (left),
including the curves, which represent 3-inch-
deep inverted pleats on the skirt and outside
back. To each of the width and length measurements, add 2 inches for a fitting allowance. The

*Inverted pleats at each corner of the seat and
at the top of the outside back account for the
slipcover's tailored look. Buttons on both sides
of the back pleat are anchored with ribbon.
When the ribbon is removed, the pleat allows
the cover to be put on or taken off with ease.*

bottom fitting allowance on the skirt
and outside back pieces will become
the hem allowance. Fitting allowances
will later be trimmed to uniform ½ -
inch seam allowances.

Cutting the slipcover

Using your measurements, including
fitting allowances, cut one piece for
each chair area, plus one more skirt
side. If using a large floral print, cut
the pieces so that the major motifs
are centered within each area. For
stripes and plaids, match the lines at
the top of the backs, the seat back
and seat front seams, and from skirt
seam to skirt seam. Making these
concessions for particular prints
may require more fabric, but the
professional-looking results will be worth it.

Fitting the slipcover

As you fit the fabric pieces to the chair, place
all the pins exactly where the pieces will join,
in effect creating the seam with the pins.
1 Following Diagram 1 (p.144), center the inside
back piece over the chair, wrong side out. Pin
a dart at each top outside edge to form a
boxing along the top and sides.
2 Following Diagram 2 (p.144), center the seat
piece wrong side up on the seat. Pin its back
allowance to the bottom of the inside back,
pinning from edge to edge of the seat; mark
the pin lines with tailor's chalk on both layers

DIAGRAM 1
*fitting the
inside back*

darts

wrong side

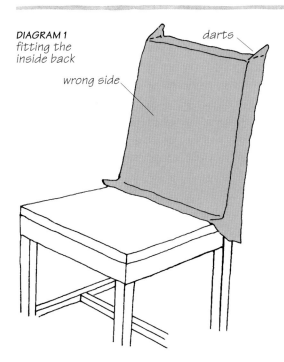

DIAGRAM 2
*inside back
and seat*

wrong side

pins

wrong
side

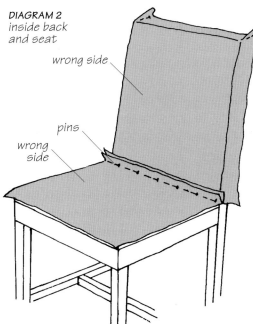

DIAGRAM 3
*pinning skirt
to seat*

front corner pleat

back corner
half pleat

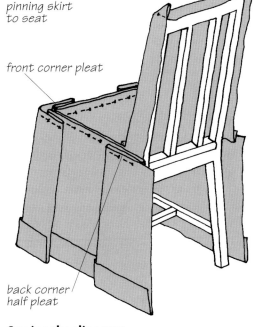

so that you will have a seam line to follow.

3 On the three skirt pieces, press the 2-inch hem allowance to the wrong side, finish the hem edges, and baste the hem in place. Repeat for the outside back.

4 On the side skirt pieces, form and pin one 3-inch-deep pleat 5 inches from each end (half the inverted pleat). Center a side skirt, wrong side out, over the side of the chair. With the hemline level at the floor and the pleat folds at the corners, pin its top allowance to the side allowance on the seat. Turn up the bottom edge of the inside back within the boxing area and continue pinning the skirt to this allowance to the end of the allowance. Leave the front area of the skirt loose beyond the front corner. Repeat Step 4 for the side skirt on the opposite side of the chair.

5 With the wrong side out, center and pin the skirt front to the front allowance of the seat with the hemline at the floor. At each corner, fold the pleat allowance back toward the center and pin.

6 Finish pinning the side skirt in place by layering the front extension over the front skirt area that was folded inward. These two layers form the second side of the inverted pleat (see diagram 3). Pin the vertical fitting allowances of the side and front skirt together 3 inches from the corner.

7 Fold the outside back in half lengthwise, right sides together. Measure 6 inches from the fold and place three pins parallel to the fold. Arrange the fabric into an inverted pleat, with half the fabric on each side of the pins.

8 Pin the top fitting allowances of the inside and outside backs together. Starting 2 inches above the seat, trim the outside back allowance to about 2 inches (see Diagram 4).

9 Pin the sides of the backs together from the top to the seat and arrange the second side of the back inverted pleat with the skirt layer on top of the outside back. Pin the vertical ends together as you did on the front.

DIAGRAM 4
*attaching
outside back*

pleat

2 in.

2 in.

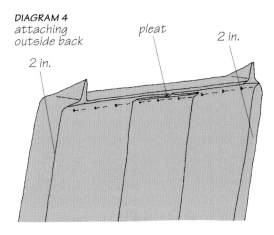

Sewing the slipcover

1 Chalk-mark all seam lines on each layer of fabric, following the pin marks. Clip or notch the top folds of pleats and seam lines. Remove all the fitting pins.

2 With the right sides of the fabric facing, sew the slipcover together in the same order that you fitted the pieces to the chair.

3 Trim all seam allowances to ½ inch and finish the raw edges with zigzag stitches, if desired (if the fabric tends to ravel, you will need to).

4 Topstitch the hem 1¾ inches from the fold.

5 Press the slipcover with a steam iron and arrange it on the chair.

6 Cover two buttons with the fabric; sew one to each pleat edge 10 inches from the top.

7 Sew the ribbon ends together, right sides facing, to make a circle. Press seam open and turn ribbon right side out Twist the circle of ribbon to form a figure eight, and fit one loop around each button to close the back of the slipcover.

Create an oasis of privacy with chairs fashionably refurbished in covers that match the handsome folding screen. Vary the fabric patterns and colors, and the decorative possibilities are limitless.

Folding screen

A screen can disguise a study area in a living room or provide privacy when curtains aren't an option. This simple folding screen is inexpensive to make—just a few hinges, some upholstery tacks, some fiberboard panels, and your choice of covering. Wallpaper is used here, but you can also paint the panels. If you pick prepasted wallpaper, follow the manufacturer's instructions for activating the paste.

- ◆ **3 pieces ¾ -inch medium-density fiberboard (MDF), each 64 x 16 inches**
- ◆ **sandpaper (120 grit)**
- ◆ **latex undercoat or wood sealer**
- ◆ **1 scissors**
- ◆ **1 paintbrush (4-inch)**
- ◆ **2 rolls wallpaper of choice**
- ◆ **1 box wallpaper paste**
- ◆ **1 paste brush**
- ◆ **1 clean paintbrush or roller**
- ◆ **wallpaper seam roller**
- ◆ **craft knife**
- ◆ **pencil**
- ◆ **tape measure**
- ◆ **electric drill**
- ◆ **screwdriver**
- ◆ **6 brass butt hinges, ¾ inch wide**
- ◆ **120 brass upholstery tacks**
- ◆ **rubber mallet**

Applying wallpaper

1 Give a light sanding to each panel of the fiberboard, especially along the edges.

2 Paint an undercoat on both sides of each panel. Allow to dry, and lightly sand again.

3 Cut the wallpaper to fit one side of one screen panel, allowing an additional 2-inch margin around all sides.

4 Lay the wallpaper on a flat surface and apply wallpaper paste all over, using a paste brush. Apply right to the edges.

5 Lay the panel flat. Carefully pick up the wallpaper and lay it paste side down on the panel. This is easier if you have someone to help you. With a clean, dry paintbrush or paint roller, press the paper down, working from the center outward and pushing any air pockets to the edge (below). If air pockets occur, lift the paper from the ends and brush down again.

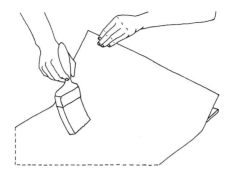

6 Form a crease around the panel edges by running your thumb and forefinger firmly along each edge (below). Though there is paste around the wallpaper edges, these edges will not stick well to the edge of the panel. Let the panel sit for 30 minutes before pasting the edge down.

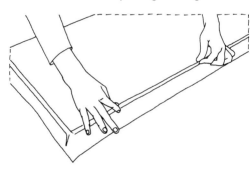

7 After 30 minutes, apply paste to one long edge of the panel and to the wallpaper that will cover it. Gently press down the paper with the seam roller. Stand the panel on the opposite edge and, with a utility knife (the blade must be very sharp), cut along the edge to remove excess paper (below). Paste and trim the short sides of the panel; then turn the panel over to paste and trim the other long

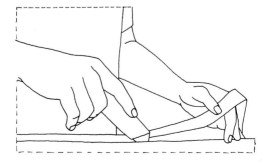

side. At corners, fold and glue a miter or trim off completely.

8 When the wallpaper is completely dry, turn the panel over and repeat Steps 3 to 5 to cover the other side of the panel (this time omitting the 2-inch margin for the sides). When pasting the edges of the wallpaper on the second side, to avoid getting paste on the paper that has already been affixed, remove any oozing paste immediately with a wet sponge. Trim paper at the edges with a sharp utility knife.

9 Repeat the wallpaper-application process for the two other panels.

Applying hinges and tacks

1 Once the wallpaper is completely dry, mark the positions for the hinges on the edges of each panel with a pencil. The middle screw hole of the top and bottom hinges should be 8 inches from the top and bottom. The third hinge will be centered between them.

2 Mark the positions for the upholstery tacks. On the left-hand edge of each panel, make a mark every 4 inches. On the right-hand edge, make a mark 2 inches from the top and then every 4 inches (the last mark will be 2 inches from the bottom). This ensures that when the edges are hinged together, the heads of the upholstery tacks will alternate neatly.

3 Take two panels that will form the left-hand and central sections of your screen and place them side by side, standing them lengthwise on their edges.

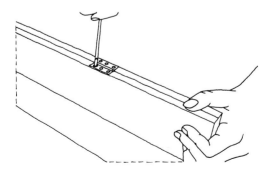

4 Place the hinges in position over the hinge marks. Using an electric drill, make a gentle impression in the wood for the screws.

5 With a screwdriver, screw the three hinges first to one panel, then to the second (above).

6 Attach the last panel to the central panel with the hinges (repeating Steps 4 and 5). These hinges should open in the opposite direction from those on the other side of the center panel: when all three panels are together, they must open like an "N"; otherwise the screen will not stand up properly.

7 Once the screen is hinged together, you are ready to tap in the upholstery tacks. This should be done with the screen folded and standing lengthwise on the edges of the panels. Use a rubber mallet to gently tap the tacks into the screen (below), as noted in Step 2.

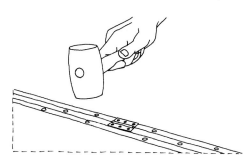

8 To complete the screen, tap four tacks into the top edge and the bottom edge of each panel. If your screen is to stand on a hardwood floor, you may want to substitute rubber stoppers for the tacks on the bottom of the panels to prevent scratching. Start 2 inches from the side and space the tacks at 4-inch intervals. If you use striped wallpaper for the screen, the stripes can help mark the equal spacing.

PRACTICAL IDEAS

STARTING RIGHT

MDF board (medium density fiberboard) is a stable building material that is less likely than plywood to warp and has finished edges. Sold in 4 x 8-foot sheets, it can be cut to size by your lumber dealer. Save scraps for other projects or for practicing with new painting techniques.

While a blazing open fire in winter is a fine sight, a cold, empty grate is not. When not in use, hide it with this attractively decorated fireboard.

Fireboard

A fireboard covers the fireplace to keep furnace-warmed air from escaping up the chimney in winter and to hide an empty grate in summer.

- **paintbrush (2 ½-inch)**
- **latex undercoat or sealer**
- **1 sheet medium-density fiberboard (MDF), ½ inch thick, cut to fit the fireplace**
- **fine sandpaper (120 grit)**
- **latex paint in two colors**
- **scumble medium, available at art-supply stores**
- **natural sea sponge**

TO DECORATE
- **gift-wrapping paper of choice**

- **small scissors, craft knife**
- **pencil**
- **white craft glue**
- **clean cloth or squeegee**
- **pattern for stencil (p.148)**
- **stencil acetate or board stencil**
- **fine-tip permanent marker**
- **small stencil brush (½-inch)**
- **gold paint**
- **plastic molded rosettes for corners (optional)**
- **water-based varnish**

1 Using the paintbrush, apply the undercoat or sealer to the fiberboard. When the coat is dry, give the surface a light sanding.
2 Clean the paintbrush and apply two coats of the background color; let to dry.

3 Make a glaze of 1 part paint (your second color), 1 part scumble medium, 1 part water. Wet the sponge and squeeze until it is just damp. Dip the sponge in the paint mix and then remove most of the paint by dabbing the sponge on newspaper. Dab lightly over the background color, changing direction all the time to avoid making any sort of regular pattern. Allow some background color to show through. Let dry.

4 With small, sharp scissors, carefully cut out decorative motifs from the wrapping paper. We used one large motif of a vase of flowers; scissors were used for most of the cutting, and a scalpel or craft knife for the areas that could not easily be reached with scissors. If your chosen image is large and difficult to handle, you can cut it into smaller pieces along the lines of the pattern and reassemble it later, when you glue it onto the board.

5 Position the motifs carefully in a design that pleases the eye and mark a few key points lightly with a pencil on the board.

6 Coat the backs of the motifs with glue and stick them onto the board. Press a damp cloth firmly on the motifs to get rid of any air bubbles or use a squeegee, working from the center out.

7 For the gold border, use a photocopier to enlarge the stencil pattern (see below) 200 percent (to enlarge without copying, see p.276). Lay the acetate on the enlarged design, trace with a marker, and cut out with a craft knife. Or buy a compatible border stencil at a crafts store.

8 With the stencil brush, apply a gold border around the board, with the outer edge of the border about ¾ inch from the board edge.

9 To add plastic moldings, paint them with gold paint and allow to dry. Glue them at the corners of the gold border.

10 Coat the finished fireboard with the varnish and let dry completely before using.

Firescreen

With the same motif as the fireboard (p.147), the firescreen achieves quite a different effect.

- ◆ **1 sheet medium-density fiberboard (MDF), ½ inch thick, 22 x 28 inches**
- ◆ **ruler, pencil**
- ◆ **tenon saw**
- ◆ **compass**
- ◆ **jigsaw drill, with 1⅛-inch bit**
- ◆ **sandpaper (fine & medium grades)**
- ◆ **dressed pine, 2 x 1 x 16 inches**
- ◆ **¼-inch chisel**
- ◆ **white craft glue**
- ◆ **paintbrush (2-inch)**
- ◆ **latex undercoat or sealer**
- ◆ **latex paint in three colors**
- ◆ **scumble medium, available from art-supply stores**
- ◆ **natural sea sponge**
- ◆ **½-inch low-tack masking tape**
- ◆ **craft knife or scalpel**
- ◆ **stencil acetate**
- ◆ **fine-tip permanent marker**
- ◆ **small stencil brush (½-inch)**
- ◆ **small scissors**
- ◆ **gift-wrapping paper of choice**
- ◆ **clean cloth or squeegee**
- ◆ **water-based varnish**

Making the screen

1 Use the diagram on the facing page as a guide for cutting the top of the screen. First, measure and mark in pencil a rectangle (4 x 3 inches) at each top corner of the fiberboard. Use a tenon saw to make cuts.

2 Set your compass to draw a 2-inch-radius circle; put the compass point at "A" on one corner and draw the corner curve. "A" is 2 inches in from both edges (see diagram). Repeat for the three other corner curves, placing the compass

point at "A" each time. Cut out each curved corner with a jigsaw.

3 For the handle, drill two 1⅛-inch holes as indicated on the diagram. Use a jigsaw to cut out the fiberboard between the two holes.

4. Sand all cut edges to a smooth finish, first with medium sandpaper, then with fine.

5 To make the "feet" of the screen, cut the pine in half, so that you have two pieces 8 inches long. To make the slots in which the board will fit in, mark two vertical lines ½ inch apart and 1 inch deep at the center of each piece (for measurements, see below). With a tenon saw, cut down halfway through each piece at the marked lines. Use a chisel to remove the wood between the cuts.

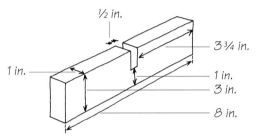

6 Round off the curved ends of the feet (below) by marking a pleasing curve and cutting with a jigsaw. Sand to a smooth finish first with medium sandpaper, then with fine.

7 Coat the slots with glue and insert the screen (above), placing each foot about 2 inches in from the side. Allow to dry completely before picking up the firescreen.

The stencil pattern below creates a charming geometric border for the firescreen shown on p.147.

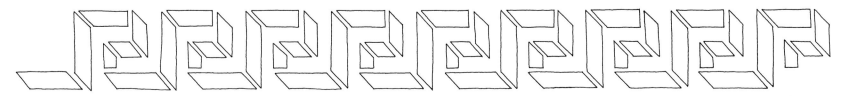

This beautiful freestanding firescreen will make your fireplace as much a focal point in summer as it is in winter when you light a roaring fire on a chilly night.

Decorating the screen

1 To paint the front, follow steps 1 to 3 of the Fireboard directions (p.145), using your chosen colors. Paint the back a single color.

2 To mark straight border areas, place ½-inch masking tape along each side with its inner edge ½ inch up from the firescreen edge. Add a second row of tape inside and against the first row, and a third row inside and against the second. Remove the center row of tape; this untaped space becomes the border. Square the inner corners on the third row of tape using a ruler and a craft knife.

3 Follow instructions on page 102 for cutting a stencil for curved borders. Make a stencil for the curves between the top and the side straight areas. Space the ½-inch-wide border ½ inch from the curved edge.

4 To stencil, paint the taped areas with your third color using the stencil brush. Align the stencil with one curved area and paint. When the paint is dry, remove the tape. Wipe the stencil with a paper towel and flop it to paint the other side.

5 Lay the screen flat on a table with the feet over the table edge. To apply the floral motif, follow steps 4 to 6 of the Fireboard directions.

6 Coat the finished firescreen with varnish.

TIPS FROM THE EXPERTS

When cutting out paper motifs, hold the scissors at an angle to give a slanted cut to the underside of the paper edges. This makes a flatter edge, with no white paper showing.

To apply the glue to each motif, turn it facedown on a pasting board and brush the glue on, working from the center out to the edges.

To make positioning and moving of paper motifs easier, dilute the glue with up to 50 percent water.

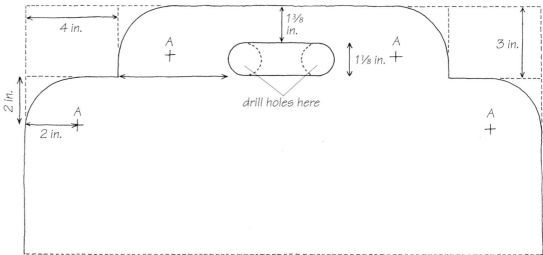

◆ Candlemaking ◆

Candles help to commemorate birthdays, and celebrate holidays, and create romantic moods. They will help set a festive tone for any event. You can make special times—and special gifts—even more memorable with the warm glow of candles you've lovingly made yourself.

Rolled candles

Honey-scented rolled beeswax candles are not only easier to make than molded candles, but they also burn longer. Use sheets of pliable honeycomb-textured wax, available in natural pale colors and in bright dyed hues. Supplies are available at crafts shops.

- ◆ **scissors**
- ◆ **wicking**
- ◆ **beeswax**
- ◆ **utility knife**
- ◆ **ruler**
- ◆ **butter knife**

1 To make the wax easier to work with, heat it on a radiator or with a hair dryer until it's pliable (a minute or two). Cut a piece of wicking; it should be ¾ inch longer than the length of the candle. Place the wicking along one long edge of the wax; fold the wax over the wicking and press tightly to seal it in.
2 Carefully roll up the wax sheet with the wicking inside. Make sure the top and bottom

CANDLE SAFETY

Making candles. Melt paraffin wax, which is highly flammable, in a double boiler. Never let the wax exceed 200°F. Use pot holders or mitts to handle hot wax and molds; these get hot enough to cause bad burns.

Using candles. Never leave a burning candle unattended. Drafts can blow flames dangerously close to drapes or furniture and ignite them—so always position candles away from flammable materials. Before lighting a candle, make sure it is secure in its holder and won't tip over. Above all: keep candles out of the reach of children.

edges remain even and that the wicking stays securely in place.
3 When the candle is the diameter you want, cut off the excess wax with a sharp utility

knife. Use a ruler as a straightedge to make sure that you get a neat, clean edge.
4 Smooth the cut end by pressing a warmed butter knife (hold it under running hot water and dry it or warm it with a hair dryer) along the seam. Don't press too hard; beeswax is delicate and you can easily crush the candle. To prime the end of the wick, press a tiny bit of wax around it just before lighting it.

VARIATIONS Vary the height of your candles by cutting the beeswax into strips of different heights before rolling the candles in different widths as well. You can group candles of varying widths and heights for an elegant display.

To make a tapered candle, cut a right triangle from a sheet of beeswax. Roll from one of the equal sides.

Make beehive-shape candles by rolling a tapered candle, then adding layers of sheet wax, each layer slightly shorter than the last.

For square candles, gently press the candle against a hard, smooth surface after each quarter turn.

MAKING ROLLED CANDLES

1 *Heat the sheet of beeswax with a hair dryer on the low setting for a few minutes to make it more pliable. Overdoing the heat can prematurely melt the wax.*

2 *Lay the wicking on the edge of the beeswax. Roll the wax around the wick against a flat surface. Keep the roll tight and even as you make each turn.*

3 *Use a ruler as a straightedge to get a sharp, straight cut. Put a fresh blade in your utility knife, and hold the ruler with one hand while you cut with the other.*

4 *To finish the candle, warm a butter knife in hot water, dry it, and press the seam closed. The heat is more important than the pressure for fixing the seam.*

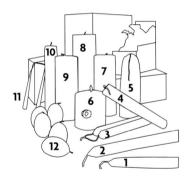

1 *Dipped tapered candle;* **2, 3, 4** *Rolled beeswax candles;* **5** *Large molded candle;* **6** *Molded cylinder with sealing-wax ornament;* **7, 8, 9** *Rolled beeswax pillars;* **10** *Molded pillar candle;* **11** *Small dipped tapered candles;* **12** *Molded egg-shaped candle.*

Molded candles

Candle molds come in a range of shapes, from fruits and vegetables to geometric. You can also improvise molds with household items, such as tin cans, tart pans, and flowerpots.

- ◆ **candle mold and wicking**
- ◆ **double boiler**
- ◆ **paraffin wax**
- ◆ **wax paper**
- ◆ **mold seal**
- ◆ **nonstick cooking spray**
- ◆ **candy thermometer**
- ◆ **wax dyes or crayons**

1 With scissors, cut a length of wicking 3 to 4 inches longer than the height of the mold. In a double boiler, melt some of the wax over very low heat and soak the wick in it for 5 minutes. Lay the wick on a piece of wax paper to dry; make sure it's straight. If your mold isn't watertight, seal it with mold seal. Lightly spray inside the mold with nonstick cooking spray.
2 Secure the wick to the bottom of the mold with a bit of mold seal. Tie the other end to a small stick or skewer. Pull the wick taut and lay the stick across the mouth of the mold.
3 Melt the rest of the wax in a double boiler; don't let it exceed 200°F (use a candy thermometer). Then lower the heat and add the dye or crayon; stir until dissolved. Pour the wax into the mold, stopping ½ inch from the top.

4 Using pot holders or mitts, place the mold in a bowl of cold water. Don't let any water splash onto the wax. Let cool for 1 hour.
5 As the wax cools, a hollow will appear near the wick. Use a fork to prick small holes in the candle; then fill the area with melted wax.
6 When the wax is completely cool, grab the stick and pull the candle from the mold. Trim the wick and smooth the bottom of the candle by standing it in a pot of warm water.

VARIATIONS To make scented candles, add a few drops of sandalwood, vanilla, almond, cinnamon, pine, or citrus essence to the melted wax. Or perfume your candles with a drop or two of essential oil of lavender, rose, jasmine, lilac, or another favorite flower. Add a few drops of citronella oil to candles you make for outdoor use to help keep bugs at bay.

Emboss candles with sealing wax. Use a few drops of melted wax to attach the seal.

◆ Finishes for Frames ◆

*Framing pictures can be extraordinarily expensive. Recycling old frames that you
rescue from garage sales or secondhand shops is a more economical option—and gives you a
chance to show your creative flair. Look for finishing supplies at an art-supply store.*

Gilded frame

Turn a basic frame into an instant "antique."

- **plastic molded segments (from arts and crafts shops)**
- **low-sheen red latex paint**
- **2 soft nylon brushes**
- **sandpaper (220-grit)**
- **water-based quick-size sealer**
- **white cotton gloves**
- **book of Dutch metal leaf**
- **white craft glue**
- **water-based varnish**

1 Paint the frame and molded segments with two coats of red paint. Let each coat dry and sand lightly. Dust with clean cloth and tack rag.
2 Apply quick-size sealer to the segments. Leave for 15 minutes (it will still be tacky). Wearing white gloves, cut the spine from the book of Dutch metal leaf. Cut enough sheets to cover the segments. Quarter each sheet, leaving the protective paper.
3 Move the top piece of paper from one sheet so that about ¼ inch of gold leaf protrudes. Turn the leaf and paper over and lay the protruding leaf at the top of the segment. Slide

the paper from beneath as you position the leaf. Then peel off the top paper. Apply the next quarter sheet the same way, overlapping the previous sheet about ¼ inch. Continue until the segments are covered.
4 Tamp gold leaf down with a soft, clean brush, taking care not to touch the size with the brush and making sure that all the size—and the segments—are covered with gold.
5 Arrange the gilded segments on the frame, glue down, clamp, and leave overnight to set.
6 Finish frame with a water-based varnish.

Pearlized frame

Achieve the opalescent effect of mother-of-pearl with layers of four different colored glazes.

- **four glazes, mixed in these proportions: 1 part latex paint (red, green, blue, or mother-of-pearl), 1 part scumble mix, 1 part water**
- **nylon paintbrush, steel wool**

1 Brush on one spare and uneven coat of each glaze in order. Allow each coat to dry before applying the next.
2 Rub lightly with steel wool.

Tortoiseshell frame

The brushes help create the authentic look.

- **yellow low-luster latex paint**
- **round nylon brushes, nos. 1, 3, and 6**
- **glaze 1: equal parts burnt umber paint and scumble mix**
- **glaze 2: equal parts burnt umber paint, raw umber paint, and scumble mix**
- **glaze 3: equal parts black paint and scumble mix**

1 Paint the frame with the yellow paint.
2 Apply the glazes in small diagonal strokes on the yellow. Start by applying glaze 1 with the no. 6 brush. Then apply glaze 2 with the no. 3 brush, and then glaze 3 with the very fine

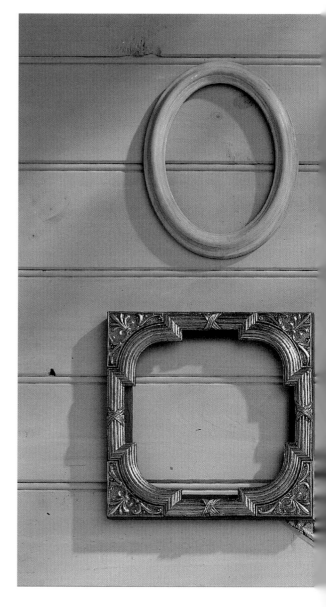

SURFACE PREPARATION

If the frame you have chosen to work on has already been finished with paint or varnish, clean it using steel wool and mineral spirits and, when dry, sand it with 220-grit sandpaper.

Sand raw wood surfaces with 220-grit sandpaper until smooth and then seal with a water-based sealer or shellac.

If the surface is uneven, sand with 220-grit sandpaper or steel wool. Wipe clean with a cotton cloth, then a clean tack cloth (p.101).

no. 1 brush. Work with all three glazes inter-changeably. Dip the brushes into water to soften and move the glazes around. Blend some of the colors, and keep others separate. Allow a little yellow to show through. As an accent, pick out fine details with glaze 3.

Spectacular frame finishes are shown top row, from left: two distressed effects; a plaster ceiling molding, and a tortoise shell finish. Seen in the bottom row are a gilded frame with plastic moldings; a pearlized finish; and a combination of distressing and gilding.

Distressed finish

Layers of paint, with sanding, produce this "weathered" finish.

- ◆ **2 or 3 foam brushes (2-inch)**
- ◆ **latex paint or artist's acrylic in white, green, pink, and blue**
- ◆ **sandpaper (220-grit)**
- ◆ **tack cloth**
- ◆ **paste wax**

1 Apply a coat of white paint sparingly and unevenly to create areas of light and dark; do not completely cover the frame. Allow the paint to dry.

2 Sand the surface, then wipe thoroughly with the tack cloth.

3 Apply one coat each of green, pink, and blue paint, sanding each time and allowing to dry. Do not completely cover the frame with any one color. There are no strict rules for this finish; if desired, continue applying colors and sanding until satisfied with the appearance. The look you want is one of wear and age.

4 To finish, rub the whole surface lightly to a soft sheen with the paste wax.

153

◆ Découpage Framed Mirror ◆

The word découpage *is derived from the French word* découper, *meaning "to cut out."*
An art form in former times, it traditionally involved up to 100 layers of varnish. This project uses
far fewer layers but still achieves a beautiful finish for a frame from a crafts store.

Transform an unfinished-wood mirror into an heirloom with a little paint, paper, and glue.

- **mirror, framed in unfinished pine or other wood**
- **screwdriver**

PREPARATION AND PAINTING
- **wet-and-dry sand-paper (600 grit)**
- **foam brushes (2 ¾ -inch and ¼ -inch)**
- **¾ -inch low-tack masking tape**
- **low-sheen black latex paint**
- **pencil, ruler, French curve**
- **fine-tip permanent marker**
- **red latex background paint**
- **small stencil brush**
- **gold latex paint**
- **absorbent cotton rags**
- **size 0 liner brush**
- **water-based sealer**

CUTTING AND GLUING
- **sheets of plastic**
- **gift-wrapping paper of choice**
- **cutting mat**
- **craft knife (new blade)**
- **small, straight-edged scissors**
- **glue-tack pen**
- **paper paste**
- **white craft glue**
- **4-inch rubber roller**
- **white vinegar**

VARNISHING AND SANDING
- **no. 12 sable varnishing brush**
- **clear water-based gloss varnish**
- **1200-grit wet-and-dry sand-paper**
- **tack cloth**
- **clear satin oil-based varnish**

Preparation and painting

1 Remove the screws from the mirror backing and keep in a safe place. Remove the mirror and store flat, protecting the back.

2 Sand all surfaces of the wooden frame, using a dry 600-grit sandpaper.

3 Using the large foam brush, apply a coat of black paint to both sides of the frame. Let dry and sand again. Apply a second coat; let dry.

4 To mark straight areas of the border, place one strip of ¾ -inch masking tape along each straight side. Add a second row of tape inside and against the first and a third row inside against the second. Remove the center row of tape; this untaped space becomes the border.

5 Follow instructions on page 103 for cutting a stencil for curved borders. Make one stencil for the top curves, from the center to the taped straight side border; likewise, make another stencil for the bottom. On each stencil, space the ¾ -inch-wide border ¾ inch from the curved edge.

6 To stencil the border, paint one coat of red in the taped areas with the stencil brush. Tape the top stencil on half of the frame top and connect it to the taped side border; repeat for the bottom stencil. Use the stencil brush to stencil red. When dry, flop the stencils and complete the border. (Wipe stencil with a paper towel before using the reverse side.)

7 When red is dry, paint the border again with gold paint. When that dries, remove the tape.

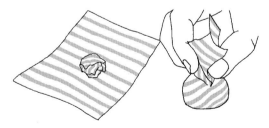

8 Make a "swab" by putting a small ball of absorbent cotton cloth in a larger piece (above) and twisting the larger piece around the ball. Dip into a little red paint and wipe around the inside beveled edge (near mirror), shelf edge

To carry through a particular theme, this elegant découpage mirror could be decorated with motifs from color photocopies of your upholstery fabrics.

(if your frame has a shelf), and side of frame (edge between the front and the back). Let dry. Make another swab; repeat with gold.

9 Fix imperfections with the liner brush and black paint. When dry, apply sealer over the paint, using the small foam brush.

Cutting and gluing

1 On a plastic sheet, apply sealer to your paper by gently brushing over its front surface with a foam brush. Allow at least 1 hour's drying time. If the paper is very thin, wait until the front dries, then turn over and seal the back.

2 When the paper is dry, select the sections you wish to use. Place on a cutting mat, and use a craft knife to cut out the inside areas of the design that are hard to reach with scissors. For outside areas, cut less closely with the knife, then finish off with scissors. Hold scissors at an angle (below) to cut the underside of the edge diagonally, so that when the paper is in place, no white edges show.

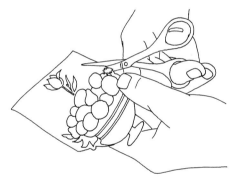

3 Arrange the motifs on the frame and position with the glue pen. Step back from the project to make sure the design is balanced.

4 Before proceeding, make up a glue mixture of 3 parts paper paste to 1 part white craft glue.

5 Work on one motif at a time. Spread the glue on the back of the motif and on the surface of the frame where it will lie. Once it is in position, dab a little glue on the top of the motif so that you can slide your fingers over the surface to push out excess glue mixture and air bubbles. Finish off with the rubber roller, cleaning the roller after each use.

6 With a clean, damp cloth, dab up excess glue. Gently wipe the area around the motif. Press lightly so as not to damage the edges.

7 Repeat for the other motifs. When all are glued down, dab all over with a little vinegar on a cloth, to ensure a fresh, clean surface.

8 When motifs are dry, prick any air bubbles with a craft knife and apply a little more glue.

9 Using the liner brush and diluted black paint, touch up any white paper edges that show against the black background. Let dry.

10 Apply sealer to the frame with foam brush.

Varnishing and sanding

1 Dip the bristles of the varnishing brush three-quarters of the way into the water-based varnish; then, starting at the top of the frame and working downward, apply one coat. Let dry. Apply the next coat from side to side and let dry. Repeat, changing direction each time, until 20 coats of varnish have been applied. Allow 30 minutes between coats.

2 When thoroughly dry, rub back gently with wet 1200-grit sandpaper, using plenty of water. Use the tack cloth to remove dust particles.

3 Continue to apply varnish as before, building up five or six coats and then sanding gently and wiping with the tack cloth; repeat until the surface is smooth and level.

4 After the final sanding, wipe with the tack cloth and apply two coats of oil-based varnish. (Make sure the brush is completely dry before using it for the oil-based varnish.) Allow the first coat to dry for 24 hours before applying the second one. Allow the work to cure (harden) for a two weeks before you reassemble the mirror.

FOR THE BEST RESULTS

Use only unfolded paper for the motifs; creases and folds will show through the varnish. Roll and store sheets of paper you may want to use on cardboard cylinders.

Never varnish on a wet or humid day—the varnish may cloud. Use a top-quality brush and work in an airy, dust-free area. Always wear a mask.

Never sand in circles; always use a left-to-right and top-to-bottom cross-hatching method.

• On Display •

*A pair of matching shelves are a novel feature in their own right while giving
you ample space to show off your favorite knickknacks or a revolving exhibit of
prized photographs and other works of art.*

*These display shelves are made of inexpensive
pine. Pacific maple was chosen for the front faces,
as it is free of knots and blemishes that can show
through a painted finish. When buying lumber at
a lumberyard, ask for the width and thickness
measurements given below, but customize the
length to your needs. Our shelves are 10 feet long,
a standard lumber size. You can have the lumber
cut at the lumberyard or do it yourself at home,
using a T square to mark the cut line. Don't worry
if purchased wood measures ¼ inch less in width
and thickness than it is said to be; shrinkage
occurs during curing.*

- **steel brackets: four 3 x 3 inches
  and four 6 x 6 inches
  (these come with screws)**
- **stud finder**
- **1 piece radiata pine, 10 inches
  x 1 inch x 10 feet**
- **1 piece radiata pine, 4 inches
  x ⅝ inch x 10 feet**
- **2 pieces Pacific maple, 4 inches
  x ⅝ inch x 10 feet**
- **pencil and ruler**
- **tenon saw**
- **chisel (¾ inch or less)**
- **screwdriver, hammer**
- **white craft glue**
- **1 ¼ -inch finishing nails**
- **nail set**
- **putty or wood filler**
- **fine sandpaper (120 grit)**
- **paintbrush (2-inch)**
- **latex undercoat**
- **satin acrylic enamel**
- **level**
- **anchors appropriate to
  your walls**
- **drill, with bits to match screws
  and anchors**

1 Mark the wall studs, located with the stud
finder. Mark the position for the brackets on
each shelf to match the spacing of the studs
(usually 16 inches or 24 inches). Mark a groove
(equal to the width and depth of the bracket)
in the back edge of the shelf for each bracket
(below). Saw the sides of the groove with a
tenon saw and use a chisel to take out the
depth. Test that the brackets fit flush to the
back edge of the shelf so that the shelf will sit
lightly against the wall. Screw the brackets to
the shelves.
2 Apply a smear of white craft glue to the
front edge of one shelf. Fix a front face to this
edge with finishing nails—about 12 inches apart
(below). Make sure to center the front face
accurately so that it protrudes an equal
amount above and below the shelf (diagram,
above right). Repeat for the other shelf.
3 Use a nail punch to countersink the head of
each nail slightly below the surface; then use
putty or wood filler to fill the holes. When dry,
smooth the surface with fine sandpaper.

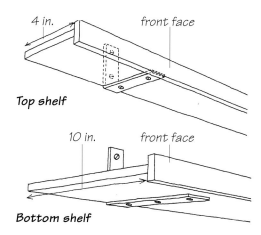

Top shelf

Bottom shelf

4 Sand the edges and faces of each shelf, and
apply a coat of latex undercoat. Leave the
shelves to dry for 2 hours.
5 Lightly sand any rough spots on the shelves
and apply two coats of satin acrylic enamel,
allowing the first to to dry completely before
applying the second.
6 Using a level to ensure level mounting, mark
the spots for the bracket screws and anchors

MAKING THE SHELVES

1 *Mark positions for the brackets
on the shelf. Mark a small groove at
the back of the shelf. Saw the sides,
then chisel out the depth.*

2 *Glue the front face (maple) to
the shelf (pine), then nail every 12
inches. Countersink the nails, fill
with putty, and, when dry, sand.*

3 *Sand the shelves. Apply undercoat to wood and brackets, then
two coats of paint (paint wall section of brackets in the wall color).*

along the wall studs. Drill holes in the wall to accept the anchors. For masonry walls, use appropriate plugs to hold the screws securely (ask for choices at your hardware store).

7 Screw the brackets of the two shelves firmly to the wall.

8 To finish off the shelves, paint the part of each bracket that is attached to the wall in the wall color. Although the paint dries in a couple of hours, it's a good idea to leave it overnight before putting items on the shelves.

PRACTICAL IDEAS

FITTING TO A CUPBOARD

If your shelves butt a cupboard, you have to make sure the doors will open easily. A solution is to cut a triangular section off the end of the shelf. Mark and cut this section before you start. Also adjust the length of the front face.

It is surprising what a difference a pair of simple wall-to-wall shelves can make in a room, particularly when one is stepped back from the other to give a sense of perspective. The shallow top shelf is ideal for narrow objects, such as picture frames, while the broad bottom shelf suits bulkier ornamental items (use these to hide the wall brackets). With this design, you can make appropriate shelving for any room.

◆ Tiles in Bloom ◆

Your favorite blossoming herbs can adorn tile markers for a potted garden or an outdoor herb patch.
Giant sunflowers, hand-painted on a white background, dramatically
enhance plain tiles on a kitchen wall and even, with felt backing, become handy trivets.

Tile herb markers

These hand-painted tiles make wonderful markers for plants, or they can be a lovely kitchen wall decoration. Buy your materials at a crafts store or art-supply store. One 2-ounce bottle of paint is sufficient for painting many tiles. White can be used to create highlights on any leaf or flower.

- **6 or more 6 x 2-inch edging tiles in pale sage green**
- **black carbon paper, pencil**
- **sealant for tile surface preparation and protective coating**
- **2-ounce bottles acrylic paints in the following colors: poetry green and bayberry (leaves); orchid and rose pink (chives); lavender sachet and plum chiffon (peppermint); light periwinkle and light blue (rosemary); light periwinkle and plum chiffon (sage); moon yellow (sweet basil); rose pink (thyme); white (highlighter)**
- **brush sizes 00, 0, 1, and 2**
- **palette or clean plastic meat tray**
- **6 aluminum garden markers or other weatherproof stakes**
- **glue gun and glue sticks**

1 Enlarge the drawings to fit your tiles, with a photocopier or by hand, following the directions on page 276.

2 Prime the surface of each tile with the sealant; it will become dull. Place the carbon side of the paper against the tile and transfer the herb drawing to the center of the tile.

3 With a pencil, write the name of the herb, either freehand or by tracing it from the drawing, then paint the letters in the darker green, using the largest brush.

These drawings illustrate the blossoms and leaves of six favorite garden herbs. If you enlarge the drawings with a photocopier, you can use the enlarged labels under each as a guide for painting the names of the herbs on the tiles.

peppermint

sage

rosemary

sweet basil

chives

thyme

4 Paint the leaves the lighter green, with shading and veins in the darker green. On rosemary, paint a white center vein.

5 Paint the flower petals the lighter color. Paint any feathery strokes and shading in the darker color. Finish with another coat of the sealant after the paint has dried.

6 Use the glue gun to attach a garden marker or stake to the center back of each tile. Let glue dry thoroughly before using the tiles.

Pretty tile markers identify the herbs in this tiny kitchen garden, so the cook's helpers can pick the right sprigs.

Sunflower tiles

The 6-inch-square tiles are easily interspersed within a wall of 2-inch or 3-inch tiles. They also look great as a border above a chair rail in a breakfast alcove or sun room.

- ◆ **6-inch-square white tiles**
- ◆ **black carbon paper, pencil**
- ◆ **sealant for tile surface preparation and protective coating**
- ◆ **2-ounce bottles acrylic paints in the following colors: thicket green, clover green, and lemon custard green (leaves); medium yellow, school bus yellow, and butterscotch (petals); nutmeg, maple syrup, and brown sugar (center)**
- ◆ **brush sizes 0, 4, and 5**
- ◆ **palette or clean plastic meat tray**

1 Enlarge the sunflower (below) to fit your tile, with a photocopier or by hand, using the directions on page 276.

Sunflower pattern

2 Prime the surface of each tile with the sealant. It will become dull. Place the carbon side of the paper against the tile and transfer the sunflower drawing to the center of the tile, as shown below.
3 Use the order of painting shown below to make the sunflowers. Wash your brush with cold water and soap when changing colors.

Hand-painted tiles reflect the splashy colors of their inspiration—showy sunflowers, freshly picked from a late-summer garden.

Blot it with paper towels to remove all the moisture, to avoid diluting the paints.
4 Finish each painted tile with another coat of the sealant.

PAINTING THE SUNFLOWER TILES

1 Prime the surface of each tile with sealant. Place the carbon paper, carbon side down, on a tile and trace the sunflower pattern onto the tile's center.

2 Fill all the leaves with the darkest green, shade with the medium green on half or parts of the leaves, and use the lightest green for the veins.

3 Paint all the petals first with the lightest yellow and then shade them with the two darker yellows, letting the first dry before adding the second one.

4 Paint the center with the lightest brown and shade it with the two other browns. Add dark brown and yellow dots to the center last.

◆ Kitchen Blackboard ◆

A blackboard is a practical addition to any kitchen—just the thing for leaving messages or jotting down items for the grocery list. It's all the nicer if the blackboard is framed with a cheerful stenciled pattern that picks up the colors of the kitchen decor.

Start with an empty frame—new or recycled—and stencil it with a pear or other motif.

- **mdf (medium-density fiberboard) frame with a 4-inch-wide border and an mdf insert**
- **sandpaper (120 grit), tack cloth**
- **all-purpose sealer**
- **blackboard paint**
- **2 nylon brushes (1½ to 2 inches)**
- **artist's acrylic paints: smoked pearl, storm blue, yellow oxide, pine green, crimson, burnt umber**
- **paint palette**
- **acetate, for stencils**
- **fine-tip permanent marker**
- **surface for cutting**
- **craft knife**
- **hard pencil**
- **masking tape**
- **6 stencil brushes (⅜ to ¾ inch)**
- **water-based varnish**
- **varnish brush**

1 Remove the insert from the frame, sand both frame and insert, and wipe with a tack cloth to remove dust.
2 Coat both the frame and the insert with the all-purpose sealer, using a flat brush.
3 For the blackboard surface, use a flat brush to apply 2 or 3 coats of blackboard paint to the insert; set this aside while you prepare the frame.
4 Mix even quantities of smoked pearl and storm-blue paint, making enough to give the frame two coats. Apply the two coats, allowing the first to dry completely before starting the second one.
5 Using the pattern on the facing page, trace and cut out a pear stencil, as described below.
6 Position pears on the frame, as shown below. On the finished frame (facing page), each alternate pear is reversed simply by turning the stencil over.
7 Place the yellow, green, crimson, and burnt umber paints separately on the palette. Begin stenciling the pears, as shown below. Make sure the brush is barely moist,

FOR A PLEASING RESULT

Keep the stencil clean to prevent smudging around the motif's outline. It's particularly important to wipe the stencil clean each time you turn it over to paint a reversed-image pear.

If you switch to fabric stencil paints, you can add matching pears to a seat cushion, table linens, or a curtain border. And remember, pears come in a variety of colors, not just yellow!

The stencil design can be altered to reflect motifs already present in your kitchen, such as flowers in a china pattern or a border of wallpaper used around the ceiling.

so that paint doesn't seep under the edges of the stencil. The paint dries very quickly, allowing you to add a second and third color in fairly rapid succession.

STENCILING THE PEARS

1 *Trace the pear motif onto a sheet of acetate using a fine-tip permanent marker. Place the acetate on the cutting surface and use the craft knife to cut out the pear shape.*

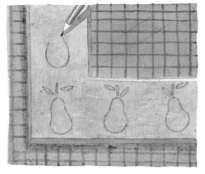

2 *Using a pencil, lightly mark the positions of the pears around the frame. The exact number of pears and the amount of space between them will depend on the size of your frame.*

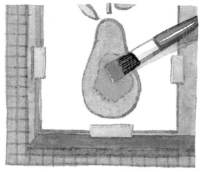

3 *Place the stencil on one pear outline. Use tape to hold it in place. Dip a stencil brush in yellow paint, keeping the brush quite dry. Gently stipple the paint over the pear until it is covered.*

4 *Using a separate stencil brush for each color, dab a little green and crimson paint on each pear for a natural look. Work around the frame, repeating the process for the other pears.*

Family life revolves around the kitchen, so give the room a warm, welcoming atmosphere with colorful touches, such as this stenciled blackboard frame.

8 Using the photograph at left and the step-by-step illustrations on the facing page to guide you, shade the pears with other colors. Then apply green for the leaves and burnt umber for the stems.

9 Continue stenciling around the frame. It will go more quickly if you first stencil all the pears that face one direction, then wipe the stencil clean, turn it over, and stencil all the pears that face in the other direction.

10 Allow the frame to dry completely; then give it two coats of varnish, letting the first dry before you apply the second one. When the second coat is dry—at least 24 hours—replace the insert in the frame.

11 Hang the blackboard in a convenient place for leaving messages and put some chalk on the frame or in a nearby basket.

Pear pattern for a stencil

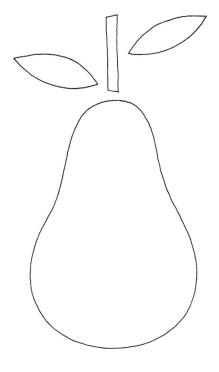

◆ Clean and Gleaming ◆

Cleaning, deodorizing, and disinfectant products need not contain harsh, toxic chemicals to get the job done—there is a natural solution for every household cleaning job. By making your own from simple household staples, you'll not only help the environment—you'll save money, too.

All-purpose cleansing paste

This paste is effective for most household cleaning chores and contains no harsh abrasives to harm surfaces. The paste resembles a gray putty, except that it is slightly softer and has a bubbled surface. The chalk or diatomaceous earth provides a fine sheen without scratching. You can find diatomaceous earth in garden, pool, and hardware stores. Use store-bought brands of pure soap flakes, such as Ivory or Dreft, or make your own by grating a bar of pure soap.

- ½ **cup pure soap flakes**
- **1 cup chalk or diatomaceous earth**
- ½ **cup baking soda**
- **3 tablespoons glycerin**

1 In a small bowl, crush the soap flakes into a powder with the back of a spoon (or whirl them in a blender if you wish). Thoroughly mix in the chalk or diatomaceous earth and the baking soda.
2 Stir in enough of the glycerin to form a thick paste. Spoon the mixture into a widemouthed screw-top jar or other container.
3 Keep the paste covered when not in use, to prevent it from drying out.

Lemony furniture polish

This furniture polish protects the wood surface and makes it shine. Mix it fresh before each use.

- **1 cup olive or vegetable oil**
- **1 teaspoon lemon essential oil (available at health-food or aromatherapy stores)**

Mix the oils together thoroughly and apply sparingly with a soft rag. Wipe dry with a clean, soft cloth, buffing to a gleaming finish.

Nonstreaking spray glass cleanser

Use crumpled newspaper instead of paper towels for lint-free results.

- ¼ **cup white vinegar**
- **1 tablespoon cornstarch**
- **2 cups warm water**

Mix the ingredients in a spray bottle and shake well to dissolve cornstarch. Spray liberally onto glass surface. Wipe dry with a clean cloth or newspapers, buffing to a streak-free shine .

Eucalyptus tile cleanser

This fresh, tangy powder leaves kitchen and bathroom tiles shiny and clean.

- ½ **cup pure soap flakes**
- **1 cup chalk or diatomaceous earth**
- **1 cup baking soda**
- **1 teaspoon essential oil of eucalyptus (available at health-food or aromatherapy stores)**

1 In a small bowl crush the soap flakes with the back of a spoon until powdered (or whirl them in a blender). Mix in the chalk or diatomaceous earth and the baking soda, breaking up any lumps.
2 Sprinkle the essential oil over the surface of the powdered mixture and stir in with the spoon. Continue stirring for several minutes to disperse the oil throughout the mixture, then spoon the mixture into a screw-top jar or can that has had small holes punched in the lid.
3 Cover the holes in the lid with masking tape to keep the powder dry while it is stored. Let the mixture sit for a week before using so that the essential oil is thoroughly dispersed.

Pine floor cleanser

Washing soda, available at grocery-store laundry sections, is an inexpensive yet effective cleansing agent that quickly cuts grease and removes stubborn stains. Mixed with soap and salt, it makes an excellent cleanser for most hard floor surfaces.

- ½ **cup soap flakes**
- ¼ **cup washing soda**
- **1 cup salt**
- **2 cups water**
- **2 teaspoons pine essential oil (available at health-food or aromatherapy stores)**

1 In a saucepan, place the soap, washing soda, salt, and water and heat gently, stirring until soap, soda, and salt have dissolved.
2 Cool the mixture to lukewarm, then add the essential oil. Stir well and pour into a jar or other container.
3 To use, pour two to three tablespoons of the mixture into half a bucket of hot water, stirring well. For large areas, you may need to double the amount.
4 After cleaning, rinse the floor with half a bucket of clean water into which you have poured a cup of white vinegar.

Nontoxic toilet bowl cleanser

Clean and sanitize your toilet bowl without harmful chlorine! For no-scrub convenience, simply pour in and leave overnight.

- **1 cup borax**
- ½ **cup white vinegar**

1 Flush the toilet to wet the sides of the bowl.
2 Sprinkle the borax around the toilet bowl, then drizzle with the vinegar. Leave for several hours before scrubbing with a toilet brush.

Oven cleanser

The best defense against a dirty oven? Prevent spills before they happen. If you suspect a dish will bubble over during baking, place it on a cookie sheet before putting it in the oven. For tough, baked-on grease, use this remedy.

- ◆ **1 box baking soda (16 ounces)**
- ◆ **¼ cup washing soda**

1 In a container, mix the ingredients well.
2 Wet the floor and walls of the oven (you can use a wet rag or paper towels) and generously sprinkle the mixture on the surface. Repeat and let sit overnight.
3 In the morning, wipe the mixture and the grease away, rinsing well to remove any filmy residue.
4 For stubborn, burned-on stains, scour with salt and an abrasive pad.

Fabric gel wash

The old-fashioned method of washing clothes in pure soap is still one of the most reliable ways of getting them clean. This fabric gel, with its built-in water softener, is particularly good for washing in hard water.

- ◆ **2 cups pure soap flakes**
- ◆ **1½ cups borax**
- ◆ **1½ quarts (6 cups) water**
- ◆ **½ cup glycerin**
- ◆ **2 teaspoons essential oil of eucalyptus, lemon, or lavender (available at health-food or aromatherapy stores)**

1 In a saucepan, stir together the soap flakes, borax, and water. Heat gently and stir until the liquid is clear. Add the glycerin and cool to lukewarm.
2 Add the essential oil and stir thoroughly.
3 Pour into a widemouthed jar or other container and cover until needed. Add a cupful to the washing machine, making sure that the soap is fully dissolved before adding any clothing. For best effect, use this gel with warm or hot water.

NATURAL STAIN STOPPERS

Stubborn stains need extra care. But that doesn't mean you have to make a costly investment in store-bought products. Look no further than your household shelves for these stain stoppers.

BLOOD, CHOCOLATE, OR COFFEE. Soak soiled article overnight in a solution of ¼ cup borax and 2 cups cold water. Wash as usual the next day.

GREASE. Apply a paste of cornstarch and water. Let dry, then brush away the powder and grease.

RED WINE. Sprinkle stain with salt; let sit for several hours. When dry, brush away salt and wash, or clean immediately with club soda or seltzer.

GRASS. Soak stain in a 3 percent solution of hydrogen peroxide, then wash.

INK ON A WHITE SHIRT. Wet fabric with cold water and apply a paste of cream of tartar and lemon juice one hour before washing.

SCORCH MARKS. Rub area with a cut raw onion. After the onion juice has been absorbed, soak the stain in water for a few hours.

Fabric softener

Use this simple treatment to make fabrics soft and fluffy.

- ◆ **¼ cup baking soda**
- ◆ **½ cup white vinegar**

1 Fill the washing machine with water.
2 Add the baking soda and then the clothing.
3 During the final rinse cycle, add the vinegar (pour it into the softener dispenser, if your washing machine has one).

VARIATIONS You can also soften clothes by adding ½ cup baking soda during the wash cycle or simply use one part soap flakes and one part borax to wash the clothes, putting the mixture in the water in the washing machine before you add the clothes.

All-purpose cleanser and disinfectant

This spray is great for both kitchen and bathroom surfaces. It works double duty, cutting grease and grime while killing germs.

- ◆ **1 teaspoon borax**
- ◆ **½ teaspoon washing soda**
- ◆ **2 tablespoons lemon juice**

1 In a pint spray bottle, combine the ingredients. Add 1 cup very hot water and shake well to mix and dissolve the dry ingredients.
2 To use, simply spray on the surface and wipe off with a sponge or rag. This solution can be stored indefinitely.

Mildew remover

Stubborn mildew on material often resists ordinary washing. Use this solution to get rid of it. Do not use it on dark or colored items, however, as lemon juice can bleach fabric.

- ◆ **2 parts salt**
- ◆ **1 part lemon juice**

1 Wash the fabric in warm soapy water, then mix salt and lemon juice, enough to cover the mildewed area, and apply it.
2 Place the article in full sun, rinsing it after several hours. If the stain persists, repeat.

Homemade soft scrubber

This nonabrasive scrub disinfects and helps eliminate mold.

- ◆ **¼ cup borax**
- ◆ **vegetable oil–based liquid soap (available at health-food stores)**
- ◆ **½ teaspoon lemon essential oil (available at health-food or aromatherapy stores)**

In a small bowl, mix the borax with enough soap to form a creamy paste. Add the lemon oil and blend well. Scoop a small amount of the mixture onto a sponge, wash the surface, and rinse well.

Mold remover

Borax is a natural mold retardant. If you live in an area where the humidity levels are high, try adding a cupful to your soapy water whenever you wash down the walls.

- ½ **cup borax**
- ½ **cup vinegar**
- **1 cup water**

In a spray bottle, combine the ingredients and spray generously on moldy surfaces. Wipe clean with a damp sponge.

Septic toilet activator

If persistent odors from a septic system indicate the absence of sufficient sewage-digesting bacteria, flush this mixture down the toilet.

- **1 quart hot water (105° to 115°F)**
- **1 pound brown sugar**
- **2 teaspoons dried yeast**

Dissolve the brown sugar in the hot water and leave until it is lukewarm. Stir in the yeast, then immediately flush the mixture down the toilet.

Air-freshener spray

This spray is strong and needs to be applied judiciously. You want a room to have a hint of this spicy scent, not an overpowering perfume. You'll find these essential oils at health-food or aromatherapy stores.

- ¼ **cup isopropyl alcohol**
- **25 drops bergamot essential oil**
- **8 drops clove essential oil**
- **5 drops lemon essential oil**
- **1 cup distilled water**

1 In a spray bottle, combine the alcohol and the essential oils and shake well to disperse the oils. Add the distilled water and shake for a minute or two more to thoroughly blend all the ingredients.
2 Let sit for at least a few days before using, to allow the fragrance to mature. A quick spritz is usually all that is needed to freshen a room.

Herbal carpet freshener

Many commercial air and carpet deodorizers work to mask odors by deadening the nerves associated with your sense of smell. To freshen carpets, opt for this natural formula instead.

- **1 cup baking soda**
- ½ **cup lavender flowers**

1 Crush the lavender flowers to release their scent.
2 Mix well with the baking soda and sprinkle liberally on carpets.
3 After 30 minutes, vacuum carpets.

Upholstery shampoo

Use this shampoo on a regular basis to freshen up furniture fabric that gets a lot of use.

- **6 tablespoons pure soap flakes**
- **2 tablespoons borax**
- **1 pint boiling water**

1 In a large bowl, mix the soap flakes and borax together. Slowly add the boiling water, stirring well to thoroughly dissolve the dry ingredients.
2 Let cool, then whip into a foamy consistency with an egg beater.
3 Brush dry suds onto the furniture, concentrating on soiled areas. Quickly wipe them off with a damp sponge.

Simple silver polish

Clean your silver with good old toothpaste! You can even use the recipe for our homemade toothpaste (p.182), but be sure to omit the food coloring and, if you wish, the minty flavoring.

- **white toothpaste (do not use a gel variety)**
- **old soft-bristle toothbrush**

1 Apply the toothpaste to the surface of the silver with an old soft-bristle toothbrush and gently scrub away the tarnish.
2 Rinse silver with warm water and dry immediately with a soft cloth.

ROOM FRESHENERS

Tuck lavender or southernwood sachets into clothing and linen drawers to repel moths and keep contents smelling clean and fresh.

Put a drop of your favorite essential oil directly onto the wood in dresser drawers. The wood absorbs the oil and releases the scent gradually.

Hang sachets of aromatic herbs from door handles or in a sunny window. Pack a small decorative pillow with pine needles; put it among the sofa pillows to freshen the den.

Place a porous pottery jar filled with essential oil near a sunny window. The heat will dissipate the oil, releasing the scent. Replace oil often.

Simmer a blend of cloves, cinnamon sticks, and dried orange peel in 4 cups of water to give a warm, spicy scent to your home on winter days.

Top a lightbulb with a drop or two of your favorite essential oil or scent. The heat from the bulb will release the aroma for hours.

Drain cleanser

Slow drains? Use this drain cleanser once a week to keep drains fresh and clog-free.

- ½ **cup baking soda**
- **1 cup white vinegar**
- **1 gallon hot water**

Pour baking soda down the drain, then vinegar. Allow the mixture to foam for several minutes before flushing the drain with hot water.

Disposal cleanser

Keep your garbage disposal smelling fresh with this useful tip.

- **half of a used lemon**

Drop the lemon into the disposal and run the motor until the lemon is pulverized and washed down the drain.

Dishwashing liquid

You don't need expensive detergents to get dishes clean. Used with hot water, this liquid gel cleans dishes beautifully without creating unnecessary suds. Do not use in dishwashers.

- ¼ **cup soap flakes**
- **2 cups hot water**
- ¼ **cup glycerin**
- ½ **teaspoon lemon essential oil (available at health-food or aromatherapy stores)**

1 In a bowl, combine the soap flakes and the water and stir until the flakes have dissolved. Cool to lukewarm.
2 Stir in the glycerin and the essential oil and leave to cool. As the mixture cools, it forms a loose gel. Stir with a fork to break up the gel and, using a funnel, pour into a narrow-necked plastic bottle. (An old shampoo bottle makes an excellent storage container.)
3 To use, squirt two to three teaspoonfuls under running water into the sink.

Automatic dishwater soap

If you live in a hard-water area, add the spotless dishwasher rinse (below) to the machine before washing.

- **2 cups borax**
- **2 cups washing soda**

Mix the borax and washing soda and store in a closed plastic container. To use, add 2 tablespoons to the dishwasher soap compartment.

Spotless dishwasher rinse

You can get dishes spot-free in your automatic dishwasher without using chemical rinsing agents.

- **1 to 1½ cups white vinegar**

Add the vinegar to the rinse compartment of your automatic dishwasher, being careful not to overfill. Wash dishes as usual.

The Home Car Wash

Taking your car to a commercial car wash can be a costly habit to maintain—and the results are never as satisfying as when you do it yourself. A car wash also uses up to 10 times the amount of water you would use cleaning the car at home. Try the following solutions to pamper your car— and its finish—in style.

Car wash

This soap is gentle to the car but tough on grime.

- **1 tablespoon vegetable oil– based liquid soap (available at health-food stores)**
- **2 gallons warm water**

1 Combine soap and water in a large pail.
2 Cleaning one section at a time, apply the solution with a large sponge, concentrating on heavily soiled areas. Rinse immediately before moving to a new section.
3 To avoid spotting, dry the car with a chamois or soft flannel cloth.

Car-interior cleanser

This solution is great for cleaning vinyl and leather upholstery. For cloth interiors, try the homemade upholstery shampoo (p.164)

- **2 tablespoons vegetable oil–based soap**
- ¼ **cup olive oil**
- **1 teaspoon lemon essential oil (available at health-food or aromatherapy stores)**

Mix the ingredients well and apply with a sponge. Wipe the windows dry with absorbent towels or a soft flannel cloth.

Windshield cleanser

For streak-free results, always clean your car windows in the shade.

- ½ **cup cornstarch**
- **2 quarts warm water**

Mix the ingredients well and apply with a sponge. Wipe the windows dry with absorbent towels or a soft flannel cloth.

All-natural car wax

Commercial automotive waxes often contain petrochemicals. Try this natural alternative. Please note that turpentine is flammable and can be toxic if swallowed. Store away from heat sources and out of the reach of children.

- **7 tablespoons yellow beeswax**
- **12 tablespoons carnauba wax**
- **2 cups mineral oil**
- **4 tablespoons turpentine**
- **1 tablespoon pine oil**

1 Using a double boiler, melt the waxes together.
2 Remove from the heat and allow to cool slightly before stirring in the turpentine and the oils.
3 Pour into metal cans that have secure lids (old coffee cans with plastic lids work well). Cool, uncovered, to room temperature. When cool, close the cans securely.
4 To use, scoop a small amount of wax onto a soft cloth or rag. Using a circular motion, rub the wax into the car's finish. Allow to sit for several minutes before buffing to a show-room shine.

VARIATION Don't throw those old cotton socks away! Save to use as perfect waxing and buffing cloths—then discard.

Chrome polish

All you need to make your automobile's chrome shine is a handful of aluminum foil and a little elbow grease.

- **aluminum foil**

To remove rust from chrome bumpers, simply wad up a piece of aluminum foil and rub it over the spot vigorously.

Looking Good Feeling Good

*B*eauty and body-care products based on plant extracts instead of synthetic ingredients are growing in popularity. You may have discovered that natural skin- and body-care products can be expensive. But the good news is that at home in your own kitchen you can make beauty products that are every bit as effective as the commercial versions—the ingredients are readily available and relatively inexpensive.

Preparations for women, men, and children; bath oils and lotions for the skin and hair; and even fragrances are included in this compendium of time-honored formulas. Because they are made of herbal extracts and infusions, these products are kinder to the skin than many factory-prepared products. Best of all, you know exactly what each contains because you have made it yourself.

This chapter also contains eight pages of home remedies to treat such common complaints as stuffy noses, calluses, and minor burns. So choose from among these traditional recipes to help yourself and your family to look good and feel good, too.

BEFORE YOU BEGIN...

*Making your own cosmetics and remedies offers many satisfactions. All of our recipes
are quick, easy, and inexpensive to make. Because you control the content of your health and beauty
regimen, you can be sure the products you use are pure, natural, and entirely suitable for you.*

MOST of the ingredients used in these recipes can be obtained easily. Look in pharmacies, health food stores, plant nurseries, or special mail-order outlets recommended by health food stores: buy the best-quality ingredients that you can find. It's even possible to grow some ingredients yourself—we provide details for growing scented herbs in Chapter 5.

Read and follow the recipes carefully. Take note of the ingredient lists and don't exceed the recommended amounts. In particular, don't confuse "oils" with "essential oils." Oils, such as almond, olive, and vegetable oils, are derived primarily from seeds. They are nonvolatile and are often called fixed oils. Essential oils, which are obtained by distilling leaves or flowers, are volatile and flammable; they evaporate at low temperatures and are potentially toxic if inhaled or used incorrectly. Most essential oils must be diluted in a fixed oil before they are applied to the skin. Lavender and tea-tree oils are exceptions but should be used sparingly.

Equipment
You need only basic kitchen equipment for making beauty and skin-care products. To avoid any chance of contaminating food, it's better not to use your everyday cookware. If possible, buy secondhand equipment and store it separately. If this is not practical, clean your kitchen equipment thoroughly before and after use. Any wooden spoons or other tools made of absorbent materials should be purchased new and used solely for the purpose of making skin-care products. Store them away from the spoons and tools you use for cooking.

For heating and boiling, avoid using uncoated aluminum, iron, or copper pots and pans. They can react chemically with the materials you are using and affect their color and odor. Safe, nonreactive cooking materials include stainless steel, glass, coated aluminum, and ironware that is protected with an enamel or nonstick surface. Take care that enamel and nonstick surfaces are not seriously chipped or scratched.

Spoons should also be of a nonreactive material. Use a stainless-steel spoon for measuring and a wooden or stainless-steel spoon for stirring the mixtures.

Any bottles and jars you use for storing materials and products must be cleaned and sterilized properly before filling. Lids should be nonporous, to prevent evaporation—metal or plastic screw-on tops, glass stoppers, or plastic lids that snap on securely are fine. A cork stopper on its own may be too porous for storing some products satisfactorily. Make a cork stopper airtight by covering it with plastic wrap.

A stainless-steel funnel is ideal for straining and pouring liquids into bottles; some plastics are damaged by concentrated essential oils. Be sure that you clean the funnel well immediately after use.

Sterilizing and labeling
To sterilize jars and bottles for cosmetic products or for foods that you are putting up, follow the step-by-step method that is illustrated below. If you are using plastic containers or lids that cannot withstand very high heat, wash them well in hot, soapy water, then dry them thoroughly. Keep them covered with a cloth until needed. Also wash and dry all bowls, saucepans, and utensils before using them. Keep in mind that it is easier to keep metal and glass bowls and utensils scrupulously clean and oil-free than it is plastic products.

STERILIZING JARS

1 *Wash the jars and their lids thoroughly in warm, soapy water. Use a bottle brush to be sure you scrub all the surfaces.*

2 *Rinse the bottles and lids in a separate step. You want to rid them of any soap or detergent scum—for taste as well as chemical reactions.*

3 *Place clean jars and lids in a pot of water (use a canning pot and rack, if you have them). Bottles must be totally submerged. Bring water to a full boil.*

4 *Boil 10 minutes at altitudes of 1,000 feet above sea level or less. Add 1 minute for each extra 1,000 feet. Use jars direct from the pot, or drain on a clean towel.*

SAFETY TIPS

You can use an electric mixer to blend ingredients, but be sure to clean the beaters thoroughly before using them for cooking.

Use bottles that hold exact amounts of a product in order to minimize contact with air. When you have used a good portion of the product, transfer the remainder to a smaller bottle.

Use amber-colored bottles to protect products against light. Store in a cool, dark place; for the long term, a refrigerator is best.

When making products as gifts, be sure to include a list of the ingredients on the label. If possible, check beforehand whether the recipients of your gifts are allergic to any of the ingredients you may be using.

You need very little specialized equipment to make beauty and health products at home. All that's required is basic kitchen equipment plus bottles and jars for storage, some common herbs and flowers from your garden or a nursery, and a few ingredients from your health food store or pharmacy.

Be sure to label everything you make with its name and/or ingredients and the date on which it was prepared and bottled. Labeling is important because many oils and preparations look very similar. Some products must be used within a certain period of time.

Storing natural products

Heat, moisture, light, and contact with air can all cause natural products to deteriorate. Keep the products in a cool, dark place such as the refrigerator, or in a closed cupboard if you are storing in quantity.

Because these recipes do not include preservatives, you must check products regularly to be certain they have not deteriorated. Pronounced discoloration or an unusual smell will indicate that a product's constituents may have broken down. If this should occur, discard the product immediately without using it. In general, unless you intend the product for family use, it is best to make only small batches of a product that will last for only a short period of time.

A word of caution

While skin reactions and other side effects are not common with natural products, some can occur because of allergies. Effects can include rashes, nausea, sneezing, skin irritation, and breathing difficulties. If you experience any of these, stop using the product.

When making your own skin- and hair-care products:

1 Do not exceed the recommended amount of ingredients.

2 Do not swallow or even taste essential oils. Keep bottles and jars sealed and out of the reach of children.

3 If an essential oil is accidentally swallowed, do not induce vomiting. Give the affected person a glass of water and seek medical advice and/or take the person to a hospital immediately.

4 Do not use essential oils without professional advice if you have a chronic or acute disorder such as heart disease, epilepsy, asthma, diabetes, or kidney disease. Do not use essential oils on young children or while you are pregnant.

5 Certain herbs may cause allergic reactions in some people. Should this be a cause for concern, patch-test each herb or product before using it. Apply a small amount of the product to the tender skin under the upper arm above the elbow or in the crease of the elbow and wait several hours or overnight. If redness, swelling, or any other form of irritation occurs, do not use the herb or product.

◆ Total Body Treatment ◆

Soothe your skin and indulge your senses with creams and lotions you can make yourself. You'll feel silken and scented all over—naturally.

Soothing footbath

At the end of the day, give tired feet a real treat— soak them in a reviving footbath. Relaxing the feet can have a calming effect on the whole body.

- ◆ **1 tablespoon sea salt**
- ◆ **2 drops lavender essential oil**
- ◆ **1 drop rosemary essential oil**
- ◆ **1 drop bay essential oil**
- ◆ **1 drop geranium essential oil**
- ◆ **rose petals (optional)**

You will need a large basin or wide-bottomed bowl and a bath towel.

1 Fill the basin with enough warm water to cover the feet.

2 Stir the sea salt into the warm water until it dissolves (use your toes to stir, if you wish). Add the essential oils, mixing them in well. For a little luxury and a pleasant aroma, float scented rose petals on the surface.

3 Soak your feet in the basin for about 10 minutes, or until the water has cooled. Pat your feet dry with the towel. Finish off by massaging the feet with Eucalyptus Foot Lotion (recipe at right), taking time to massage the toes well.
MAKES ENOUGH FOR 1 FOOTBATH

Leg massage cream

This soothing cream will help to firm and moisturize the skin, keeping it soft and supple. Massage it over your toes, feet, ankles, legs, and knees, using firm upward strokes.

- ◆ **3 tablespoons anhydrous (water-free) lanolin**
- ◆ **1½ ounces olive oil**
- ◆ **2 tablespoons apricot oil**

To start, you will need a nonreactive double boiler, a wooden spoon, and a steril-ized 4-ounce jar with a tight-fitting lid.

1 In the top of the double boiler, over low heat, warm all the ingredients together until the lanolin has liquefied. Stir for several minutes with the wooden spoon.

2 Pour the mixture into the jar and allow to cool. Keep in a cool, dark place.
MAKES ABOUT 4 OUNCES

Eucalyptus foot lotion

The feet are very often neglected when it comes to moisturizing, and the skin can easily become cracked. Rubbed regularly into the heels and feet, this lotion will soften the skin.

- ◆ **1 tablespoon almond oil**
- ◆ **1 teaspoon avocado oil**
- ◆ **1 teaspoon wheat-germ oil**
- ◆ **10 drops eucalyptus essential oil**

Put all of the ingredients in a small, sterilized glass bottle with a tight-fitting stopper. Shake the liquid vigorously until it is completely combined. Store the bottle in a cool, dark place. Shake well before using.
MAKES ABOUT 1 OUNCE

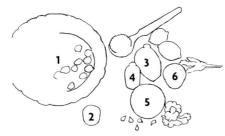

Give the skin and body protection and nourishment with these natural products: **1** *Soothing footbath,* **2** *Lemon hand cream,* **3** *Quick and easy hand lotion,* **4** *Eucalyptus foot lotion,* **5** *Leg massage cream, and* **6** *Gardener's hand cream.*

170

Lemon hand cream

A fresh-smelling, soothing, and smoothing cream to protect and help repair damaged skin.

- ◆ **1 to 2 tablespoons fresh or 1 to 2 teaspoons dried lemongrass**
- ◆ **1¼ cups boiling water**
- ◆ **2 tablespoons apricot oil**
- ◆ **4 teaspoons avocado oil**
- ◆ **1 teaspoon wheat-germ oil**
- ◆ **½ ounce beeswax**
- ◆ **2 teaspoons lemon juice**

You will need a heatproof ceramic or glass bowl, a fine sieve, 2 nonreactive saucepans, a nonreactive double boiler, a wooden spoon, and two sterilized 6- to 8-ounce glass jars with tight-fitting lids.

1 In the ceramic bowl place the lemongrass and add the boiling water to make an infusion. Cover and allow to steep for 15 minutes.

2 Into one of the saucepans, strain the water and heat to lukewarm. In the other saucepan, heat the oils to lukewarm.

3 In the top of the double boiler, over simmering water, melt the beeswax completely. With the wooden spoon, stir in the warmed oils; then, drop by drop, stir in 4 teaspoons of the warmed infusion.

4 Remove from the heat, add the lemon juice, and beat until thick and smooth.

5 Pour into the jars. Keep one handy for use and the other in the refrigerator until needed.

MAKES ABOUT 15 OUNCES

Moisturizing body lotion

Soothe and repair dry, scaly skin with this easily prepared lotion. Shake well before use.

- ◆ **3 tablespoons glycerin**
- ◆ **3 tablespoons rosewater**
- ◆ **1 tablespoon almond oil**
- ◆ **1 teaspoon wheat-germ oil**
- ◆ **1 teaspoon jojoba oil**

Put all ingredients in a sterilized 4-ounce jar with a tight-fitting lid. Shake vigorously until mixed. Store in a cool, dark place.

MAKES ABOUT 4 OUNCES

FOOT CARE

For all-day comfort, it's important to take special care of your feet. Hardened skin around the heels and odor from perspiration are common problems. You can minimize their effects with a few easy steps:

To deodorize shoes, sprinkle the insides with a small amount of powdered camomile every day, brushing the powder out before wearing. Another trick is to fill a spare pair of socks with a mixture of coarsely crushed dried herbs and spices—any combination of rosemary, bay leaves, cinnamon sticks, whole cloves, orange peel, lemon peel, thyme, lavender, and pine needles. Tie the socks at the top and leave them in the shoes between wearings. For a gift, fill a new pair of socks with the mixture and tie with ribbons.

To soften hard skin on the soles of the feet or the backs of the heels, massage in equal quantities of olive oil and apple cider vinegar.

Treat a fungal infection between the toes with applications of cider vinegar diluted with an equal amount of water over the affected area. Or use a fungicide made by diluting 2 drops tea tree essential oil with ½ teaspoon water.

For a quick foot treatment, when you don't have time for a separate footbath, rub the feet with a mixture of apple cider vinegar and water in equal amounts. Or you can massage 1 to 2 drops of rosemary essential oil diffused in a teaspoonful of vegetable oil into the feet for 5 minutes before you take your bath.

Gardener's hand cream

Apply this special cream before bedtime after a day in the garden, and your hands will be cared for while you sleep. Rub some into your hands each time you set out to work in the garden for added protection.

- ◆ **2 tablespoons avocado oil**
- ◆ **1 tablespoon honey**
- ◆ **2 teaspoons glycerin**
- ◆ **about 1½ cups finely ground almonds or rolled oats**

You will need a ceramic bowl, a spoon, and a pair of washable cotton gloves.

1 In the bowl, thoroughly mix the avocado oil, honey, and glycerin. Stir in a sufficient amount of almonds or oatmeal to form a thin paste.

2 Rub the paste over the hands; then put on the gloves and wear them overnight. The gloves can be washed and reused. Store the excess in a small jar with a tight-fitting lid.

MAKES ENOUGH FOR A FEW APPLICATIONS

Rose and honey body lotion

Apply this gentle lotion regularly to protect your skin and to replace natural oils lost through swimming, bathing, and exposure to the sun.

- ◆ **¼ to ½ cup fresh or 1 to 2 teaspoons dried rose petals**
- ◆ **1¼ cups boiling water**
- ◆ **1 cup distilled or boiled water**
- ◆ **1 teaspoon quince seeds, available through mail order**
- ◆ **⅓ cup almond oil**
- ◆ **2 teaspoons avocado oil**
- ◆ **2 teaspoons wheat-germ oil**
- ◆ **1 teaspoon honey**
- ◆ **5 drops geranium essential oil**

You will need a medium-size heatproof ceramic or glass bowl, a fine sieve, a cup, a nonreactive saucepan, a stainless-steel spoon, a dessert bowl, and a sterilized 8-ounce glass jar with a tight-fitting lid.

1 In the bowl, place the rose petals and add the boiling water to make an infusion. Cover and leave for 15 to 20 minutes.

2 Strain the infusion into the cup.

3 In the saucepan, over moderate heat, bring the distilled water and quince seeds slowly to a boil. Simmer for about 15 minutes, stirring to prevent sticking. The mixture will thicken into a gel. Using the back of the spoon, push the gel through the sieve into the dessert bowl. The seeds can be dried and used again.

4 In the saucepan, combine the infusion and the almond, avocado, and wheat-germ oils. Warm over low heat; then stir in the honey until combined. Remove from the heat and allow to cool.

5 Add 2 ½ ounces of the quince gel. Then add the geranium essential oil, 1 drop at a time. Finish by stirring the mixture until smooth.

6 Pour the body lotion into the jar. Store in a cool, dark place.

MAKES ABOUT 8 OUNCES

Cellulite massage oil

Good diet and regular exercise are the first defenses against cellulite, but an effective massage oil may also be beneficial. Regular massage with this oil may help increase circulation and break down fatty deposits.

- ◆ **2 tablespoons almond oil**
- ◆ **½ teaspoon jojoba oil**
- ◆ **½ teaspoon carrot oil, available through mail order**
- ◆ **14 drops geranium essential oil**
- ◆ **6 drops lemongrass essential oil**
- ◆ **4 drops cypress essential oil, available through mail order**

You will need a sterilized 1-ounce glass jar with a tight-fitting cover.

1 Put all the ingredients in the jar and shake vigorously to combine.

2 After a bath or shower, pat the skin dry and massage a small amount of the oil on cellulite-affected areas, using circular movements. Use ¼ to ½ teaspoon, depending on the size of the area you are treating. Apply only once a day and do not exceed the recommended amount.

MAKES ABOUT 1 OUNCE

Herbal deodorant

This pleasant deodorant will control odor and inhibit the growth of some microorganisms that thrive on perspiration. Choose from rosemary, thyme, lavender, sage, spearmint, eucalyptus leaves, marjoram, and scented rose petals.

- ◆ **⅓ cup cider vinegar**
- ◆ **⅓ cup distilled or boiled water**
- ◆ **3 tablespoons dried herbs or flower petals of choice**
- ◆ **⅓ cup rosewater**

You will need a nonreactive saucepan, heat-proof ceramic or glass bowl, and a sterilized 10-ounce bottle with a tight-fitting stopper.

1 In the saucepan, heat the cider vinegar and water to just below boiling.

2 Place the herbs or flower petals in the bowl, and pour the heated liquid over them. Cover and allow to steep for 15 to 20 minutes.

3. Strain the liquid into the bottle, then add the rosewater. Shake to combine. Store in a cool, dark place. Use within a few days and make more as needed. When making more, vary the herbs to prevent bacteria from developing a resistance to the deodorant.

MAKES ABOUT 10 OUNCES

Summer body splash

An invigorating body splash for those hot, humid days and nights of summer.

- ◆ **⅓ cup vodka**
- ◆ **10 drops lavender essential oil**
- ◆ **10 drops lime essential oil**
- ◆ **5 drops lemon essential oil**
- ◆ **5 drops lemongrass essential oil**
- ◆ **2 cups distilled or boiled water**

You will need a sterilized 20-ounce bottle with a tight-fitting stopper (or several small sterilized bottles), a ceramic or glass bowl, a sieve, and a paper coffee filter.

1 Pour the vodka and essential oils into the bottle. Seal and shake for several minutes.

2 Add the distilled or boiled water and shake for several minutes. Set aside for at least 48 hours (3 weeks for a better fragrance).

3 Place the coffee filter in a sieve and let the liquid drip through it into the bowl. Then pour the liquid back into the bottle or into a few small sterilized bottles. Keep one bottle in the refrigerator and store others in a cool, dark place until needed.

MAKES ABOUT 20 OUNCES

Quick and easy hand lotion

An old favorite valued by generations of women long before the advent of cosmetics companies and commercial hand creams. Massage regularly into your hands.

- ◆ **⅔ cup rosewater**
- ◆ **⅓ cup glycerin**

Pour the ingredients into a sterilized 8-ounce bottle with a tight-fitting stopper. Shake vigorously to combine. Keep the lotion in a cool, dark place.

MAKES 8 OUNCES

PRACTICAL IDEAS

HAND-CARE HINTS

Wipe the hands with the cut flesh of a lemon to lighten skin discolorations. Add granulated sugar to the lemon juice and rub into the backs of the hands to remove dead cells.

Massage a little avocado flesh into the hands and cuticles as a moisturizer.

When using rubber gloves for chores, wear a pair of cotton gloves inside to keep hands dry.

To shine nails, dust with cornstarch and polish vigorously with a chamois cloth.

Rub untidy cuticles with Lemon hand cream (facing page), then gently push back.

Eat lots of seafood, nuts, lean meat, and raw fruit and vegetables to promote nail health.

File toward the center of the nail in one direction only. Use an emery board, not a metal nail file.

◆ Bath time Indulgences ◆

Sink into bliss as you spoil yourself with these delightfully scented bath salts, bubble baths, soaps, and scrubs. You know they're pure because you've made them yourself. Presented in a pretty bottle, any one of them would make a wonderful gift.

Almond-oatmeal body scrub
This natural body scrub will remove dead skin cells, improving skin tone and texture.

- ◆ **2 to 3 aloe vera leaves**
- ◆ **2 tablespoons honey**
- ◆ **2 drops geranium essential oil**
- ◆ **2 drops palmarosa essential oil, available through mail order**
- ◆ **1 cup almonds, ground**
- ◆ **1 cup rolled oats, ground**

You will need 2 ceramic or glass bowls, a small stainless-steel spoon, and a sterilized 8-ounce bottle or jar with a tight-fitting lid.
1 Cut the aloe leaves in half lengthwise and scoop out 1 to 2 tablespoons of the clear gel (the pigmented gel can be irritating) into a bowl. Mix in the honey and essential oils.
2 Place the almonds and oatmeal in the second bowl. Stir in the liquid, adding a little water as needed to make a thick paste.
3 Use half the paste to rub all over your body, paying special attention to dry-skin areas. Rinse off in the shower. Apply an aromatic body oil (box, opposite page).
4 Put the remaining paste in the sterilized jar and store in the refrigerator.
MAKES ENOUGH FOR 2 APPLICATIONS

Fragrant bath powder
A delightfully aromatic powder to use after a bath. Choose your favorite essential oil.

- ◆ **⅓ cup rice flour**
- ◆ **⅓ cup cornstarch**
- ◆ **5 to 10 drops essential oil**

You will need a food processor or blender, a spoon, and a container for storage.

1 Blend all the ingredients in the processor or blender for 1 minute (or shake the ingredients in a clean, covered jar for several minutes).
2 Allow the powder to settle. Spoon into a clean, dry container and set the mixture aside for 2 weeks before use.
MAKES ABOUT ⅔ CUP

Rose-scented bubble bath
A mixture that feeds and softens the skin. Shake it well and add a teaspoonful to your bath while the water is running, then lie back and relax.

- ◆ **1 to 2 tablespoons dried rose petals**
- ◆ **1 quart boiling water**
- ◆ **1 cup pure soap flakes**
- ◆ **1½ ounces glycerin**
- ◆ **2 teaspoons almond oil**
- ◆ **1 teaspoon wheat-germ oil**
- ◆ **1 teaspoon geranium essential oil**
- ◆ **2 tablespoons witch hazel lotion**

You will need a large heatproof ceramic or glass bowl, a fine sieve, a nonreactive saucepan, a stainless-steel spoon, and 1 or more clean, airtight plastic bottles.
1 Place the petals in the bowl and pour the boiling water over them. Cover and leave for 15 to 20 minutes. Then strain into the saucepan.
2 Heat the water over medium heat; add the soap and stir until it dissolves.
3 Place the glycerin, almond and wheat-germ oils, the geranium essential oil, and witch hazel lotion in the bowl. Mix well, then add the soap mixture and stir well.
4 Pour into small bottles. Keep one in the bathroom and the others in a cool, dark place until needed.
MAKES ABOUT 32 OUNCES

Bubble bath for kids
Wash away grime and make bath time fun with this fresh bubble bath. Shake, then add three tablespoonfuls while the tap is running.

- ◆ **2 tablespoons dried rose petals**
- ◆ **2 tablespoons dried lavender flower heads**
- ◆ **1¼ cups boiling water**
- ◆ **1¼ cups natural baby shampoo**
- ◆ **12 drops lavender essential oil**

You will need 2 bowls, a fine sieve, and 1 or more clean, airtight plastic bottles.
1 Place the rose petals and lavender in a bowl and add the boiling water. Cover and allow to steep for 15 to 20 minutes.
2 Strain the water into the other bowl, squeezing all liquid out of the petals and flower heads. Add the shampoo and essential oil.
3 Pour into bottles and shake for several minutes. Keep a bottle handy by the bathtub. Store extra bottles in a cool, dark place.
MAKES ABOUT 20 OUNCES

Rosemary shower gel
For a gentle cleansing and softening effect, rub this rosemary gel all over your body while showering.

- ◆ **4 to 6 teaspoons dried lavender flower heads**
- ◆ **4 to 6 teaspoons dried rosemary**
- ◆ **4 to 6 teaspoons dried chamomile**
- ◆ **1 quart boiling water**
- ◆ **1¼ cups pure soap flakes**
- ◆ **10 to 20 drops lavender essential oil**

You will need a nonreactive saucepan, 2 heat-proof ceramic or glass bowls, a fine sieve, a wooden spoon, a potato masher, and 2 or 3 clean, widemouthed plastic bottles with tight-fitting lids.

1 Put the lavender flowers, rosemary, and chamomile into one bowl and add half the boiling water to make an infusion. Cover and steep for 15 to 20 minutes. Strain this water into the other bowl, squeezing all liquid from the herbs.

2 Place the soap flakes in the saucepan, and pour the remaining water over them. Stir continuously over low heat to dissolve the soap (use a potato masher if necessary); keep below the simmering point. Add the infusion and stir until well blended. Remove from the heat.

3 When the mixture has started to cool, stir in the lavender essential oil, a drop at a time, until sufficiently scented. Pour into the bottles and allow to set until a soft gel has formed. Keep in a cool, dark place until needed.

MAKES ABOUT 1 ½ CUPS

Almond-rose soap

Use this fragrant soap to clean the skin gently and remove dead cells from its surface.

- ◆ **2 tablespoons dried red rose petals**
- ◆ **8 ounces pure soap flakes**
- ◆ **⅔ cup boiling water**
- ◆ **½ cup rosewater**
- ◆ **2 tablespoons ground almonds**
- ◆ **9 drops geranium essential oil**

You will need a mortar and pestle, a metal mixing bowl, a wooden spoon, and wax paper.

1 Pound the petals with a mortar and pestle.

2 In the bowl, mix the soap, petals, and water and stir until smooth (if the soap starts to solidify, place the bowl over near-boiling water). Stir in the rosewater and ground almonds; leave to cool.

3 Mix in the essential oil. Shape into 6 balls and flatten them slightly; allow the soap to harden between sheets of wax paper. Keep unused soap in a cool, dark place until needed.

MAKES 6 SOAP CAKES

Relaxing bath salts

These bath salts are easy to make and a joy to use. Add two handfuls to the bath.

- ◆ **1 pound baking soda**
- ◆ **1 tablespoon dried lavender or rose petals**
- ◆ **8 drops lavender essential oil**
- ◆ **8 drops geranium essential oil**

You will need a ceramic or glass bowl, a wooden spoon, and a large, sterilized glass jar with a tight-fitting lid.

1 Place the baking soda and dried petals in the bowl, add the essential oils, and mix thoroughly with the wooden spoon to combine.

2 Pour the salts into the jar and keep in a cool, dark place, handy to the bath.

MAKES ENOUGH FOR ABOUT 5 BATHS

Invigorating bath salts

Use these salts to refresh your body and lift your spirits after a long, hard day.

- ◆ **1 pound baking soda**
- ◆ **8 drops rosemary essential oil**
- ◆ **4 drops rosewood essential oil**
- ◆ **4 drops tangerine essential oil**

Follow the directions for preparing and storing relaxing bath salts (left).

MAKES ENOUGH FOR ABOUT 5 BATHS

AROMATIC BODY OILS

USED regularly after a bath or shower, body oils moisturize the skin and keep it feeling smooth and silky and looking great. Choose the oil blends suited to your skin—and your nose—from the list on the right.

Put the ingredients in a small, sterilized glass jar and shake the mixture well. Pour a little oil into your palm, rub your hands together, and apply to the rest of your body, skipping the eye area. Use firm, circular movements on the chest, stomach, and buttocks, and firm upward strokes on the arms and legs.

Each blend is sufficient for four body rubs. Store in a cool, dark place. To 4 teaspoons of almond oil, add an essential oil appropriate for your skin type.

NORMAL SKIN
8 drops lavender
6 drops geranium
2 drops chamomile

OILY SKIN
10 drops lemon
6 drops geranium
4 drops sandalwood

DRY SKIN
8 drops patchouli
4 drops geranium
2 drops carrot

SENSITIVE SKIN
3 drops geranium
2 drops patchouli

◆ A Pampered Face ◆

The range of natural possibilities seems endless when it comes to facial care.
There's a recipe here to suit every skin type and meet every skin care need—all free of
the chemicals and preservatives that can aggravate allergies.

Rose moisturizing cream

Here is an everyday moisturizer that is especially good for dry or sensitive skin.

- ◆ **2 tablespoons rosewater**
- ◆ **½ cup almond oil**
- ◆ **⅓ ounce beeswax, finely chopped**
- ◆ **2 tablespoons lanolin**
- ◆ **1 vitamin E capsule, 400 IU**
- ◆ **4 drops geranium essential oil**
- ◆ **2 drops red food coloring (optional)**

You will need a nonreactive saucepan, double boiler, wooden spoon, and 6-ounce sterilized widemouthed jar with a tight-fitting lid.
1 Warm the rosewater in the saucepan.
2 Warm the almond oil in the double boiler. Stir in the beeswax and lanolin until melted and combined. Remove from the heat.
3 Add the rosewater, drop by drop, and beat until the mixture is cooled and smooth.
4 Stir in the contents of the vitamin E capsule, the geranium essential oil, and the food coloring, if desired. Stir well until blended.
5 Spoon into jar. Store in a cool, dark place.
MAKES ABOUT 6 OUNCES

Cleansing milk

Suitable for regular use, this gentle cleanser will remove all traces of oil and makeup.

- ◆ **⅔ cup buttermilk**
- ◆ **1 tablespoon each dried elder flowers and lime flowers, available through mail order**
- ◆ **1 teaspoon dried chamomile**
- ◆ **1 tablespoon honey**

You will need a nonreactive saucepan, a spoon, a fine sieve, and a sterilized 2-ounce glass bottle with a tight-fitting lid.
1 In the saucepan, over low heat, bring the milk and dried ingredients to a simmer. Leave on low heat for 30 minutes.
2. Remove from the heat, stir in the honey, and allow to cool.
3 Strain into the bottle and store in a cool, dark place. Use within 7 days. Shake before use.
MAKES ABOUT 1½ OUNCES

Everyday facial moisturizer

This moisturizer will replace natural oils. Choose essential oils to suit your skin type (box, p.179):
normal—6 drops lavender, 2 drops lemon;
dry—6 drops sandalwood, 4 drops geranium;
oily—16 drops geranium, 4 drops juniper;
sensitive—6 drops lavender.

- ◆ **2 tablespoons apricot kernel oil**
- ◆ **1 teaspoon jojoba oil**
- ◆ **1 teaspoon wheat-germ oil**
- ◆ **essential oils of your choice**

Place all the ingredients in a sterilized glass jar with a tight-fitting lid and shake well. Store in a cool, dark place and use within 2 months.
MAKES ABOUT 1½ OUNCES

Galen's cold cream

The original cold cream recipe is believed to have been invented by the Greek doctor and philosopher Galen in the second century A.D.

- ◆ **1 ounce beeswax**
- ◆ **⅓ cup light olive oil**
- ◆ **2 tablespoons distilled water or rosewater**
- ◆ **3 drops geranium essential oil**

You will need a nonreactive double boiler, nonreactive saucepan, wooden spoon, and 5-ounce widemouthed jar with tight-fitting lid.
1 In the double boiler, melt the beeswax. In the saucepan, heat the oil slightly, then pour it into the melted wax. Beat until combined.
2 In the saucepan, heat the water or rosewater, then stir it, drop by drop, into the oil and wax mixture. Remove from the heat and stir until the mixture is cooled and thick. Blend in the essential oil.
3 Spoon mixture into jar and store in a cool, dark place.
MAKES ABOUT 5 OUNCES

Ideal face cleanser

This beautifully scented cleanser is beneficial for all skin types.

- ◆ **¼ cup almond oil**
- ◆ **2 tablespoons sesame oil**
- ◆ **2 teaspoons wheat-germ oil**
- ◆ **4 drops lavender essential oil**
- ◆ **1 drop geranium essential oil**

Place all the ingredients in a 4-ounce sterilized glass bottle with a tight-fitting lid and shake for several minutes. Store in a cool, dark place.
MAKES ABOUT 3⅓ OUNCES

NATURAL FACIAL CARE

If skin tends to be oily, add a few drops of lemon juice to cleansing creams and lotions.

Keep an aloe vera plant on hand. Smooth the gel from the leaves onto the face to refresh the skin.

To make a gentle face cleanser, cover 2 tablespoons crushed soapwort root with 1 quart boiling water and leave for an hour. Strain and bottle.

Crush petals of calendula until they are juicy and rub gently onto irritated areas of skin to relieve irritation and help healing.

If using soap on the face, choose a gentle one containing natural oils, such as Dove. Follow with an herbal toner to remove all traces of soap.

Brush the skin regularly with a soft cosmetic brush designed especially for the face, to stimulate the circulation and remove dead skin.

If your eyes are sensitive to mascara, a small amount of petroleum jelly applied to the lashes with a fingertip gives them the appearance of thickness.

To reduce puffiness under the eyes, soak a couple of tea bags in boiling water for a moment. Let cool; then place over the eyes for 10 to 15 minutes.

Use these preparations to give your face a fresh, healthy glow: **1** *Galen's cold cream,* **2** *Rose moisturizing cream,* **3** *Antiwrinkle eye cream,* **4** *Peppermint moisturizing lotion,* **5** *Basic skin toner, and* **6** *Cleansing milk.*

Antiwrinkle eye cream

Avoiding the eye itself, gently apply this cream around the eye area with small, circular strokes.

- **2 tablespoons elder flower water, available through mail order**
- **¼ cup avocado oil**
- **2 tablespoons almond oil**
- **4 teaspoons wheat-germ oil**
- **2 tablespoons lanolin**
- **2 teaspoons glycerin**
- **2 drops geranium essential oil**
- **1 vitamin E capsule, 400 IU**

You will need a nonreactive saucepan, a nonreactive double boiler, a wooden spoon, and a sterilized, widemouthed 6-ounce glass jar with a tight-fitting lid.

1 In the saucepan, over low heat, warm the elder-flower water.

2 In top of double boiler, over simmering water, warm the avocado, almond, and wheat-germ oils. Stir in the lanolin until melted, then remove from the heat. Gradually beat in the warmed elder-flower water.

3 Stir in the glycerin, geranium essential oil, and the contents of the vitamin E capsule. Pour into jar and store in a cool, dark place.

MAKES ABOUT 6 OUNCES

Treatment for large pores

After washing face, morning and night, gently dab this mixture on the skin to tighten large pores.

- **1 teaspoon dried sage leaves**
- **1 teaspoon dried yarrow leaves**
- **1 teaspoon dried witch hazel**
- **1¼ cups boiling water**

You will need a small bowl, a fine sieve, and a sterilized 10-ounce glass bottle with a stopper.

1 Place all the dry ingredients in the bowl and add the boiling water. Cover, and allow to steep for 15 minutes.

2 Strain into the bottle and store in a cool, dark place. Use within 7 days, checking daily to ensure that it is clear and smells fresh.

MAKES ABOUT 10 OUNCES

Peppermint moisturizing lotion

Moisturizing lotions are more easily absorbed than creams because they contain more water. Peppermint gives this lotion a refreshing aroma.

- **1 teaspoon dried peppermint**
- **1⅛ cups boiling water**
- **⅓ cup almond or vegetable oil**
- **1 ounce beeswax, finely chopped**
- **2 drops peppermint essential oil**
- **1 drop green food coloring (optional)**

You will need 2 cups, a fine sieve, a nonreactive double boiler, a wooden spoon, and a sterilized, widemouthed 6-ounce glass jar with a tight-fitting lid.

1 Place the dried peppermint in a cup, and add the boiling water. Cover, and allow to steep for 15 minutes. Strain into the other cup.

2 In the top of a double boiler, over simmering water, warm the almond or vegetable oil. Add the beeswax and stir until melted.

3 Remove from the heat and gradually add about 2 ounces of the infusion, beating continuously until well combined. Stir in the peppermint essential oil and food coloring.

4 Pour into jar and store in a cool, dark place. Apply sparingly, massaging in gently with small, circular strokes.

MAKES ABOUT 6 OUNCES

Rich neck moisturizer

The neck is often neglected, yet it can show the first signs of aging. This recipe has oils that keep the skin supple. Massage in a small amount, from the neckline up to the chin, at least once a day.

- **1 teaspoon dried chamomile**
- **1⅛ cups boiling water**
- **3 tablespoons avocado oil**
- **3 tablespoons almond oil**
- **2 teaspoons jojoba oil**
- **1 ounce beeswax**
- **2 teaspoons glycerin**
- **20 drops lemon essential oil**

You will need 2 cups, a fine sieve, a nonreactive double boiler, a wooden spoon, and a sterilized, widemouthed 6-ounce glass jar with a tight-fitting lid.

1 Place the chamomile in a cup, and add the boiling water. Cover, and allow to steep for 15 minutes. Strain into the other cup.

2 In the top of the double boiler, over simmering water, warm the avocado, almond, and jojoba oils. Add the beeswax. Stir until melted.

3 Remove from the heat and beat in 1 ounce of the warmed infusion, drop by drop, until the mixture thickens and cools. Thoroughly mix in the glycerin and the lemon essential oil.

4 Spoon into jar. Store in a cool, dark place.

MAKES ABOUT 6 OUNCES

APPLYING FACE CREAM

1 *Press the fingers of both hands into the center of the forehead and work the cream slowly outward. Pat gently around the eyes.*

2 *Work the cream in evenly around the jawline, chin, mouth, and cheeks, using small, firm, circular movements.*

3 *Massage the cream over the throat. Use upward strokes, starting from the collarbone and moving up to the chin.*

Basic skin toner

This toner stimulates circulation, reduces oiliness, and refines the pores. Choose essential oils that suit your skin type (box, far right): normal—neroli, geranium, lavender, or palmarosa; dry—neroli, patchouli, sandalwood, or geranium; oily—rosemary, lavender, lemon, or geranium; sensitive—neroli or lavender.

- ◆ **1 teaspoon dried chamomile**
- ◆ **⅓ cup boiling water**
- ◆ **2 drops essential oil**

You will need a cup, a fine sieve, a sterilized 4-ounce glass bottle with a tight-fitting lid, and a paper coffee filter.

1 Place the chamomile and boiling water in the cup. Cover, and allow to steep for 15 minutes.

2 Strain into the bottle. When cool, add the essential oil and shake well to mix. Allow to stand for 48 hours, shaking periodically.

3 Pour the liquid through the filter paper into the cup. Resterilize the bottle and fill. Seal and keep in a cool, dark place until needed.

MAKES ABOUT ⅓ CUP

Scented vinegar toner

Diluted vinegar is an effective toner that also helps protect the skin from infections. Choose herbs or flower petals to suit your skin type (see box, far right): normal—chamomile, lemon balm, spearmint, or rose; dry—violet, rose, jasmine, or borage; oily—lavender, peppermint, rosemary, or marigold; sensitive—borage, violet, parsley, or salad burnet.

- ◆ **1 teaspoon dried or 1 table-spoon fresh herbs or flower petals**
- ◆ **⅓ cup cider vinegar**

You will need 2 sterilized bottles with tight-fitting stoppers, a fine sieve, and a bowl.

1 Place the herbs or flower petals in one bottle and cover with the vinegar. Seal and set aside for about 10 days, until the vinegar is perfumed.

2 Strain the vinegar into the bowl, then pour it into the second bottle. (If you want a stronger fragrance, add fresh herbs or petals and leave for another 10 days; then strain.) Store in a cool, dark place.

3 To use, dilute 1 tablespoon of the scented vinegar with ½ cup distilled or boiled water. Splash liberally on the face as required.

MAKES ABOUT ⅓ CUP

Lip gloss in a tube

Lip gloss protects the lips from cracking and drying. It can be used on its own or over lipstick, in which case it helps extend the life of the lipstick. This recipe shows you how to recycle a used lipstick holder that would usually be thrown away.

- ◆ **2 teaspoons beeswax, finely chopped or grated**
- ◆ **1 teaspoon jojoba oil**
- ◆ **1 teaspoon liquid paraffin**
- ◆ **3 drops geranium essential oil**
- ◆ **1 vitamin E capsule, 400 IU**

You will need a used lipstick holder, paper towels, baking parchment, a small cup, a saucepan, and a thin skewer for stirring.

1 Remove any lipstick residue from the holder—put the residue aside for possible use ("Variations," below). Using a paper towel, wipe the tube clean.

2 Screw the tube downward until the small plastic insert that holds the lipstick is at the bottom. Roll a 2½-inch square of baking parchment into a tube and insert it into the holder until it touches the bottom.

3 Place the cup in the saucepan. Pour water into the saucepan so that it comes partially up the side of the cup. Place the beeswax, jojoba oil, and paraffin in the cup. Gently heat until the beeswax has melted. Remove the cup from the water and allow to cool slightly, stirring continuously.

4 Add the essential oil and the contents of the vitamin E capsule and stir until combined.

5 Pour the mixture into the lipstick holder. Leave in a cool place until the gloss has set.

6 Screw the tube upward and carefully take off the baking parchment (if the stick lifts off,

pour a little melted gloss onto the insert and quickly replace the stick). Test the texture of the gloss. If too soft, remelt and add a little more beeswax. If too hard, remelt and add a little more jojoba oil. You will then need to repeat the process of rolling and inserting the baking-parchment tube.

VARIATIONS To color lip gloss, use some of the residue lipstick—an amount about the size of two peas. Add after the beeswax has melted (Step 3). Stir until the lipstick has melted and the mixture is evenly colored.

To give your lip gloss a little flavor, replace geranium essential oil with a drop of clove or cinnamon essential oil at the end of Step 4.

For a quick but effective lip gloss, melt 2 teaspoons grated beeswax over hot water. Stir in 1 teaspoon jojoba oil and mix well. Let cool slightly and pour into a small sterile container.

KNOW YOUR SKIN TYPE

It's important to know your skin type and how best to care for it. The four main types are normal, dry, oily, and sensitive. Most people have a combination of skin types—for example, basically normal with some oily areas on the forehead, around the nose, and on the chin.

Normal skin is clear, supple, and soft, neither too dry nor too oily. It is not overly sensitive to sun, climate, or the environment.

Dry skin looks dull, feels tight after washing, and needs constant protection and moisturizing to avoid flaking and peeling.

Oily skin might feel soft and supple, but it looks shiny and needs to be cleansed several times a day. Pores are larger than those of either normal or dry skin. This type of skin is often prone to outbreaks of acne.

Sensitive skin reacts badly to sunlight or irritants. It burns easily and may develop rashes, blotches, or spots when exposed to new substances, such as the chemicals often found in commercial skin-cleansing products.

Green herb steam facial

Choose herbs to suit your skin type (box, p.179): normal—lemon balm, spearmint, chamomile; dry— parsley, violets, rose petals; oily—peppermint, sage, lavender. Do not use on sensitive or inflamed skin.

- ◆ **2 handfuls herbs or flowers**
- ◆ **6 cups boiling water**

You will need a large bowl and a towel.
1 Coarsely chop the herbs or flowers and place them in the bowl. Add the boiling water.
2 Lean over the bowl and cover your head and the bowl with a thick towel. Close your eyes and remain under the towel, with your face just above the hot water, for 10 minutes.
3 To finish, splash your face with lukewarm, then cool water. Stay out of the sun for an hour or so.

Honey-almond face scrub

This scrub is good also for areas such as elbows, legs, and hands.

- ◆ **1 tablespoon honey**
- ◆ **2 tablespoons ground almonds**
- ◆ **1 drop geranium essential oil**

You will need a cup, a saucepan, a bowl, and a small stainless-steel spoon.

1 Place the cup in a saucepan of hot water. Warm the honey in the cup. (Alternatively, place the honey in the cup and warm in the microwave.)
2 Place the almonds in the bowl and stir in sufficiently warmed honey to make a spreadable paste. Stir in the essential oil.
3 To apply, first rinse your face with tepid water. Then carefully massage in the scrub, paying attention to any flaky skin. Keep any leftover mixture in the refrigerator, covered with plastic wrap.
MAKES ENOUGH FOR 1 OR 2 APPLICATIONS

Lip balm

Lips often react quickly to extreme forms of weather. This balm will soothe and soften lips affected by sun, dry wind, or cold.

- ◆ **aloe vera leaves**
- ◆ **2 teaspoons distilled water**
- ◆ **2 tablespoons hazelnut oil**
- ◆ **1 teaspoon jojoba oil**
- ◆ **1 teaspoon wheat-germ oil**
- ◆ **1 teaspoon beeswax, finely chopped**
- ◆ **½ teaspoon anhydrous (water-free) lanolin**
- ◆ **2 drops lavender essential oil**
- ◆ **2 drops sandalwood essential oil**

You will need two nonreactive saucepans, a heatproof ceramic or glass bowl, a small stainless-steel spoon, and a sterilized 2-ounce glass jar with a tight-fitting lid.
1 Cut the aloe leaves in half lengthwise and scoop out 2 teaspoons of clear gel. In one saucepan, warm the gel, water, and the three oils over low heat.
2 In a bowl set in hot water in the second saucepan, heat the beeswax and lanolin. Stir until the beeswax is liquefied. Stir in the aloe mixture until combined.
3 Remove the bowl from the water and allow the mix to cool slightly. Stir in the lavender and sandalwood essential oils and beat until cool.
4 Spoon the balm into the sterilized jar and store in a cool place.
MAKES ABOUT 2 OUNCES

REFRIGERATOR FACIALS

S OME of the best cosmetics can be found in the refrigerator. For example, roll an avocado stone around in your hands; then massage the residue into your face and hands to leave them supple. Or use a teaspoonful of mayonnaise to achieve the same almost instant lubricating effect.

Process a few cabbage leaves in a food processor and strain to collect the juice. Use on oily skin to cleanse and tighten the pores. Or mash very soft pears and apply to the face to help clear up oily skin.

Another effective cleanser and pore tightener is watermelon juice. Strain, to remove pulp and seeds; then pat the juice all over the face.

Fresh corn kernels, blended with the corn silk to produce a milky slush, are a skin soother. Strawberries will also soothe the skin—mash two and apply to the face.

Wipe some cut pieces of cucumber or halved grapes over your face for a pleasant, refreshing feel. Or, for a real pick-meup, puree some cucumber in a blender and use the juice as a bracing skin cleanser.

To soften the skin, apply a small amount of mashed pawpaw to the face and leave for a few minutes only; then wash off. This solution is not recommended for sensitive or problem skin.

◆ Face Masks ◆

*Whether you wish to tighten pores or simply refine the skin, there is a natural
product that will work wonders for you. Follow our directions, and these masks will, over
time, give you a glowing complexion. Each recipe makes one mask.*

Strawberry yogurt mask

*Strawberries and yogurt have long been used for
bleaching and refining the skin.*

- ◆ **1 handful ripe strawberries**
- ◆ **1 tablespoon ground almonds**
- ◆ **2 tablespoons plain yogurt**

Mash the strawberries and ground almonds in a
bowl until completely blended together. Stir in
the yogurt to make a spreadable paste. Apply
immediately, as directed in the box, far right or
refrigerate and use within 1 day.

Fresh herb mask

This mask is especially beneficial for oily skin.

- ◆ **1 tablespoon freshly chopped
  peppermint**
- ◆ **1 tablespoon freshly chopped
  cabbage leaf**
- ◆ **1 tablespoon apple juice**
- ◆ **1 tablespoon ground almonds**
- ◆ **1 egg white**

You will need a mortar and pestle, a fine sieve,
a cup, and a spoon.
1 Place the peppermint and cabbage in the
mortar. Use the pestle to pound them to a
paste. Strain excess juice into a cup; set aside.
2 Add the ground almonds and egg white
to the paste and beat to combine; apply immediately, according to directions in the box,
far right.
3 Once the mask has been removed, tone the
skin with the excess juice diluted with a little
boiled water or refrigerate and use within a day
or two.

VARIATION Similar masks will suit other skin
types. For normal skin, substitute lemon balm

and cucumber for the peppermint and sage.
For dry skin, substitute calendula flowers and
finely grated carrot for the peppermint and
cabbage, and egg yolk for the egg white.

Aloe and honey mask

*This combination of aloe and honey is just right
for soothing and nourishing dry skin.*

- ◆ **aloe vera leaves**
- ◆ **1 egg yolk**
- ◆ **1 teaspoon warmed honey**
- ◆ **about 1 tablespoon
  powdered milk**

Cut the aloe leaves in half lengthwise and
scoop 1 teaspoon of gel into a cup. Beat in the
egg yolk and honey with a spoon. Add sufficient powdered milk to make a thin, spreadable paste. Apply immediately as directed at
right or refrigerate and use later in the day.

Green clay (kaolin) mask

*Clay masks leave skin feeling firm and smooth.
Although green clay suits all skin types, for oily
skin substitute brown clay for green, and 1 teaspoon of egg white for the honey. Don't apply
a clay mask more than once a week.*

- ◆ **1 teaspoon honey**
- ◆ **2 tablespoons green clay
  powder**
- ◆ **1 to 2 tablespoons warm water**

In a bowl, mix the honey into the clay with a
spoon and add sufficient water to make a
spreadable paste. Apply as directed below.

APPLYING A MASK

FACE masks have been used for centuries to
cleanse and tone the skin. Used regularly,
they leave the skin glowing with vitality.

Cover your shoulders with a clean towel. Make
sure you have a damp towel or facecloth available to wipe up any drips.

Use a cotton ball or your fingers to spread the
mask, covering your skin up to the hairline and
down to the chin, avoiding the area immediately
around the eyes. Leave it on for 15 minutes
(you can gradually increase the duration of
future applications, up to 30 minutes, depending
on the sensitivity of the skin and the effective-
ness of the mask). For maximum relaxation, lie
down and shut your eyes while allowing the
mask to set.

Next, use your fingers to remove as much of
the mask as possible. If it has dried, splash your
face with warm water and remove the mask with
your fingers. Use a wet facecloth, if needed, to
clean away the remainder. To finish, splash your
face with running water and apply a toner.

◆ A Winning Smile ◆

Ensure a fresh-tasting mouth and white,
healthy-looking teeth with these preparations, all of
which are made from purely natural ingredients.

Cinnamon mint tooth powder

Peppermint and cinnamon essential oils in this
tooth powder help to relieve the discomfort
of sensitive teeth. Simply dip a toothbrush into
the powder, wet slightly, and clean your teeth,
paying particular attention to chewing surfaces
and the gum line.

- ◆ **13 tablespoons calcium carbonate (from a pharmacy)**
- ◆ **4 tablespoons baking soda**
- ◆ **1 teaspoon salt**
- ◆ **25 drops peppermint essential oil**
- ◆ **12 drops cinnamon essential oil**

You will need a food processor or blender, a
spoon, and a sterilized, widemouthed 10-
ounce glass jar with a tight-fitting lid.
1 Place all the ingredients in the processor or
blender and blend for 1 minute to combine
well. Set aside to allow the powder to settle.
2 Spoon the powder into the jar and store in a
bathroom cabinet. It keeps well if the lid is
always replaced after use.
MAKES ABOUT 10 OUNCES

Citrus antiseptic mouthwash

Use this refreshing homemade mouthwash to
help fight bacteria. Dilute it and rinse your mouth
or gargle after you brush your teeth. Do not swal-
low the liquid.

- ◆ **¾ cup vodka**
- ◆ **30 drops lemon essential oil**
- ◆ **25 drops bergamot essential oil**
- ◆ **1¼ cups distilled water**

You will need a sterilized 16-ounce glass bottle
with a tight-fitting lid.
1 Place the vodka and the lemon and bergamot essential oils in the bottle and shake
vigorously to combine.
2 Add the distilled water and shake until well
mixed. Leave for 1 week to mature, shaking
from time to time.
3 To use, shake the bottle and mix 1 part of
the mixture with 3 parts lukewarm distilled
water in a small tumbler.
MAKES ABOUT 1 PINT (16 OUNCES)

Minty-fresh toothpaste

This natural toothpaste is easy to make and
a pleasure to use for adults and children alike.
If you want the toothpaste to look as "minty"
as it tastes, add a drop or two of green food
coloring.

- ◆ **3⅓ ounces calcium carbonate (from a pharmacy)**
- ◆ **1½ ounces baking soda**
- ◆ **1 teaspoon salt**
- ◆ **about 7 tablespoons glycerin**
- ◆ **3 to 4 drops peppermint essential oil**
- ◆ **2 drops green food coloring (optional)**

You will need a small ceramic or glass bowl, a
spoon, and a sterilized, widemouthed 5-ounce
glass jar with a tight-fitting lid.
1 Place the calcium carbonate, baking soda,
and salt in the bowl. Stir in sufficient glycerin
to make a thick paste.
2 Stir well and add the peppermint essential
oil, drop by drop, until the paste is pleasantly
flavored. Add the 2 drops of green food coloring at this stage if desired.
3 Spoon the paste into the jar and keep in
a bathroom cabinet. Make sure the lid is always
replaced after use.
MAKES ABOUT 5 OUNCES

Herbal mouthwash

The herbs in this mouthwash will keep your breath sweet and your mouth feeling fresh and clean. It can also be used as a soothing gargle.

- ◆ **1 teaspoon dried sage**
- ◆ **1 teaspoon dried rosemary**
- ◆ **1 teaspoon dried peppermint**
- ◆ **1 cup boiling water**
- ◆ **¼ cup cider vinegar**

You will need 2 bowls, a fine sieve, a funnel, a paper coffee filter, and a sterilized 10-ounce glass bottle with a tight-fitting stopper.

1 Place the herbs in a bowl and add the boiling water. Cover and steep for 15 to 20 minutes.
2 Strain the liquid through the sieve into the second bowl, discarding the herbs.
3 Line a funnel with a coffee filter and place in neck of bottle. Drip the liquid through the filter into the bottle. Add the vinegar and shake. Store in a cool, dark place. Use within a few days, shaking the bottle well before use.
MAKES ABOUT 10 OUNCES

PRACTICAL IDEAS

REFRESH YOUR MOUTH

Rub two or three fresh sage leaves over your teeth regularly to whiten and clean them.

The oil from cashew nuts has been shown to fight tooth decay. Chew cashews after a meal to help prevent the production of plaque acids.

Clean teeth and fresh breath can easily be achieved with such homemade products as: **1** *Cinnamon mint tooth powder,* **2** *Citrus antiseptic mouthwash,* **3** *Lip balm (p.180),* **4** *Minty-fresh toothpaste, and* **5** *Herbal mouthwash.*

◆ Especially for Men ◆

Homemade products can be strikingly successful in meeting men's special skin-care requirements. The soothing properties of some of the herbal components are perfect for such uses as preparing skin for the razor and calming aftershave irritation.

Tangy body cologne

Pat on this invigorating lotion to refresh the skin and revive the spirits.

- ◆ 1 cup vodka
- ◆ 10 drops lime essential oil
- ◆ 10 drops lavender essential oil
- ◆ 5 drops lemon essential oil
- ◆ 3 drops lemongrass essential oil
- ◆ 1 cup distilled water

You will need a sterilized 16-ounce glass bottle with a tight-fitting stopper.

1 Pour the vodka and essential oils into the bottle and shake well to disperse the oils. Set aside to mature for 4 weeks.

2 Add the distilled water to the bottle and shake for several minutes. Set aside to mature for another 2 weeks, shaking periodically.

3 Store in a cool, dark place. Shake before use.

MAKES ABOUT 1 PINT (16 OUNCES)

Fragrant shaving soap

Rinse the face, then lather with this gentle soap.

- ◆ ⅔ cup rosewater
- ◆ 4 ounces pure soap flakes
- ◆ 4 drops rosemary essential oil
- ◆ 3 drops lemon essential oil
- ◆ 2 drops bay essential oil
- ◆ 1 drop sage essential oil

You will need a nonreactive saucepan, a non-reactive double boiler, a wooden spoon, a potato masher (optional), and a sterilized, shallow 7-ounce glass jar with a tight-fitting lid.

1 In the saucepan, over low heat, warm the rosewater.

2 In the top of a double boiler, over simmering water, place the soap flakes. Add the warmed rosewater and stir to moisten. Stir the mixture until the soap has melted to a smooth

To keep the skin in good condition and make shaving easy, use these simple preparations: oatmeal body scrub (left), fragrant shaving soap (center), aftershave splash (right).

gel (if necessary, use a potato masher to help dissolve the soap). Remove from the heat and cool to lukewarm.

3 Stir in the essential oils and spoon the soap into the jar. Set aside to harden for 3 to 5 days. Keep handy in a cool, dark place.

MAKES ABOUT 6 ½ OUNCES

Aftershave splash

Delightfully aromatic, this mildly antiseptic lotion can be used as an aftershave or to protect the skin before using an electric razor. Simply dab it on with a cotton ball before shaving.

- ◆ 5 tablespoons orange flower water
- ◆ 5 tablespoons cider vinegar
- ◆ 3 tablespoons witch hazel lotion
- ◆ 18 drops bergamot essential oil
- ◆ 18 drops lemon essential oil
- ◆ 6 drops neroli essential oil

Place all of the ingredients in a sterilized 7-ounce glass bottle with a tight-fitting lid and shake well. Set aside to mature for several days, shaking each day. Store in a cool, dark place. Shake before using.

MAKES ABOUT 6 ½ OUNCES

Oatmeal body scrub

Removes dead skin cells to give the skin a smooth texture and natural color.

- ◆ 1 handful brown lentils
- ◆ 1 handful coarse rolled oats
- ◆ ½ teaspoon carrot oil
- ◆ ½ teaspoon jojoba oil
- ◆ water

You will need an electric blender, a spoon, and a small bowl.

1 In the blender, reduce the lentils to a coarse powder. Add the rolled oats and process again to make powder; then add the oils and process again. Blend in water by the teaspoonful until the mixture becomes a thick paste.

2 Spoon the mixture into the bowl. Massage the scrub all over the body before a shower or bath, paying particular attention to dry areas.

MAKES ENOUGH FOR 1 APPLICATION

Shaving-cut lotion

A little razor nick needn't cause discomfort. Dab a drop of this lotion on the cut to help stop the bleeding and prevent infection.

- ◆ 4 teaspoons witch hazel lotion
- ◆ 13 drops lavender essential oil
- ◆ 7 drops geranium essential oil

Place all the ingredients in a sterilized 1-ounce glass bottle with a tight-fitting lid and shake well to combine. Keep in a cool, dark place. Shake before using.

MAKES ABOUT 4 TEASPOONS

Pre-shave moisturizer

Shaving can be made so much easier and more effective with a little preparation. Massage in this moisturizer to soften bristles and avoid razor cuts.

- ◆ 3 tablespoons orange flower water
- ◆ 2 teaspoons beeswax
- ◆ 1 teaspoon anhydrous (water-free) lanolin
- ◆ ¼ cup almond oil
- ◆ 1 teaspoon wheat-germ oil
- ◆ 12 drops lemon juice
- ◆ 6 drops bergamot essential oil

You will need a cup, a nonreactive double boiler, a wooden spoon, and a sterilized 4-ounce jar with a tight-fitting lid.

1 In a cup sitting in hot water, warm the orange flower water.

2 In the double boiler, melt the beeswax, lanolin, almond oil, and wheat-germ oil. Stir in the warmed orange flower water. Remove from the heat and stir well.

3 When the mixture has cooled, stir in the lemon juice and essential oil. Beat until creamy.

4 Pour into the jar and keep handy in a cool, dark place.

MAKES ABOUT 4 OUNCES

◆ Hair-care Secrets ◆

For glossy, healthy hair, free from dandruff and split ends, you can't beat natural
substances such as honey, chamomile, lavender, and rosemary. These shampoos and treatments
can be used on any type of hair every day, if you wish, with complete safety.

Chamomile shampoo

Chamomile makes a mild shampoo that is gentle to the hair and the pocketbook. You need only one tablespoonful for one wash. Use leftover pieces of pure soap instead of soap flakes, if you prefer.

- ◆ **1 handful fresh or dried chamomile flowers**
- ◆ **1¼ cups boiling water**
- ◆ **3 tablespoons pure soap flakes**
- ◆ **1 tablespoon glycerin**
- ◆ **5 drops yellow food coloring**

You will need 2 heatproof bowls, a sieve, a wooden spoon, and a clean 14-ounce bottle with a tight-fitting cover.
1 Place the flowers in a bowl and add the boiling water. Let stand for 15 minutes, then strain into the other bowl.
2 Clean the first bowl. Combine the soap flakes and hot infusion in it. Let stand until the soap softens—a few minutes. Beat in glycerin and food coloring until well blended.
3 Pour the mixture into the bottle. Keep in a cool, dark place.
MAKES ABOUT 13 ⅓ OUNCES

Instant dry shampoo

Perfect for those occasions when you don't have time to wash your hair or when washing facilities are not available, such as on camping trips.

- ◆ **1 tablespoon cornstarch or finely ground oatmeal**

1 Sprinkle small amounts of cornstarch or oatmeal onto the hair, lifting up the hair in sections to let the powder get to the scalp. Rub it through the hair to absorb excess oil.
2 Comb the hair to remove tangles; then

spend 5 to 10 minutes brushing (depending on the length and thickness of the hair) to remove all traces of the powder and prevent the suggestion of dandruff. Shake and blow on the brush to clean it while brushing the hair.
ENOUGH FOR 1 APPLICATION

Dandruff treatment

This strong infusion of rosemary and thyme can help eliminate dandruff. Shampoo and rinse the hair thoroughly; massage a small amount into the scalp. Between shampoos, massage in a small amount before going to bed.

- ◆ **2 teaspoons dried rosemary**
- ◆ **2 teaspoons dried thyme**
- ◆ **⅔ cup boiling water**
- ◆ **⅔ cup cider vinegar**

You will need a heatproof ceramic bowl, a fine sieve, and a clean 10-ounce plastic bottle with a tight-fitting cover.
1 Place the herbs in the bowl. Pour in the boiling water. Cover and allow to steep for 15 to 20 minutes.
2 Strain into the bottle, add the vinegar, and shake. Store in a cool, dark place.
MAKES ABOUT 10 OUNCES

Soapwort shampoo

Soapwort root can help relieve itching and dermatitis. Use 3 to 4 tablespoonfuls to clean hair and scalp without a lather. Choose herbs from the box on the opposite page.

- ◆ **1½ tablespoons chopped dried soapwort root**
- ◆ **2 cups water**
- ◆ **2 teaspoons dried herbs**

You will need a nonreactive saucepan with a lid, a fine sieve, and a 16-ounce bottle with a tight-fitting cover.
1 Place the soapwort root and water in the saucepan and bring to a boil. Cover and simmer for 20 minutes.
2 Remove saucepan from heat and add dried herbs to mixture. Cover and set aside to cool.
3 Strain the mixture into the bottle and store in a cool, dark place handy to the shower. It must be used within 7 to 10 days, so be generous and share it with the family. Check the shampoo regularly to make sure it has not deteriorated.
MAKES ENOUGH FOR 6 TO 8 SHAMPOOS

Herbal rinse

After shampooing, give your hair a lingering fragrance with this rinse. For an itchy scalp, double the quantity of herbs and use daily. Choose herbs from the box on the facing page.

- ◆ **1 tablespoon dried herbs**
- ◆ **1 quart boiling water**
- ◆ **2 tablespoons cider vinegar**
- ◆ **1 drop green food coloring (optional)**

You will need 2 large heatproof ceramic or glass bowls, a fine sieve, and a cup.
1 Place the herbs in a bowl and pour the boiling water over them. Cover, and allow to steep for 15 to 20 minutes.
2 Strain the infusion into the other bowl and add the vinegar and food coloring, if desired.
3 After shampooing and rinsing your hair in your usual fashion, hold your head over the bowl and pour cupfuls of the herbal rinse through your hair.
MAKES ENOUGH FOR 1 APPLICATION

Constant shampooing can cause hair to lose its natural shine. For a gentle alternative to the strong chemicals that are found in many commercially available products, try these simple homemade preparations: Chamomile shampoo (left), Prewash honey treatment (center) and Herbal rinse (right).

HERBS FOR HAIR

CATNIP	Traditionally believed to promote hair growth.
CHAMOMILE	Can help to keep the scalp and hair follicles healthy, so that new hair grows well.
COMFREY	Can soothe and heal scalp irritations.
ELDER BERRIES	Have traditionally been used to add color tones to graying hair.
LEMON BALM	Leaves a fresh citrus fragrance on the hair.
LEMON-GRASS	Has astringent properties and can be effective in toning the scalp.
LEMON VERBENA	Leaves a fresh citrus fragrance on the hair.
NETTLE	An astringent herb that is beneficial in the treatment of skin irritations and itching.
PARSLEY	This common plant can be helpful in relieving skin irritations.
ROSEMARY	Is said to enhance the color of dark hair and to help control dandruff.
SAGE	An astringent for oily hair. Can also be beneficial for damaged or fragile hair.
THYME	Has antiseptic, tonic, and astringent properties.
YARROW	Acts as a tonic for the hair.

Prewash honey treatment

Your hair can become damaged by exposure to the sun or harsh chemicals. Before a shampoo, use this special treatment to condition the scalp and repair damaged hair. Use the treatment regularly if your hair is dry or ends are split.

- ◆ **2 tablespoons olive oil**
- ◆ **2 teaspoons honey**
- ◆ **5 drops rosemary, lavender, or geranium essential oil**

You will need a small cup, a ceramic or glass bowl, a small stainless-steel spoon, a plastic shower cap, and a comfortably hot towel.

1 In a cup sitting in hot water, warm the olive oil and the honey (or you can use the microwave for heating). Stir in your choice of essential oil and mix well.

2 While the mixture is still warm, apply it all over your hair, massaging well into the scalp. Cover your hair with the shower cap, wrap the towel around your head, and leave on for 10 to 15 minutes.

3 Remove the towel and shower cap, and wash your hair with a mild shampoo, such as the chamomile shampoo (on the facing page) or a baby shampoo.

MAKES ENOUGH FOR 1 APPLICATION

◆ A Splash of Fragrance ◆

*These days, when commercial colognes are so costly, it's a true luxury to wear a scent
made especially for you. Making your own splashes and colognes lets you vary ingredients to create
subtle fragrances that suit every mood and your personal taste.*

Essential eau de cologne

*Eau de cologne was favored by Napoleon.
He is said to have used more than 50 bottles
a month!*

- ⅔ cup vodka
- 60 drops orange essential oil
- 30 drops bergamot essential oil
- 30 drops lemon essential oil
- 6 drops neroli essential oil
- 6 drops rosemary
  essential oil
- 3 tablespoons distilled or
  boiled water

You will need a sterilized 8-ounce glass bottle
with a tight-fitting stopper, a bowl, and a paper
coffee filter.
1 Pour the vodka and essential oils into the
bottle. Let stand for 1 week, shaking daily.
2 Add water, shake, and leave 4 to 6 weeks.
3 Strain through the filter into the bowl, then
pour into the bottle. Keep in a cool, dark place.
MAKES ABOUT 7 OUNCES

Lavender toilet water

*The old-fashioned scent of lavender is one of the
most popular and is perfect for gift giving.*

- ¾ cup vodka
- 25 drops lavender essential oil
- 5 drops bergamot essential oil
- 3 tablespoons distilled water
- 2 drops blue and 1 drop red
  food coloring (optional)

Pour the vodka and both essential oils into a
sterilized glass bottle with a tight-fitting lid.
Shake well. Add the water and food coloring.
Let stand for 2 weeks, shaking frequently.
MAKES ABOUT 1 CUP

Fruity body splash

If you like a citrus scent, this one is for you.

- 1 tablespoon finely chopped
  lemon peel
- 1 tablespoon finely chopped
  orange peel
- 3 tablespoons vodka
- 10 drops mandarin
  essential oil
- 10 drops orange essential oil
- 5 drops lemon essential oil
- 5 drops grapefruit essential oil
- 3 tablespoons white wine
  vinegar
- 2 cups distilled or boiled
  water

You will need a fine sieve and a sterilized 20-
ounce glass bottle with a tight-fitting stopper.
1 Place the peels and the vodka in the bottle.
Cover tightly with the stopper and let stand
for 1 week.
2 Press the mixture through the fine sieve to
extract all the liquid.
3 Pour the liquid back into the resterilized
bottle. Add the essential oils, vinegar, and
water. Let stand for 2 weeks, shaking often.
Keep in a cool, dark place.
MAKES ABOUT 20 OUNCES

Rosewater perfume

*Sprinkle a few drops onto your handkerchiefs
for a delightfully scented drawer, handbag,
or pocket.*

- 2 tablespoons vodka
- 2 tablespoons rosewater
- 8 drops bergamot essential oil
- 4 drops geranium essential oil
- 2 drops patchouli essential oil

You will need a sterilized 2-ounce glass bottle
with a tight-fitting top, a bowl, and a paper
coffee filter.
1 Place all the ingredients in the bottle, shake
vigorously, and set aside for 2 weeks.
2 Strain the liquid through the filter into the
bowl; then pour back into the bottle. Store in a
cool, dark place.
MAKES ABOUT 2 OUNCES

Carmelite water

*Carmelite nuns in 14th-century France invented
one of the earliest scents. Use sparingly as a perfume, or dilute with distilled water for cologne.*

- 2 tablespoons lemon balm leaves
- 1 tablespoon finely chopped
  lemon peel
- 1 sprig sweet marjoram
- ½ cinnamon stick
- 5 whole cloves
- 1 teaspoon nutmeg, grated
- ¾ -inch piece angelica stem
- 1¼ cups vodka

You will need a mortar and pestle, two 10-ounce
sterilized glass bottles with tight-fitting stoppers,
a fine sieve, a paper coffee filter, and a bowl.
1 Using the mortar and pestle, crush the dry
ingredients. Place in a small bottle, add the
vodka, and set aside for 10 days, shaking daily.
2 Strain the liquid through the sieve into a
bowl. Then drip the liquid through the coffee
filter into a freshly sterilized bottle. Let stand
at least 2 weeks. Keep in a cool, dark place.
MAKES 10 OUNCES

*Clockwise from back: Carmelite water, Rosewater
perfume, and Lavender toilet water—three delightful
fragrances you can make using your own ingredients.*

• Natural Home Remedies •

The earliest cures were based on herbs, and for centuries healers turned first to the herbaria,
where the plants for their work were grown. Today, people are again realizing that many complaints respond
well to herbal treatments, which may have fewer side effects than commercial remedies.

Acne and pimples

Herbal steam facial Place one handful each of fresh thyme and calendula flowers in a heat-proof bowl. Add 1½ quarts of boiling water. Lean over the bowl, covering your head and the bowl with a thick towel. With eyes closed, remain for 10 minutes. Then gently splash your face with lukewarm water and pat dry.

Medicated steam facial Put 2 drops of essential oil—lemon, tea tree, lavender, rosemary, geranium, or cedarwood—in a bowl and pour in 1 quart of boiling water. Proceed as directed in the Herbal steam facial (above).

Essential oil treatment Rub 1 to 2 drops of tea tree or lavender essential oil on the affected area. For a wide area, dilute with 20 to 40 drops of light olive oil. Use once or twice a day.

Aloe vera gel Cut a fresh aloe vera leaf and scoop out the gel. Rub in twice daily.

Witch hazel infusion Dab the affected area 3 times a day with an infusion (box, opposite page) of witch hazel leaves.

Athlete's foot

Quick treatment Using a cotton swab, apply 2 drops of tea-tree essential oil directly on the skin. For an extensive area, apply an oil blend made by mixing 3 drops of tea-tree essential oil in 1½ teaspoons light olive oil.

Healing ointment Warm 3 tablespoons of vegetable oil in a cup placed in hot water. Add ⅓ ounce of finely chopped beeswax to the warmed oil and stir until the wax melts. Remove the mixture from the heat and stir until it cools. Beat in 50 drops of tea-tree, gera-

An enormous range of herbs, flowers, and natural oils can be used to make safe and effective remedies to relieve any number of common ailments.

nium, lavender, pine, or peppermint essential oil (or make a combination of tea tree with any of these, not exceeding 50 drops total). Spoon the ointment into a small, sterilized, wide-mouthed jar with a tight-fitting stopper. Keep in a cool, dark place. Massage a small amount into the affected area twice a day.

Bad breath

Herbal breath sweetener Chew 1 or 2 fresh leaves of spearmint, peppermint, fennel, or parsley for a minute or two, or chew several fresh or dried seeds of caraway, cardamom, or fennel. Alternatively, make an infusion (box, right) with any of these herbs or seeds. For seeds, you will need to infuse 1 teaspoonful for 30 minutes. Allow to cool before using. Gargle with the infusion several times a day.

Bee stings and insect bites

First remove the stinger from your skin by grasping it near the base with tweezers and pulling carefully or by pushing it out with a fingernail. Then you can use any of the following recipes to relieve the pain. Anyone prone to severe allergic reaction should follow the treatment recommended by their doctor.

Instant relief As an immediate step, you can apply some crushed leaves or flowers of chamomile to relieve the pain and prevent swelling. Simply applying ice to the spot will also provide quick relief.

Baking soda paste To relieve itching, apply a paste that is made by combining ¼ teaspoon baking soda with a little water.

Essential oil soother Essential oils have both soothing and healing properties. Fill a bowl with enough cold water to moisten a small washcloth or cotton pad. Swirl 1 drop of lavender, eucalyptus, or tea-tree essential oil through the water; then soak the cloth or pad. Squeeze gently to remove any excess water and apply the cloth to the skin. Hold it in place with your hand for as long as possible, or cover it with plastic wrap and leave in place for about 1 hour.

CAUTION

THE remedies given on these pages are not suitable for acute or chronic conditions. If an ailment fails to respond to a home remedy, consult your doctor immediately.

MAKING AN INFUSION

MAKING an herbal infusion is similar to making a cup of tea. In a cup, place 3 rounded teaspoons (½ ounce) fresh herb leaves or 1 rounded teaspoon dried herb leaves. Pour ½ cup boiling water over the leaves, cover with a saucer, and allow to steep for 5 to 10 minutes. Strain the infusion through a fine sieve or a doubled piece of cheesecloth; then discard the herbs. Drink the infusion while it is hot, or leave it to cool if you are going to use it as a lotion or gargle. Most infusions can be stored in the refrigerator for up to 24 hours and reheated whenever you want to use them.

Blisters

Essential oil application Place 1 drop of tea-tree or lavender essential oil on a blister, gently massaging it in. Take care not to break the skin. Do not use this treatment on open blisters.

Calendula treatment For open blisters, make an infusion (box, above) of calendula flowers. Dab on and let dry. For foot blisters, apply a small amount of Simple calendula ointment (box, p.193) to a clean piece of gauze, and cover the blister. Remove the gauze when not wearing shoes.

Body odor

Fresh herb bath Put a large handful of herbs in a doubled piece of cheesecloth. Choose from rosemary, lovage, lavender, lemongrass, sage, parsley, and peppermint, individually or combined. Gather up the corners of the cheesecloth and tie securely. Toss the bundle into a hot bath to soften and to scent the water. Rub the herbal pouch all over the skin, paying particular attention to areas where odor is a problem.

Almond massage oil In a small bowl, mix 2 tablespoons of almond oil with 10 drops of lavender essential oil, 10 drops of eucalyptus essential oil, 5 drops of peppermint essential oil, and 5 drops of pine essential oil. Massage the body with the oil once or twice a week.

Boils

Compress Put 4 teaspoons of hot water in a bowl. Swirl 2 drops of lavender, lemon, tea-tree, or nutmeg essential oil through the water, then soak a cotton ball or gauze pad. Gently squeeze out excess fluid and apply the cotton ball or pad directly to the area of the boil. Cover with plastic wrap and secure with a bandage or tape. Leave in place for at least 1 hour. Repeat the treatment twice a day.

Bruises

Circulation stimulant Use two washcloths, cotton pads, or a piece of cheesecloth large enough to cover the bruise. Put 3 to 4 drops of tea-tree, lavender, geranium, or rosemary essential oil into a bowl of cold water and swirl it around to disperse evenly. Swirl 3 to 4 drops of one of the essential oils in a bowl of hot water. Soak a cloth in each bowl, and gently squeeze out excess fluid. Apply the hot and cold compresses alternately, directly to the area of the bruise, leaving each one for 2 to 3 minutes. Repeat several times.

Fragrant massage oil Mix 5 drops of essential oil with 1 teaspoon of vegetable oil, and massage into the bruise. For the essential oil, choose from lavender, geranium, rosemary, or tea tree, using one or a combination of them.

Burns and sunburn

These suggestions are for the treatment of mild burns. For severe burns, seek medical attention immediately. Before applying any treatment, immerse the burned area of skin in cool, but not ice-cold, water. Alternatively, soak a clean cloth in water and apply to the burn to reduce the sensation of heat; then pat dry with a towel.

Calendula juice Apply the juice of crushed calendula petals several times a day. Crush the petals in your fingers or use a mortar and pestle for a larger amount.

Aloe vera gel Cut a leaf of the aloe vera plant, scoop out the clear gel, and apply it directly to the burn.

Soothing paste Mix a little baking soda with water to make a thick paste and apply to the burn. Do not use on broken skin.

Quick oil rub Apply 1 drop of tea-tree or lavender essential oil to the skin and gently massage it in. For a more extensive area, dilute 1 drop of essential oil with ¼ teaspoon olive oil and apply when the skin is cool. Use several times a day, but do not apply more than 10 drops of essential oil in 24 hours.

Infusion for broken skin If the skin is broken, dab on a cooled infusion (box, p.191) of calendula flowers, raspberry leaves, or ordinary tea leaves.

Chili burns

Natural treatment For burns caused by chilies, first wash the area with milk or cream. Then apply mashed avocado or banana flesh to the skin. Leave on until the pain subsides. After eating chilies, alleviate the burning sensation in your mouth by drinking milk or eating a piece of avocado or banana. Do *not* drink water, which can make the sensation worse.

Colds

Fragrant oil bath Fill a bath with comfortably hot water. Swirl in 6 to 8 drops lavender or peppermint essential oil, and then relax in the bath for 10 minutes. Gently pat yourself dry, to retain essential oils on the skin.

Cinnamon soother Stir a teaspoon each of powdered cinnamon and lemon juice into a cup of hot water and sip slowly.

Traditional herbal remedy Mix 2 parts dried peppermint leaves, 2 parts dried lemon balm leaves, and 1 part dried yarrow leaves; store in an airtight container. Make an infusion (box, p.191) with these, as needed, and drink three times a day.

Cold sores

Herbal mouthwash Make an infusion (box, p.191) of thyme or sage leaves or marigold flowers. Or make an infusion using equal amounts of thyme leaves and marigold flowers. Add ¼ cup of cider vinegar. Use either liquid as a mouthwash three times a day.

Colic

Fennel tea. Make an infusion (box, p.191) with 1 teaspoon crushed fennel seeds. Give to baby by spoon or bottle; the licorice taste of fennel appeals to many infants. The oils found in fennel seeds help expel gas, relieving abdominal cramps.

Thyme tea. Alternatively, make an infusion using 1 teaspoon crushed thyme leaves to 1 cup boiling water. Give to baby by spoon or bottle. Thyme contains an oil that calms the gastrointestinal tract.

Constipation

Fruit and fiber Soak about 5 prunes in orange juice or water overnight. Eat the prunes and drink the liquid before breakfast.

Linseed drink Stir 1 to 2 teaspoons of whole linseeds into a glass of water and drink. Follow with a second glass of water (always drink at least 2 cups of fluid when ingesting whole linseeds). Use the drink three times a day as a gentle laxative.

Corns

Natural removal Crush a small dandelion leaf or a clove of garlic and scrape the inside of a banana or fig skin (about a teaspoonful) or use the flesh of a squeezed lemon. Apply the pulp to the corn, binding it in place with a small adhesive bandage. When the skin is soft, gently rub the top layer of the corn away with an emery board. Repeat daily until the corn disappears. For several days after, massage the area with a small amount of Simple calendula ointment (box, opposite page).

Coughs

Violet cough syrup Place 2½ ounces of fresh violet flowers in a heatproof bowl, pour in 2 cups of boiling water, and cover. Let stand until cold. Strain through a fine sieve into a saucepan. Stir in 1½ cups of sugar and cook, still stirring, on low heat, until dissolved. Simmer, without stirring, for 10 to 15 minutes until syrupy. Pour into a sterilized 16-ounce glass bottle with a tight-fitting lid. The cough syrup will keep for about a year in the refrigerator. Take 1 teaspoonful, as needed.

Herbal honey Place 1 tablespoon of dried rosemary, thyme, aniseed, or horehound in a sterilized glass jar with a tight-fitting lid. Warm 14 ounces of honey in a bowl placed in hot water and pour it over the herbs. Let stand in a warm place for about a week. Strain through a sieve and pour into a freshly sterilized jar. Sip a teaspoonful as required.

Cuts and abrasions

Antiseptic wash Make an infusion (box, p.191) using calendula flowers, garlic cloves, or leaves of thyme, winter savory, blackberry, or sage. Cool; keep the wash in a cup or bottle. Bathe the cut or abrasion with the antiseptic wash several times a day.

Traditional calendula ointment To heal the skin, apply a small amount of Simple calendula ointment (box, right) twice a day.

Gentle tea-tree ointment Warm 3 ⅓ ounces of olive oil in a double boiler. Add ¾ ounce of beeswax, and stir until the wax has melted. Remove from heat and continue stirring until the mixture cools and thickens. Add 1 teaspoon of tea-tree essential oil; beat until cold. Spoon into a small jar. Gently spread the ointment onto the skin.

Diarrhea

Berry leaf tea Make an infusion (box, p.191) of dried raspberry or blackberry leaves. Drink a small cup 3 times a day, and make sure you drink plenty of other fluids to prevent dehydration. If diarrhea persists for more than 24 hours, see your doctor.

Eczema and dermatitis

Calendula flower lotion For quick relief, crush several calendula flower petals between your fingers (for larger amounts use a mortar and pestle) until the petals are juicy. Then rub both petals and juice onto the skin.

Soothing bath oil Choose from pine, geranium, or lavender essential oils and add 6 to 8 drops to a hot bath. Swirl the water around to disperse the oil, and relax in the bath for 10 minutes. After the bath, massage in any essential oil that is still left on the skin. Do not take this bath more than once in 24 hours.

Anti-itch ointment To ease symptoms of itching and dryness, apply a small amount of Simple calendula ointment (box, below) to the affected area twice a day or as needed.

Floral infusion Dab a cooled infusion (box, p.191) of fresh or dried calendula flowers onto the irritated area several times a day.

Headaches and tension

Lavender water To ease tension after a hard day, soak a washcloth in Lavender toilet water (p.188) and squeeze out the excess. Lie down, place the washcloth on your forehead, and relax for at least 15 minutes.

Herbal tea Make an infusion (box, p.191) using chamomile or lemon balm leaves. Take a few minutes to sip a cup of the hot tea slowly while sitting in a quiet spot. Sweeten the tea with a teaspoon of honey, if desired.

SIMPLE CALENDULA OINTMENT

named cultivars or African, French, or Mexican marigolds *(Tagetes* spp.*)*.

Place 3 tablespoons fresh calendula petals in a double boiler, and crush them slightly with the back of a spoon. Add ⅓ cup of light olive oil and cook for two hours over low heat. (Alternatively, place the crushed petals and the oil in a sterilized glass jar, seal, and keep in a warm place for 2 weeks.)

Strain the liquid into a bowl, pressing against the strainer with the back of a spoon to extract it all. Return the oil to the double boiler. Over medium heat, add 2 tablespoons of chopped beeswax and stir until it melts. Remove the bowl from the double boiler and beat the mixture until it cools and becomes thick and creamy. Mix in the contents of one vitamin E capsule (400 IU)

Spoon into a sterilized 4 ½ -ounce jar, seal, and keep in a cool, dark place. Or divide the ointment between two smaller jars; keep one handy and store the other in the refrigerator. This recipe makes about 4 ½ ounces of calendula ointment.

CALENDULA is highly regarded as a soothing and healing herb and is used in a number of commercially available preparations for the treatment of skin problems. For this ointment, use only the old-fashioned variety *(Calendula officinalis)*, which has several rows of bright orange or yellow petals around a circular center. Do not use the modern

CHICKWEED VARIATION Chickweed is renowned for treating inflamed skin. To make chickweed ointment, replace the calendula petals with 4 tablespoons chickweed leaves.

Feverfew Chewing a leaf of the feverfew plant can bring relief.

Essential oil freshener Place 2 drops of lavender, peppermint, or geranium essential oil in a small bowl of lukewarm water. Swirl the water around to disperse the essential oil, and then leave a washcloth in the liquid until it's fully soaked. Gently squeeze out any excess water, lie back, place the washcloth on your forehead, and relax for as long as possible.

Hunger pangs

Stomach settler To alleviate hunger pangs at inappropriate times and to control stomach rumbling, chew on a few fennel seeds or a small piece of fennel cut from the bulb. The flavor of fennel is similar to that of licorice and often appeals to children.

Indigestion and flatulence

Seed remedy Chew 1 teaspoon of aniseed, dill, or caraway seeds for a minute 3 times a day. Do not swallow the seeds.

Digestive brew Place 1 teaspoon of dill, aniseed, or caraway seeds in a cup, crush with the back of a spoon, and add 3 ⅓ ounces of boiling water. Cover and let stand for 30 minutes; strain. Drink three times a day.

Peppermint tea A cup of peppermint tea is a traditional remedy for gas pains and is also a pleasant drink to enjoy at the end of a meal. Make an infusion (box, p.191) of peppermint leaves, strain, and drink hot, as needed. For persistent flatulence, drink three times daily for 2 to 3 days.

Insomnia

Herbal nightcap Before going to bed, sip an infusion (box, p.191) of chamomile or lemon balm. When sleep comes more easily, halve the concentration of the herb (continued use of the stronger concentration can cause sleeplessness to return). Stop taking the tea for a week after each 3 weeks of continual use.

Quick lavender rub Massage a single drop of lavender essential oil into the temples (that is, 1 drop for the two temples, not 1 drop each) before going to bed.

Fragrant lavender pillow Dry a bunch of fresh lavender in a pillowcase kept in a warm linen closet. When needed, remove the lavender and insert a pillow into the case (put the lavender in another pillowcase for future use—it can be used like this for up to a year). The herb's sedative properties will help to induce a good night's sleep and will last until the pillowcase is washed. Alternatively, you can place a single drop of lavender essential oil on the corner of your pillowcase each night.

BACK MASSAGE

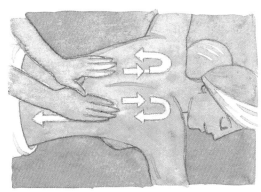

1 *Pour a little massage oil onto one palm and warm it by rubbing the hands together. With a gliding movement, slide the hands up and down the back to spread the oil, repeating this process once to spread it evenly.*

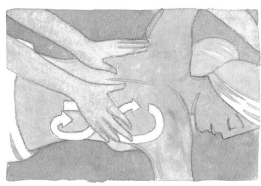

2 *Using small, circular movements, move your hands slowly from the buttocks up to the neck, pressing firmly but not too deeply. Repeat for 5 to 10 minutes, increasing pressure gradually as the muscles relax.*

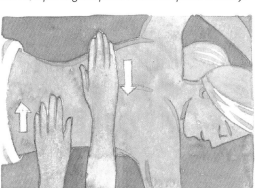

3 *Place one hand on each side of the back. Using small, circular movements, move each hand across to the other side, then back again. Repeat twice. Continue to Step 4, then repeat the whole process several times.*

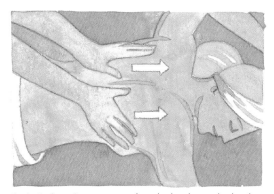

4 *As in Step 2, move your hands slowly up the back to the neck, using small, circular movements. Repeat several times, decreasing pressure. Finish with some light gliding strokes up and down the back.*

Itching

Anti-itch infusion Bathe the affected area with a cooled infusion (box, p.191) of calendula flowers. This remedy is particularly effective in relieving the itchiness associated with childhood diseases such as chickenpox. Bathing with cooled chamomile or chickweed infusion also provides relief.

Total body soak For extensive itching, mix 2 cups of cornstarch to a paste with a little water. Then add this mixture and 1 cup of baking soda to a lukewarm bath. Swirl the water around to disperse the mixture, and immerse your body in the bath.

Low spirits

Bath oil Fill the bath with comfortably warm water. Add no more than 6 drops of essential oil—any combination of lavender, geranium, pine, sandalwood, or bergamot— and swirl the water around. Relax in the bath for about 10 minutes. The warm bathwater and inhaled essential oils will help to calm the mind and lift the spirits.

Menstrual cramps

Ginger tea Make an infusion (box, p.191) with ½ teaspoon minced fresh ginger and 1 cup boiling water. Drink just before menstruation (ginger inhibits the production of prostaglandins, hormones associated with menstrual cramps) and then as needed.

Peppermint tea Make an infusion (box, p.191) with 1 tablespoon chopped fresh mint leaves and 1 cup boiling water. Sip the tea to soothe cramps; peppermint is an antispasmodic.

Morning sickness

Ginger tea Make an infusion (box, p.191) with ½ teaspoon minced fresh ginger and 1 cup boiling water. Sip in the morning on waking. Ginger calms the stomach and reduces nausea without making you sleepy.

Muscular aches

Herbal massage oil Place a large handful of fresh rosemary or lavender in a widemouthed jar. Add 16 ounces of vegetable oil, cover, and let stand for 10 days. Strain and store in a sterilized glass bottle in the refrigerator. It should keep for up to 6 months.

Quick massage oil In a glass or ceramic bowl, dilute 5 drops rosemary, tea-tree, or eucalyptus essential oil in ¼ ounce of vegetable oil. Massage into aching muscles.

Massage cream for sore muscles Pour 1 ½ ounces of vegetable oil into a cup, and place it in hot water to warm. Finely chop ⅓ ounce of beeswax and stir it into the oil until melted. Remove the cup from the hot water and stir the mixture until cool. Beat in 50 drops of tea-tree, rosemary, or eucalyptus essential oil, or a combination of these, not exceeding 50 drops total. Spoon the cream into a small wide-mouthed jar. Massage a little into the painful area twice a day.

Neck massage oil Pour 1 ounce of vegetable oil into a small jar. Add 30 drops of rosemary, lemon, ginger, or peppermint essential oil or a combination of these, not exceeding 30 drops. Shake well for several minutes and store in a cool place. Massage the oil into the neck as required. For an effective neck massage technique, use the step-by-step method detailed below.

Back massage oil Pour 1 ounce of vegetable oil into a small jar. Add 30 drops of pepper-mint, eucalyptus, lemon, or rosemary essential oil or a combination of these, not exceeding 30 drops total. Shake the mixture vigorously for several minutes. Store the bottle in a cool, dark place until needed. For an effective back-massage technique, use the step-by-step method detailed on the opposite page.

Massage for tired feet Put 1 ounce of vegetable oil into a jar and add 30 drops of rosemary, juniper, peppermint, or lavender essential oil or a combination of these, not exceeding 30 drops total. Shake well for several minutes. Massage gently into the feet.

Treatment for muscle cramp To soften the immediate effects of muscle cramping, mix ⅓ ounce of vegetable oil with 10 drops lavender or rosemary essential oil or a combination of these oils, not exceeding 10 drops total. Massage a little into the muscles. To relieve the pain that follows a cramp, make a poultice by mixing 2 teaspoons of chili or mustard powder with 1 tablespoon of cornstarch or rice flour. Add a little hot water, and stir to form a thick paste. Or you can mix the chili or mustard powder with any leftover mashed vegetable. Place the mixture in a cloth and fold to form a pad. While the cloth is still comfortably hot, apply it to the site of the cramp. Leave the cloth in place for up to 1 hour.

NECK AND SHOULDER MASSAGE

1 *Lay the person face down with a pillow under the chest. Pour a little massage oil onto one of your palms and warm it by rubbing your hands together. Spread the oil over the shoulders and neck, repeating once to spread it evenly.*

2 *Place your hands on the shoulders as shown. Squeeze and knead the shoulders, moving from the outside to the center. Repeat this movement for 5 to 10 minutes, as needed, gradually increasing the pressure as the muscles relax.*

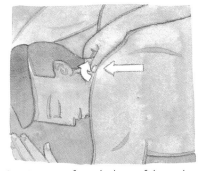

3 *Moving up from the base of the neck, massage the left side of the neck with your right hand, using small, circular thumb movements. Continue for 3 to 4 minutes, gradually increasing pressure. Repeat on right side, with your left hand.*

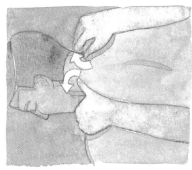

4 *Place your hands on the edge of the shoulders and massage across to the base of the neck. Continue up each side of the neck, using circular thumb movements. Repeat several times, decreasing pressure to wind down the massage.*

A steaming inhalant made from chopped fresh thyme is excellent for clearing nasal congestion. Acne and pimples also respond well to herbal steams.

Nasal congestion

Fresh steam inhalant Place 3 teaspoons of finely chopped fresh thyme, sage, peppermint, or pine needles in a small heatproof bowl and add boiling water. Lean over the bowl, covering your head and the bowl with a thick towel, and inhale for 10 minutes. Repeat 2 to 3 times a day, as needed.

Inhalant for sinusitis Put 2 drops of tea-tree, eucalyptus, or pine essential oil in a heatproof bowl with 1 quart of boiling water. Lean over the bowl, covering your head and the bowl with a thick towel, and inhale for 10 minutes.

Stop before the 10 minutes are up if you feel uncomfortable. Sinusitis sufferers may find that difficulty in breathing is eased if they smear 2 drops of tea-tree essential oil over their palms, cup their hands over their nose, and inhale deeply through the nose.

Instant decongestant Place 1 drop of tea-tree, peppermint, or rosemary essential oil on a handkerchief and inhale as needed.

Nosebleeds

Healing aid for bleeding With the head tilted forward, pinch the lower part of the nostrils. Hold for 5 minutes or longer until the bleeding stops. Then soak a cotton ball in an infusion (box, p.191) of witch hazel leaves or ca-lendula flowers, and gently insert the cotton ball into the nostril.

Rashes

Healing oil Put 1 drop of lavender or tea-tree essential oil directly onto the rash, gently smoothing it over the surface. To treat a large area, apply a blend made by mixing 3 drops of essential oil in ¼ ounce of light olive oil.

Gentle diaper rash treatment For diaper rash, wash the baby's bottom with an infusion (box, p.191) of calendula or chamomile flowers. Pat the skin dry, then massage in a small amount of Simple calendula ointment (box, p.193). Alternatively, combine ⅓ ounce of almond oil, 15 drops of wheat-germ oil, 5 drops of borage oil, and 1 drop of lavender essential oil (note that, of these, only the lavender is an essential oil), and massage into the affected area. Leave the baby without a diaper or for as long as possible.

Rheumatism and arthritis

Relieving compress For temporary relief of aching joints, fill a small bowl with warm water. Swirl in 2 drops of lemon, lavender, rosemary, or eucalyptus essential oil. Soak a cotton pad or cheesecloth, gently squeeze out excess fluid, and apply directly to the affected area. Cover with plastic wrap or a bandage and leave the compress on for at least an hour.

Soothing bath To relieve pain, soak in a comfortably hot bath in which 4 drops of rosemary, lavender, or eucalyptus essential oil have been swirled. Gently massage in any oil still left on the skin after the bath.

Cabbage leaf wrap Bruise a cabbage leaf with a rolling pin until soft. Wrap it around the painful joint and bind with a bandage.

Bracing massage oil With a mortar and pestle, pound together 1 tablespoon of chopped rosemary leaves, 3 teaspoons of celery seed, and 1 teaspoon of fresh chili. Spoon into a jar with a tight-fitting lid and add 8 ounces of vegetable oil. Shake vigorously, then leave for 10 days, shaking periodically. Strain through a paper coffee filter into a sterilized glass bottle and keep in a cool, dark place. Rub 1 to 2 drops onto the skin to test for any adverse reaction. If there is no reaction, gently massage a little of the oil onto the aching joint twice a day.

Sore throat

Soothing gargle Make an infusion (box, p.191) with sage or thyme leaves and gargle warm, as needed. Gargling with a simple solution of ½ teaspoon salt in 1 cup of warm water can also be helpful.

Sprains

First soak the sprained limb in a bucket or sinkful of icy water or cover the sprain with an ice pack for 15 to 20 minutes. Repeat several times during the first 4 hours; then use any of the following remedies.

Cold compress Fill a bowl with water, and add 3 to 4 drops of lavender, rosemary, eucalyptus, nutmeg, or pine essential oil. Swirl the water to blend in the oil. Thoroughly soak a washcloth or gauze pad, squeeze gently to remove excess liquid, and apply to the sprain. Cover the pad with plastic wrap, then with a bandage. Leave on for at least an hour and repeat twice a day.

Olive oil massage Pour 1 ounce of light olive oil into a small jar and add 15 drops of rosemary, 10 drops of nutmeg, and 5 drops of eucalyptus essential oils. Shake well for several minutes, then massage into the sprained area.

Fresh leaf poultice Bruise several fresh leaves of comfrey, cabbage, and plantain with a rolling pin. Place the leaves in a clean cloth and fold to form a pad. Dip in comfortably hot water, squeeze, apply to the skin, and secure with a bandage. When cool, remove, dip in hot water, and reapply (or keep in a hot-water bottle.

Tiredness

Bath oil If you are tired and want to relax, put 6 to 8 drops of essential oil into a comfortably hot bath, swirl the water to disperse the oils, and relax in the bath. Choose from among lavender, geranium, or cinnamon-leaf oils. If you are tired and want a lift, use peppermint or rosemary essential oil instead.

Rosemary and ginseng Slowly drink a cup of an infusion (box, p.191) made from ½ teaspoon dried rosemary leaves and ½ teaspoon dried ginseng root, sweetened with a little honey.

Tired, achy eyes

Cucumber treatment Soothe tired eyes by placing a slice of fresh cucumber on each eye for several minutes.

Eyewash infusion Make an infusion (box, p.191) of calendula or chamomile flowers or borage leaves, strain twice through paper coffee filters, and cool to lukewarm. Use in a sterile glass eye bath, or soak a cotton ball in the infusion and wash it into the eyes. Alternatively, soak two cotton balls and place them on the eyes for 10 minutes.

Toothache

Clove rinse For relief until you can see a dentist, rinse with an infusion (box, p.191) using ¼ ounce whole cloves.

Simple oil rub As a temporary measure, place 1 drop of clove essential oil on a cotton swab, dip the cotton ball in water, and rub on the aching tooth and gum area. See a dentist as soon as possible.

Travel sickness

Simple ginger remedy An effective remedy is to chew on a lump of crystallized ginger, as needed. This is particularly effective for children. Always keep a packet in the car so it is on hand when you need it.

Lemon settler Make a warm, tummy-soothing drink by squeezing the juice of 1 lemon in a cup of water sweetened with a teaspoon of honey. Sip, as needed. Keep the drink warm in a thermos when traveling.

Warts

Milky sap treatment Use the milky sap that exudes from freshly cut dandelion stalks or fig leaves. Apply the sap once or twice a day for several days or until the wart pulls away from the skin. Keep the sap away from the skin around the wart and from sensitive areas such as the eyes. If you are using this treatment on a child, cover the wart area with a bandage to prevent spreading the sap to sensitive skin.

USING MEDICINAL PLANTS

ALWAYS make sure you use the correct species of plant. You can't tell from a plant's common name because several may be called the same thing. If in doubt about identification, find the botanical, or Latin, name and check with a local nursery. Plants mentioned in this chapter are listed here with their botanical names.

ALOE VERA *Aloe vera*

ANISEED *Pimpinella anisum*

BLACKBERRY *Rubus* spp.

BORAGE *Borago officinalis*

CALENDULA *Calendula officinalis*

CHAMOMILE *Chamaemelum nobile or Matricaria recutita*

CARAWAY *Carum carvi*

CARDAMOM *Elettaria cardamomum*

CHICKWEED *Stellaria media*

CINNAMON *Cinnamomum zeylanicum*

COMFREY *Symphytum officinale*

DANDELION *Taraxacum officinale*

DILL *Anethum graveolens*

FENNEL *Foeniculum vulgare*

FEVERFEW *Chrysanthemum parthenium*

FIG *Ficus carica*

HOREHOUND *Marrubium vulgare*

LAVENDER *Lavandula angustifolia*

LEMON BALM *Melissa officinalis*

PARSLEY *Petroselinum crispum*

PEPPERMINT *Mentha piperita*

PETTY SPURGE *Euphorbia peplus*

PINE *Pinus sylvestris, P. palustris, P. pinaster, P. radiata*

PLANTAIN *Plantago major, P. lanceolata*

RASPBERRY *Rubus idaeus*

ROSE *Rosa* spp.

ROSEMARY *Rosmarinus officinalis*

SAGE *Salvia officinalis*

SPEARMINT *Mentha spicata*

SWEET CICELY *Myrrhis odorata*

THYME *Thymus vulgaris*

VIOLET *Viola odorata*

WINTER SAVORY *Satureja montana*

WITCH HAZEL *Hamamelis virginiana*

YARROW *Achillea millefolium*

Pets and Wildlife

Whether you are a dog or cat owner, an avid bird-watcher, or simply a conscientious gardener looking for new ways to keep a healthy balance of nature in your yard without using toxic chemicals, this chapter will offer you plenty of practical and useful ideas.

If your best friend is a country dog, you can build a well-insulated outdoor house that will keep your furry companion warm in winter, cool in summer, and out of the rain all year round. If yours is a city dog, you can—with minimal sewing skills—make a cozy, fresh-smelling bed that not only matches your decor but stashes into a corner to keep people from tripping over it. We also include instructions for a snappy, warm, washable dog coat for winter. For cat owners, we offer a stylish window perch to satisfy your pet's curiosity about the passing scene and a handsome sling bed. Pet owners with a sense of fun will like our fanciful holiday collar covers. There are also recipes for healthful animal foods and nostrums.

Bird lovers may be inspired by our plans for birdhouses, bird feeders, and birdbaths and the ideas for mixing up food mixtures to attract your favorite species. Gardeners should welcome the bat house and butterfly house, which attract these creatures. Bats are voracious insect eaters, and butterflies make sure your flowers get pollinated.

BEFORE YOU BEGIN ...

Many skills—from sewing to cooking to carpentry—come into play when you make comforts for your pets or the wildlife in your neighborhood. While some woodworking demands special equipment and skills, many of these projects are simple enough for youngsters to make.

Tools for building projects

For the building projects in this chapter—doghouse, cat window perch, birdhouses, bird feeders, hanging birdbath, bat house, and butterfly house—you will need the following common tools: electric drill, hammer, coping saw, hand saw, keyhole saw, miter box, paint brush, pliers (regular and long-nose), screwdriver, stapler, utility knife, wire cutters, wood chisel, and wood vise. Having an electric saw, a machinist's vise, and a router will make some of the work easier and quicker, but they aren't essential. One project, the Stump birdbath, requires a router.

Simplifying the projects

Some of the wood projects have sophisticated plans with angled sides and beveled edges. You can make a perfectly serviceable birdhouse, however, by using right angles and straight sides. Also, if you don't have a router, you can skip the beveling, which is simply a fancy way of finishing the edges. Butt the corners of trim rather than mitering them, if you don't have the tools for making miter cuts. The nesting shelf for robins will attract birds just as well without curved sides.

Buying materials

If you have a workshop in your home, chances are that you will have scrap materials left over from other projects for putting together such small structures as the birdhouses or feeders. If not, take the materials list at the beginning of each project to a lumberyard and ask for guidance in what to buy. Many lumber yards will also make some basic cuts for

you with their power equipment, which will save you time and effort if you don't have power equipment of your own.

Cutting wood pieces

For a more durable structure, cut out wood projects so that the grain of the wood runs parallel to the longest dimension of a piece. For the wood projects in this chapter, the grain runs with the length of the wood unless stated otherwise. That doesn't always make the most efficient use of your board, but it does result in a stronger birdhouse or feeder.

Preparing for painting

Use a sanding block and 120 grit paper to lightly sand all sides of any wood pieces that you plan to paint. Sand with the grain. You can use emery cloth or an emery board to sand any hard-to-reach places. Sanding smooths the surface and removes dirt and fingerprints that might interfere with the paint's adhesion. Sand any sharp edges just enough to "break" or round the edge so that paint will adhere better.

For outdoor projects, spot prime any knots with an exterior-grade knot primer. This will prevent the knots from "bleeding through" the paint and discoloring it. When the spot primer has dried, brush an exterior grade wood primer (water-based is less harmful to wildlife) on all surfaces and edges of the wood, and let the primer dry overnight. On a birdhouse, prime the inside edge of the entrance hole, but leave the interior bare (you don't want birds eating paint), and take care to keep primer from clogging up the drainage slits in the floor.

TECHNIQUES FOR INSTALLING A POLE

1 *Dig a 24-inch deep hole for the pole (or a post of pressure-treated wood). Use a post-hole digger or a shovel. Place a large flat rock at the bottom of the hole.*

2 *Fill the hole with 5 to 6 inches of gravel before you put the pole (or post) in place. This will ensure proper drainage around the pole once it is set.*

3 *Set pole in hole; check its plumb with a level. Fill hole with alternate layers of gravel (3inches) and soil (4 inches), tamping after each, to 6 inches from. top.*

4 *Check plumb of pole again and fill top 6 inches of hole with concrete, overfilling so that the concrete slopes away from the pole for good drainage.*

GLOSSARY

LUAUN PLYWOOD: A smooth grade of mahogany plywood used for interior walls.

MACHINIST'S VISE: A heavy-duty vise with steel jaws that is bolted to a workbench for extra strength.

MITER BOX: A device for making accurate angled cuts in wood and other materials with a handsaw to create a mitered joint.

ROUTER: A woodworking power tool used to make bevels and other decorative edges and fine joinery.

SABER SAW: A portable electric saw that can make straight or curved cuts in wood, metal, plastic and other materials.

TABLE SAW: A stationary power saw mounted in a table.

The basic carpentry and sewing tools you need for the projects in this chapter are found in most home tool kits or sewing baskets. Certainly, such basic power tools as an electric drill and a sewing machine have many home maintenance uses.

Beveling the edges with a router

For a professional finish, you can round over, or bevel, the edges of your bird houses and feeders with a router. Dry assemble all the pieces, then rub a pencil or a dark crayon along the edges you wish to round over. Set up the router. Use a round-over bit with a pilot bearing, and make a couple of test cuts on scrap pieces of wood before starting on the real thing. Clamp the pieces to a workbench as you run the router along the edges. Touch up the cut surfaces as needed with 100 grit sandpaper.

Safety for wildlife.

The nicest houses for dogs, birds, bats, and butterflies are made of naturally weather-resistant woods, such as cedar, cyprus, or redwood, which age well without toxic preservatives. You can safely paint the exterior of wildlife houses with exterior latex paint, if you leave the interior untreated. All of the wildlife structures in this chapter are designed to be opened easily for cleaning. You should plan to scrub houses out once a year. Clean and restock bird feeders and baths more frequently; moldy food isn't healthy for birds and mosquitoes don't hatch in fresh water.

Making your own bird food

What you put in your bird feeder determines the species of birds you attract to your yard. There are many seed eaters. Experiment with different seeds, such as hulled sunflower seed, thistle, safflower seed, black oil sunflower seed, and white millet. Woodpeckers love suet. Hang a suet ball in a net bag, such as oranges come in. Chickadees, titmice, and nuthatches love the high fat and protein of peanuts. Orioles like apples, grapes, or oranges. For humming birds, stir ½ cup granulated sugar into 2 cups water until dissolved. Serve in a nectar feeder with a red opening.

Why our doghouse doesn't look like Snoopy's

Although a gable roof connotes the traditional image of a doghouse, we chose a flat roof for several reasons. Many dogs like to perch atop the house for a view of the neighborhood. Also, the flat roof reduces the volume inside the house, so that in cold weather the dog's body heat can warm it better. The roof and floor are exceptionally strong, allowing you to move the house without harming it. The roof will also support a child who happens to climb on it. An extended eave over the front door keeps rain out and offers shade. The smooth interior surfaces are easy to clean. Ventilating channels just beneath the roof are for summertime cooling (they can be blocked off with scraps of rigid insulation in the winter). A flap can be fit over the door to retain heat in cold weather.

◆ The Comfortable Dog ◆

*Here is an all-weather industrial-strength house for outdoor dogs and a handsome
corner bed for indoor canines, accustomed to central heating, who might also benefit from
a good-looking winter coat that is warm, washable, and a snap to make.*

Doghouse

*This house was designed for a medium-size dog,
but it can easily be scaled up to fit a bigger one.
An expert suggests that the length and width of
the house's floor should be 1½ times the length
of the dog. The ceiling height should be about 1⅓
times the shoulder height of the dog. Site the
house in the shade atop bricks.*

- three 2 x 3 x 30-inch joists
- two 2 x 3 x 27-inch header joists
- two pieces ½ x 27 x 33-inch
  CDX plywood for floor top
  and bottom
- four 2 x 3 x 33-inch front and
  back wall plates
- four 2 x 3 x 21½-inch side
  wall plates
- seven 2 x 3 x 13-inch wall studs
- four 2 x 3 x 15-inch wall studs
- 2 x 3 x 11½-inch door header
- ¼ x 18 x 33-inch luaun plywood
  for front interior wall
- ¼ x 16 x 33-inch luaun plywood
  for back interior wall
- two ¼ x 16 x 21½-inch luaun
  plywood for side interior walls
- four 2 x 3 x 36-inch roof rafters
- two 2 x 3 x 38-inch eaves
- ½ x 38 x 39-inch CDX plywood
  for roof sheathing
- three 2 x 8-foot pieces
  1-inch-thick R-5 extruded
  rigid insulation
- construction adhesive
- ¼ x 38 x 39-inch luaun plywood
  for ceiling
- nails: 8d sinker, 10d sinker,
  6d galvanized common, 4d galvanized finishing, 1-inch roofing
- 1 x 5 tongue-and-groove pine
  siding: 8 courses, 27 inches,

and 9 courses, 34½ inches
- 7 feet corner guard molding
- 1½-inch metal corner braces
  with screws
- 13 feet ¼-inch pine for roof trim
- exterior latex primer and
  paint, brush
- 6½ feet aluminum drip edge
- asphalt roll roofing
- asphalt mastic

Building the floor

1 All the framing is made of 2 x 3's. Cut three
floor joists to 30 inches and two header joists
to 27 inches. Use 8d sinker nails to attach the
header joists to the joists, centering one joist
between the headers (Framing diagram).
2 Cut two pieces of CDX plywood to 27 x 33
inches. Put construction adhesive on one side

*A comfortable home of its own allows your dog
protection from bad weather—even if you're away
and there's no one to put your pet in a safe place.*

of the floor frame and attach one plywood piece to it with 8d galvanized common nails.

3 Flip the floor over and use a utility knife and metal straightedge to cut insulation into panels that fit snugly between joists. Push panels into place, and put a few 8d nails into the sides of the joists to secure the panels. Attach the second piece of plywood to the exposed side of the frame with nails and adhesive.

Building the walls

1 Cut four plates to 33 inches for the front and back walls and two plates to 21 ½ inches for each side wall. Cut seven studs to 13 inches for the side and back walls and four studs to 15 inches for the front wall. Cut the door header to 11 ½ inches. (The taller front wall creates the roof pitch.) Use 8d sinker nails to attach the plates to the studs as shown. Note that the back wall gets a center stud. Form the door opening with two studs in the corner and another stud 11 ½ inches away. Attach the door header between the door studs with a 1-inch space between the header and the top plate.

2 Install the interior walls. Trace the door opening on the luaun for the front wall and cut

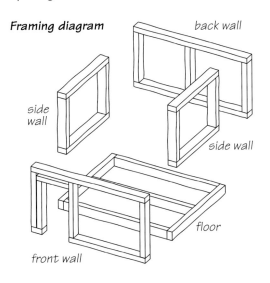

Framing diagram

back wall

side wall

side wall

floor

front wall

it out. Put construction adhesive on one side of each framing assembly and fasten the luaun with galvanized finish nails.

3 Nail the front wall to the floor with 10d sinker nails. Nail the side walls to the floor,

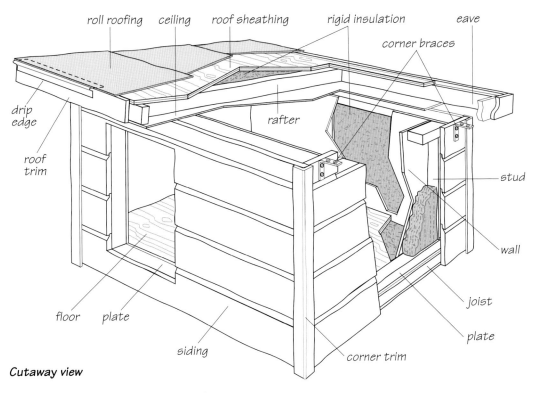

roll roofing   ceiling   roof sheathing   rigid insulation   eave

corner braces

drip edge

rafter

roof trim

stud

wall

floor   plate

joist

plate

siding   corner trim

Cutaway view

making sure the studs are tight against the front wall. Nail the back wall to the floor. Nail each wall to its neighbor. Use a handsaw to remove the "sill" of the door.

4 Cut insulation panels to fit into each wall, including the small space above the door.

Installing roof and siding

1 Fasten the eaves to the rafters with 8d sinker nails. Place one rafter at each end of the eaves and center the remaining rafters 11 inches from the ends. Cut a piece of CDX plywood and a piece of luaun, each to 38 x 39 inches. Attach the CDX to the roof with adhesive and common nails. Cut insulation to fit between rafters. Attach the luaun to the ceiling side with adhesive and galvanized finishing nails.

2 You'll need four full courses of siding for each side of the doghouse, plus a 2-inch-wide course for the top of the front wall and two small pieces to cover the ends of the front top plate, which protrude over the side walls. Start the siding, tongue side up, at the base of each wall. Put 1 galvanized finish nail in each end of the boards, 1 ½ inches up from the bottom

edge. Cut the top board on each wall flush with the top plates.

3 Cut two pieces of corner guard molding to 21 ¾ inches for the front corners and two pieces to 19 ½ inches for the back corners. Use galvanized finish nails to secure the molding.

4 Attach the roof with the corner braces (Cutaway view, above) so that you can remove it for cleaning the interior. Set the roof with an 8-inch overhang at the front. Drill pilot holes for the screws in the ceiling and siding, then attach the roof with the corner braces.

5 Cut roof trim: two side pieces to 39 ¾ inches, a back piece to 38 inches, and a front piece to 39 ½ inches. Position the pieces as shown in the drawing above, flush with the top of the roof, and attach with finishing nails.

Finishing

1 To paint the house, first prime the siding and trim, then apply two coats of paint.

2 Install drip edge on eaves with roofing nails. Apply double-coverage rolled roofing, bedded in asphalt mastic. This roof requires three pieces run horizontally.

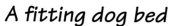

A fitting dog bed

By custom making a bed for your dog, you can tailor it to suit your decor as well. The inner liner, which holds the filling, and the outer cover are made in exactly the same way.

THE LINER
- **2 yards muslin, at least 45 inches wide**
- **24 inches ¾ -inch-wide hook and loop fastener tape**
- **1 bag (10 pounds) cedar shavings**

THE COVER
- **2 yards fabric, at least 45 inches wide**
- **24 inches ¾ -inch-wide hook and loop fastener tape**

To start

Measure your dog from nose to base of tail; add 10 inches to the measurement for a comfortable bed size. Our bed is for a 34-inch-long dog, so the sides are 44 inches long. Adjust the measurements accordingly for your dog.

Make the liner first; it allows you to practice, and the cover will be easier to sew together.

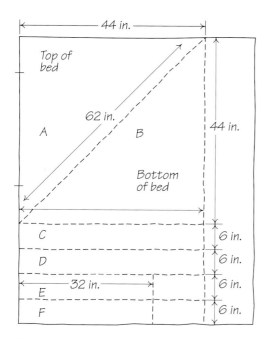

Dog bed pattern

This handsome navy-and-white checked dog bed allows the family pet to snuggle up in the living room, where an easy chair sports matching checked pillows.

Cutting

1 For the top and bottom of the bed: Cut a 44-inch square of fabric. Fold it diagonally and cut along the fold (A and B in pattern).
2 For the short side panels: Cut two pieces 6 inches wide and 44 inches long or length to equal the side (C and D in pattern).
3 For the long side panel: Measure the long side and add 2 inches for seam allowances (a total of 64 inches for our bed). Cut two 6-inch-wide pieces to equal the measurement. For our bed, the two pieces (E and F in pattern) are 32 inches long.

Closure and assembly

1 Select top piece A. Fold a ¼ -inch hem toward the wrong side of the fabric along one short side. Machine-stitch and press.
2 With the right side of the fabric facing you, center a hook strip of the fastener tape along the hemmed edge (covering the raw edge of hem). Pin and machine-stitch on four sides.
3 Repeat Step 1 on side panel C.

4 On the right side of panel C, center the loop strip of fastener tape over the hemmed edge, pin, and machine-stitch on four sides.
5 With the right sides of A and C facing, match and close the tape strips (they will form the inside of the seam allowance). Complete the seam on either side of the tape, leaving ½ inch open at the outer edges.
6 To make the side panel: With right sides together, pin and sew panels E and F together at one short end; press seam open.
7 With right sides together, pin and sew one end of panel D to the E-F panel; press seam open. Then sew the opposite end of panel D to panel C (the piece with the fastener tape), matching the bottom edges; press seam open. Finally, to complete the circle of side panels, sew the opposite end of panel C to the E-F panel; press seam open.

8 With right sides together, pin and sew side panels to piece A (panel C is already sewn). Clip corners; press seam toward side panels.

9 With right sides together, pin and sew piece B to the side panels. Clip corners; press seams toward the side panels.

10 Turn right side out. Repeat process to make bed cover.

11 To finish: Fill the liner with cedar shavings and close hook and loop strip. Fit the liner into the cover, matching corners for a smooth fit.

Polarfleece dog coat

Your dog can feel as cold as you do on a frosty winter walk. This coat will keep the chill away.

- ◆ **1 yard polarfleece**
- ◆ **6 yards 1-inch trim (bias-cut or flexible trim works best on curves and corners)**
- ◆ **4 buttons for decoration**
- ◆ **8 inches ⅝ -inch-wide hook and loop fastener tape**

Making the coat

1 Measure the dog around its neck and chest; then from neck to rump. Our coat is made for a dog with a 17-inch neck, a 27-inch chest, and a length of 27 inches.

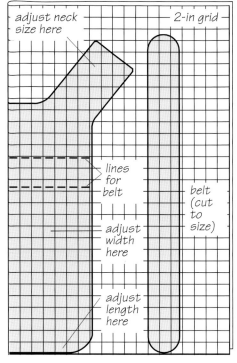

adjust neck size here   *2-in grid*

lines for belt

belt (cut to size)

adjust width here

adjust length here

DIAGRAM 1

2 Enlarge pattern (Diagram 1) on 2-inch graph paper (p.276). Cut out fabric using the pattern but adjusting it to your dog's measurements.

3 For the trim around the edge of the coat: Begin at the belt line on the wrong side of the coat. Pin the trim, right side down, ½ inch in from the edge. (To start, fold in the end of the trim ½ inch to prevent raveling. To finish, overlap folded trim ends by ½ inch.) On low heat, press the trim toward the edge of the coat.

4 Fold the trim over the edge. Pin in place on the right side of the fabric, making neat folds around angles. Stitch edge of trim and press.

5 Pin two 3-inch hook strips of fastener tape to the wrong side of the fabric on the left collar tab. Pin two 3-inch loop strips to the right side of fabric on the right collar tab (Diagram 2). Make sure strips line up evenly. Stitch all the edges of the strips.

hook tape on right side of fabric

loop tape on wrong side of fabric

DIAGRAM 2

6 With right side of the coat facing you, sew decorative buttons on the left collar tab, covering the outline of the tape strips (Diagram 3).

7 To make the belt, follow Steps 3 and 4 for applying the trim to the belt.

8 Pin the belt in place on the coat, letting the extra length hang off to the left (Diagram 3). Machine-stitch the belt to the coat along the edges of the belt trim.

9 Place a 2-inch strip of hook tape on the belt end attached to the coat. Cut it to match the curve of the belt and stitch it in place.

10 Check to make sure the belt fits the dog. Position the loop tape accordingly on the wrong side of the loose belt end and stitch in place.

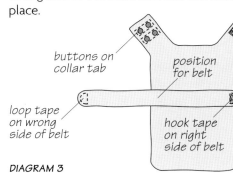

buttons on collar tab

position for belt

loop tape on wrong side of belt

hook tape on right side of belt

DIAGRAM 3

More than just a canine fashion statement, this polarfleece dog coat is as warm as it is handsome.

· The Happy Cat's Meow ·

*Thoughtful cat owners, who may also want to save their upholstery, can make a cozy bed
to keep their kitty out of drafts and off the sofa. If your house doesn't have window seats for
viewing the world, your cat will consider our window perch the next best thing.*

Cat sling

*A cozy spot for the favored feline, this perch calls
for modest woodworking and sewing skills.*

THE FRAME
- **4 oak stair balusters**
- **3 wooden dowels, ½-inch
  diameter and 4 feet long**
- **sandpaper (120 grit)**
- **yellow wood glue**
- **clear urethane sealer**
- **4 self-adhesive floor protectors**

THE SLING TOP
- **1 yard polarfleece**
- **½ yard 1-inch elastic**
- **2 yards matching double-fold
  bias binding**

Constructing the frame

1 For the legs: Cut the tenon off the bottom
of each baluster, then cut each baluster to 16
inches. The squared section of each baluster—
which will be the bottom of the leg—should
be at least 7 inches long.
2 Put a ½-inch spade bit in your drill. Working on one flat face of each leg, center and drill

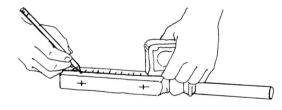

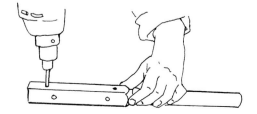

two ⅝-inch-deep holes, one 2 inches, the
other 6 inches, from the bottom. On an adjacent face, center and drill two ⅝-inch-deep
holes, one 1½ inches, the other 6½ inches,
from the bottom.
3 Cut eight dowels 15⅞ inches long. Sand the
ends to fit easily into the leg holes.
4 With sandpaper, smooth any sharp edges on
the legs, and round the tops of the legs.
5 To assemble the frame: Put a light dab of
glue into each hole before inserting a dowel.
Use a hammer and a block of wood to seat the
dowels firmly. When the glue is dry, apply a
coat of the urethane sealer, let it dry, and apply
a second coat. When the finish is dry, attach a
floor protector to the bottom of each leg.

Constructing the sling

1 For the sling, cut out a 17-inch square of
polarfleece. For the pockets (for hanging the
sling from the frame), cut out four 8-inch
squares and fold each in half diagonally.
2 Cut four pieces of elastic ½ inch longer
than the top of a leg. Wrap each piece of
elastic into a ring that
will fit tightly over the
leg. Stitch one elastic
ring onto the long
side of each pocket
triangle (right).

3 Arrange the triangles, ring side down and
ring inside, at each corner of the sling. Pin and
machine-stitch in place, rounding the corners
slightly. Trim the corners.
4 To finish the edges of the sling with the bias
binding, follow Steps 3 and 4 for the Polarfleece dog coat on page 205. (The edging reinforces the soft edges of the fabric and gives
the sling a finished look.)
5 To assemble the cat sling, slip an elastic ring
over the top of each leg for security. Then let
the sling hang from the legs by the pockets.

Window perch for cats

*This project is sized to fit a window that is at
least 24½ inches wide.*

- **¾ x 10 x 22-inch plywood base**
- **two 1 x 2 x 23½-inch front
  and back rim pieces**
- **two 4-inch mending plates**
- **two 1 x 2 x 10-inch side
  rim pieces**
- **25-inch piece screen molding
  for the front (optional)**
- **two 12-inch pieces screen
  molding for the sides (optional)**
- **yellow wood glue**
- **4d finishing nails**
- **sandpaper (120 grit)**
- **1-inch brads (optional)**
- **1 x 4 x 12-inch brace**
- **two 1⅝-inch wood screws**
- **6 inches foam weatherstripping**

1 Cut the base of the perch from plywood.
Measure the depth of the window stool
(below). Bend one end of each mending plate
so that it hooks over the outside of the stool.
To bend a plate, secure it in a machinist's vise.
Use a hammer and a block of wood to pound
the plate until it makes a 90-degree angle.

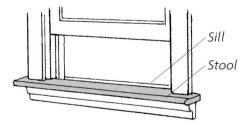

Sill

Stool

2 The perch has a rim made of 1 x 2 pine
(actual dimensions, ¾ x 1½ inches). The rim
pieces are mitered at the corners. Place pieces
of 1 x 2 against the base and mark the inside of
the miter cuts. Make the cuts in a miter box.

Drill those holes, too. Using a ³⁄₁₆-inch bit, drill a seed hole 1½ inches above each perch hole.

3 Cut a 1½ x 2½-inch-high hole for the seed-viewing window. Start by drilling a hole with a spade bit. Complete the cuts with a saber saw or keyhole saw. Make the window itself from a 3 x 4-inch piece of clear plastic, cut from a food container. Hold the window in the pipe with masking tape, and drill ¹⁄₁₆-inch-diameter holes through the pipe into the window. Secure the window with machine bolts, lock washers, and nuts, then remove the tape.

4 Make the feeder cap by cutting the utility bucket down to 2½ inches. Mark an even line and use shop scissors to cut it.

5 Rest the bucket upside down atop the pipe, center it, then drill two ³⁄₁₆-inch holes through the bottom of the bucket just beyond the outside edge of the pipe on opposite sides of the bucket. Drill another pair of holes ½ inch below the top of the pipe. Remove the wire handle from the bucket to make the hanger.

6 Cut three dowel perches 9¼ inches long. Round over ends with sandpaper. Line up highest perch so an equal length extends on each side of the pipe. Mark 2 points on the dowel just inside the tube wall. Remove perch and drill a hole through each mark to accommodate a 1-inch brad. Repeat with other perches. Slip perches back into place, and use needle-nose pliers to maneuver a brad into each hole. Once each perch is locked into place this way, give it a quarter turn so that the brads squeeze against the inside of the tubing. Dab silicone caulk over brads to seal base of each perch.

7 Install bottom cap with ABS cement.

8 To install top cap, work ends of wire handle into holes in the cap and then into holes at top of tube; bend ends of wire over with pliers. To fill feeder, lift cap, pulling it up the wire handle until the opening is clear.

9 Use a chain to hang the feeder by the wire handle from a tree branch or a porch frame.

Hanging bird feeder

Here's a bird feeder that calls for a handful of materials that you may already have and some very basic skills. It's a perfect parent-child project.

- 4-inch-diameter x 18-inch-long lightweight plastic drainpipe
- 4-inch plastic pipe cap
- four No. 6 ½-inch-long machine bolts with toothed lock washers and nuts
- 80-ounce plastic utility bucket
- three ³⁄₈ x 9¼-inch wood dowels
- ABS cement
- six 1-inch brads
- silicone caulk

1 Use a hacksaw to cut the drainpipe to 18 inches. Keep the cuts as square as possible. Sand off burrs with 80-grit sandpaper.

2 Mark the height and location of three perch holes, as shown in the photograph. Use a ³⁄₈-inch spade bit at slow speed to drill one hole at each height, spaced equidistantly around the diameter of the pipe. Put a scrap of dowel into the hole and mark the location for an opposing hole on the other side of the pipe.

• Birdbaths •

To attract birds to your feeding station or your birdhouses, you also need to provide a ready source of water— for drinking and for cleaning. After you watch some birds clowning around in a birdbath, you will swear they come just for the fun.

Stump birdbath

This is an inexpensive project that calls for a minimum of materials. It can be built using any stump of wood you have handy—the one shown here is maple. The stump serves as a shallow, rustic birdbath that fits well into any garden. Fill it with fresh water every day to discourage mosquitoes. If your log isn't cut square on both ends, dig out a hole that will hold the top of it level.

- ◆ **a log at least 14 inches in diameter**
- ◆ **12-inch-diameter ceramic or plastic saucer used under plant pots to catch water**
- ◆ **grease pencil or marker**
- ◆ **router with flat cutting bit**

1 Find a likely stump, then trace the diameter of the saucer at the center of its top surface with a grease pencil or marker, as shown at right. If the bottom of the saucer is slanted, turn it upside down, trace the outline of the top lip, then mark a second outline within the first.

2 Set up a router with a flat-cutting bit.

3 Don't try to dig out all the wood at once— you'll have to make at least three or four passes, depending on the power of your router, each slightly deeper than the previous one. Start by making a 4-inch-diameter hole at the center of the log, and work your way down to the depth of the saucer (right).

4 Reset the router for a shallow cut and begin to enlarge the hole outward. This technique ensures that the base of the router will always have firm support while cutting.

5 Test-fit the saucer and adjust the hole as needed (right). To keep water from collecting in the area beneath the saucer, run a bead of clear silicone caulk around the lip of the saucer and set it in place.

6 To slow the rotting of the log where it meets the earth, brush wood preservative on the bottom end before you set it in place.

Hanging birdbath

This is an easy project, but working with wire takes a little practice. Site the birdbath in a sheltered area—it will attract more birds and it will be buffeted less by breezes. A hanging birdbath should not be left out in high winds.

- ◆ **coated clothesline wire (a 50-foot roll is more than enough)**
- ◆ **2 feet 14-gauge galvanized wire**
- ◆ **8 feet light gauge chain**
- ◆ **4 ¾-inch S-hooks**
- ◆ **12-inch diameter plant saucer (glazed ceramic or plastic to hold water)**
- ◆ **O-shaped metal key ring**

1 Cut a length of clothesline wire long enough to fit around the saucer just beneath the lip, plus 4 inches for overlap and securing it. Form a ring; then, to secure the ring at the overlap, use pliers to twist galvanized wire tightly around the clothesline wire (below). Make 5 turns, then clip off the excess.

Fold each end of the clothesline wire over the galvanized wire (below).

MAKING THE STUMP BIRDBATH

1 *Find a likely log, then trace the diameter of the saucer, roughly centered, on the log. If the sides of the saucer are slanted, the hole in the log will have to be large enough to hold the saucer's widest part.*

2 *Start by routing a 4-inch hole at the center of the log. Make at least 3 or 4 passes (depending on the power of your router), each slightly deeper than the previous one, then enlarge the hole outward.*

3 *When the hole reaches full dimension, test-fit the saucer. Widen the hole as needed. Run a bead of clear silicone caulk around the lip of the saucer, and set it in place. The caulk protects the wood below.*

2 Cut three 5-inch lengths of galvanized wire to serve as guards for holding the saucer inside the clothesline ring. Form a loop in one end of each guard using needlenose pliers. Hook the loops over the clothesline ring at three equidistant points and crimp the loops tight to the ring with pliers (below). Bend the ends to fit over the sides of a ceramic saucer, if that is what you are using, as shown below. If you are using a plastic saucer, leave the ends straight for now.

3 Midway between the guard wires, slip three S-hooks over the clothesline wire at three equidistant places. The open top of the S should be facing outward. Crimp the S-hooks tight on the clothesline ring with pliers.

4 Place a ceramic saucer in the clothesline ring and slip the three bent galvanized-wire guards over the lip. They will prevent the saucer from slipping out of the ring when birds land on it or a gust of wind catches it. Clip the wire guards with wire cutters just short of the base of the saucer. If you are using a plastic saucer, drill holes in the saucer's rim directly above each guard piece. Put the straight ends of the guard pieces through the holes and bend them back over the rim for security.

5 Cut three 2-foot lengths of chain and slip the end of each over the open end of each S-hook. Crimp the hook to retain the chain.

6 Connect the opposite ends of the chains to the O-shaped key ring (or a large S-hook) for hanging the birdbath on a tree limb. Use weatherproof cord to tie the birdbath to an overhanging branch. Fill with fresh water daily.

Two birdbaths blend into the landscape of a backyard. Both have shallow ceramic basins for water. In one case, the basin sits on a tree stump (near right); in the other, it hangs from a wire and chain support (far right).

◆ Homes for Bats and Butterflies ◆

Sometimes, the best way to attract helpful wildlife to your yard is to build suitable living quarters.
Bats, once associated only with horror movies and Halloween, are now appreciated as the voracious
insect eaters that they are. Butterflies are more than pretty; they help pollinate plants

Bats enter this house at the peak of a barn from the open bottom and hang from the partitions to rest.

Bat house

A small structure can house a surprising number of bats; this model, for example, holds up to 50.

- **two ¾ x 6 ¾ x 24-inch plywood siding or pine board for sides**
- **¾ x 7 ½ x 26-inch plywood siding or pine board for back**
- **¾ x 7 ½ x 20 ¼ -inch plywood siding or pine board for front**
- **¾ x 7 ½ x 10-inch plywood siding or pine board for roof**
- **¼ x 6 ½ -inch luaun plywood, cut to fit five grooves, for partitions**
- **½ x ¾ -inch x 12-feet pine for trim**
- **1 roll 24-inch-wide, 19-gauge, ½ -inch-square galvanized hardware cloth**
- **heavy-duty staples**
- **1 ½ -inch galvanized finishing nails**
- **exterior-grade wood glue**

Exploded view

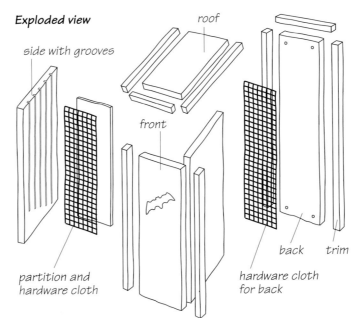

side with grooves

roof

front

partition and hardware cloth

hardware cloth for back

back   trim

1 Cut the sides, back, front, and roof to the dimensions in the materials list. When cutting the roof, cut one short side with the saw set for a 30-degree bevel (Exploded view).

2 Drill four ¼ -inch-diameter mounting holes in the back piece. Locate the holes 1 inch from the top or bottom and 1 inch from the sides. These holes will allow you to hang the house from a tree or mount it to a building.

3 As shown in the Side pattern (right), each side has five stepped grooves to hold the partitions. It's easiest to cut these grooves before you make the angled cuts at top and bottom. Lay out the grooves so that the left side of each groove is 1 inch from the left side of the next. Use a router with a ¼-inch-diameter straight bit and make the grooves ¼-inch deep.

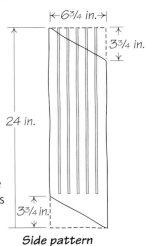

|←6¾ in.→|

3¾ in.

24 in.

3¾ in.

Side pattern

4 Make the angled cuts on the top and bottom of the side pieces, as shown in the Side pattern (above).

5 Cut five pieces of luaun plywood to 6 ½ inches wide. Make the lengths fit the five groove lengths on the sides.

6 To give the bats something to cling to, cut six pieces of wire hardware cloth to fit to within an inch of the edges of the partitions. Staple these pieces in place.

7 Place the partitions in the

grooves. Position the top of the sides 2 inches from the top of the back. Attach the front, back, and top to the sides with the finishing nails and glue.

8 Sand the outside of the house, then prime with exterior primer. Apply two coats of exterior paint.

9 Cut the trim to fit and attach with glue and finishing nails.

10 Mount the house on a tree or building 20 feet or more above the ground.

11 The bat on the front of the house is optional. Sketch your own from the photograph or look through your Halloween decorations. Use a saber saw or coping saw to cut the bat from a piece of ¼-inch luaun plywood.

Butterfly house

Some butterflies migrate long distances, while others hang around the neighborhood. This house provides a safe haven for nonmigrating butterflies, and is a cool shelter for them in hot weather.

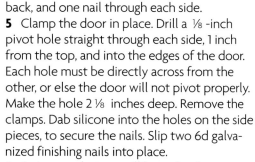

- ◆ ⅞ x 3 ½ x 3 ½ -inch cedar base
- ◆ **two ⅞ x 3 ½ x 18- inch cedar sides**
- ◆ **two ⅞ x 3 ½ x 20 ½ -inch cedar front and back**
- ◆ **scraps of cedar shingles**
- ◆ **¾ x 1 x 6 ¾ -inch corner molding for roof ridge**
- ◆ **6d galvanized finishing nails**
- ◆ **cabinet knob (or handle) with mounting bolt**
- ◆ **1-inch-long aluminum brads**
- ◆ **zinc turn button**
- ◆ **1 x 10-inch mending plate**
- ◆ **1-inch no. 10 galvanized screws**

1 The butterfly house is made of cedar boards that are smooth on one side, rough on the other. Assemble with smooth side out. First cut the base, sides, front, and back to the dimensions in the materials list. Lop off each corner of the base at 45 degrees for drainage.

2 Lay out the front and back pieces, as shown in the exploded view (right). When laying out the slots in the front piece, note that the measurements are to points at the centers of holes

to be drilled. Drill into each mark with a ½ -inch spade bit, then connect each pair of holes using a saber saw. Sand smooth the face of the front piece and edges of the holes.

3 Assemble the house. Nail the back and front to one side with 6d galvanized finishing nails.

4 Install the base, putting two nails each through the front and back, and one nail through each side.

5 Clamp the door in place. Drill a ⅛ -inch pivot hole straight through each side, 1 inch from the top, and into the edges of the door. Each hole must be directly across from the other, or else the door will not pivot properly. Make the hole 2 ⅛ inches deep. Remove the clamps. Dab silicone into the holes on the side pieces, to secure the nails. Slip two 6d galvanized finishing nails into place.

6 A zinc turn button will keep the door closed. Drill a hole for the turn button's screw, and attach the turn button.

7 Drill a hole for a knob near the bottom of

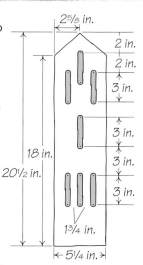

Side pattern

Exploded view

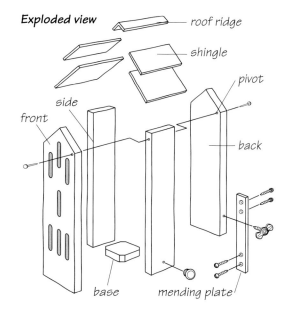

A butterfly house should be situated at a height under 5 feet and near the flowers that feed the butterflies.

the door. This knob called for a ½ -inch diameter countersink hole and a ³⁄₁₆ -inch through hole for the bolt. Attach the knob.

8 The roof consists of four pieces of scrap wood shingle in two layers. Cut the pieces to the shapes shown in the Exploded view. Use 1-inch aluminum brads to attach them with equal overhangs at the eaves. Install the corner molding as the ridge with silicone caulk.

9 Stand strips of bark upright inside the house to give butterflies a place to cling.

10 A butterfly house is best placed in the garden, atop a short pole or fence post. For post mounting, attach a 1 x 10-inch mending plate to the back of the house with galvanized screws, then screw the plate to the side of the post.

Yard and Garden

A kitchen garden full of fresh herbs and vegetables for healthful family meals, a carefree flower bed with colorful blossoms to fill every room in the house, a patio container brimming with red, ripe, ready-to-pick strawberries—these are among the pleasures you can enjoy by following the instructions in this chapter.

We offer lots of creative ideas for making the most of your precious outdoor space, not only as a setting for plants but also as a restful spot for you and your family. You'll discover ways to integrate man-made structures into the natural landscape: how to turn half a barrel into a tiny pond, how to build an arbor for your climbing roses, and how to improvise a rustic fence. You'll learn how to create a topiary animal out of a common garden shrub— step by step—and how to lay a curved brick or gravel path. You'll also find instructions for building a receding trellis that alters perspective and magically extends the horizon of your garden.

In addition, this chapter explains how to maintain your garden the easy and healthy way. Follow our instructions for making your own humus with an efficient compost pile and our tips on discouraging destructive garden pests—from whiteflies to fungi and moles and rabbits— without using toxic chemicals.

BEFORE YOU BEGIN...

You can turn an ordinary yard into a tranquil retreat from the workaday world. While nurturing your plants and garden beds, add shape and ornamentation to the landscape with benches, arbors, pools, and containers that you have made yourself. In this chapter we show you how to do just that.

TRANSFORM your garden into an outdoor space that is as inviting as any room in your home. With the help of pathways, containers, ornaments, furniture, and structures, you can shape and unify the natural landscape. A stone pathway, for example, lends a fluid sense of motion to a flower border. A trellis swathed in blooms becomes a majestic centerpiece. Handmade rustic seats invite visitors to linger. When you make the pieces yourself, you put your own stamp on the garden. Indeed, most of the projects in this chapter can be varied to suit your garden's special needs and features and your own personal preferences.

A little planning is a good investment
When planning the design of your garden, let fences, pathways, trellises—even the house—serve as a framework for the plants. Surround a bench with hedges to create a private reading room. Dig a pond to hold delicate aquatic plants. Build frames to contour topiary. You might even use natural elements to shape your garden. Trained hedges, for example, do the work of fences. Grapevines can be fashioned into trellises. Border plants serve as garden boundaries.

Drawing up a plan, no matter how rough, will guide you in bringing together all the different elements you want in your garden. Take a clear-eyed look at your choices and the amount of space you can allocate to them. Sketch in the hard framework items first: walls, fences, steps, and

paths. Indicate renovations you want to make, such as a new path. A straight concrete path is the least expensive and the simplest to create, but a curved walkway of brick or stone (directions below) is far more inviting. In the same way, a square hedge is easy to trim, but a handsome topiary shaping along the top will lift your garden out of the ordinary.

Following the sun: exposure
Understanding the position of the sun in different seasons allows you to take optimal advantage of it in your yard. It helps you find the best location for a deck, swimming pool, or barbecue, as well as the proper orientation for a vegetable garden, which needs lots of sun, and a reading nook, which should be shady and cool.

Throughout most of the year, the sun shines from the southeast in the morning and the southwest in the afternoon; trees planted on the east or west of a house can help to shade and cool it in summer. The angle of the sun is low in winter, enabling sunlight to penetrate below the lowest branches, but it also creates longer shadows. In summer, the sun is higher in the sky and more directly overhead.

Always keep in mind that the north side of a house is more shaded than the south side and that winds from the north are generally cooler than those from the south. Plants chosen for a northern exposure must be hardy and tolerant of shade and wind.

LAYING A PATH OF BRICKS OR STONES

1 *For best results, temporarily frame the path with a removable wooden edging, called formwork. Use 6-inch-wide strips of ¾ - inch plywood or scrap board. For a permanent edging, use preservative-treated lumber.*

2 *For a curved path, mark the perimeter with a string line (p.247) and stakes at 18-inch intervals. Before nailing the edging to the stakes, make it flexible enough to bend with a series of saw cuts halfway through the inside surface.*

3 *Dig between the framed edges deep enough to allow the bricks to sit level with the surface on top of a 2½ -inch layer of sand or stone dust. Spread the sand with a rake, checking for evenness with a spirit level before tamping down.*

4 *Starting in a corner and kneeling on a piece of flat board, pack bricks tightly in position according to your chosen pattern. When all are laid, sweep fine sand into cracks and crevices and hose down the path with a fine spray.*

Understand your climate

For the successful gardener, the secret of growing healthy plants can be summed up in a sentence: Work *with* nature, not against it. To start, identify your United States Department of Agriculture (USDA) hardiness zone (right), which is determined by average minimum winter temperatures. Also consider the average rainfall in your area; you don't want to be dependent on an irrigation system in an area with frequent water shortages. Choose plants native to your region or those that are suited to your zone. Your local nursery or Cooperative Extension Service will help guide you; mail-order plants are usually marked with zone limits.

Taking care of your soil

Healthy, fertile soil is the foundation of successful gardening. Adding organic matter when starting a garden bed will save future woes. Your first step—even before you plant—is to dig in a 4-inch or deeper layer of compost mixed with well-composted animal manure. Repeat this procedure at least twice a year and mulch the soil with organic matter, such as salt hay, leaves, or even newspapers, each time you dig in the compost. Doing so will increase water and nutrient retention in sandy soil and help open the pores of clay soil, thus allowing excess water to drain away.

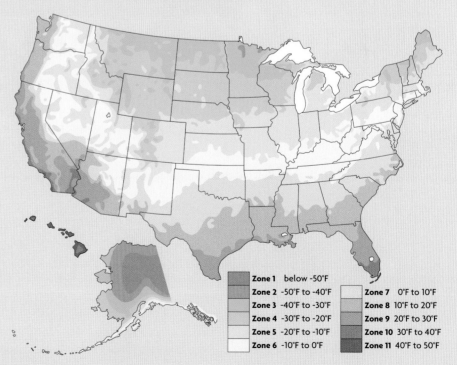

Zone 1 below -50°F	
Zone 2 -50°F to -40°F	**Zone 7** 0°F to 10°F
Zone 3 -40°F to -30°F	**Zone 8** 10°F to 20°F
Zone 4 -30°F to -20°F	**Zone 9** 20°F to 30°F
Zone 5 -20°F to -10°F	**Zone 10** 30°F to 40°F
Zone 6 -10°F to 0°F	**Zone 11** 40°F to 50°F

223

◆ The Kitchen Garden ◆

*What could be easier than stepping out the back door and plucking fresh cherry tomatoes
or snipping a handful of chives to sprinkle over a hot breakfast omelet? With a little basic preparation
and regular maintenance, you can have the makings of a meal always on hand.*

A *potted garden*

If you are a gardener with limited space or limited time, you can still grow some commonly-used herbs and salad vegetables in a sunny spot near the back door and enjoy fresh ingredients all summer long. You can use several different-size planters and stack them together (below right) or construct the simple three-tiered stand to hold them (opposite page). Terra-cotta containers are handsome but can be expensive; terra-cotta-colored plastic pots are lighter, easier to move, and relatively inexpensive.

- ◆ **3 bowl-shape planters (15 to 24 inches wide in descending sizes)**
- ◆ **2 small flower pots (at least 5 inches high)**
- ◆ **fiberglass window screening**
- ◆ **clippers for cutting screening**
- ◆ **small bag of gravel**
- ◆ **large bag of potting soil**
- ◆ **herb and vegetable seedlings**

1 Start with the largest bowl planter. Cover the drainage hole with small piece of screening and a ½-inch layer of gravel. Place a small flower pot upside down in the center.

2 Keeping the small flower pot centered, fill the bowl planter with potting soil to within 2 inches of the top. A few handfuls of composted manure and a sprinkling of slow-release fertilizer will encourage growth.

3 Place the medium-size bowl planter in the center of the large bowl planter (below) and repeat the procedure described above. Top with the smallest bowl and fill it with potting soil. You are now ready to plant.

4 Plant low-growing or cascading plants in the bottom and middle tiers. Reserve the top for a single, larger plant, such as a tomato. Apply liquid fertilizer twice a month and remove dead leaves to stimulate the growth of new foliage.

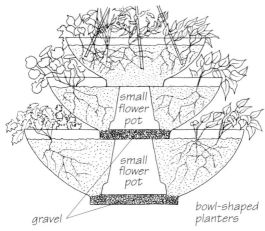

small flower pot

small flower pot

gravel

bowl-shaped planters

For the main planting, we mixed a variety of salad greens, including watercress, arugula, endive, and leaf lettuce, with popular herbs, such as basil, parsley, and chives. Flowering edibles, including nasturtiums, marigolds, and violas, make a colorful addition. You might also try planting dwarf varieties of such vegetables as cucumbers, carrots, tomatoes, squashes, peppers, and eggplants.

HERBS IN THE KITCHEN GARDEN

THE modern kitchen garden has its origins in the walled gardens of medieval monasteries. In the Middle Ages, gardens were set out in rows with paths between the ranks of espaliered fruit trees, herbs, and vegetables. Such a plan is a good basis for a kitchen garden today.

Herbs are a good starting point when you are planning a garden, for not only are they important for seasoning and cooking, but they can be planted to define borders, deter insects, and encourage the growth of other plants. Many herbs are compact in size and make ideal plants for pots and other containers and small garden plots. Some, such as creeping thyme, can even double as a ground cover to replace lawn in low-traffic areas of the yard.

Most herbs are decorative, with small scented leaves and simple, tiny flowers in white, pink, blue, or silver that create a pleasant contrast with ornamental plants. They can also be planted to help soften the edges of formal gardens and can be positioned behind low hedges of boxwood, lavender, or santolina, where their tendency to spread is easily controlled.

As a general rule, herbs need full sun (at least six hours a day) and good drainage. Many scented herbs, such as oregano, rosemary, and thyme, originated on stony Mediterranean hillsides where their roots found relief from hot, dry conditions in cracks under boulders. Most such herbs are not overly particular about soil fertility, but beds should be enriched before planting with a 2-inch layer of well-composted manure or leaves.

An application of a complete fertilizer and a layer of mulch in summer is beneficial. Where summers are wet, you can reduce humidity by using a gravel mulch around herbs. Another solution is to put herbs in pots and raised beds.

Tiered bowls make a pretty planting. If you are growing sun-loving plants, rotate the bowls periodically to let all the plants receive light. Or plant the shadier side with mint or other shade-tolerant plants.

A bed of herbs

With a little preparation, you can realize a cook's dream and pick herbs straight from the garden.

- ◆ **tape measure**
- ◆ **string and wooden stakes**
- ◆ **carpenter's square**
- ◆ **2 x 6-inch cedar edging**
- ◆ **galvanized or plastic bolts or brackets**

1 Use a tape measure, string, and stakes to mark out a rectangular bed of the desired size. Indicate the perimeter by tying the string to a stake at each corner. Use the carpenter's square to ensure the corners make 90-degree angles.
2 Set the edging in place and bolt the corners together or join them with galvanized or plastic brackets.
3 Dig the bed thoroughly to at least the depth of a spade blade, incorporating a 2-inch layer of composted manure or leaves.
4 Plant tall varieties in back and ground covers at the edges, where they can spill onto paths.

Make use of the decorative qualities of herbs: marjoram, thyme, and oregano perform handsomely in a raised bed (above). Catmint, lavender, bronze fennel, and dill all mix happily with calendulas (bottom right). The herb garden at top right is made ornamental by the variety of its shapes and leaf forms and a show of vivid color from salvia and edible nasturtiums.

A raised bed

Vegetables and herbs need soil that has good drainage. The most effective way to achieve it is to raise the garden bed. Doing so creates plenty of room for incorporating manure and compost into the soil to encourage healthy, fast-growing plants. In the large garden below, we've made divisions between the planted areas with wooden shingles, but you can use any attractive, natural material, such as slates, paving bricks, wood blocks, or smooth stones.

- ◆ **graph paper, pencils, and ruler**
- ◆ **string line and hammer**
- ◆ **wooden stakes**
- ◆ **2 x 6-inch cedar edging**
- ◆ **galvanized bolts or brackets**
- ◆ **cedar shingles**

1 Draw your garden plan to scale on paper. Include paths, beds, walls, and other features.

2 Translate the plan to the ground, marking the beds with string and stakes (Step 1, facing page). Hammer in a stake at each corner and dig a shallow channel connecting the four corners so that the edging boards will sit firmly when put in place. In heavy soil, lay 2 inches of coarse sand or road gravel in the channel.

3 If the ground slopes, as in the garden bed below, lay the first pieces of edging on a level

Tightly packed cedar shingles laid end to end make handsome, hard-wearing bed dividers that prevent soil runoff. Used in this way, the shingles should last about 10 years. A plan for this bed is shown on page 228.

Surrounding a bed with raised edging makes it easy to build up the soil with the rich organic matter that crops, such as the peppers, endives, and oregano in the garden above, need in order to thrive. Dividers within the garden bed allow you to cater to the individual soil, nutritional, and watering needs of different plants.

surface and add additional edging in a stepped or terraced fashion to follow the natural slope (right). Bolt or bracket the edging together at the corners.

4 Create individual planting areas within the bed by setting shingles on end in shallow channels. Press firmly in place and tap the edges together lightly so that they fit side by side.

5 Dig and turn over the soil thoroughly to spade-blade depth and add plenty of composted organic matter.

6 Leave the narrow access paths between beds as bare earth so that width of the beds can be varied readily as required. Alternatively, create individual small beds with cedar edging (right) and leave grass paths between them.

Edged and divided bed

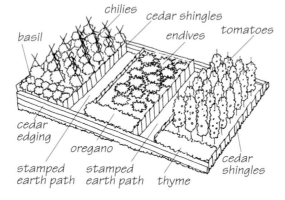

chilies
cedar shingles
basil
endives
tomatoes
cedar edging
oregano
stamped earth path
stamped earth path
thyme
cedar shingles

Small beds

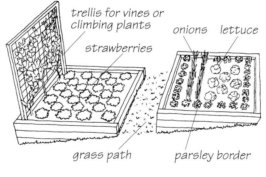

trellis for vines or climbing plants
strawberries
onions
lettuce
grass path
parsley border

FAVORITE HERBS AND VEGETABLES

BASIL differs from many popular herbs in its preference for moist, rich soil conditions. It's a summer-growing annual and is frost-sensitive.

BEANS produce a generous bounty with little labor. The climbing "pole" varieties need support, but bush beans thrive in freestanding rows. In cool areas, grow scarlet-flowered runner beans for an attractive show.

CILANTRO, or coriander, a pungent herb of tropical Asian origin, is related to parsley. It requires warmth and plenty of water in the summer growing season. The plant tends to run to seed, so make sure you buy a nonbolting variety.

CUCUMBERS are invaluable for summer salads. Left to themselves, the plants can take over a garden. Trailing cucumbers, however, can be trained to climb a trellis; the bushier varieties can be planted in raised beds or large tubs.

LETTUCES are many and varied and include romaine, redleaf, black simpson, and Bibb. Most varieties prefer a cooler climate but need at least six hours of sunlight a day.

MINT is a flavoring herb with many varieties, tastes, and aromas. Popular varieties include apple, spearmint, and peppermint. Mint spreads profusely, so keep the plants contained.

OREGANO and marjoram are very similar and are often confused: Marjoram is the milder tasting of the two. Use either one in stuffings or in dishes with a Mediterranean flavor. Golden and variegated forms are useful ground covers.

PEPPERS thrive in the heat. You can easily grow hot chili peppers in a patio container as long as they get plenty of sun and warmth. If you want to keep your green peppers sweet, grow them far away from their hotter relatives.

SAGE, particularly common sage, is a major culinary herb, but most other members of the Salvia family have cosmetic uses.

SQUASH can be grown on a trellis if space is a concern. Pick summer squash when it is young and small for maximum sweetness.

TOMATOES are a must in the home garden. Where space is limited, grow cherry or "patio" varieties in containers.

VARIATION Many flowers and herbs make good plant companions because they either enhance the growth of the plants around them or provide protection against certain pests and diseases. Some successful combinations include: French marigolds with most vegetables, to repel nematodes; garlic and other onion-family members with roses, to encourage vigorous growth; basil with tomatoes, to deter white flies, which spread fungal diseases.

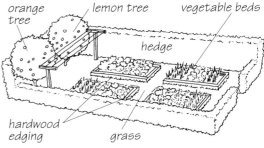

Solid edging clearly defines a bed (left) and helps prevent soil runoff. Landscape ties laid in a stepped profile are best for a sloping site (bottom left). Herbs will thrive on the gradient's low side, where drainage is best.

GETTING THE BEST FROM YOUR PLANTS

Select a site that is open but sheltered and gets at least six hours of sun a day. For best results, choose a southern or southeastern exposure.

The ideal loam is moisture-retentive but free-draining and can be made from either sandy or clay soils with the addition of plenty of composted organic matter.

Regular, thorough watering is a must. Water at cool times of the day, especially in summer, and mulch to prevent moisture evaporation.

Remove weeds regularly. Weeds compete with vegetables and may harbor diseases.

Keep plantings away from trees. Not only do trees shade precious sunshine, but their large root systems also compete for water and nutrients.

◆ The Home Orchard ◆

Few pleasures can compare with that of walking into your backyard and picking fresh, sweet fruit from the trees or bushes you planted yourself and nurtured over the years. Many fruiting plants are ornamental as well and are well suited to small-scale cultivation.

A citrus hedge

The bushy growth of some citrus trees makes them ideal for a scented, fruiting screen—whether grown informally or pruned into a formal shape. Try kumquats for a small hedge and Seville oranges or Lisbon lemons for a large hedge. (The open-growth habit of most other lemon varieties makes them unsuitable for hedging.) North of USDA zone 9 (p.223), plant trifoliate orange; this thorny shrub is hardy through zone 7.

- ◆ **spade**
- ◆ **string**
- ◆ **hammer or mallet**
- ◆ **stakes**
- ◆ **young hedge trees**

1 Mark out the perimeter of the hedge bed with a string line tied to short stakes. For a large hedge, stop periodically as you hammer in the stakes to look along the string line and make sure that all are properly aligned.

2 Plant young orange and grapefruit trees no

Planted close enough for the branches to intertwine and trimmed to a convenient height for picking fruit, bush lemon trees make an almost impenetrable evergreen fruiting hedge.

less than 4 ½ feet apart and kumquat trees no less than 2 feet apart. Mark the placement for each tree with a small stake. The spacing between plants is determined by the vigor of the variety chosen, the type of rootstock onto which the plants have been grafted, and local growing conditions. So check with your nursery before making a choice.

3 Using the spade, dig a planting hole that is approximately 4 inches deeper than the root ball of the tree. Loosen the soil at the base of the hole to allow roots to spread out readily. Remove any plastic wrapping from the root ball. Center the tree in the hole and gently loosen the roots. Fill in around them with soil. Make sure the stem of the tree is planted to the same level in the soil as in the nursery pot.

Citrus in containers

A number of citrus plants can be displayed to great advantage in containers. Kumquats, with their small fruit, are traditional pot specimens; 'Meyer' lemons and mandarin oranges also make handsome pot plants.

- ◆ **1 large pot or tub (minimum 12-inch diameter)**
- ◆ **fiberglass window screening**
- ◆ **large bag of potting mix**
- ◆ **pelletized cow manure; citrus fertilizer**
- ◆ **trees: kumquat, lime, mandarin orange, or 'Meyer' lemon tree**

1 Select a container roughly as wide as it is deep. A squat pot or tub with a diameter of at least 12 inches is more stable than a deep, tapered container. An old barrel is ideal because the wood provides good insulation against summer heat. Paint the inside of a terra-cotta, stone, or concrete pot with asphalt to reduce evaporation.

2 Position the container in a sheltered place that gets at least six hours of sun a day. To ensure free drainage, use supports to raise it slightly above the ground.

3 Place screening over the drainage hole to prevent soil loss. Fill with enough potting mix to bring the root ball to the desired level. Place the root ball in the container so that the bottom of the stem sits about 2 inches below the rim; lightly tease out the roots. Center the plant and fill in around the roots, mixing in a little fertilizer.

4 Gently tamp down the potting mix to remove any air pockets. Soak the mix with water and continue to water every three or four days. Mulch the surface to the rim of the container.

STARS OF THE ORCHARD

CITRUS trees have many virtues, for not only are they prolific fruit bearers but they're aesthetically pleasing as well, with handsome foliage and scented blossoms. Most are also easy to grow. Oranges and lemons thrive in much of zone 9. Limes and grapefruits are especially cold-sensitive and need a climate that is virtually frost-free. A sheltered position, out of the path of strong winds, is ideal.

General care: Citrus trees require well-drained soil to flourish. You can improve drainage by digging an area at least 1½ feet square to a depth of about 1 foot. Add compost or rich garden loam. After planting, apply a thick mulch to retain moisture and suppress weeds. Apply small amounts of nitrogen-rich fertilizer every two months. Pruning is usually unnecessary.

Most citrus tree pests and diseases are easily controlled by spraying. Always read the instructions and follow the dosage carefully when using any type of chemicals.

Trim the lower stems from potted kumquat and lemon trees so that they develop elegant shapes, reminiscent of those in Mediterranean gardens.

A waist-high boxwood hedge provides a stylish division between a lawn area and the berry bushes and fruit trees growing on the other side.

Tie string close to the ground to connect the outer stakes and dig 8 to 12 inches deeper than the depth of the hedging plants' nursery pots; dig deeper if using large plants. Mix a handful of fertilizer through each square yard of removed soil.

4 When the trench is ready, tie a string line to the center stakes as a planting guide. Before planting, soak potted plants in a bucket of water. Plant them with the stem at the same level as it was in the pot.

5 Fill in the trench and lightly firm soil around the roots with your hands to remove any air. Water and apply a mulch over the root area away from the stems.

6 As plants grow, lightly prune new growth with shears, using a string line to maintain an even height. The base of the hedge must be wider than the top, or leaves on the lower branches will die from lack of light.

Selecting a suitable hedge

Choose hedging plants with modest root systems that will not spread to compete with your fruit trees. Plants should be low-growing and a type that can be trimmed regularly.

The most versatile plants for hedging are the members of the boxwood family. Once established, they will survive drought, frost, and snow. In dry, warm climates, consider substituting myrtle *(Myrtus commanis)*, an attractive plant similar in style to boxwood but with glossier, darker green leaves. Alternatively, plant lavender, rosemary, or lavender cotton *(Santolina)*. All have attractive foliage or flowers and are drought-hardy.

Framing hedge

One way to turn an orchard into a "garden room" is to plant a bordering hedge.

- ◆ **tape measure**
- ◆ **hedge shears**
- ◆ **spade**
- ◆ **compost or decomposed manure**
- ◆ **short stakes**
- ◆ **string**
- ◆ **hammer or mallet**
- ◆ **hedge plants**

1 Select a site that receives at least six hours of sunlight a day. Test drainage by digging a hole about 12 inches deep and filling it with water. If the water does not drain away after 30 minutes, you may need to consider laying drainage tile or raising the beds.

2 Calculate the number of plants needed by measuring the total distance around the orchard perimeter and dividing this by the distance between plants (ask about this at your local nursery). Small to medium-size plants need to be at least 12 inches apart.

3 Mark out the hedge's position with a string line. At each corner, hammer in three short stakes about 8 inches apart. The two outer stakes are width guides for a planting trench.

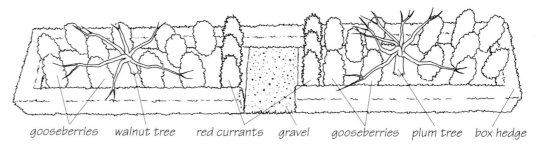

gooseberries   walnut tree   red currants   gravel   gooseberries   plum tree   box hedge

Strawberries in pots

Pots and cans are the perfect space-saving containers in which to grow this favorite fruit. The potting process is quite simple and takes only minutes. If you feed and water the plants regularly, you'll have juicy strawberries for the picking all summer long. You may turn the cans into hanging containers, if you like, by placing them in wire holders (page 234).

◆ **strawberry crowns (certified disease-free)**
◆ **pots or cans**
◆ **bag of potting mix**
◆ **fiberglass window screening**
◆ **slow-release fertilizer**

1 If using cans, hammer three large nail holes in the base of each one and place the screening over the holes to prevent soil from washing out. If using a strawberry pot (at right in the photograph below left), fill it to the lowest pocket; fill cans to within 1 ½ inches of the rim.

2 Plant crowns in the pocket and thread the stems through the opening from the inside to the outside. Make sure the crown—the point at which roots and leaves join—is just above the level of the soil.

3 Fill the pot to the level of the next opening and repeat the planting procedure. Plant two or three crowns in the top of the pot.

4 Place containers in a sunny position and turn them 180° twice a week so that the plant is evenly exposed to sunlight.

5 In the summer, feed the plants every second week with a liquid fertilizer that has a high phosphorus content to encourage flowering. Water whenever the top ½ inch of potting mix appears to have dried out; water the pockets of strawberry pots individually.

A STRAWBERRY PRIMER

STRAWBERRIES are ideal for the home orchard: the fruit is delicious, the plant has few pests, and on a space-to-yield ratio, strawberries are unbeatable. Growing your own means you can choose the most vigorous and flavorful varieties for your climate. For best results:

1 Dig the strawberry bed to spade-blade depth and add manure, dried blood, and bonemeal before you set out the plants.

2 Cover the bed with black plastic sheeting to warm the soil and reduce competition from weeds. Plant through slits in the plastic.

3 Buy certified-disease-free plants only. Plant in low mounds about 1 foot apart, cover roots with soil, and firm gently, ensuring that the crowns stay above the surface.

4 Pinch out runners as they form to en-courage the growth of a strong central plant.

Plump strawberries are a cheerful sign of summer. Potted plants can easily be moved to follow the sun—and when the fruit appears, it is easily harvested.

Strawberry hangers

Plant strawberries in cans, then hang them up with these attractive wire hangers. Make the basic hanger first, then tackle the decorative variations (photo, p.233). Paint the hangers if you wish. Read the section on wirework techniques (p.223) before proceeding.

- ◆ **large cans (20-ounce tomato juice or coffee cans), tops removed**
- ◆ **wire: 14, 16, or 18, and 22 gauge,**
- ◆ **ruler or measuring tape**
- ◆ **felt pen**
- ◆ **pliers, hammer, gloves**
- ◆ **saucepans of various sizes**
- ◆ **vise**
- ◆ **piece of 2-inch-diameter galvanized-iron pipe**
- ◆ **drill**
- ◆ **optional: high-gloss spray paint or small can of enamel paint and paintbrush**

Basic hanger—cutting to length

1 To make the three hoops that encircle the can, bend a length of 14-gauge wire around a saucepan with a diameter ½ to 1 inch larger than that of the can. Allowing about 3 inches for an overlap, cut each piece of wire. Form the hoops and wrap two small pieces of 22-gauge wire around each overlap to secure the hoop. Mark four points an equal distance apart around the circumference of each hoop.

2 Two pieces of wire in a cross shape form the hanger base. To make them, cut 14-gauge wire to equal the hoop diameter plus 1 inch.

3 For the uprights, cut four straight pieces of 14-gauge wire to match the height of the can. Mark each upright at its midpoint.

4 For handles, cut four straight pieces of 14-gauge wire, each 16 inches long. With pliers, bend ½ inch around the ends of each piece to make a hook; at one end leave the hook open.

Assembling the basic hanger

1 Form the base by joining the two pieces of wire (Step 2, above) with 22-gauge wire so that they form a cross with segments of even lengths. Hook about ½ inch of each cross

piece around a hoop at the marked points and close the hooks with pliers.

2 Hook one end of each upright wire to the base hoop next to the cross-piece joins. Turn the hooks inward around the base hoop and close them with pliers.

3 To form the top of the hanger, hook the tops of the upright wires to the second hoop.

4 Insert the third hoop into the frame and tie it with 22-gauge wire to the midpoint of the uprights (the marked points on the hoop wire and the upright wire should meet).

5 Attach the handles to the top hoop, closing the hooks with pliers. If desired, paint the hanger.

6 A can planted with strawberries placed in the hanger will stand 1 inch taller than the top hoop (photo, p.233). Bend the tops of the handles into large hooks and tie the handles together just below the hooks with 22-gauge wire for ease of handling. Remove this wire when taking the can out of the hanger.

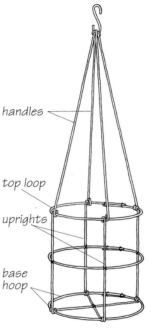

handles

top loop

uprights

base hoop

VARIATION Frilled hanger

1 Make the basic hanger as above, but with handles 2 feet long. Use pliers to bend the tops of the handles into scrolls approximately 2 inches in diameter (photo, p.233).

2 To make a frill around the top hoop of the hanger, drill a hole in the galvanized-iron pipe, about 5 inches from one end. Secure one end of a 12-foot piece of 16- or 18-gauge wire in a vise. Stretch the wire out to its full length and put the free end in the hole in the pipe. Holding the pipe at each end and keeping the wire taut, slowly walk toward the vise, coiling the wire around the pipe as you go. When the wire

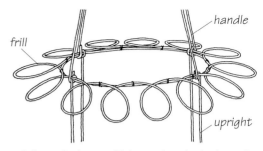

frill

handle

upright

is fully coiled, cut off the end in the hole and release the tension; remove the other end from the vise. Spread out the wire and flatten it as it uncoils so that it forms a series of loops that make a frill (above).

3 Use 22-gauge wire to attach the frill to the top hoop at regular intervals.

4 Attach the handles to the top hoop. Tie the tops of the handles together with wire.

VARIATION Flat-topped hanger

1 Cut upright wires 10 inches longer than those for the basic hanger, and mark where the extra length begins. Fix in a vise at this mark; with gloved hands, bend the wire to a right angle; tap gently with a hammer to form a neat angle. Use pliers to make a 2-inch-diameter coil at the free end.

2 Make three hoops as for the basic hanger, increasing the diameter of each by ½ inch. Attach to the shaped uprights, this time placing the uprights inside the hoops (below).

3 Make two more hoops, one 10 inches in diameter and one 12 inches.

4 Using 22-gauge wire, attach these hoops to the horizontal part of the uprights (below).

5 Attach handles as for the basic hanger.

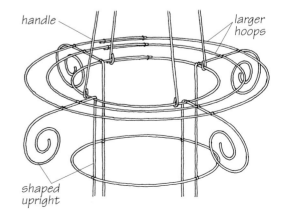

handle

larger hoops

shaped upright

◆ Flowers to Cheer the House ◆

*Nothing brightens a home more than or provides as much satisfaction for a gardener
as a vase brimming with fresh, colorful, homegrown flowers. Even better: you don't have to be a master
gardener to grow all you need for year-round floral arrangements.*

The classic flower arrangement is made up of three elements: focal flowers, filler flowers, and foliage. Your cutting garden should include a mix of shrubs and perennials as well as seasonal annuals and bulbs. Since annuals can be grown readily from seed, they offer a cost-effective way to ensure a steady supply of summer flowers.

- **spade**
- **compost and manure**
- **sand or lime**
- **4 or 5 packets of flowering annuals (preferably with long stems)**
- **bulbs of daffodils and tulips for spring flowers**
- **organic fertilizer**

For best results, set aside a garden area devoted exclusively to growing flowers for cutting. A plot about 2 yards by 3 yards will provide all the rooms of your house with plenty of floral beauty.

To ensure vigorous plant growth and sturdy stems, a flower bed should receive at least 6 hours of sunlight a day. If this is not possible, try growing shade-tolerant plants, such as astilbes, foxgloves, violas, or impatiens.

1 About two weeks before planting, prepare the soil by digging and turning it over to the depth of a spade blade. Add a 4-inch layer of compost and manure. Allow the ground to settle before planting.

2 Map out your planting plan on the ground by making a thin trail of sand or lime around the area where each variety is to grow. Plant within these boundaries.

3 Water lightly with a fine mist from the garden hose.

4 Once your plants are established, fertilize them regularly with an organic fertilizer according to the manufacturer's instructions.

The flowers of a large and densely planted bed of annuals can easily withstand regular cutting to provide flowers for the house—in fact, picking blooms generally encourages the formation of others. In order to have a house and garden full of flowers, reserve a plain rectangular bed similar to the one at left solely for the production of cutting flowers in your favorite varieties and colors.

◆ Displaying the Rose ◆

*Few flowers can match the popularity of the rose—and few rose types can match
the spectacular beauty of a climbing one in full bloom. A simply made arbor in metal or
wood allows the plant to display its splendor to dramatic effect.*

*This inexpensive rose arbor has a simple, classical
shape that unobtrusively allows the showy rose
to take its place as the main garden ornament.*

◆ **20 feet of concrete reinforcing
mesh (available at lumberyards
and large home centers)**
◆ **wire cutters**
◆ **cement**

1 Mesh is usually sold in 10-foot lengths; you
will need to buy two pieces. The taller the
arbor, the more impressive the display (the one
in the photograph at right is nearly 10 feet tall).
The standard width for mesh strips is 5 feet,
which is ideal for a freestanding arbor.

2 Place the two mesh sections on the ground
and bend each to form a curved top similar to
the one shown at right. Shape one section first
and use it as a template for bending the other.
(You can make the curves as simple or dramatic
as you like, as long as the arbor is symmetrical.)

3 The first curve begins approximately 7 feet
from the ground and can be measured as about
a 30 degree angle from the horizontal.

4 The second curve follows the first at an
angle of between 100 and 110 degrees. A final
minor bend occurs about 1 ½ feet higher again,
at 30 to 40 degrees from the horizontal.

5 Fashion a decorative scroll or finial at the
top of the arbor by cutting off the last cross
piece on each section and bending the vertical
mesh wires outward around a piece of pipe to
form an almost-closed circle (note the example in the photograph at right). Wire the two
sides tightly together at the top.

6 To be sure the arbor is secure enough to

*Train a profusely flowering rose, such as 'Climbing Ice-
berg,' on a graceful arbor, and the plant will provide
you with an eye-catching focal point.*

support a large climbing rosebush, bury the base at least 20 inches and cement it in place (p.200).

VARIATIONS Arches, arbors, and pergolas are much the same in principle; the main difference is the shape of the overhead support. Whereas an arch is curved at the top, an arbor may be flat or curved. A pergola commonly has a pitched roof. All can be used in a series to create a tunnel effect or to highlight

Use sturdy posts cemented well into the ground (p.200) for an archway or pergola to support the vigorous growth of an old-fashioned climbing or rambling rose.

an entranceway. A dramatic effect can be achieved by attaching heavy ropes or chains loosely to the tops of tall posts or along a wall to form a series of loops that will support the rose. This is particularly effective along a pathway or to define a particular area.

TO TWIST OR TIE?

How should a climbing rose be attached to its support? Some rose growers suggest twisting shoots around the supporting structure, while others prefer simply to tie them flat against it. On balance, tying makes more sense because it is easier to prune a straight stem than one that has grown in a spiral.

◆ Topiary: Living Sculpture ◆

Encouraging selected plants to assume the ornamental shapes of topiary adds a distinctively stylish look to your garden. Better yet, it's surprisingly easy to do. This ancient garden art form is as fascinating a diversion for gardeners today as it was in Roman times.

A hedged globe

Share in the revival of the ancient craft of topiary. It's easy, especially if you start with simple forms, such as a pyramid, a globe, or a standard "lollipop" shape. For a formal subject, try this boxwood hedge with a globe topiary set inside it.

- **40 to 60 well-established, bushy boxwood plants for hedge**
- **1 large globe-shaped boxwood or contrasting plant, already clipped and trained**
- **small wooden stakes, dowels, or thin metal rods**
- **pruning shears**
- **hedge shears**
- **string and stakes for string line**
- **spade**

1 Begin by marking out a 12 x 18-foot rectangle. Place wooden stakes at the corners and run diagonal string lines from the stakes to find the center. To be sure the corners form 90-degree angles, check that the measurements from the center to each corner are equal.

2 Dig the trench for the hedge plants and a hole in the center for the globe plant (in zone 8 and south, *Camellia sasanqua* is a good choice for the globe). For detailed instructions on how to prepare the trench, see Framing hedge on page 232.

3 Plant the hedge, placing the boxwood plants about 12 inches apart. (If your hedge will be high, make a path through it to reach the globe plant.) To create a flat, even top, use a string line made from two stakes and a taut length of string tied at the desired height. Using the string as a guide, trim the tops of all the plants with hedge shears.

4 Plant the globe plant. Begin shaping it by trimming the top and snipping off any protruding stems. Maintain a regular pruning schedule throughout the year, cutting any loose shoots back to the basic, oval shape.

5 Apply an organic fertilizer according to the product label in spring and summer.

STARTING A POT TOPIARY

1 *For best results, train a potted topiary plant in a simple, classical shape. Use your eye to judge the shape for the first trimming.*

2 *After 12 months, use a pruning guide, such as this one, made from canes and wire rings. Trim any growth outside the guide.*

3 *Once the plant has developed the desired shape, trim it at least once a year with pruning shears to maintain a well-defined outline.*

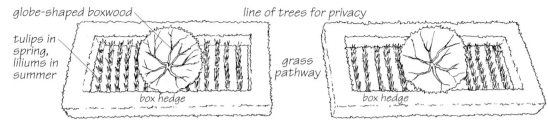

globe-shaped boxwood

line of trees for privacy

tulips in spring, liliums in summer

grass pathway

box hedge

box hedge

The beds, bounded by twin box hedges (below left and plan at left), provide cool soil in which bulbs flourish in all seasons. The hedges are connected by a grass pathway and a line of trees. The camellia below shows topiary in the making. It forms a plinth with a top portion that will be developed into a more complex shape as the plant matures.

PLANTS: THE RAW MATERIAL

For successful topiary, be sure to choose evergreen plants with small leaves and a thick, dense growth habit. Good topiary candidates should also be fast-growing and able to produce new shoots fairly quickly after clipping. Conifers, such as cypress or juniper, are fine choices for topiary. Boxwood, a traditional and popular plant for hedges, is also ideal for topiary because it lends itself readily to shaping. In northern regions, however. be sure to use hardy Korean boxwood.

Other useful topiary plants include honeysuckle (particularly *Lonicera nitida*), *Camellia sasanqua*, English or Japanese yew, small-leafed privet, arborvitae *(Thuga* spp.), figs *(Ficus benjamina* and *F. microcappa*), and pittosporum. Rosemary works well for miniature topiaries. Climbing plants, such as ivy and wisteria, are effective when trained on frames in pots.

Bring a sense of play to your topiary garden by training plants into such whimsical shapes as the chicks (left foreground) or the dinosaur (left background).

TENDING TOPIARY

When pruning, work from the top of the plant down. Cutting guides can be made from chicken wire placed over the plants and tied to stakes.

Pinch off shoots every second week while the plant is growing strongly. Trimmings of topiary made with such culinary herbs as rosemary or bay can be dried or used fresh in the kitchen.

Some woody plants from dry climates, such as rosemary, may not reshoot if they are cut below a leaf bud. When pruning, make sure you always leave several leaves on the stem.

Container-grown topiary should be removed from the pot once a year to prune the roots.

Fertilize your topiary in spring and summer only, the main growing seasons. Apply liquid fertilizer monthly and slow-release fertilizer pellets in early spring and again just before the onset of fall.

Bird topiary

To create a dramatic display of topiary in amusing or imaginative shapes, train plants to grow on wire frames or templates.

- ◆ **topiary plants**
- ◆ **chicken wire**
- ◆ **wire cutters**
- ◆ **pruning shears**
- ◆ **wooden stakes and hammer**
- ◆ **blocks of softwood**
- ◆ **file or plane**
- ◆ **paint and brush**
- ◆ **fine-gauge wire**

1 Select a plant with a bushy growth habit and two main branches. The best plants to use are small-leaved varieties with strong but pliable stems, such as rosemary, small-leaved privet, lonicera, or ivy. The height of the plant can vary from 1 to 3 feet.

2 Dig a hole of appropriate size, hammer a supporting stake into the ground, and plant the topiary, tying it lightly to the stake.

3 Remove lower leaves to an appropriate level

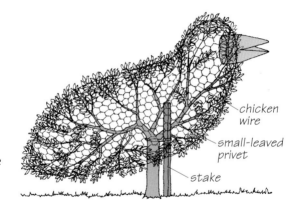

chicken wire

small-leaved privet

stake

so that the trunk suggests the bird's legs.

4 Cut the chicken wire to the desired size, position it over the plant and form it into a rounded body shape as a pruning guide (left). Tie the wire to the stake in several places to keep it steady.

5 As the plant grows, loosen its ties to the stake. Pinch out stems that grow through the wire. This encourages new stems and shoots to form increasingly denser foliage.

6 Once the plant has reached the desired size, add the beak. Cut it from a small block of soft wood, rounding the edges with a file or plane until the desired shape is achieved. Paint with enamel. Drill small holes on either side of the beak and thread fine-gauge wire through the holes before tying the beak to the head section of the wire frame.

◆ Water in the Garden ◆

*Imagine a warm summer garden in which a shimmering ornamental pond lies
beside a spreading shade tree or a rustic bench. A pond, planted properly to keep
it clear, brings both beauty and tranquillity to a garden.*

Ornamental pond

Few garden features have the charm and allure of a pond. Even a small pool can give your garden a boost in color and texture.

- ◆ **hose**
- ◆ **20-mil flexible PVC liner**
- ◆ **spade**
- ◆ **wooden plank**
- ◆ **spirit level**
- ◆ **rocks or bricks, for edging**
- ◆ **sand and cement**
- ◆ **a selection of water plants**

How much liner?

A light, flexible pond liner is installed more quickly and is far less difficult to work with than concrete. It's important, however, to calculate exactly how much liner you will need. Multiply the maximum planned depth of the pool by two, add the number to the length, and then add it to the width. For example, for a pond that will be 2 feet deep, 6 feet long, and 3 feet wide, you will need a liner measuring 10 x 7 feet.

Choosing the best location

Ponds need sunlight for at least half a day. Site the pond away from overhanging trees that provide too much shade and may foul the water with leaves or send out roots that punc-

ture the liner. Water plants should provide enough shade to inhibit algal growth; fish help create an ecological balance.

Position the pond where it can be seen from the house. Doing so not only will increase your pleasure but also will allow you to keep an eye on children playing nearby. Local laws may require fencing of any large pond, so check with city or county officials before you begin.

Constructing the pond

Pool liners and preformed ponds make installing a water feature an easy and relatively inexpensive weekend project. Flexible liners should be of PVC at least 20 mils thick.

A liner allows you to build a large pond. A minimum size to aim for while maintaining a healthy ecological balance is 3 square yards. To reach this capacity, a pond should be about 3 x 9 feet and no less than 18 inches deep. The slope of the sides should not exceed a 60-degree angle.

1 Using a hose or a length of rope, mark the outline of the excavation site. Remove the soil, making sure you dig out roots or rocks that could puncture the liner. Dig several ledges, or "shelves," in the pond sides, about 10 inches from the top, to hold pots containing water plants (Step 3, below).

2 Lay a plank across the excavation, first lengthwise and then crosswise, and use a spirit

level to check that the opposite edges are the same height. Line the bottom with 3 inches of moist sand to protect the liner.

3 Evenly stretch the liner over the excavation and lay heavy weights, such as rocks or bricks, around the edges to prevent it from slipping (illustration 2, below left). Trim the edges of the liner, leaving an 8-inch overlap around the perimeter. As you fill the pond, smooth out creases, and gradually release the weights as water fills the hole.

4 Cement your choice of stone or paving material around the edge of the pond so that it covers the overlap and hangs far enough over the water that the liner cannot be seen.

Starting an underwater garden

Not only do plants make a pond more attractive, but they also provide a natural environment for fish, release oxygen into the water, and control the spread of algae (the presence of algae is a sign that the water is unhealthy; see step 6 in Barrel Pond, facing page).

Water lilies and other underwater plants are best grown in submerged containers. For water lilies, allow 1 square yard of surface per lily and place them on the bottom; stand other plants on the ledges dug into the sides when the pond was excavated.

A special water-plant basket is the best type of container, but a terra-cotta or plastic pot with a few slits cut into the side will do. Use 7 parts garden loam to 3 parts composted cow manure for your potting medium. Water lilies are heavy feeders and may need to be repotted regularly. To add nutrients without repotting, wrap a handful of organic fertilizer in a sheet of newspaper and slip it down among the plant's roots.

Introducing fish

Goldfish are the most popular fish for garden ponds. Do not overstock your pond, however, because too many fish will result in polluted water. For every square yard of pond surface, allow approximately ten 3-inch goldfish. In a large, established pond, fish forage for themselves, but supplementary feeding is recommended. Fish require more food in spring and summer, when they are most active.

MAKING A POND

1 *Use a hose to mark out the area for the pond. Excavate a hole, making sure to remove roots and rocks that could puncture the liner. Line the bottom with 3 inches of moist sand to act as a soft bed.*

2 *Evenly stretch the liner over the hole and weigh down edges to prevent it from slipping. Trim the liner, leaving an 8-inch overlap. Cement stone or brick edging in place so that it hides the edge of the liner.*

3 *After the pond has been filled, introduce plants in the water by first planting them in open-sided pots and then standing the pots either on the bottom (water lilies) or on ledges around the sides.*

Barrel pond

If you long for the refreshing presence of water in the garden or the pleasure of growing aquatic plants but don't have enough room for a conventional pond, try a barrel minipond. Check your local liquor store for the half barrel or get a barrel-size planter from a garden center.

- ◆ **half a whiskey barrel**
- ◆ **sealant or liner (optional)**
- ◆ **a selection of water plants**
- ◆ **potting mix**
- ◆ **small fish**
- ◆ **coarse gravel**
- ◆ **pump (optional)**

1 Place the barrel half in what will be its permanent position—once it has been filled with water, it will be very difficult to move. The water may have to be siphoned off at some point, which can be a messy procedure, so be sure there is a garden bed or a drain nearby to receive the stale water.

2 To test the barrel for leaks, fill it with water and leave for several days (use a spirit level to make sure that the water is level). If the water level drops or the outside becomes damp, empty the barrel, allow it to dry, and seal the inside with an asphalt-based sealant.

3 Fill the pond and wait a week for the water to warm and the chlorine to dissipate. Then stock your barrel with both submerged and floating plants to help maintain a healthy environment. Submerged plants grow completely underwater on the bottom of the pond. They keep algae in check by adding oxygen to the water. Floating aquatic plants have roots in soil but leaves that float on the water, providing shade, which also inhibits the growth of algae.

4 Pot water plants in water-plant baskets or, as an economical alternative, use black plastic pots with slits cut into the sides. Hold each plant by the crown, allowing the roots to hang down into the container, and fill with potting mix. Make sure the crown of the plant is not covered, or the plant will rot. Cover the surface of the potting mix with coarse gravel. Most water plants are heavy feeders, so make sure that about one-third of the mix is composted cow manure.

5 Slowly submerge the pots in the water, letting air bubbles escape gradually so that the soil is not disturbed. If the leaves of floating aquatic plants are totally submerged when the pots are placed on the base of the barrel, elevate the pots, using a brick or two, until the leaves are on the surface.

6 Allow time for the pond environment to stabilize before introducing fish. Barrel aquatic plants like a warm, stagnant water environment but it may take two to three weeks for the water to clear.

Aquatic plants, such as the water lilies above, will thrive in a cut-off whiskey barrel filled with water. Cover potting mix with gravel to keep the water clear.

7 If you should have reason to drain the barrel, you can buy a simple plastic siphon with a bulb to do the job. You will find such a siphon at an aquarium store. Your barrel pond is, in effect, just a big aquarium, and you may get recommendations for a healthy mix of plants and fish there as well.

◆ Creating Paths and Edgings ◆

Paths and edgings make eye-pleasing frames for the various elements of a garden.
If you invest a little time in planning and provide the labor yourself, you can quite inexpensively
create distinctive designs that show off your plantings.

Sandstone path

Capitalize on the sculptural qualities of irregularly shaped sandstone slabs by combining them with fine gravel to make a straight path.

- ◆ **string, wooden stakes, and hammer**
- ◆ **shovel**
- ◆ **sandstone or other stone slabs**
- ◆ **coarse builder's sand**
- ◆ **cement**
- ◆ **fine gravel or stone dust**
- ◆ **rake, tamper, leveling board, spirit level, rubber mallet**

For basic information on laying paving, see step-by-step instructions on page 222.

1 Determine the best position and stone pattern by laying out the stones on the ground prior to making the path. Hammer in a stake on either side at the start of the path; add corresponding stakes at the other end of the path. String a line from end to end on each side to mark the outer edges of the path.

2 Dig out the path area to a depth equal to the depth of the stone slabs plus 2 to 4 inches. Mix 6 parts damp sand to 1 part dry cement and spread a 2- to 4-inch layer of the mix as a bed for the stones. If the path is on soft ground, dig the path area 2 inches deeper, spread fine gravel or stone dust to a depth of 2 inches, and compact it with a tamper before spreading the sand-cement mix.

3 Level the sand-cement mix with a rake, tamp it down, and then smooth it with a leveling board. It may help to frame the path site with narrow boards laid flush with the level of

The character of a sandstone path is enhanced over time by oxides in the stone that meld with tiny lichens to form patterns on the surface.

the sand as a guide for leveling.

4 Stretch a third line down the path site halfway between the other string lines to serve as a center line.

5 Place the stones on the sand; use a spirit level to ensure that they lie flat. Line one edge along the center line to give the path a rough symmetry; you can break the symmetry if desired by laying stones on either side of the string line. As each stone is placed in position, gently tap it down with a rubber mallet. When all the stones are laid, brush a dry mixture of 10 parts sand to 1 part cement between them and gently mist the path with a garden hose.

In an informal or natural garden, create the simplest path of all with organic materials, such as shredded bark or wood chips. These materials keep the path relatively dry underfoot and, as long as they are laid a minimum of 1 inch deep, will discourage the growth of weeds. Allow informal paths to meander (left) rather than follow a straight line. Let the edges be similarly unstructured so that they become softer as low-growing plants creep over them.

Shredded bark or wood chips can also be used as an alternative to gravel to fill the level landing sections of a stepped path, such as the one shown below. See p.248 for instructions on building brick steps that deceive the eye and extend the garden.

Add variety to a series of steps or to a path that traverses a gentle slope by combining natural materials. Weathered railroad ties laid flat make an interesting focal point in a gravel path (above). Allow border plants to grow so that they overflow onto the path; this helps to soften the look of the hard edging. Most types of paving stones combine well with gravel. At right, landings filled with gravel complement the stone and brick steps perfectly.

Block-edged path

Edgings of paving blocks neatly confine loose paving, such as gravel, and prevent soil from spilling from a plant bed onto the path.

- ◆ **string and stakes**
- ◆ **spirit level, tape measure**
- ◆ **shovel**
- ◆ **dry premixed concrete (optional)**
- ◆ **square paving blocks**
- ◆ **gravel**
- ◆ **plywood and wooden strips about 5 inches wide (optional)**
- ◆ **wooden tamper (optional)**

1 Stretch a string line (Step 1, p.244) along each side of your chosen gravel-path area. Outside these lines on each side, stretch another string line for the edging. The distance between the lines on each side should be the the width of your chosen block.

2 Between the lines on each side, dig a trench as deep as the thickness of your block. If desired, lay concrete (Variation, below).

3 Along each outside string line, stand blocks in the trench, leaving small gaps between each. Along each inside line (next to path), lay blocks flat to form a gutter.

4 For the path, excavate the area between the two inner string lines to about 1 inch below the level of the block gutter. Compact the soil with a wooden tamper, to form a solid base for gravel. For drainage, form a slight camber or slope from the center to either side of the path.

5 Lay gravel over the earth. For a firm surface, water the gravel, then press with a roller or mechanical tamper, if desired.

VARIATION To create a firm base for paving blocks, dig the trench another 2 inches deep, mix concrete, lay it in the trench, and then bed the blocks while the concrete is wet. If desired, build formwork for the concrete along the string lines, using strips of plywood or scrap lumber (for step-by-step information on laying a brick or paved path, see p.222).

Large paving blocks are ideal for giving garden borders a formal appearance. The curb and gutter (above) provide a neat, clear-cut division between garden bed and pathway as well as help channel water away from the path during a heavy rainstorm. A boxwood hedge planted along the path's other edge heightens its formality. If the cost of paving blocks and gravel seems prohibitive, pave with asphalt instead (left). Keep the edges of an asphalt path neat by laying house bricks end to end and allowing them to protrude about half their width above the path's surface.

◆ Illusions of Space ◆

A little ingenious trickery in the form of subtle optical illusions can create the impression that any garden is bigger than it really is. With a few basic tools—and at a fraction of the professional cost—you can use these ideas to help push back your garden perimeter.

A *curved path*

The principle on which this simple path's construction is based can be used in any small garden.

- ◆ **stakes and string**
- ◆ **coarse sand**
- ◆ **40 to 50 flat-topped stones**
- ◆ **shovel, spirit level**
- ◆ **wooden tamper**
- ◆ **gravel**

1 To form a semicircle, hammer a stake into the ground well back from the path site (near the fence; photograph at left) and attach a length of string to it. At the desired distance, tie a stake to the other end, stretch the line taut, and use it to mark a semicircle for the path's outer edge. Repeat, with the string 1 to 1½ feet shorter, for the inside edge of the path. The area between the two lines will form a bed for the stones.

2 Calculate the bed's depth, allowing 1½ to 2 inches for a sand base plus the thickness of the stone. The stone should protrude 1 to 1½ inches above ground level. Dig to the required depth and even out the surface with a shovel. Firm the base by compacting the soil with a wooden tamper.

3 Lay sand on the base, compact with a tamper, and then level it off. Place the stones on the sand and adjust the height of each so that they will be about flush with the gravel when it is added. A spirit level is useful for this.

4 Lay gravel to a depth of 1 to 1½ inches in the surrounding courtyard area. If desired, you can allow the stones to protrude slightly for an irregular effect (as shown at left).

Use materials like stone in an informal fashion to lead the eye away from the rigid surroundings of a small courtyard and create a feeling of spaciousness.

Brick steps

When building steps on a sloping site, the right technique can create the illusion that there is more to the garden than meets the eye.

- ◆ **string and stakes**
- ◆ **bricks, coarse gravel**
- ◆ **sand-cement mix**
- ◆ **tape measure**
- ◆ **shovel**
- ◆ **cement trowel**
- ◆ **stiff brush**
- ◆ **muriatic acid**

1 Select a site in your garden with a slope. Place stakes at the top and base of the slope and run a string line between them.

2 Using the string as a guide, dig out the basic shape of each step. The riser (vertical face) of each step should be the depth of two bricks; the tread (horizontal face) should be 1½ brick lengths or more, depending on the slope. The base step's width should be 6 feet, and each successive step should be narrower (by about 3½ inches, the height of a brick), up to a top step of about 4½ feet (the standard width at which two people walk side by side).

3 Starting at the base step, dig a trench the shape of the step and about 4 inches deep. Lay 2 inches of gravel, then 2 inches of wet, pre-mixed cement. Bed the first layer of bricks in this, with the bricks at the front lying end to end. Lay a second layer of bricks on top, using premixed cement for mortar, with the front bricks side by side.

4 Repeat for each step. When done, brush the bricks with a stiff brush. Dissolve any stains with a solution of muriatic acid. Use acid with caution and according to the product label.

Build a special effect into a flight of practical brick steps (top left). Make it gradually narrower as it rises, and the steps will appear to recede further into the distance than they actually do. Another simple illusion is to make a lawn path (bottom left). Mow the whole lawn to about 2 inches in height; then lay down a garden hose to mark the chosen shape of your path. Set the mower a few notches lower and mow the path.

◆ Lattice Style ◆

*Used as a framework or a trellis to display pretty climbers, lattice panels from the garden center
are inexpensive and charming garden accessories. A lattice you make yourself—with perspective built
into the pattern—will fool the eye and make a small garden seem to go on and on.*

An awareness of the intriguing way that manipulation of perspective can fool the eye is the inspiration behind this lattice project. To buy the lattice strips (laths), try lumberyards or garden centers. The strips come 1⅛ inches wide by ¼ inch thick in random lengths and are sometimes used as trim.

- ◆ **280 feet lattice strips**
- ◆ **quart exterior stain or paint**
- ◆ **three 4 x 8-foot sheets ¼-inch plywood**
- ◆ **packet ¾-inch roofing nails**
- ◆ **11 wood screws (1½-inch size)**
- ◆ **9 feet string**
- ◆ **compass and pencil, measuring tape, saw, electric drill, hammer, steel block (or second hammer), T square, sandpaper**

Getting ready

1 Apply two coats of exterior latex paint or stain to all strips of lattice.
2 Lay the plywood sheets on the floor, as shown in Diagram 1, to be a layout board.
   This lattice is made of three parts that go around the window: two side panels and a top panel. Make the side panels first.

Drawing a plan for the side panels

1 Measure the height from the ground to the top of the window (including trim) you want to frame. At the top of the layout board, draw a rectangle—the long sides equal to your window height (7 feet here) and the short sides its width (2½ feet here). Draw a basic plan of a side panel within this rectangle (Diagram 1); this takes time but ensures that the panels will be in proportion. Use a long piece of lattice to draw six evenly spaced strips across the rectangle and a strip at each short end, as shown.
2 Mark a point ⅝ of the way along the bottom edge of the rectangle. Using the T square, draw a perpendicular line (the "center line") 5 feet long from the point; hammer a nail at the end (Diagram 1).
3 Attach the string to the nail; then tie the pencil to the string 3 feet from the nail and draw an arc (Diagram 1). Fix the compass at 3 inches. Put the compass point at A and draw a mark on the arc; draw eight points on the arc toward B and five toward C (Diagram 2).

Making the side panels

1 For the first side panel, cut six lengths equal to window height and three laths of 2½ feet. Lay two long pieces and two short pieces in the

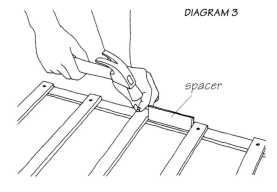

DIAGRAM 3

spacer

shape of a rectangle (on the plan), with the long lengths on top. Drill ¹⁄₁₆-inch-diameter holes for nails at the four corners. Hammer the nails in place (the points will pierce the board beneath).
2 Drill and nail the remaining four long pieces, using the plan as a guide. To make nailing accurate, cut a small piece of lattice as a "spacer" between the strips (Diagram 3). The length of the spacer depends on the width of the lattice strip.
3 Now the radiating lattice strips can be added (Diagrams 4 and 5, p.251). Pull the string taut along the center line and lay your third 2½-foot length on the frame (under, and centered on, the string). Nail the ends of the strips to the frame's top and bottom strips.

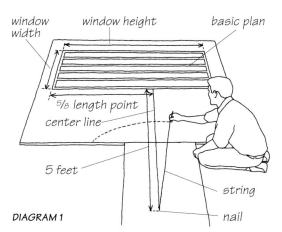

window width *window height* *basic plan*

⅝ length point
center line
5 feet
string
nail

DIAGRAM 1

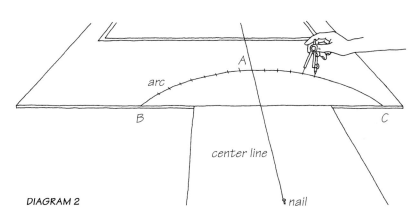

A
arc
B
center line
C
nail

DIAGRAM 2

You can dress up the exterior of a window and enlarge the perspective of your yard with this lattice. which has strips attached at angles to create an illusion of both depth and space.

DIAGRAM 4

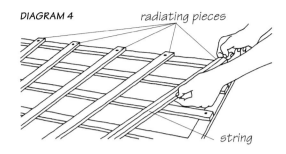

radiating pieces

string

4 Pull the string taut in line with the next mark along the arc. Measure the lattice strip length needed to fit on the frame at this point—the length of string between top and bottom strips of the frame—and cut a piece slightly longer. Lay the strip, centered under the string (Diagram 4) and overlapping the ends, then nail in place. Trim off excess at the ends. Repeat for the other radiating lengths (Diagram 5).

DIAGRAM 5

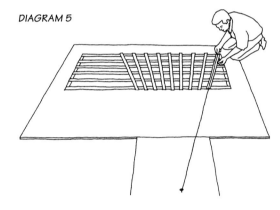

5 Drill holes and nail all the radiating lengths to the four other long strips of the frame.
6 To save time later, mark on the layout board where the edges of the radiating lengths meet the bottom and top strips of the frame.
7 Turn the panel over—it will come away easily from the layout board. Place the panel on the steel block (or on the head of a hammer) so that the block is under the flat head of one nail. Hammer the nail point flat; this is "clenching," to secure the nails. Clench all the nails.
8 The second side panel is the reverse of the first. To make it, first drill, nail, and clench the basic rectangle (Steps 1 to 3) and lay it— with the long lengths underneath—on the plan of the first side (lengths are marked underneath because the panel is a mirror image of

the first panel). Transfer marks for the radiating lengths of the first panel onto the top and bottom of the frame. Turn it over; drill, nail, and clench radiating lengths at these positions.
9 Sand all cut ends and paint.

Making the gabled top panel
1 To make a frame for the top panel, which has a pointed, or "gabled," top, cut one strip to the length of the width of the window (including trim) plus 5 feet, and cut two 6 feet long.
2 Lay them in the form of a triangle on the same plan that you used for the side panels (Diagram 6). The long piece is on the bottom of

DIAGRAM 6

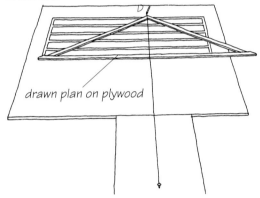

drawn plan on plywood

the rectangle, with its midpoint on the center line. At the two lower corners, the long length should sit on top of the short lengths. The shorter pieces will meet at the top (point D, on the center line), where they will overlap each other slightly.

DIAGRAM 7

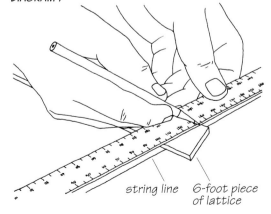

string line   6-foot piece of lattice

3 Stretch the string taut and secure it at the top, above point D. Use the string line as a guide for cutting the ends of the 6-foot lengths (Diagram 7). After being cut, they will fit neatly together with no overlap. Drill and nail the two lower corners of the triangle.
4 Lay a short piece across the top corner at 90° to the string line (Diagram 8). Drill and nail

DIAGRAM 8

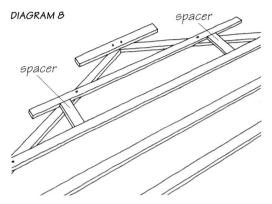

spacer

spacer

the joint as shown. Add four evenly spaced horizontal lengths between the top and the bottom of the frame; use the plan on the layout board as a guide for placing these pieces, and cut them so they overlap slightly at the sides. Cut spacers if desired and use when nailing. Drill and nail each piece, then trim the ends (the top piece is trimmed to a small triangle the shape of the top of the frame).
5 The radiating lengths for the top panel are added in much the same way as the side panels. The difference is that the top panel has six radiating lengths on either side of the center line (the side panel had eight on the left and five on the right). Make marks for the radiating lengths by using the string-line method as before (for most of the radiating lengths, you can save time by using the marks that you drew on the rectangular plan).
6 Drill and nail each radiating length to the outer pieces of the triangular frame. When all have been nailed, drill and nail all the remaining joints. Clench the nails. Saw off excess ends flush with the outer strips of the frame.
7 Paint or stain all cut ends and touch up the nails on both sides. The frames are now ready to be attached to your wall. Use a screw at each corner of each panel. On a masonry wall, use appropriate plugs for the screws

• Garden Trimmings •

Some of the most interesting materials for use in a garden come from the garden itself. With minimal preparation, such natural materials as fallen branches, saplings, and grapevines can provide the basis for garden structures that blend harmoniously with their surroundings.

Rustic arbor

An arbor provides a restful place to sit, particularly when it's covered with vines. This one is a three-sided structure with side and back sections made of branches and logs. Dimensions are not specific, as the size of the structure depends on the size of your materials and your space. Use the instructions as a guide only. You may need some assistance with the heavy work.

- **posts (see Cutting the posts, below)**
- **wood preservative**
- **bricks**
- **galvanized nails, 2 to 3 inches long**
- **14-gauge wire**
- **10-gauge wire (available at large hardware stores and home centers)**
- **tape measure**
- **chain saw or bow saw, spade, large paintbrush, staple gun, fencing staples, electric drill, hammer**

Cutting the posts

Use a chain saw or bow saw to cut the posts you need; what you use will depend on what you have available on site. The wood may be dry or green, but remember that green wood shrinks as it dries. Leave bark on or remove it.

If you do not have enough posts to fill in the upper part of the side walls, you can use strong wire mesh for the walls and ceiling, and train vines to cover the mesh. You can even omit the lower walls.

You will need the following lumber:

Corner posts: four lengths—ours were about 9 feet long and up to 8 inches thick at the base, with forks near the top (Diagram 2); they don't have to be perfectly straight.

Roof beams: four trimmed straight branches 4 inches thick or more, long enough to reach between the corner posts with a 16-inch overhang at each post (Diagram 2).

Base walls: enough logs to fill between the posts at the back and sides of the arbor (Diagram 3). The thickness of the lower walls is 4 to 6 inches, so cut logs of this width; alternatively, split thicker logs lengthwise into pieces of about this thickness—the pieces will have one flat side and one curved side with bark on. We cut logs for the back wall to about 3 feet long and logs for the sides to about 2 feet long (the sides are lower than the back wall (Diagram 3). Cut a few extra logs to trim the wall tops.

Roof: 12 to 15 straight branches, about 2 inches thick and of various lengths, to stretch over the top in all directions.

Upper side panels: 10 (or even more) limbs no more than 4 inches thick and 5 feet long, some with long branches still attached. Use Diagram 4 as a guide.

Getting ready

1 Apply wood preservative with the paintbrush to each corner post, covering to about 4 inches above the 12 to 18 inches that will be in the ground. Allow to dry according to the manufacturer's instructions.

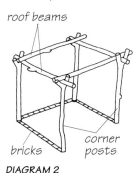

DIAGRAM 1

2 Stake out and prepare the site (Diagram 1). Vary these proportions to suit the site and the wood that you have available.

Building the basic structure

1 Dig holes 12 to 18 inches deep for each of the corner posts.

2 Place the four corner posts in the holes. Fill the holes with earth and compact the soil. If your log posts have a natural bend in them, make sure they lean slightly outward, not inward toward the center of the arbor.

3 Place a roof beam in the forks of one front post and one back post; if your posts do not have forks, tie the beam to the posts. Wrap 10-gauge wire around each joint several times, then staple the wire end out of sight. Secure a beam to front and back posts on the other side. Lay a beam across the back and one across the front, resting on the two beams already in place, and secure to complete the top of the frame (Diagram 2).

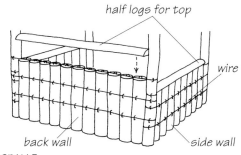

DIAGRAM 2

Making the base walls

1 Dig a trench and lay a single row of bricks, end to end, between the corner posts at the back and sides (Diagram 2); these help prevent water damage to the wooden base. You may need to break some bricks in half or smaller, to fill in gaps. (For a neat break, place one brick on top of another lengthwise, so that half its length hangs over the bottom brick. Hold the top brick firmly in place with your foot and hit the overhanging piece sharply with a mallet.)

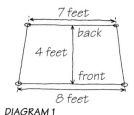

DIAGRAM 3

2 Start with the back base wall. Trim all branches from the 3-foot-long logs so that they fit neatly together. Stand them side by side on the row of bricks, to fill the space between the two back posts (Diagram 3, facing page). As mentioned, you can use split instead of whole logs. If using split logs, stand them with flat sides to the rear and out of sight.

3 Secure each log by stapling 10-gauge wire on top; this wire should pass across the wall and around each corner post and then be stapled to the posts. Also run two rows of wire along the back of the wall and staple to the corner posts (Diagram 3, facing page).

4 To make an attractive curved top for the base walls, saw a log in half lengthwise.

Choose a good viewing spot for your arbor so that you can look out on the garden while you relax inside. This natural—and economical—shelter will gradually lose its starkness as climbing plants take hold on the walls.

Measure the length of the back wall and cut a piece the same length from the halved branch. Place it, flat side down, on the top of the wall (Diagram 3, p.252). Drill holes and nail the half log in place.

5. For the side walls, repeat steps 1 through 4 using the 2-foot logs.

Filling in the sides and the top

1   For the arbor roof, lay the straight branches across the beams from front to back, side to side, and also diagonally. You may want to overhang the front beam by 20 inches or more for extra protection from the sun or rain (once your arbor is covered with creepers). Lash branches together with 14-gauge wire where they cross. Where the branches meet the roof beams, it's better to nail them together, though wiring may suffice. Drill before nailing.

2   There are no strict rules on filling in above the side walls; diagram 4 shows how one area was covered. As for the top section, wire branches together where they cross but use

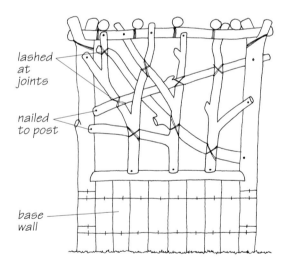

DIAGRAM 4

nails where they meet the roof beams, corner posts, and base walls. In front, some angular pieces were added to frame the entrance; these extend from about the midpoint of the roof beam to about one-third of the way down each front post and are filled in with smaller branches.

3   The arbor is now complete. For the final touches, place a garden bench near the back wall and plant vines around the outside so that they can grow up and fill in the spaces between the branches.

VARIATION Rustic fence

Using some of the basic techniques from the rustic arbor, you can build a practical and attractive rustic fence. It can stand on its own to mark off a part of the property, or you can use it to disguise an existing chain-link fence.

Cut as many long, straight branches—about 2 inches thick—as you need posts. Expect to use 1 branch every 6 feet or so for the length of the fence plus others for crossbars and diagonal pieces to stretch between the posts.

Treat the bottoms of the posts with wood preservative and, when dry, set 12 to 18 inches deep in the ground and compact the earth around them (for the fence below we pushed some saplings into the ground and tied them around existing metal posts to hide them).

Attach four or five horizontal rows of 10-gauge wire between the posts, spaced evenly from the ground to the top of the posts. (If you are hiding a chain-link fence, just use the fence as a base.) With 14-gauge wire, lash crossbars to the tops of the posts; these form the top edge of the fence. Lash diagonal pieces between the posts to form a cross, then weave branches in and out of the wire rows in a pleasing pattern . Lash another post at the point where the diagonals cross, placing it in the ground if necessary to keep the fence sturdy.

Finally, use sticks and trimmed branches up to ¾ inch thick to fill in the spaces between the posts in an attractive arrangement. Weave the sticks and branches in and out of the wires, and secure them with 14-gauge wire where necessary.

Build a fence that blends in with its surroundings by using natural materials. Such a fence is very effective in a garden where you want to attract wildlife.

Pyramid frame

This three-sided pyramid structure makes a surprisingly strong and inexpensive support for all kinds of plants. You can buy bamboo poles at your local garden center.

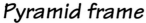

- ◆ **3 bamboo poles, 10 feet long and 1 to 2 inches in diameter**
- ◆ **bamboo lengths as required, ¼ to ½ inch in diameter**
- ◆ **green garden twine**
- ◆ **heavy-duty shears or saw**
- ◆ **leather gloves, marker pen, tape measure, scissors**

Making one side of the pyramid

1 Lay two 10-foot pieces of bamboo on the ground. Using a tape measure and marker pen, make a mark at points A, B, and C on each pole (Diagram at right). The dimensions are a guide only; if you have a good eye for proportion, you can construct the frame without making precise measurements.

2 Tie the poles together at A. When tying, wind the twine around the poles until secure, then finish with a nonslip knot (a clove hitch is good). Spread the bottom ends of the poles apart so that the distance from C to C is about 48 inches.

3 Using shears and wearing gloves, cut a thin piece of bamboo 56 to 64 inches long. Tie it to each pole at C and allow it to overhang at each side by 4 to 8 inches.

4 Measure the distance from B to B, cut a piece of bamboo—once again allowing a small overhang—and tie it to each pole at B.

5 Continue to cut and tie the four other pieces of bamboo shown in the diagram. It is

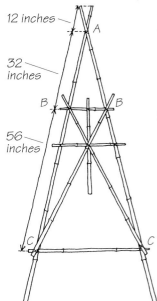

12 inches — A

32 inches

B — B

56 inches

C — C

Bamboo canes make an attractive and inexpensive support for small climbing roses or for tall, weak-stemmed plants, such as tomatoes or pole beans.

255

best to do the two diagonal pieces next; follow those with horizontal and vertical pieces that are attached at the point where the two diagonal pieces of bamboo cross.

6 When all the pieces have been tied to the poles, go over the joints with extra twine to be sure the structure is secure.

7 If desired, trim overhanging ends at 45-degree angles so that they are roughly even.

Completing the pyramid

1 Mark positions A, B, and C on the third upright. Tie it to the other uprights at A.

2 Set the three feet of the pyramid on the ground to form an equilateral triangle. Repeat Steps 3 to 5 (above) for the two incomplete sides.

3 When all pieces are attached, strengthen the main joins with extra twine.

Flexible frame

This bamboo frame is ideal for supporting plants and flexible enough to be used as a temporary barrier around a damaged or newly planted lawn or a freshly poured concrete path. It is made of identical panels, so that you can make as many as needed. Vary the dimensions to suit your garden. You may need to buy bamboo in standard lengths and cut it to size

- ◆ **lengths of ¼ - to ¾ -inch bamboo: 1 piece 70 inches long (crossbar)**
  2 pieces 65 inches long (diagonals)
- ◆ **2 pieces ¾ -inch bamboo, 50 inches long (uprights)**
- ◆ **green garden twine**
- ◆ **leather gardening gloves**
- ◆ **heavy-duty pruning shears**
- ◆ **scissors**
- ◆ **tape measure**

1 Using the shears and wearing gloves, cut the bamboo to the required lengths.

2 The best way to put the panel together is by eye. Use the diagram below as a guide; you don't have to be too precise about measurements. Bear in mind that pieces overhang at the corners by about 10 inches. First, lay the crossbar on the ground, then lay the uprights on it and tie them together. When tying, wind around until secure, then finish with a nonslip knot.

3 Lay the diagonals in place; they should meet the crossbar roughly one-third of the way from each upright. Tie the diagonals to the crossbar and uprights.

4 Trim all ends of the bamboo. If desired, cut the tops of the diagonals so that they are neatly in line with the tops of the uprights.

Use a flexible frame as an in-bed support for annuals. Four panels in a zigzag formation (bottom left) display a row of sweet peas to good effect. The triangular arrangement of panels (above left) supports a smaller clump of the same flowers.

◆ Scarecrow ◆

Scarecrows have been used since early times to scare pesky birds away from crops. Making one is easy—just use your imagination and whatever old clothing you have on hand. Even if your mock farmer doesn't frighten the birds, he's guaranteed to make the neighbors smile.

Decorate your scarecrow's clothes and hat before putting them on. Spoons, cloth patches, and decorative stitching make amusing embellishments.

- **6-foot garden stake (upright)**
- **5- to 14-foot garden stake or an old rake or spade (arms)**
- **screw (to go through 2 stakes)**
- **burlap bag**
- **straw**
- **tie wire (20 or 18 gauge)**
- **assorted clothes and accessories**
- **fabric glue**
- **needle and thread**
- **electric drill, screwdriver, scissors, pliers, hammer**

1 Lay the longer stake on the ground and center the shorter one (or rake or spade) on it, 1 foot from the top. Where the stakes cross, drill a hole for the screw that will hold them together. Fasten the screw through the stakes.

2 Put the bag over the top of the long stake; cut the bag to a suitable size for the head. Stuff it with straw, fastening it at the neck with wire.

3 Create a face on the head. We glued on a piece of felt for a mouth, sewed on buttons for teeth, and attached pieces of plastic with wire for the eyes. Glue on straw for hair before wiring the hat to the head.

4 Put a shirt on the frame and fill with straw. Knot the bottom of the shirt to hold straw in.

5 Make a hole in the overalls for the stake to pass through. Put the overalls on the scarecrow and stuff them with straw.

6 Hammer the stake into the ground in the center of the garden.

Add a whimsical touch to your garden—and keep the birds out of the vegetable patch and the home orchard—with an old-fashioned scarecrow.

◆ Party Lights ◆

Garden lighting can help to create a magical atmosphere for an outdoor party. It doesn't have to involve expensive equipment or complex installations. With a little imagination, you can create gentle luminescence with your own festive lights, made from simple, everyday materials.

Glass jar lights

Here are three ways to hang jars using wire. The specifications are for the ones we used; you can vary them as desired. Read the section on wire-work techniques, p.223, before proceeding.

- ◆ **selection of glass jars**
- ◆ **lengths of copper or brass wire**
- ◆ **20- and 22-gauge tie wire**
- ◆ **vise, pliers, thick screwdriver**
- ◆ **drill and cup hook**
- ◆ **measuring tape**
- ◆ **candles, sand**
- ◆ **glass paints, paintbrush**

Basic hanger

1 Measure circumference of jar neck, add 3 inches, and cut a piece of copper wire to this length. Bend the wire around the jar neck to form a loose circle and use pliers to hook the two ends securely together. With a screwdriver, twist the wire to form two eye loops on opposite sides of the jar (left).

hanging loop

eye loop

2 For the hanger, cut another piece of wire, 3 feet long. At its midpoint use pliers to twist a loop (for hanging).

3 Thread 1 inch of each end of the hanger wire through the eye loops; secure by twisting the ends back on themselves.

Twisted-wire hanger

1 Loop a piece of 20-gauge wire, about 6 ½ feet long, into a circle and use pliers to hook

the two ends together. Shape the wire around the top of the jar, just below the lip (below) so that there are two loops of about 3 feet in length on either side of the neck.

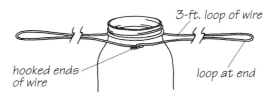

3-ft. loop of wire

hooked ends of wire

loop at end

2 With pliers, twist the left-hand loop hard up against the neck of the jar. Insert a cup hook in the drill and slip the right-hand loop over the cup hook.

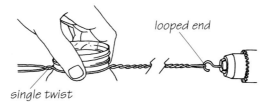

looped end

single twist

3 Hold the wire firmly on either side of the jar's neck as shown above and run the drill at its lowest speed so that it twists the wire tightly right up to the jar. Repeat this procedure on the left-hand side.

4 Neatly cut off the two end loops from the twisted wire. Bend the two strands up above the jar and, about 4 inches from their ends, bind them together with 22-gauge wire. Use

pliers to form decorative coils of about 1-inch diameter at the ends (see cage hanger, below).

Cage hanger

1 Take two pieces of 20-gauge wire, each 3 feet long. Cross them at their midpoints (right) and bind them together at this point, using 22-gauge wire.

2 Center the base of the jar over the joint and, holding it firmly in place, bend the wire up over the sides (right). Bind the four pieces together, 6 inches from their ends, using 22-gauge wire. Form a decorative coil on each end by twisting the wire in on itself with pliers.

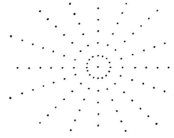

loop

cross

3 Cut a piece of 20-gauge wire to the circumference of the jar plus an inch. Loop it around the four wire strands just below the lip of the jar. Bind each of the four strands with 22-gauge wire.

Finishing off

1 Paint the glass jars, if you like, following the glass paint manufacturer's instructions.

2 Make a bed of sand 2 inches deep in each jar to hold the candles steady.

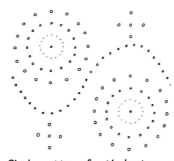

Circle pattern for tin lanterns

Radiating sun design

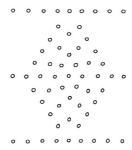

Diamond pattern

Tin can lights

Candlelight glints through the holes in these cans. To make the designs, transfer marks from a paper pattern and then drill holes in the can.

- ◆ **clean tin cans**
- ◆ **paper, pencil, and compass**
- ◆ **ruler and measuring tape**
- ◆ **adhesive tape**
- ◆ **thick piece of doweling**
- ◆ **vise, pliers, hammer, drill**
- ◆ **20- and 22-gauge wire**
- ◆ **paint and paintbrush**

1 Make a pattern of holes on paper to wrap around your can by using a photocopier to enlarge one of the designs shown at the bottom of the facing page. Alternatively, cut a piece of paper to size and copy the designs onto it freehand.

2 To copy the circle designs from the patterns, use a compass and pencil to draw concentric circles and mark equidistant points around the outer circumference. Draw lines from the center to these points to divide the circle into even sectors. A dot at each intersection indicates where a hole is to be made.

3 For the diamond design, draw a small diamond shape made of two equilateral triangles and enclose this in two proportionately larger triangles. Add dots to the outlines at evenly spaced intervals to indicate holes.

4 Tape the paper pattern to the can.

5 Place one end of the dowel lengthwise in the vise; slip the can over the other end.

6 At each dot on the pattern, tap a small hole with a large nail and then enlarge the hole with a drill. Make holes for the handles near the top of the can in the same way.

7 Make a handle by bending a 20-inch length of wire at its midpoint, then bending small hooks at each end to attach to the can. Twist the other end into a small loop for hanging. Paint the cans if desired.

Create a special atmosphere with glass jar candle holders and twinkling tin lanterns, perforated in the patterns shown on the facing page.

Pots with a Difference

*Here are some unconventional yet charming containers that will introduce individual touches to
your garden. With a little spit and polish and the right planting, such items as broken pots, old buckets,
or a not-used-very-often wheelbarrow can be given a new lease on life.*

Recycled pots

*When an attractive clay pot is cracked or broken,
its useful life need not necessarily be over. An
imperfect object can be recycled to add its own
special charm and character to your garden.*

- **a broken pot (with enough bowl remaining to hold some potting mix) and shard**
- **small piece of fiberglass window screening**
- **potting mix**

1 If you don't have a cracked or broken flower pot, look out for a "second" at your local nursery or pot shop. Damaged items are usually available at a greatly reduced price. Use a hammer to carefully chip any sharp points or irregular or jagged pieces off the shard (the piece that has broken away).

2 Cover the drainage hole with a piece of fiberglass window screening to prevent potting mix from being washed out. Add potting mix to the damaged pot up to the level of the lowest point of the break.

3 Press the shard upright into the potting mix, placing it about one third from the rear of the pot. Press the potting mix around the shard to keep it in place.

4 Fill the pot with plants. Those that require good drainage are best placed at the rear; those that prefer moist conditions, at the front. Plants with large root balls should also be positioned at the rear where their roots have more room to grow. For dry-climate plants or cactus, add some coarse sand to the potting mix to further improve drainage.

VARIATION To age a newly bought "second" pot, smear it with dirt and moss or a handful of peat moss and white glue.

*Use a large pottery shard to create a minuscule terrace
and restore a broken pot to a useful container that can
be planted in two levels (above and left). The shard
also helps hold potting mix in place until plant roots
are well established enough to do the job. Creeping
plants spill out of the container above, turning its
imperfections into attractions. The pot at left becomes
a miniature frivolity with its use of a water-worn
aquarium stone as a makeshift replacement for a missing shard. The impact of the display of a true geranium
(Pelargonium), stonecrop, and daisy fleabane (Erigeron)
is enhanced by placing the pot on a weathered sandstone step.*

Mock stone pots

A stone trough is one of the most handsome—but expensive—garden containers. A cheap and easy alternative is mock stone, or hypertufa. This material, which you make yourself, simulates the texture of real stone at a fraction of the cost.

- ◆ **peat moss, packaged sandcement mix**
- ◆ **containers with rigid sides (cardboard boxes, plastic containers, or Styrofoam coolers)**
- ◆ **5-inch length of 1-inch-diameter doweling**
- ◆ **small sheet of plywood, bricks**
- ◆ **whisk broom or wire brush**
- ◆ **potting mix**
- ◆ **variety of ground covers or similar plants**

1 Combine the dry peat moss and the sand-cement mix using two parts peat to one part sand-cement. When thoroughly mixed, add small quantities of water until the mixture is the consistency of dough—sticky but not wet.

2 To make a simple mold from a box, insert two 2½-inch lengths of 1-inch-diameter dowel through the box's bottom to form drainage holes. Line the bottom of the box with 1½ inches of the mix. For the inner walls of the mold, cut four lengths of plywood 1½ inches shorter than the outside dimensions of the box and stand them corner to corner inside the box to mimic its shape. Support the plywood pieces on the inside with a layer or two of bricks or half-bricks.

3 Fill the space between the plywood inner walls and the sides of the box with the mix, pressing it down firmly as you go with a thin, blunt stick to eliminate air bubbles.

4 Allow to dry in a covered place for 24 hours.

5 The next day, slide out the inner sides and tear away the cardboard outer walls. Remove the doweling drainage plugs.

Add cement dyes (available at building-supply stores) to boost the natural look given to the mock-stone mix by the peat moss. Add a dye to the wet mix and stir it in only once or twice; it will introduce haphazard, sedimentlike streaks to the pot.

6 Rub the sides of the container with a small whisk broom or wire brush to roughen the surface slightly, giving it the appearance of natural hewn stone.

7 Leave the container unplanted for three to five days (depending on the weather) to ensure that the mix firms properly.

VARIATION For a round pot, line the bottom of a plastic container of the desired diameter and height with 1½ inches of the mix around a short dowel for drainage. Center a second round container with a diameter 1½ inches less than the first one on the mix so that the gap between the two is even all around.

Painted pots

These decorative pots are as practical as they are good-looking. They can be used as highlights to bring color to a garden corner, and they make excellent gifts. Painted as subtly or as boldly as you like, they are a cheerful ingredient in giving the garden your own individual touch.

- ◆ **metal buckets or pails and terra-cotta pots of various sizes**
- ◆ **sandpaper**
- ◆ **hole punch for metal**
- ◆ **tinsnips and emery cloth (optional)**
- ◆ **metal primer (spray can or can)**
- ◆ **semigloss exterior alkyd paints (spray can or can)**
- ◆ **paintbrushes, if needed**
- ◆ **mineral spirits for cleanup**

1 Make sure all containers are scrubbed clean, sanded free of rust, and in good condition.

2 Some of our metal containers were purchased with rims already scalloped. If yours are straight-edged and you would like them to be scalloped, draw a semicircular pattern around the top rim with a sharp pencil, using a jar lid as a template. Cut the design out with sharp tinsnips, then rub with emery cloth to dull sharp edges.

3 If you wish to use a metal container for planting (it can also serve as a vase), punch three or four drainage holes in the base.

4 Spray or brush the metal containers inside and out with a metal primer. Allow to dry.

5 Working in an airy, dust-free environment, spray or brush each container with two or three coats of paint. Make sure each coat is dry before you start the next one. The number of coats required will depend on the color of the paint you choose. Allow the containers to dry thoroughly before use.

Use a simple coat of paint to bring style to inexpensive metal or terra-cotta containers or to blend a variety of pots in a particular color scheme.

Where space is limited, plant bulbs and annuals in galvanized bowls, tubs, and buckets (below) for displays that can be moved readily from place to place. Ensure that containers have drainage holes before planting.

Novelty planters

Just about any type of container that will hold soil and can be drained will serve as a novel, eye-catching planter. Old galvanized buckets or watering cans are particularly interesting; new ones can be "aged" with wet soil to give them character.

- ◆ **potting mix**
- ◆ **slow-release fertilizer**
- ◆ **range of flowering plants**
- ◆ **containers, such as old galvanized buckets and watering cans**

1 To give an aged look to a shiny new galvanized bucket or watering can, smear a handful of moist soil haphazardly over the surface. Let this dry and then use a gloved hand to scrape or wipe off any lumps that have stuck to the surface. Don't wash it off or you will remove the layer that dulls the silver gloss finish of the galvanizing process.

2 If an old container is still watertight, punch two or three ¼-inch-diameter holes in the

Use found or discarded objects such as this old wheel-barrow (above) as feature planters. Grouping small and large containers together in a corner or against a wall makes an effective display.

bottom with an awl or metal punch. Cover the holes with a layer of fiberglass screening so that they don't become clogged with potting mix or allow the mix to wash away. If the bottom of the bucket or can has disintegrated through rusting, you may want to slip a plastic pot (with drainage holes) inside to keep the soil from escaping.

3 Fill the containers with a good potting mix, add a handful of slow-release fertilizer pellets, and plant as you would any other container.

VARIATION If you have a large container, such as a galvanized tub, make drainage holes and fill the bottom with several inches of gravel. Then use the container to hold a changing display of seasonal flowers—from spring bulbs to fall mums—in individual pots.

QUIRKY INSPIRATIONS

HOLLOW LOGS, wooden crates, metal coffeepots, or even old birdcages can be adapted to hold plants; you can attach a length of chain or weatherproof cord to the top of a birdcage to make an unusual hanging basket.

Look around the basement, garage, or attic for ideas. Baskets with plastic liners and several inches of gravel can hold pots of flowers handsomely. So can large decorative tins—the kind that come full of popcorn at Christmas—if you punch holes in the bottom. A pair of brightly colored children's rain boots—long outgrown—could make clever containers.

◆ Wire Pot Stands ◆

*The ancient craft of wirework produces a novel form of decoration.
Choose either of two versions of this handsome and sturdy wire pot stand, or tailor the style
and proportions to suit a particular pot you want to display.*

Read the section on wirework techniques on page 223 before proceeding with this project.

- **rolls of 10-, 12-, 20-, 22-gauge wire**
- **saucepan, 10-inch diameter or less**
- **ruler or measuring tape, felt pen**
- **vise, pliers, screwdriver, gloves**
- **piece of 1½-inch diameter galvanized iron piping**
- **jar, about 3 inches in diameter**
- **electric drill and cup hook**
- **high-gloss spray enamel or small jar of enamel paint and paintbrush**
- **mineral spirits for cleanup**

Making the base

1 To make a cross-shaped base, take two pieces of 2-foot-long, 10-gauge wire and mark the midpoint of each and a point 3½ inches on either side of the midpoint.

2 To shape the four rings that sit beneath the crosspiece for feet, secure the iron pipe horizontally in a vise (Step 1, below). Rest one cross-piece on the pipe at one of the 3½-inch marks, holding it in place with your thumb. With the other hand, bend the long end of the wire around the pipe so that it overlaps the shorter end and forms a 2-inch-diameter ring. When released, the long end should spring back to form a neat ring (practice with spare wire a few times).

3 Make a second ring at the other 3½-inch mark. Make rings at the 3½-inch marks on the other piece. Bend a kink into one crosspiece at its midpoint (below), rest the second piece in it, and secure the joint with 22-gauge wire.

4 To make an outer hoop to sit on the cross-shaped base, wear gloves and unwind enough 10-gauge wire to go around the saucepan—approximately 32 inches—plus 2 inches for making hooks, or 34 inches total. Use pliers to hook the ends together to secure the hoop.

5 Lay the hoop on top of the base, cutting

back the four ends of the crosspiece so that only ½ inch extends beyond the hoop. Secure the two together by hooking the crosspiece ends around the hoop with pliers.

6 Use pliers to bend 10 feet of 12-gauge wire into a spiral of an outer diameter to fit within the 32-inch-circumference hoop. Leave ½ inch free at each end.

7 Lay the spiral on the base. Hook the ½ inch of wire at the spiral's center around the center of the crosspiece and the ½ inch at the other end around the outer hoop.

8 Secure the spiral to each crosspiece with a 32-inch length of 22-gauge wire (Step 3, below). Wind the wire across so that it loops around each point where the two pieces intersect. Secure neatly at each end to the outer hoop.

Decorating with petals

1 Use the drill to twist 3-foot double strands of 20-gauge wire into plaits (p.258) and cut these into sixteen 12-inch lengths with ½-inch hooked ends (Step 4, below).

MAKING THE POT STAND

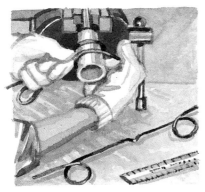

1 *To start the base, take two lengths of wire and make two rings in each by bending the wire around a pipe. Place a kink at the midpoint of one piece, rest the other in it, and join the two here.*

2 *Next, make a 32-inch-diameter hoop, place it on the crosspiece, and secure by hooking the ends of the crosspiece around it. Wind a piece of 12-gauge wire into a spiral that fits inside the hoop.*

3 *Lay the spiral within the hoop. Tie it to the crosspiece with 22-gauge wire at each place where they intersect. Also tie the spiral to each of the foot rings with the 22-gauge wire.*

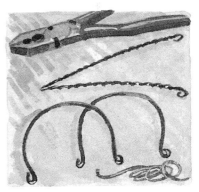

4 *For a decorative trim, make 16 V-shaped petals of plaited 20-gauge wire and press each over a jar to make a curve. Alternatively, use 12-gauge wire scallops bent on the pipe in the vise.*

2 Bend each length into a V-shaped petal, then press each petal over a jar on its side to give it a gentle curve.
3 With curve and hooks facing out (above), connect a petal to the base hoop with its hooks 4 inches apart. Close the hooks with pliers. Attach the next petal, overlapping the first. Continue around the hoop back to the start. Where petals cross, secure with 22-gauge wire.

Decorating with scallops
1 Cut 18 lengths of 12-gauge wire, each 10 inches long. Make ½-inch hooks at each end.
2 Bend each piece of wire around the iron pipe secured in the vise until it forms almost a complete hoop. Remove from the pipe and let it spring out to make a half-ring or scallop shape (above), with ends about 4 inches apart. Repeat for each length.

Use these sturdy stands to support pots on the veranda or patio or for vases indoors. Paint them with a metal primer before coating in your favorite color.

3 Attach in the same way as Step 3 of Decorating with petals but with hooks facing in.
4 Finish either stand by painting, if you like. Use a metal primer and exterior acrylic paint.

265

◆ On the Veranda ◆

*Day-to-day gardening chores are easy to put off if you have to go to the garage
or the basement to find the tool you need. A rack that holds all the tools where you
can quickly pick them out will make you a much more efficient gardener.*

A hanging rack

*A rack hung on the veranda or just inside the back
door provides a convenient place not only to
hang hats and bags as you go in and out but also
to keep all your gardening paraphernalia at the
ready for quick bouts of weeding or trimming.*

- **24 feet of lattice strips**
- **one quart exterior stain or paint in color of choice**
- **paintbrush (about 2 inches wide)**
- **half sheet ¼ -inch plywood**
- **one packet 1-inch roofing nails**
- **four screw-in coat hooks**
- **two screws (2-inch) to attach rack to wall**
- **tape measure**
- **pencil**
- **T square**
- **tenon saw**
- **electric drill**
- **hammer**
- **steel block (or a second hammer)**
- **sandpaper**

1 Apply stain or two coats of paint to all
the wood.

2 Cut the wood strips to the lengths spelled
out below; the horizontal pieces are of different lengths because the rack tapers slightly
from bottom to top, which gives it a more
graceful appearance. For the horizontal pieces,
cut two strips at 23 inches, one strip at 23 ½
inches, and one strip at 24 inches. For the vertical pieces, cut four strips at 19 ½ inches and
three strips at 24 inches. For the diagonal
pieces, cut four strips at 19 inches.

3 Lay the plywood on a flat surface. Place the
horizontal pieces on it with the shortest at the
top and longest at the bottom; then place the
vertical pieces over them. Arrange all these
pieces by eye following the pattern shown in

the diagram below. Overhanging end pieces
can be be trimmed off later, if you like. Keep in
mind that although most pieces don't meet at
a right angle because of the taper, the central
vertical piece does cross each of the horizontal pieces at a right angle. Use a T square to
align this piece with each of the horizontal
pieces. Mark each juncture with a pencil; this
alignment is the key to the whole design.

4 Drill holes for the nails with a bit slightly
smaller than the nails at each of the points
shown in the diagram. Hammer in a nail at each
hole; the nail points should slightly pierce the
surface of the plywood board.

5 When the pieces are nailed together, turn
the rack over and remove the plywood
board—it should come away quite easily. Place
the steel block (or the head of a second hammer) under the rack so that the flat head of
one nail is on the steel block. Bend down the

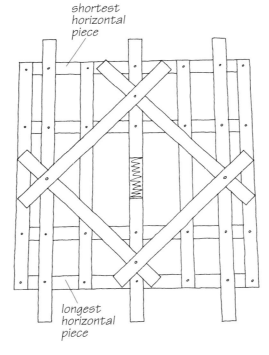

shortest
horizontal
piece

longest
horizontal
piece

point of the nail and hammer it flat (the steel
block supports the nail as you do this). This
is known as "clinching" and is shown below.
Repeat this step for each of the nails.

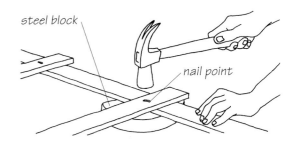

steel block

nail point

6 Turn the rack back over to face you, then
lay down the diagonal laths as shown in the
diagram. To secure the diagonals in place, first
drill holes for the nails at the points shown.
Then hammer in the nails and clinch them as
shown above.

7 Trim overhanging strips, if you like, to make
neat edges for the rack. Sand any rough edges.

8 Stain any raw surfaces, if you are using stain.
On a painted rack, paint over the nails and any
raw surfaces, such as the trimmed ends.

9 To install the coat hooks, drill holes at the
four points where the diagonals cross each
other (photograph, facing page), making sure
you are not too close to the nails. Screw in the
coat hooks.

10 To mount the rack, drill two holes in the
second horizontal from the top between the
first two and last two vertical strips for the
screws. Use long (2 ½ -inch) screws for stucco
walls, to reach through to the framing or studs.
On plaster walls, use expanding plugs for the
screws, to get a tight hold.

*Keep your veranda or hall tidy with this hanging rack—
you can make it larger than shown—that holds all
manner of small tools and other odds and ends..*

Garden carryall

Lots of pockets on one side and a divider compartment in the middle of this gardening bag give you plenty of places to store all your tools, seeds, and other supplies. It's made with strong green canvas, the traditional material for such a tote. You can buy canvas at large fabric stores, sail makers, or upholstery-fabric stores.

- **2 feet of 72-inch-wide canvas**
- **scissors**
- **sewing machine**
- **heavy-duty sewing machine needle**
- **masking tape**
- **heavy-duty thread in color to match canvas**
- **one large heavy-duty snap**

1 Cut the following pieces from the canvas (below): one 8 x 20 ½ -inch pocket piece; one 22 ½ x 20 ½ -inch front piece; one 28 ½ x 20 ½ -inch back piece; and two 36 x 3-inch strap pieces.

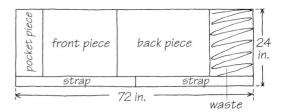

2 With the sewing machine, make a row of stitches approximately ½ inch from the edge of one long side of the pocket piece. Fold over at the line of stitches, press, and stitch close to the fabric edge to make a hem. Repeat this hemming process with the short edges of the front piece, turning one edge under and the opposite one up.

3 Tape the pocket piece, hem turned under, to the front piece, with the top (hemmed) edges 3 inches apart, as shown in Diagram 1. Machine-stitch through both layers ½ inch from the bottom (raw) edge of the pocket piece.

4 To form the bottom pockets, fold the front piece up 7 inches, as shown in Diagram 1. Machine-stitch close to each side edge, from top to bottom, to hold both rows of pockets

in place. Stitch two rows, from top to bottom, 6 inches from each side edge, to make the pocket dividers.

5 On the short sides of the back piece, stitch two hems as described in Step 2, turning both

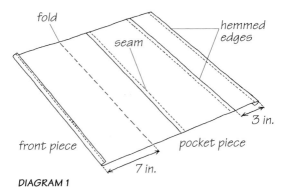

DIAGRAM 1

edges under. To form a divider for the inside of the bag, fold the back piece up 14 inches from the bottom hem with the raw edges of the

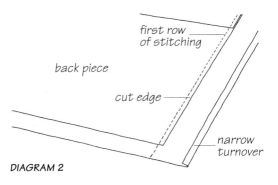

DIAGRAM 2

hem in the inside. Place front and back pieces together with the divider between them and stitch together ¾ inch from one side edge.

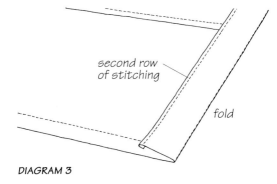

DIAGRAM 3

6 Cut the edge of the front piece close to the seam and fold the edge of the back piece over narrowly, as shown in Diagram 2.

7 Fold it over again at the row of stitching, as shown in Diagram 3, and machine-stitch through both pieces close to the folded edge of the back piece. Join the edges of the other side in the same way. Stitch along the bottom of the bag close to the edge.

8 Fold the short ends of the straps under narrowly, then fold the strap pieces in half lengthwise so that each has a width of 1 ½ inches. Stitch around all four sides of each strap close to the fabric edge. Position and double-stitch each strap 1 inch below the top edge of the bag and just outside the stitching of the pocket dividers, as shown in Diagram 4.

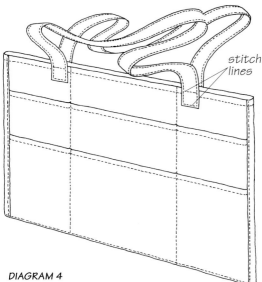

DIAGRAM 4

9 Hand-sew the two sides of the snap in the center of the bag close to the top hem edge, one side on the front piece and the matching one on the back piece. Be sure the two pieces meet comfortably.

VARIATION You can customize the bag to your own particular needs by changing the width and number of pockets. You can also embroider or appliqué a friend's name or initials on the front of the bag—in the center of the front piece where it turns up to make pockets—before you sew the pieces together. Such a personalized bag would make a lovely gift.

✦ Homemade Compost ✦

*The best additive for your garden beds is the compost you make yourself, and the best place
to make it is in a no-nonsense, homemade compost bin. These straightforward projects show you how
quick and easy it is to turn garden and kitchen waste into valuable nutrients for your plants.*

Compost bin

*Proper composting depends on good aeration.
This stake-and-wire-mesh bin allows a continuous free flow of air, while at the same time it
gives you access through a door on one side to
turn the buried contents with a fork.*

- **9 wooden stakes (cedar
  if possible), 4 feet long**
- **12 x 3-foot roll of light
  welded mesh fencing**
- **40-inch-square piece of
  ¼ - inch exterior-grade
  plywood, for lid**
- **5 wooden stakes, 2 feet long
  (buy two cedar tomato
  stakes and cut to length)**
- **thick (14-gauge) tie wire**
- **thin (18-gauge) tie wire**
- **6 galvanized bolts, 2 ½ inches
  long, with nuts and washers**
- **exterior paint or stain**
- **paintbrush**
- **measuring tape**
- **long ruler (optional)**

Making the bin

1 To make the stakes, shape the bottom end
of each 4-foot length to a point using a plane
or sharp knife. If you have bought precut
stakes, this step isn't necessary.

2 Drill three holes in each stake, one about
4 inches from the top, another 14 inches below
this, and a third 12 inches from the bottom. Be
sure that the holes are slightly larger than the
diameter of the heavy wire.

*Make a bin with straight wire sides to allow the air
to circulate, and your garden need never be short of
compost, an essential ingredient for healthy plants.*

3 Dig holes about 12 inches deep for the stakes and insert them in the ground. Place the stakes 1½ feet apart to form a 3-foot-square bin (Diagram 1). Put two stakes at the most accessible corner—one of these will form the opening edge of the bin's "door." Twist the corner stakes by about 45° (Diagram 1) so that a flat

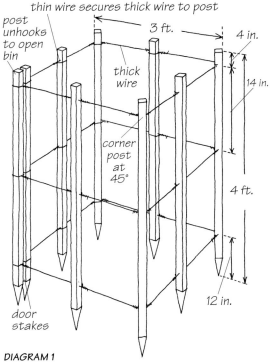

DIAGRAM 1

surface faces inward diagonally—this allows for ease of wiring later. Fill in the holes and tamp down the soil.

4 Starting with one of the stakes at the double-stake, or door, corner and ending with the other door stake, thread three rows of the thick tie wire through the holes in the stakes. At each hole, secure the thick wire with thin wire anchored on either side of the pole. The row at the bottom of the stakes should be at ground level or even a bit below; digging a small trench around the bottom of the bin will make it easier to attach this row.

5 Wrap one end of the mesh around one of the door stakes and secure it with thin wire to the three rows of thick wire.

6 Roll the mesh around the square on the inside of the stakes (Diagram 2). As you work,

connect the mesh to the top row of thick wire with the thin wire, making a tight weave every 4 inches or so (Diagram 2). Do not take the mesh past the second door stake, as this is the edge of the door.

7 Run thin tie wire along the two other rows of thick tie wire, weaving through the mesh and thick wire as before.

8 Anchor the mesh to the top of each stake with a loop of thick tie wire (Diagram 2).

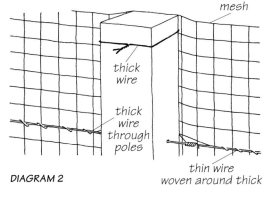

DIAGRAM 2

Making the lid

1 Mark out six holes for bolts to attach the handle to the plywood lid. To do this, mark a point 10 inches from each corner—you should have two marks on each edge, 20 inches apart. Rule straight lines across the lid to join each mark to its opposite, and the result should be a 20-inch square in the middle of the lid. Mark

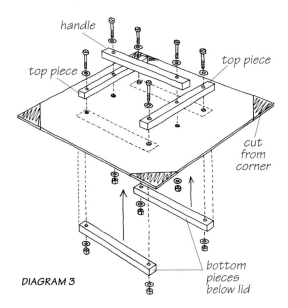

DIAGRAM 3

drilling holes where the lines intersect, then mark two more holes halfway between these holes (Diagram 3). Drill holes big enough for the bolts at the six marked points.

2 For the handle, mark drilling holes 2 inches from each end of each 24-inch-long piece of cedar—be sure that these correspond to the drill holes on the lid. Drill the holes. Also mark and drill a hole at the midpoints of the two top pieces (Diagram 3).

3 With the lid sandwiched between, position the two top pieces and the two bottom pieces at right angles to each other and bolt them together (Diagram 3). Lay the handle across the two top pieces and bolt it to them through the holes at their midpoints.

4 Shape the lid by sawing small triangles off the corners of the plywood (shaded areas on Diagram 3) to let in air.

Finishing off

1 Stain the lumber and the plywood lid with an exterior wood finish; doing so will increase the life of the bin.

2 Start your compost by following instructions for Making a heap on the facing page.

MAKING THE BEST OF A BIN

Position your heap in a reasonably sunny place. The sun will provide extra heat to encourage the decomposition process.

If you can't turn the compost regularly, drill holes in a wide plastic drainage pipe the height of the bin and place it in the center of the heap to encourage aeration.

Avoid trees when positioning your heap: shade will lower the heap's temperature, and any roots under the compost will quickly pilfer its nutrients.

More is compostable than you might think. While you should avoid all animal products except shells—egg and shellfish—don't forget to add wine corks, chewing gum, nutshells, and the cotton balls from medicine bottles.

Compost heap

The rich humus formed by composting is not only a vital part of good soil but also the cheapest soil conditioner available and the easiest to obtain because you make it yourself. Without it, plants will not flourish no matter how much love and attention are lavished upon them.

How a compost heap works

The basic ingredients of a compost heap are nitrogen, carbon, oxygen, and water. Nitrogen-rich materials include most fresh, green forms of vegetable matter, such as kitchen peelings, green leaves, and grass clippings. Carbon-rich materials include those that have already started to decompose by drying out: straw, dried leaves, and bark. Paper is also rich in carbon. Green materials also contain some carbon, but an effective heap requires at least twice as much dry, carbon-rich material as green, nitrogen-rich matter.

Oxygen is absorbed from the air, so the heap must be turned regularly, or, if it is enclosed, provision should be made for air to penetrate through the sides (facing page). Too much water is as bad as too little—excess water will decrease the amount of oxygen in the heap. To keep the heap damp but not wet, cover it. If it starts to dry out, you can add moisture for a few minutes by fine spraying with a hose.

The interaction of all these elements, combined with the heat generated by microbe activity, breaks down the organic matter. Regular turning of the heap helps maintain a high temperature and adds fresh oxygen, which reacts with the nitrogen to provide additional heat. A fresh heap takes about two weeks to reach its maximum temperature, and, if it is well maintained, will mature in two to three months. The result should be a dark-colored, sweet-scented, crumbly medium for mixing into garden soil.

Heaps versus bins

A simple, open heap is the traditional and most common way to compost materials, but its exposure to the elements means that heat build-up is slow. Bins such as the one described on the facing page are more efficient. A series of three containers will ensure a regular supply: one in the process of being filled, a full one with waste left to decompose, and a third with fully decomposed waste being used as needed on the garden.

Making a heap

1 In a sunny position, measure out an area at least a yard square (this is the minimum size necessary to generate the required heat in the shortest possible time). The bigger the heap, the more rapidly it generates heat.

2 Arrange coarse materials, such as sticks,

prunings, and bark pieces, to form the base. These will allow air to filter into the center of the heap without smothering the soil surface. You want worms to enter the heap, and smothering the soil discourages them.

3 Place 2 to 4 inches of other organic matter, such as kitchen waste, grass clippings mixed with dry leaves, animal manure, or weed-free garden loam, over this.

4 Lightly water each layer with a fine spray and build further layers of material 4 inches deep. Turn the heap once every two weeks with a pitchfork.

MAKING A COMPOST HEAP

1 *Start your heap on an open, sunny site a minimum of 3 feet square. For the base, spread a loose layer of twigs and bark over the soil.*

2 *Build up the heap with layers of organic matter—vegetable peelings, leaves, and grass. If it starts to dry out, spray with a hose until it is just damp.*

3 *For every 4 in. layer of waste, add a handful of blood meal and bonemeal or a spadeful of manure. Use a fork to turn the heap every two weeks.*

VARIATION *A plastic compost bin, store-bought or improvised from a bottomless garbage can, is useful in limited spaces. Alternate soil layers with waste layers.*

⋄ Keeping Your Garden Healthy ⋄

*Every gardener knows that beautiful flowers and bountiful vegetables depend on
good rich soil, regular doses of fertilizer, and protection from harmful pests and diseases.
Here's how to do it all with a little ingenuity and no toxic chemicals.*

Homemade soil

*With the proper mix of compost and fertilizers,
you really can almost customize the soil in your
planting beds for the flowers and vegetables you
want to grow. To be sure that everything you do
adds up to good soil, first have it tested.*

Soil testing

A complete soil test—available from your
local Cooperative Extension office or your
state agricultural university—costs less than
$20 and is the best investment you can make
in your garden. The results will provide an
exact prescription for fertilization, liming,
and adding trace elements. Knowing what
your soil needs allows you to furnish your
plants with ideal conditions with no wasted
effort.

Seed-starting mixes

All-natural: Mix one part sifted garden loam,
one part sphagnum peat, and one part coarse
sand. To eliminate soil-borne diseases, place
mix in a shallow baking pan with a small
potato and bake at 200°F until the potato
is cooked.

   Lightweight potting soil: Mix thoroughly
1 part vermiculite, 1 part milled sphagnum
moss, and 1 part perlite. Moisten before using.

Homemade fertilizers

*No matter where you live, good sources of
fertilizer, free for the hauling, are probably available right around the corner. Is there a riding
stable nearby? Does your neighbor's child have
a pet rabbit? All you have to do is ask for animal
manure to enrich your compost (p.271). Here are
some other possibilities.*

Seaweed

Seaweed is actually richer in nitrogen and potassium than most animal manures. Many municipal-
ities with beaches are glad to have you haul it
away. To cleanse seaweed of salt, stack it on the
driveway or another place where the runoff won't
go into your lawn or garden. Let several rains wash
through it before adding it to the compost heap
or digging it directly into the garden in late fall.

Wood ashes

Wood ashes from the fireplace are also an
excellent source of potassium and a way to
improve the hardiness of plants and the flavor
of their fruits.

Coffee grounds

Coffee grounds may be applied as a light
mulch around acid-loving plants to provide a
mild but complete food.

PLEASE TAKE NOTE
SOIL SOLARIZING

Soil-dwelling pests and diseases, such as para-
sitic nematodes and fungal wilt, attack a wide
variety of garden plants and once in a bed will
persist for years, reducing your crops of flowers
and vegetables year after year. There is a solution—solarizing, an easy home method of sanitiz-
ing your soil.

Wait until hot weather before you clear the bed
of vegetation, water it thoroughly, and cover it
with a sheet of clear plastic. Tuck the sheet's
edges securely into the soil around the bed's edge
and hold it in place with rocks. If the bed requires
two sheets or more, piece them together with
clear heavy-duty tape. Leave the plastic in place
for six weeks. Heat from the sun will destroy any
pests and diseases in the soil.

WHIPPING UP A HOMEMADE PESTICIDE

1 *To make a spray for getting rid of
aphids, whiteflies, and similar garden pests, puree 8 to 10 cloves of
garlic in a blender with 1 tablespoon
vegetable or mineral oil.*

2 *Strain the mixture through a
sieve into a quart storage jar. Add
3 cups hot water and a teaspoon
liquid dishwashing soap. Cap the jar
and shake to mix thoroughly.*

3 *Decant the mixture into a spray
bottle (scrub out and use an old
cleaning spray bottle) and spray the
affected plants, making sure to
cover both sides of the leaves.*

For a balanced fertilizer with a 2-4-2 formula of nitrogen, phosphorus, and potassium, mix four parts coffee grounds with one part wood ashes.

Houseplant food

For an organic food for houseplants, dump two bucketfuls of fresh horse or cow manure (or one bucketful of poultry manure) into a burlap sack. Tie the sack shut with one end of a long rope and place it in an empty barrel. Fill the barrel with water and leave the sack to steep for one week, using the rope occasionally to jerk it up and down and mix the liquid. Apply the resulting "manure tea" monthly to the soil around plant roots.

Green manure

After clearing vegetables or annual flowers from a bed in fall, sow hairy vetch or winter rye. Often called green manures, these plants thrive in cool weather, protecting the beds from soil erosion and weeds. In early spring, three to four weeks before planting time, dig the green manure right into the soil. As it decomposes, it adds humus to the soil and acts as fertilizer for next year's crop.

Homemade Pesticides

There are many nontoxic tricks for discouraging pesky animals around the yard and garden.

Ants

To keep a pet's food from attracting ants, set the food dish in a pie pan filled with soapy water.

To destroy invading ant colonies, mix three cups water with one cup sugar and four teaspoons boric acid. Loosely pack several small screwtop jars half full with cotton balls, saturated with the mixture. Pierce jar lids with two to three small holes (large enough to admit ants) and screw back onto jars. Place jars in areas where ants are active but out of the reach of children and pets.

KNOW THE ENEMY

To successfully identify a pest that is attacking your plants, first study the scene of the crime. If you suspect an animal marauder, look for a trail of footprints or shed fur samples. You can't fight a deer with a mousetrap.

Collect samples of damaged plant parts and take them to your Cooperative Extension office—the number is in the government listings section of your telephone book. Specialists there will tell you (without charge) what the problem is—pest or disease—and the most effective remedy.

Aphids, mealybugs, mites, scales, and thrips

Soap spray: Mix one tablespoon dishwashing soap, such as Ivory Liquid or Shaklee's Basic H, in one gallon of water. Test spray a few leaves of the affected plant; if no damage results, spray the whole plant.

Ammonia spray: Mix one part household ammonia with seven parts water.

Oil spray: Stir one tablespoon of liquid dishwashing soap into one cup of vegetable oil (peanut, safflower, corn, soybean, or sunflower). Mix 1 to 2g teaspoons of the soap and oil blend with one cup water, and apply to affected plants.

Fungal diseases

To control fungal diseases, such as powdery mildew and blackspot, mix one teaspoon of baking soda in one quart warm water. Add one teaspoon liquid dishwashing soap. Apply to leaves as a spray or drench the leaves of smaller plants with a watering can.

Mice

Inexpensive snap traps from the hardware store are quite effective when deployed in large numbers. Set baited traps at two-foot intervals along the base of walls where mice run. To kill both young and old mice, set traps out twice: once to trap the adults, and then two weeks later to trap maturing young. Bait traps with peanut butter or with a small cotton ball. Mice pull at the cotton when they are collecting nesting material and so trigger the trap; unlike food baits, cotton doesn't spoil in hot weather. To avoid leaving a telltale human odor, always wear gloves when handling traps.

Moles

Dump several scoops of used cat litter into the mole's tunnel; moles find it offensive and will leave. Don't, however, spread cat litter near a food garden because it can carry infections harmful to humans.

Protect a garden from moles with wire mesh fencing, set into a 12-inch or deeper trench, all around the bed; such a fence will also help to fend off other ground-level pests, such as rabbits or woodchucks.

Predator bugs

To attract predacious insects—the kind that eat other insects—dot your garden with sweet alyssum, asters, daisies, marigolds, sunflowers, yarrow, and members of the parsley family, such as parsley, fennel, and dill. These flowers offer the nectars and pollens that predacious bugs need to supplement their insect diet.

Rabbits

Marigolds: Plant French marigolds amid rabbit delicacies, such as lettuce and carrots, in the vegetable garden. The marigolds' strong odor repels rabbits.

Black pepper: Sprinkle ground pepper around plants to repel rabbits—renew after every rain.

Slugs

Countersink tin cans (such as tunafish cans) in the garden and bait them with beer.. Slugs are drawn to the beer, fall in, and don't get out again. Replenish the bait beer after a rain.

Loving Touches

*H*ere is a wide-ranging collection of inspiring ideas and easy-to-follow instructions for things you can make yourself, from cutout stamps for children to elegant, handmade greeting cards. Personal items, gifts for friends and family, ornaments, decorations for the home—you can give them all your own individual cachet, crafting them to suit your particular taste or that of the intended recipient.

Make a reversible sundress for your favorite niece or a classic sunsuit for your nephew. Knit yourself a sweater. Make a quilt and bumper guards for the new baby in the family. Fashion an evening bag from satin ribbon. Make your own raffia baskets and trim your own straw hats.

Create bright-colored piñatas for festive birthday parties, and dry your favorite garden flowers to make one-of-a-kind wreaths and bouquets.

For holidays and special occasions, there are home-made wrapping papers, gift tags, and cards—you can even make and decorate your own gift boxes. And you'll be especially proud of a toy-filled Advent calendar that can be used year after year to help the children wait for Christmas. With these and many other ideas, there are endless possibilities for creativity and fun in making items that are both beautiful and practical.

BEFORE YOU BEGIN …

*Nothing compares to the thrill of satisfaction you experience when a friend admires a piece
of handiwork and you can say, "I made it myself." The projects in this chapter call for a range of skills
and inspirations. Your confidence should increase with each new project you undertake.*

To make most of the projects in this chapter, you will need only basic materials and tools. Each project gives a full list of what is required, and you should read it carefully before you start. To buy the materials, look in art-supply stores, crafts shops, hardware stores, stationery stores, and supermarkets. Occasionally, you may have to go to a specialty shop to find the right materials.

For some of the projects, you will need to protect your work surface with a drop cloth, newspapers, or a sheet of scrap wood. When using paints, varnishes, and glues, always work in a well-ventilated area, as the fumes may be toxic.

The instructions accompanying each project explain the specific steps you will need to follow. A few basic craft techniques and skills are described in more detail below and on the following five pages.

Applying color

To achieve the various effects in the projects that call for paint, you will need a range of brushes. A stiff brush is good for stenciling, for example, while a soft round one is better for delicate designs. If a particular brush is specified, it is advisable to match this as closely as possible, asking your art-supply dealer for help if needed. For other projects, the type of brush is not important, and you can use whatever you have on hand. You may choose to experiment with different brushes or with everyday objects, such as kitchen sponges, to vary the methods given. Always work out a new technique on scrap wood before tackling a whole wall.

Paper—more versatile than it looks

A sheet of paper is the beginning point for any design or image used in crafts, but this versatile material has many other applications as well and lends itself to more than its traditional roll as a surface for pen, pencil, or brush. Paper has been cut, folded, and molded by everyone from artisans in the Renaissance Venetian court to origami craftsmen in Japan to small children everywhere, amusing themselves with strings of cutout figures.

Specialty paper shops or art-supply stores provide the best selection of paper types. If you are prepared to buy in bulk, paper merchants are also a good source (10 sheets is usually the minimum order). The charm of paper craft is that the raw material is generally inexpensive and readily available; sometimes the most rewarding projects are those made from found or recycled paper. Some outlets sell clean industrial wastepaper; call your local government for the number of a recycling center.

The large variety of papers available means that this is a craft that lends itself well to creative innovation. While different textures and strengths mean that certain papers will be preferred for particular crafts, experimentation is the key to your own style.

Placing your image where you want it

There are a number of ways of placing a picture, outline, or design on the material you will work with. Stenciling is a relatively easy way of achieving an accurate reproduction, particularly for an image that is to be used repeatedly. For stencils, use stencil acetate, a transparent plastic that you

ENLARGING WITHOUT A PHOTOCOPIER

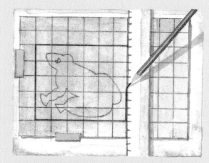

1 *Decide how large you want the design to be, noting the width. Trace the design onto tracing paper, tape it to a flat surface, then draw a grid over it with a ruler. Mark the perimeter of the design in thick pencil.*

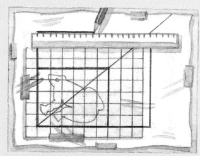

2 *Tape a second piece of tracing paper over the design. Rule a diagonal line and extend it as shown. Extend the rectangle's base to the desired width. Rule a line from this point up to the diagonal. Complete the large rectangle.*

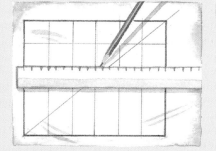

3 *Remove the underlying tracing paper. On the enlarged rectangle, measure and rule the same number of rows and columns as you ruled over the original design, so that you have an identical grid but with larger squares than the original.*

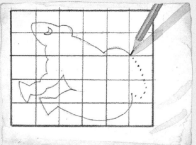

4 *Working square by square, copy the design lines from the original grid onto the corresponding squares on the larger grid. It's easier if you mark a dotted line first, making dots particularly where the design lines intersect the grid's squares.*

With just a few basic materials—and a little creativity—you can make a whole range of beautiful craft projects.

can buy at art supply or crafts stores. Place your design underneath and trace it directly onto the acetate. You can also use opaque waxed stencil paper, which is quite firm and comes in very large sheets, handy for large stencils. Place the design on top and transfer it, using one of the techniques explained in the next section.

Many of the stenciling projects in this chapter give you specific designs to copy, but you may like to choose your own—designs from other projects may also provide inspiration. Any design can be enlarged or reduced by a photocopier or graph paper, as shown facing page.

You will need a sharp craft knife to cut stencils. A backing board or self-healing cutting mat should be placed underneath. Cut toward you, turning the stencil and backing around as you work. To make the cutting out easier, you can use masking tape to secure the stencil.

To stencil, use an almost dry brush and don't thin the paint; runny paint can slip under the stencil and make a mess. Apply paint to the tip of the brush only, hold the brush upright, and apply to the stencil cutout with a light circular motion, moving from the center to the edges.

To trace or to transfer?

Two simple ways of moving an image from a sheet of paper to another material are tracing and transferring. The method you choose depends on what material you are using.

To trace a design onto plastic, such as a stencil acetate, place the plastic over the design and trace the design onto it using a fine-tip permanent marking pen. Permanent ink is important; if some of the lines remain on the acetate, permanent ink won't bleed into your stenciling paint. To trace onto transparent or semitransparent fabric, place the fabric over the design and trace the lines with a water-soluble pen or a fade-out pen for fabric that cannot be washed (marks last up to 48 hours). Backlighting can help you to outline a design: place the fabric and design on a light box or tape them to a window.

To trace onto opaque surfaces, such as cardboard or wood, first trace the design onto tracing paper. Using small pieces of masking tape at each corner, attach the tracing paper to the surface to be decorated. Then slip transfer (graphite) paper underneath the tracing paper and, using light pressure, trace over the design lines with the end of a stylus or an empty ballpoint pen. Later, you can remove any lines on the finished product with a pencil eraser. To transfer design lines onto opaque fabric, use a similar method. Trace the design onto tracing paper; then place the tracing paper in position on the right side of the fabric and pin at the corners. Slip dressmaker's carbon paper, carbon side down, between the fabric and the design. Draw over the design lines using a dressmaker's tracing wheel or a stylus. You can remove any marks when the project is finished.

Knitting

Knitting is one of the world's favorite crafts, dating back to at least the middle of the third century. The variety of yarns and colors available today has added extra interest to the craft for modern knitters: wool, cotton, cashmere, alpaca, linen, and various synthetic yarns allow you to broaden your skills with all manner of garments. As with yarns, many different types of knitting needles are also available. Plastic, metal, bamboo, and the highly prized tortoiseshell needles come in a variety of lengths and sizes. In general, if you are knitting an adult's garment, you will need longer needles than for a child's or baby's garment. Circular needles are good for working a large number of stitches and for neckbands.

Knits with inset designs feature a charted pattern that is either knitted in with one or more added yarn colors during the making of the garment or is embroidered on top of the finished piece. If you are knitting the design into the garment, wind small amounts of the charted colors onto plastic or cardboard bobbins. The bobbins prevent the extra colors of yarn from tangling and help you keep an even gauge in your knitting stitches as you change yarns. For best results, do not carry yarns over too many stitches and keep the carried yarn quite loose across the back of the work. If this is not done, the knitting will not lie flat.

Blocking and pressing

To make a good fit, some knitted garment pieces require blocking and pressing before being sewn together. Blocking is the shaping of knitted sections to the required size. To block a piece of knitting, lay it wrong side up on a padded surface, such as a clean towel or blanket. Pin the knitted piece around its edges to the correct measurements, without any overstretching or distortion. Fewer pins are usually better, but not if the edges become scalloped.

Press with a steam iron, lifting (not dragging) the iron each time you press each part of the knitting. Leave to cool and dry before removing the pins. Always check the yarn label, as many synthetics and some blends do not respond well to blocking and pressing.

Instructions

To understand knitting instructions, see "Knitting abbreviations" box on page 298. A single set of instructions often covers several sizes. The requirements for the smallest size are listed first. Then the requirements for each other size that the instructions cover are given in parentheses in order from smaller to larger. Thus k 6 (8, 10) rows means knit 6 rows for size "small," 8 rows for size "medium," and 10 rows for size "large."

Casting on

Casting on is the first step in knitting. It forms the first row of stitches and one selvage of the finished article, usually the bottom, or hem edge. Stitches of the cast-on row should be equal in size or the edge will be untidy.

There are many methods of casting on; three common ones are shown here. For all methods, form the first stitch by making a slip knot. To form a slip knot, make a loop six inches from the end of the yarn. Insert the needle into the loop, draw the yarn from the ball end of the wool through the loop and tighten the knot.

KNITTING ON

The knitting-on method forms a versatile selvage that you can make soft or firm, as you choose. It is soft when worked through the front of the loops and firm when worked through the back.

1 *Hold the needle with the slip knot in the left hand. Insert the right needle through the front of the loop and take the yarn around the needle.*

2 *Draw yarn through to form second loop. Transfer new loop to left needle and knit into it to form next new stitch. Continue for desired number of stitches.*

CABLE CAST-ON

The cable cast-on method is done the same way as for knitting on, but for each new stitch, the needle is inserted between the two previous stitches instead of into the last loop. The resulting edge is decorative and elastic.

1 *Make knot and first stitch as for knitting on. For each new stitch, insert right needle between two previous stitches.*

2 *Take the yarn around the needle as for knitting on, draw through a new loop, and transfer it to the left needle.*

3 *Continue forming new stitches, inserting the right needle between the loops until you have made the required number. If you want a really firm edge for stocking stitch, knit the first row after the cast-on into the back of the stitches.*

SINGLE-NEEDLE CAST-ON

Unlike knitting on and cable cast-on, the single-needle method requires only one needle instead of two. It forms a loose selvage that is particularly good for hem edges, buttonholes, or lacy knitting patterns. It is a very easy cast-on technique but can be somewhat difficult to work off the needle evenly in the first row. A beginner may find that one of the cast-on methods using two needles is easier to control for a neat and even effect in the first two rows.

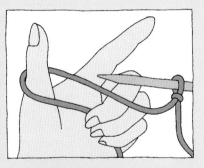
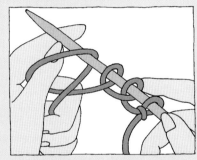
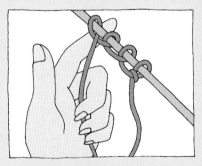

1 *Make a slip knot on the needle, held in your right hand. Wrap the yarn from the ball around your left thumb, then grasp the yarn firmly between the palm of your hand and the tips of your fingers.*

2 *Turn your thumb around so that the back of the thumb is facing you, as shown. Insert the needle from front to back through the loose loop of yarn that is formed by twisting the thumb.*

3 *Slip your thumb out of the loop, at the same time pulling the yarn downward to close the loop around the needle. Continue forming new stitches in this way until you have the required number.*

Basic stitches

There are two fundamental stitches in knitting—the knit stitch and the purl stitch. All knitting stitch patterns are made by combining and varying these two stitches. Basic knitting alternates rows of knit and purl stitches, producing the stockinette stitch. The knit stitch and the purl stitch described on this page follow one method; there are others that can be used.

CHECKING THE GAUGE

Knitting instructions always specify a gauge—the exact number of stitches and rows per 4 inches, using the specified needles, yarn, and stitch pattern. It is worth taking time to get the gauge correct, as even small variations add up.

Before beginning a project, make a sample piece about 6 inches square, using the specified yarn and needles. To measure the horizontal gauge, insert two pins 4 inches apart on a row and count the stitches between them. It is easier to count stitches on the knit side of stockinette stitch, where each loop represents one stitch.

To check the vertical gauge, place two pins 4 inches apart and count the rows between them. It is easier to count rows on the purl side of stockinette stitch, where every two ridges equal one row.

If you count more stitches or rows than the pattern specifies, knit another sample using needles one size larger. If you count fewer stitches or rows, try needles one size smaller.

KNIT STITCH

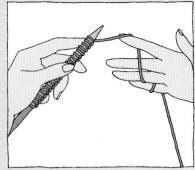

1 *Hold needle with cast-on stitches in your left hand. The first stitch should be about ½ inch from the tip. Take the yarn around the little finger of your right hand, under the next two fingers, and over the index finger, extending it 2 inches from the first stitch on the needle.*

2 *Holding the yarn behind the work, insert the right needle into the front of the first stitch from left to right (the needle tip pointing toward the back of the work). With your right index finger, take yarn forward under the right needle, then around and back over the top, as shown.*

3 *Draw the loop that is on the right needle forward through the stitch, at the same time pushing the stitch on the left needle toward the tip. These basic steps take some getting used to, but with practice you'll be able to coordinate them easily and increase your knitting speed.*

4 *Let the first stitch slip off the left needle. The new stitch (the one just made) remains on the right needle. Repeat Steps 2 to 4, pushing stitches forward on the left needle with thumb, index, and middle fingers and moving stitches back on the right needle with the thumb.*

PURL STITCH

A purl stitch is the reverse side of a knit stitch. Purl stitches tend to be looser than knitted ones, as the yarn must be cast farther. With experience, a compensation develops, especially if the index finger is kept close to the work.

1 *Hold the needle with the cast-on stitches in your left hand. The first stitch should be about ½ inch from the tip. Wind the yarn around the fingers of your right hand in the same way as for a knit stitch (p.279, Step 1).*

2 *Holding the yarn in front of the work, insert the needle into the front of the first stitch, from right to left (the needle tip pointing upward). With your right index finger, take the yarn back over the right needle, then forward and under it.*

3 *Draw the loop on the right needle back through the stitch, at the same time pushing the stitch on the left needle toward the tip. With practice, you will be able to coordinate these two movements smoothly and increase your speed.*

4 *Let stitch on left needle slip off; new stitch remains on right needle. Repeat Steps 2 to 4, pushing stitches forward on left needle with thumb, index, and middle fingers and moving stitches back on right needle with your thumb.*

Casting off

Casting off is the removal of stitches from a needle in such a way that they will not unravel. It forms the last row of finished work. There are several methods of casting off; the one given here, plain cast-off, is the simplest and most frequently used.

1 *Work the first two stitches at the beginning of the row in the stitch pattern you have been following.*

2 *Holding the yarn behind the work, insert the left needle into the first of the two stitches just worked.*

3 *Pull first stitch back over second stitch with left needle and then let it slip off under the needle. Work the next stitch.*

4 *Continue the cast-off row by repeating Step 3 until you have cast off the desired number of stitches.*

Increasing, or adding, stitches

KNIT INCREASE

Bring yarn forward, in front of right needle. Insert needle knitwise in first stitch and knit a new stitch through the first stitch. Put new stitch back onto left needle and knit it in the normal way, placing it, at this stage, on right needle as usual.

PURL INCREASE

For a purl increase, hold yarn behind right needle, insert needle purlwise in the first stitch, and purl a new stitch through it. Place new stitch back onto left needle and purl it, placing it on the right needle as usual.

Decreasing, or reducing, stitches

KNIT DECREASE

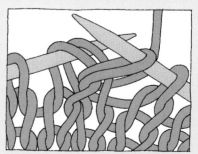

A decrease is a reduction of one or more stitches. Its purpose is to shape work by making it narrower. A common method for a knit decrease is to knit two stitches together (K2 tog) through the front of both loops, as shown above.

PURL DECREASE

This method of purl decrease, like the one shown for knit decrease at left, uses two stitches worked together. For this method you need to purl two stitches together (P2 tog) through the front of both loops, as shown above.

Sewing and needlework

There are many sewing stitches, each with its own special uses. For the projects in this chapter, the hand stitches you will need are shown on this page. In addition, you should know that to tack two or more pieces together, you simply repeat a large running stitch several times in the same holes and to baste a seam, just use large running stitches.

SLIPSTITCH

Uneven slipstitch is used to join a folded edge to a flat surface. Work the stitching from right to left, as shown below.

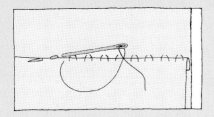

Knot the thread and bring the needle and thread out through the folded edge. Take a small stitch into the single layer, catching one or two threads of the fabric. Insert the needle back into the fold. Slide the needle along the inside of the fold for about ¼ inch, then bring the needle out and draw the thread through. Continue alternating stitches from the single layer to the fold, keeping them even and ensuring that the thread is not pulled too tight so that the stitches on the right side are as invisible as possible.

BLANKET STITCH

Blanket stitch is used to neaten raw or edges of thick fabrics. Work from left to right, with the point of the needle and the edge of the fabric toward you.

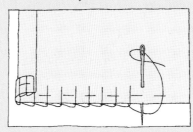

Baste hem in fabric. Bring the thread out below edge of hem. Insert a needle from the right, bringing it down below hem. With thread from the previous stitch under the needle point, draw the needle through to form a stitch over the edge.

RUNNING STITCH

Running stitch is a very short, even stitch used for fine seaming, tucking, mending, gathering, and other such delicate sewing. Work from right to left.

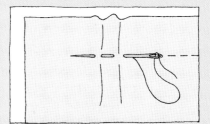

Weave the point of the needle in and out of the fabric several times before pulling the needle through. Keep the stitches and the spaces between them small and even. Unlike basting, this stitch is usually meant to be permanent.

STEM STITCH

Primarily an outlining stitch, stem stitch is often used for embroidering plant stems and other solid lines.

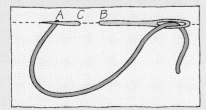

1 Working from left to right, bring the needle out at A. Insert it at B and bring it out at C, half a stitch-length back.

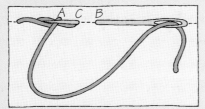

2 Repeat this sequence, keeping the thread below the needle and to the left. Keep stitches even in length.

STRAIGHT/SATIN STITCHES

The straight and satin stitches have the basics in common, only the finished effect varies. The straight stitch is used to cover straight design lines or scattered to make an open filling, seen in the far half of the drawing at right. The satin stitch (near area of drawing at right) is a series of adjacent straight stitches worked in any length and in any direction to fill an area solidly.

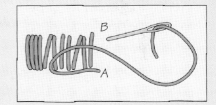

Bring needle up at A and take it to the back at B, then to another point A for the next stitch. Work as many stitches as needed for the design. Embroidered flower buds are two to three straight stitches on top of one another.

Tearing rag strips

Rectangles or squares of fabric—new or left over from other projects—can easily and quickly be torn to create a continuous rag strip suitable for braiding or knitting rag rugs (pp.112–115). The torn strips are rolled into balls, ready for use. Prints and solids are equally appropriate for this rag-making technique, since the strip is folded, wrong side inside, and held in that position for the work.

Prepare fabric for making rag strips by tearing across one of the cut edges to get a straight side. Before starting the tearing process (right) begin at the torn end and mark off along one selvage with the "A measurement" given in the directions for the project you want to make. Then make a short clip over that mark that stops inside the selvage. You are now ready to start tearing across the fabric.

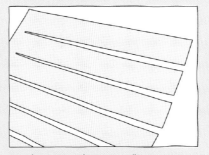

1 Along one selvage, tear "A-measurement" intervals from the outside edge of that selvage to within ½ to 1½ inches of the opposite selvage.

2 Along the opposite selvage, offset the "B-measurement" intervals by half the measurement of A. Tear to within ½ to 1½ inches of the first selvage.

◆ Novelty Stamps ◆

*Children will have fun using these easy-to-make stamps with acrylic paint or ink,
but they will need help with cutting the blocks and the foam shapes. The stamps can be applied to a wide
variety of surfaces—even fabric. If stamping on cardboard, seal it first with an all-purpose sealer.*

These supplies and directions apply to making any shape stamp, such as the stars on the cover.

- **small scraps of wood or plywood**
- **saw (optional)**
- **⅛-inch- or ³⁄₁₆-inch-thick craft foam (available at crafts and art stores)**
- **tracing paper**
- **pencil**
- **craft knife**
- **spray foam adhesive**
- **newspaper**
- **artist's acrylic paints**
- **small roller (brayer) or brush**
- **large ink stamp pad (optional)**

1 Trim four small pieces of wood to accommodate the stamp design at right and the three designs on page 284. The pieces should be slightly larger than the designs. Some lumberyards will cut wood for you.

You may also be able to get free scraps of plywood or other wood from a crafts shop or lumber-yard.

2 Using the craft knife, cut four pieces of foam large enough to accommodate each of the designs.

3 Trace the designs onto tracing paper.

4 Cut each piece of tracing paper to fit the corresponding piece of foam. Place the tracing paper over the foam and set on the block of

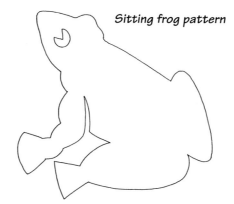

Sitting frog pattern

wood for a safe cutting surface. Use tape at the sides to hold the paper in place.

5 Using a craft knife, cut around the designs, through the paper and foam. Remove the excess paper and foam. Carefully trim the edges so they are smooth and even.

6 Spread some newspaper. Place the foam cutouts face side down on the newspaper. Working with one cutout at a time, spray the back with foam adhesive and then glue the cutout to its corresponding piece of wood, pressing down firmly to make sure it bonds securely. Repeat the process with the other foam cutouts.

7 The stamps are now ready for use. They can be applied in many ways—with paint or ink—and on surfaces from paper to walls and even fabric. See p.284 for an explanation of stamping techniques and the effects they produce.

Use a pencil to trace the frog outline at left onto tracing paper. Allow excess paper on all sides of the tracing to make it easy to tape the outline to the foam.

MAKING THE FROG STAMPS

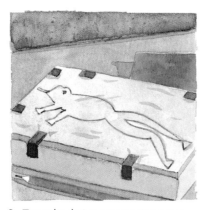

1 *Cut a piece of plywood or wood slightly larger than the stamp design. Then cut a piece of craft foam to fit the piece of wood.*

2 *Trace the design onto tracing paper. Cut the tracing paper to the shape of the foam, then place it over the foam and attach to the block using pieces of tape.*

3 *Use a craft knife to cut around the design outline, cutting through both the tracing paper and the foam. Work slowly with a steady hand for best results.*

4 *Remove the tracing paper and excess foam and tidy up the edges. The neater the outline, the clearer the final stamped image will be.*

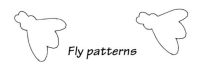

Fly patterns

Application

To apply paint to foam stamps, you can use a small roller (brayer) or a brush. If you want to print with ink, you'll need a large ink stamp pad. Each applicator has its own effects.

A roller provides even coverage without a buildup of color at the edges. Applying paint to a stamp with a brush is also easy, particularly when applying more than one color to the same stamp. You may need to blot brush-applied paint before you use the stamp.

An ink stamp pad allows you to work quickly. Ink stamping is best applied to paper or cardboard and produces crisp, even-colored designs. Stamped designs appear more translucent when they are worked with ink.

Acrylic fabric paints are usually stickier than artist's paints, but since fabric is absorbent, it will take up a lot of paint. You may need to experiment with fabric paints and different applicators—a roller or brush—to achieve the best result. Make sure you don't overload a foam stamp with paint or it will bleed and make the edges uneven.

APPLYING THE STAMP

For even paint coverage when stamping a large area such as a wall, use a roller to apply paint to the stamp. Reapply the paint each time you use the stamp.

Ink pads come in a variety of colors. They are less messy to use than paint and make crisp images. Experiment first by stamping the design onto white paper.

Applying several colors is best done by brushing the paint onto the stamp. Squeeze some paint in a saucer before brushing it onto the appropriate section of the stamp. Use a different brush for each color.

Apply fabric paint to your stamp with a brush or roller, being sure not to use too much paint. Check the stamp before you use it to be sure that it is evenly covered or the results may be blotchy.

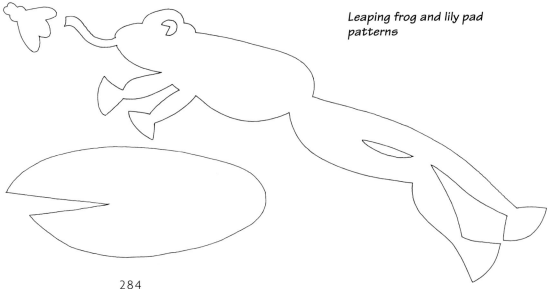

Leaping frog and lily pad patterns

◆ Baby's Patchwork Quilt ◆

*These traditional patchwork designs are simple, restful patterns, especially suitable
for a baby's crib. The quilt can double as a wall hanging in a child's room when it's no longer
needed in the crib; quilted bumper guards protect a baby in style.*

*We've chosen blue and white for our quilt, which
measures 38 ½ inches by 47 inches when finished.*

- ◆ **⅔ yard of 44-inch-wide
  blue cotton print fabric**
- ◆ **1 ½ yards of 44-inch-wide
  white cotton fabric**
- ◆ **1 ½ yards of 44-inch-wide
  cotton fabric for backing (coordinating print or plain color)**
- ◆ **matching thread**
- ◆ **thin batting**
- ◆ **quilting hoop**
- ◆ **quilting needles**
- ◆ **quilting thread**
- ◆ **rotary cutter**
- ◆ **self-healing cutting mat**
- ◆ **ruler**
- ◆ **small scissors**
- ◆ **thimble**
- ◆ **tracing paper**
- ◆ **pencil**
- ◆ **quilter's pencil**
- ◆ **cardboard**
- ◆ **blue washout pen**

Cutting

All cuts are across the width of the fabric. Use
a rotary cutter, mat, and ruler. A ¼ -inch seam
allowance is included in all measurements.

1 Cut 11 strips of blue print fabric 2 ½ inches
wide; put 4 strips aside for binding (p.287). Cut
two of the remaining strips in half crosswise.

2 Cut 10 strips of white fabric 2 ½ inches
wide; put four strips aside for a border. Cut
two of the remaining strips in half crosswise.

*This project, a patchwork quilt for a baby's crib, is
well within the scope of the first-time quilter. Make
it for your child or grandchild and it may well become
a precious heirloom, a reminder of fond family ties.*

Cut two strips 6 ½ inches wide; cut each into six 6 ½ inch squares (12 squares total). Cut one strip 7 ⅜ inches wide; cut into four 7 ⅜ -inch squares. Cut these squares diagonally twice to make 16 triangles (14 are needed). From the remaining fabric, cut two 5 ¼ -inch squares; cut each square diagonally, once, to make the four corner triangles.

Sewing

1 Make two triple strip A's, stitching a long blue strip on either side of a white strip. Make a third strip A using the short blue and white strips. Press *all* seams toward the darker color.

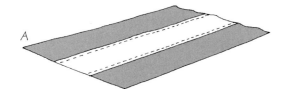

A

2 Make one triple strip B, stitching a long white strip on either side of a blue. Make a strip B with the short white and blue strips.

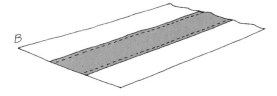

B

3 Cut all triple strips at 2 ½ -inch intervals. In all, you will need 40 cut sections of triple strip A and 20 sections of triple strip B.

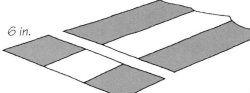

6 in.

4 Sew one triple strip A to either side of a triple strip B to make a patchwork square. Sew 20 squares in this way.

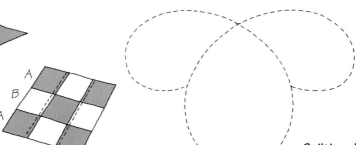

A
B
A

The design above shows the layout of the quilt. The quilting pattern is shown as dotted lines. The binding is attached after all the hand quilting has been completed.

Quilting design

Assembling

1 Position the patchwork squares, white squares, and white triangles on a flat surface. Machine-stitch the squares and triangles together, one row at a time, to make eight diagonal rows, as indicated below. Press seams. Join the diagonal rows to form the quilt top.

2 Place the quilt top flat and measure down each long side to make sure the measurements are the same. Cut the side borders to this length from two of the reserved white strips, matching the center of each strip to the center of each side. Pin and sew the side borders to the quilt top. Repeat with the top and bottom borders, which should extend to the outer edges of the side borders (design, facing page).
3 Press the quilt top on the wrong side, pressing the border seams toward the borders. Turn right side up and mark the quilting lines (design, facing page).
4 Leave the backing and batting slightly larger than the quilt top and sandwich the three layers together with several rows of basting stitches—working out from the center.
5 Fold the excess backing to the front and baste around all four sides; this will protect the edges during quilting.

Quilting

Quilting is an even running stitch that is worked through all layers of fabric and batting. Use a single strand of quilting thread about 20 inches long with a small knot tied at the end. To protect your finger from the needle—and

provide extra control—use a thimble on the middle finger of your sewing hand.
1 Position the quilting hoop in the middle of the quilt and work out toward the edges. Make sure the tension of the fabric is even on the top and the backing, with no puckers.
2 Insert the needle into the top only, about 1 inch away from where you want to make your first stitch. Gently pull on the thread until the knot pops through into the batting. Take a small backstitch, then make a small running stitch. Continue to take several small, even running stitches at a time, making sure the thread is going through all layers. Aim to have the stitches the same length on both the top and the bottom. Quilt whatever is within the hoop—when doing the long, straight vertical and horizontal lines, you can leave the thread dangling when you reach the edge of the frame, if you wish, and rethread your needle as you move the hoop to the adjoining area.
3 To finish off each piece of stitching, make a knot in the thread near the last stitch, make a single backstitch, and pull the knot into the batting; pass the needle through the batting and away from the stitch. When you cut the thread, this end will disappear into the batting.

Binding

1 Join the four 2½-inch-wide blue strips together to make a continuous length; fold in half lengthwise, wrong sides together, press.
2 Trim the excess backing and batting so that all three layers are the same size.
3 Using a ¼-inch seam allowance, pin and machine-stitch the cut edges of the binding to the front of the quilt. Begin 6 inches from one corner, and sew through all layers; stop sewing ¼ inch from the next corner, backstitch, lift the machine foot, and pivot the quilt. Fold the binding back to form a 45° angle, then fold the binding forward to the next side along the raw edge—a mitered corner should form automatically. Lower the foot and continue sewing.
4 When you reach the starting point, overlap the binding ends by 1 inch, turning the first cut end under before finishing.
5 Turn the binding to the back and hand slip-stitch along the machine line, mitering each corner to match the front. Remove basting.

QUILTING DESIGN

TRACE the quilting design (facing page) and transfer it to cardboard; cut out. With a washout pen, draw around the shape onto the quilt as indicated in the diagram on the facing page (test the pen on a scrap of fabric before using). Trace the border design (below) in the same way. Use a design of your choice, if you prefer.

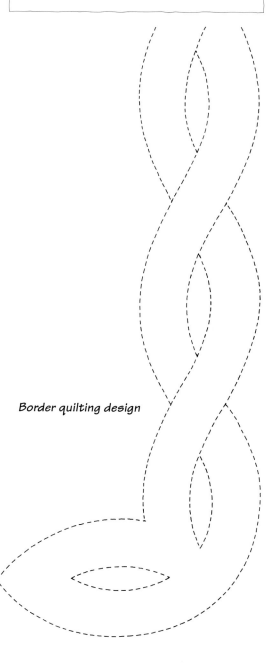

Border quilting design

◆ A Cozy Guardian ◆

*This thick, soft set of bumper guards not only protects the baby from the crib slats but
also enlivens the nursery with the bright color and lively pattern. When you team them with the
patchwork quilt on page 285, you have a charming homemade crib set.*

*A thin layer of batting allows machine-quilting in
this easy patchwork project. Loftier batting is
used only as stuffing. Made in four parts for easier
washing, the finished bumper has two end panels
(9 ⅜ x 27 ½ inches) and two side panels (9 ⅜ x
55 ½ inches). All seam allowances are ¼ inch.*

- ◆ **3 ¼ yards 44-inch-wide
  calico fabric**
- ◆ **2 ½ yards 44-inch-wide
  white fabric**
- ◆ **1 ¾ yards 48-inch-wide low-loft
  batting (cotton or polyester)**
- ◆ **1 yard 90-inch-wide high-loft,
  extra thick polyester batting**
- ◆ **4 ¾ yards 1 ½ -inch-wide
  pregathered white eyelet**
- ◆ **rotary cutter or scissors**
- ◆ **self-healing cutting mat**
- ◆ **transparent ruler**
- ◆ **threads to match fabrics**
- ◆ **dressmaker's pins**
- ◆ **scissors**

Cutting

1 From the print fabric, cut two pieces
7 x 29 inches for the end panels and four
pieces 7 x 58 inches for the side panels.
2 From the remaining print, cut two pieces
10 x 29 inches and two pieces 10 x 58 inches for
the backs of the bumper guards, six pieces
1 x 58 inches for the ties, and two 7 ½ -inch
squares to piece the corners of the panels
(Step 5, Sewing). Cut the squares diagonally in
each direction to yield eight triangles. Set all
these pieces aside.

*Pretty and practical, these bumper guards come in four
pieces, so you can wash individual ones if there are
unexpected spills. The four parts also balance better in
a washing machine than does one continuous strip.*

PRACTICAL IDEAS

QUILTING SECRETS

Rotary dressmaker's cutters can be bought at any good fabric store that also sells notions. They are a particular boon to quilters because they make quick work of cutting out a stack of pieces in the same size. They are also efficient in cutting out other patterns. Some come with a pinking blade. Rotary cutters should be used with a self-sealing mat because they are very sharp and could mar other surfaces.

Always wash and iron the fabric used in patchwork and quilting before cutting the pieces out. You don't want to discover after you have the quilt made that some of the fabric shrinks in the wash and some of it doesn't. When cutting out quilting pieces, place the longer measurement along the lengthwise grainline of the fabric.

3   From the white fabric cut one piece 7 x 29 inches for the two end panels and two pieces 7 x 58 inches for the two side panels.

4   From the remaining white fabric cut two pieces 10 x 29 inches and two pieces 10 x 58 inches. These will be used as the backing layers, under the batting, for the quilted front panels of the bumper guards.

Sewing

1   Match the print and white strips in groups of equal lengths, with two print strips for each white strip.

2   With right sides together, sew one print strip to each side of a white strip (below) and press the seam allowances toward the print.

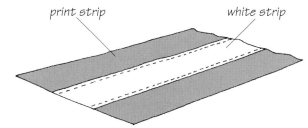

print strip   white strip

3   Cut at right angles across the seams on each of the patchwork units at 7-inch intervals (below) to yield 3 strips per each end panel and 6 strips for each side panel—a total of 18.

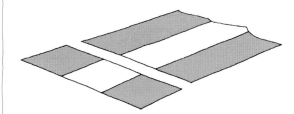

4   For each panel, sew together its allocated number of strips so that the corners of the white squares meet the seamlines "on point," beginning to make the diamond pattern of the finished bumper guards. The ends of the strips will be staggered, forming points, as seen in the drawing below.

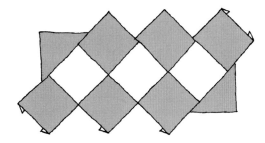

5   With right sides together, center, pin, and stitch the long edge of one triangle over the unstitched edge of the white squares on the ends of the panels. Press these outer seams inward and all other seams in one direction.

6   Trim the pointed edges of each panel into a straight line by placing the edge of the transparent ruler ¼ inch outside each white point; align the ruler carefully over the full length of the edge before cutting. The rectangular end panels now measure 9 ⅝ x 28 inches, and the side ones, 9 ⅝ x 56 inches.

7   Using the backing rectangles cut from the white fabric as a pattern, cut out a matching low-loft piece of batting.

8   Layer the batting on top of the white backing fabric. Center a patchwork piece, right side up, on top of each batting piece of comparable size. Pin the layers together. Then use long stitches to

hand-baste them together, following the grain line, through the center of each square in each direction. Also baste around the edges together ¼ inch inside the edges of the patchwork layer.

9   With the patchwork side up, machine-quilt ¼ inch inside each white square. Pull the thread ends to the wrong side and knot them together. Remove the center basting.

10   From the eyelet, cut two pieces 29 inches long and two 58 inches long. With right sides together, pin the center of one strip to the center of the basted top seam of a panel of comparable size and match the eyelet binding edge to the cut edge of the patchwork. Continue pinning along the top. When nearing the corners, turn the cut ends of the eyelet outward so that the embroidered top edge of the eyelet is at the corner basting line; ease the fullness of the cut edge into gathers. Machine-baste the eyelet to the panel.

11   To sew the ties, press ¼ inch to the wrong side on each long edge and then fold and press again so the long edges meet; edge-stitch each tie piece. Cut each length into 19-inch pieces to yield 16 ties. Finish each cut end with a tight slip knot.

12   Fold the length of each tie in half and pin the fold ½ inch inside each top and bottom corner. Secure the knotted ends with pins to keep them away from the seamlines.

13   With right sides together, pin a print back rectangle to each quilted front panel of comparable size; place the pins on the side with the white backing fabric. Following the perimeter basting lines, stitch the layers together, starting and stopping about 10 inches inside the bottom corners. Trim away the excess batting and print to a ¼-inch width and diagonally trim the corners. Turn the panels right side out and remove the pins holding the ends of the ties.

14   From the high-loft batting, cut two pieces 17 x 27 inches and two 17 x 54 inches. Fold each piece so that the 17 inches become 8 ½ inches. Insert the batting, stuffing it through the bottom seam opening into its comparable cover size. Slipstitch the openings closed.

15   To dress the crib with the bumper guards, place one guard inside the slats on each end and side with the eyelet edging at the top. Secure the ties to the corner posts of the crib.

• Traveler's Game Bag •

*Make this novel game board and playing pieces and give them pride of place on a table
in your family room. Or keep them safely in their own bag and take them with you on trips.
The felt board is easy to roll and store and will add little weight to your luggage.*

*The button playing pieces are used flat side up for
checkers, but when they become kings, pieces are
turned over to reveal the decorative center. Use
¼ -inch-wide seams unless otherwise specified.
For stitching techniques, see p.285.*

- ◆ **15-inch-square brown felt**
- ◆ **15-inch-square beige felt**
- ◆ **scissors**
- ◆ **1 yard 44-inch-wide plaid fabric**
- ◆ **white craft glue**
- ◆ **10-inch-square cream fabric**
- ◆ **tracing paper**
- ◆ **fine-point fabric-marking
  pencil**
- ◆ **red, yellow, and brown
  6-ply embroidery floss**
- ◆ **four ½ -inch brown buttons**
- ◆ **1½ yards ¼ -inch-wide ribbon
  to match plaid**
- ◆ **1 yard ½ -inch-wide ribbon
  to match plaid**
- ◆ **1-inch buttons with recessed
  centers, 24 cream and 24 brown**
- ◆ **small flat buttons to sit inside
  recesses, 12 red and 12 brown**

Board

1 From the brown felt cut eight strips 1½ x
12½ inches. Cut like strips from the beige felt.
2 From the plaid fabric cut the following, as
shown in Diagram 1: one 13½ -inch square for
the board backing and binding, one ¾ x 24-
inch strip for the board tie, one 18 x 26-inch
piece for the large bag, one 8 x 14-inch piece
for the small bag, two 1¼ x 18-inch strips for
the large bag casings, two 1 x 14-inch strips for
the small bag casings.

*Style and practicality combine in this checkers set.
The bag for storing the playing pieces fits inside the
larger bag, along with the rolled-up board.*

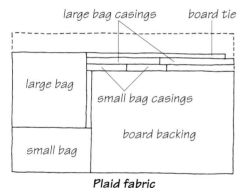

large bag casings   board tie

large bag

small bag casings

board backing

small bag

Plaid fabric

DIAGRAM 1

3 Press the board tie in half lengthwise, with right sides together and cut edges even. Stitch together along one short end and the long edge. Turn right side out, turn in seam allowance on remaining end, and slipstitch closed. Stitch the center of the tie to the middle of the board-backing square, 6¾ inches down from one edge.

4 Line up, center, and stitch the brown felt strips on the wrong side of the board backing, using the same method described in Step 2 for woven ribbon bag on page 292. The short ends will be ½ inch and the sides will be ¾ inch inside the fabric's cut edges. Weave the beige strips over and under the brown strips following directions in Step 3 on page 292.

5 Press under ¼ inch on all the backing edges. Fold the pressed backing edges over the felt edges to form the binding; pin. Fold a miter at each corner. Slipstitch the edge by hand or edge-stitch by machine. If desired, the felt edges can be stitched to the backing.

Bag and men

1 From the cream fabric cut one 4¼ x 6½-inch piece and one 1¾ x 5-inch piece (Diagram 2). Press a ¼-inch hem to the wrong side on

label for small bag

label for large bag

Cream fabric

DIAGRAM 2

all edges of both pieces. Trace the words from the patterns (above right) and transfer these to the center of the cream pieces.

2 Using two strands of embroidery

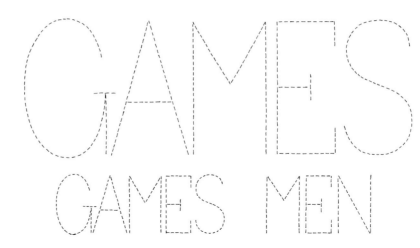

floss, embroider the letters in colors, as shown, using a running stitch. Work a border above and below GAMES in fly stitch (p.295).

3 Make both bags in the same way. Fold the fabric in half, wrong sides together. Allowing for the side seam, center the embroidered label on the front. Using floss in a running stitch (p.281), sew the label in place—stitching through the top layer of fabric only. Sew ½-inch brown buttons to the corners of the label on the large bag.

4 Turn the bag so that right sides are together. Stitch the side and bottom edge of each bag together. Turn under and stitch a ¼-inch double hem around the top edge of each bag.

5 Press ¼ inch to the wrong side on all edges of the casing strips that will hold

the ribbon drawstrings. Pin then stitch the appropriate casing strips to each bag, positioning the top edge of each strip 2 inches below the top edge of the large bag and 1 inch below the top edge of the smaller bag. There should be a ½-inch gap between the casing strips at the side seams.

6 For the large bag, cut the ½-inch-wide ribbon in half and thread one piece all the way through the casing. (Use a safety pin to pull the ribbon through, if necessary.) Tie the ribbon ends together. Repeat with the other length of ribbon but with the ends hanging from the opposite side of the bag. Tie the ends together.

7 Cut the ¼-inch-wide ribbon in half and thread through the casings on the smaller bag in the same way.

8 Place pairs of cream buttons together with a red button in the top recess. Pass six strands of yellow embroidery floss through the holes, tie together with a knot on top of the red button, and cut the ends. Repeat with the brown buttons using red floss.

MAKING THE BOARD AND BAG

1 *On the wrong side of the board backing, weave the felt strips following the method described on page 292 for the ribbon bag.*

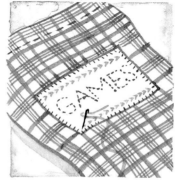

2 *Using two strands of embroidery floss, stitch label words in running stitch (p.281). Position labels, allowing for seams, and stitch in place.*

3 *Secure pairs of matching large buttons together with a small button in the recess by threading six strands of floss through the holes.*

◆ Luxury Bags ◆

The luxurious feel of silk and satin lends elegance to these special accessories.
One of the stylish evening bags would be nice for a bridesmaid, made in the colors of her dress.
The embroidered lingerie case shown on the next page is a traditional part of a bride's trousseau.

Woven ribbon bag

This elegant bag, designed for evenings out, has a detachable strap, so it can be used as a shoulder bag or a clutch. A ¼-inch seam allowance is used throughout the project.

- ¼ **yard 44-inch-wide Thai silk or similar fabric**
- **thread to match fabric**
- **2½ yards ¾-inch-wide ribbon**
- **2½ yards ¾-inch-wide ribbon in a contrasting color**
- **8 x 17¾-inch piece of fleece interfacing**
- **4¼ yards satin rat-tail cord**
- **2 clear snaps**

1 From the silk cut one piece 8½ inches square, one piece 8 x 10¼ inches, and one piece 8 x 17¾ inches.

2 Place the 8½-inch-square fabric on a flat working surface. Cut one ribbon length into eleven 8-inch-long pieces. Center them side by side on the fabric with their edges touching; the edges will be ¼ inch inside the fabric's cut edges. Stitch ¼ inch inside the cut edges of the ribbon (below).

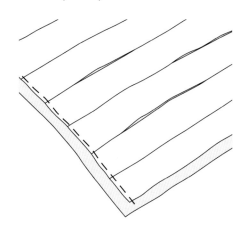

3 Cut the contrasting ribbon into eleven 8-inch lengths. Weave these pieces at right angles through the first rows of ribbon to create a checkerboard effect (below). It is important to weave the ribbons as straight as you can. Stitch across the ends of the second ribbons.

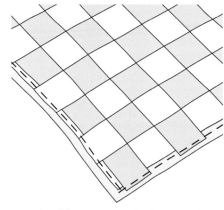

4 Trim the fabric even with the cut edges of the ribbon.

5 With right sides together, stitch the woven ribbon layer to the 8 x 10¼-inch piece of silk along one 8-inch side. Press seam open.

6 Stitch the interfacing to the wrong side of the remaining piece of silk. You will now have two pieces 8 x 17¾ inches.

7 Place the two pieces of silk right sides together and pin. Machine-stitch the ribbon end and both long sides, leaving the plain end open. Trim the corners diagonally. Turn the bag right side out, turn in cut edges ¼ inch, and slipstitch together.

8 With the ribbon panel face down, turn up the opposite end of the bag approximately 5 inches to create the interior pocket; slipstitch the side seams.

9 Cut the cord into three equal lengths and braid them together. Cut the braid to the length you want and knot the ends. Attach the ends to the inside of the flap with snaps.

Evening backpack

This easy-to-make bag, with its fun combination of woven ribbons on the flap, can be coordinated to match a favorite outfit. Bright colors will make the bag look more casual, whereas more subtle colors create an elegant effect. A seam allowance of ¼ inch is used throughout.

- ¾ **yard 44-inch-wide Thai silk or similar fabric**
- **thread to match fabric**
- **2¼ yards 1-inch-wide ribbon**
- **2¼ yards 1-inch-wide ribbon in a contrasting color**
- **8-inch square fleece interfacing**
- **1 clear snap**

1 From the silk fabric, cut two pieces 8 inches square (for flap and lining), two pieces 3 x 12 inches (for gussets), two pieces 10 x 12 inches (for front and back), two pieces 3 x 28 inches (for straps), one piece 1 x 40 inches (for drawstring), and one piece 1½ x 7 inches (for finish). See cutting guide below—the grain of the fabric runs vertically.

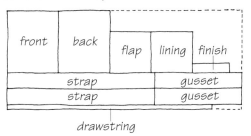

drawstring

2 For the flap, place one piece of 8-inch-square fabric on a flat working surface. Cut one ribbon into eight 8-inch lengths, then position the ribbon strips on the flap fabric as described in Step 2 for the woven ribbon bag (left).

3 Cut the contrasting ribbon into eight 8-inch lengths. Weave and stitch these ribbon pieces into place as described in Steps 3 and 4 for the

woven ribbon bag. Trim the fabric even with the cut edges of the ribbon.

4 Stitch the interfacing to the wrong side of the second 8-inch-square piece of fabric.

5 Place both squares of fabric—the ribbon square and the square with interfacing—right

sides together and pin. Round off the two lower corners of the flap evenly. Machine-stitch around three sides, leaving the top open. Trim the seams and interfacing close to the stitching. Turn the flap right side out, then edge-stitch the raw edges together at the top.

Clockwise from top left, a glamorous satin lingerie case, nice for a bridal-shower gift (or as a special treat to pamper yourself); a woven ribbon bag, made to match a special outfit; and an evening backpack, for those social occasions when you want to keep a few personal belongings close by.

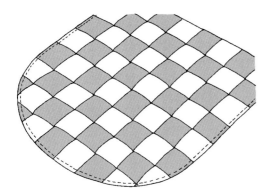

6 Make the straps by folding each 28-inch length in half, right sides together. Machine stitch, leaving the ends open, then turn right side out, press, and topstitch close to the folded edge and the joined edge.

7 For the back piece: Measure across the 10-inch width, mark the center of the back with thread. Match to the center of the straight edge of the flap and stitch, ribbon side out, 3 ½ inches down from the top edge.

8 Place one end of each strap on the top of the flap with the end level with the flap's straight edge, 2 inches in from each side. Stitch the straps into position. Make a small button-

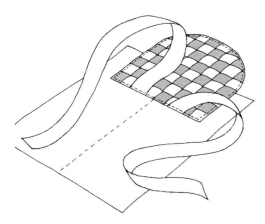

hole in the center of the back piece 1 ¾ -inches down from the top, for the ends of the draw-string to pass through.

9 Press under ¼ inch on all edges of the 1 ½ -inch by 7 ½ -inch piece of fabric. Center it over top edge of the flap and straps; edge-stitch.

10 Sew the other ends of the straps to the bottom of the back piece, approximately 2 ½ inches on either side of the center.

11 Evenly round off the two lower corners of the front and back pieces.

12 Seam the ends of the two gusset pieces to make one length. Press the seam open. With right sides together, pin one side of the gusset carefully to the front piece and the other to the back and machine-stitch, easing the gusset around the corners as you work. Turn the bag right side out.

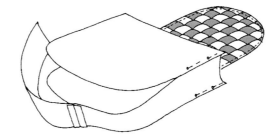

13 Turn over the raw edge around the top of the bag and make a casing about 1 ¼ inches deep, being careful to avoid the flap.

14 To make the drawstring, fold the 1-inch by 40-inch piece of fabric lengthwise, right sides together, and machine-stitch close to the edges, leaving ends open. Turn right side out, fold ends in, and slipstitch to close. Using a safety pin to pull it, thread the drawstring through the casing and knot each end.

15 Sew the snap on to secure the flap.

Creamy satin, gold-toned thread, and a dainty embroidered floral motif have been chosen for this satin lingerie case, a detail of which appears below.

Satin lingerie case

Bridal satin is ideal for this beautiful lingerie case. It is easier to embroider than lighter satin and does not require any interfacing. We chose a cream-on-cream color scheme; you might like to try another scheme, such as pink ribbon buds on gray satin or cream buds on coffee satin.

- ⅔ **yard 40-inch-wide bridal satin**
- **2 ¼ yards 7-millimeter-wide cream silk embroidery ribbon**
- **2 ¼ yards 7-millimeter-wide coffee silk embroidery ribbon**
- **1 skein DMC embroidery floss, color number 738**
- **chenille needle size 18 or 20**
- **crewel needle size 10**
- **4-inch embroidery hoop**
- **tracing paper, pencil**
- **transfer pencil**
- **1 yard ¾ -inch-wide double-face cream satin ribbon, cut into two equal lengths**
- **2 ¼ yards cream satin piping**
- **thread to match fabric**

1 Cut two strips of satin, each 24 x 10 ½ inches; cut two more, each 21 ½ x 10 ½ inches .

2 Press the smaller strips in half crosswise and embroider Motif 1 (Ribbon embroidery, p.295) on one side of each strip, centered about 1 inch from the fold (below).

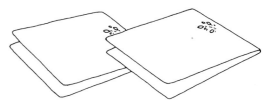

3 Embroider Motif 2 on one side of one of the larger strips, centered about 1 inch from the end (below).

4 With embroidery completed on these three strips, press out hoop marks (iron on the wrong side and around the embroidery).

5 Lay the unembroidered larger strip right side up with the folded strips on top, embroidery at the center. Machine-stitch these strips together using a ½-inch seam allowance. Sew ribbons, right side up, in place (below).

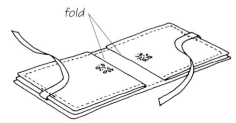

fold

6 With the same side up, and using the zipper foot on the sewing machine, sew the satin piping over the previous stitching line, aligning the new stitches over the previous stitches. Overlap the piping ends to join (or abut them as shown on page 134) and clip at the corners to make smooth curves (below). Be careful not to clip the stitching.

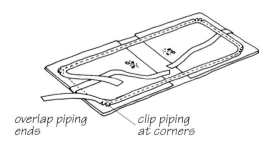

overlap piping ends

clip piping at corners

7 Place the remaining strip on top of the pockets, right sides facing. Using the zipper foot and following the previous stitching line, sew this strip to the pockets, leaving a 4-inch opening at one end (below).

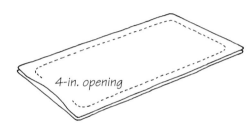

4-in. opening

8 Trim the seams to ¼ inch, and turn the bag right side out. Slipstitch the opening closed.

Ribbon embroidery

Motif 1 (shown actual size) for lingerie pockets has 3 buds and 8 leaves (below).

MOTIF 1

Motif 2 (shown actual size) for outside flap has 9 buds and 12 leaves (below).

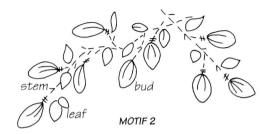

stem

bud

leaf

MOTIF 2

Work buds, then stems, and finally the leaves. For stitches, see Sewing and needlework, p.281. Use a pencil to trace the motifs onto tracing paper. Turn the paper over and retrace the designs with transfer pencil; iron the transfers onto fabric.

1 For ribbon work, thread a 12-inch length of cream embroidery ribbon through the chenille needle, pass the needle through the ribbon, then pull the ribbon up firmly (below).

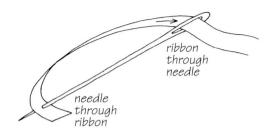

ribbon through needle

needle through ribbon

2 Starting at the base of the first bud, push the needle through from the back of the work to the front, leaving about ½ inch of ribbon hanging on the wrong side. Make a stitch from the tip of the bud and back up through the base, passing through the end of the ribbon to

anchor it. Make one or two more stitches on top of one another (below). Without cutting the ribbon, push the needle through at the base of the next bud and repeat. When the buds are finished, pass the needle through the ribbon on the wrong side to secure. Cut the ribbon ½ inch from the work.

3 With the crewel needle and one strand of embroidery floss, make a fly stitch around the base of the bud, anchoring the stitch under the base (below).

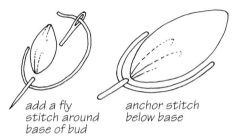

add a fly stitch around base of bud

anchor stitch below base

4 Add two or three straight stitches through the ribbon, meeting at the base. Add two small straight stitches across the base (below).

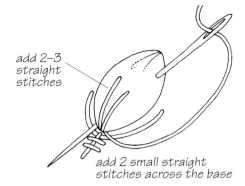

add 2–3 straight stitches

add 2 small straight stitches across the base

5 For stems, thread the crewel needle with one strand of embroidery floss and work in stem stitch, following the lines shown on the motifs. After this, add small, straight stitches to represent the thorns.

6 For the leaves, work as for the buds, using the coffee satin ribbon. Make a single straight stitch for each leaf, smaller than the buds.

◆ Straw Hat Trimmings ◆

*There's no need to buy an expensive new hat every summer when there's probably
plenty of life left in your old ones. All you need is a fresh idea or two, a few pieces of ribbon, raffia,
or artificial flowers, and you can make yourself an exciting new creation for very little cost.*

Raffia sun hat

*Raffia trim—available natural and in colors—can
be used on a variety of straw bases. We have
used an unblocked Panama straw. Shells or coral
can be substituted for the starfish.*

- ◆ **1 straw hat base**
- ◆ **raffia**
- ◆ **3 to 5 starfish**
- ◆ **large crewel needles**
- ◆ **thread**
- ◆ **hat pins or long
  pins (optional)**

1 Take a handful of raffia, not too thick, with lengths graduated so they don't all finish together. When arranging the raffia, don't be too neat. Odd strands poking out or unraveling are part of the charm.

2 Wind the raffia around the base of the crown, firmly but not too tightly. It may help to twist it slightly as you go. Use hat pins to pin in place, if necessary, and weave the ends into the rest of the raffia. Try the hat on and check the effect in the mirror.

3 Using a crewel needle with a doubled thread or a fine strand of raffia, attach the woven raffia to the hat crown at intervals. This can be done using "tie" stitches—stab through from the inside of the hat, catch a few strands of raffia, and stab back, tying the ends together firmly inside the hat. Try to use as few stitches as possible.

4 Arrange the starfish around the hat at irregular intervals to achieve the desired effect.

5 To attach the starfish, carefully make a small hole through the center of each with a needle. Thread the needle with a thin strand of raffia and make a double knot a couple of inches from the end—the knot must be large enough not to slip through the hole in the starfish. Pass the raffia through the center of the starfish,

with the knot at the front. Attach the starfish to the hat by stabbing through from the outside of the hat and securing in the desired position with a few backstitches on the inside. Cut and fray the knot end, if desired.

Flowered sun hat

*Bright silk flowers and a bow of raffia and ribbon
make this sun hat smart and contemporary.
Experiment with color and texture as you choose
your flowers, ribbons, and straw hat base.*

- ◆ **1 straw braid hat base**
- ◆ **20 inches 4-inch-wide grosgrain
  ribbon to match hat**
- ◆ **raffia**
- ◆ **3 silk flowers**
- ◆ **thread to match ribbon**
- ◆ **needle**
- ◆ **hat pins or long pins
  (optional)**
- ◆ **white craft glue (optional)**

1 Fold the grosgrain ribbon into a bow by looping the two ends to meet in the center. Secure the loops by wrapping lengths of thread around the middle where the ends overlap and finishing with a couple of backstitches (p.281).

2 Wrap several strands of raffia around the wings of the bow and secure at the center with thread.

3 Lightly twist several strands of raffia around the crown and knot at the front of the hat, leaving the ends to be trimmed just beyond the front of the brim.

4 Lightly pin the bow and flowers to the straw base with hat pins. Try the hat on and check the effect in the mirror. Adjust the flowers and other trim as necessary before you attach them permanently.

5 When you are satisfied, attach the trim to the straw base using a needle and double thread. Make "tie" stitches, stabbing through the crown from inside the hat and catching the trim in places where it lies flat against the straw. Try to use as few stitches as possible. Tie off the individual stitches securely. Alternatively, you can use craft glue to attach the trim. This method isn't as secure as sewing and once you apply the glue, the decorations can't be moved around anymore.

PRACTICAL IDEAS

NOT JUST FOR HATS

Decorative raffia can spruce up a headband or a ponytail elastic as well as a hat. So can many other of the accessories you may find for trimming a straw bonnet.

Colored raffia, for example, can be braided to make a multicolored headband or a hat band. You can also decorate packages with it.

Choose a fairly crisp or stiff ribbon for decorative bows; otherwise, they won't hold their shape. Or try wired ribbon, which is widely available in trim departments of fabric and crafts stores.

A hat box is the ideal way to store your hat, but a stack of pretty hatboxes can store other items as well. Use the smallest for your hair accessories, for example; the middle one for scarves and ribbons; and the bottom one for a hat. Line the box with tissue paper and stuff the crown of the hat with more tissue to help hold its shape.

*Two charming summer hats to keep the sun off
your face. Make them for yourself or trim one as
a practical and pretty gift for a friend.*

◆ Knits for the Family ◆

*Keep the family snug in chilly weather with this trio of sweaters. For best results,
use only the yarn specified. The recommended quantities, however, are approximate; the amount of
yarn needed varies from knitter to knitter. Knitting techniques are shown on pages 278–280.*

His-and-her crewneck

*One pattern makes a warm crewneck pullover for
either a man or a woman.*

- **sportweight wool or acrylic yarn
  (50-gram or 1.75-ounce balls):
  15 (16, 17, 17, 18, 19) balls**
- **1 pair each sizes 4 and 5
  knitting needles**
- **2 stitch holders**
- **knitter's sewing needle**

Measurements

Fits bust/chest: woman, 30–32 (34–36, 38–40);
man, 36–38 (38–40, 42–44) inches. Garment
measures: 41 (45 ¼ , 48 ¾ , 48, 51 ½ , 55 ¾)
inches. Crewneck length: 26 (26 ⅜ , 26 ¾ , 37 ⅛ ,
37 ½ , 37 ⅞) inches. Cropped sweater length: 18
(18 ⅜ , 18 ¾) inches. Sleeve length: 17 ¼ (17 ¼ ,
17 ¼ , 19 ¼ , 19 ¼ , 19 ¼) inches, or length
desired. These garments are designed to be a
generous fit; about 10 inches of ease allowed.

Gauge

23 sts and 31 rows to 4 inches over stockinette
st, using size 5 needles. Use smaller or larger
needles to adjust your knitting to gauge.

Back

Using size 4 needles, cast on 118 (130, 138, 138,
146, 158) sts.
   1st row. K2, *P2, K2; rep from * to end.
   2nd row. P2, *K2, P2; rep from * to end.
   Rep last 2 rows 9 times more, inc 0 (0, 2; 0, 2,
2) sts evenly across last row 118 (130, 140; 138,
148, 160) sts, 20 rows rib in all.
   Change to size 5 needles.
   Work in stockinette st until work measures
25 ⅜ (25 ¾ , 26 ⅛ ; 26 ½ , 26 ⅞ , 27 ¼) inches
from beg, ending with a purl row.
   Shape shoulders. Cont in stockinette st, cast
off 10 (11, 12; 12, 13, 14) sts at beg of next 6 rows,

ABBREVIATIONS

alt	alternate
beg	beginning
cont	continue, continuing
dec	decrease
foll	follow, following
inc	increase, increasing
incl	including
K	knit
P	purl
rem	remain, remaining
rep	repeat
rnd	round, rounds
st/sts	stitch, stitches

then 10 (12, 13; 12, 13, 15) sts at beg of foll 2 rows.
Transfer rem 38 (40, 42; 42, 44, 46) sts to a stitch
holder.

Front

Work as for Back until there are 22 (24, 24; 24,
24, 26) rows less than Back to beg of shoulder
shaping, ending with a purl row.
   Shape neck. Next row. K49 (55, 60; 58, 63, 69)
sts, turn.
   **Cont in stockinette st on these 49 (55, 60,
58, 63, 69) sts, dec one st at neck edge in every
row until 47 (53, 56; 56, 59, 65) sts rem, then in
alt rows until 40 (45, 49; 48, 52, 57) sts rem.
   Work 5 rows.
   Shape shoulder. Cast off 10 (11, 12; 12, 13, 14)
sts at beg of next and foll alt rows 3 times in all.
   Work one row.
   Cast off rem 10 (12, 13; 12, 13, 15) sts.**
   With right side facing, slip next 20 (20, 20;
22, 22, 22) sts on a stitch holder and leave.
   Join yarn to rem 49 (55, 60; 58, 63, 69) sts and
knit to end.
   Work as from ** to **, working 6 rows
(instead of 5) before shaping shoulder.

Sleeves

Using size 4 needles, cast on 50 (50, 54; 54, 58,
62) sts.
   Work 20 rows rib as for Back, inc 12 sts
evenly across last row 62 (62, 66; 66, 70, 74) sts.
   Change to size 5 needles.
   Work in stockinette st, inc one st at each end
of 5th and every foll 4th row, until there are 74
(92, 96; 70, 74, 78) sts, then every foll 6th row
until there are 98 (104, 108; 104, 108, 112) sts.
   Cont straight in stockinette st until the work
measures 17 ¼ (17 ¼ , 17 ¼ ; 19 ¼ , 19 ¼ , 19 ¼)
inches (or length desired) from beg, ending
with a purl row. Cast off loosely.

Neck band

Using small running st (p.281), join right shoulder seam. With right side facing you and using
size 4 needles, pick up 110 (114, 118; 118, 122, 126)
sts evenly around neck, incl sts from stitch
holders.***
   1st row. P2, *K2, P2; rep from * to end.
   2nd row. K2, *P2, K2; rep from * to end.
   Work 15 more rows in rib and cast off
loosely in rib.

To assemble

With a dampened cloth and a warm iron, press
the pieces lightly on the wrong side. Using running st, sew the left shoulder and Neck band
seam. Tie colored threads 8 ⅝ (9, 9 ⅜ ; 9 ¾ ,
10 ¼ , 10 ½) inches down from the beginning of
the shoulder shaping on the side edges of the
Back and Front to mark the armholes.
   Sew in the Sleeves evenly between the colored threads, placing the center of each Sleeve
at a shoulder seam. Sew the side and Sleeve
seams. Fold the Neck band in half to the wrong
side and slip-stitch loosely in position. Lightly
press all seams, if necessary.

Cropped sweater

The abbreviated pullover is always fashionable, and this roll-necked version is easy to make.

- ◆ **sportweight wool or acrylic yarn (50-gram or 1.75-ounce balls): 11 (12, 13) balls**
- ◆ **1 pair each sizes 4 and 5 knitting needles**
- ◆ **2 stitch holders**
- ◆ **knitter's sewing needle**

Measurements and tension

Same as for His-and-her crewneck, but the women's sizes only

Back

Using size 4 needles, cast on 118 (130, 140) sts.

Work 10 rows stockinette st.

Change to size 5 needles.

Cont in stockinette st until work measures 18 (18 ⅜, 18 ¾) inches from beg, ending with a purl row (¾ inch has been allowed for roll at lower edge).

Shape shoulders. Complete as for Back of His-and-her crewneck, noting to foll instructions for corresponding women's sizes only.

Front

Work as for Back until there are 22 (24, 24) rows fewer than Back to beg of shoulder shaping, ending with a purl row.

Shape neck. Complete as for Front of His-and-her crewneck, noting to follow instructions for corresponding women's sizes only.

Sleeves

Using size 4 needles, cast on 62 (64, 68) sts.

Work 10 rows stockinette st.

Change to size 5 needles. Cont in stockinette st, inc one st at each end of 5th and every foll 6th (4th, 4th) row until there are 90 (70, 74) sts, then every foll 8th (6th, 6th) rows until there are 98 (104, 108) sts.

Any child, boy or girl, would be delighted with this Ice Cream Sweater, while older members of the family are in style with the crewneck or the cropped versions.

Follow the chart on page 301 to create the ice-cream cones on this child's sweater. Each square on the chart equals one stitch. Choose bold or soft shades.

Cont straight in stockinette st until work measures 18 inches (or length desired) from beg, ending with a purl row (¾ inch has been allowed for roll at lower edge).

Cast off loosely.

Neck band

Work as for corresponding women's sizes of Neck band of His-and-hers crewneck to ***.

Work 17 rows in stockinette st, beg with a purl row.

Cast off very loosely.

To assemble

With a slightly damp cloth and a warm iron, press lightly. Using a running stitch (p.281), join left shoulder and Neck band seam, reversing seam for half of stockinette st rows on Neck band. Tie colored threads 8 ⅝ (9, 9 ⅜) inches down from shoulder, shaping on side edges of Back and Front to mark armholes. Sew in Sleeves evenly between colored threads, placing the center of each Sleeve at a shoulder seam. Sew side and Sleeve seams, reversing seam at lower and Sleeve edges for ¾ inch. Allow lower and Sleeve edges and Neck band to roll to right side. Press seams.

PRACTICAL IDEAS
GIVING AND WEARING IDEAS

The unisex sweaters on page 298 make thoughtful gifts for husband and wife or brother and sister. Choose a color that suits the individual.

Knit the cropped pullover in several different colors. It will become a can't-do-without item in any woman's wardrobe because it can be worn with skirts, slacks, and jeans.

The child's sweater is made with short sleeves for easy summer wear. In cooler weather, team it with a long-sleeved T-shirt in a contrasting color.

Ice-cream sweater

Lightweight baby yarn makes this a great choice for a warm-weather sweater. Its distinctive ribbing comes from knitting a twist stitch (TW2). In this version of the stitch, you knit into the front of the second stitch on the left-hand needle, then knit into the front of the first stitch, slipping both stitches off the needle together.

- ◆ **4-ply baby wool (25-gram or 1.75-ounce balls): 7 (7, 8) balls of yellow, 1 (1, 1) ball of red, 1 (1, 1) ball of blue**
- ◆ **one pair each sizes 2 and 3 knitting needles**
- ◆ **one size 2, 16-inch circular needle**
- ◆ **two stitch holders**
- ◆ **yarn bobbins, if desired**

Measurements

To fit age: 4 (6, 8) years. Fits chest: 22 ¾ (23 ⅛ , 23 ½) inches. Garment measures: 26 ⅜ (27 ⅞ , 30 ¼) inches. Length: 16 ⅛ (17 ⅝ , 20) inches.

Gauge

29 sts to 4 inches of width in stockinette st, using size 3 needles.

Back

Using size 2 needles and yellow, cast on 90 (98, 106) sts.

1st row. P2, *K2, P2; rep from * to end.

2nd row. K2, *P2, K2; rep from * to end.

3rd row. P2, *TW2, P2; rep from * to end.

4th row. As 2nd. These 4 rows form the twisted rib.

Rep last 4 rows 3 times more.

Rep 1st and 2nd rows once more, inc 8 sts

evenly across 2nd row to 98 (106, 114) sts, 18 rows rib in all.

Change to size 3 needles.

Cont in stockinette st until work measures 15 ¾ (17 ¼ , 21 ¾) inches from beg, ending with a purl row.

Shape neck. 1st row. K38 (41, 44) sts, turn.

Cont in stockinette st on these 38 (41, 44) sts only.

2nd row. Cast off 3 sts, purl to end.

3rd and foll alt rows. Knit.

4th row. Cast off 2 sts, purl to end.

6th row. Cast off 1 st, purl to end and break off yarn.

Leave these 32 (35, 38) sts on circular needle.

Right side facing you, slip next 22 (24, 26) sts on a stitch holder and leave. Join yarn to rem 38 (41, 44) sts and work to correspond with side just completed, reversing shaping. Leave rem 32 (35, 38) sts on circular needle.

Sleeves

Using size 2 needles and yellow, cast on 66 (70, 74) sts.

Work 14 rows twisted rib as for Back.

Change to size 3 needles.

Cont in stockinette st, inc one st at each end of 3rd and every foll 4th (6th, 8th) row until there are 78 (82, 86) sts.

Work 3 rows stockinette st.

Cast off loosely.

Starting Front

Work as for Back until 6 ¼ (6 ¾ , 7 ¼) inches from beg, ending with a purl row.

Working in the design

Use the chart at right to work the ice-cream cone design into the front of the sweater. Work 16 (20, 24) stitches at each end of every row in yellow stockinette stitch. Then pick up the pattern from the chart, row by row. Each square on the chart represents one stitch. Read the knit rows (right side) from right to left, and the purl rows (wrong side) from left to right.

Choose whatever colors you want for the cones and ice cream. When changing colors in the middle of a row, twist the color to be used (on wrong side of work) underneath and to the right of the color just used to avoid leaving

holes in work. Use a separate ball of yarn for each section of color or wind yarn into smaller balls or onto yarn bobbins, if desired. Work rows 1 to 54 incl from Graph.

Finishing Front

Cont straight in yellow stockinette st until work measures 14 (15, 16) inches from beg, ending with a purl row.

Shape neck. 1st row. K42 (45, 48) sts, turn.

Cont in stockinette st on these 42 (45, 48) sts.

2nd row. Cast off 4 sts, purl to end.

3rd and foll alt rows. Knit.

4th row. Cast off 3 sts, purl to end.

6th row. Cast off 2 sts, purl to end.

8th row. Cast off 1 st, purl to end.

Cont straight in stockinette st on these 32 (35, 38) sts until Front measures same as Back to shoulders, ending with a purl row.

Join shoulders. Place Back and Front pieces tog with right sides tog. Using a third needle, cast off both sets of sts at the same time by knitting tog one st from each needle.

Right side facing you, slip next 14 (16, 18) sts of Front piece on a stitch holder and leave. Join yarn to rem 42 (45, 48) sts and work to correspond with side just completed, reversing shaping and joining to Back shoulder (as before).

Neck band

With right side of work facing, and using the circular needle and yellow wool, knit 100 (108, 116) sts evenly around neck, incl sts from stitch holders.

Work 8 rnds in twisted rib, then work 8 rnds in stockinette st (knit every rnd).

Cast off loosely.

To assemble

Using running stitch (p.281), sew in Sleeves, placing the center of each Sleeve at a shoulder seam. Join the side and Sleeve seams.

The pattern for three ice-cream cones, below, allows you to knit the motifs right into the child's sweater.

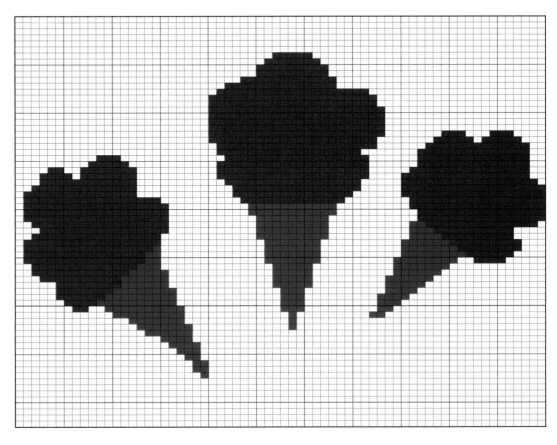

✦ Sundresses and Sunsuits for Toddlers ✦

*Our cool and comfortable outfits include a reversible dress and a classic sunsuit.
To dress them up, we've included designs for four colorful appliqués, each of them suitable
for use on either outfit. The one-size pattern is for toddler's sizes 3 to 4.*

Easy appliqués

The directions for our sundress and sunsuit indicate when to add the appliqués, which can be made with scraps of fabric. Enlarge the appliqué patterns on 1-inch graph paper (p.276).

- ½ yard 22-inch-wide paper-backed fusible webbing
- small embroidery scissors
- dressmaker's tracing paper
- needle

FOR THE TURTLE:
- green, floral print, pink, and yellow cotton remnants; 6-inch piece of ½-inch-wide lace edging; green and pink thread

FOR THE WHALE:
- white-background print and pink cotton remnants; turquoise thread; 1 package white jumbo rickrack

FOR THE SAILBOAT:
- blue, red, and yellow fabric; black thread; 1 package blue jumbo rickrack; blue thread

FOR THE BEACH BALL:
- yellow, hot pink, and green-dot cotton fabric; white thread

1 Enlarge the appliqué design of your choice.
2 Cut pieces of fusible webbing slightly larger than each part of the appliqué. Using a steam iron, fuse the webbing to the wrong side of each piece of fabric. Use dressmaker's tracing paper to transfer the pattern pieces onto the fabric (right). Cut out the pieces.

fusible webbing

fabric with pattern traced on

3 The dotted lines on our patterns indicate where one piece will be covered by another when all the pieces are in place. Starting with the pieces that have dotted lines, fuse the pieces onto the dress or sunsuit.
4 Appliqué the motifs in place. Use a dense, medium-width zigzag stitch to cover the edges and to stitch the sailboat's mast. With a needle and doubled thread, embroider the eyes and mouth of the turtle and whale and the center of the flower and the starfish.

Reversible sundress

Use coordinating fabrics to make this charmer. Be sure to choose fabrics that will not bleed.

- 1-inch graph paper, ruler, pencil
- scissors
- ¾ yard 44-inch-wide solid or print fabric
- ¾ yard 44-inch-wide coordinating print fabric
- thread to match fabrics
- needle
- 1½ yards ½-inch-wide lace edging or 1 package piping
- 2 buttons, 1⅛ inches in diameter (optional)
- 4 large snaps (for lapped-shoulder dress only)

1 Using 1-inch graph paper, enlarge the dress pattern as directed on page 276.
2 Choose between long, tied shoulder straps or shorter straps with snaps. Cut out two pieces from each of the fabrics, adding a ½-inch seam allowance to all cut edges.

Ready for a summer outing are a toddler girl's two choices of appliquéd sundresses and a toddler boy's two choices of appliquéd sunsuits.

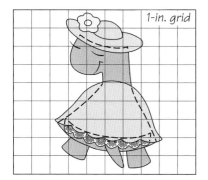

Flirtatious turtle appliqué

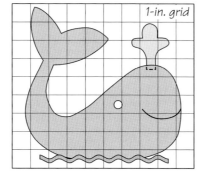

Spouting whale appliqué

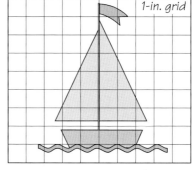

Sporty sailboat appliqué

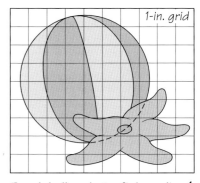

Beach ball and starfish appliqué

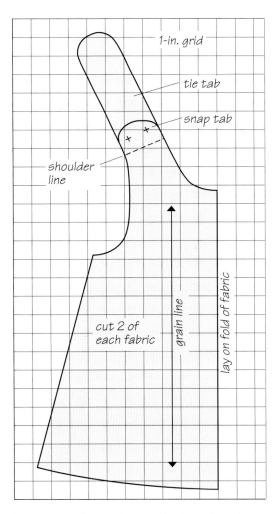

The pattern—for both front and back—outlines the dress without a ½-inch seam allowance all around.

3 Follow Step 4 of Easy appliqués to apply a motif to one front piece, 3 inches above the hemline. For the boat or whale, sew one side seam of the dress before adding the rickrack. A single row of rickrack goes across the front and around the back of the dress (below).

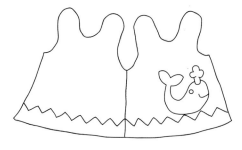

4 For each set of dress pieces, sew and press open the side seams.

5 Select one dress layer. With the right side facing you, pin the lace edging or piping along the hemline, matching the flat edge of the trim with the raw edge of the hem. Sew in place, lapping the ends of the trim. Fold under the edges to the wrong side of the fabric.

6 With right sides together, pin and sew the two dress layers together all the way around the top; clip curves and trim the seam allowances (below). Turn the dress right side out and press. Topstitch along the top seam.

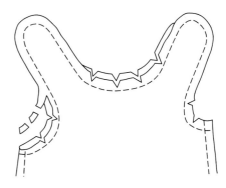

7 Matching the side seams, pin the hems of the dress layers together, turning under ½ inch on the layer without the trim. The trim should be visible from both sides. Edgestitch the newly turned hem (below).

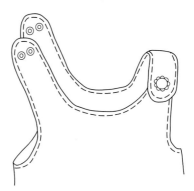

8 For the lapped shoulders, sew on snaps to close the dress. Add buttons on one side, if you like. For the other sundress, tie the straps.

Reverse sides of girls' dresses, refreshingly different, literally give two dresses for the price of one.

Sunsuit

This carefree summer suit has snap shoulders and crotch, making it easy to put on and take off.

- ◆ **1¼ yards 44-inch-wide fabric**
- ◆ **thread to match fabric**
- ◆ **4 buttons, ½-inch diameter**
- ◆ **4 large snaps**
- ◆ **¼ yard ¾-inch-wide snap tape**

1 Using 1-inch graph paper, enlarge pattern as directed on page 276. For sunsuit, add 1½-inch hem allowances to the legs and ½-inch seam allowances to the other edges. For the facings, retrace front and back from the facing line up and add ½-inch seam allowances.

2 Cut two pieces each of the front and back. Cut one piece each of the facings, placing the centers on a fold of fabric.

3 Apply motif, following Step 4 of Easy appliqués. Sew center seam first to center motif.

4 With right sides together, sew the front center seam. Repeat on the back. With right sides facing, sew the front and back together along the sides. Sew the facings together on the side seams. Turn under the bottom edge of the facing ¼ inch and stitch. Press all seams open.

5 Follow Step 6 of the sundress instructions to sew the top seams, using the facings for the second dress layer. Sew two snaps at each shoulder to fasten and buttons for decoration.

6 Fold and press the leg hems under ½ inch and then 1 inch; stitch the hem edges.

7 Press front crotch edge under ½ inch. Press back crotch edge ½ inch toward right side of fabric. Pin half of the snap tape to cover the raw edge on either side, centering snaps and turning the ends under; sew the tape along each edge.

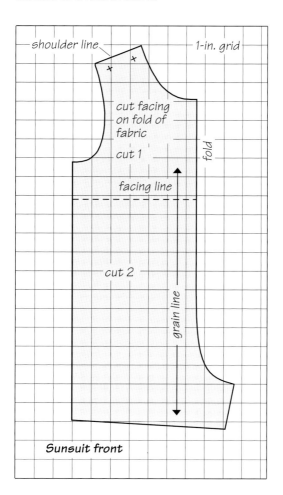

Sunsuit front

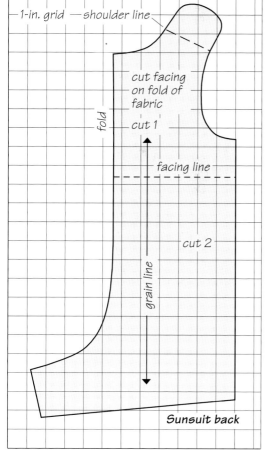

Sunsuit back

◆ Great Ideas for the Table ◆

*Personalize your entertaining with linens and serving bowls you make yourself. Our directions
show you how to use a simple photocopying technique or cutouts from printed fabric to make
appliqués or borders for papier-mâché bowls, table linens—anything that strikes your fancy.*

Table linens

*Make this set of placemats and napkins for six as
a gift or as an addition to your own table. Finished size: placemats, 20 x 15 inches; napkins, 20
inches square. A ½-inch seam allowance is used.*

- **3 yards 44-inch-wide print fabric**
- **2 ¾ yards 44-inch-wide solid-color fabric**
- **2 yards 22-inch-wide fusible medium-weight interfacing**
- **thread to match fabrics**

Making the napkins

1 Cut six 22-inch squares of print fabric.
2 Sew ½ inch inside each edge; press edges
to the wrong side along the stitching and then
press under again for a double hem.
3 Open out each corner and fold the point
inward so that a diagonal fold aligns with the
inner pressed point; press. Refold sides, forming a mitered corner.
4 Edge-stitch the pressed hems.

Making the placemats

1 For the front, cut six 17 x 12-inch pieces of
print fabric with the long sides across the grain.
Cut six pieces of interfacing, 16 x 11 inches.
2 Following the manufacturer's directions,
center and fuse the interfacing to the wrong
side of the fabric.
3 Along the length of the solid fabric, cut
twelve 12 x 3-inch strips and twelve 17 x 3-inch
strips. With right sides facing, center, pin, and
stitch a 17-inch strip to each long side of the
placemats, leaving ½ inch unstitched at
each corner. To miter the corners, mark a fold
line from the end of each strip back toward
the corner of the placemat at a 45-degree
angle (as shown in the diagram, above right).
4 Repeat with the 12-inch strips on the short

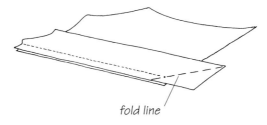

fold line

sides, stitching the long strips to the corners of
the mat. Mark as before.
5 At each corner, pin and stitch a seam joining
the marked lines at each strip (below). Press
seams open and trim excess fabric to ½ inch.

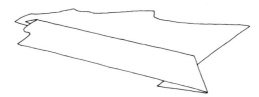

6 For the backs of the placemats, cut six
21 x 16-inch rectangles of solid-color fabric.
With right sides together, stitch fronts to
backs, leaving a 4-inch-wide opening on one
side; press. Trim the corners diagonally and
turn right side out. Press the edges and slip-
stitch the opening closed.

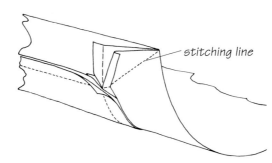

stitching line

7 With right side up, edge-stitch the inner
seamline through all the layers to keep the
inside seam allowances flat.

Decorative bowls

*Match these papier-mâché bowls to your linens
by photocopying the fabric in color. Varnishing
offers some protection, but such bowls should
not be used for holding liquid.*

- **2 circular items with different diameters, such as a mug and a large plate**
- **1 large sheet cardboard**
- **marking pen**
- **scissors**
- **masking tape**
- **newspaper**
- **white craft glue (diluted 3 parts glue to 1 part water)**
- **white paper**
- **photocopies of chosen images**
- **artist's acrylic paints**
- **spray varnish**

To make the form

1 Trace the outline
of the plate onto card-
board. Measure the
diameter to find the
center point, then draw
a straight line from the
center to the edge of
the circle (right).
2 Cut out the circle,
then cut down the line to the center point.
3 Overlap the cut edge to form a cone
(above right). When you're happy with the
shape, cut away the overlap and tape the two
edges together.

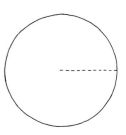

*This fully coordinated table is set with our attractive
handmade Table linens—napkins and placemats—and
Decorative bowls made of papier-mâché patterned
with photocopied motifs.*

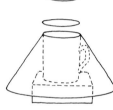

4 Place the point of the cone inside the mug, adjusting it until the top of the cone is level (below left). Trace a line around the cone, using the top of the mug as a guide.

5 Untape the joint, cut around the small circle to remove the center, then retape the joint firmly.

6 To make the base, place the mug top side down on the cardboard, then trace around the top of the mug and cut out the circle (left).

7 Upend the cone onto the mug, taping loosely. Then tape the cardboard base into position. Carefully remove the mug, cutting tape if necessary.

To make the bowl

1 Tear the newspaper into strips. Place the diluted glue in a bowl and, dipping each piece of paper as you go, apply 5 to 8 layers to the inside of the form. Allow each layer to dry before applying the next. A hair dryer can speed up the process.

2 When the inside is dry, repeat the process on the outside of the form. Allow to dry.

3 Tear the white paper into narrow strips, dip them into the diluted glue, and apply two layers over the newspaper.

4 Cut out the photocopied images or fabric motifs. Position around the outside of the bowl, taping to the bowl with masking tape, if necessary. Once you are happy with the placement, glue each to the bowl. Allow to dry.

To finish

1 To achieve a color-washed look, paint the bowl with acrylic paints mixed with a little glue. Apply two or three coats.

2 When the paint is dry, apply four coats of varnish. This will help seal the bowl so that when you need to clean it, you can wipe it with a damp cloth.

◆ Pretty Placemats at Your Service ◆

*These generously sized placemats are quilted for good looks and durability. One is made
with two compatible fabrics; just flip it over for a new look. The other is styled with a colorful
pocket for holding a matching napkin. Be sure to use washable fabrics that will not bleed.*

Octagon mats

*The materials listed below are enough for two
mats and two napkins. For the greatest variety,
make the placemats with a print on one side and
a solid color on the other. We made our napkins
from the solid-color fabric.*

- ◆ **1-inch graph paper**
- ◆ **⅝ yard 44-inch-wide
  print fabric**
- ◆ **1⅔ yards 44-inch-wide
  solid color fabric**
- ◆ **⅝ yard 44-inch-wide fusible
  fleece interfacing**
- ◆ **thread to match fabrics**
- ◆ **buttonhole twist**
- ◆ **½ yard 22-inch-wide paper
  backed fusible webbing**
- ◆ **transparent ruler, pencil**
- ◆ **air-soluble marking pen**
- ◆ **scissors, needle, pins**

1 With the graph paper, ruler, and pencil,
enlarge the pattern following the directions on
page 276. Draw a 6-inch square pattern for the
napkin rings. When cutting out the fabric, add
a ½-inch seam allowance to all edges.

2 For each placemat: Cut one piece of each
fabric and the fleece. For each napkin ring: Cut
one piece of solid fabric plus a 2 x 6-inch piece
of fleece.

3 For the mat: Trim away the seam allowance
on the fleece. Fuse the fleece to the wrong
side of the solid-color fabric.

4 For the napkin ring: Fold the 6-inch square
of fabric in half, right side in. Stitch a ½-inch
seam along the long edge; press open. Turn the
piece right side out, with the seam centered on
the back. Slide interfacing inside and fuse it in
place. Topstitch along both long sides, ½ inch
from the edge. Fold napkin ring in half crosswise, and center it, loop side in, on one side of

the octagon. Match the raw edges.

5 With right sides together, pin and stitch the
mat, attaching the napkin ring along one edge
and leaving 4 inches open on another edge.
Trim the corners diagonally and turn the mat
right side out; press. Slip-stitch the opening.

6 Use buttonhole twist as the top and bobbin
threads on your sewing machine to quilt the
placemat. Use the ruler and marking pen to
draw the quilting lines.

7 Beginning 1 inch from the edge, draw three
concentric octagons, 1 inch apart. Stitch the
octagon lines while the markings are still fresh.
When machine quilting, leave long threads at
each stitching end. Finish ends by pulling them
between the fabric layers and hand-sewing
several backstitches in the seam line.

8 Cut out and sew the matching napkins, following the instructions on page 306.

*This octagonal floral placemat with attached napkin
ring (above) can be flipped to a solid-color mat. Each
square of the pattern grid (below) equals 1 square inch.*

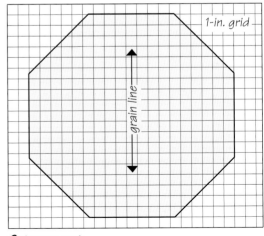

Octagon mat

Pear pocket placemat

The materials given are enough for two place-mats and two napkins. Double the amount of fabric and interfacings for four of each.

- ◆ **1-inch graph paper**
- ◆ **transparent ruler, pencil**
- ◆ **½ yard 44-inch-wide yellow fabric**
- ◆ **1½ yards 44-inch-wide green fabric**
- ◆ **½ yard 44-inch-wide fusible fleece interfacing**
- ◆ **7-inch square of interfacing**
- ◆ **thread to match fabrics**
- ◆ **4½ yards ¼-inch piping cord**
- ◆ **air-soluble marking pen**
- ◆ **scissors, needle**

1 With the graph paper, ruler, and pencil, enlarge the placemat pattern following the instructions on page 276. Enlarge the pear pattern by the same method. Add a ½-inch seam allowance to all sides on each piece.

2 For each placemat, cut 2 pieces of green fabric and 2 pieces of fleece interfacing. Cut two 22-inch squares for napkins from the green. From the yellow fabric, cut enough 1⅝-inch-wide bias strips to equal the length of the piping cord when seamed end to end. Also cut two pear pieces of yellow fabric and one of interfacing for each pear pocket.

3 To make the pear pocket: With right sides together and interfacing pinned to one side, stitch around the pear, leaving an opening between the marks on the pattern. Trim the interfacing. Clip the curves and trim the seam allowance. Turn the pear right side out and press. Embroider pear bottom design with satin stitch (p.281). Do it freehand or use transfer paper to draw the pattern on the fabric.

4 Select a fabric piece for a placemat's front. Use the pen to make placement marks on mat front and pear. Pin the pear in place, then edge-stitch the sides and bottom between the straight marks, leaving the pocket top open.

An outdoor summer supper can be made very festive with green and yellow placemats that sport a pear pocket for a napkin and silverware.

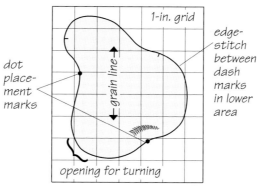

Pear pocket

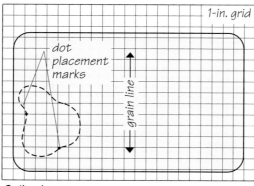

Quilted mat

5 Select a fabric piece for the placemat's back. Trim ½ inch from edges of a piece of fleece interfacing; fuse it to the wrong side of the placemat's back.

6 To make the piping, follow the instructions on page 134. Stitch the piping to the right side of the placemat front, matching the raw edges. Clip the seam allowance around the curves. To join the piping ends in a neat abutment, follow the instructions given on page 134.

7 With right sides together, pin and stitch the back of the placemat to the front, leaving a 4-inch opening. Trim and clip the curved corners.

8 Turn the mat right side out through the opening and press. Slip-stitch (p.281) the opening closed.

9 Repeat Steps 3 to 8 to complete each subsequent placemat.

10 To make the matching green napkins, follow the napkin instructions on page 306.

Patterns for the placemat and pear pocket (below) are drawn on grids in which each square represents 1 square inch; enlarge the patterns on 1-inch graph paper for correct size.

• Party Animals •

It's fiesta time whenever these adorable critters are around.
Based on traditional Mexican piñatas, the colorful bear and pig both have an
oatmeal-box body, a balloon head, and egg-carton-cup legs, hands, and nose.

Fill a brightly-colored piñata in your child's favorite animal shape with wrapped candies and small, unbreakable toys. Hang it from a doorway or the branch of a tree, and let partygoers break it open with sticks to scatter the contents.

- 18-ounce oatmeal box
- 2 yards fishing line
- large sewing needle
- 1 medium-size round balloon
- masking tape
- 1-inch graph paper
- 6-inch square lightweight cardboard
- 5 cups from an egg carton
- 1½ x 6-inch strips newspaper
- 1½ x 6-inch strips white paper towels
- flour, water, white craft glue, and a whisk for mixing
- two plastic bowls, one with lid
- small paintbrush
- cookie sheet
- four packages tissue paper, each a different color
- scissors, craft knife
- transparent ruler, pencil
- fine-tip black permanent marker
- 9 x 12-inch white poster board
- small pieces white and black construction paper
- 1 yard 1½- to 2-inch-wide wired ribbon

FOR THE PIG PIÑATA
- two ¼-inch black pom-poms
- 1-inch purple pom-pom
- pink pipe cleaner stem
- 10-inch gold paper doily

FOR THE BEAR PIÑATA
- 1-inch black pom-pom
- 1-inch red pom-pom
- 9 x 12-inch piece of printed gift wrap paper

Our piñatas get a festive look from contrasting colors of tissue paper. We show how to make a pig and a bear; improvise any animal you choose.

1 Discard the oatmeal-box lid. Thread the needle with the fishing line. For the pig, push the needle into the box 1½ inches from the open end and have it exit about 1 inch to the left or right. For the bear, push the needle into the box ½ inch from the open end and have it

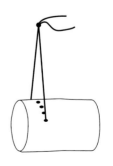

Pig hangs from side   *Bear hangs from top*

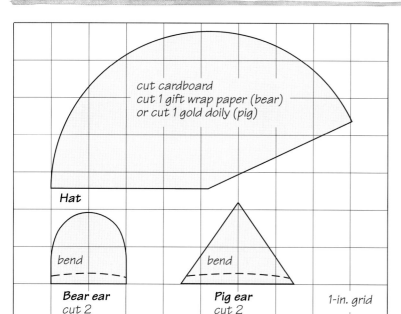

cut cardboard
cut 1 gift wrap paper (bear)
or cut 1 gold doily (pig)

Hat

bend

Bear ear
cut 2

bend

Pig ear
cut 2

1-in. grid

Tissue-paper fringe

1 Cut 3-inch-wide strips of tissue paper along the long edge.

2 Fold the strips in half lengthwise. To cut the fringe: Cut from the fold to within ½ inch of the opposite edge. To save time, several strips of tissue paper can be folded and cut together.

3 Pour a small amount of craft glue in a clean plastic bowl. Working on one layer of fringed tissue at a time, open out the fold. Use the paintbrush to apply a thin line of glue to one edge of the tissue paper.

4 Refold the strip, reversing the fold so that the fringe has a rounded, fluffy edge. Glue the long unfringed edges together.

5 Paint a ring of glue around the bottom end of the box; attach the uncut edge of the fringe, trimming as necessary. Continue gluing overlapping rings of fringe around the body and head, changing colors as desired.

6 For each egg-cup leg or nose: Glue a circle of tissue over the end as a base, then build up rings of fringe around the sides.

Finishing

1 For eyes, cut two black dime-size circles and two white quarter-size circles; glue a black circle to one edge of the white. Glue to the face.

2 Cut the hat pattern from poster board. Glue either the gift wrap paper or the paper doily over the poster board as trim. Roll hat into a cone shape; lap and glue the edges together. Glue a pom-pom to the tip. Glue the hat to the head.

3 Wrap the ribbon around the piñata's neck and tie a bow.

4 To fill a piñata just before a party, use a craft knife to cut a 2 x 1-inch flap just behind the head. Gently lift the flap, fill the piñata, and glue the flap closed.

PLEASE TAKE NOTE

PAPIER-MÂCHÉ TIPS

Don't worry about spaces between the egg-cup features and the box or balloon. The papier-mâché strips will cover the gaps.

Torn paper strips are preferred to cut strips because their edges blend more smoothly against other layers of paper.

Work on a cookie sheet: Papier-mâché glue does not stick to metal. When glue thickens, add a little water; if it's too thin, add more flour.

---

exit on the opposite side of the box. Tie ends together for hanging up the piñata.

2 Blow up the balloon to a 5-inch diameter. Insert the knotted end into the open end of the box. Tape the balloon in place.

3 Enlarge the pattern pieces (above) to full size, using the 1-inch graph paper and the directions on page 276. Cut out two ears from cardboard. Bend the pieces along the dotted lines. Stand the ears on the top of the balloon head; tape in place

4 Tape two egg-cup legs to one side of the box and two to the other. Tape an egg-cup nose to the center front of the balloon.

Papier-mâché

1 For the papier-mâché glue: In a plastic bowl, whisk together ½ cup flour and ¾ cup water until smooth. Blend in 1 to 2 tablespoons of craft glue. Keep covered, if you are interrupted, so that the glue doesn't dry out.

2 Dip one newspaper strip at a time in the glue mixture. Pull the strip through two fingers to get rid of excess glue. Position strips over the junctures of the balloon and the box, then cover the remainder of the animal. Keep the strips smooth. In small areas, such as ears, tear the strips into smaller pieces. Allow to dry.

3 Repeat Step 2, using paper-towel strips.

MAKING PAPIER-MÂCHÉ PIÑATAS

1 *Blow up a balloon to a 5-inch diameter and tie a knot. Insert into the open end of the box. Use masking tape to attach the egg-cup features to the box and balloon.*

2 *Glue strips of torn newspaper over the junctures of the balloon and the box, and then over the remainder of the animal. Let dry; repeat with paper-towel strips.*

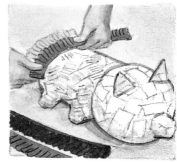

3 *Fold tissue-paper strips lengthwise and cut the fringe. Reverse the fold and glue the uncut edges together. Then glue rows of overlapping fringe to the form in a pattern of colors.*

◆ Flying High ◆

The joy of flying a kite can be surpassed only by flying a kite you've made yourself.
Our kites are made with ripstop nylon, which is extremely light, flexible, and strong. A "hot knife"
is used to cut the nylon, giving it clean, sealed edges and eliminating any fraying.

Kite-making basics

The tools and basic techniques listed below are essential to making all kites, including ours.

- **1-inch graph paper**
- **pencil, chalk**
- **metal ruler, French curve**
- **dressmaker's carbon paper, tracing wheel (to transfer design onto poster board)**
- **4 to 6 pieces of poster board (for making pattern templates)**
- **masking tape**
- **craft knife**
- **"hot knife," pencil-type, flat- or sharp-tip soldering iron, to cut ripstop nylon fabric**
- **scissors**
- **water soluble glue stick**
- **newspaper**
- **sewing machine with zigzag capabilities**
- **white nylon or dacron (polyester) sewing thread**
- **12-inch square 200-denier nylon or 3.9-ounce dacron flag fabric for frame sleeves**
- **spindle of kite string, no. 20 or no. 30 test nylon or dacron cord, for bridle and for flying**

Template Preparation

1 Enlarge the design to its full size, using 1-inch graph paper and the instructions on page 276. Add the perimeter hem measurements required by the design.

2 Make a separate template for each section of the design; such pieces as tail bows or teeth, which are repeated, need only one template. Make the large templates first, taping poster boards together to achieve the needed size.

3 To make a template, place the carbon side of the dressmaker's paper against the poster board and center a section of the enlarged design on top. Trace the section, including dotted line edges and perimeter hem allowances. Remove

We've made our kites in two favorite styles—diamond and delta. One brings a blazing comet to an afternoon sky, the other might cause a sensation on the beach.

the pattern and carbon paper and cut out the poster board template using the craft knife with the ruler for straight edges and the French curve along curves. On asymmetrical pieces, mark "up" on the template to indicate the right side.

Comet kite

This traditional diamond-shape kite finishes to a 40-inch height, with another 10 feet or so of tail.

- **basic tools, at left**
- **60- inch-wide ripstop nylon:**
  1⅓ yards royal blue;
  ¾ yard orange; ⅔ yard each fuchsia, red, and yellow;
  ¼ yard gold
- **¼ - inch wooden dowels; one 40 inches long and one 36 inches long**

1 Arrange the templates right side up on the right side of the fabric. For the main portion of

the kite, cut 1 piece of fabric from each template, including the large star, using the color fabric indicated in Diagram 1. In addition, cut out 2 small gold stars; 8 tail-bow halves from mixed colors; and 3 tail strips 2 x 45 inches (not shown in diagram)

2 To make the multicolored comet: Spread newspaper on a work surface. Place the top section of orange fabric face down and apply the glue stick in a thin line along the top and bottom edges. Turn right side up and glue in position on the blue background fabric.

3 Apply the remaining comet sections in the same manner, lapping each new piece over the former by ¼ inch until the bottom orange section is in place.

4 Set the sewing machine with a long, wide zigzag stitch. Zigzag each edge of the comet sections from the outer to the inner edge.

5 Turn the kite wrong side up. Using scissors, trim away the blue layer of fabric from behind each comet tail section, leaving about ³⁄₁₆ inch of fabric beyond the stitches.

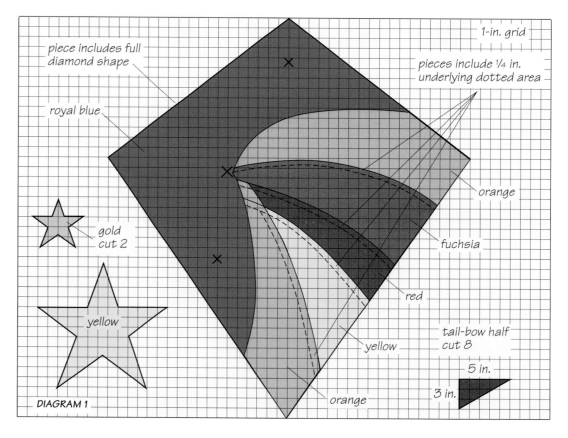

1-in. grid

piece includes full diamond shape

pieces include ¼ in. underlying dotted area

royal blue

orange

gold cut 2

fuchsia

red

yellow

yellow

tail-bow half cut 8

5 in.

3 in.

orange

DIAGRAM 1

6 Turn the kite right side up. Using the same gluing technique, glue the large star over the large *X* mark and the small stars over the small *x* marks. Zigzag the stars to the kite, switching to a straight stitch at the top of each point.

7 Turn the kite face down and trim away the background fabric from behind the stars.

8 Working on one outside edge of the kite at a time, double-fold a ¼ -inch-wide hem and stitch with straight stitch.

9 From the flag fabric (see materials list under Kite-making basics) cut out four 1 x 3-inch "frame sleeves," to hold the dowels in place at the kite corners (Diagram 2).

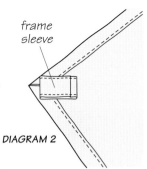

Fold each frame sleeve so that the bottom of the fold extends ¼ inch beyond the top. Position a sleeve at each corner with the fold overlapping the hemmed edges. Edge-stitch the sides.

frame sleeve

DIAGRAM 2

10 To make the tail of the kite: Seam the 3 tail strips together, end to end, using a ¼ -inch seam allowance. On one end, fold 1 ½ inch to the wrong side twice and edge-stitch. Use the hot knife to burn a ⅜ -inch hole at the center of the hemmed end.

11 To make the bows for the tail: Select 2 triangular bow halves and overlap the long points about 2 inches. Position 1 bow over a seam in the kite tail and stitch in place (Diagram 3); repeat, covering the other seam. Position and sew the remaining bows equally spaced between the first two.

12 Place the kite on a protected work surface. Chalk a dot 8 ¾ inches down from the top corner of the kite and another 7 ½ inches up

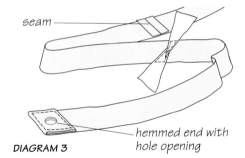

seam

DIAGRAM 3   *hemmed end with hole opening*

from the bottom corner. Use the tip of the hot knife to burn a ⅛ -inch hole at each mark for the kite bridle string.

13 To assemble the kite: Select the longer dowel. Insert one end through the hole in the tail piece and then into the bottom frame sleeve. Insert the opposite end in the top sleeve, bowing the dowel slightly. Insert the ends of the shorter dowel in the side sleeves. If necessary, reduce the dowel lengths so there is no distorted tension. Knot string around the dowels where they cross.

14 Using the hot knife, cut a length of string for the bridle, 60 inches long. Insert 1 end through each of the prepared holes and tie the ends to the vertical dowel. Turn the kite right side up and pull the center portion of bridle string to the front of the kite. Measure 19 inches along

PRACTICAL IDEAS

CUTTING TIPS

Cut one layer of ripstop fabric at a time. The dull side of ripstop is considered the right side.

For symmetrical pieces, make a vertical half-template. Before cutting the fabric, chalk a fold-line on the fabric. Align the template edge that represents the piece's center along one side of the line and cut that half; flip the template to the other side of the line and cut the other half.

Use a hot knife to cut ripstop fabric on a glass-top table or another safe, hard, work surface. Move the hot knife swiftly and smoothly along the edge of the template. Gently pull the excess fabric away; if the cut is not clean, retrace the area with the hot knife.

If the template and fabric edges become joined during the cutting process, insert a ruler between the two layers and gently pull it around the edges to separate them.

Position templates on the ripstop fabric along the grain of the fabric, following the selvage. The symmetry of the grain will give the kite optimum strength, which is critical for good construction and long life.

the string from the top hole and make a looped slipknot for attaching the kite's flying string. The loop can be repositioned higher or lower on the bridle string for different wind conditions. Lower the knot for stronger winds.

15 Tie the spindle of string to the bridle loop.

Jaws kite

This delta-wing kite finishes to a 36-inch height. Read Kite-making basics and the Comet kite instructions to familiarize yourself with kite-making materials and techniques before you begin.

- ♦ **basic tools (p.313)**
- ♦ **60-inch-wide ripstop nylon in the following colors and yardage: green ⅔ yard; blue, white, orange, and purple ¼ yard each; black ¼ yard**
- ♦ **four ¼ -inch wooden dowels, each 24 inches long**

1 After enlarging the pattern (Diagram 1), add ⅝ inch to each perimeter line on kite body and keel pieces before making the cutting templates.

2 Place the templates right side up on the right side of the fabric. Cut out 1 piece from each template in the color indicated except for the following: 16 orange teeth; 2 black eyes; 2 each of the 2 blue triangles; 2 each purple bottom fins and side fins.

3 Using the methods described in Steps 2 to 4 of the Comet kite, glue and stitch the following pieces in the order described: orange teeth on top of white mouth; mouth and teeth on top of green head; black eyes on head.

4 Turn the kite face down and trim away the green fabric within the edge of the mouth.

5 Lap the sides of the purple top fin over the sides of 2 blue top fin triangles and zigzag. Center this piece at the top of the kite, lapping it under the edge so that it forms a continuous line with the sides of the kite. Zigzag the edge.

6 Lap one edge of each purple side fin over the edge of a blue side fin triangle and zigzag. Position these pieces at the lower sides of the kite, lapping them under the edge. They should form a continuous line with the sides and bottom of the kite. Zigzag the edges.

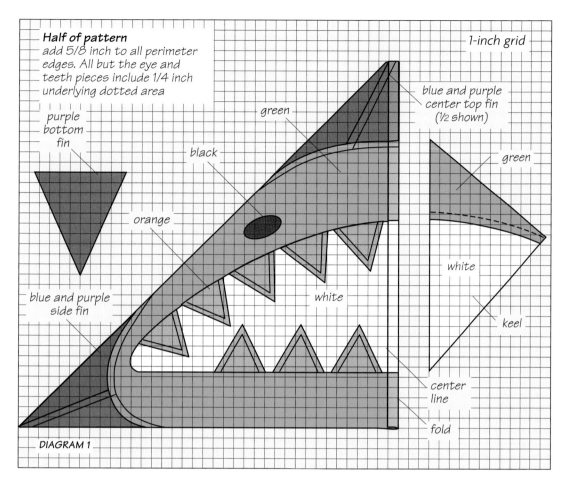

Half of pattern
add 5/8 inch to all perimeter edges. All but the eye and teeth pieces include 1/4 inch underlying dotted area

1-inch grid

purple bottom fin

green

blue and purple center top fin (½ shown)

black

green

orange

white

white

blue and purple side fin

keel

center line

fold

DIAGRAM 1

7 For the 2 bottom fins: Turn under ¼ inch on 1 side edge and hem; repeat on other side edge. With right sides together, align the top edge of the fin with the bottom edge of the kite so that, when the edge is turned under ½ inch, the side and bottom fins meet at the corner. Stitch the fins ¼ inch in from the edge.

8 From the flag fabric (see materials under Kite-making basics) use a hot knife to cut: 1 tri-angle with 2-inch sides for the keel reinforcement and one 3-inch square. Cut the square in half diagonally; fold the long edge of each portion in half and stitch 1 inch from the fold to create 2 frame sleeves (Diagram 2).

9 The side hems of the kite double as dowel casings. Fold the side edges ⅝ inch to the wrong side. Tuck a frame sleeve into each fold, 16 inches from the bottom of the kite: The opening of the frame sleeve should face upward, as shown in Diagram 3. Stitch each hem casing as follows: Start-

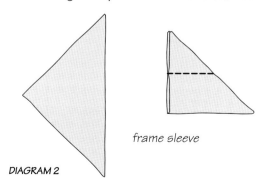

frame sleeve

DIAGRAM 2

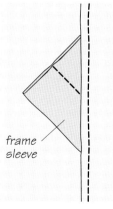

frame sleeve

DIAGRAM 3

ing at the bottom, stitch for 2 inches; skip 1 inch (for a dowel opening). Backstitch at both ends of the dowel opening. Continue stitching to the top of the kite. Make sure the frame sleeve is caught in the stitching. About 26 inches up from the bottom, stitch across the casing to prevent the dowel from riding up.

10 On the bottom edge of the kite, fold under and stitch a ¼ -inch double hem (the bottom fins will hang downward). Trim any excess hem at the corners. Seal the corners by running the hot knife over the edges.

11 Lap the curved edge of the green keel piece over the white keel piece and zigzag. Tape the keel reinforcement triangle just inside the corner where the pieces meet. Stitch ¼ -inch double hems on the 2 sides, as shown in Diagram 4. Catch the reinforcement corner inside as you sew.

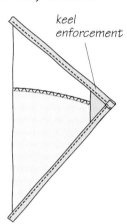

keel enforcement

DIAGRAM 4

12 Use the hot knife to burn three ⅛ -inch holes in the keel reinforcement triangle; 1 at the point, the others ⅝ inch away along the sides. Hot-cut an 8-inch piece of kite string. Fold the string in half and knot the ends together. Thread the looped end of the string through the hole at the point of the keel and pull the knotted end through the loop; tighten.

13 To make the center dowel casing: Turn the kite wrong side up. Using a ruler, chalk a line vertically down the center of the kite. Then chalk a parallel line, ⅝ inch away, to one side of the center. With the right side of the kite facing, align the long edge of the keel along the center: match the colored sections, as shown in Diagram 1. Tape the keel in place.

14 On the wrong side, fold the kite along the center line. Stitch across the bottom end between chalk lines, pivot and stitch along the second chalk line for ½ inch. Leave a 1-inch opening and continue stitching to the top and across the casing area.

15 Insert the dowels into the casings and tie the flying string onto the keel string.

• Dried Beauty in a Basket •

What a wonderful focal point these dried roses will make on a buffet or hall table.
Their beauty will last a whole season. You can dry flowers from your garden or from the florist
yourself and keep fresh-looking blossoms in the house all year.

A bouquet of roses

This lovely dried floral display is appropriate at any time of the year in any decor. Dried flowers add warmth to any room.

- **36 large rosebuds**
- **2 to 3 bunches nigella leaves (or other narrow, fine-leaf foliage)**
- **2 bunches small-petal flowers**
- **1 bunch small contrasting flowers**
- **2 bunches white statice**
- **large wicker basket with handle**
- **3 yards ⅜ -inch-wide red satin ribbon**
- **2 yards ¼ -inch-wide white satin ribbon**
- **one sheet florist's moss**
- **2 or 3 bricks green florist's foam**
- **kitchen knife, floral scissors**
- **florist's wire, wire cutters, tapestry needle**
- **3 yards 2-inch-wide wired white moiré ribbon**

1 Pinch off the leaves on all the flower stems. Dry as shown below.
2 On the basket, wrap the narrow satin ribbons in opposite directions from one side of the handle to the other. Tie bows at the sides.

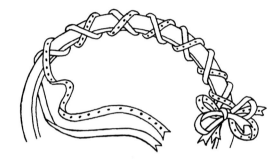

3 Line the basket with moss up to the top edge. Lay the foam bricks in the bottom of the basket to cover the entire area. Trim the bricks with the knife as necessary to contour them to the shape of the basket.
4 Wire each section of foam to the basket in two perpendicular directions. Use the tapestry needle to pull the wire through the moss and the bottom and sides of the basket. Cover the top of the foam with moss.
5 Arrange the roses throughout the basket, starting with the longest stems in the middle and tapering to shorter ones near the sides of the basket. Trim the stems as necessary.
6 Repeat Step 5 with the other flowers, finishing with the leaves.
7 Wrap the moiré ribbon around the top edge of the basket; overlap the ends 1 inch and trim the excess with an angled cut. Wire the lapped ends to the basket.
8 Make one large white moiré bow and one small red satin bow. Place the red bow over the white one, and wire both bows together over the lapped ends of the moiré ribbon.

VARIATION Be on the lookout for interesting containers for your dried flowers, such as a brass bucket, wooden bowl, or pewter mug.

Lush arrangements of dried flowers make a welcoming statement in any part of the house.

EASY STEPS FOR DRYING FLOWERS

1 Pick flowers, such as hydrangeas, just at their peak or a little before. Choose blooms in a variety of sizes, but make sure that each has at least a 12-inch stem. Remove all the leaves, including the small ones at the base of the flower.

2 Using spring clothespins or a piece of string to tie them, hang each stem upside down in a cool, dark, dry area for about 7 days, or until they are completely dry. Don't attempt to dry flowers in very humid weather.

3 Select a deep rectangular basket to hold your arrangement. Make a stabilizing bed of broken flower heads in the basket. Then arrange larger blooms around the rim and fill in with the remaining flowers.

4 As a decorative option: When you are happy with the floral arrangement, spray the flowers with a lavender or mauve floral paint, available at crafts stores. Protect the basket with aluminum foil or newspaper while you spray.

◆Dinosaur Magnets ◆

Cheerful monsters like these will brighten any spot from the fridge door or a magnetized bulletin board to the side of a filing cabinet. Children will love them and, with a little help from an adult, they'll be able to make a set of these lovable lizards for themselves

To avoid moving the soft clay too much, assemble the dinosaurs on a baking sheet.

- ◆ **tracing paper, pencil**
- ◆ **lightweight cardboard (shiny surface is best)**
- ◆ **transfer (graphite) paper**
- ◆ **stylus**
- ◆ **small scissors**
- ◆ **rolling pin**
- ◆ **white modeling compound**
- ◆ **craft knife, short dowel**
- ◆ **sandpaper (600 grit)**
- ◆ **artist's acrylic paints**
- ◆ **small artist's paintbrush**
- ◆ **magnet**
- ◆ **white craft glue**

1 Using tracing paper and a pencil, trace the dinosaur patterns shown above and on the opposite page, drawing the basic body shapes and the extra body parts (legs and frills, for example) separately. Numbers on the patterns tell you how many parts there are for each dinosaur, and the dotted lines indicate where the pieces overlap.

Give your imagination free rein when decorating your collection of Dinosaur Magnets—the brighter the colors and patterns you choose, the more fun they are.

2 Lay a piece of lightweight cardboard on a flat surface. Place a piece of transfer paper on it and place the tracing paper with the dinosaur patterns on top. Use a stylus to trace the individual shapes onto the card, leaving a little space between the shapes. Cut out all the shapes with scissors.

3 Using the rolling pin, roll out the modeling compound approximately ⅛ inch thick.

4 Place the cardboard stencil of the dinosaur body on the rolled compound and cut out the shape with the knife. Do the same for the smaller body parts. Smooth raw edges with your fingertips.

5 Place the dinosaur bodies on the baking sheet. Arrange the separate smaller body parts on each base shape (frills are attached beneath the body; head and legs are attached on the surface). Gently press the pieces together. For a more rounded shape, place extra compound under the body. Using the knife, clean up the cut edges and then smooth them with your fingertips.

6 Using a small dowel or rolling pin and pressing very lightly, roll over the dinosaur figures to make the legs, frills, and other parts adhere to the base body shapes.

7 Roll a small piece of compound between your fingertips to make an eyeball. Gently position on the figure.

piece 2 includes underlying dotted area

piece 2 includes all frills and underlying dotted area

8 Bake, following the compound manufacturer's instructions. Allow to cool and use sandpaper to smooth the rough surfaces.

9 Refer to the picture of the dinosaurs as a guide for drawing decorations on your creations, or use your imagination to design your own decorations.

10 Paint with artist's acrylic paints. When dry, attach a magnet to the back of each dinosaur with white craft glue.

MAKING THE DINOSAURS

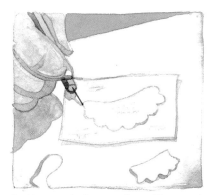

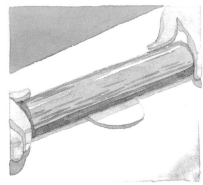

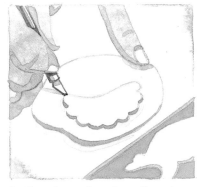

1 *Trace each dinosaur shape. Place cardboard (with a shiny surface to prevent sticking) on a flat surface, cover with transfer paper, and lay the tracing paper on top. With a stylus, trace each shape onto the cardboard.*

2 *Remove the tracing and transfer papers, and cut out the cardboard shapes with scissors. Roll out a piece of modeling compound to about ⅛ inch thick, working carefully so that the compound is perfectly even in thickness.*

3 *Place the cardboard stencils on the compound and press down slightly. Cut out the shapes with a knife, slowly and accurately cutting around all curves and corners. When finished, remove the surrounding compound.*

4 *Assemble the parts of the dinosaurs on a baking sheet. Using a small dowel and pressing lightly, roll over the assembled bodies to make the parts adhere. Bake in the oven for the time specified by the manufacturer of the compound.*

◆ Easter Baskets for Everyone ◆

*The young and the young at heart can enjoy the pleasures of a hand-knitted
Easter basket. Knit from the bottom up using raffia straw or jute twine in either round or oval
shapes, the baskets can be filled with edible goodies or potted springtime blossoms.*

Round twine basket

*These directions are for a 6-inch-round basket.
For an oval, purchase two rolls of twine, use the
oval base, and cast on 90 stitches.*

- **400-foot roll of sisal twine
  (hardware and variety stores)**
- **2 yards ecru 6-strand
  embroidery floss**
- **size 8 circular knitting needle,
  16 inches long**
- **size 10 straight knitting needle**
- **ruler or 6-inch gauge**
- **6-inch can or round form**
- **6-inch circle cut from ¼-inch-
  thick grade A plywood
  (ask supplier to cut to shape)**
- **1 yard 1-inch-wide wire edge
  ombré ribbon**
- **size G crochet hook**
- **drill with ⅛-inch bit**
- **2 tapestry needles**
- **four small safety pins**
- **glue gun and glue sticks**

Gauge for all baskets

10 sts = 3 ½ in. of stockinette stitch. Using the
circular needle, cast on 15 sts and work 4 in. of
stockinette stitch (knitting every row) and measure the gauge away from the cast-on edge.
Make a swatch to get a feel for the sisal and
raffia; they don't have the give of regular yarns.
If you have fewer stitches than stated, use
smaller needles; if more stitches, use larger
needles. For abbreviations, see page 298.

*Knit Easter baskets of twine with its subtle natural
color or of jute in seasonal pastel shades. The baskets
are eye-catching centerpieces, whether they are filled
with a toy collection, sweet treats, or potted plants.*

Knitting the tube

1 Loosely cast on 55 sts. Taking care not to twist the cast-on stitches, knit the first row and then continue knitting until you have 5 inches.
2 Switch to P sts and cont for 5 rounds. This forms basket's rolled top rim. Using the straight needle, cast off very loosely. Cut twine.

Blocking

1 To straighten basket sides, thoroughly wet tube. Blot excess water using a towel. Pat until the curling disappears. Do not press.
2 Slide the knitted tube over a coffee can or canister of the appropriate size, with the rim rolling outward. Let it dry overnight.

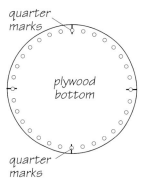

quarter marks

plywood bottom

quarter marks

Finishing

1 Drill ⅛-inch holes in plywood bottom ¼ inch from edge and ½ inch apart. Mark the edge in four equal parts.
2 Divide bottom edge of tube into four equal parts and mark with safety pins. Tie the tube to the marks on the bottom with scraps of floss; remove the pins.
3 To sew the tube to the base, thread the floss in a tapestry needle; knot the end. Starting on the inside, *bring the needle to the outside, pick up a stitch through the cast-on band, and go back through the same hole. Move to the next hole.* Cont from * to * around the perimeter. Finish with a slip stitch; weave in the floss end.
4 Use the crochet hook to pull the ribbon under and over several stitches about ½ inch below the rim; end with a bow on the outside.
5 For a handle, cut eighteen 36-inch-long pieces of twine. Glue-gun one group of ends together. Braid three groups of six strands each for the full length. Glue other ends together.
6 To finish handle ends, wrap and glue a strand of twine for 1 inch above cut ends.
7 Glue the ends of the handle to opposite sides of the plywood bottom, inside the basket; add dots of glue between the handle and the tube.

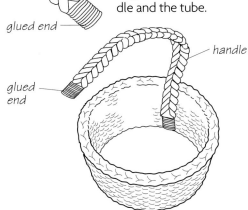

glued end

glued end

handle

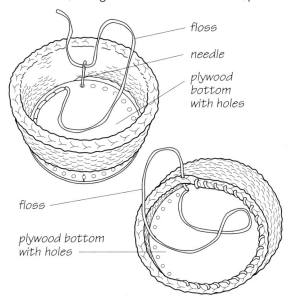

floss
needle
plywood bottom with holes

floss

plywood bottom with holes

Round raffia basket

Collect the same materials as for the twine basket but omit the twine, floss, and ribbon. Use two strands of raffia as one throughout, and pull them from the hanks; don't wind into a ball.

- **four 24-yard hanks of white raffia straw**
- **two 24-yard hanks each of baby pink and bright pink raffia straw**

1 Follow the basic directions for the twine basket except leave a 24-inch end to use for sewing the tube to the plywood, and cast on 58 sts with white raffia; K for 1½ in. *Cut white and knot on one strand of each pink color; K for 1¼ in.*

2 Rep between * with white.
3 Rep between * with pink.
4 Switch to white and P for 1¼ in. to form the rolled top rim.

Oval raffia basket

Collect the same materials as for the twine basket but omit the twine, floss, ribbon, and round plywood bottom. Use 24- or 29-inch circular needles and treat two strands of raffia as one throughout.

- **four 24-yard hanks each of purple, lavender, and yellow raffia straw**
- **one 24-yard hank of grass green raffia straw**
- **two 5 x 18-inch pieces of purple poster board**
- **6 x 12-inch oval cut from ¼-inch-thick grade A plywood (ask supplier to cut to shape)**

1 Follow the basic directions for the twine basket except leave a 2-yard end to use for sewing the tube to the plywood, and cast on 90 sts with purple raffia. K for 5¼ in.
2 Switch to yellow and K for 1 round. P for 5 rounds to form the rolled rim.
3 After blocking and sewing the basket to the base, cut the green raffia into 10-inch lengths. Holding two pieces together, fold them in half and insert the crochet hook through the loop; pull the loop downward through a purple stitch below the rim and hook it in place.
4 Braid two handles using 10 strands in each of the three groups.
5 Place the poster board liners inside, between the handles, to support the sides.

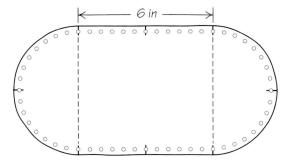

6 in

• Pressed-Flower Cards •

Every sign of the zodiac and every calendar month has its own flower. For a homemade birthday card that will be treasured long after the celebrations are over, use the flower symbolizing the recipient's birth date as a decoration. The pressing and drying of the flowers is a joy in itself.

Pressing flowers by hand

Specially designed flower presses are available at crafts shops, but if you aren't doing a lot of pressing, there's no need to buy one; this simple method will work just as well.

- ◆ **newspaper**
- ◆ **blotting paper**
- ◆ **flowers and leaves of choice**
- ◆ **2 telephone directories or heavy books**

1 Lay 3 to 4 sheets of newspaper on a flat work surface (for very succulent flowers, use several more sheets). Top with a sheet of blotting paper.
2 Carefully place the flowers on the blotting paper, making sure they do not overlap.
3 Cover with another sheet of blotting paper, then 3 to 4 more sheets of newspaper (use extra for succulent flowers).
4 Place the books on top.
5 Leave for 3 weeks in a cool, dry place, such as a cupboard. Check the pressed flowers daily for the first week, straightening out any petals or leaves as necessary. When checking the flowers, peel away the blotting paper carefully; place your fingernail (or the curved side of a teaspoon) on the blotting paper and run it along as you pull up the paper, to prevent flowers or leaves from sticking. Replace the newspaper daily during the first week, as it absorbs moisture from the flowers. After the first week, check the flowers and replace the newspaper 2 to 3 times a week.
6 After 3 weeks, test whether the flowers are sufficiently dry. To do so, check for the following: The flowers should feel dry, they should be rigid, not limp, and the paper should be dry. Almost all types of flowers will be dry in 3 weeks, but leave for 1 week extra, if necessary, to be certain.

Pressing flowers by microwave

Use a medium to low microwave setting: Flowers dry too quickly if set on high, and become brittle. Microwave ovens get hotter the more they are used. If you are drying several batches of flowers, later batches will take less time to dry. Watch carefully and adjust your timing.

- ◆ **paper towels**
- ◆ **blotting paper**
- ◆ **flowers and leaves for pressing**
- ◆ **heavy, flat microwave dish**

1 Lay 3 to 4 paper towels on a work surface or on the removable turntable of a microwave (if drying particularly succulent flowers, use a few more towels). Top with a sheet of blotting paper.
2 Carefully place the flowers on the blotting paper, making sure they don't overlap.
3 Cover with another sheet of blotting paper, and place 3 to 4 more paper towels on top (and extra for succulent flowers).
4 Place the flowers and paper in the microwave, placing a dish or casserole lid on top of the paper to keep it flat.
5 Heat on medium (or low-medium for dark flowers) for 3 to 4 minutes. Check at 1-minute intervals, straighten any flowers or leaves, if necessary, and check for dryness: The flowers should feel dry, and they should be rigid, not limp. Note that the paper towels may still be slightly damp. Usually 3 to 4 minutes is enough, although times will vary according to the flowers being dried—an extra minute or so may be needed for some flowers. Be careful, however, not to microwave the flowers too long. It's a good idea to err on the side of underdrying them. When the flowers feel dry or very nearly dry, leave them in the microwave for a few minutes with the power off. This will safely finish the drying process.

Making the card

Some flowers may be too large for a card. You can still press these flowers and use the petals to create free-form designs.

- ◆ **tweezers**
- ◆ **pressed flowers and leaves**
- ◆ **plain card (available at stationery or crafts shops) or card stock, folded in half**
- ◆ **white craft glue, scissors**
- ◆ **small paintbrush, for glue**
- ◆ **felt-tip pen with chisel tip**
- ◆ **waxed paper**
- ◆ **telephone directory or heavy book**

1 Using tweezers, place the flowers on the card, trying different arrangements if using several specimens. Smaller flowers and leaves can be used to fill any gaps, if desired.

2 Leave space for any writing at the top or bottom of the card.

3 Remove the flowers from the card with the tweezers. For delicate fronds or flowers, it may be easier to leave them on the card when applying glue, using tweezers to lift each segment gently.

4 Starting with the plant material that is featured or that will lie closest to the surface of the card, dab a little glue on the back of the petals, stem, and leaves with the paintbrush.

5 Stick in place, applying a little more glue, if necessary, after the final positioning.

6 Repeat until all the flowers and leaves are in place, cutting away the stems if too bulky.

7 Remove excess glue from around the flowers. Leave for five minutes to allow the glue to set. Place a piece of waxed paper over the top and a heavy book. This will prevent the petals and leaves from curling.

8 Leave for several hours or overnight in a cool, dry place.

9 Using a chisel-tip pen, write the flower name and month, if you wish.

These pretty pressed-flower cards can be reminders of a bouquet received on a happy occasion or of a friend's garden in which the flowers were picked.

◆ Decorations for Christmas ◆

The holiday season provides lots of opportunity to create decorations for the home.
Try a novel Advent Calendar, make a wreath you can use year after year—or even personalize
the Christmas Party Favors that might adorn your dinner table on Christmas Day.

Advent calendar

This beautiful wall hanging can be used year after year. Children will enjoy putting the decorations in place each day. At the end of the season, the calendar can be rolled up for storage.

- ◆ **1 ¼ yards 72-inch-wide cream felt**
- ◆ **cream thread**
- ◆ **6-strand embroidery floss to match cream, green, brown, and red felt, and all small felt squares**
- ◆ **crewel needle**
- ◆ **tracing paper**
- ◆ **12 x36-inch rectangle green felt**
- ◆ **4-inch square brown felt**
- ◆ **5-inch square red felt**
- ◆ **3-inch felt squares in a variety of colors for decorations**
- ◆ **variety of glass beads, sequins, gold cord, and ribbons to trim decorations**
- ◆ **white craft glue**
- ◆ **24 small gold safety pins**
- ◆ **two 11 ½ -inch lengths of ½ -inch wooden doweling**
- ◆ **1 yard of thin silk cord**

1 Cut two 40 x 25-inch pieces cream felt to form the background. From the remaining cream felt, cut two 24 x 2 ¾ -inch pieces for the doweling pockets.
2 Center the pocket pieces across the top and bottom edges of one background piece, 1 inch inside the edges. Using cream thread, machine-stitch the pockets to the background, leaving the ends open. Put this piece aside.
3 Trace the tree pattern on page 326 and enlarge on a photocopier until the measurement from the base of the pot to the top of

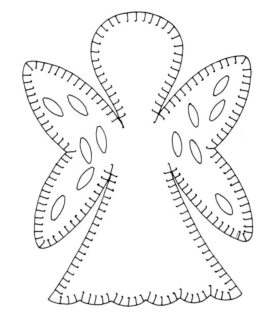

the tree is 21 inches. To enlarge without a photocopier, see page 276. Pin patterns to the green felt and cut out the tree. Cut out the tree trunk in brown felt and the tree stand in red felt. Position the felt shapes on the remaining background piece, with the top of the tree 5 ½ inches down from the top edge, and the bottom of the tree stand about 3 ½ inches from the bottom edge. Pin in place, with the pieces tightly butted. Using two strands of matching floss, sew each shape to the background with blanket stitch (see page 281 for all stitches used in this project).
4 Trace the decoration patterns (above and on page 326). For each decoration, cut two identical pieces from colored felt—50 pieces in all. Decorate the front of each shape as desired, using glue to attach the trimmings. Join the front and back of each pair with the blanket stitch, using two strands of matching embroidery floss. Take a small safety pin and hand-tack the side with the catch head to the back of the decoration.

5 Trace the outlines of all the decorations onto tracing paper. Pin to the tree, then, using two strands of yellow embroidery floss, work the outlines in running stitch). These indicate the positions for each decoration.
6 Pin the two cream background pieces together, with the tree to the front and the doweling pockets to the back. Using two strands of matching embroidery floss and the blanket stitch, sew the two pieces together around the four sides.
7 Insert the doweling pieces in the pockets and glue the silk cord to the ends to hang up the calendar.
8 Place the decorations along the sides of the background. Beginning December 1, place one decoration on the tree each night until, on Christmas Eve, the tree is complete.

CALENDAR TRIM

Decorate the tree with gold cord for sparkle.

For a quick alternative, mimic the embroidery stitches in the ornaments with tube puff paints (available at crafts and art stores) in a variety of colors. Sequins and rhinestones can be pushed into the wet paint with tweezers to add sparkle. Use craft glue to attach the second felt layer to the back of the decorated layer.

The doweling can be painted to match your wall, extended beyond the width of the calendar, and decorated with fancy tassels or cords.

The personal touch for the holidays includes an Advent calendar for the children, a Christmas wreath to welcome family and friends, and a box of Christmas party favors to add some fun to the festivities.

Dried fruit—slices of apples and oranges—mixed with lemon leaves and dried flower pods creates an impressive indoor wreath for a wall or door.

Fruited grapevine wreath

Making vine wreaths is a casual process. There is no right or wrong way, and they can be any desired diameter. For this version, vary the types of oranges and apples you select so that the fruit and skins will yield a variety of colorful decorations when dried. Follow the directions in the box (p.330) for drying your own.

- **bunch of grapevines (wisteria vines may also be used)**
- **8 branches glycerin-cured lemon leaves**
- **spool of florist's wire, wire cutters**
- **8-inch piece 20-gauge wire**
- **florist's scissors**
- **24 slices of dried apple**
- **24 slices of dried orange**
- **3 small bunches each of dried green and pink flower pods (8 to 10 per bunch)**
- **2 yards ½-inch-wide wired iridescent organza ribbon**
- **glue gun, glue sticks**

MAKING THE GRAPEVINE WREATH

1 *Loosely bend vines to the size circle you want for the wreath. At several spots, wrap florist's wire around the vines to secure them. Tuck in loose ends. Weave in more vines until the desired thickness is formed.*

2 *Arrange the fruit on the front of the wreath as desired, alternating or mixing types. Use the glue gun to attach each slice of fruit to the vine. Twist a hanging loop from 20-gauge wire, if desired, and secure ends to the top back of wreath.*

3 *Cut the lemon leaves from the branches and glue them under the fruit clusters. Alternating colors and sides of the wreath, glue the small pod clusters around the fruit, tucking their cut ends inside the vine.*

4 *Finish with a decorative bow, if desired. Lap the ribbon in 6-inch-wide zigzags, in rows on top of itself, for the desired number of loops. Secure the center with florist's wire, leaving long ends. Position the bow and wire it to the vine.*

Welcome the holiday season with a miniature wreath of dried baby roses for display inside or on a sheltered porch and a garland of juniper branches, handsome on a fence outdoors or a mantel in the house..

Miniwreaths of roses

The following directions are for making two small wreaths; you will need two 9-inch grapevine wreaths and the flowers and materials listed here.

- ◆ **72 dried red baby rose buds**
- ◆ **2 bunches each dried dock, statice, celosia, rice flowers, and straw flowers**
- ◆ **glue gun, glue sticks**
- ◆ **florist's scissors**

1 Trim the rose stems to 1 inch or less. Using half the roses on each wreath, stick them around the top and sides randomly until the color is balanced throughout. Glue the roses to the vines.

2 With the remaining flowers, work from the largest to the smallest size and repeat step 1 until the entire visual surface of each wreath is covered. Leave the back undecorated.

PRACTICAL IDEAS

PREPARING YOUR MATERIALS

VINES: If you buy vines, soak them in a bucket of water overnight or until they become pliable.

DRYING FRUIT: Dry like fruit slices together, since more time may be needed for one. Slice oranges ¼ inch thick and apples ⅛ inch. Leave seeds in place. Arrange like fruit on a cookie sheet. Place in a 110°F oven until the fruit is bone dry, about 12 to 24 hours; check and turn fruit every 5 to 8 hours.

CURING LEAVES: Mix equal parts glycerin and water in a jar. Insert freshly cut branches. Allow them to stand in a dark place until the leaves turn a deep reddish-brown. They will still retain their softness.

DRYING FLOWER PODS: Wire together 8 to 10 like pieces about 2 inches below the base of the pod. Trim the stems below the wire. Hang the bunches upside down in a cool, dark, airy place until dry.

Garland of greenery

We used juniper, but pine also makes a beautiful garland. Customize your garlands to drape a mantel, festoon a stairway, or set off a gate.

- ◆ **jute or twine cord**
- ◆ **juniper branches**
- ◆ **florist's scissors**
- ◆ **florist's wire, wire cutters**

1 Cut the cord to the desired garland length.

2 Trim the juniper from its heavy branches into small sprigs of greenery.

3 Starting at one end of the cord, wire several sprigs of greenery to the cord. Without cutting the wire from the spool, continue to wire on sprigs of greenery, covering the wire of the previous round. To wire, hold the spool of wire tightly in one hand while wrapping it around the greenery and cord held in the other hand. If desired, twist the unwrapped part of the cord into a ball or a figure-8 and secure it with a rubber band until more cord is needed. Packing the rounds of greenery closer will make a fuller, heavier garland. Spreading them out a little will make a thinner, lighter garland.

4 When you reach the last inch or two of the cord, wind several sprigs from the opposite direction, carefully filling out the juncture where they meet so that this end has the same appearance as the starting end.

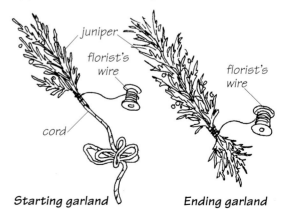

juniper

florist's wire

cord

florist's wire

Starting garland   **Ending garland**

◆ Tags, Cards, and Boxes ◆

Many techniques are used in making homemade cards and gift tags: stenciling, stamping, cutting, and pasting. Two unusual ideas are suggested below. You can mix or match them with wrapping paper you make yourself and even devise a clever box for your gift.

Greeting cards

You can make lovely cards from everyday things, such as magazine art, fabric, and colored paper.

Magazine-weave card

The impact of this type of card comes from the blend of tones—it's like a woven carpet.

- **6 x 10-inch card stock**
- **colored paper**
- **glue stick**
- **colorful magazine images**
- **craft knife**
- **grid ruler**
- **cardboard**
- **dressmaker's pins**

1 On the card stock, score a center line from one long side to the other. Fold in half, creating a 5 x 6-inch card.

2 Cut two pieces of colored paper 4 ¾ x 5 ¾ inches. Apply glue to the back of one piece; center and glue it to the card front.

3 Using the knife and ruler, cut eight strips ½ x 5 inches from the magazine images. Arrange them, long edges together and desired image face down on the cardboard. Stab a pin in the end of each strip.

4 Cut 10 strips ½ x 5 inches. Hold one strip in a horizontal position and weave it under and over the pinned strips; push it against the top pins. Weave the next strip over and under and push it against the first woven strip. Weave all the strips in this alternating arrangement.

5 Apply the glue stick to the second piece of colored paper and press it to the back of the woven strips. Remove the pins from the strips.

6 Turn the weaving right side up. Use the knife and ruler to trim away the unwoven ends. Glue the weaving to the card front, centering it on the colored paper.

Fabric-covered card

Use motifs from fabric to create a floral montage.

- **thick cardboard**
- **fabric and colored paper**
- **length of ribbon**
- **craft knife**
- **ruler**
- **scissors**
- **white craft glue**
- **hole punch or awl**

1 Using the craft knife, cut out two 5 x 7 ½-inch pieces of cardboard.

2 On one piece draw a 3-inch-square window 1 ½ inches down from the top and 1 inch in from each side. Using the craft knife and ruler, cut out the window.

3 With the scissors, cut a 7 x 9-inch piece of fabric. Apply glue to one side of the cardboard with the window. Center and glue the cardboard to the wrong side of the fabric.

4 Trim the fabric diagonally at the corners. Fold the fabric borders over the edges of the cardboard and glue them down.

5 From corner to corner, cut an X in the fabric covering the window. Wrap the fabric triangles over the edges of the window, trim as necessary, and glue to the back of the cardboard.

6 Cut a 4 ¾ x 7 ¼-inch piece of fabric. Apply glue to the back of the cardboard with the window, ensuring that it is coated to the edges. Center the wrong side of the fabric over the cardboard. Press firmly and allow to dry.

7 Turn the cardboard window side up. Use the knife to cut a hole in the backing

The elaborate Fabric-covered card (blue flowers) takes a little time to make, but the Magazine-weave card (orange background) and others made with stencils or paper cutouts, are very quick.

fabric, following the edges of the window.

8 Cover the second piece of cardboard with the colored paper, front and back.

9 Determine the center point on the left long side of both pieces of cardboard. Punch a hole on either side of the center point on each piece, ½ inch in from the edge.

10 Thread the ribbon through the holes and secure with a bow. Do not make the bow too tight, as the card needs to open easily—experiment until you have the right amount of give.

11 Center a picture, photograph, cutout, greeting, or sticker in the window and write your message inside the card beneath it.

A great variety of paper and fabric gift wraps, cards, and tags can be made using the projects on these pages as a start. Make them as simple or as elaborate as you like, from a quick thank-you card to a stunning gift wrap for a special friend: **1** Potato-print wrap, **2** Stenciled tag and card, **3** Variety tags and cards, **4** Ribbon Christmas Tree, **5** Corrugated Wrap.

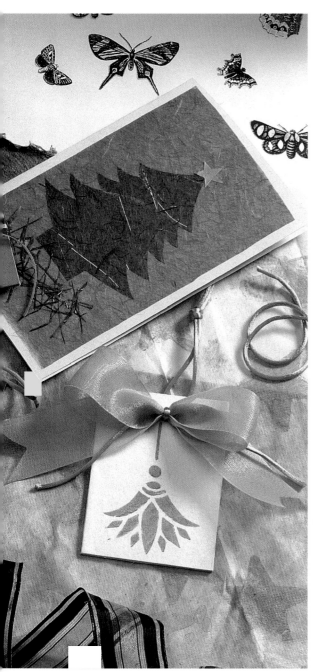

Gift wraps

Take any plain paper and dress it up to make imaginative wrapping for Christmas, Chanukah, or other special-occasion gifts

Potato-print wrap

Get the children to help make wrapping paper using this simple but effective technique.

- ▸ **sheet of tracing paper**
- ▸ **potato**
- ▸ **craft knife**
- ▸ **sheets of paper appropriate for wrapping paper**
- ◆ **artist's acrylic paints**
- ◆ **artist's paintbrush**

1 Trace the outline of the star motif from page 132. Choose a potato that, when cut in half, will have a surface area large enough to accommodate the motif. Place the tracing on top of the cut side of the potato. With the craft knife, cut along each line of the star to a depth of about ½ inch. Turn the potato on its side and carefully cut away the area outside the star by slicing horizontally ½ inch deep between the star points.
2 Lay the sheets of paper on a flat surface. Using the paintbrush, dab paint on the potato star to cover. Firmly stamp the motif on the paper, then, holding the paper with one hand, carefully lift the potato off. Repeat until the sheet is covered. Allow the paper to dry.

Scribble wrap

Making candle scribble paper is quite easy and quick. Vary wax applications for different effects.

- ◆ **sheets of paper (the paper will be wet with a sponge, so it cannot be too thin)**
- ◆ **white candle**
- ◆ **artist's acrylic paint**
- ◆ **sponge**

1 This technique can be quite messy, so spread plenty of newspaper on your work surface before you start. Lay the sheets of paper to be colored on top.

2 Take the candle and scribble wax all over the paper until the paper is well covered.
3 Dilute the paint with water to a watery consistency: You will need enough to cover all the sheets you intend to color. Dip the sponge in the paint and draw it over the paper to cover the sheet completely. Allow each sheet to dry.
4 For a deeper color, you will need about three layers of paint. Allow the paper to dry between each coat. Alternatively, for a more subtle effect, you can add more wax scribbles over the first layer of paint and each subsequent layer. Allow each layer to dry.

Corrugated wrap

The texture of corrugated paper gives dimension to a gift wrap. Even the smallest gift can look special. It is best if the present is a rectangular shape, such as a book, but with a little imagination, most objects can be wrapped in this way.

- ◆ **sheet of colored paper**
- ◆ **sheet of thin, colored corrugated cardboard (or color it with acrylic paint)**
- ◆ **sheet of tracing paper**
- ◆ **craft knife**
- ◆ **awl**
- ◆ **ribbon and 5 inches of cord**

1 Wrap a gift with the colored paper. Place the wrapped gift on the corrugated cardboard and cut a piece large enough to wrap around it.
2 On the piece of tracing paper, trace the star motif on page 132 and lay the tracing on the cardboard in the position you want the cutout to appear. Using the knife, carefully cut out a star. Repeat so that you have two corrugated star cutouts to decorate the top.
3 Wrap the corrugated cardboard around the present; tie and knot the ribbon to hold the edges of the corrugated cardboard in place.
4 With the awl, pierce a hole through the center of both corrugated stars. Thread the cord through one and tie a knot in the end. Thread the other end of the cord through the other star and knot. Push both stars against the knots. Attach the center of the cord to the knot of ribbon.

Make an assortment of gift tags in your spare time throughout the year so that when Christmas comes, you have a good supply to choose from.

Spatter wrap

Use richly colored paper and gold or silver paint to impart a seasonal richness with this technique.

- **colored sheets of paper appropriate for wrapping**
- **acrylic paint**
- **large brush**

1 This technique can be messy, so spread plenty of newspaper on your work surface. Lay the sheets of paper to be spattered on top.
2 Wet the brush with plenty of paint and, with a flicking action, spatter the wrapping sheet. The size of spatters and coverage of the paper will depend on the size of brush, the viscosity of the paint, and the flicking technique. It is a good idea to experiment with scrap paper until you have a result you are happy with.
3 Allow the paper to dry.

MAKING THE JOB EASIER

Make photocopied wrapping paper by copying on colored papers, or by adding color highlights with acrylic paints and a brush.

A hole punch is useful for punching holes in thin cardboard and paper, especially if you are making a large number of tags.

A dressmaker's awl or an ice pick is useful for piercing holes in thick cardboard and cardboard covered with fabric. Or you can use a nail and hammer. Place the nail tip at the hole position and hit the head until the nail protrudes through the card. Do this on some scrap wood or a few sheets of scrap cardboard so that you don't punch holes in your table or floor.

Ribbon is available at crafts stores as well as fabric stores. You can buy it by the yard or by the roll, which is usually less expensive.

Gift tags

Use the wrapping paper for your gift as material for the tag, or adapt our Christmas card ideas to this use. Below are more suggestions.

Novelty tags

Tags can be made from any number of found objects, photocopies, cutouts of fabric or colored paper, magazine pictures, tassels, ribbons—the key is your imagination.

- **card stock**
- **glue stick**
- **white craft glue**
- **ribbon or cord**
- **craft knife**
- **scissors**
- **ruler**

1 Cut the card to a suitable shape. If the tag is to be shaped (a Christmas bell, for example, as shown on page 326), glue all the elements onto the card first, then cut out the shape.
2 Arrange colored paper, photocopies, magazine pictures, or found objects on the card until you are happy with the result.
3 Glue the elements to the card, using the glue stick for paper and white craft glue for sequins, beads, or bulky items.
4 Punch a hole in the top or corner of the tag and attach the ribbon or cord for the tie (see the box on decorative ties, facing page).

Stenciled tags

Stenciling is one of the quickest ways to make gift tags. You can buy stencils at crafts stores, or you can design and cut your own.

- **card stock**
- **artist's acrylic paint**
- **stencil brush**
- **ribbon or cord**
- **craft knife**
- **ruler**

1 Cut the tags to the size and shape required and position the stencil on a card.

2 Wet the brush with a small amount of paint (to avoid bleeding around the edges of the motif, it's best if the brush is not saturated). Being careful not to wipe the paint under the stencil edges, dab the paint over the cutout until the area is covered. Holding the paper with one hand, carefully lift off the stencil and allow the tag to dry.

3 Punch a hole in the top or corner and attach the ribbon or cord for the tie.

Ribbon Christmas tree

Vary the colors of this Christmas gift tag, perhaps blue and silver or green and gold, for a change from the standard green and red. Or coordinate the colors with your gift wrap.

- ◆ **poster board in the colors of your choice**
- ◆ **craft knife**
- ◆ **ruler**
- ◆ **scissors**
- ◆ **for each tree, 1⅓ yards ⅛-inch-wide ribbon**
- ◆ **for each tree, 12 inches ¼-inch-wide ribbon**
- ◆ **tapestry needle**

1 From the poster board, cut triangles 4 inches wide at the base and 5 inches high.
2 On a scrap of card, mark 11 intervals, ⅜ inch apart, along one edge. This will be the template for cutting the notches for the ribbon.
3 Lay the template along one side of the triangle. Starting ½ inch from the base, snip a ⅛-inch notch at each mark on the template. Repeat on the other side. Using the tapestry needle, make a small hole between the two notches at the top of the triangle.
4 Fold the length of narrow ribbon in half to determine the center point. Place the center point midway between the first two notches at the base of the triangle and start crisscrossing the ribbon around the tree, pulling it into the notches and crossing each end over as if you were threading shoe laces. Pull the ribbon tightly into each notch as you go.
5 When you have reached the last two notches at the top of the triangle, thread both

ends of ribbon through the eye of the tapestry needle and push them through the hole.
6 Fold the wider ribbon in half to determine the center point. Cross the two ends at the center point to form a loose bow. Pass the double strand of narrow ribbon from the top of the tree around the center of the bow and back through the hole. Pull the needle through until the bow is held tightly—this forms the "knot" of the bow as well as secures the bow to the card.
7 Remove the needle and tie the two ends in a knot behind the hole. Trim the ends of the narrow ribbons about 6 inches above the top of the tag and knot them together to make a loop for hanging.

Paper tassels

You can use these paper tassels as festive napkin rings for the Christmas table, to coordinate with your gift wraps, or as an attractive trim for the tree.

- ◆ **thick cardboard**
- ◆ **craft knife**
- ◆ **awl**
- ◆ **sheet of white paper of the length you want your "cord"**
- ◆ **white craft glue**
- ◆ **artist's acrylic paints**
- ◆ **brush**

1 Cut out 2 cardboard tassel shapes and punch a hole in the top of each.
2 Roll and twist the white paper to look like a cord. (If you want cords that are longer than your paper, tape strips together and roll them with the tape on the inside.)
3 Thread one end of the cord through one of the cardboard tassels, repeat with the other tassel and the other end of cord. Glue the ends of the cord to the back of each tassel with craft glue.
4 Cross the cord over until the tassels are sitting side by side. Glue the cord together at the point of crossing. When the glue is dry, paint the cord and cardboard with acrylic paint. Add black lines as shown in the photograph on the facing page to give the tassels definition.

DECORATIVE TIES

TIES made from ribbon or cord can finish off a card or tag with flair. Ribbon comes in many colors, textures, and widths. When making a card with a specific theme and in specific colors, it's a good idea to take samples to the store so that you can choose a ribbon that suits. A few strands of raffia also make an effective tie for a parcel wrapped in something as simple as white butcher's paper or plain brown paper.

Attaching a bow to a gift tag

Method 1—one wide and one narrow ribbon
Fold the wide ribbon in half to determine the center point. Cross the two ends at this point to form a loose bow. Thread one end of the narrow ribbon through the hole in the tag from the back and pass it around the center of the loose bow. Thread the narrow ribbon back through the hole, pull it tight, and tie a knot. This will secure the bow to the tag.

Method 2—two equal ribbons
Punch two holes in the top of a tag, ½ inch apart. Thread ribbons into the large eye of a needle. Insert the needle into the front of one hole and pull several inches to the back. Insert the needle into the second hole and bring the ribbons to the front. Remove the needle. Adjust the ribbons so that the ends are equal at the front of each hole. Tie a bow.

Attaching cord and ribbon ties

Tie the ends of a ribbon together in a firm knot. Pass the loop through the hole in the card or tag, pull it through a short way, and thread the knotted end through the loop. Let go of the loop and pull the knotted end firmly. Alternatively, simply pull a length of ribbon or cord through the hole and tie the ends together in a knot.

Finishing touch

Don't forget to finish off your ribbon ends, using sharp scissors to cut either a diagonal or a fishtail. This is not only a decorative element but also a practical one because it will minimize fraying at the end of the ribbon.

Gift boxes

Bright and imaginative presentation gives a thrill of pleasure even before the gift itself is revealed.

Wrapped and painted

Gift boxes can be recycled from former gifts or bought inexpensively at card and crafts shops.

PAINTED BOX
- **artist's acrylic paints**
- **paintbrush**
- **white craft glue**

FABRIC-COVERED BOX
- **fabric to cover**
- **white craft glue**
- **ribbon**

PAPER-COVERED BOX
- **paper to cover**
- **glue stick**
- **acrylic paint**
- **stencil**
- **stencil brush**

Painted box

1 Paint the box in colors the recipient will like. You may need up to three coats of paint for even coverage.
2 When the paint is dry, glue a cheerful figure—made or purchased—to the top of the lid. The bear shown facing page is made with papier-mâché (see page 311 for this technique).

Covered boxes

1 Cover each box with fabric or paper. To achieve the neatest finish, experiment with the corner folds before you glue them.
2 Decorate the paper-covered box with stencils and allow to dry. Glue ribbon to the lid of the fabric-covered box with craft glue. Push-pins are useful for holding the ribbon in place while the glue dries. Tie the ribbon bow and glue it to the top. For contrast, we painted parts of the fabric on the lid with acrylic paint mixed with a little glue.

NOTE: As an alternative, when covering the lid, you might reverse the fabric, if the wrong side provides a pleasing contrast.

Doric column box

This intriguing container may have the recipient puzzled for a few moments about how to open it —the bottom pulls out. Fill it with candy sticks, colored pencils, or rolled-up paper items.

- **corrugated cardboard**
- **thick cardboard**
- **craft knife**
- **ruler**
- **pencil**
- **gold acrylic paint**
- **white craft glue**
- **brush**
- **2 small paper clips**
- **hair dryer (optional)**

1 Cut out the corrugated cardboard as shown below (note the direction of the corrugations): one piece A, 7 ½ x 12 ½ inches.; one piece B, 7 ½ x 1 ¾ inches; two pieces C, 2 ⅛ x 5 ½ inches. Cut out two pieces of the thick cardboard 2 ¾ inches square (D). Paint one side of pieces A and B, and both sides of pieces C and D with gold paint and allow to dry.
2 On pieces A and B, mark a line ⅜ inch from one end. Score this line with the blunt side of the craft knife on the corrugated side. Clip out triangle shapes along the scored border, leaving the last ¾ inch clear for overlap.

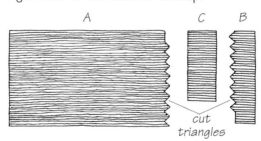

cut triangles

3 Apply glue on one long edge of piece A and fit the two edges together with a ¾ -inch overlap, to form a tube. Hold in place with paper clips while glue dries—use a hair dryer to speed up the process. Repeat with piece B, with an overlap of a little more than ¾ inch, so that the tube it makes fits inside the tube formed by A.
4 On each cylinder, bend triangles inward, apply glue to them, and press each cylinder onto the center of piece D. Allow to dry.

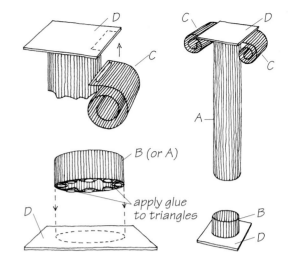

B (or A)

apply glue to triangles

5 Take two pieces C and curl into a spiral by rolling them tightly and then releasing the spiral. When you are satisfied with the spiral, apply glue to the top of the edge and attach to the column, as shown above. Hold firmly with clips while drying with a hair dryer.

Simple box

You can make this perfect cube any size you wish.

- **cardboard**
- **craft knife**
- **ruler and pencil**
- **white craft glue**

1 Decorate one side of a piece of cardboard with potato prints or stencils or cover with some attractive paper. The side you have decorated will be called the "right side."
2 Using the template (facing page), mark the dimensions you require on the wrong side of the cardboard with a pencil and ruler.
3 Using the craft knife and ruler, cut around the outside edges. Score the fold lines on the right side with the blunt side of the craft knife for thin cardboard, and lightly with the sharp side for thicker cardboard.
4 Fold into a box along the score lines with all the tabs inside. Glue the two top tabs down over the side tabs. It is not necessary to glue the side tabs in place. Paper clips are excellent for holding the top tabs in place while they dry.

This selection of boxes of all sizes and shapes is quite within the scope of even a beginning handicrafter. Covered with fabric or paper, decorated with stencils, and tied with ribbon, they are dressed-up enough to go to any party.

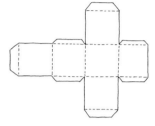

Diagram of whole piece

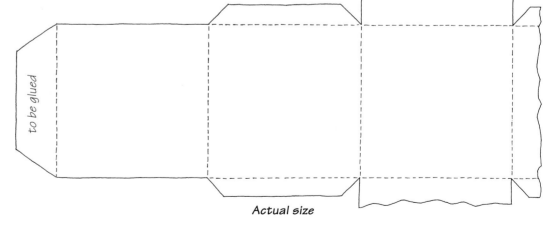

to be glued

Actual size

A PROFESSIONAL FINISH

When gluing awkward objects, use paper clips to hold the layers together while the glue dries.

For a clean fold on a card, score the fold line first. With the blunt edge of a craft knife, score a line on the right side of the card. The idea is that you are not cutting the card, just indenting it.

On thick cardboard, score the fold line first to achieve a clean fold. With the sharp edge of a craft knife, lightly score a line on the right side of the cardboard. This will cut it just deep enough to allow the cardboard to fold easily.

To make a simple box, use this template, extending it to its complete shape using the small diagram as a guide. Note that there are 7 tabs, 3 slightly larger (to be glued) and 4 smaller (no need to glue).

◆ Innovative Gift Wraps ◆

With some of these novel ideas, the wrapping can become part of the gift. Give a little thought to coordinating the wrap and gift—you might choose a rose-patterned fabric to make a cover for a book on roses, for example, or a wine-colored napkin to wrap a bottle of red wine.

Kitchen gift wrap

Choose a colorful kitchen towel for this practical and pretty bridal shower idea.

- **new kitchen towel**
- **sewing needle**
- **thread to match kitchen towel**
- **rope, enough to go around package twice and leave 2½ inches at each end**
- **2 cookie cutters**
- **2 wooden cooking spoons**

1 Wrap the item with the kitchen towel as you would with a sheet of paper. Fold over the ends neatly and tack them with the needle and thread—don't stitch too securely.

2 Make a knot at each end of the rope. Tie the package with the rope, looping the cookie cutters and spoons into the final tie. For a homespun touch, make a knot instead of a bow.

Japanese gift wrap

Choose filmy fabric or scarves for this project. Fabrics of different textures and thicknesses will add interest to your wrap.

- **2 squares fabric or 2 scarves**
- **needle and thread, or sewing machine**

1 Hem all edges of the fabric by hand or machine (not necessary if using scarves).

2 Lay one piece of fabric on top of the other and place the item to be wrapped on a diagonal in the center of the fabric. Bring two opposite corners of the fabric together and fold neatly over each other. Bring the other opposite corners together and tie. Tuck in all the edges to make a neat parcel.

Book gift wrap

For a special book, create a wrapping that will later act as a decorative and protective envelope. A book for a gardener could be wrapped in a floral print; a country-style cookbook, in gingham.

- **rectangular piece of fabric, for pocket (see step 1)**
- **contrasting fabric, for flap (see step 2)**
- **fabric scissors**
- **needle and thread, or sewing machine**
- **2 buttons, about 1 inch diameter**
- **silk cord, about 12 inches**

1 Measure the height, width, and thickness of the book. Cut a rectangle of fabric. The length should double the book's height plus the thickness plus ½-inch seam allowance on each side. The width should be the book's width plus the thickness plus 1 inch. One of the rectangle's short ends should be on the selvage.

2 Cut a square of contrasting fabric to equal the width of the rectangle. With right sides facing, stitch one side of the square to the nonselvage end of the rectangle. Press. Turn under a ½-inch hem on the opposite side of the square. Press.

3 Fold each end of the combined strip in to meet at the join, right sides facing (below). Pin, then stitch each side, ½ inch from each edge.

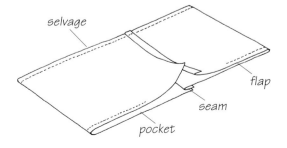

selvage

flap

seam

pocket

Turn the pocket and flap right side out. Slip-stitch the pressed hem to close the open end of the flap.

4 Slip the book into the bag and mark the position of the two buttons, one on the flap and one on the pocket, centered. Sew on the buttons. Tie one end of the cord around the thread of the flap button and tie a knot in the other end of the cord.

5 With the book inside the bag, wind the cord around the buttons in a figure 8 pattern to secure the parcel.

Flower pot gift wrap

This is a quick way to dress up a potted plant.

- **2 large new bandannas or colorful square napkins**
- **cloth tape**

1 Fold one bandanna diagonally in half and tie it around the rim of the pot with a simple knot (the folded edge runs around the rim and the loose points of the handkerchief hang down). Tuck the pointed end of the triangle under the pot and tape it in place.

2 Repeat with the other handkerchief, tying the knot on the opposite side of the rim.

Baby gift wrap

The wrapping on this baby gift may prove as useful as the present itself.

- **cloth diaper**
- **3 diaper pins**
- **small teddy bear for trim**
- **ribbon for bow**

1 Lay the diaper flat on a table with a corner toward you. Place the gift item (a square or rec-

tangular shape is best) in the center of the diaper, at a 45-degree angle to the sides. (For a gift that is too large to be accommodated this way, use a baby's bath towel.)

2 Fold the top corner of the diaper down over the gift, then fold in the two side corners. Finally, fold up the bottom corner to overlap the other corners. Pin the four corners together with two diaper pins, making sure you don't damage the item inside.

3 Tie a ribbon bow around the teddy bear's neck. Thread the ribbon through the hole at the end of the remaining diaper pin, and attach the teddy bear to the gift.

Bottle gift wrap

Turn a bottle of wine or sparkling cider—or a bottle of flavored oil or vinegar—into an elegant gift with this easy gift wrap.

- ◆ **colorful cloth napkin**
- ◆ **cloth tape in matching color**
- ◆ **contrasting ribbon, for bow**

1 Lay the napkin on a table. Place the bottle on one edge of the napkin with the bottom of the bottle about 1½ inches from the bottom of the napkin. Secure the napkin to the bottle with cloth tape, about halfway down the bot-

The extra thought that has been given to the wrapping of these gifts has added greatly to their charm. Clockwise from back left: Baby gift wrap; Bottle gift wrap; Japanese gift wrap; Kitchen gift wrap; Book gift wrap; and Flower pot gift wrap.

tle, and fold down the top edge of the napkin a little above the top of the bottle.

2 Roll up the bottle tightly in the napkin and secure the end of the napkin with tape.

3 Tuck the bottom of the napkin under the bottle and secure with tape. Tie a bow around the neck of the bottle.

Index

Credits

Pp.107-109:
Designed by Zuelia Ann Hurt and created by Gallery Y, New York, NY.

Pp.112-115:
Designed by Zuelia Ann Hurt; knitted rug created by Sigrid Etter; braided rug created by Marie LaFevre.

Pp.118-119:
Designed by Zuelia Ann Hurt and created by Plaid Enterprises, Inc., Norcross, GA, using Gallery Glass Paint and Gallery Glass Simulated Liquid Leading.

Pp.120-121; 122-123; 134-137:
Designed by Zuelia Ann Hurt and created by Barbara Fimbel, using Waverly Fabrics "Candlelight Chintz," "Caprice," "Melissa," "Folly," and "Mortimer."

Pp.136-137:
Designed by Zuelia Ann Hurt and created by The Pink Flamingo, Staten Island, NY, using Waverly Fabrics "Polka" and "Market Place."

Pp.158-159:
Designed by Zuelia Ann Hurt and created by Plaid Enterprises, Inc., Norcross, GA, using Folk Art Glass and Folk Art Acrylic Color.

Pp.202-203:
Designed and created by Mark D. Feirer.

Pp.204-205:
Designed and created by Catherine Alston.

Pp.206-207:
Cat bed frame and window perch designed and created by Mark D. Feirer; cat bed sling designed and created by Catherine Alston.

Pp.208-210:
Pet collars designed and created by Catherine Alston.

Pp.211-219:
Designed and created by Mark D. Feirer.

Pp.292-293:
Designed by Virginia Wells Blaker and created by Judith Sandstrom, using quilt battings from Fairfield Processing Corporation, Wilton, CT.

Pp.302-305
Designed by Zuelia Ann Hurt and created by Ginger Kean Berk

Pp.308-309:
Designed by Zuelia Ann Hurt and created by Maureen Klein.

Pp.310-311:
Designed by Zuelia Ann Hurt and created by Connie Matricardi.

Pp.312-315:
Designed by Virginia Wells Blaker and created by T. C. Powers, TC Ultra Co. at Sails & Rails, Savannah, GA.

Pp.316-317; 326-327; 338-339:
Designed by Zuelia Ann Hurt and created by Zabel Meshigian.

Pp.320-321
Designed by Zuelia Ann Hurt and created by Beth MacDonald, Brain Strorms, Sioux Falls, SD.

Bibliography

Cooking and cleaning

Ball Blue Book Guide to Home Canning, Freezing & Dehydration, Alltrista Corporation.

Bread Dough Creations, Susan Roach, Sally Milner Publishing.

Better Than Store-Bought, A Cookbook, Helen Witty and Elizabeth Schneider Colchie, Harper & Row.

The Cook's Bible, The Best of American Home Cooking, Christopher Kimball, Little Brown and Company

How to Clean Absolutely Everything, Barty Phillips, Avon Books.

Made for Giving: Gifts from the Kitchen, Pamela Westland, Reader's Digest.

Crafts

Art School: an Introduction to Acrylics, Ray Smith, DK.

Art School: an Introduction to Pastels, Michael Wright, DK.

Art School: an Introduction to Perspective, Ray Smith, DK.

The Book of Candles, Miranda Innes, DK.

Crafts & Hobbies, A Step-by-Step Guide to Creative Skills, Reader's Digest

Decorative Frames & Labels, Carol Belanger-Grafton, editor, Dover.

Decorative Paint Effects – A Practical Guide, Annie Sloan, Putnam.

Decorative Papercrafts Workstation, Susan Niner Janes, Grosset & Dunlap.

Découpage, Nerida Singleton, Sterling Publishing Co., Inc.

55 Country Dough Craft Designs, Linda Rogers, Sterling Publishing Co., Inc.

Papercraft School, Clive Stevens, Reader's Digest.

Practical Craft Ideas from Your Garden, Janet Taylor, Seven Hills.

Practical Guide to Decorative Antique Effects, Annie Sloan, Reader's Digest.

The Rag Doll Kit, Alicia Merrett, Running Press.

Singer Creative Gifts & Projects, Cy DeCosse, Cowles Creative.

Stencil Book, Louise Drayton and Jane Thomson, DK.

3,800 Early Advertising Cuts, Carol Belanger Grafton, Dover.

Tonia Todman's Paper-Making Book, Tonia Todman, Sterling Publishing Co., Inc.

Tricia Guild on Colour, Tricia Guild, Rizzoli International.

25 Kites That Fly, Leslie L. Hunt, Dover.

Ultimate Christmas, Jane Newdick, DK.

Victorian Crafts Revived, Caroline Green, Reader's Digest.

Victorian Splendour, Suzanne Forge, Oxford University Press.

Wirework, Mary Maguire, Lorenz Books.

Woodcraft of the World, Thunder Bay Press.

A World of Beads, Barbara Case, Sterling Publishing Co., Inc.

Wreaths and Garlands, Malcolm Hillier, DK.

Health and Beauty

The Complete Medicinal Herbal, Penelope Ody, DK.

Encyclopedia of Medicinal Plants, Andrew Chevallier, DK

Home Herbal, Penelope Ody, DK.

Magic and Medicine of Plants, Reader's Digest.

Home and Garden

Complete Home Decorating Book, Nicholas Barnard, DK.

Home Accessories with Style, Cowles Creative.

House Style Book, Deyan Sudjic, Gallery Books.

1001 Hints & Tips for the Garden, Reader's Digest.

Singer Home Decorating Projects, Cy DeCosse, Cowles Creative.

The Stenciled House, Lyn LeGrace, DK.

Terence Conran's DIY by Design, Terence Conran, Conran Octopus.

Treasures in Your Home, David Battie, Reader's Digest.

Upholstery Techniques and Projects, David James, Sterling Publishing Co., Inc.

Pets and Wildlife

Attracting Backyard Birds, Inviting Projects to Entice Your Feathered Friends, Sandy Cortright and Will Pokriots, Sterling Publishing Co., Inc.

The Backyard Bird Watcher, George H. Harrison, Simon and Schuster.

Beastly Abodes, Homes for Birds, Bats, Butterflies & Other Backyard Wildlife, Bobbe Needham, Sterling Publishing Co., Inc.

Birdfeeders, Shelters, and Baths, Edward A. Baldwin, Storey Communications, Inc.

Birdhouses, 20 Unique Woodworking Projects for Houses and Feeders, Mark Ramuz and Frank Delicata, Storey Communications, Inc.

Birdwatching, Dr. Janann V. Jenner, Friedman/Fairfax Publishers.

Feed the Birds, Helen Witty and Dick Witty, Workman Publishing.

How to Attract Birds, Ortho Books

An Illustrated Guide to Attracting Birds, Sunset Publishing Corporation.

The Joy of Birding, A Guide to Better Birdwatching, Chuck Bernstein, Capra Press.

Natural Health for Dogs & Cats, Richard H. Pitcairn, D.V.M., Ph.D., and Susan Hubble Pitcairn, Rodale Press, Inc.

The National Audubon Society North American Birdfeeder Handbook, Robert Burton, DK.

Sewing and Needlework

Butterick Fabric Handbook, Irene Cumming Kleeberg, editor, Butterick.

Celtic Cross Stitch, Gail Lawther, Reader's Digest.

Complete Book of Embroidery, Melinda Coss, Reader's Digest.

Complete Guide to Needlework, Reader's Digest.

Complete Guide to Sewing, Reader's Digest.

Country Quilts, Linda Seward, Grove Press.

Cross Stitch Country Christmas, Brenda Keyes, Sterling Publishing Co., Inc.

Decorating with Traditional Fabrics, Miranda Innes, Reader's Digest.

Decorative Needlepoint: Tapestry and Beadwork, Julia Hickman, Reader's Digest.

Design and Make Curtains, Heather Luke, Storey Communications.

The Ehrman Needlepoint Book, Hugh Ehrman, Reader's Digest.

The Essential Quilter, Barbara Chainey, David & Charles.

Fabrics: The Decorative Art of Textiles, Caroline Lebeau, Thames and Hudson.

The Patchwork Planner, Birte Hilberg, David & Charles.

Patchwork, Quilting, & Appliqué, The Complete Guide to All the Essential Techniques, Jenni Dobson, Reader's Digest.

Quilting School, Ann Poe, Reader's Digest.

Ribbon Embroidery, Daphne J. Ashby & Jackie Woolsey, Sterling Publishing Co., Inc.

The Sampler Motif Book, Brenda Keyes, Putnam.

The Sasha Kagan Sweater Book, Sasha Kagan, DK.

Singer Sewing Step-by-Step, Cy DeCosse, Cowles Creative.